THE INSIDERS' GUIDE TO
Washington, D.C.

by
Nicole McGehee
and
Mary Jane H. Solomon

Insiders' Guide
105 Budleigh St.
P.O. Box 2057
Manteo, NC 27954
(252) 473-6100
www.insiders.com

Sales and Marketing:
Falcon Publishing, Inc.
P.O. Box 1718
Helena, MT 59624
(800) 582-2665
www.falconguide.com

•

THIRD EDITION
1st printing

•

Publications from The Insiders' Guide®
series are available at special discounts for
bulk purchases for sales promotions,
premiums or fundraisings. Special editions,
including personalized covers, can be
created in large quantities for special
needs. For more information, please write
to Karen Bachman, Insiders' Guide, P.O.
Box 2057, Manteo, NC 27949, or call
(800) 765-2665 Ext. 241.

ISBN 1-57380-053-8

Insiders' Guide

Publisher/Editor-in-Chief

Beth P. Storie

Advertising Director/
General Manager

Michael McOwen

Creative Services Director

Giles MacMillan

Art Director

David Haynes

Managing Editor

Dave McCarter

Project Editor

Bridget Millsaps

Project Artist

David Todd

Insiders' Guide
An imprint of Falcon Publishing Inc.
A Landmark Communications company.

Preface

Setting about the task of writing *The Insiders' Guide® to Washington, D.C.*, is every bit as daunting as it is exciting. Perhaps no other region in the country is as diverse, dynamic, intriguing and, for that matter, misunderstood as the Nation's Capital.

All of us, no doubt, have strong perceptions of Washington. It is, after all, a city that lives and breathes under an international microscope. The idealist in us views Washington as a great shrine to the American heritage, a beacon reinforcing the beliefs in freedom and democracy for all nations. We are awed by the inspiring landmarks, monuments and memorials, the broad avenues, sprawling parks, world-class museums and galleries, and stately embassies.

At the same time, the cynic in us might see Washington as a place of freewheeling politicians, lethargic bureaucrats, pampered diplomats and petty special-interest groups. We are dismayed by the sight of homeless people sleeping on steam grates and park benches within earshot of the White House, and alarmed by grave crime statistics.

In the last decade or so, we all have come to view Washington in a dramatically new light. This once largely one-dimensional government town has blossomed into a premier national and global business center; it is in Washington where the rules are made for the complex game of international trade and commerce. The decision-makers are here. The information is here. The communication channels are here. It might surprise you to learn that only about 17 percent of the area's residents are employed by the federal government. The rest have jobs in Washington's burgeoning service industries, including tourism, law, banking, medical research, telecommunications, publishing and higher education. Indeed, these factors might be why you are, or soon to be headed, here.

And you're not alone.

Metro Washington's population now stands at some 4.65 million, and its annual visitor count tops 20 million.

Despite the area's growth, Washington doesn't have the sprawling metropolitan feel of other large cities. There are no skyscrapers, the streets are clean, and flowers and trees abound. The city is alive with outdoor cafés, colorful neighborhoods and inviting parks. Visitors are more likely to compare it to Paris than New York.

The neighborhood feeling isn't limited to the 63-square-mile stretch of federal land bounded by the Potomac River, Virginia and Maryland. "Washington" has come to mean much of Northern Virginia, including Fairfax, Arlington, Loudoun and Prince William counties as well as the City of Alexandria. "Washington" also is the fast-growing Suburban Maryland counties of Montgomery, Prince George's and Anne Arundel. Residents of each area can be fervent advocates of their own stomping grounds, but what holds the vast array together is the District of Columbia.

For practical purposes, this book concentrates primarily on the District and the aforementioned core counties of Northern Virginia and Suburban Maryland. They encompass what we view as Metro Washington, D.C., or the Nation's Capital.

In the pages that follow, you will find what we hope is a fresh, insightful and comprehensive guide to our region. It is our goal that *The Insiders' Guide® to Washington, D.C.*, proves to be an invaluable source for newcomers, as it sketches the nuts and bolts of touring the area or even relocating here.

About the Authors

Nicole McGehee

Nicole McGehee is one of the rare few who have lived in Washington for decades. She was 10 years old when her family moved to the Maryland suburb of Chevy Chase, and since then she has lived in D.C. proper as well as Virginia. A true "inside the beltway" denizen, Nicole began her career as a lobbyist, went from there to Capitol Hill and landed at the White House. In 1986 she exited the political revolving door and became a full-time writer.

Nicole's first foray into publishing was as managing editor and founder of *Washington Report on Latin America and the Caribbean*, a biweekly publication for banks, international businesses, government officials and diplomats interested in the effects of Washington policy on business, trade and travel in Latin America and the Caribbean. When the threat of terminal seriousness began to loom too large, she turned her attention to fiction and travel writing and has never regretted her decision to stick with the "fun topics."

Her debut novel, *Regret Not a Moment*, was released in hard cover in 1993 by Little, Brown, and in paper by Warner Books in November 1994. Her most recent novel, *No More Lonely Nights*, was published in hard cover by Little, Brown in 1995. Nicole's works have been translated into French, German and Spanish and have been published in the United Kingdom and Canada. She describes her fiction as "beach reading for thinking women."

Nicole's travel articles have appeared in daily newspapers such as *The Miami Herald* and *The Washington Post*, as well as in national travel magazines such as *Honeymoon*.

Her college years prepared her in no way for her current profession. She is the first to admit that her parents undoubtedly squandered their money sending her to Georgetown University for a B.A. in international relations, and to the Fashion Institute of Technology for an A.A. in advertising and communications. Nicole also maintains to this day that the three summers she spent in Paris were devoted to studying the French language, and that the breadth of her vocabulary and her fluency are not a result of contact with French gentlemen.

Mary Jane H. Solomon

A native of Dayton, Ohio, Mary Jane H. Solomon left the Buckeye State for the Old Dominion 14 years ago. She is well-acquainted with Metro Washington, having lived in Washington, D.C., Rosslyn, Old Town Alexandria, Leesburg and Reston before settling with her family in Annandale, Virginia, three years ago.

She began her journalism career at Miami University in Oxford, Ohio, where she got her big break covering a dining-hall salmonella outbreak. Another assignment led to an even bigger story: While interviewing students taking a special-interest class, Mary Jane met her future husband, Steve Solomon.

After graduating with a bachelor of philosophy degree in 1982, she worked as a classified advertising manager and society editor at the *Urbana Daily Citizen*, where she received an Ohio Associated Press Honorable Mention award for lifestyle writing. Following her soon-to-be husband to Northern Virginia in 1984, she found a position at *The Alexandria Gazette*, at that time the nation's oldest daily newspaper. As a lifestyle editor and feature writer there and later for the *Loudoun Times-Mirror* in Leesburg, Mary Jane received nine Virginia Press Association awards, including a first-place honor for an article about the effects of Alzheimer's Disease on families. She also served as the *Times-Mirror*'s deputy editor, helping the paper earn the National Newspaper Association's top award for general excellence.

After a job producing themed advertising supplements and the company newsletter for Arundel Communications Inc., Mary Jane decided to freelance so she could stay home with her then-infant daughter. During the past eight years, she has written more than 250 features and film and theater reviews. Her articles appear in *The Washington Post*'s "Weekend" section, and in such other publications as *Sesame Street Parents* and *Virginia Parent News*.

Mary Jane and her husband live with daughters Rachel and Anna and cat Macaroon in the heart of Fairfax County. She enjoys exploring area attractions with her family, playing basketball and helping with classroom writing projects at her children's elementary school.

Acknowledgments

Mary Jane H. Solomon

Many people contributed information and encouragement to help make this book a reality. Thanks to the Insiders' Guide staff, especially editors Bridget Millsaps and Dan DeGregory, for their patience and constructive suggestions; and to Brian T. Cook and Stephen Soltis for laying the foundation for this new edition.

Laura Bergheim's *The Washington Historical Atlas: Who Did What When and Where in the Nation's Capital* and Suzanne Hilton's *A Capital Capital City, 1790-1814* served as helpful and entertaining references regarding Washington history.

The Washington, D.C. Convention and Visitors Association supplied invaluable maps and important facts. The Greater Washington Board of Trade shared numerous statistics and detailed transportation studies. Several area agencies on aging offered insight into Metro Washington's "senior scene."

Thanks also to all those who promptly and cheerfully provided piles of helpful information, especially Carol Ann Cohen of the Northern Virginia Regional Park Authority, Adrien F. Creecy at the United States Army Military District of Washington, Paul Eno with the Fairfax County Department of Transportation, Merni Fitzgerald of the Fairfax County Park Authority, Phyllis Gittleson and Ellen Greenberg with the Jewish Council for the Aging, Bruce Lawson at Manassas Regional Airport, Sally A. McDonough at Mount Vernon, Joan Morris with the Virginia Department of Transportation, Marca Piehuta of IONA Senior Services, Christi Ruhstorfer of the Sports Network and Trish Shuman of George Mason University.

On a personal note, I'm grateful for the many dedicated, enthusiastic teachers who nurtured my interest in pursuing a writing career, particularly Oda Wilkey, Andrew Ballauer, Hugh Morgan and the late Herbert Erbaugh. The assignments and good advice I've received from several editors contributed to my "insider's" knowledge. Special thanks to George L. Barton IV, Patti Snodgrass, Linda Cross, Nora B. May and John F. Kelly.

I'm blessed with wonderful friends who provide unlimited encouragement and patience, not to mention lots of great ideas. Thank you, Sheryl and Jim Alexander, Judy and Andy Bramnick, Donna Klinger, Marie and Jeff Mee, Barbara Ruben, Gayle and Rob Weiss and my many friends from Wakefield Forest, the JCCNV, Springfield Christian Church and elsewhere who always ask what I'm working on and give me terrific story tips.

Finally, I couldn't have come this far without my loving, understanding family. My heartfelt thanks go to my parents, Donald and Johanna Hoak, for their faith, love and wisdom; and to Sheldon and Sharon Solomon, for always making me feel like a special "daughter." Thanks also to my siblings, Susan Hoak (your screenplay's next!) and Terry Layne and Jeff and Rachael Solomon; and to the many aunts, uncles and cousins who always show interest in my work. Most of all, love and deepest gratitude to my greatest gifts: Steve, Rachel and Anna, whose unconditional love, support and patience give me strength and enable me to fulfill my dream to be a mom who works inside the home.

This book is dedicated to Steve, Rachel, Anna and Macaroon; and to the memory of Jean Kelly, Abel Solomon and my grandparents.

Nicole McGehee

I would like to thank my late husband, my mother and my mother-in-law for years of unflagging support, love and encouragement. Without their confidence in me, and their strength, my writing career would not be possible. Michael, I miss you more each day.

Table of Contents

Directory of Maps

Washington, DC and Surrounding Counties

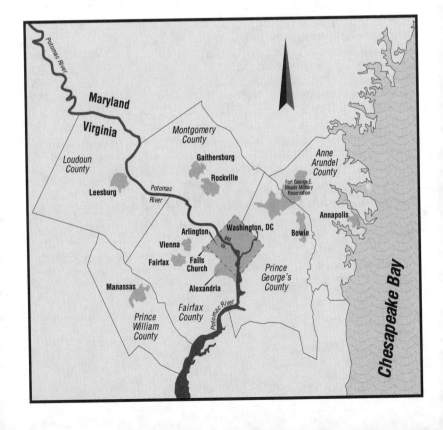

Metro Washington, DC

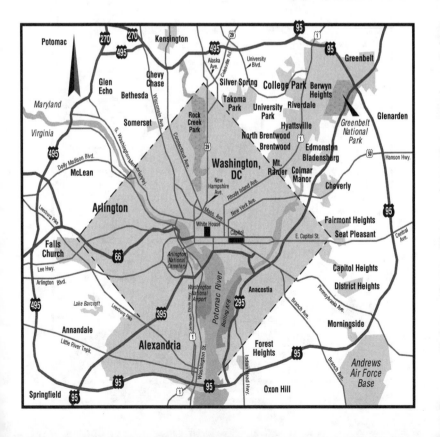

The Mall and Vicinity

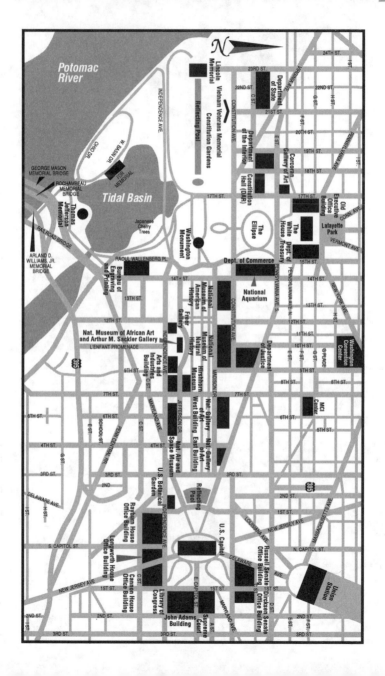

Metrorail
System

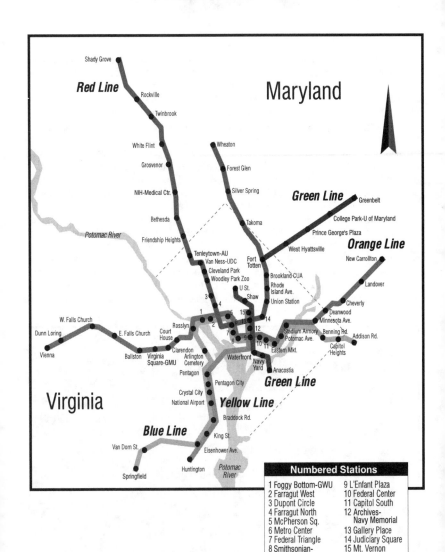

Red Line

Shady Grove
Rockville
Twinbrook
White Flint
Grosvenor
NIH-Medical Ctr.
Bethesda
Friendship Heights
Tenleytown-AU
Van Ness-UDC
Cleveland Park
Woodley Park Zoo

Maryland

Wheaton
Forest Glen
Silver Spring
Takoma
Fort Totten

Green Line

Greenbelt
College Park-U of Maryland
Prince George's Plaza
West Hyattsville

Orange Line

New Carrollton
Landover
Cheverly
Deanwood
Minnesota Ave.
Benning Rd.
Addison Rd.
Capitol Heights

U St.
Shaw
Brookland-CUA
Rhode Island Ave.
Union Station

W. Falls Church
Dunn Loring
E. Falls Church
Court House
Rosslyn
Ballston
Virginia Square-GMU
Clarendon
Arlington Cemetery
Pentagon

Virginia

Stadium Armory
Potomac Ave.
Eastern Mkt.

Waterfront
Navy Yard
Anacostia

Green Line

Pentagon City
Crystal City
National Airport

Yellow Line

Braddock Rd.

Blue Line

Van Dorn St.
King St.
Eisenhower Ave.
Springfield
Huntington

Potomac River

Vienna

Potomac River

Numbered Stations

1 Foggy Bottom-GWU	9 L'Enfant Plaza
2 Farragut West	10 Federal Center
3 Dupont Circle	11 Capitol South
4 Farragut North	12 Archives-
5 McPherson Sq.	Navy Memorial
6 Metro Center	13 Gallery Place
7 Federal Triangle	14 Judiciary Square
8 Smithsonian-	15 Mt. Vernon
National Mall	Square-UDC

How to Use This Book

Whether you're visiting the Nation's Capital for a business trip or family vacation, relocating to the Washington Metro area or just looking for new ways to spend your leisure time, you'll find something of interest in this book. As longtime local residents, the authors are well-acquainted with the area, from its awe-inspiring landmarks to its diverse educational and cultural opportunities. We know firsthand the joy of hearing the National Symphony perform at the Kennedy Center, and the frustration of almost being late for the concert because of a Beltway traffic tie-up! We relish the chance to dine out at one of the city's exquisite restaurants — when we're not bargain-hunting at Potomac Mills.

We've designed this book as a portable, accessible guide to Washington, D.C., and its surrounding suburbs: Northern Virginia and Suburban Maryland. The paperback is small enough to stuff in a suitcase or backpack, yet detailed enough to give you an overview of this vast region's best cultural, historical and recreational attractions, as well as tips on how to get around and where to dine and sleep. If you're planning to stay awhile, check out the chapters on real estate, education, retirement, child care and healthcare. We also describe a variety of weekend getaways, ideal for travelers extending their vacations or residents in need of a quick escape.

In most chapters, you'll find information organized in a listing format under the three regional headers. Northern Virginia listings encompass the cities of Alexandria and Fairfax and the counties of Arlington, Fairfax, Loudoun and Prince William. Suburban Maryland includes Montgomery and Prince George's

counties, as well as occasional notable attractions in nearby Anne Arundel and Howard counties.

Wherever possible, we include an address and phone number, followed by a description of the attraction, event or organization, often including admission costs and hours of operation. For Restaurants, Accommodations, and Bed and Breakfasts and Country Inns, we include a price code with each listing. Please be aware that prices and hours are subject to change. Check the price-code keys in those chapters for explanations. Please note that you'll find some attractions mentioned in more than one chapter, and cross-referenced accordingly. For instance, we describe Smithsonian Institution museums in Attractions, but highlight their family programs in Kidstuff and detail their art collections in Arts.

Throughout the book, you'll also find Insider's Tips, helpful or entertaining tidbits of information that appear at the bottom of some pages. We've also included occasional "Close-ups," informative profiles and accompanying photos of special events and attractions.

We hope you'll find this guide to be a handy reference book. We also appreciate hearing from our readers. Tell us what you find helpful and let us know if something is missing. We update the book annually, and find your comments invaluable.

Write to us at:
Insiders' Guides
P.O. Box 2057
Manteo, NC 27954.

Life is never dull in Washington, D.C. The nation's capital regularly makes headlines, not only for its role in the national and international political scenes, but also for its local events.

History

The history of Washington, D.C., is a subject that fills countless volumes. From local happenings to international incidents, Washington, D.C. makes history regularly. Here, we offer a thumbnail sketch of Washington history, featuring many of the city's landmark events from its shaky beginnings to now. For more about the economics and lifestyle of today's city, see the Overview chapter.

Creating a Capital

He's not only the Father of Our Country: George Washington also is the Father of Washington, the District of Columbia, in the sense that our first president chose the site for the nation's capital that would be named in his honor.

During the years immediately following the Revolutionary War, Northerners and Southerners had fierce debates over where to put the permanent capital city. Philadelphia was a top contender, as were New York and Charlestown. The two sides finally struck a deal in 1790, a concession forged between two of the greatest political leaders in America: Alexander Hamilton, a New York Federalist and fiscal conservative, and Thomas Jefferson, a Virginia agrarian liberal. The terms were straightforward; Jefferson's Southerners agreed to support Hamilton's proposal that the federal government assume the war debts of the 13 original states if, and only if, Hamilton's Northerners would agree to move the capital city (which then was in Philadelphia) to the South, to a veritable wilderness along the banks of Potomac River.

President George Washington, a surveyor by profession, honed in on what he deemed an ideal site in 1791, chosen for its convenient central location to the states and its proximity to the Potomac River, considered a likely boon for commerce. Never mind that the area consisted of scattered farms and murky riverside

corridors that resembled swamps to most who saw them. Washington could picture in its place a magnificent city, and he knew just the person to put his dream to paper: Pierre Charles L'Enfant, a French-born architect who had volunteered in the American Revolutionary army. When presented with the task, L'Enfant — who had spent his childhood in the palace at Versailles, where his father served as an artist — conjured up visions of grandeur that rivaled royal European cities, and raised the eyebrows of government officials. The plan he mapped out contained wide, tree-lined streets, including a mile-long avenue with a Congressional building at one end and a presidential "palace" at the other. He imagined large parks adorned with statues and fountains. L'Enfant had his own ideas of how to do things and he increasingly ruffled feathers as he refused to follow government-ordered instructions and deadlines. Eventually, Washington had no choice but to fire him. L'Enfant's original plan remained largely intact, however. Surveyor Andrew Ellicott and his African-American assistant, Benjamin Banneker, who had mapped out the district's 10-mile-square boundaries, continued laying out the city's grid-like street designs.

The City Slowly Takes Shape

The grand city L'Enfant and Washington envisioned didn't spring up overnight. On the contrary, people were in no great rush to settle into a place characterized by damp, mosquito-infested areas, free-roaming farm animals and more muddy roads than elegant boulevards. Even in 1800, with the Capitol's north wing completed and the government relocated from its temporary Philadelphia headquarters, one local citizen described the capital as "a town of streets without houses." George Washington also had selected the location for the White House, and although he laid the cornerstone in 1792 and lived to see the building's completion, he never occupied the presidential residence. The honor of being first to live at the historic address fell upon second President John Adams and his wife, Abigail, who found the mansion to be an inconvenient work in progress for quite some time after they arrived in 1800. Washington, D.C., received its city charter in 1802, along with a local government that included a mayor appointed by the president and a council chosen by the residents. Although officially a city, it remained a scourge to many Congress members, who found it crowded, dirty and unbearably hot and humid in the summer. Even Thomas Jefferson, president from 1801 to 1809, retreated to his Charlottesville home to escape the heat. From 1800 to 1803, the population rose from 3,000 to only 8,000 people.

A Devastating Fire

The city still possessed an ambiance of incompleteness in 1814, when, two years after the start of the War of 1812, British troops invaded the city and set fire to most of the public buildings. They set the Capitol on fire, as well as the President's House, as the White House was called until the Roosevelt administration. First Lady Dolley Madison, waiting for husband James to return from a trip, hesitated to leave their home even after James sent orders for her to evacuate. She refused to go before securing several of her husband's papers and Gilbert Stuart's portrait of George Washington, which has continued to hang in the White House throughout the years. Although rainy weather helped contain the fires, the Capitol and President's House received exten-

sive damage. The Madisons finished out James' term in temporary residences, as the President's House repairs weren't complete until James Monroe took office in 1817. The Capitol took even longer to rebuild: It wasn't finished until 1830.

The Capital Grows

As the city was rebuilt over the next few years, more and more people began to move there. By 1822, the population had increased to more than 15,000 people, including many freed blacks. Over the next several years, citizens saw the beginnings of what would become some of the area's best-known attractions.

An Act of Congress in 1821 created George Washington University, which would grow into a nationally recognized school of higher education (see our Education chapter for more on the university today). The National Theater, founded in 1835, was one of the city's first cultural attractions. It suffered through five fires and a partial collapse over the years, but still continues to entertain Washingtonians with plays and concerts. In 1846, the government founded the Smithsonian Institution with money willed to the country by James Smithson, a British scientist who wanted the United States to build an establishment to promote knowledge.

Construction began in 1848 on the Washington Monument, deviating greatly from the proposed equestrian statue included in L'Enfant's original plan. Due to a lack of finances, the 555-foot-tall obelisk wasn't completed until 1884, and didn't open to the public for four years after that. The city's first art gallery, the Corcoran Gallery of Art, got its start in 1859. Today it ranks not only as the oldest, but also as one of the finest and largest. (See the Attractions chapter for more about visiting these places.)

The Birthnight Ball, a social celebration of George Washington's birthday, began during his lifetime and still takes place every year in Alexandria.

Photo: Courtesy of The Fairfax Economic Development Authority

Colvin Run Mill is one of the many historic sites in the Washington area.

On a sad historical note, 1841 saw the first death of a president in office. William Henry Harrison delivered his inaugural address while standing outside in cold drizzle — for about 90 minutes. One month later, he succumbed to pneumonia and Vice President John Tyler was sworn in, during in indoor ceremony.

The Civil War Takes Its Toll

Washington, D.C., found itself in a precarious position as the Civil War raged from 1861 to 1865. Located 60 miles south of the Mason-Dixon Line and just 100 miles north of Richmond, the Confederate capital, the city was pulled in both directions. Washington became overcrowded with camps, temporary shelters and hundreds of soldiers and escaped slaves who flocked to the city. Housing grew scarce and disease ran rampant. (See the Civil War

chapter for a more detailed description of the war's effects on Washington and its neighboring states.) Even though the war ended in 1865, the year proved tumultuous for the city. The budding Smithsonian Institution lost its original collection of artifacts in a fire at its castle headquarters. And the country suffered a devastating loss: President Abraham Lincoln, attending a performance at Ford's Theatre, was fatally shot by the deranged Confederate activist John Wilkes Booth.

Changes in Government

Through the remainder of the 1800s, the city took shape, in terms of government and appearance, as a capital in which the nation could feel proud. In 1871, Congress took control of the District, initiating plans to improve the streets and add sewers and water and gas lines. It also annexed the neighboring tobacco port town of Georgetown, popular for its tav-

INSIDERS' TIP

Edward Kennedy Ellington — better known as "Duke" — was born in Washington D.C. in 1899. Today a public magnet school for the arts and a bridge are named in honor of the jazz composer, musician and band leader, whose boyhood home still stands in northwest Washington.

erns and residential district. The city in 1872 began planting trees systematically, creating the beginnings of many of Washington's current vistas. The White House brightened up with electric lights in 1890, the same year that cable cars began operating. Congress changed the city's government again in 1878, creating a municipal corporation with three Presidential-appointed, Senate-approved commissioners. Washington and the nation endured yet another tragedy in 1881, when angry civil servant Charles Guiteau shot President William Garfield. Although the president hung on for two months while doctors tried to help him recover, he eventually died as a result of his two wounds, and Guiteau was executed.

On the cultural front, this period saw the 1871 founding of Howard University, now the nation's largest predominantly African-American university (see the Education chapter). The Smithsonian expanded with the addition of artifacts from Philadelphia's Centennial Exposition of 1876, the National Zoological Park found a home at Rock Creek Park in 1890 and the Library of Congress opened in 1897. *The Washington Post*, now the city's oldest daily newspaper, first went to press in 1877 (see the Media chapter).

A New Century

The 1900s brought more changes to the nation's capital. Cars took to the now-paved roadways, and in 1908 the city opened a splendid, new railroad terminal, Union Station. The city's first park commission, created in 1901, strove to improve the city's appearance, in accordance with L'Enfant's original plan. In 1912, Washington received what would become one of its internationally known trade-

marks: Japanese cherry trees, a gift from the city of Tokyo. The delicate blossoms continue each spring to transform the shores of the Tidal Basin — created in 1900 — into a frothy cloud of pink and white. By 1910, Washington's population had grown to 330,000. As the country entered World War I in 1917, new workers arrived in the city in droves, driving the population up to more than 430,000 by 1920.

Another famous landmark made its debut in 1922: The Lincoln Memorial, with its majestic statue of the seated president, designed by American sculptor Daniel Chester French. (Seventeen years later, the memorial steps served as a concert stage for contralto Marian Anderson, who performed a free concert after the DAR refused to allow a black woman to sing in their Constitution Hall.) The year 1922 also brought the city's worst tragedy: As Knickerbocker Theater patrons watched the final few minutes of a silent movie, the building's roof suddenly collapsed under the weight of piles of heavy snow. Caught off-guard, the audience was unable to escape, and 96 people perished.

A New Deal and Beyond

In 1932, following the Great Depression, President Franklin D. Roosevelt promised the nation a New Deal, and his Works Progress Administration program did indeed create many new jobs in the city. The '30s marked a boom in Washington construction, and many of the city's familiar landmarks opened during this time. In 1932, the Folger Shakespeare Library opened, and the Supreme Court moved into its majestic new quarters in 1935. The National Archives Building — which houses our country's most treasured documents, the Declaration of In-

---

INSIDERS' TIP

Historical societies and offices can help you dig up facts about local people and places. Following are some local resources: Historical Society of Washington, D.C., (202) 785-2068; Montgomery County Historical Society, (301) 762-1492; Prince George's County Historical Society, (301) 464-0590; Office of Historic Alexandria, (703) 838-4554; Arlington Historical Society Museum, (703) 892-4204; and Historical Society of Fairfax County, (703) 246-2123.

dependence, Constitution and Bill of Rights — also opened its doors in 1935. The government work force grew again when we entered World War II in 1941, ushering in the city's modern era. The West Building of the National Gallery of Art, containing some of the world's greatest art treasures, opened in 1941. (The East Building addition opened 30 years later, fittingly exhibiting more modern works.) In 1943, the Pentagon, the nation's largest office building, sprung up just across the river in Arlington, Virginia. In 1942, another striking monument, The Jefferson Memorial, joined the ranks of the city's best-loved landmarks. Renovations of the Capitol and White House ushered in the '50s.

Civil Rights

With the nation still divided on issues regarding race, Washington became a major player in the civil rights struggles of the 1950s and '60s. In 1954, the U.S. Supreme Court's ruling in the Brown v. Board of Education case led to Washington became one of the first major cities to integrate its schools. In 1963, around 200,000 civil rights supporters participated in the peaceful, historic March on Washington, which culminated at the Lincoln Memorial, as Martin Luther King Jr. delivered his stirring "I Have A Dream" speech.

Later in 1963, the assassination of President John F. Kennedy in Dallas cast a pall over Washington and the entire nation. Five years later, King again offered a memorable speech in the capital city: his final sermon. Just days after addressing the congregation of Washington National Cathedral, King was assassinated in Memphis. The sad event triggered deadly, destructive riots here and in other cities.

It is worthy to note that King's event in 1963 set the stage for later, larger marches, from the 250,000-person anti-Vietnam war demonstration in 1969 to the Million Man March staged by 800,000 or more African-American men and boys in 1995. In 1997, approximately 500,000 Christian men converged on the National Mall for a six-hour Promise Keepers' rally, perhaps the country's largest religious gathering ever.

The Watergate Era

What began as a 1972 break-in by Republican campaign workers at the Democratic Party headquarters in the Watergate Hotel launched an embarrassing tale of corruption that reached all the way to the White House. Washington Post reporters Carl Bernstein and Bob Woodward earned a Pulitzer Prize for their investigative work uncovering the country's biggest political scandal. The revelations forced President Richard M. Nixon to resign from office in August of 1974.

Along with the nationally oriented changes that took place in Washington in the '60s and '70s came an evolution in the city's government. In 1961, the 23rd Amendment to the Constitution granted District residents the right to vote in national elections. Three years later, they voted in their first presidential election. A charter change in 1967 allowed the city a chief executive, assistant and nine council members. In 1970, Washington residents elected a nonvoting representative to the U.S. House of Representatives, and 1973 brought about the Home Rule Charter, allowing the city to elect a mayor and 13-member council, but giving Congress the power to veto legislation. Under the charter, the president appoints local judges, and local criminal cases fall under the jurisdiction of the U.S. Attorney General's Office.

The 1970s also brought positive cultural additions to Washington. The beautiful Kennedy Center for the Performing Arts opened in 1971, and the National Air and Space Museum — now the Smithsonian's most popular museum — began welcoming visitors in 1976.

Photo: Courtesy of Mark Downey, Virginia Tourism Corporation

Officially known as the U.S. Marine Corps War Memorial, the Iwo Jima statue is the largest bronze statue in the world.

The nation held its collective breath in 1981, when President Ronald Reagan was shot by John Hinckley Jr. outside the Washington Hilton. The assassination attempt failed, and the president recovered quickly, but his press secretary, James Brady, was shot in the head and suffered permanent brain damage. The incident was the catalyst for the Brady Bill, which led to the passage of a law requiring a waiting period before handgun purchases.

The following year brought the District a pair of tragedies. An Air Florida plane crashed into the Fourteenth Street Bridge shortly after takeoff, killing most of the passengers. That same day, a Metro train crashed, causing three fatalities.

Washington Today

Life is never dull in Washington, D.C. The nation's capital regularly makes headlines, not only for its role in the national and international political scenes, but also for its local events. In 1990, stunned TV audiences watched a surveillance videotape of Washington Mayor Marion Barry caught smoking crack cocaine in a Washington hotel room. Not surprisingly, Barry lost re-election, as voters chose instead Sharon Pratt Dixon, the first African American woman to become mayor of a major U.S. city. Barry made a comeback though, winning re-election in 1994, even after having served time in federal prison.

Violence, drug use and city mismanagement continue to plague Washington, and the troubled District government is, for all intents and purposes, being run by a Congressionally mandated control board.

Washington remains a city of contrasts, however, and problems aside, the nation's capital deserves to be in the spotlight for many of its innovations and contributions. The '90s have witnessed the Washington Redskins football team win their third Super Bowl championship, the opening of the distinguished National Holocaust Memorial Museum and the 150th birthday of the Smithsonian Institution. Last year alone saw the grand reopening of the renovated Library of Congress, dedication of the inspiring Franklin Delano Roosevelt and Women in Military Service memorials, a $400 million facelift for Ronald Reagan Washington National Airport and a brand new 20,000-seat sports/entertainment arena. So, whether you live here or are just passing through, now's your chance to take a closer look at Washington, D.C., and create your own personal history in this intriguing city.

The District's Neighbors

The areas that lie just beyond the District's borders — Montgomery and Prince George's counties in Maryland and Alexandria and Arlington and Fairfax counties — are themselves rich with history. Alexandria was, until 1846, included in the Washington boundaries. Founded in 1749 by Scottish merchants along the banks of the Potomac, Alexandria served as a chief port of trade during the Revolutionary years. George Washington was a prominent town figure, active in Christ Church Parish and other civic organizations. Another resident, esteemed soldier and statesman "Light-Horse" Harry Lee, in 1799 delivered the now-famous eulogy that described Washington as "First in war, first in peace, and first in the hearts of his countrymen." Lee's son Robert Edward, commander in chief of the Confederate armies during the Civil War, spent his childhood in Alexandria. His "Boyhood Home" remains a tourist attraction. Much of colonial Alexandria still stands, and its brick side streets and quaint townhouses make Old Town Alexandria a popular tourist destination. Amidst the residential developments, shopping centers and office buildings that proliferate in the modern-day counties of metro Maryland and Virginia, one still finds traces of the prehistoric wilderness discovered by English settlers in the 1600s. A few remaining plantations offer a view of the Colonial lifestyle. The Civil War's profound impact on the region is chronicled in this book's Civil War chapter.

In the '90s, for better or for worse, Washington remains the single most important political center in the world — the unquestioned, dominant political force.

Metro Washington
Overview

Like the elected officials that come and go, Washington is in perpetual transition. It's a markedly different creature today than it was just 10 years ago — let alone in 1800, the year it became the nation's capital. It is fitting that Washington's growing pains reflect America's. It was almost destroyed in the War of 1812, and in the Civil War it reflected the nation's hotly divided sentiments. It celebrated the arrival of the Second Industrial Revolution and the success of the great barons who transformed the nation's economic landscape. It teemed with energy and a sense of sacrifice during World Wars I and II. It grew wary and then outright divided over the Korean and Vietnam wars. It became cynical in the wake of Watergate; hopeful, then pessimistic during the Carter years; and a bit overconfident during the Reagan/Bush tenure. Now, in the latter part of the Clinton era, Washingtonians — and the newcomers who arrived with his administration only to face a new-look Congress brought about by the landmark midterm elections of 1994 — seem to be girding themselves for change.

The downtown area and many of the surrounding suburbs are in the midst of a building boom, even a cultural renaissance. Trend-setting restaurants and retailers, which in past years eschewed Washington as too stodgy, now compete for hot metro locations. High-ticket designer boutiques are represented here, as are star conglomerates like Planet Hollywood and Hard Rock Cafe.

To really understand where the District and its surrounding suburbs are today and where they're headed in the 21st century, it's helpful to go back a few decades, to at least the beginning of the post-World War II years. As the 1940s gave way to the '50s, Washington's population soared. In the nearby countryside of Maryland and Virginia, forests of oak and pastures of blue grass yielded to subdivisions and shopping centers. Business was booming. The future looked bright. As the federal government continued to grow dramatically during the '60s, so did the physical size (and, some may say, the ego) of the region.

Then came a bombshell, a watershed event that changed the face of Washington and impacted the entire country: the 1968 assassination of the Rev. Martin Luther King Jr. Parts of Washington erupted into a riot zone. Many residents who could afford to, fled to suburban enclaves. The city became a ghost town by night. The suburbs ballooned farther out, and the resulting polarization was both psychological and physical. On the one hand were the commuters, a daily influx who increased traffic problems exponentially, but paid no taxes that might have helped the D.C. infrastructure meet new demands placed on it. Remaining in Washington were the riot survivors, who lived in burned-out neighborhoods a few blocks from the White House. Amidst the downtown chaos were pockets of extreme affluence: Georgetown, Foxhall Road, Embassy Row. The lines of demarcation were clear and rarely crossed.

The Vietnam war and the Watergate era, culminating in President Richard Nixon's resignation in 1973, only added to the divisiveness in Washington. But those events also indirectly revitalized D.C. because they brought about a new era of grassroots activism. The activism resulted in closer interaction between government and industry as consumer advocates and environmental groups demanded that Washington investigate and regulate U.S. business. No large company or industry in America could afford to be without a presence in the nation's capital. Some opened government relations offices, some funded industry coalitions, and some even moved their companies' headquarters to the area. Big government started to get strong competition from big business for the Metro D.C. labor force. In reality, each was fueling the growth of the other as business realized that it would have to answer to government. At the same time, government experts on industry were a labor pool in high demand by the very companies they oversaw. Many were and are wooed by the private sector, thus the infamous Washington "revolving door."

Today, 75 percent of the world's multinational corporations have a foothold here, and a third, or nearly 2,500, of the nation's trade and professional associations are headquartered in Metro D.C.

The Washington area claims more than 200 telecommunications and information giants, including MCI, Bell Atlantic and COMSAT. Journalism is big business here as there are some 4,100 correspondents, newspapers, wire services, news agencies and radio and television networks (the highest concentration of journalists in the world is here). Fortune 500 companies as diverse as Mobil, Gannett, General Dynamics, USAir, Marriott and Lockheed Martin also call the metro area home.

But Washington's growth hasn't all been a facile, downhill coast. In the mid to late 1980s, local business development officials used to talk of Washington's "recession-proof" economy. They touted the fact that the federal government's employment and spending base had a stabilizing effect on the economy, and that the diversity of business here was too great to allow for any major slowdowns.

Well, things didn't quite turn out that way. Washington, like everywhere else, was hit hard by the recession. Commercial real estate, already dangerously over-built, took a beating in 1990 and '91, primarily due to unleased existing space and a dramatic slowdown in new development. Defense contractors awoke to a post-Cold War new world order and an anticipation of scarcer federal outlays. Banks failed. Engineers, architects, technicians and journalists, among others, were handed pink slips faster than Congress writes checks. Unemployment jumped. Local governments wrestled with fiscal problems. Those accustomed to the prosperity of the '80s were thinking the world was coming to an end.

In reality, though, Metro Washington fared much better than most other parts of the United States. The recession surfaced later here, packed far less sting, and was quicker to leave. Unemployment never got much beyond 4 percent, a figure most communities would envy during the best of times. The darkest days have passed, it seems. The economy continues to improve, folks are going back to work, new houses are being built and more office space is being absorbed.

While the business-development people may have blown their recession-proof theory, they were on target as far as the diversity of the economy is concerned. The region's broad mix of industry is one of the great untold economic stories of the past decade.

www.insiders.com

See this and many other **Insiders' Guide®** destinations online — in their entirety.

Visit us today!

INSIDERS' TIP

The area climate is temperate. Here is some pertinent data: The average maximum temperature in the summer is 88 degrees, minimum is 70; average maximum winter temperature is 43 degrees, minimum is 32; average annual rainfall is 39 inches, for snowfall it's 16 inches. We average seeing 101 clear days per annum, 111 days typically bring precipitation.

Photo: Courtesy of the Washington, DC Convention and Vistors Association

The Lincoln Memorial, the Washington Monument and the U.S. Capitol mark the beginning, middle and end, respectively, of the National Mall.

In fact, since 1980, a staggering 98 percent or so of all jobs created in the metro area, or nearly 650,000 new positions, have been attributed to the private sector, in areas like high-tech and bio-tech, telecommunications, finance and construction. To be sure, federal employment has remained steady but now is only 16.7 percent of the total work force compared with 25 percent at the beginning of the Reagan/Bush era. On top of that, even when you factor in the thousands of jobs supplied by local and state governments, the private sector still comes out way ahead of the game. All told, big business employs 74 percent of metro Washingtonians. Big government, 26 percent.

So what does this tell us? First, we'd be kidding ourselves to dismiss the economic importance of the government's presence. Nobody spends money like federal Washington, and no one feels the effects of those shopping sprees more than our local economy. The feds spend upward of $40 billion in the region each year, which accounts for 65 percent of Metro D.C.'s gross regional product.

At the same time, Washington's growing stature as an international business center has brought the benefit of a more sound, more flexible economy. This also has had a stabilizing effect on the region's psyche. We're no longer all that transient. Businesses and people are staying put, thus redefining the social and economic character of the region. And Washington newcomers and visitors are once again being drawn to a revived city center.

Practically every block of the District's major, historic artery, Pennsylvania Avenue, has been renovated with new plazas, office space, retail areas, theaters, restaurants and more. The "Avenue of the Presidents," once deserted by night, has again become a thriving thoroughfare, and its renewal has sparked development throughout the rest of downtown. On Capitol Hill, Washington's historic Union Station was painstakingly restored in a years-long project, and is now the "grande dame" of all train stations. It houses Amtrak corporate headquarters and serves as their flagship station, with trains arriving and departing from beneath the magnificent, statue-lined roof.

In the District of Columbia, information and power spring not only from business and government but also from global financial institutions such as the World Bank and the International Monetary Fund. Equally vital are the city's 150-plus embassies that provide instant access to commercial and government representatives from nearly every nation.

The region's inordinate supply of research institutions and business incubators bodes well for firms aiming to diversify away from federal purse strings and into the commercial sector. Indeed, this so-called "technology transfer" remains one of the biggest challenges facing the region as it heads into the new millennium.

Washington's transformation from a government- to a private-sector information-driven economy mirrors one of the most pervasive trends in our global society. The international marketplace of the late 20th century is fueled first and foremost by information. Information is power, and Washington is a wellspring of both commodities.

Chances are, if you're a newcomer to the nation's capital, you're part of this new dynamic.

The Washington Work Force

If you're looking for a job in Metro D.C., or even if you've already landed one, it's good to know a few vital statistics about the Washington work force. Besides, a few provocative figures here and there will go a long way on the Washington cocktail-party circuit.

Let's start with the big picture: Some 2.2 million people are employed in the Washington area, 72 percent working in white-collar jobs. That's the highest such percentage in the country and a full 15 percent higher than the national average.

Sounds impressive enough, but wait . . . it gets even more striking. The region claims the largest percentage of executive, administrative, managerial, professional and technical workers among the nation's largest metropolitan areas. The proportion of scientists, technicians and Ph.D.s working in Metro D.C. is unsurpassed, and the number of computer specialists is greater than Boston and San Francisco combined. Employment in communications, finance and retail has seen a percentage increase of 47, 41 and 39 respectively since 1980. The service industry overall has gained 84 percent more jobs during that period, to total roughly 860,000 positions.

If you're a woman, you're in good company here. A full two-thirds of working-age women in greater Washington are employed, with 25 percent of them in professional and managerial positions. Again, on both accounts, these are the highest such percentages in the United States.

With three out of five of its residents African American, the District of Columbia has long been the nation's most influential and affluent predominantly black city. Today, the entire region boasts the leading percentage of black executives, administrators and managers. Little surprise then that the fast-growing cable network, Black Entertainment Television, is headquartered in the District. In recent years, Washington also has experienced a surge in entrepreneurship among its growing Asian, Hispanic, Middle Eastern and Indian communities.

Of course, at the root of Washington's white collars is education. The metro area inarguably has the best-educated work force in the United States. Nearly 40 percent of area adults age 25 and older hold college degrees, almost twice the national average. In addition, 55 percent have some college experience, and enrollment in continuing-education programs in local colleges is among the highest anywhere.

Beyond all the grand statistics, however, are some very down-to-earth implications. More and more young people are launching their careers in Metro Washington despite the intensely competitive nature of the labor force, especially for entry-level positions. Maybe more important, fewer are packing their bags after a couple of years. A full 45 percent of the region's population is between the ages of 25 and 49, making the Washington work force the youngest in the nation.

Where the Jobs Will Be

Good show, newcomers. Your timing couldn't have been better. Although it's unlikely we'll ever see the kind of economic expansion we had around here in the '80s, Metro Washington is well positioned for long, sustained growth over the next two decades. As the shift from federal to private-sector employment continues unabated, it's estimated there will be 1.3 million more workers out there by the year 2010, the vast majority in highly skilled service occupations.

We'll likely see a steady climb in the ranks of high-tech, bio-tech and telecommunications workers, as well as in manufacturing and clerical positions. By the end of the decade, the region will have nearly 32,000 more elementary and secondary schoolteachers than in 1985, 20,000 more college educators, 14,000 more nurses, 23,000 more computer specialists and 9,000 more electrical engineers. We'll also see 37,000 more secretaries, 10,000 more accountants and, yes, even 9,000 more lawyers. In a nutshell, the job market is wide open.

Growing Pains

Unfortunately, there's a dark side to the boom of the past decade — it hasn't been confined to legitimate enterprises. It has also ushered in an ominous problem that continues to plague Washington. Drug trafficking, primarily in crack cocaine, began paralyzing neighborhoods throughout the inner city. Consequently, by 1988, the District of Columbia had become the "Murder Capital of the World"; while violence indeed remains a serious problem in the District, the un-savory moniker has since been hung on other cities with greater frequency. In fact, Washington's violent crime rate ranks far below that of many cities including Atlanta, Dallas, Houston, Miami and New Orleans. The best advice for visitors to Washington, as in any big city, is to use caution and common sense. Random acts of violence in usually quiet areas are of course a reality too; yet, by simply using everyday street smarts, locals and tourists alike should feel perfectly comfortable in Washington's main tourism and business sectors.

Still, it is sad to point out that crime is common just a few blocks from Capitol Hill, that several residents of exclusive Georgetown have been mugged while taking an evening walk, and that D.C.'s red-light district is located in what is by day the thriving business corridor bordered by 14th and 15th streets NW. To sum up, don't be paranoid, but be cautious.

One of the city's most well-known bad boys — now apparently reformed — is the mayor himself, Marion Barry, who in 1990 was arrested for possessing and using the same crack cocaine that was devastating so much of his city. His actions, which were captured on film by police using a hidden camera, severely scarred, perhaps terminally, Washington's national and international image. Who would have imagined that in 1994, after serving time in a federal prison, Barry would be reelected to the same office he left in disgrace?

Washington at the Millenium

In the '90s, for better or for worse, Washington remains the single-most-important political center in the world, the unquestioned, dominant political force. In Berlin and Moscow, communism has been dismantled and the countries' entrepreneurs have embraced

The USA Today towers provide an outstanding view of Washington, D.C.

U.S.-style capitalism with gusto. In South Africa, the U.S.-initiated embargo finally has led to the abandonment of apartheid and the election of former political prisoner Nelson Mandela as president. In recent years, the U.S. has taken center stage in places like the Middle East, Bosnia and Haiti. So as Moscow fumbles over social and economic woes, and Tokyo reels from the effects of an overheated economy, no real challenge to Washington's power appears on the horizon for the remainder of the millenium.

Illustrative of Washington's power is the aforementioned revival of the city itself. A new, 20,000-seat sport/entertainment complex called the MCI Center opened in midtown in December of 1997. Local officials expect the arena to generate more than $150 million a year in economic benefits and $10 million a year in taxes. Ronald Reagan Washington National Airport's dazzling new terminal opened in 1997 after $400 million of construction to provide new air-traffic-control facilities, a moving sidewalk system, expanded parking, shops, restaurants and a network of convenient walkways (see the Transportation chapter). If you arrive at Dulles International Airport, you'll see that an expansion of equal proportions is ongoing there. In fact, almost everywhere you look in the city or the outlying suburbs, you'll see building cranes and road construction — the buzz is palpable.

Quite frankly, it's more than history that draws people to Washington, it's the vitality of the area. Whether you live here or visit, you'll feel the excitement in the air.

Northern Virginia

The Monolith That Is Fairfax County

Since 1980, the suburbs have claimed 80 percent of Metro Washington's employment growth, and two-thirds of these new jobs have been placed in Northern Virginia, principally Fairfax County. All told, there are now more than 818,000 jobs in Northern Virginia, compared with the District's 730,000 and suburban Maryland's 719,000.

Fairfax County, which encircles the self-governed municipalities of Falls Church,

Fairfax City, Vienna and Herndon, houses some of the biggest employers in the metro area including Mobil, AT&T, BDM International, EDS Corp. and Mitre. Defense giant, General Dynamics, even moved its national headquarters here from St. Louis. Fairfax County also claims the largest share of international firms in Metro D.C. Among the 100 foreign-based or affiliated companies here are France's Lafarge Corp., Japan's Canon USA, Britain's BT North America and Canada's and Australia's Molson Breweries USA. One of the nation's most populous and economically vibrant suburban areas, Fairfax County is the driving force of Northern Virginia and, for that matter, much of Metro Washington. With a population fast approaching 900,000, it has more residents than several states and almost twice the number of the District of Columbia. Moreover, nearly one in seven Virginians lives in the county.

But it's more than jobs that attract people to Fairfax County. Steeped in history — this is, after all, the home of George Washington and George Mason, father of the American Bill of Rights — the county is defined by a sense of civic orderliness and a commitment to a high standard of living. When English explorer John Smith, the first European to set eyes on the present-day Washington, D.C., ventured into the county in 1608, he was taken aback by the amount of wildlife and natural resources that graced the area — bounty he would later help claim for England.

If Smith were in Fairfax County today, he would also want to claim some of the finest public schools in the nation, a work force that is among the nation's most educated and affluent, and a public safety record that is the envy of most suburban jurisdictions.

Equally alluring to newcomers — especially families — are the county's extensive park lands, myriad shopping malls — including one of the nation's largest in Tysons Corner Center — upscale neighborhoods and abundant historical and recreational attractions.

The flip side to the county's fortunes are home costs, which as in most of the metro area, are among the highest in the nation, with affordable housing in seriously short supply. In addition, the infrastructure lags behind the pressures of a booming population. No matter what time of day, you can usually find a traffic jam somewhere in Fairfax County, though matters have improved with the construction of the Fairfax County Parkway, which winds its way from the northernmost limits of the county to the southern tip.

While the local government is largely responsive to these and other problems, Fairfax, especially to the uninitiated, must seem like a congested and hectic place. That aside, the county continues to be one of the region's most popular relocation sites. So much so that by century's end, the county's population could eclipse one million residents.

Urban Cousins: Arlington County and the City of Alexandria

Arlington County and the City of Alexandria are the alter egos to suburban Fairfax. Much more in tune with the urban pace of Washington (they were in fact part of the District of Columbia at one time), Arlington and Alexandria command a great influence on the nation's capital.

In Arlington, the self-proclaimed "Virginia Side of the Nation's Capital," you can find such Washington icons as the Pentagon, Arlington National Cemetery, the Iwo Jima Memorial and Washington National Airport. As in Alexandria, economic activity in Arlington historically has been tied to the federal government. In addition, both jurisdictions house hundreds of national and international associations, lobbyists and special-interest

INSIDERS' TIP

Before you mail a letter to an address in Chevy Chase, be sure you know whether the person lives in D.C. or Maryland. The two communities border each other.

groups, as well as a fair number of federal government offices. Nevertheless, Arlington and Alexandria contain their share of private industry. Arlington County serves as headquarters for USAir and Gannett Corporation. Other large employers include MCI, Bell Atlantic, and American Management Systems. Next door in Alexandria — one of the nation's oldest port cities and business centers — are the headquarters for the Public Broadcasting System, Crown Life Insurance USA, Time-Life Books, Inc., Softech and the Independent Insurance Agents of America.

Over the years, Arlington has assumed somewhat of a multiple personality. Self-contained communities such as Ballston, Crystal City, Pentagon City and Rosslyn, each with its own central business district, compete against each other as they bloom with shopping centers, towering offices and condos, and an inexhaustible supply of restaurants. The northern edge of the county contains upscale single-family homes, many on large lots with views of the Potomac and the District beyond, while the extreme southern end borders on seedy, with crime being a major concern. All told, some 186,000 people now call Arlington home. But unlike Fairfax County, which is the refuge of families with children, 73 percent of Arlington County's households are comprised of singles or two-adult families — perhaps the most persuasive indication of Arlington's urban atmosphere.

Mention the word "Alexandria" and most people immediately think of Old Town, the city's charming and affluent historic district that hugs the banks of the Potomac. And for sure, history is a way of life in Old Town. Settled in 1749 by Scottish merchants, the city blossomed into one of the leading ports of Colonial America, driven in good measure by a lucrative trade in Virginia-grown tobacco. George Washington conducted a lot of business here and Robert E. Lee grew up here, later moving to Arlington House, now part of Arlington National Cemetery. Alexandria's venerable Christ Church has been visited by almost every president. The Revolutionary and Civil wars played out on Alexandria's streets, some of which look much the same today as they did in the early 19th century.

Walk around and you'll find block after block of painstakingly restored Federal-style homes interspersed between curio shops, inns, bars, restaurants, parks, churches and museums. So picturesque is Old Town that it draws 1.5 million visitors a year. Old Town wasn't always so gentrified, though. From the 1940s through the early '70s, hard times set in and much of the area was blighted with boarded-up shops and dilapidated homes. When the revitalization bug kicked in some 20 years ago, entire blocks of houses could have been purchased for a fraction of the present-day cost of a single home here. As you can imagine, many a fortune was made in Old Town. Among the upscale renovations, there still exist several housing projects, and most of the crime in Old Town occurs here in the form of drug-related wrong doing. Residents of nearby homes, no matter how affluent and well-protected, are also subject to burglaries and muggings from time to time. For the most part, you can avoid trouble by sticking to the crowded commercial areas and steering clear of the shadowy residential streets, whose many trees and alleys provide strategic hiding places for mischief makers.

Alexandria is more than Old Town, though many visitors think the two are synonymous. Most of its 118,000 residents live in diverse, outlying neighborhoods, like the West End, with its many high-rise apartments, and Beverly Hills, an established community of shaded streets and gracious homes. Further confusion arises from the fact that the City of Alexandria is surrounded by Alexandria, Fairfax County. Perhaps the most famous landmark in the expanded area is the community of Mount Vernon (mailing address Alexandria), with homes ranging from modest to baronial. As the name implies, George Washington's estate — also Mount Vernon — sits smack in the middle of the area. Leading to it is a bicycle path offering Potomac River vistas, a route popular with both tourists and residents. In fact, the George Washington Memorial Parkway, and the national park land adjoining it, make this one of the most scenic and bucolic corners of the metro area.

Prince William County

With more than 40 percent of its working-age residents commuting out of the county to their jobs, Prince William County is pretty much a vintage bedroom community. In the last decade the county's population surged from 145,000 to more than 260,000, a jump of nearly 80 percent, making it one of the nation's biggest gainers.

Newcomers arrive in masses here to live in nice, relatively affordable neighborhoods with improving schools and a surprisingly large amount of cultural and recreational diversions. It's a good place for families just starting out, and that's reflected by the median age of residents: 29 years old. A home that would cost $300,000 in Fairfax County might range in cost from $200,000 to $250,000 in Prince William, depending on its proximity to the county border, Interstate 66 or Interstate 95.

Prince William still contains huge tracts of undeveloped land, and is home to sprawling national and state parks, including the Manassas National Battlefield, one of the most important sites of the Civil War. Other attractions include a minor-league baseball team, several community theater groups and museums and the Nissan Pavilion at Stone Ridge, a state-of-the-art concert amphitheater. Here you'll also find the FBI Academy, Quantico Marine Base and Quantico National Cemetery, which is actually larger than Arlington National Cemetery.

Prince William has been extremely proactive in efforts to lure more employers to the county. However, not every corporate entity is welcome. The Walt Disney Co. was sent packing in 1994 after encountering fierce — and largely unexpected — opposition to an American history theme park it had proposed for the rolling countryside near the history-rich town of Haymarket. Some of the larger corporate names that do have a presence here include IBM and GTE, which have offices in Manassas, as well as Dynatech and Virginia Power, with locations in Woodbridge. Easily the biggest attraction in Prince William, though, is Potomac Mills, one of the biggest outlet shopping centers in the world and — incredibly — the single largest tourist attraction in the entire Commonwealth.

The Virginia Exurbs: Loudoun, Fauquier and Stafford Counties

The outlying Virginia counties of Loudoun, Fauquier and Stafford are at a crossroads as Metro Washington continues to expand in its radial fashion. Not quite totally suburban but neither completely rural anymore, the counties are what may be termed "exurban."

In a way, we're hesitant to lump Loudoun County into this category, since it is easily one of the fastest-developing outer jurisdictions in either Virginia or Maryland. Since 1980, its population has more than doubled from 57,000 to 126,000. Nevertheless, with only about one-seventh the number of residents of Fairfax County, Loudoun is still mostly wide open spaces. More than 200,000 acres are devoted to agriculture, compared to just more than 71,000 for housing and 20,000 for commercial enterprises. A vocal group of natives and newcomers would like to keep it that way. That's why you'll see the heaviest concentration of commercial and residential activity kept to the eastern stretches of the county, from Leesburg to the Fairfax County line. Here is where you'll also find Washington Dulles International Airport (although a small piece sits in Fairfax), a major catalyst behind the county's growth, and a major source of employment. To the south and west of Leesburg, the county seat, is a sprawling patchwork of farms, orchards and horse pastures. It is here where Virginia's famed Hunt Country begins.

South of Loudoun is Fauquier County, with its equally beautiful horse farms and country estates. New housing developments in and around Warrenton, the county's largest community, are attracting more and more Metro D.C. commuters and even a growing number of retirees. Fauquier contains some of the most scenic land in the Old Dominion and consequently, like Loudoun, there is a considerable anti-growth sentiment here (or as some local government officials like to put it, "controlled growth").

Stafford County is a bit of a different story, however. Located just south of Prince William, it is actively wooing new residents and businesses with affordable land prices, the promise of relaxed living and easy access to Interstate 95. Folks are responding to the offer. During the '80s, the county's population recorded one of the highest percentage gains in Virginia. Stafford enjoys a close proximity to both Washington and Richmond and is bordered immediately to the south by the City of Fredericksburg, one of the most charming and historic communities in the Commonwealth. However, the access to I-95 is a mixed blessing, since the road is almost always snarled with traffic. Rush hour begins at noon on Fridays, since this is also the most widely used interstate route for tractor-trailers and others traveling along the east coast. At peak hours, the drive from Stafford County to Washington, D.C. can take up to two hours, so investigate carefully before you believe claims by Realtors of an "easy commute."

Suburban Maryland

The "State" of Montgomery County

Although diehards on both sides of the Potomac would probably never admit it, Montgomery County is to Maryland what Fairfax County is to Virginia. In terms of population, jobs, median household income and size, the two counties are strikingly similar. In other words, Montgomery County is an aberration of sorts. As Maryland's largest and most affluent county, one could argue — as do many lawmakers in Annapolis — that Montgomery is its own separate state. That might be overdoing it a bit, but this mega-county of about 820,000 residents is far more aligned, socially and economically, with the District and Northern Virginia than with Baltimore or any other part of the Free State.

At the same time, Montgomery in many ways is Metro D.C.'s most diverse jurisdiction. The southern half of the county is overwhelmingly white collar and decidedly urban. Here you'll find the posh homes and estates of Potomac and Chevy Chase, the retail meccas of White Flint and Montgomery malls, and the lost-in-time Victoriana of tiny Garrett Park (which has declared itself a nuclear-free zone). Here you'll also find an interesting mix of highly successful immigrants, with most hailing from Vietnam, India, Iran and China. Many come to work at the impressive campus of Bethesda's world-renowned National Institutes of Health or at the high-tech companies that flank Interstate 270.

The northern portion of Montgomery, or the "Upcounty" as locals emphatically refer to it, moves to a gentler, less-urban beat. Here, it's not unusual to see large dairy farms abutting business parks, or commuters coming to a halt at cattle crossings and creeping slowly behind tractors in the spring. A few years ago, a black bear cub emerged from the woods of Seneca Creek State Park and onto a heavily trafficked road. The cub returned to the wilds unscathed, but not before setting off one of the region's more memorable traffic jams. While the Upcounty is proud of its efforts to preserve open space — Montgomery has set aside more farmland than any other suburban county in the nation — the tenor of the place is rapidly changing. Subdivisions now extend north of Gaithersburg, transforming once-sleepy areas like Germantown and Damascus into bustling bedroom communities favored by young professionals seeking affordable housing. Onetime apple orchards and wheat fields increasingly are sprouting single-family homes and shopping centers.

The Melting Pot of Prince George's County

In 1988, one of the largest commercial developers in Metro Washington broke ground on an ambitious project that came with the promise of virtually reinventing the image of Prince George's County. The huge development was to be called Port America, a stately, multipurpose business and residential community that would grace the banks of the Potomac River, within earshot of the busy Woodrow Wilson Bridge. But the national recession set in, legal hassles ensued, and today Port America remains largely a dream that has yet to materialize.

While it would be unfair to draw too much of a parallel between the fate of Port America and the county it wanted to call home, it's probably safe to say that Prince George's has still not yet totally arrived, at least not to the same degree as its more prosperous neighbors to the north and west. A chronic crime problem in the urban areas closest to Washington, coupled with some highly publicized criminal cases involving local government officials, have taken their toll on the county's image. Don't count "P.G." — as it's commonly called — and its 730,000 residents out of the picture, however.

The positives far outweigh the negatives. P.G., among other things, has always been the region's — if not one of the nation's — most established multiracial communities. Black, Caucasian, Hispanic and Asian Americans live side by side and largely in harmony in Prince George's. Affordable housing isn't a catchy buzzword; it's a reality. The county's public school system has made tremendous inroads in recent years, and its multilingual education program serves as a model for the nation.

P.G. is home to the University of Maryland, the state's flagship university with more than 30,000 students and a tradition-rich athletic program. The federal government's presence is also profound. Andrews Air Force Base, which is used by the president and many other government officials, the National Agricultural Research Center, NASA's Goddard Space Flight Center and the U.S. Census Bureau all call P.G. home.

If you're into spectator events, chances are you'll be spending some time in Prince George's. USAir Arena (concerts, ice skating, gymnastics) in Landover, Rosecroft and Laurel Raceways (horse racing), the new Jack Kent Cooke football stadium less than a mile away and the Prince George's Equestrian Center in Upper Marlboro entertain many thousands of Washingtonians throughout the year (see the Sports chapter).

A Sense of Place in Anne Arundel County

There's a certain feeling that pervades Anne Arundel County. Maybe it's due to Annapolis, the splendid Maryland capital city, with its colonial waterfront homes, the oldest State House in continuous use in the United States (since the 1770s) and imposing campuses of St. John's College and the United States Naval Academy. Maybe it's the quiet coves and inlets of the Magothy, Severn and South rivers. Or maybe it's the broad, sweeping views of the Chesapeake Bay afforded from atop hilly pastures dotted with wooden tobacco barns and thoroughbred horses. From whatever it springs, it's hard not to feel an acute sense of place in Anne Arundel, a county as beautiful as its name suggests.

Not too many decades ago, Washingtonians built summer homes here and the county's economy was associated largely with the state government and the fishing and sailing trades of the Chesapeake Bay.

Today, Anne Arundel is grappling with a new identity. The past decade ushered in a surge in population, fueled in large part by the well-documented economic fortunes of nearby Baltimore and Washington. Many of the county's 450,000 or so residents now make the 25-plus-mile commute into the District and other parts of Metro Washington — a feat virtually unheard of 20 years ago. Rapid suburbanization has had its share of nasty side effects like increased crime and housing costs, but all told, Anne Arundel retains a remarkably high quality of life. Indeed, this is its main selling point. And while longtime residents vehemently resist the notion of being part of Metro D.C. or Baltimore, there is an accommodating attitude toward newcomers that are drawn to this enchanting, history-filled corner of Maryland.

Maryland's Exurbs: Frederick, Howard and Charles Counties

As suburban Maryland continues to creep farther out into the countryside, it's markedly changing the face of at least three outlying communities: Frederick, Howard and Charles counties.

Bounded by Pennsylvania to the north and Montgomery County to the south, Frederick County offers the perks of a relaxed country setting — this is the land of covered bridges, inns, vineyards and roadside produce stands — but with an undeniable air of big-city sophistication. In downtown Frederick, the county's principal city, one can munch on blue-corn tortillas and other trendy fare before taking in a gallery opening or browsing through dozens of antique shops. From here, you're about equal distance from Gettysburg, Pennsylvania, and downtown Washington, although the commute north is much easier. In winter, the ski slopes of White Tail and Liberty in Pennsylvania are only a bit more than 30 minutes away. Still, Frederick is less than an hour's drive from much of Metro D.C. and housing prices won't send your heart rate through the roof.

Howard County, lodged between Montgomery and Baltimore counties, is easily the most established Maryland exurb. Columbia, its largest community, is a planned city developed by the same folks responsible for revitalizing the inner harbors of Baltimore and Norfolk, Virginia. In Columbia, one can find the comforts of suburbia and the home-investment security that goes with intense zoning regulations. Like its Northern Virginia counterpart, Reston, Columbia may be a tad sterile for some, but its numerous tree-lined parkways and quiet residential areas give the impression of country living just 25 miles from either Washington or Baltimore. Merriweather Post Pavilion, one of the nation's first outdoor concert venues, brings top-name entertainment to the county throughout the warm-weather months.

South of Prince George's County, and just 20 miles from the District line, lies Charles County, a place where not too long ago tobacco and truck farming reigned supreme. An influx of new housing developments, especially along the U.S. Highway 301 corridor between Waldorf and La Plata, and the opening of the county's first shopping mall are helping to create a bona fide suburban atmosphere. The challenge of the future for Charles County inevitably will be forging a balance between development and preservation of its long-cherished rural lifestyle.

(Note: For information about independent cities within the above mentioned counties, consult our Neighborhoods and Real Estate chapter.)

Suggested Readings

An entire publishing subindustry has cropped up dealing with finding a job in Metro Washington. Among the better books in the genre are:

•*How to Get a Job in Washington*, *D.C.* by Thomas Camden and Karen Tracy Polk, Surrey Books Inc., 101 E. Erie Street, Suite 900, Chicago, Illinois 60611, (312) 751-7330 — An A to Z approach to landing a job in the metro area, including tips on resumes, locating the right contacts, dress and making yourself noticed.

•*How to Be Happily Employed in Washington, D.C.* by Janice Benjamin and Barbara Block, Random House, New York, New York

The U.S. Capitol looms majestically over the city as its tallest building.

— An outline of trends in employment, job options and overviews of Washington industries, including the government, tourism and hospitality sectors.

• *The Metropolitan Washington Job Bank* edited by Carter Smith, Bob Adams Inc. Publishers, 260 Center Street, Holbrook, Massachusetts 02343 — A popular job hunters' guide to the D.C. area, with comprehensive listings of companies and contacts selected by trade.

• *1,001 Great Opportunities for College Graduates: Jobs in Washington, D.C.* by Greg Diefenbach and Phillip Giordano, Impact Publications, 9104-N Manassas Drive, Manassas Park, Virginia 22111, (703) 361-7300 — A great graduation gift/survival tool for those hoping to tap into entry-level Washington. Interesting chapters on finding jobs in the media, health, education and environmental industries, plus working on Capitol Hill.

• *Find a Federal Job Fast!* by Ronald L. Krannich and Caryl Rae Krannich, Impact Publications, 4580 Sunshine Court, Woodbridge, Virginia 22192, (703) 361-7300 — Excellent resource to help you cut through the red tape that is so ubiquitous in federal Washington.

• *Federal Career Opportunities* by Federal Research Service Inc., 234 Church Street, Vienna, Virginia 22183-1059, (703) 281-0200 — A regularly updated booklet, found in virtually every bookstore in Washington, that lists all current job openings in the federal government, plus qualifications, contacts, salary structure and responsibilities.

Suggested Contacts

If you'd like to receive more specific information about the Metro Washington economy and/or labor market, we encourage you to contact the following agencies:

• District of Columbia Department of Employment Services, Labor Market Information Research Staff, 500 C Street NW, Room 200, Washington, D.C. 20001, (202) 724-7000.

• The Greater Washington Board of Trade, Office of Research, Policy, Transportation, 1129 20th Street NW, Suite 200, Washington D.C. 20036, (202) 857-5970. Or at the same address, the Greater Washington Initiative, (202) 857-5990.

• Maryland Department of Economic and Employment Development, Office of Labor Market Analysis & Information, 1100 N. Eutaw Street, Baltimore, Maryland 21201, (410) 767-2250.

• Virginia Employment Commission, 703 E. Main Street, P.O. Box 1358, Richmond, Virginia 23211, (804) 786-8223.

Selected Economic Development Authorities

If you're interested in starting or expanding a business in Metro Washington, or simply want to know more about companies in specific jurisdictions, we recommend that you contact the following economic-development groups:

• D.C. Office of Business and Economic Development, 717 14th Street NW, Washington, D.C. 20004, (202) 727-6600.

• Montgomery County Office of Economic Development, 101 Monroe Street, Suite 1500, Rockville, Maryland 20850, (301) 217-2345.

• Prince George's County Economic Development Corp., 9200 Basil Court, Suite 200, Landover, Maryland 20785, (301) 386-5600.

• Anne Arundel County Office of Economic Development, Arundel Center, Room 418, Annapolis, Maryland 21404, (410) 280-1122.

• Fairfax County Economic Development Authority, 8300 Boone Boulevard, Suite 450, Vienna, Virginia 22182, (703) 790-0600.

• Alexandria Economic Development Program, 99 Canal Center Plaza, Suite 4, River Level, Alexandria, Virginia 22314, (703) 739-3820.

• Arlington County Economic Development Division, One Courthouse Plaza, 2100 Clarendon Boulevard, Suite 608, Arlington, Virginia 22201, (703) 358-3520.

• Prince William County Office of Economic Development, 10530 Linden Lake Plaza, Suite 105, Manassas, Virginia 20109, (703) 392-0330 or (800) 334-9876.

Convention and Tourist Bureaus/ Tourist Information

Contact the following agencies to receive free, comprehensive travel and tourism information packets.

Washington, D.C.

• **Washington, D.C. Convention and Visitors Association**, 1212 New York Avenue NE, Washington, D.C. 20005, (202) 789-7000

Northern Virginia

• **Virginia Division of Tourism**, 901 E. Byrd Street, 19th Floor, Richmond, Virginia 23219, (804) 786-2051; Local office: 1629 K Street NW, Washington, D.C. 20006, (202) 659-5523

• **Alexandria Convention & Visitors Bureau**, 221 King Street, Alexandria, Virginia 22314, (703) 838-4200

• **Arlington Convention and Visitors Service**, 735 S. 18th Street, Arlington, Virginia 22202, (703) 358-5720

• **Fairfax County Tourism and Convention Bureau**, 8300 Boone Boulevard, Suite 450, Vienna, Virginia 22182, (703) 790-0600

• **Loudoun Tourism Bureau**, 108-D South Street SE, Leesburg, Virginia 22075, (703) 777-0519

• **Prince William County Tourist Information Center**, 200 Mill Street, Occoquan, Virginia 22125, (703) 491-4045

Suburban Maryland

• **Maryland Office of Tourist Development**, 217 E. Redwood Street, Baltimore, Maryland 21202, (410) 767-3400

• **Annapolis & Anne Arundel County Conference and Visitors Bureau**, 26 West Street, Annapolis, Maryland 21401, (410) 280-0445

• **Montgomery County Conference and Visitors Bureau**, 12900 Middlebrook Road, Suite 1400, Germantown, Maryland 20874, (301) 428-9702

• **Prince George's County Conference & Visitors Bureau**, 9200 Basil Court, Suite 101, Largo, Maryland 20774, (301) 925-8300

The nation's capital greets well over a million foreign visitors a year.

International Washington

The original plans for the nation's capital were drafted by a Frenchman, Pierre L'Enfant, so it seems only logical that Metro Washington would develop into a vibrant international crossroads. You don't have to look far to find some of the ingredients for this melting pot of humanity and heritage.

It's Chinatown, where the spirit of cross-cultural friendship is symbolized in the glittering archway that spans the width of a thoroughfare. It's Adams Morgan, where native Latinos, Ethiopians, Nigerians, Jamaicans and others have forged a neighborhood of extraordinary contrasts, a place where many of the 100 or so restaurants serve global cuisine. It's Embassy Row where the diplomatic corps — several thousand strong from over 150 nations — embodies the meaning of international communication, cooperation, trade and goodwill. It's Arlington, where Vietnamese, Laotians, Cambodians, Koreans, Thai, Filipinos and other Asian groups in particular have prospered as merchants and small business owners. It's virtually anywhere in the region where you'll find proud people who fled war-torn, famine-ravaged, economically distressed or brutally oppressive homelands to begin life anew here in professions as disparate as cab driver, banker, store clerk, police officer, computer technician, engineer, food and maintenance worker, craftsperson, scientist and artist. It's the presence of institutions such as the World Bank, the International Monetary Fund and the Organization of American States that speaks volumes about living and working in a global economy and a drastically shrinking world.

This chapter offers a glimpse of Metro Washington's colorful and diverse character. Note that diversions such as ethnic dining are not covered here, so please see the Restaurants chapter for suggestions on gastronomic globetrotting.

Resources for International Visitors

International Monetary Fund Visitors' Center
700 19th St. NW, Washington, D.C.
• (202) 623-7311

This intergovernmental agency's 156 member nations promote international monetary cooperation and assist in the expansion and balanced growth of global trade. The IMF also oversees the international monetary system and helps member nations overcome short-term financial problems. Scheduled to open in spring of 1998, the visitors' center will offer information on all aspects of foreign affairs.

International Visitors Information Service
733 15th St. NW, Ste. 300, Washington, D.C. • (202) 939-5566

This service offers a telephone language bank with information in some 45 languages and a reception/information center with bilingual staff and multilingual brochures.

Meridian International Center
1630 Crescent Pl. NW, Washington, D.C.
• (202) 667-6800, (202) 939-5544

This nonprofit educational and cultural institution, located in a splendid Beaux Arts mansion, has a number of educational outreach programs, both for international visitors to the United States and for United States citizens interested in other cultures. It offers seminars on international political issues, intercultural briefings for those relocating or visiting a foreign country (including those coming to the U.S.), educational workshops and arts programs.

Perhaps most valuable to the non-English speaker is Meridian's language bank, a service open during weekly business hours and providing immediate help for visitors trying to make themselves understood. Washington museums and Metrorail tap into the bank when at a loss for a translation. Meridian then transfers the tourist to a three-way telephone call with a native speaker of his or her language.

Organization of American States (OAS)
17th St. and Constitution Ave. NW, Washington, D.C. • (202) 458-3751

Formed in 1890, the OAS is the oldest international regional organization in the world, providing a forum for political, economic, social and cultural cooperation among the member states of the Western Hemisphere, including nations in North, Central and South America and the Caribbean. The headquarters are in a magnificent white marble building just opposite the Ellipse. OAS offers free tours of its beautiful grounds and gardens and also maintains a speakers bureau. Latin American art and antiquities are showcased in the OAS Gallery as well as at the Art Museum of the Americas, an OAS annex at 201 18th Street NW, between Constitution Avenue and C Street. The museum offers slide sets, videocassettes and publications on Latin American art. Admis-

sion is free, and tours are available. Call (202) 458-6016 for more information.

Travelers' Aid Society
1015 12th St. NW, Washington, D.C.
• (202) 546-3120

The society maintains information desks at all three Washington airports as well as Union Station (AMTRAK rail arrivals). Special assistance for U.S. and foreign travelers is available 24 hours a day.

Washington Convention and Visitors Association
1212 New York Ave. NW, Washington, D.C. • (202) 789-7000

This association serves as a clearinghouse for all tourist information, and can direct you to useful foreign language resources, tours and phone numbers, either in their own organization or elsewhere.

Washington Metrorail
600 5th St. NW, Washington, D.C.
• (202) 637-7000

Call this number to obtain free subway and bus maps in a variety of languages. Routes are clearly marked, as are transfer points — a useful tool for any tourist.

World Bank
1818 H St. NW, Washington, D.C.
• (202) 477-1234

Officially named the International Bank for Reconstruction and Development, the World Bank's main goal is to promote long-term economic growth that reduces poverty in developing nations. A major way of doing this is by providing loans to those countries and financing investments that contribute to economic growth. While it does not provide the community outreach and one-stop shop for resources that the IMF provides, anyone re-

INSIDERS' TIP

Don't overlook the sometimes-forgotten wealth of resources offered by embassies and numerous international organizations in Washington.

Embassy Row on Massachusetts Avenue is where the majority of the capital's 140-plus embassies are located.

searching international economic issues should contact the bank.

The Allure of Embassy Row

Few aspects of life here are more strongly identified with international Washington than the diplomatic community. The images — stereotypical but fairly accurate in most cases — are easy to conjure up: elegant residences in fashionable neighborhoods, lavish receptions and other power social functions, limousine motorcades, large and attentive staffs, instant access to political leaders and other establishment players and, of course, perhaps the ultimate perk: diplomatic immunity.

Ambassadors and their staffs do enjoy many special privileges, one of which is protection from many of the laws that the rest of us have to obey. This isn't to say that diplomats abuse the system and intentionally break laws knowing that they won't have to make amends, but in the event that things do happen, suffice it to say they receive considerations that go beyond the realm of even preferential treatment. Occasionally, you'll read stories of a particular embassy that has amassed, let's say, several thousand dollars worth of parking tickets and other minor violations and is being asked by the city to fork over the dough. Don't bet the mortgage on how those cases turn out.

It's tough to explain the degree to which diplomatic coddling is taken, so who better than the U.S. State Department to offer a summary explanation. Quoting Article 29 of the *Vienna Convention on Diplomatic Relations*, as found in the official Diplomatic List: "The person of a diplomatic agent shall be inviolable. He/she shall not be liable to any form of arrest or detention. The receiving State shall treat him/her with due respect and shall take all appropriate steps to prevent any attack on his/her person, freedom, or dignity." Make of it what you will.

Approximately 150 "embassies" (by law, the private residences of ambassadors and family) and "chanceries" (offices where all the work gets done) are in Washington, including such geographic mind-benders as Burkina Faso, Cape Verde, Myanmar, Benin, Belarus, Mali and the former Soviet republic of Kyrgyzstan. Chanceries are often staid and rather industrial looking, while many of the embassies are gracious old mansions, painstakingly restored and complete with manicured lawns and gardens and massive gates. Diplomatic residences are clustered primarily in the historic northwest neighborhood of Kalorama, located north of Dupont Circle, and along Massachusetts Avenue northwest between Sheridan and Observatory circles, thus the common reference to the area as Embassy Row. Some embassies, however, are scattered throughout other parts of town. Coats of arms and flags identify each diplomatic mission, though not all are easy to spot from the street.

While you're unlikely to have much success walking up to an embassy and asking for a peek inside, some swing their doors open to the public a few times a year during organized tours, often as important fundraisers for charitable causes (see Annual Events). The walking/bus tours are a great way to see some beautiful homes and get a rare upclose look at a unique world.

Embassies are wonderful, often overlooked sources on culture, customs, history and other facets of a nation, as well as for a broad range of travel and tourism information (usually free). Many diplomatic missions, particularly some of the larger ones like Canada, Mexico, Australia and the western European nations, also offer wonderful outreach programs, lectures, art exhibits and more that are open to the public. In any one month, you might find a series of Aboriginal films at the Australian Embassy, a symposium at the Canadian Embassy on implications of the North American Free Trade Agreement or a lecture on gourmet cooking at the French Embassy. Embassies can also direct citizens to area social clubs and various ethnic organizations.

Embassy Listings

Unfortunately, there's no central telephone number the public can call for general information on embassies and their resources. We've listed the chancery addresses and phone numbers of the 25 most prominent diplomatic missions. Public- or cultural-affairs personnel can help with questions and referrals. Since the turnover rate in the diplomatic corps is rather high (the diplomatic list is updated every three months), we didn't include names.

Argentina, 1600 New Hampshire Avenue NW, (202) 939-6400

Australia, 1601 Massachusetts Avenue NW, (202) 797-3000

Brazil, 3006 Massachusetts Avenue NW, (202) 745-2700

Canada, 501 Pennsylvania Avenue NW, (202) 682-1740

China, 2300 Connecticut Avenue NW, (202) 328-2500

Egypt, 3521 International Court NW, (202) 895-5400

France, 4101 Reservoir Road NW, (202) 944-6000

Germany, 4645 Reservoir Road NW, (202) 298-4000

Great Britain, 3100 Massachusetts Avenue NW, (202) 462-1340

Greece, 2221 Massachusetts Avenue NW, (202) 939-5800

India, 2107 Massachusetts Avenue NW, (202) 939-7000

Israel, 3514 International Drive NW, (202) 364-5500

Italy, 1601 Fuller Street NW, (202) 328-5500

Japan, 2520 Massachusetts Avenue NW, (202) 939-6700

Mexico, 1911 Pennsylvania Avenue NW, (202) 728-1600

Netherlands, 4200 Wisconsin Avenue NW, (202) 244-5300

Philippines, 1617 Massachusetts Avenue NW, (202) 467-9300

Russia, 2650 Wisconsin Avenue NW, (202) 298-5700

Saudi Arabia, 601 New Hampshire Avenue NW, (202) 342-3800

South Africa, 3051 Massachusetts Avenue NW, (202) 232-4400

South Korea, 2370 Massachusetts Avenue NW, (202) 939-5600

Spain, 2375 Pennsylvania NW, (202) 452-0100

Sweden, 1501 M St. NW, (202) 467-2600

Switzerland, 2900 Cathedral Avenue NW, (202) 745-7900

Turkey, 1714 Massachusetts Avenue NW, (202) 659-8200

The Lincoln Memorial gazes eastward upon the National Mall.

Hurdling Monetary Barriers

Besides most major banks and airports, local firms specializing in currency exchange include:

Thomas Cook Currency Services. This service is a subsidiary of the large British-based travel and currency-exchange company. Aside from the usual posts at the airports, Ronald Reagan Washington National and Washington Dulles International, there are also two offices in Washington, D.C.: Union Station, 50 Massachusetts Avenue NE, Washington, D.C., (202) 371-9219; 1800 K Street NW, Washington, D.C., (202) 872-1233

American Express Travel Service. There are several locations throughout the metropolitan area. In Washington, D.C.: 1150 Connecticut Avenue NW, Washington, D.C., (202) 457-1300; 5300 Wisconsin Avenue NW, Washington, D.C., (202) 362-4000

In Virginia: Pentagon City Mall, 1100 S. Hayes Street, Arlington, Virginia, (703) 415-5400; Springfield Mall, Exit 169A off Interstate 95, Springfield, Virginia, (703) 971-5600; Tysons Galleria, Exit 11 B off Interstate 495, 2001 International Drive, McLean, Virginia, (703) 893-3550.

Speaking the Language

If words, not money, are the problem, there are several major translation services available:

Berlitz Translation Services, 1050 Connecticut Avenue NW, Washington, D.C., (202) 331-1160; or, Tysons Corner Center, 2070 Chain Bridge Road, McLean, Virginia, (703) 883-0626.

The Interpreters Bureau, 1660 L Street NW, Washington, D.C., (202) 296-1346.

The Language Exchange, 1821 18th Street NW, Washington, D.C., (202) 328-0099.

Linguex Language Center, 2639 Connecticut Avenue NW, Washington, D.C., (202) 296-1112.

Meridian International Center Language Bank, 1630 Crescent Place NW, Washington, D.C., (202)667-6800, or (202) 939-5544.

Ethnic Neighborhoods

Adams Morgan is one of the Washington, D.C. neighborhoods you don't want to miss touring. Its hub is at 18th Street and Columbia Road NW. The area is alive with restaurants, bars, nightclubs, shops, boutiques and a host of other attractions, many of which revolve around the community's Caribbean, Latin American and African roots.

Chinatown encompasses eight blocks bordered by H Street and 6th and 9th streets NW. It is three blocks from the D.C. Convention Center, seven blocks from Capitol Hill, and sits conveniently atop the Gallery Place station on Metrorail's Red Line. You will again see restaurants and shops galore.

The social highlight of the year is undoubtedly the Chinese New Year celebration each January and February. Perhaps the neighborhood's most visible symbol, the glittering jewel-tone Friendship Archway spans H Street at 7th. Decorated in the classical art of the Ming and Ch'ing dynasties and featuring four pillars and five roofs, the $1 million project was paid for and built jointly by the D.C. government and Beijing in 1986. The two capital cities pledged in 1984 to create a mutually beneficial relationship emphasizing cultural, economic, educational and technical exchanges with a goal to make Washington's Chinatown a world-class center for Asian trade and finance.

International Landmarks

Landmarks, both natural and man-made, are as much a part of Washington's international landscape as its people. Here's a quick

INSIDERS' TIP

If you're in search of a number of international dining options near one another, consider spending an evening in Arlington, Bethesda, Adams Morgan or Chinatown.

look at a few of the monuments and landmarks that have a distinct international flavor. Countries of all sizes are an integral part of the nation's capital. Among the most prominent influences:

Japanese cherry trees were a gift from the city of Tokyo in 1909. More than 3,000 of these gorgeous specimens dot the landscape near the Jefferson Memorial, the adjacent Tidal Basin, and nearby Hains Point. Because the original trees were infected by a fungus, the Department of Agriculture had them destroyed. Replacements arrived in 1912 and were officially welcomed by First Lady Helen Taft and the wife of the Japanese ambassador.

Each April (with a little cooperation from Mother Nature), in what is surely one of the most welcome harbingers of spring, the trees sprout their brilliant pink and white blossoms. Thousands of passersby enjoy seeing the blooming trees during the week-long National Cherry Blossom Festival, but the dazzling "peak" period lasts only a few days. The weather greatly affects the arrival, brilliance and longevity of the blossoms, so listen for the National Park Service's blossom forecasts as spring approaches.

The Netherlands Carillon is an often-overlooked landmark that has strong foreign ties. After World War II the Dutch government gave the 49-bell tower to the United States in gratitude. Looming over Arlington near the Marine Corps War Memorial (Iwo Jima statue) and Arlington National Cemetery, it is surrounded by a sea of tulips. It is also the site of numerous summer and holiday concerts.

Even Washington's most famous landmark, the Washington Monument, has global influence. The 555-foot obelisk — the world's largest masonry structure — contains nearly 200 memorial stones in its interior walls. Among the stones are a block of lava from Italy's infamous Mount Vesuvius, a mosaic block from the ruins of Carthage (present-day Tunisia), a stone from the Swiss chapel of William Tell, and a stone praising George Washington in Chinese. There is also a replica of the stone given by Pope Pius IX. The original stone was stolen by a radical anti-Catholic group in 1854 and dumped in the Potomac. The replacement, a gift to the National Park Service in 1982, is Italian marble inscribed in Latin with the phrase "A Roma Americae," meaning "From Rome to America."

Heritage Festivals

What better way to honor the diverse heritage of Metro Washingtonians than with parties, parades, festivals and other such events. Each year literally starts with a bang as the colorful Chinese Lunar New Year parade draws thousands with music, firecrackers and colorful costumes. In spring, several metro-area municipalities celebrate St. Patrick's Day with their own parades where you can binge on traditional green beer, corned beef and cabbage.

Choose any month of the year and you're likely to find an ethnic celebration in Washington. The Greek, British, Hispanic — they're all ready to party in their unique ways. For a great mix of them all, catch the popular Smithsonian Festival of American Folk Life, which highlights our diverse cultural background. The annual festival is held over a 10-day period in late June and early July (always including the 4th). For more on these and other celebrations, turn to the Annual Events chapter.

Cultural Immersion

Almost every nation has an interest group located in Washington, but most of them focus on promoting their agendas to the media and the U.S. government. If you want to delve deeper into the multi-cultural side

The Pentagon is the headquarters for secretaries of the U.S. Department of Defense, Army, Navy, Air Force and Coast Guard.

of Washington, many organizations provide public outreach. For more information, contact the following:

Washington, D.C.

Alliance Française de Washington
2142 Wyoming Avenue NW, Washington, D.C. • (202) 234-7911

This organization has branches throughout the world and in other major U.S. cities. Native speakers provide French lessons and cultural and social activities are available, all at a reasonable cost.

American Association of Foreign Service Women
5125 MacArthur Blvd. NW, Washington, D.C. • (202) 362-6514

Foreign service families moving in and out of Washington are often strangers to the city and its international resources. This organiza-

tion provides a home base for such families and helps them cope with their itinerant lifestyles. As the name implies, it has close ties with the U.S. State Department and can serve as a resource for those stationed in Washington and abroad.

Goethe Institut
810 7th St. NW, Washington, D.C. • (202) 289-1200

This active nonprofit organization's mission is promoting the German language and culture worldwide. It is run with impressive Teutonic efficiency, and offers a wide variety of cultural activities, media outreach and German language classes.

Hispan-Am International
1622 Lamont St. NW, Washington, D.C. • (202) 234-4636

Hispan-Am is oriented toward those of Hispanic descent who wish to do business in Washington, and toward their U.S.-native counterparts who want to tap into the community. It is a networking organization that holds periodic social events focusing on business exchange.

Hispanic Service Center
1805 Belmont Rd. NW, Washington, D.C.
• (202) 234-3435

Not a tourist organization, nor exactly one for cultural exchange, this service center is instead a resource for Spanish speakers in America who need help with government documents, translation, housing and other daily life issues.

The Hospitality Information Service (THIS)
1630 Crescent Pl. NW, Washington, D.C.
• (202) 232-3002

THIS is like a Welcome Wagon for foreign diplomats stationed in Washington. It serves as a valuable source of information as they settle here, providing lists of schools, stores, hospitals and other crucial information. THIS also sponsors social and cultural events to help introduce diplomatic community members to one another.

Islamic Center
2441 Massachusetts Avenue NW, Washington, D.C. • (202) 332-8343

The Islamic Center's primary mission is managing the Washington mosque, which is in the same building (see the Worship chapter). The center also offers Arabic language classes and periodic cultural events.

Japan Information and Culture Center
1155 21st St. NW, Washington, D.C.
• (202) 939-6900

There is perhaps no diplomatic outlet in Washington quite like the expansive Japan Information and Culture Center, an adjunct of the Japanese Embassy and definitely the top local authority on all things Japanese. The center offers a friendly, helpful staff, permanent exhibit space for showings by a wide range of Japanese artists and a calendar of events filled with programs about Japan and its people.

Japan-America Society of Washington
1020 19th St. NW, Washington, D.C.
• (202) 833-2210

Japan is an enigma to most Americans, and the Japan-America Society seeks to bridge the gap of understanding with exchanges of information on business, culture and the arts. The society promotes several concerts and performances a year at venues throughout Washington, as well as smaller gatherings aimed at those doing business in or touring Japan. It can also direct you to Japanese language classes by native speakers.

Meridian International Center
1630 Crescent Pl. NW, Washington, D.C.
• (202)667-6800, (202) 939-5544

Please refer to the beginning of this chapter, where we have included a full listing for the Meridian International Center.

National Council for International Visitors
1420 K St. NW, Washington, D.C.
• (202) 842-1414, (800) 523-8101

The council is a national network of program agencies and community-based organizations that provide services to participants in international exchange programs. These nonprofit groups design and implement professional programs and internships, and provide cultural activities and home hospitality opportunities for foreign officials and international scholars.

Suburban Maryland

Italian Cultural Society of Washington, D.C.
5480 Wisconsin Avenue, Chevy Chase, Md. • (301) 215-7885

This group provides language lessons and once-a-month social gatherings for Italians or anyone practicing the language.

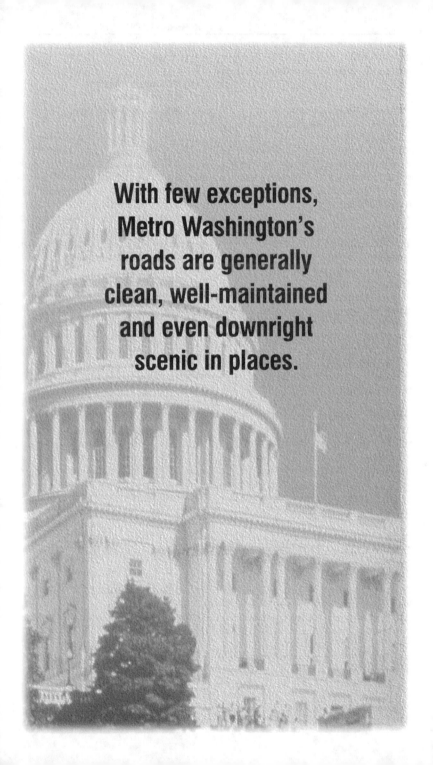

With few exceptions, Metro Washington's roads are generally clean, well-maintained and even downright scenic in places.

Getting Around the Metro Area

Natives of Los Angeles or New York may chuckle at this notion, but getting around Metro Washington can be an intimidating experience for newcomers. Even longtime residents will concede that negotiating the network of often-congested highways, byways and bridges that serves 4.65 million people often isn't the most pleasant of tasks.

In fact, recent research studies confirm that Washington, D.C. drivers suffer from headaches with good reason. According to the Texas Transportation Institute, Washington tops the list for the amount of time — roughly 59 hours annually per person — wasted during traffic tie-ups. Traffic jams also waste fuel, at the No. 1 rate of one quart per person for each work day. Only Los Angeles has worse traffic congestion, according to the report released in the fall of 1997. Meanwhile, a detailed 1997 transportation study by the Greater Washington Board of Trade cites the need for new roads and Potomac bridges to keep up with the D.C. area's steady population increase.

While the region has grown dramatically over the past 30 years or so in both population and the rate of commercial and residential development, the transportation infrastructure — due to a combination of political and bureaucratic stagnation, fiscal belt-tightening and an acute case of shortsightedness — unfortunately has not kept pace. As shopping malls, housing tracts and office parks sprouted on the landscape, road, mass-transit and other transportation improvements all too often became an afterthought. Subsequent changes in commuting patterns further challenged planners, as more and more suburban residents began driving to neighboring suburbs to go to work in-stead of into the District. While this shift took some of the strain off downtown, it resulted in rush-hour problems never envisioned in the 1960s.

On an average day, the sheer volume of traffic can make an ordinary non-rush hour journey aggravating. Toss in an accident (even a fender-bender that's been moved to the road shoulder), a few snowflakes, some rain, a holiday weekend or a Friday afternoon during the summer, and you've got the makings of a potentially harrowing ordeal that can leave you longing for the solitude of the Australian outback.

That's the bad news.

Now for the good news:

With few exceptions, Metro Washington's roads are generally clean, well-maintained and even downright scenic in places (we offer the George Washington Memorial Parkway and even the unusually green Capital Beltway in spring and fall as prime examples). Besides the usual police presence (leadfoots beware!), drivers can take comfort in knowing that many of the primary roads, notably the Beltway, are also patrolled by motorist-assistance units — a courtesy service provided by the Virginia State Police. The assorted trucks and vans are a welcome sight for countless folks confronting a flat tire, spewing radiator, empty gas tank or other vehicular challenge.

Some notable progress has also been made in improving Metro Washington's transportation network: Major stretches of roadway have been widened; once-nightmarish intersections have been transformed into the safer and far more efficient under/over configuration; the designation of HOV (high-occupancy vehicle) lanes, requiring two or three persons to a vehicle during rush hour, has encouraged carpooling; several new roads (Dulles Greenway, Fairfax County Parkway, Franconia-Springfield Parkway) are nearing completion; the Metrorail system has continued to expand toward its ultimate length of 103 miles; and inter-jurisdictional communication and cooperation have been improved in areas such as accident response and snow removal.

Another significant advancement was the inception of the Virginia Department of Transportation's (VDOT's) high-tech Smart Traffic management system, a computerized highway monitoring and control program that oversees 30 miles of Interstates 66, 95 and 395, and helps detect and clear accidents and disabled vehicles to keep traffic flowing smoothly. In this case, it's nice to know Big Brother is watching. Smart Traffic uses closed-circuit cameras to keep an eye on traffic conditions, traffic counters embedded in the pavement to convey important information, ramp meters to regulate the number of vehicles entering the roadway, and variable message signs that alert motorists to accidents and other traffic-related events ahead. VDOT personnel monitor the system at a control center in Arlington, where they communicate not only with the public but with service patrols, state police and traffic reporters. By fall of 1998, VDOT plans to extend coverage from I-95 to Prince William County and I-66 to Manassas, for a grand total of 70 miles.

In Maryland, a similar traffic-management system called CHART, short for Chesapeake Highways Advisories Routing Traffic, also uses state-of-the-art technology (message signs,

cameras and detection devices, as well as patrol vehicles) to provide quick response to accidents and other road emergencies, and help reduce congestion. When fully completed by the late 1990s, the statewide program will cover some 400 miles of highway and another 400 miles of major arterial roadways in Maryland's eight heavily traveled traffic corridors. The system currently covers roadways primarily in the Metro Washington and Baltimore areas.

Future major transportation improvement proposals include constructing bypasses to the Capital Beltway, adding bridges, and expanding rail systems and other means of getting people out of their single-passenger vehicles. While these plans have been hotly debated at times, they are nevertheless cause for optimism.

In the meantime, you've got to deal with the situation at hand, and that's where we hope this chapter proves helpful. There's no substitute for experience, and that's particularly true when it comes to trying to find your way around and drive in unfamiliar territory. We hope that the following information will give you a feel for the region's overall transportation system and perhaps make those initial journeys somewhat less intimidating.

First, here are a couple of suggestions. Before tackling Metro Washington from behind the wheel or from any other perspective, we strongly suggest that you get a good map and keep it nearby. We can't recommend enough the book-style variety produced locally by Alexandria Drafting Company (ADC), "The Map People," as they proudly bill themselves. And they truly are. ADC's detailed and easy-to-use maps of cities, counties and the region are invaluable resources, as well as

---

www.insiders.com

See this and many other **Insiders' Guide®** destinations online — in their entirety.

Visit us today!

Photo: Courtesy of Washington Dulles International Airport

A multitude of cab services are available in Metro Washington.

great providers of peace of mind. Updated frequently, they're widely available at convenience stores, drugstores, supermarkets and bookstores. For more information, call ADC at (703) 750-0510.

You'll also be wise to keep an ear tuned to the radio for the latest traffic information, both before you leave home or office and while in the car. All it takes is one nightmarish backup that could have been easily avoided and you'll soon become a devout listener. Most local stations broadcast traffic reports frequently during the morning and evening rush hours, and a few offer updates throughout the day. Some of the most comprehensive coverage is on WMAL (630 AM), WTOP (1500 AM), WARW (94.7 FM) and WMZQ (98.7 FM).

Now, fasten your seatbelt and let's hit the road.

Roadways

The Capital Beltway and Connecting Interstates

No matter how much you may wish to avoid it, as a driver in Metro Washington you're bound to travel the Capital Beltway (Interstate 495), that 66-mile, 55-interchange ring of asphalt so many people love to hate. Envisioned as a bypass to Metro Washington when construction began in the early 1950s, it became instead the area's Main Street — at once a transportation lifeline and the bane of our existence. We curse it for legendary traffic jams, ill-conceived interchanges and entrance/exit ramps (though many of these have been dramatically improved) and that confusing Inner and Outer Loop business (we'll clear this up shortly) — but we also can't imagine living here without the Beltway.

History and Statistics

The road opened in stages beginning in 1957, with the federal government picking up 90 percent of the $189 million construction tab; the four- and six-lane version that was completed in 1964 was subsequently widened to eight lanes. No matter the number of lanes, at times it never seems to be enough. One workday soon after opening, the Beltway carried about 48,000 automobiles; today, the daily figure tops 600,000, with vehicles logging some 8 million miles in an average 24-hour period.

The experts tell us that if we think Beltway traffic is bad today, it's only going to get worse unless more people start carpooling (Metro Washington already boasts the nation's highest proportion of ridesharing) and using mass transit, and until an outer bypass is built to reroute non-local traffic (the I-95 variety in particular). Estimates say that the results of inaction will be that by the turn of the century the average Beltway commuter will spend almost two more hours in the car each week, and congestion will cost users up to $180 million annually in time, gas consumption and accident losses. These are sobering thoughts indeed.

Virginia and Maryland state police have jurisdiction over the Beltway and maintain a very high profile in both marked and unmarked cruisers ready to nab drivers exceeding the 55-mph speed limit, although off-peak traffic often zooms along at 60 mph or higher speeds. Flashing lights less likely to send your blood pressure skyward are yellow and found atop specially equipped vehicles that come to the aid of stranded motorists, helping prevent ordinary breakdowns from becoming extraordinary backups.

Tractor-trailers constitute only about 6 percent of Beltway traffic, yet studies have shown that they're involved in nearly 20 percent of the accidents. Truckers, of course, are not always at fault; in fact, they're usually considered among the best drivers on the road, although police are adamant about spot safety inspections to ensure the vehicles themselves don't pose unusual risks. As a further precaution, the big rigs are prohibited from traveling in the far left fast lanes of the Beltway, and vehicles that transport hazardous materials — gasoline, chemicals, etc. — are encouraged, whenever possible, to travel in the wee hours of the night and early morning when traffic is light and the risks of a mishap are greatly reduced.

Which Loop is Which?

Sooner or later you'll hear about or see the Inner and Outer Loops, the two portions of road that comprise the Beltway. Discerning which is which is actually pretty simple. Using Washington, D.C. as a reference point (better yet, refer to your handy ADC map), with the 12 o'clock position at the top, the Inner Loop is

physically closer to the city, and traffic travels in a clockwise motion. The Outer Loop, naturally, sits a bit farther out and traffic moves counterclockwise. This is easy, right? Well, you don't have to think about it as much as you used to. To alleviate some of the confusion, the Virginia and Maryland state highway departments several years ago posted signs that tell you which loop you're traveling.

Major Roads That Intersect the Capital Beltway

You could almost say that all roads in Metro Washington lead to the Beltway. Circumnavigating Washington, D.C. like a giant lasso with numerous appendages, it slices through Fairfax County and the City of Alexandria in Northern Virginia, and Prince George's and Montgomery counties in Maryland. It crosses the Potomac River twice, via the American Legion (also called Cabin John) Bridge at the northern border of Fairfax County and southern border of Montgomery County; and the Woodrow Wilson Bridge, where eastern Fairfax County and western Prince George's County meet.

The Beltway offers access to these major thoroughfares:

Interstate 66 intersects near Tysons Corner in Fairfax County, heading east into Arlington and the District and west toward Prince William County.

Interstate 95 overlaps the Beltway's eastern side, veering south at Springfield for drivers headed toward Richmond, and north in Prince George's County for those traveling toward Baltimore.

Interstate 270 connects to I-495 in Montgomery County and leads north to Frederick, where it becomes Interstate 70.

Interstate 295, also known as the Baltimore-Washington Parkway, heads through southern sections of the District and up through Prince George's County toward Baltimore-Washington International Airport (BWI).

Interstate 395, also known as Henry Shirley Memorial Highway, heads north into Arlington and the District, where it becomes I-295.

The Beltway also provides access to the

Dulles Toll Road and the parallel Airport Access Road; the scenic George Washington Memorial Parkway; well-traveled U.S. Highways 1, 29 and 50; Routes 7, 123, 236 and 355; and numerous secondary roads.

Bridges and Traffic

No other highway in the area carries as much clout or can get us to so many places in so short a time, barring those horrendous traffic jams. While we're mentioning traffic, we'd better point out that the two bridges across the Potomac are the sites of some of the worst Beltway backups. Maryland and Virginia finally got wise and began stationing tow trucks at either end of each span during the morning and evening rush hours to remove disabled vehicles quickly. The American Legion Bridge has seen great improvement through widening, but the dreaded Wilson, a drawbridge with one fewer lane than the Beltway itself, remains a prime bottleneck and major source of motorist irritation. Drawbridge openings (always off-peak hours) are much more closely regulated than in years past, but the jams that still occur are ferocious.

Keep this in mind: Coming from Virginia, you must cross a bridge to get into the District. (If you manage to accomplish this otherwise, let us know and we'll put together an amazing magic act.) Your five choices, starting north and working south, are Chain Bridge, linking the McLean/Arlington areas with Canal Road and upper northwest; Key Bridge, named for "Star-Spangled Banner" author Francis Scott Key, joining Rosslyn and Georgetown; Roosevelt Bridge, in the shadows of Rosslyn, where I-66 runs into Constitution Avenue NW; stately Memorial Bridge, perhaps the most picturesque of all, stretching from Arlington National Cemetery to the Lincoln Memorial at Rock Creek Parkway; and the 14th Street Bridge, where I-395 winds past the Pentagon and crosses the Potomac near the Tidal Basin and the Jefferson Memorial.

If you drive to work, remember that the morning rush hour in Metro Washington can begin as early as 5 AM along some stretches of the Beltway and other heavily traveled routes, such as I-66, I-95, I-270 and I-395, and as early as 3:30 PM for the drive home. Factor in extended crunch times during inclement weather, Fridays and holiday weekends.

Beltway Safety Tips

Now that you know a little bit about the major thoroughfares, keep in mind some pointers to lessen aggravation and enhance safety:

• Leave earlier and know where you're going.

• Gas up before you go — remember that traffic jams can eat up a lot of fuel.

• Drive courteously and be alert.

• Learn alternate routes to avoid traffic jams.

• Don't rubberneck!

To avoid confusion on roads that intersect the Beltway, remember that the same highway can have several different names. Here are a few prime examples: Route 7 is called Leesburg Pike in the Tysons Corner area, Broad Street in the City of Falls Church, and King Street in Alexandria. Route 236 is known as Duke Street in the Alexandria area, Little River Turnpike in Annandale, and Main Street in Fairfax City. Route 123 is Ox Road in southern Fairfax County, Chain Bridge Road in the Fairfax City area and again in Tysons Corner, Maple Avenue in the Vienna town limits, and Dolly Madison Boulevard in McLean. Nothing like a little variety to enhance your driving pleasure, eh?

Toll Roads

Dulles Toll Road
P.O. Box 9430, McLean, VA 22102
• (703) 383-2696

The Dulles Toll Road (Route 267), the region's only toll road except for the connecting Dulles Greenway, exceeded popularity expectations almost immediately after opening in 1984. Despite today's heavy traffic burden, commuters in the corridor, primarily from western Loudoun County and the Fairfax County communities of Herndon, Reston, Tysons Corner, Vienna and McLean, are much better off with the road than they were before it was built.

The 26-mile highway runs parallel to the airport-only Dulles Access Road and feeds into

I-66. The toll road consists of three lanes in each direction, and fourth lanes are scheduled for completion in the fall of 1998. The far left lanes will then be reserved for carpoolers.

The main toll plaza, between Spring Hill Road and Route 7, is staffed 24 hours a day. Booths at other entrances and exits are attended 16 hours a day (5:30 AM to 9:30 PM Monday through Friday); outside of these hours, automatic toll machines are in operation and motorists need exact change. The toll is 50¢ at the main plaza except for Spring Hill Road commuters, who ride through a designated lane and pay 25¢. The fee is 25¢ at all other gates except Route 28, where it costs 35¢.

Drivers who frequent the toll road may want to buy a high-tech Smart Tag (formerly called Fastoll), an electronic receiver that attaches to your car's windshield. When you drive through a designated toll lane, your car's signal is automatically read and deducted from your pre-paid account, enabling you to avoid stopping at a toll booth. For information on signing up for the program, call (888) 327-8655 or (703) 736-9300, or ask for an application at the toll booth.

Dulles Greenway
109 Carpenter Dr., Ste. 200, Sterling, Va.
• **(703) 707-8870**

This privately operated, 14-mile extension of the Dulles Toll Road opened in September of 1995 and still hasn't lived up to its high expectations. With a 65 mph speed limit, the scenic road offers a quick route to Leesburg, but many motorists balk at the tolls, ranging from $1 to $1.25. Still, it's a welcome addition for folks who commute into the city from bucolic Loudoun County: You can get from Leesburg to Herndon in about half the time required for the same commute relying on routes 7 and 28. The four-lane highway has seven interchanges.

Major Parkways

Fairfax County Parkway
Rt. 7100, Fairfax County, Va.
• **(703) 324-1100**

This 35-mile, cross-county road has opened gradually in connecting sections since September of 1987. It's especially handy for folks commuting between communities in different parts of the county. The road starts in Reston, north of the Dulles Toll Road, and crosses over U.S. Rt. 50, I-66 and Rt. 123 before turning into the Franconia/Springfield Parkway (Route 7900) at Rolling Road in Springfield. Travelers can follow Rt. 7900 to I-95, then hop back on an as-yet unconnected section of Rt. 7100 to Newington Road. The newest unconnected section runs from Telegraph Road to Rt. 1 south of Alexandria. Construction should begin in late 1998 on a segment running from the current beginning in Reston to Rt. 7 near the Loudoun County line. Total estimated cost of the entire project, funded through the county and Virginia Department of Transportation (VDOT) is $560 million.

George Washington Memorial Parkway
Turkey Run Park, McLean, Va.
• **(703) 285-2598**

This parkway along the Potomac is one of the prettiest routes to travel into the District, but it can also be one of the most dangerous. Watch out for aggressive drivers and treacherous curves, but don't allow our words of caution to steer you away from this road, which runs from George Washington's home, Mount Vernon, to Great Falls, Maryland. For more about the parkway's abundant natural, recreational and historic sites, see our Parks and Recreation and Attractions chapters.

HOV Restrictions

If you can get people to ride with you, the HOV lanes often get you home or to work faster, although a shorter trip is never guaranteed, given the unpredictable nature of our roads. Still, when you consider the chances of having a shorter ride plus the certainty of reduced auto and fuel expenses, air pollution and traffic congestion, you can see why the HOV program is so popular with many commuters.

If you're a newcomer and wonder how you'll be able to distinguish the HOV lanes, fear not; they're well-marked with signs and

Washington is served by three major airports: Ronald Reagan Washington National, Washington Dulles International, and Baltimore-Washington International.

either physical barriers (gates, concrete dividers) or diamond-shaped lane markings. Members of the law-enforcement community will be more than happy to remind you as well. Don't take HOV restrictions lightly. Scofflaws face healthy fines plus several points on their licenses for moving violations. You'll pay $50 for a first offense, $100 for a second, $250 for a third within two years of the second and — take a deep breath — $500 for a fourth violation within three years of the second! Forget about putting a mannequin or some other human substitute in your car to get around the passenger requirements. The police have seen it all and don't take kindly to motorists trying to put one over on them.

Here's a summary of the regional HOV scene (restrictions apply Monday through Friday only, excluding holidays).

I-395/I-95: HOV-3 (three or more people)

Where: A 30-mile stretch of road runs from the 14th Street Bridge in the District to Route 234 in Prince William County.

When: Two lanes, separated by barriers, operate northbound from 6 AM to 9 AM, and southbound from 3:30 PM to 6 PM.

I-66, inside the Capital Beltway: HOV-2 (two or more people)

Where: A 10-mile length of road stretches from Theodore Roosevelt Bridge to the Capital Beltway eastbound.

When: Two eastbound lanes are designated HOV-2 from 6:30 AM to 9 AM. Two westbound lanes are designated HOV-2 from 4 PM to 6:30 PM.

I-66 outside the Beltway: HOV-2

Where: An 18-mile stretch runs from the Capital Beltway to Rt. 234 in Manassas.

When: Outside the Beltway, the far left lane in each direction is painted with diamonds to designate HOV travel from 5:30 AM to 9:30 AM eastbound and from 3 PM to 7 PM westbound. During these times, the far right "lanes" (note the electronic green and red control signals overhead) that run for about seven miles are open to traffic; otherwise, these stretches

INSIDERS' TIP

The U.S. Transportation Department, 400 7th Street SW, Washington, D.C., (202) 366-4000, offers toll-free consumer hotlines on such topics as air travel, truck and bus complaints, and auto, aviation and boating safety.

of dark pavement (to distinguish them from the regular lanes) are used as shoulders ONLY, and traffic is strictly prohibited, so please heed the signs. It can make for a dangerous situation if drivers aren't paying attention or choose to ignore the restrictions. To alleviate the nasty bottleneck conditions that have long plagued I-66, the road is being gradually widened to the west, but the project is far from complete. Expect to see construction work and experience some related traffic tie-ups during off-peak hours along this heavily traveled corridor for quite some time.

A Washington Driving Primer

Washington is indeed one of the most beautiful and well-planned cities anywhere — with its broad avenues, abundant parks and open space — but that doesn't mean it's a pleasure to drive in, especially for newcomers.

Confusing one-way streets, traffic circles, a critical shortage of on-street parking spaces, outrageous prices for parking garages (expect to pay $10 or more a day), and other factors can frustrate the uninitiated. Finding a place to park can be both costly and aggravating, and police don't hesitate for a moment to hand out tickets. Ignore those pieces of paying paper and you may find your car towed or perhaps wearing a boot, a heavy steel clamp attached to a front wheel, preventing the car from being driven and ensuring the car owner a bit of embarrassment. All of this underscores the beauty of walking and using public transportation such as Metrorail, Metrobus or one of the 9,000 or so taxicabs. Fortunately, the city's relatively small size and its grid system street layout are helpful to newcomers. With a good map, some patience and a bit of practice, Washington is actually not a difficult place to get around.

When pondering Washington's street system, remember that the U.S. Capitol is the geographic center. The city is arranged in four sections — Northwest, Northeast, Southwest and Southeast — with the dividing lines being N. Capitol Street, S. Capitol Street, E. Capitol Street and the National Mall, radiating like spokes of a wheel from the Capitol building. The NW, NE, SW and SE used in addresses are very important. An address on M Street NW could also be found on M Street SE, so keep this in mind when mailing something, much less trying to get somewhere.

Streets that run north-south (14th, 15th, 18th, etc.) are numbered in sequence, while those going east-west are lettered (H, M, R and so forth) in alphabetical order. There are no J, X, Y or Z streets. Streets with state names (Pennsylvania, Connecticut) are all diagonals. Circles and squares occur at the intersections of diagonal avenues and numbered and lettered streets.

The MetroSystem and Other Ground Transportation Networks

The Metro

Washington Metropolitan Area Transit Authority (Metro)
600 5th St. NW, Washington, D.C.
• (202) 637-7000, (202) 638-3780 TDD

Metro Washington is blessed with a first-rate rail and bus system, Metro, short for the Washington Metropolitan Area Transit Authority (WMATA). The award-winning Metrorail is clean, efficient, inexpensive and, yes, even attractive. Good luck finding any graffiti, but you will see some spectacular concrete work, dramatic arched ceilings, graceful lines and towering escalators, giving the primarily underground system a futuristic appearance.

Metro is generally safe, but be careful not to ensnare loose clothing in the moving steps of the escalators. Keep a cautious distance from the platform edge, and make sure to enter and exit quickly. When you hear a loud electronic bell-like tone, watch for the doors to snap open or shut.

"America's Subway" first opened in 1976, and has grown to link a large portion of the National Capital Area. It's especially loved by commuters and tourists, as it offers superb access to the major business districts as well as such popular destinations as the Smithsonian, the Pentagon, the National Zoo, Ronald Reagan Washington National Airport and Arlington National Cemetery.

Metro's general manager reports to the Metro Board, whose members include representatives from the District, Maryland and Virginia. Area jurisdictions served by Metro pay a subsidy to the system, and residents pay a few cents extra per gallon of gasoline to help fund Metro's operation, maintenance and expansion. Believe us — it's money well spent.

Each of Metrorail's five lines — Orange, Red, Green, Blue and Yellow — passes through the District at some point. The Green Line (the shortest, with most of it still to be built), never leaves the District, but it will, once fully extended into Prince George's County. The Orange Line stretches from Vienna, Virginia, to New Carrollton, Maryland; the Red, from Shady Grove, Maryland, to Wheaton, Maryland, but that will change to Glenmont when the line is completed in mid-1998. The Green Line runs from U Street-Cardozo to Anacostia, and from Fort Totten to Greenbelt; on completion, it will begin and end in Maryland, linking Greenbelt with Branch Avenue. The Blue Line runs from Addison Road in the District to the newest station, Franconia-Springfield, which opened in June of 1997 at Frontier Drive, right off the convenient Franconia/Springfield Parkway. The Yellow Line goes from the Huntington area of Fairfax County to Mt. Vernon Square-UDC (University of the District of Columbia) in the District. Once fully developed, Metrorail will boast 83 stations along 103 miles of track; the current system includes 75 stations along 92.35 miles of track.

The system operates from 5:30 AM to midnight, Monday through Friday, 8 AM to midnight Saturday and Sunday. The last trains leave some stations prior to midnight; refer to signs in stations for details. Trains as well as buses run on a reduced schedule on certain holidays.

Large brown pylons topped with Metro's distinctive "M" logo mark all station entrances. There's also very good signage along roads for those stations accessible by auto.

Instead of cash or tokens, Metro operates on a farecard system. Every passenger must have a farecard to enter and exit, except children younger than age 5, two of whom may travel free with a paying rider. Fares start at $1.10 and vary depending on the time of day and distance traveled. To determine your fare, look at a hard-to-miss map to determine your destination, and then check the posted fee schedule for the peak and off-peak fares to that station. Peak (rush) hours of operation are 5:30 AM to 9:30 AM and 3 PM to 8 PM, Monday through Friday. Off-peak occurs all other times and on federal holidays. While the system is far busier during the peak periods, the trains also run more often — the wait any time of day is rarely longer than 15 minutes.

Purchasing a farecard may seem confusing at first, but it's easily mastered with just a few minutes of study. Farecard machines, located in every station, accept nickels, dimes, quarters and $1 and $5 bills; some machines also accept $10 and $20 bills. Be aware, however, that change comes in coins only, and machines provide no more than $4.95 in change. Put your money in the machine, and when you've pushed the "+" and "-" buttons to reach your desired fare amount, press another button to receive your card. To avoid having to run to an Addfare machine to get in or out of a station, you should consider purchasing a little more fare than you think you might need for a roundtrip. Better still, just keep a farecard with $10 or $20 worth of travel stashed in your wallet or purse at all times. You never know when it might come in handy.

When you buy a farecard for $20 or more, you receive a 10-percent bonus. You also can purchase special passes, such as a $5 one-day pass geared toward tourists and various large-denomination passes that save time and expense for commuters. Visit the sales offices

Photo: Courtesy of the Washington, DC Convention and Visitors Association

The Jefferson Memorial was constructed in the style of
Jefferson's Rotunda at the University of Virginia.

at Metro Center, the Pentagon or Metro's head-quarters, or stop by Giant, Safeway or Superfresh. Passes also are available through TicketMaster at (202) 637-7000; the Commuter Stores at Ballston, Crystal City and Rosslyn; and the White Flint Transit Store.

Metrobus goes everywhere the rail system does, and then some, reaching far into suburban areas as well as the inner city. Metro is gradually replacing aging buses, and plans to have 85 percent of its 1,300-plus fleet equipped with wheelchair lifts by 1998. Bus routes and schedules are coordinated with rail routes and schedules to provide a comprehensive transportation system. Individual bus routes are detailed on brochures available at Metrorail stations and in various town, city and county transportation offices. You need exact change or a Metrobus pass for bus fare, which generally costs approximately $1 to $2, de-

pending on the route; drivers do not carry cash and cannot make change.

Parking is available at many Metrorail stations, but be forewarned that it often fills up quickly on weekdays. It costs $1 to $2.50 on weekdays and is free on weekends and holidays. Some stations also feature a limited number of metered spaces, as well as short-term parking for driver-attended vehicles picking up passengers. If you're dropping off someone, follow signs to the "kiss and ride" lane.

If you have questions while at a Metrorail station, don't hesitate to ask an employee in the information booth near the entrance gates. Otherwise, for general Metrorail and Metrobus details and timetables, call the ridership information line listed above. Operators are on duty daily from 6 AM to 10:30 PM weekdays, and 8 AM to 10:30 PM weekends. Transit Police can be reached in emergencies at (202) 962-2121.

Did you leave something behind? Call Lost and Found at (202) 962-1195.

Bus Systems

Greyhound Bus Lines
1005 1st St. NE, Washington, D.C.
• **(202) 289-5154**

Greyhound offers a less expensive, albeit more time-consuming, alternative to air and rail travel. The automated phone line lists departure times and fares for Atlanta, Boston, New York, Newark, Norfolk, Philadelphia, Pittsburgh and Richmond. Greyhound offers package express and charter services, and the buses also travel to and from these suburban stations:

3860 S. Four Mile Run Road, Arlington, Virginia, (703) 998-6312

4103 Rust Road, Fairfax, Virginia, (703) 273-7770

6583 Backlick Road, Springfield, Virginia, (703) 451-5800

18518 Jefferson Davis Highway, Triangle, Virginia, (703) 221-4080

8100 Fenton Street, Silver Spring, Maryland, (301) 588-5110

Northern Virginia

Alexandria Transit Company's DASH
116 S. Quaker Ln., Alexandria, Va.
• **(703) 370-3274**

DASH buses offer daily service in the City of Alexandria and provide links to Metrobus, Metrorail, Virginia Railway Express and the Fairfax Connector bus system. DASH takes rush-hour passengers to all Alexandria Metrorail stations, as well as the nearby Pentagon station. Base fares are 85¢, with a 25¢ supplemental charge for Pentagon service. Kids younger than age 5 ride for free, with up to two per paying customer. A $28 DASH PASS, available at Alexandria City Hall and other locations, is good for unlimited rides for a month; a Pentagon Pass costs $38 a month. To arrange for pickup by a bus equipped with a wheelchair lift, call by 3 PM the day before your trip. Call the city at (703) 838-3800 for information about door-to-door service for mobility-impaired passengers.

City of Fairfax CUE Bus Service
10455 Armstrong St., Fairfax, Va.
• **(703) 385-7859**

This daily service offers rides in the city and to the Vienna Metrorail Station and George Mason University. Regular fares are 50¢. You can purchase convenient 10-ticket booklets through the City Treasurer's Office, (703) 385-7900. High-school students with school IDs, elementary and intermediate students and ID-carrying seniors age 60 and older ride for 25¢, and George Mason students, faculty and staff with University IDs ride for free. On weekdays, passengers can ride for free from the Vienna station by presenting to the driver a Metro rail-to-bus transfer, available at the station. Disabled persons should call the service to arrange City Wheels or Metro Access transportation.

Fairfax Connector
12055 Government Center Pkwy., Ste. 1034, Fairfax, Va. • **(703) 339-7200, (703) 339-1608 TDD**

One of the largest community bus systems, the daily Fairfax Connector serves much of Fairfax County, supplementing Metrobus routes. Riders need exact cash or Metrobus flash passes, tokens or commuter tickets, and most rides cost 50¢ to $1. All buses in the Reston/Herndon area are wheelchair lift-equipped. To schedule a lift-accessible ride elsewhere, call a day in advance. Pick up timetables at food stores, post offices, libraries, drugstores, governmental centers and various Metro stations.

Loudoun Ride-On
741 Miller Dr. SE, Leesburg, Va.
• **(703) 777-2708**

This bus service, operated by the nonprofit Loudoun County Transit, offers a fixed route in Leesburg and door-to-door service throughout the county on weekdays and Saturdays. Fixed-route service includes travel from Leesburg to the new county hospital east of town and from the hospital to Reston in western Fairfax County. Door-to-door fares are $2 in Leesburg, and $3 town-to-town; and fixed-route fares are $1.

OmniRide
3460 Commission Ct., Woodbridge, Va.
• **(703) 490-4811**

This Prince William County-based commuter bus service is managed by the Potomac and Rappahanock Transportation Commission. The service goes to Franconia-Springfield, West Falls Church, the Pentagon, Crystal City and the District.

Suburban Maryland

The Bus
Prince George's County Department of Public Works & Transportation, 9400 Peppercorn Pl., Ste. 320, Landover, Md.
• **(800) 486-9797 in Maryland,**
(301) 883-5656

The county's newest bus service covers 12 routes from Upper Marlboro to the New Carrollton and Addison Road Metrorail stations. Fares are 75¢ for adults, 35¢ for senior citizens age 55 and older and disabled persons, and free for children younger than age 5.

Call-A-Bus
Prince George's County Office of Transportation, 9400 Peppercorn Pl., Ste. 320, Landover, Md.
• **(301) 499-8603, (800) 899-2287**

This curb-to-curb bus service is available to all Prince George's County residents who are unable to use existing bus or rail service. Seniors and the disabled receive priority. The service runs weekdays, 8:30 AM to 3:30 PM, with fares of $1; seniors and disabled persons pay 50¢. You can make a reservation up to 14 days in advance; same-day requests are subject to availability.

Ride-On
110 N. Washington St., Rockville, Md.
• **(301) 217-7433, (301) 217-6434**

This Montgomery County bus service runs daily, supplementing Metrobus service. Fares are $1.10 during the peak weekday hours of 6 AM to 9:30 AM and 3 PM to 6:30 PM; all other times, fares are 90¢. Children age 4 and

younger ride for free, up to two per fare-paying passenger. Fares for seniors and persons with disabilities are 50¢ at all times with valid IDs. You can obtain special passes, such as the Montgomery Mover All-day transfer, for $1.50 after 9:30 AM weekdays and all day weekends, and a 20-trip ticket for $18, at local Giant supermarkets, government service centers and libraries.

Train Service

Amtrak
Union Station, 50 Massachusetts Ave. NE, Washington, D.C. • **(202) 484-7540, (800) 872-RAIL, (800) 523-6590 TDD**

The 125-mph Metroliner service runs between Washington's grandly restored Union Station (Massachusetts Avenue and N. Capitol Street NE) and New York, offering frequent departures and few stops. Passengers can also travel to such cities as Baltimore, Philadelphia, Boston, Richmond and Atlanta. Call to obtain detailed schedule and fare information. See our Shopping chapter for more information about Union Station.

Dial any of the phone numbers listed above for further information about picking up Amtrak trains at Union Station or at the following suburban stations:

110 Callahan Drive, Alexandria, Virginia
Railroad Avenue, Quantico, Virginia
1040 Express Way, Woodbridge, Virginia
4300 Garden City Drive, New Carrollton, Maryland
Hungerford Drive and Park Street, Rockville, Maryland

Maryland Commuter Rail Service (MARC)
(800) 325-RAIL, (301) 850-5312 TDD

Trains operate Monday through Friday between Washington's Union Station and Baltimore (including Oriole Park at Camden Yards for you baseball and Inner Harbor fans), serving many of the key commuter corridors of Prince George's County. Fares vary according to your destination; you can travel from Union Station to the Camden Yards station for $5.75 one way, and $10.25 roundtrip; $43 for a week's fares or $143 for a month's worth.

MARC also links the region with Martinsburg, West Virginia. Call the numbers listed above for detailed, automated information about stations, schedules and fares.

Virginia Railway Express (VRE)
1500 King St., Ste. 202, Alexandria, Va.
• **(703) 684-0400, (800) 743-3873**

The region's newest commuter rail service hit the tracks in 1992. It's a unique public-private transportation partnership, offering convenient, economical alternatives to car commuting. VRE operates two lines: the Manassas Line, between Manassas and the District, and the Fredericksburg Line, from Fredericksburg to the District.

Manassas Line stations are located in Manassas, Manassas Park, Burke, Springfield, Alexandria, Arlington and the District. Fredericksburg Line stations are in Fredericksburg, Falmouth, Stafford, Quantico, Woodbridge, Lorton, Springfield, Alexandria, Arlington and the District. As with Metro, VRE has easy-to-spot roadside directional signs to help guide travelers to the stations, four of which are just a short walk from easy connections with Metrorail at L'Enfant Plaza and Union Station in the District, and at Crystal City and King Street (Alexandria) in Northern Virginia. Single-ride fares range in price from $2.05 to $6.70, depending on your travel route. You can buy discounted 10-trip and monthly passes. Call for detailed trip information.

Taxicabs

If you opt for a taxi in the District, you'll likely be pleasantly surprised by the cost. Periodic rumblings indicate that drivers want to switch to a metered system, but for now, anyway, the fares are based on a zone pricing system, starting at $3.50 for one person and $1.25 for each additional passenger. The total price varies depending on where you go. Cabs in the suburban jurisdictions still use a traditional meter system.

You shouldn't have any trouble hailing a cab in the District. In the suburbs, you'll most readily find them at Metro stops and the airports; otherwise, you'll need to call to arrange a pickup.

Contact the D.C. Taxicab Commission, 2041 Martin Luther King Jr. Ave. SE, Washington, D.C., (202) 645-6005, with questions or complaints.

Commuter Aids

Commuter Connections
Metropolitan Washington Council of Governments, 777 N. Capitol St. NE, Ste. 300, Washington, D.C.
• **(800) 745-RIDE**

Are you interested in joining a carpool? Missed your ride home because you had to work late? Need information about local mass transit? Commuter Connections, a regional transportation information network, is ready to come to the rescue with solutions to common dilemmas. The Guaranteed Ride Home program provides registered commuters, who regularly travel to work via car alternatives, with free rides home from work, up to four times annually, in cases of emergencies, illnesses or unscheduled overtime. The network's rideshare database helps people find carpools or vanpools in their neighborhoods. Commuter Connections also helps companies implement commuting and "telework" programs; provides information about Park-and-Ride lots, HOV locations and public transit options; and publishes a quarterly newsletter.

Prince George's County Ride Finders
Prince George's County Department of Public Works & Transportation
9400 Peppercorn Pl., Ste. 320, Landover, Md. • **(800) 486-RIDE, (301) 925-5167 TDD**

Fill out an application and you'll receive a

carpool/vanpool match list with names of other commuters with whom you may wish to arrange transportation.

SmarTraveler Information System
400 Virginia Ave. SW., Washington, D.C.
• (202) 863-1313

Call this automated service before you leave for work or home and you'll have an idea of what to expect in traffic and transit conditions. The free service — operated by Partners in Motion, a partnership of several public agencies and private businesses — provides constant updates from 5:30 AM to 7 PM on weekdays, as well as construction and events information all the time. Mobile phone users can dial #211.

Airport Options: National, Dulles and BWI

Washington ranks as one of the top five domestic and international air travel markets, according to the Greater Washington Board of Trade. When traveling requires you to leave the ground — something you'll likely relish after enduring a few Beltway traffic nightmares — you'll be glad that Metro Washington is served by not one, but three major airports: recently-renamed Ronald Reagan Washington National and its sister facility, Washington Dulles International, and Baltimore-Washington International, commonly called BWI. This enviable situation offers travelers some real advantages in terms of choices in scheduling, carrier selection and, to a lesser degree, fares. Combined, the three airports handle about 42 million passengers annually and are served by nearly 50 scheduled airlines. The region is a major cargo hub as well, with more than a billion pounds of air freight transported annually. Dulles, with four air cargo buildings, gets most of the region's cargo business.

While BWI is state-owned and operated, National and Dulles are managed by the Metropolitan Washington Airports Authority (MWAA), an agency created by an act of Congress in 1987. Before the dawn of MWAA, whose Board of Directors features equal representation by Virginia, Maryland and District residents, National and Dulles were the only

two civil airports in the nation run by the federal government. Fortunately for the traveling public and the airline industry, Uncle Sam decided to get out of the civil airport business. Contrary to public perception, MWAA is self-financed; no state or local tax revenues are used to fund airport activities or construction. Oh yes, and don't forget, National and Dulles are very much in Northern Virginia, despite the announcement you may hear on the plane flying in, or the occasional Washington, D.C. address or phone number you may see. The latter are just vestiges of the days of federal control.

For general information on National and Dulles, call the Metropolitan Washington Airports Authority's Airport Information Line at (703) 419-8000. Both National and Dulles are served by the authority's Washington Flyer Ground Transportation System, (703) 685-1400, a network of buses, taxis and limousines. Regular bus service is offered between each airport, to and from the Downtown Terminal at 15th and K streets NW, as well as to and from the West Falls Church Metrorail station. Read on for more information about each individual airport.

Baltimore-Washington International Airport
Maryland Aviation Administration,
P.O. Box 8766, BWI Airport, MD 21240
• (301) 261-1000, (800)-I-FLY-BWI

Baltimore-Washington International often seems overshadowed by National and Dulles, but that's changing. BWI is modern, easy to get to, easy to use and ably serves both of its namesake markets with all major domestic carriers. A new 370,000-square-foot International Pier opened recently, garnering high praise from the local media. Recently completed projects include parking garage expansion, moving pedestrian walkways and a recreational trail.

Arlington-based USAirways in particular offers extensive service, and BWI is the only local airport served by wildly popular Southwest Airlines. The airport also boasts a handful of foreign airlines, including Air Aruba, Air Jamaica, British Airways, El Al Israel and Icelandair. BWI also has taken the lead in offering regional residents the most choices in

Photo: Courtesy of Washington Dulles International Airport

Washington Dulles International Airport is the area's
full-service domestic and international hub.

low-cost flights, with Southwest and Continental in particular slugging it out in fare wars. Low-fare ProAir in 1997 began offering two daily flights to Detroit.

The fact that BWI is so user-friendly, boasts ample parking and is served by both the Amtrak and MARC rail lines gives the airport added clout with the flying public. Garage parking is free for the first half-hour, a welcome bonus if you're just dropping off a passenger. Rates after the first 30 minutes are $2 per half-hour, with a maximum $15 for the day. Other parking options include ESP Parking close to the terminal, with on-demand shuttle service at $4 per hour, with a $13 daily maximum; Daily Express, with frequent shuttle service at $2 per hour, with a $9 daily maximum; and Satellite Parking, with many shuttles at $1 per hour, with a $6 daily maximum, and the seventh day free. Seven car rental companies are on the premises, and visitors will find plenty of taxis and limousines.

While you wait, grab a bite to eat at one of the airport's fast-food restaurants or bars, or browse one of the speciality shops like the Smithsonian Museum Shop. The airport also has a game room and observation gallery to keep fidgety kids happy.

Count on nearly an hour's drive to BWI from downtown Washington or Northern Virginia — and that's without heavy traffic! The airport is in Anne Arundel County just off the Baltimore-Washington Parkway, but is also easily accessible from I-95. Ample signs are posted along the Maryland portion of the Capital Beltway, clearly showing you which exit to take for BWI, a great help for some of us provincial Northern Virginians who don't wander into the Free State very often except for the occasional sporting event, concert or trip to the beach.

Ronald Reagan Washington National Airport
Arlington County, Va. • (703) 417-8000

The $400 million main terminal that opened at National in July 1997 is a dazzling new landmark — the cornerstone of the airport authority's hefty modernization and improvement program for both National and

---

INSIDERS' TIP

Superstitious? You won't find a Gate 13 at Ronald Reagan Washington National Airport!

Dulles. Designed by award-winning architect Cesar Pelli, the spacious terminal, with its scalloped roof and striking control tower, proves as convenient as it is eye-catching. As passengers follow clearly marked paths to their gates, they can enjoy the sky-lit views in the high, vaulted ceiling; admire tiled floor medallions, colorful railing panels, murals, glass friezes and sculpture designed by nationally known artists; browse in shops like The Disney Store and Victoria's Secret; and grab snacks or meals at various sit-down and take-out restaurants.

Joined to the terminal by a covered walkway, one of three new parking garages offers quick access. A stone's throw from the pedestrian bridge, Metro's Blue and Yellow lines pick up and deposit riders. Add a revamped road network to these innovations and you've got an airport that's finally reversing its long-held reputation for being difficult. National, which has served the region since 1941, will only get better, not bigger, as airport officials like to say.

National is the region's close-in, short-haul airport; it handles domestic traffic only, with nonstop flights limited to 1,250 miles — the number of landings and takeoffs each day is tightly controlled by federal regulations to limit noise. In Arlington County just off the George Washington Memorial Parkway and abutting the Potomac River (from which much of National's land mass was claimed), it couldn't be much closer to the heart of Washington, D.C. Under normal traffic conditions, it's about a 10-minute ride from the airport, up the parkway, over the 14th Street Bridge and into the District. It's only about another five minutes to Capitol Hill. National is unbeatable for convenience. Just ask a member of Congress or anyone who works or lives in nearby Crystal City, Rosslyn or Alexandria. National is served by all the major domestic carriers and a host of commuter airlines, as well as the popular USAirways and Delta shuttles that ferry passengers hourly between Washington, New York and Boston.

Hourly parking is $2 per half-hour, with a $26-per-day maximum. Park in the daily garage for $2 per half-hour, with a $10 daily maximum. Parking at long-term lots, with plenty of free shuttles, costs $1 an hour, and $8 maximum per day.

Washington Dulles International Airport
Fairfax and Loudoun Counties, Va.
• **(703) 417-8000**

Dulles, at the end of the airport-only access road 26 miles (about 45 minutes) from downtown Washington, is the area's full-service domestic and international hub. Dulles was the first airport built for the jet age, opening in 1962 and named after John Foster Dulles, secretary of state under President Eisenhower. Finnish-born architect Eero Saarinen sought to convey the movement of flight in his design of the stunning main terminal, which the American Institute of Architects has recognized as one of the greatest architectural achievements of the 20th century. Beauty wasn't a harbinger of immediate success, however. Plagued by a "white elephant" label virtually from day one, Dulles languished severely until the mid-1980s when a concerted effort was made to market and promote the airport and its rich, untapped potential.

Airlines and passengers have since been flocking to Dulles in increasing numbers as the airport further establishes itself as a major player in international aviation. All major domestic airlines (United has a substantial presence) and more than a dozen foreign carriers serve Dulles. The roster continues to grow as the airport expands and bolsters its role as an East Coast hub for travel to Europe and the Far East. Its 10,000-acre site on the Loudoun/Fairfax border, a broad expanse of meadows and forest near established residential areas and a booming business corridor, provides room for enlargement that few airports in the world can match.

And grow it will as Dulles prepares to meet the challenges of the 21st century. The airport authority's $2 billion Capital Development Program, targeting 159 improvement projects at National and Dulles, is producing splendid results: Dulles boasts a new International Arrivals Building, expanded parking, new roads and overpasses and, most notably, doubling of the main terminal's length to 1,240 feet. More new projects are in the works, with work expected to continue until the early 21st century.

With any luck, a rail line will be constructed in the median of the airport access road just as was intended when the property was purchased by the federal government in the late 1950s. Such a line would conceivably link up with Metrorail's West Falls Church station, providing Dulles with the long-needed access befitting of an airport that's billed as the world's gateway to the nation's capital.

Meanwhile, many people still find Dulles easily accessible, thanks to the access road, which connects to I-66. Parking proves relatively hassle-free, with close-to-terminal and various reduced price satellite options available. The terminal houses a variety of eateries and shops to keep passengers occupied while waiting.

Other Area Airports

Northern Virginia

Leesburg Airport
1001 Sycolin Rd. SE, Leesburg, Va.
• (703) 777-9285

The Leesburg Airport — also known as Godfrey Airport as a tribute to famous former resident Arthur Godfrey — boasts an FAA Automated Flight Service Station, three professional flight schools and a variety of aircraft available for rent. A Reliever Airport for nearby Dulles International, Leesburg has a 5,500-foot runway. The airport offers full aircraft maintenance services, an on-site conference room and courtesy features for both passengers and flight crews.

Manassas Regional Airport
Off Rt. 28, 4 miles SE of Manassas, Va.
• (703) 361-1882

One of the busiest airports in the Commonwealth, this 830-acre airport founded in 1963 handles about 140,000 takeoffs and landings annually. It has a 5,700-foot by 100-foot primary runway with Instrument Landing System and a new terminal building that opened in September 1996. A proposed upcoming project calls for reconstructing a secondary runway and extending a parallel taxiway. The airport boasts more than 300 based aircraft, the most of any airport in the state.

The FAA Level 2 Tower is open 6:30 AM to 10:30 PM, and the facility is open 24 hours a day. Two fixed-base operators, Falconhead FBO, (703) 361-7267, UNICOM frequency 122.95; and Dulles Aviation Inc., (703) 361-2171, UNICOM frequency 123.0, offer flight instruction and other services. Other flight schools on the premises include Flightech, (703) 257-9999; Metropolitan Helicopters Inc., (703) 361-4684; and Manassas Aviation Center Inc., (703) 361-0575. Other amenities include three pilot supply shops, a restaurant, maintenance services and hangar space for rent. Owned and operated by the city of Manassas, the airport generates a $41.5 million annual economic impact.

Suburban Maryland

College Park Airport
6709 Corporal Frank Scott Dr., College Park, Md. • (301) 864-5844

This airport in Prince George's County boasts a museum dedicated to its storied past. College Park is the world's oldest continuously operating airport and plays nearly as important a role in aviation history as does Kitty Hawk, North Carolina. In 1909, Orville Wright came here to teach the first Army officers how to fly, and between 1909 and 1934, the airport was the site of many aviation firsts.

For More Info

For answers to questions about highway travel in the region, we suggest you contact the following offices:

• Virginia Department of Transportation, 1401 East Broad Street, Richmond, Virginia, (804) 786-5731

• Maryland Transportation Authority, 303 Authority Drive, Baltimore, Maryland, (410) 288-8400

• District of Columbia's Department of Public Works, 7th Floor, 2000 14th St. NW, Washington, D.C., (202) 939-8000.

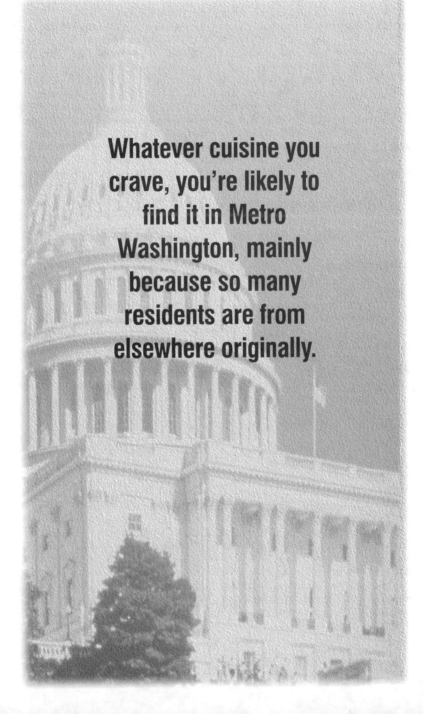

Whatever cuisine you crave, you're likely to find it in Metro Washington, mainly because so many residents are from elsewhere originally.

Restaurants

From Chinatown to Adams Morgan, Capitol Hill to Georgetown, Rockville to Old Town Alexandria, and Tysons Corner to Bethesda, a veritable dining world in miniature awaits you. Whatever cuisine you crave, you're likely to find it in Metro Washington, mainly because so many residents are from elsewhere originally; yet Washington has only recently begun to be recognized as a city for fine dining. Compared to San Francisco, say, or New Orleans, the Metro area's culinary stars are few, but they are growing in prominence.

Magazines like *Gourmet*, *Bon Appétit* — and their readers — have begun to sit up and take notice, and several Washington chefs have won international reputations. It had to happen sooner or later, given the area's demographics. Metro Washington offers a customer base that is diverse, well-traveled and affluent. Suffice it to say that there are plenty of folks here who appreciate good food and who can afford to dine out regularly. Not to say that you can't dine reasonably. There are some bargains, especially among Washington's ethnic eateries. You'll also find the national chains, from the economical Chili's to the deluxe steak houses like the Palm, Morton's and Ruth's Chris Steak House. But if you're from anywhere except New York, Tokyo or London, get ready for sticker shock. Even the most folksy eateries are likely to be pricier than you'll find back home.

Before we get into the meat of this chapter, though, a few words about the ingredients.

Please keep in mind: This is in no way an exhaustive listing. We'd probably still be writing if that was the objective! Instead, we've dished up an eclectic buffet, if you will — a little of this and a little of that — to give you a taste for what's available. Still, we've barely scratched the proverbial surface — or rather, removed that first delicious layer — of what Metro Washington has to offer in the way of calories, carbohydrates and cholesterol.

The restaurants that made the cut are a mix of recognized local favorites (in some cases, institutions), very personal choices and a smattering of others in the District, Suburban Maryland and Northern Virginia. With a few exceptions, none of the major national chain establishments (including fast-food outlets, sandwich/pizza joints and full-service family restaurants such as Bennigan's, Ruby Tuesday, Chi-chi's, Outback Steakhouse, etc.) are represented. We want to introduce you to places you're unlikely to find anywhere else.

Be sure to check out our "Close-up" on kids' dining in the Kidstuff chapter also.

Price-Code Key

To give you an idea of what to expect price-wise, we've provided the following scale as a very general guide. Prices shown are for a complete dinner for two including appetizers, wine, beer or spirits, and dessert, but excluding tax and tip. All, of course, are subject to change.

$	$40 or less
$$	$40 to $65
$$$	$65 to $100
$$$$	More than $100

All establishments listed accept most major credit cards unless otherwise noted.

Restaurants are divided first by jurisdictions: Washington, Northern Virginia and Maryland. Within each jurisdiction, we've broken down the list by ethnic cuisine, and restaurants in each ethnic heading are in alphabetic order. One final note — seafood restaurants used to be a separate category, but fish is now so prevalent on most menus that we've simply grouped these restaurants according to the type of ethnic cuisine they specialize in.

Bon appétit!

Washington, D.C.

American/Continental

Aquarelle
$$$ • Watergate Hotel, 2650 Virginia Ave. NW, Washington, D.C.
• (202) 298-4455

This spot in the notorious Watergate Hotel offers great views of the Potomac River (ask for a window-side table) and pre-theater bargains, thanks to its location next door to the Kennedy Center. The food is a creative blend of top-quality American ingredients with a Continental accent. There are several hard-to-find items on this gourmet menu, including game and, at times, fresh foie gras. Aquarelle serves breakfast, lunch and dinner daily. During the day, the room has the casual feel of a hotel restaurant, but it dresses up at night — and you may want to also.

Blackie's House of Beef
$$ • 1217 22nd St. NW, Washington, D.C.
• (202) 333-1100

Opened in 1946, Blackie's has established itself as a Washington landmark, and it's an easy one to find. A white building dripping with New Orleans-style black wrought iron, Blackie's sits just off M Street between Georgetown and downtown. This place is a bit kitschy and very cozy, with fireplaces and all the warming touches you could ask for. Not a gourmet mecca, but rather a place for hearty appetites, Blackie's features generously thick steaks and roast beef, as well as some

standard seafood dishes. They are open for lunch weekdays and dinner nightly.

Capital Grille
$$$$ • 601 Pennsylvania Ave. NW, Washington, D.C. • (202) 737-6200

Yes, Capital Grille is part of a chain, but since it was only the third link, we've decided to include it. Why? In a very short time it has become one of the trendiest places around Capitol Hill, the kind of establishment where you're likely to run into the town's top lobbyists, along with the legislators they're trying to pitch. Nowadays, some of Washington's most important powerbrokers are women, and you'll find them here, too, but this place has the atmosphere of a men's club — dark wood, dark green and, yes, even hunting trophies. From the street, you're greeted with a view of the meat-aging room, complete with moldy rinds that will be expertly cut away to provide you with flavorful —and humongous — cuts of beef. Even vegetarians will find something to like here if they are able to overlook the carnivorous atmosphere. The baked potatoes weigh a pound and salads are a meal in themselves. Capital Grille is open for lunch weekdays and dinner nightly.

Cashion's Eat Place
$$$ • 1819 Columbia Rd. NW, Washington, D.C. • (202) 797-1819

Ann Cashion is one of the town's most innovative chefs, and she has won many honors to prove it, both locally and nationally. Her namesake restaurant serves dinner nightly and Sunday brunch, but is closed Mondays.

The dining room is curved, and spills into the street on warm summer evenings, thanks to a front wall of windows. The crowd is as eclectic as the Adams Morgan neighborhood which is home to the restaurant. There are

---

INSIDERS' TIP

Dining havens such as Arlington, Bethesda, Adams Morgan and Georgetown have scores of restaurants of every nationality in short distances of one another.

Nora Pouillon: A Pioneer in Healthy Cooking

Nora Pouillon is a ground-breaker. When she was named 1996 Chef of the Year by the San Francisco-based American Tasting Institute, she became the first woman ever to receive the award. That was only one in a long career of firsts, though. Twenty years ago, when Pouillon opened her small Restaurant Nora in a Washington, D.C. townhouse, it immediately became all the rage. No other fine chef in the city insisted on organic vegetables or meats unadulterated by hormones and antibiotics. Nora's was crowded for lunch and crowded for dinner. Two decades later, its popularity hasn't waned a bit. If anything, it's grown. Maybe it's the fact that President Clinton dined there soon after his election. Or maybe it's Nora herself.

The Viennese-born chef is always on a mission, always striving to get out the message about organic foods, even now that they are so popular. Typical of Pouillon is her role as a founding member of Chef's Collaborative 2000, which promotes the use of food from growers who practice organic agriculture. The water she uses at her newest restaurant, Asia Nora, comes from an Aquapure system especially designed for Pouillon. "It is essential that our water is free of chlorine, calcium, magnesium, bacteria and all metals. We feel that our water is better than any bottled brand. Just taste it!" says Pouillon. One thing is certain, after the recent scares in D.C. resulting from bacteria-contaminated water, systems like Pouillon's are more important than ever.

As for the wine list at Nora's restaurants, many offerings are organic. And it doesn't

— continued on next page

Photo: Courtesy of Camilla Rothwell, Assistant to Nora Pouillon

Nora Pouillon strives to get the message out on organic foods.

end there. Her dairy products are from The Organic Cow of Vermont. Her herbs come from her own patio garden at Restaurant Nora, a little patch of green carved out of the sidewalk near the entrance. The beef she serves is from cattle fed a high fiber diet of organic hay and cereal grains. Her soft-shell crabs are still moving when they're delivered each morning. Pouillon is quick to stress that she practices what she preaches, even in her private life. Chefs are notorious for their late hours and indulgent diets, but Pouillon, a mother of four, says she has always been conscious of a healthy lifestyle for the sake of her family. Her daily ritual begins with either yoga or aerobic dance, and she's a regular participant in sports ranging from Rollerblading to swimming.

Fitness magazine recently honored her as one of America's healthiest chefs and her unique organic lifestyle was the topic of a feature article in Japan's top food and living magazine. Such accolades are nothing new to Pouillon, who in recent years has been praised in publications as diverse as *Gourmet*, *USA Today*, *Travel & Leisure*, *The Washington Post*, *Food & Wine*, the *San Francisco Examiner* and *Vegetarian Times*. Recently, Pouillon's career was crowned by two events monumental in the life of any chef: the publication of her first cookbook and her Chef of the Year award from the prestigious International Association of Culinary Professionals. Pouillon's goal in writing *Cooking With Nora* (Park Lane Press, May 1996) is to demonstrate how easy it is to cook foods that are both organic and low in fat. "I hate hidden calories in restaurants and try not to do the same to my customers," she told *Washington Woman* magazine. "Being a woman I think makes me more sensitive to the 'fat' subject." And that's a philosophy we can all appreciate.

---

sleek women in black dresses — and black lipstick to match — along with young execs in khakis and the occasional business-suited lawyers. The real attraction, however, is the food. It has a down-home, southern touch, but there's always an interesting fillip, often in the chef's choice of vegetable accompaniments.

The menu changes regularly, but once recently, the salmon was served on buttery summer cabbage with a sherry vinegar beurre blanc; the grilled swordfish in tomato-lime salsa came with a side of fried yucca and cubanelle peppers. There are all kinds of exotic meats, like buffalo, sweetbreads and guinea hen. What really makes dining here memorable, though, is Cashion's flair for seasoning. She manages to make her dishes distinctive, but she's so skilled at combining flavors, that you're not quite sure what the ingredients are.

Chadwicks
$$ • 3205 K St. NW, Washington, D.C.
• (202) 333-2565
It's tough to avoid comparisons with the local Clyde's chain (see subsequent entry), but Chadwicks should view it as a compliment.

It's easy to find something to like in this warm, inviting Georgetown saloon/restaurant, be it the woodsy atmosphere, the selection from the bar or the hamburgers. Indeed, this may be one of the best burgers in town, thick and charbroiled to your taste. The rest of the menu is the usual saloon fare, served in generous portions: seafood, soups, salads, pasta and the like. Chadwicks serves lunch and dinner daily, and Sunday brunch. The only hard part for the uninitiated may be finding this place, which sits literally beneath the Whitehurst Freeway near the foot of Wisconsin Avenue.

Clyde's of Georgetown
$$ • 3236 M St. NW, Washington, D.C.
• (202) 333-9180
Here's a D.C. institution that was smart enough to bring its success to the suburbs. Although all of the locations outside the Beltway have proven to be a hit, none have quite the charm as this recently renovated street-front saloon in the very crux of trendy Georgetown. Serving lunch and dinner daily, and Sunday brunch, it's a raucous, lively place — a little bit meat market, a little bit family fun

Photo: Courtesy of Clifton — The Country Inn

Whether dining at an elegant country inn or an eclectic Adams Morgan restaurant, you'll find unlimited dining options.

center — all housed in nooks and alcoves that feature touches of stained glass, extravagant art and, often, wall-to-wall people. Beyond the irresistible bar area, Clyde's beckons with its own brand of award-winning chili, steaks, burgers, salads, sandwiches and homemade desserts. Clyde's makes a special effort to buy its produce from local farmers, so the veggie dishes can be among the freshest in town. The food's not always perfect — and almost never exceptional — but the place is a blast, and its appeal is broad. Patrons include college students, families and business types.

Dean & DeLuca Café
$ • 3276 M St. NW, Washington, D.C.
• (202) 342-2500

Shopping in Georgetown and want to grab a quick bite? Do you need some takeout to stock your hotel room? This self-service counter, serving lunch and dinner daily in one of D.C.'s premier gourmet markets, will fit the bill with passable-to-yummy soups, sandwiches, salads and fresh baked goods. For those who need an extra shot of energy, there's also an espresso bar.

Georgia Brown's
$$$ • 950 I St. NW, Washington, D.C.
• (202) 393-4499

If upscale soul food's your bag, this is the place, but if you prefer traditional preparations, you may be startled by some of the innovations at Georgia Brown's. You'll find black-eyed peas, grits and collards — but they may not taste familiar. A few years back, in fact, Washington's food community was embroiled in debate about Georgia Brown's crispy collards, anathema to southern cooks who leave 'em simmerin' all day 'till they melt in your mouth. In response, Georgia Brown's added the traditional collards to their menu, but kept the crispy greens for those who preferred them. Try Georgia Brown's at lunch and you're likely to run into D.C. government bigwigs, including the mayor himself. Georgia Brown's serves lunch weekdays, dinner nightly and Sunday brunch.

The Jockey Club

$$$$ • ITT Sheraton Hotel, 2100 Massachusetts Ave. NW, Washington, D.C. • (202) 659-8000

This is Washington tradition at its best. Power dining defined since it opened more than 30 years ago, The Jockey Club has endured as a gathering spot for the town's movers and shakers. Some may not feel comfortable in the highbrow, clubby atmosphere or the tony Embassy Row locale, but it's gracious and elegant nevertheless, and you're sure to enjoy what the kitchen produces. Open for breakfast, lunch and dinner daily, The Jockey Club serves familiar standards made properly, which is often not the case elsewhere: French onion soup, Dover sole, crabcakes and, best of all — their special pommes soufflés, heavenly crisp puffs of potato filled with fragrant air. Here, also you'll rediscover the drama of tableside preparation abandoned by most modern restaurants. It's a great place to propose marriage . . . or anything else you have in mind.

Kinkead's

$$$ • 2000 Pennsylvania Ave. NW, Washington, D.C. • (202) 296-7700

Seafood is the specialty of imaginative Robert Kinkead, one of Washington's premier chefs, and a Boston transplant. This casual restaurant serves lunch Monday through Saturday, Sunday brunch and dinner nightly. Just four blocks from the White House, Kinkead's is always packed, and the wooden booths and floors make for some noisy rooms. The atmosphere, however, is beside the point in a place that transforms seafood into such a melting, rich, heavenly experience. Kinkead runs this restaurant with military precision, as you can see through the open kitchen. The kitchen staff wear headphones to communicate above the clatter, turning out seafood timed to perfection. Try the skate wing if they have it or, in season, the soft-shell crab. The seasonings are bold and exotic, and the appetizers are almost too pretty to eat.

Maine Avenue Wharf

$ • 1100 Maine Ave. SW, Washington, D.C. • (202) 488-0823

Looking for local color? You won't find anything more authentic than this spot down the road from the Jefferson Memorial — just a hop away from the embarkation point for all the cruise tours. This is nothing more than a row of stalls selling all kinds of fresh seafood, some of it ready to cook, some already cooked. You can get fish sandwiches, softshell crabs and those famous Maryland blue crabs. There are even lobsters and just-shucked bivalves. Tote your meal to the water's edge and dangle your feet over the Potomac, or find a bench and . . . presto, you're in seafood heaven.

Melrose Park Hyatt Hotel

$$$$ • 1201 24th St. NW, Washington, D.C. • (202) 955-3899

Melrose breaks the mold of hotel restaurants, which aren't generally regarded as serious eateries (though that is changing). There's an Asian influence to some of the cooking here, but also several traditional, luxe Continental dishes. Every ingredient is top quality, as are the artistic presentations. On a warm day, the outdoor terrace garden with its wide canvas umbrellas is great for people-watching, thanks to its location on a busy corner of M Street. The marble and brass dining room, with its plush banquettes and floor-to-ceiling windows makes you feel pampered, as does the gracious service. The prices are as high as the very best restaurants in town, and although Melrose is very good, you may not feel it warrants a budget-busting evening. They are open for breakfast, lunch Monday through Saturday, dinner and Sunday brunch.

Mr. Smith's

$$ • 3104 M St. NW, Washington, D.C. • (202) 333-3104

You won't be able to see the lovely patio garden from the street, yet it's the main draw at this saloon/eatery in Georgetown. You'll find standard pub fare at reasonable prices and, at night, a piano bar. If you like fancy cocktails, this place features daiquiris and other frozen drinks in a dozen varieties. Mr. Smith's serves lunch and dinner daily, and Sunday brunch.

Music City Roadhouse

$ • 1050 30th St. NW, Washington, D.C. • (202) 337-4444

It's hard to get much more "American" than this in D.C., although you'll think you're in Tennessee. A typical dinner begins with homemade soup and fresh garden salad. The main course may include fried Delta Pride catfish, chicken and biscuits, or smoked pork ribs, collard greens, creamed corn, cheese grits and corn bread hot from the oven. Choose what you like, and eat as much as you want, since it's served "boardinghouse style." Filling and tasty it is, healthful and low fat it's not, but this fun, unique dining concept indeed feels down-home, even in a building that used to house the Georgetown Foundry restaurant.

One of the proprietors says the cuisine at Music City Roadhouse is designed to be "like Sunday supper at Grandma's, seven days a week." That may be a stretch, but it is a refreshing change of pace for Washington, right down to the mismatched linoleum and wooden tables, photos of country music stars and the hodgepodge of rummage-sale artifacts hanging from the walls, columns and ceilings. If you happen to go on a Sunday, time it to experience the Sunday Gospel Brunch, complete with live gospel performances and a spread with such delights as silver dollar blueberry pancakes, smoked sausage, scrambled eggs and buttermilk fried chicken. Music City Roadhouse is open for lunch Tuesday through Saturday, dinner Tuesday through Sunday, and Sunday brunch. They are closed on Monday.

New Heights

$$$$ • 2317 Calvert St. NW, Washington, D.C. • (202) 234-4110

This second-floor charmer overlooks the massive Omni Shoreham Hotel and Rock Creek Park. Serving dinner nightly and Sunday brunch, it has the warm, casual feel of an artsy neighborhood bistro, but don't be deceived. It has been home to some of the hottest young chefs in the country, including the latest at press time — Matthew Lake — nationally recognized by several gourmet organizations and magazines. As befits such an avant-garde kitchen, the menu is full of surprising combinations, most of which succeed. It's hard to recommend any particular dish, since the menu is revised on a regular basis, but be assured whatever you order will be cooked properly. Hope and pray that the hot chocolate cake is still in the repertoire when you go. It is a dream of dark chocolate and caramel. New Heights is open for dinner nightly and Sunday brunch.

Old Ebbitt Grill

$$ • 675 15th St. NW, Washington, D.C. • (202) 347-4801

When they say old, they mean it — since 1856. Old Ebbitt Grill bills itself as "Washington's oldest saloon," and while that may be subject to argument, especially since its renovation (handsome forest green upholstery, mahogany booths and Victorian lamps), its stellar reputation and prime location are not. Just two blocks from the White House, this casually elegant establishment long ago made a name for itself with roasts, steaks, fresh seafood, homemade pastas, soups, burgers, deli-style sandwiches and homemade desserts. Check out the famed Oyster Bar — even if you don't a have a taste for this particular Chesapeake Bay delicacy.

Old Ebbitt Grill is open for lunch Monday through Saturday, dinner nightly, and Sunday brunch. With a 3 AM closing time on Friday and Saturday, it's understandably popular with the hungry after-theater crowds. In the Grill's atrium you'll find Ebbitt Express, serving freshly prepared, wholesome takeout food for breakfast, lunch and dinner.

Old Glory

$ • 3139 M St. NW, Washington, D.C. • (202) 337-3406

Great barbecue, sandwiches and burgers, a lively, casual atmosphere and fascinating history-rich decor combine to make Georgetown's Old Glory something to shoot fireworks about. If you take your barbecue seriously, you'll want to sample all eight of the sauces here: each follows the recipe of a different barbecue region like Memphis and Texas. Corn muffins, biscuits and hush puppies here are the real thing, but save room for the mouth-watering desserts. This is a noisy, fun spot, so be sure to add it to the list of places to consider for birthday celebrations or other get-togethers. Old Glory is open for lunch Monday through Saturday, dinner nightly and Sunday brunch.

Prime Rib

$$$$ • 2020 K St. NW, Washington, D.C. • (202) 466-8811

This is a place for high-rollers, and you'll sense it as soon as you see the flashy blondes

Beyond the historic homes and bustling nightlife of Georgetown lies Washington Harbour, an enclave of shops and restaurants situated on the Potomac River.

at the lively bar and lots of fit, fiftyish men . . . with lots of money. People dress up for dinner here: dark suits, slinky black dresses and even a bit of glitter. The dining room has the feel of an old-time lovers' rendezvous, with its draperies and martinis and baby-grand piano — but it's too crowded for an effective hideaway. The food here is as much an attraction as the ambiance. You won't find better prime aged beef, and there's live Maine lobster and fresh Florida seafood flown in daily. Don't forget the traditional accompaniments either: mouth-watering mashed potatoes and creamed spinach. Prime Rib is open for lunch weekdays and dinner Monday through Saturday.

Restaurant Nora
$$$$ • 2132 Florida Ave. NW, Washington, D.C. • (202) 462-5143

Nora Pouillon, the chef and founder of Restaurant Nora, was one of the first in the city to insist on organic ingredients. From free-range poultry to farm-fresh chévre, Nora has always produced the best and most healthful food. Her cozy restaurant has the same honest, farmhouse feeling, with its decorative handicrafts, dark wood floors and Windsor chairs. As is often the case with simple beauty, this eatery attracts the rich and famous, from President Clinton to media

mogul Barry Dillard. Dishes are sophisticated without necessarily being too calorie-laden, with influences from India, France and, of course, the U.S. In general, the cuisine will suit those who prefer their foods less seasoned. Those who savor strong flavors may even find some dishes a bit bland. If you go, be sure to save room for one of the special fresh fruit desserts. Restaurant Nora is open for dinner Monday through Saturday, and closed on Sunday. See our "Close-up" on Nora in this chapter.

Rupperts
$$$$ • 1017 7th St. NW, Washington, D.C. • (202) 783-0699

This top-notch restaurant is in a part of town that is, to put it kindly, in transition. On the plus side, it's only a couple of blocks from the Washington Convention Center. On the minus side, the block is almost entirely boarded up and there is an empty lot across the street that can attract an unsavory element. So how does Rupperts continue to draw well-heeled customers from all over the city? It's simple — the food is irresistible.

Step through the front door and you're greeted by a romantic refuge complete with flowers, crisp white linens and candlelight. But the food is what's important here. The menu changes according to what's available at market, and that can mean foie gras, osetra caviar with tiny French green beans, squab and several kinds of uncommon fish. Vegetarians will have no trouble eating here, thanks to all sorts of interesting produce. Stop right now if you're getting full though, because you are forbidden to miss dessert! It's worth every calorie. Though the dessert menu changes as often as the dinner menu, and what we had may not be available when you go, do not pass up the brown sugar ice cream swamped in plump raspberries and apples. The other members of your party will just have to settle for the sculpture of blackberries and white chocolate mousse or the figs and chocolate.

Lunch is served on Thursday only. Dinner is served Tuesday through Saturday, and they are closed on Sunday and Monday.

1789 Restaurant
$$$$ • 1226 36th St. NW, Washington, D.C. • (202) 965-1789

Perhaps it's the location, a two-story Federal townhouse in a quiet residential area of upper northwest in the shadows of Georgetown University. Then, once you treat your palate to the food, that immediately carries equal weight. Whatever the reason, 1789 captivates with its country-inn charm and elegance and the efficient, first-class service. Although named for the year the university was founded, 1789 offers a truly Modern American menu, serving dinner nightly, with such classic treats as pheasant, venison, fish, veal, soft-shell crabs, lobster and homemade soups. Top Washington chef Ris Lacoste makes daily menu changes to accommodate what's fresh at market. Be sure to leave room for the breads and desserts, all whipped up on-premises. 1789 is open for dinner nightly.

Sholl's Colonial Cafeteria
$ • 1990 K St. NW, Washington, D.C. • (202) 296-3065

This Washington institution is a great place for a quick bite when you're out sight-seeing — or on a budget. Unlike most cafeterias, Sholl's serves fresh veggies — lots of them — and simple, old-fashioned entrées that can be very tasty. Like most other cafeterias, there are scads of desserts, but at Sholl's lots of them are made in-house and are real treats. If you like pudding, this is the place to go. Doughnuts and biscuits? They're homemade at Sholl's. Serving breakfast and lunch daily, and dinner Monday through Saturday, Sholl's does not accept credit cards or checks.

Vidalia
$$$ • 1990 M St. NW, Washington, D.C. • (202) 659-1990

You'd never guess there was a sunny farmhouse dining room in the basement of this midtown office building, but that's just the impression you'll get when you walk through the door of Vidalia. The bright yellow surroundings pique the appetite, as do the heavenly aromas from the kitchen. Here you'll find haute southern cuisine with accents of whatever else inspires the chef, and whatever is fresh at market. Unlike much southern cooking, which relies on frying and slow-simmering, Vidalia serves dishes with real finesse and its own creative touches. You'll be off to a good start with a bread basket of corn muffins and sweet potato biscuits so sinful you may be tempted to make a meal of them. For a main course, you'll find all sorts of great, rich southern-influenced dishes. The seafood is juicy and prepared just right, and these may be the best sweetbreads in town. Vegetable accompaniments are always unusual, but rarely low-cal, so don't look for salvation here. In fact, wear something loose here because you'll be waddling away at meal's end. Vidalia is open for lunch weekdays, dinner Monday through Saturday and closed on Sunday.

West End Café
$$$ • Washington Circle Hotel, 1 Washington Cir. NW, Washington, D.C. • (202) 293-5390

A great place for a pre- or post-theater dinner, the West End Café is an adventurous but comfortable dining spot. One of the two dining rooms features plenty of greenery and glass; the other doubles as a piano bar, and has a darker, more intimate feeling with its earth-toned walls and upholstery. There's a lot of leeway for mixing and matching meals here, and many types of cuisine influence the menu. There is simple fare like pizzas and omelets, but also more elaborate main courses that highlight interesting spices and exotic ingredient mixes. Vegetarians, too, will appreciate the extra effort that has gone into dreaming up some of the meatless dishes. There's a little something for everyone at the West End Café, serving breakfast, lunch and dinner daily, and Sunday brunch.

Willard Room
$$$$ • Inter-Continental Hotel, 1401 Pennsylvania Ave. NW, Washington, D.C. • (202) 637-7440

The Willard Room is almost daunting in its grandeur: soaring ceilings decorated with medallions and carved moldings, elaborate chandeliers, silken draperies and table settings fit for royalty. The cooking is also rich and elaborate — a cuisine that hearkens back to the turn of the century when course after lavish course was served. You'll find all the rare epicurean treats here — game, truffles and vegetables in fancy shapes and combinations. Eye-popping desserts are wheeled to your table on a dessert cart that looks like it came straight from Paris, both in its construction and its contents. It's all lovely, and yet no one dish is a standout. If you're out to impress a client or a date, you couldn't choose better surroundings, but if it's a truly memorable meal you're after, there may be better choices for the money. The Willard Room is open for breakfast and lunch weekdays, and dinner nightly.

African

Fasika's
$ • 2447 18th St. NW, Washington, D.C. • (202) 797-7673

This newest entry into the Ethiopian restaurant scene offers an upscale atmosphere. In summer, the patio, with its linen-covered tables, offers a fascinating vantage point for people-watching. Inside, the room is decorated with huge African baskets and tambours covered in colorful prints. The lights are flat-

tering and there are plenty of plants in the front windows. Go for the fixed price, eight-course dinner accompanied by live music. The food is standard for Ethiopian — spicy stews of seafood, meat or poultry, large flat breads, greens, yams and other vegetarian main courses. Lunch and dinner are served daily.

Meskerem
$ • 2434 18th St. NW, Washington, D.C. • (202) 462-4100

National recognition and awards galore have done a lot to enhance the reputation of this Ethiopian restaurant, which some critics rank as the nation's finest. If you enjoy such dining adventures, one visit will have you singing its praises too. Enjoy the big floppy crepe-like bread for scooping up the various hot and mild meat dishes including beef, lamb and chicken, the lentils and green vegetables, and all that glorious sauce. You can't beat the prices. Meskerem would be justified charging more, but it's nice that they don't. Lunch and dinner are served daily.

Red Sea
$ • 2463 18th St. NW, Washington, D.C. • (202) 483-5000

Serving lunch and dinner nightly, Red Sea is also a heavyweight contender in the local arena of award-winning Ethiopian kitchens. Succulent lamb and beef, delicious poultry and seafood, irresistible spices and stews, and an excellent vegetarian menu combine to rank Red Sea as yet another Adams Morgan stalwart. To enhance what the palate enjoys, traditional music is performed on Friday and Saturday nights.

Zed's Ethiopian Cuisine
$ • 3318 M St. NW, Washington, D.C. • (202) 333-4710

Only alphabetical order put Zed's at the end of the list for recommended Ethiopian dining. Although it offers less ambiance than some

INSIDERS' TIP

Those with a palate for beer may like to try one of the tasty regional microbrews, such as Virginia's Dominion Lager and Maryland's Wild Goose Amber, that are offered at many local bars and restaurants

of its competitors, it always scores high where it matters the most for a restaurant: food. In particular, the rich sauces, beef dishes and a unique offering of broiled short ribs help place Zed's ahead of many of its contemporaries. Zed's serves lunch and dinner daily.

Asian (includes Chinese, Japanese, Indian, Vietnamese and Thai)

Asia Nora
$$$$ • 2213 M St. NW, Washington, D.C. • (202) 797-4860

Before the sushi craze, Americans equated Asian restaurants with budget fare, and most do still prove relatively economical. This is not so at Asia Nora, a prime example of the new designer Asian that has become all the rage in cities from Los Angeles to New York. The setting is a breathtaking cocoon of rosy wood, gold pillars, intimate lighting and eye-catching art — and the food lives up to the surroundings. You'll find precious Japanese-style plates decorated with art of the edible kind.

Since the owner is the same Nora (see the close-up in this chapter) who began the organic food craze in Washington two decades ago, you can be sure of fresh fish and vegetables. You'll find dishes that tend more toward the Japanese or Thai, like the steamed prawn and scallop dumplings with sesame spinach and daikon relish, as well as those with a more Indian influence, like the curry served with traditional accompaniments like chutney and basmati rice. Asia Nora is open for dinner, but closed on Sundays.

China Inn
$ • 631 H St. NW, Washington, D.C. • (202) 842-0909

Lemon chicken, orange beef, stir fry and an ocean's worth of seafood specialties . . . China Inn focuses its efforts on Cantonese-

style cooking, and the results can be yummy. This Chinatown favorite for more than half a century has built a foundation on customer loyalty that newcomers can only dream about. China Inn serves lunch and dinner daily.

Germaine's
$$ • 2400 Wisconsin Ave. NW, Washington, D.C. • (202) 965-1185

With its fashionable upper Georgetown location and a grand atrium dining room, Germaine's has indeed distinguished itself as a beautiful dining spot for the last two decades. The food and open-hearth grill have garnered equivalent raves. Pan-Asian specialties include whole fish cooked in a variety of styles, fragrant curries, and an assortment of rarely found Vietnamese specialties from the chef-owner's home country. If none of these appeal to you, though, don't despair. The menu seems to go on and on and everything is high quality. Germaine's is open for lunch and dinner.

Haad Thai
$$ • 1100 New York Ave. NW, Washington, D.C. • (202) 682-1111

Not only is this one of the most popular Thai restaurants in downtown Washington, it's also one of the most vibrantly decorated. Big windows, room-sized murals and artistic fixtures make for a lively, trendy atmosphere, and being near the Washington Convention Center is a big plus. The food is just as vibrant as the space. Flavors explode in your mouth, not just with hot chilis, but also with lemon grass and all those other wonderful Thai spices. Like most Asian restaurants, the menu seems to have so many selections that it is hard to choose, but any of the curries and coconut based dishes will please lovers of Thai cuisine. Haad Thai is open for lunch Monday through Saturday, and dinner nightly.

Hunan Chinatown
$$ • 624 H St. NW, Washington, D.C. • (202) 783-5858

The competition is fierce in the Asian restaurant-rich H Street thoroughfare, but Hunan Chinatown is a standout for its refined atmosphere and its high-quality ingredients. Serving lunch and dinner nightly, their specialties include smoked duck and plump, juicy dumplings. The sauces are excellent, without the greasiness you may find in lesser Chinese cuisine.

Japan Inn
$$$ • 1715 Wisconsin Ave. NW, Washington, D.C. • (202) 337-3400

Serving lunch weekdays and dinner nightly, this authentic Japanese inn has been a Washington mainstay for years, and it remains an elegant landmark at the edge of Georgetown, in an unmistakably Japanese building. Inside, you'll find serene rooms, each offering a different dining option, such as tabletop grilling or sushi — unusual for Japanese restaurants in Washington, which are often cramped. The cuisine is standard fare, and the setting makes for a complete Japanese experience. An evening here is an event.

Makato
$$$ • 4822 MacArthur Blvd. NW, Washington, D.C. • (202) 298-6866

It's likely no one will recommend this tiny Japanese gem, but that's because few people know of it. It's hard to find, even when you do know where to look, but it's worth the trouble. The door is your first hint that this is the real thing. It's made of pale wood and rice paper and is unmistakably Japanese. Inside, you must remove your shoes before you enter the minuscule dining area. The seats are padded stools unless you sit at the sushi bar. Here, your best bet is to go for the tasting menu, a seven-course meal of specialties that you may never see outside Japan. You'll get a chance to sample everything from soup to a delicate, perfect serving of exotic fruit or homemade fruit ice at meal's end. Lunch is served Tuesday through Saturday, dinner is served Tuesday through Sunday and they are closed on Monday.

Oodles Noodles
$ • 1120 19th St. NW, Washington, D.C. • (202) 293-3138

They are open for lunch Monday through Saturday and dinner nightly. Please see the Maryland listing.

Perry's
$$$ • 1811 Columbia Rd. NW, Washington, D.C. • (202) 234-6218

An Asian restaurant named Perry's? Well, yes, in a way. Perry's, at the throbbing heart of Adam's Morgan offers pretty darned good sushi and other Asian dishes along with international standards like pasta. Some dishes are a wonderful fusion of East and West, like the wasabi potato salad. Yep, you heard right. Perry's is for those who like to party hearty and, in summer, there's no better place than the rooftop garden sparkling with fairy lights. Inside, there's sleek decor reminiscent of those decadent '80s. Speaking of decadence, there's a drag show (by the waiters) at Sunday brunch. They are open for dinner and the Sunday brunch.

Sarinah Satay House
$$ • 1338 Wisconsin Ave. NW, Washington, D.C. • (202) 337-2955

This may be the prettiest dining room in Georgetown — it is certainly the most exotic. It looks like a jungle, with a riot of plants throughout and a tree growing in the center of the back room. If you've never tasted Indonesian cooking, this is a fun place to start. The natural choice is to order one of the traditional rijsttafel spreads, which consists of about a dozen small dishes that you mix and match. Indonesian cooking features lots of peanut or coconut sauces, as well as hot chilis, and the combinations are appealing. Indonesia was occupied by the Dutch, so you'll find that beer compliments the food; however, you'll also find some great buys on the short wine list. Sarinah Satay House is open for lunch Tuesday through Saturday, dinner Tuesday through Sunday and is closed Monday.

Star of Siam
$ • 1136 19th St. NW, Washington, D.C. • (202) 785-2838
$ • 2446 18th St. NW, Washington, D.C. • (202) 986-4133

Competition in the Thai restaurant scene has become considerably stiffer in recent years, but Star of Siam hasn't been fazed. It's consistently good, consistently popular and consistently top-rated region-wide — hard to improve on that. Whether the location is downtown (19th Street), Adams Morgan (18th Street) or in Arlington at 1735 N. Lynn Street in Rosslyn, expect satisfaction at Star of Siam. The fish and curry selections are especially good, and happy hour sushi bargains are quite good for a midtown location. They are open for lunch weekdays at 19th Street, and open for dinner nightly at both locations.

Sushi-Ko

$$$ • 2309 Wisconsin Ave. NW, Washington, D.C. • (202) 333-4187

As the name implies, sushi is the word at Sushi-Ko, and few in town do it better: eel, toro, sea urchin, shrimp, salmon, quail eggs, flying-fish roe and even monkfish liver. In fact, when Japanese dignitaries come to Washington for official visits, Sushi-Ko does the catering. Although many people have been converted by the "Try it, you'll like it" urging of their fellow diners, not everyone has embraced the sushi phenomenon. Not to worry — Sushi-Ko also offers decidedly tasty and non-sushi creations, many of which are the chefs' own fusions of Japanese and American cooking styles and ingredients. This is a cramped, no-frills place, but it's always packed with people who know Japanese cuisine. Sushi-Ko is open for lunch Tuesday through Friday and dinner nightly.

Tony Cheng's Mongolian Barbecue

$ • 619 H St. NW, Washington, D.C. • (202) 842-8669

To be certain, there's no shortage of barbecue joints in Metro Washington, but you'll be hard pressed to find the Mongolian style (yes, Mongolian) offered anywhere but Tony Cheng's. Here's how it works: you fill your plate with the raw ingredients of your choice from a buffet, then you take it to the chef who grills it. It's as good as it is different, but don't just take our word as gospel. Tasting is believing. Expect generous offerings of meat, vegetables and tangy sauces, and if you have trouble deciding, opt for the all-you-can-eat deal. Tony Cheng's is open for lunch Monday through Saturday, dinner nightly and Sunday dim sum (chinese dumplings filled with a variety of delectable meats and vegetables).

Vietnam-Georgetown

$$ • 2934 M St. NW, Washington, D.C. • (202) 337-4536

This was one of the first Vietnamese restaurants in Washington, and it remains popular, perhaps in part because of the appealing garden in back that, on summer evenings, is strung with fairy lights. The food is unexceptional, but tasty — the usual Vietnamese restaurant fare of spring rolls and sweet and sour dishes. If you enjoy Southeast Asian food and the high-energy air of Georgetown, then you won't be disappointed. They are open daily for lunch and dinner.

Hispanic/Caribbean/ Tex-Mex

Cactus Cantina

$ • 3300 Wisconsin Ave. NW, Washington, D.C. • (202) 686-7222

Lively crowds flock to this funky Cleveland Park retreat with their sights set on Tex-Mex delights, and Cactus Cantina doesn't disappoint. Standard fare includes generous portions of enchiladas, tacos, ribs and fajitas. There's also a mesquite grill that turns out tasty salmon, shrimp, ribs and quail. They are open daily for lunch and dinner.

Coco Loco

$$ • 810 7th St. NW, Washington, D.C. • (202) 289-2626

Coco Loco is such a hopping night spot (see nightlife chapter) that some may forget it is also a top-notch choice for Latin American cuisine. The decor immediately spells fun: floors are Mexican tile, asymmetrical pillars are painted in bright colors, and festive paper lanterns and green plants hang from the rafters. You can start off the evening with Mexican tapas, those mini-dishes that give you the chance to taste a bit of everything. The array is seemingly endless, ranging from familiar quesadillas to a Latin American version of lobster.

When it comes to main courses, you'll find the Brazilian influence heavy, and it's a welcome one. If you've never tried churrascaria — a banquet of Brazilian roasted meats and salads — then this is the place. It's an eye-popping buffet of cold dishes, as well as a variety of rotisseried meats circulated to tables by a contingent of waiters. It's an experience not to be missed, especially on Saturday nights, when the dancers emerge at eleven. They are open for lunch Tuesday through Friday, dinner Monday through Saturday and are closed on Sunday.

Enriqueta's

$$ • 2811 M St. NW, Washington, D.C.
• (202) 338-7772

This charming whitewashed restaurant decorated with Mexican crafts has endured in Georgetown far longer than most of the surrounding restaurants, and there's a reason. The food is authentically Mexican, refined Mexican. The menu may even seem unfamiliar if you've only frequented those chains that heap their plates with a melange of sauces, beans and tortillas. Even the familiar standards here, such as enchiladas, will taste different than in the Americanized Mexican restaurants. Enriqueta's food, while not exactly gourmet fare, is a cut above, and certainly worth a try if you've never tasted the real thing. Enriqueta's is open for lunch Monday through Saturday, and dinner nightly.

Gabriel Radisson Barcelo Hotel

$$ • 2121 P St. NW, Washington, D.C.
• (202) 956-6690

Gabriel is a surprise for a hotel restaurant, and a chain hotel at that. It doesn't look like a Latin restaurant — the furnishings are standard hotel dining room, yet there's a tapas buffet at lunch and during the cocktail hour, and the menu is unmistakably south of the border. The seafood has been very good, and the empanadas stuffed with plantains and a variety of other fillings are interesting and tasty. All fried dishes are not executed with equal skill however. If you want to sample it all and decide for yourself, go for the buffet at lunch or brunch. Both are a bargain. Breakfast, lunch and dinner are served daily.

Hibiscus Café

$$ • 3401 K St. NW, Washington, D.C.
• (202) 965-7170

The biggest challenge at Hibiscus is finding the place. It is tucked away under the Whitehurst

Freeway on the Georgetown end of K Street — the very end. But once you've found it, you'll step into a funky, vital enclave reminiscent of a sophisticated Caribbean café in . . . not the islands, but perhaps Paris. It just has that air about it. The food here is worldly rather than down home: rack of lamb with Caribbean spices, jerk quail, seafood that explodes with the flavors of tropical fruit and chili salsas, and fried dishes that are airy rather than leaden. They are open for dinner, but closed Sunday and Monday.

Red Sage

$$$ • 605 14th St. NW, Washington, D.C.
• (202) 638-4444

All the rage since debuting in 1992, Red Sage quickly established a distinctive presence at Washington's ever-growing table of dining spots. How did it happen? Quite simply through a compelling combination of super Southwestern-style food — savor especially the shrimp, tuna and steak offerings — served in what has been called a "showplace" of museum-quality architecture, design and handicrafts. There are light fixtures encircled by metal buffalo silhouettes, Indian wool rugs on the hardwood floor, alcoves for wine displays lit with an amber glow, and russet leather booths. If nothing else, Red Sage, serving lunch weekdays and dinner nightly, is worth a try just to see if so many people could possibly be so right in their bountiful praise.

Taberna del Alabardero

$$$$ • 1776 I St. NW, Washington, D.C.
• (202) 429-2200

Taberna del Alabardero, in the minds of many critics and everyday patrons alike, is considered a serious candidate for the title of nation's finest Spanish restaurant. While traditional cuisine from Spain may be a new dining experience for many, one visit will reveal a cuisine of refinement and elegance unimagined by those who think Spanish food is pretty much like Tex-Mex. Recipes are from the Iberian peninsula, which means fresh sardines, roasted duck, whole suckling pig, rabbit and several kinds of paella. The setting is as upscale as in any French restaurant, and the service is top drawer. This is not casual dining. Lunch is served weekdays, dinner is served Monday through Saturday and they are closed Sunday.

Xing Kuba

$$ • 2218 Wisconsin Ave. NW, Washington, D.C. • (202) 965-0665

We weren't sure whether to put this restaurant in the Latin American category or in the Asian category because it serves both. Seasonings range from ginger and peanut sauce to bacon and southwestern chilis. Soups and seafood are the standouts here, but it's all a dining adventure. In the busy restaurant district at the North end of Georgetown, Xing Kuba attracts Georgetown University students and well-heeled residents of the surrounding neighborhood. It's a casual, cute place with decor accenting all the nations represented here. Lunch is served weekdays, dinner is served daily and brunch is offered on Saturday and Sunday.

French

Gerard's Place

$$$$ • 915 15th St. NW, Washington, D.C. • (202) 737-4445

Chef and owner Gerard Pangaud is a true luminary, having won two Michelin stars in France at a very young age. In the U.S., he has won equal acclaim and is a huge favorite of *The Washington Post's* own food critic, Phyllis Richman. His namesake restaurant near the White House is a pretty, unpretentious, very pleasant place in which to spend an evening, but it's not where you'd bring a date you want to impress with fancy surroundings.

Gerard's is for serious gourmets. The food is as refined and as carefully prepared as in the most highbrow eatery. Roasts are juicy; seafood is cooked to that perfect temperature at which its retains its moisture but imparts its full flavors. Dessert may offer some items you've never seen before, like fruit soups or unusually flavored soufflés. This is the place to try something different, safe in the knowledge that it will be a pleasurable experience. Lunch is served weekdays, dinner Monday through Saturday, and they are closed on Sunday.

La Chaumiére

$$ • 2813 M St. NW, Washington, D.C. • (202) 338-1784

This country inn/bistro in the heart of Georgetown is a perennial favorite in the competitive, come-and-go world of French restaurants. With its mid-room fireplace and its walls of antique farm tools and copper molds, this is the perfect spot to come in out of the cold. Expect attentive and warm service, hearty and reliable French peasant fare like cassoulet and couscous, tripe, blood sausage, quenelles of pike and choucroute garnie. If these earthy offerings don't tempt, there is more conventional fare, often rich with garlic, butter and other delicious staples of French country cooking. Lunch is served weekdays, dinner is served Monday through Saturday and La Chaumiére is closed on Sunday.

La Colline

$$$ • 400 N. Capitol St. NW, Washington, D.C. • (202) 737-0400

This Capitol Hill restaurant lacks a bit in atmosphere — it's more businesslike than romantic — but makes up for it with reliable, classic French cooking. It's been around for more than twenty years, but the menu is regularly updated and always fresh. The rich, traditional French standards are there along with some modern innovations, like creative pastas and lively salads. For the quality, the prices are very good and if you're sight-seeing on Capitol Hill, this a good place to stop for a break. La Colline serves breakfast and lunch on the weekdays, dinner Monday through Saturday and is closed on Sunday.

La Fourchette

$$ • 2429 18th St. NW, Washington, D.C. • (202) 332-3077

You'll think you're in Montmartre at this quaint little spot in Adams Morgan. Walk past the entrance and the garlic wafts out, inviting you in. As befits a French restaurant, there are tables outside where you can watch the wide cross-section of humanity on busy 18th Street. Inside, murals of café scenes dominate the walls. The tables are tiny and the chairs are the kind you'd find in a Paris bistro. The menu, too, looks like it came straight from Paris: cheese-filled onion soup, crepes, bouillabaisse, escargots and pâtés.

You can't go wrong. La Fourchette is open for lunch weekdays and dinner nightly.

Lavandou
$$ • 3321 Connecticut Ave. NW, Washington, D.C. • (202) 966-3002

This adorable neighborhood restaurant, serving lunch weekdays and dinner nightly, is tucked away in a strip of old shops north of the zoo, but don't let the facade fool you. Inside, you'll find hearty Provençale bistro cooking in a dollhouse setting that may be a little too close for those seeking complete privacy, but just right for those who want the full flavor of casual French dining. This is the kind of homey cooking that carries the punch of garlic and balsamic vinaigrette, cured meats, white beans and wine. The pork tenderloin is wrapped with bacon and served with a hearty red wine sauce. The daube provençale is beef marinated in red wine and oranges, and then cooked with bacon and walnuts; or try the carbonado, a lamb stew with artichokes, beans, tomato and celery. You may even want to order extra to reheat at home tomorrow.

Le Rivage
$$$ • 1000 Water St. SW, Washington, D.C. • (202) 488-8111

For some reason, fine cuisine seems to elude those waterfront restaurants with the great views, but not at Le Rivage. This little gem, tucked away among the tour group meccas on the Maine Avenue wharf, offers seafood dishes that are absolutely reliable in quality and taste. There is some creativity among the daily specials, but even if you choose a traditional favorite, you are sure to enjoy it at Le Rivage. As a special treat, the restaurant offers a dessert sampling that consists of several of its homemade goodies in one dish. They are open for lunch weekdays and dinner nightly.

Provence
$$$$ • 2401 Pennsylvania Ave. NW, Washington, D.C. • (202) 296-1166

Provence is the creation of one of Washington's most renowned chefs, Yannick Cam, so you'll often hear it recommended. The problem is that it doesn't always live up to Cam's sterling reputation. It's a lively, warm, bustling spot — a place to see and be seen — with stone floors, umber walls, vintage armoires and wooden chairs with rush seats. The food is usually excellent, making use of top quality ingredients and lots of fresh veggies. There's plenty of variety, with some of the best dishes being the country-style fusions of flavor that seem so very Provençale.

Specialties include fresh lobster with white truffle olive oil, loin of rabbit and pheasant stew with bay leaves and figs. If you want to experience a Washington hot spot with a glamorous southern French ambiance, this is the place to come — but if you're saving your bucks for a big splurge, and you don't want to risk any disappointments, you might think twice. They serve lunch weekdays, dinner Monday through Saturday and are closed on Sunday.

German

Cafe Berlin
$$ • 322 Massachusetts Ave. NE, Washington, D.C. • (202) 543-7656

No, you haven't been transported back to Germany; it just feels that way when you step into Cafe Berlin. Like most restaurants located in townhouses, this one has that cozy, warm feeling that immediately charms. The hearty fare — good and reasonably priced, if unspectacular — and, of course, the beer selection make this eatery worth a try for those who enjoy German food in an Old World setting. Lunch is served Monday through Saturday and dinner is served daily.

Old Europe
$$ • 2434 Wisconsin Ave. NW, Washington, D.C. • (202) 333-7600

Praise and popularity are old hat for Old Europe, unwavering in its appeal, at the same spot for nearly half a century. This place, some will contend, embodies all that an Old World German restaurant should be, except maybe for the American locale. Just use your imagination, though, and enjoy various wursts, schnitzel, dumplings, pork and other filling creations, not to mention the homemade pastries and an extensive wine and beer list. And we can't forget the lively, infectious music. Lunch and dinner are served daily at Old Europe.

Italian

Al Tiramisu
$$$ • 2014 P St. NW, Washington, D.C. • (202) 467-4466

You'll feel like you're in one of those white-washed underground wine cellars that they so cleverly convert into restaurants in Europe. The effect is romantic and oh-so-intimate. This Dupont Circle restaurant is the brainchild of chef Luigi Diotaiuti, Italian born, and trained in some of the best restaurants in the world, not to mention the Ritz Escoffier Ecole de Gastronomie Française in Paris. Your first course should be pasta — it's like silk here, both in terms of the subtle melding of flavors and the just-right texture. You might, for example, try the mushroom-stuffed ravioli. Next should be a dish of veal, lamb or fish. It's hard to decide which is best, so you might want to go with a group and taste a bit of everything. Finally, ask for a sampling of the several desserts offered — they are all delicious and this small, friendly place is eager to accommodate. They serve lunch on the weekdays and dinner nightly.

Bice
$$$ • 601 Pennsylvania Ave. NW, Washington, D.C. • (202) 638-2423

Yes, this is yet another exception to our no-chains claim, but for good reason. Honest. There are only a dozen or so branches anywhere of Bice, a Milan-based operation that emphasizes upscale decor, food and service — and it didn't take long for Bice to garner critical acclaim and win over new customers shortly after opening in 1991. Now, a few of those same critics say it has lost some of its original luster, but you wouldn't know it by the clout Bice still carries with lovers of northern Italian food. The pasta, duck, quail and red snapper are especially good, and the herbs used impart them with a hearty, fresh flavor that brings out the best in them. They are open for lunch weekdays and dinner daily. They are closed from July 1 to September 15.

Galileo
$$$$ • 1110 21st St. NW, Washington, D.C. • (202) 293-7191

Galileo's Roberto Donna is one of Washington's stars. He is in demand all over the world as a guest instructor, speaker and — of course — chef. Aside from Galileo, he owns a slew of other restaurants in town, many less expensive. Galileo is his flagship, however, and it continues to be one of the city's premier Italian restaurants. You cannot be certain that every detail of every meal will be flawless, but when this restaurant is on point, it's stellar. What's more, Donna is a trend-setter, a visionary, and that makes his restaurant worth a splurge. As for specifics, if you love vegetables, you won't be able to resist some of the versions here, such as the asparagus in black truffle vinaigrette or the grilled exotics. If you're a fan of risotto, you won't find any better version outside of Italy. They are open for lunch weekdays and dinner nightly.

Geppetto's
$ • 2917 M St. NW, Washington, D.C. • (202) 333-2602

Imagine pepperoni piled so high it's hard to see the pizza itself. While such generosity seems terribly wasteful except for perhaps eaters of above-average girth, it's tough for lovers of deep-dish pizza and pasta not to adore Geppetto's. The pleasure begins from the moment you step inside this casual Georgetown café and take in the delightful aroma. This is not a place for those seeking delicate refinements in Italian cooking. It's Italian-American abbondanza at its best. Maryland residents can also enjoy the location at 10257 Old Georgetown Road, in Bethesda's Wildwood Shopping Center, (301) 493-9230. Lunch and dinner are served daily.

i Ricchi
$$$ • 1220 19th St. NW, Washington, D.C. • (202) 835-0459

Why go to Florence when you can taste the fortunes of her cuisine right here in the District? This bright, airy restaurant takes pride in serving an authentic taste of Tuscany. The setting is inviting country-casual with some luxurious touches: pink tablecloths, flowers, wooden chairs with rush seats, and lots of copper and plants. As for food, it's tough to go wrong here . . . the cheeses, the pasta, the olive oil, the quail, veal, rabbit and the pork. Especially popular, though, is the fish cooked on a wood-burning grill. i Ricchi has taken Tuscan cuisine in a classy setting to new heights. They are open for lunch weekdays, dinner Monday through Saturday, and closed Sunday.

Marrocco's

$$ • 1120 20th St. NW, Washington, D.C. • (202) 331-1354

If you like the warmth of a family-run operation, Marrocco's fits the bill. After 50 years, and with the third generation at the helm, the food remains consistently steady as well. Pick your favorite Italian province and Marrocco's will likely have a selection to match. Look for reliably good salads (featuring ingredients that are fresh here, but hardly ever elsewhere), homemade pastas, fresh seafood, and assorted dishes featuring chicken, veal and beef. Lunch is served weekdays, and dinner Monday through Saturday. They are closed Sunday.

Obelisk

$$$ • 2029 P St. NW, Washington, D.C. • (202) 872-1180

Now, for something completely different. You won't find a wide range of choices here; in fact this restaurant offers a fixed price menu from which you choose one of three items for each course. How can they get away with such restraint? This tiny townhouse dining room is always full, so it must be the cooking. You sense that the people who put this together take artistic pride in their creation, and so they should, from the decor of elegant rusticity to the food. Let's start with the bread: it's crusty and aromatic, accompanied by top-shelf olive oil. It's also, of course, made in-house. It's hard to recommend any one dish since the menu changes all the time, and if you're looking for flashy, extravagant cooking, you won't find it here. For subtle, genuine quality, Obelisk is a sure bet. They serve dinner Monday through Saturday and are closed on Sunday.

Sesto Senso

$$$ • 1214 18th St. NW, Washington, D.C. • (202) 785-9525

This chic restaurant of dark wood and mirrors has a split personality. At lunch and weeknight dinners, it's crowded with suits from the surrounding office buildings. Weekend diners may be either pleased or disappointed (depending on the company) to discover that they're eating alone. But wait an hour or two and the long, polished bar will be jumping with a crowd of young Europeans and Euro-look-alikes who are there to flirt, drink and party. Make no mistake, though, Sesto Senso has serious dining. The carpaccio here is the real thing, thin-sliced filet rather than beef cut from a pre-pressed loaf. It is garnished with exquisite olive oil and huge shavings of parmesan — it may be the best in town. The menu is extensive and tempting, but make friends with any of the kindly staff — the maître d', the waiter, the bartender — and they'll persuade the chef to concoct something just for you. Your new friend will play 20 questions to discover your likes and dislikes, and then you'll be treated to a custom-made meal that contains all your favorite ingredients. They are open for lunch weekdays, and dinner Monday through Saturday.

Middle Eastern/ Mediterranean/Indian

Bacchus

$$ • 1827 Jefferson Pl. NW, Washington, D.C. • (202) 785-0734

In the minds of many Washingtonians, the art of Middle Eastern cooking — in this case Lebanese — begins and ends at Bacchus, whether you choose the original location here or the offshoot in Bethesda, Maryland (7945 Norfolk Avenue). Count on quality and satisfaction in whatever menu selection catches your eye at this whitewashed, bustling restaurant. Bacchus specialties include the creative kebabs of beef, chicken and lamb, savory sausages, stuffed cabbage and baby eggplant. Bacchus knows how to mix spices and textures for a knockout effect. The absolute must here is the assortment of mezze, appetizers like fragrant hummus with ground beef and toasted almonds on top, baba ghanouj, or hot, flaky phyllo stuffed with cheese. Dessert? You won't have room. Bacchus is open for lunch weekdays, dinner Monday through Saturday and closed Sunday.

Bombay Club
$$ • 815 Connecticut Ave. NW, Washington, D.C. • (202) 659-3727

That a restaurant this elegant should also be something of a bargain is remarkable, especially when you consider it's just a block from the White House. Bombay Club is not what we in America think of as your typical Indian restaurant. Imagine instead colonial India and all its privilege, and you'll have it right. You can find the "usual" Indian fare here, and it is good, but why not zero in on the dishes that you don't find in other Indian restaurants, such as the seafood appetizers/salads? Seafood also stars as a main course, especially when cooked in a tandoori oven. So often tandoori dishes are overcooked in other Indian restaurants, but here you'll find an unusual refinement. The Bombay Club is an exotic way to spend an evening, and your pocketbook won't feel the punch as much as in other restaurants of this caliber. Lunch is served weekdays, and dinner daily.

Cities
$$$ • 2424 18th St. NW, Washington, D.C. • (202) 328-7194

We've categorized this as a $$$ restaurant, but you could get away with spending a lot less by composing a meal of hot and cold appetizers. Cities, which used to change the national origin of its menu every six months, has reopened as a snazzy new Mediterranean restaurant. The space is unique in Adams Morgan — a sleek, sophisticated den of fine leather, intimate alcoves and provocative art. It has a romantic, candlelit atmosphere perfect for special evenings. The menu is a mix of Middle Eastern dishes like stuffed eggplant and lamb kofte, along with some fusion cuisine, such as the New York Strip loin with gorgonzola-polenta cake. Cities doesn't shrink from the authentic Middle Eastern touches either, and that means organ meats. There's ciger tava — sautéed veal liver cubes with parsley-

onion salad; or beyin salata — poached veal brain with lemon, olive oil and capers. If that doesn't sound like your cup of tea, don't worry, there are pizzas and pastas, too. The desserts are a nice mix of East and West: you'll find baklava, but there's also a chocolate hazelnut tartlet with white chocolate and orange cream sauce. They serve dinner Monday through Saturday and are closed on Sunday.

Lebanese Taverna Restaurant
$$ • 2641 Connecticut Ave. NW, Washington, D.C. • (202) 265-8681

This lively, attractive establishment has served notice as a serious contender in the Middle Eastern market, a category that seems either to enchant diners or completely turn them away. For the faithful, Lebanese Taverna will surely please with its own brand of "moussaka" (a Greek staple) — sans the usual ground beef — and other delicious eggplant dishes, the spicy sausages, a variety of vegetable kebabs and, of course, a wood-fired oven that brings out all the right aromas. Also, be sure to sample the wonderful Lebanese breads. It's hard to complain, given the reasonable prices, good cooking, and the cordial and efficient service. (There's also a Virginia location at 5900 Washington Boulevard, Arlington.) Lunch is served Monday through Saturday and dinner nightly.

Marrakesh
$$ • 617 New York Ave. NW, Washington, D.C. • (202) 393-9393

Dinner at Marrakesh is an event, and a festival of new sensations. First, there are the low, cushy sofas and the equally low tables; then, there's the bit about eating with your hands. At the beginning of the meal, the waiter brings water and towels to accommodate the custom. Finally, there's the teasing belly-dancer who, of course, selects several men from the audience as stage props to the hilarity of everyone else. The food? Oh, yes, it's mighty good, too. The roasted chicken in preserved lemons and olives, the lamb bursting with spices, the flaky bastilla (a savory-sweet concoction of phyllo pastry and meat dusted with sugar), all serve to make the seven-course meal an exotic foray. Marrakesh is open for dinner daily and will open at lunch for parties of ten or more. This restaurant does not accept credit cards.

Mykonos
$$ • 1835 K St. NW, Washington, D.C. • (202) 331-0370

Mykonos almost looks too contemporary to fit the stereotype of a Greek restaurant. There are mirrors and Art Deco sconces, but there are also comfortable cane-backed chairs and modern paintings of Greece. Being in the heart of Washington's business district guarantees a busy lunchtime crowd, but the delectable food is what draws people at nights. Don't miss the tzatziki spread — garlicky cucumber with yogurt — served with warm, crusty Mediterranean-style bread. In fact, all the cold appetizers are a must, from the smoky eggplant to the pungent Greek olives. Main courses feature aromatic lamb, stuffed grape leaves, and the usual Greek casserole dishes, all very well executed. Save room for homemade baklava, redolent with nuts and sticky with sugar sauce. They are open for lunch weekdays and dinner Monday through Saturday. They are closed on Sunday.

Taj Mahal
$ • 1327 Connecticut Ave. NW, Washington, D.C. • (202) 659-1544

The vegetarian crowd won't have any complaints about this place; yet Taj Mahal also does right by non-vegetarians, serving imaginative selections of Mogul and tandoori cuisine with all the right spices. This casual Dupont Circle-area favorite lays out a tremendous lunch buffet weekdays. Perhaps the overall appeal has something to do with Taj Mahal's claim to being "Washington's oldest authentic Indian restaurant" (since 1965). Taj Mahal serves lunch weekdays and dinner nightly.

Northern Virginia

American/Continental

Carlyle Grand Cafe
$$ • 4000 28th St., Shirlington, Va. • (703) 931-0777

One of the cornerstone establishments in the tidy, compact urban village of Shirlington, Carlyle Grand Cafe is convenient city dining without parking headaches (ample, free and convenient spaces nearby). Just a stone's throw from I-395, the restaurant features fresh, modern and simple decor and quality food (meats, seafood, pasta, sandwiches, etc.). The hot beignets served in lieu of bread are impossible to resist. As for the menu, it offers a wide variety of New American cuisine, from Thai-flavored dinner salads to garlicky pastas. Choose to dine downstairs, where the popular bar limits the seating and makes for a livelier time, or upstairs where it's decidedly quieter but equally enjoyable. Carlyle Grand Cafe is open for lunch weekdays, dinner nightly and Sunday brunch.

Clyde's
$$ • 11905 Market St., Reston, Va. • (703) 787-6601
$$ • 8332 Leesburg Pike, Vienna, Va. • (703) 734-1900

These suburban versions of the original District Clyde's have done well, to say the least. The older Tysons location and the newer one in Reston — a cornerstone establishment in the impressive and still-developing Town Center — have faithful patrons and are wildly popular happy-hour, late-night and brunch destinations. (See the Washington listing for details.) Like the downtown and Chevy Chase, Maryland branches, these two, especially Tysons, are decorated with lavish amounts of glossy wood and glass. The menus are pretty much alike at all branches. Clyde's is open for lunch and dinner nightly and Sunday brunch.

Evans Farm Inn and Sitting Duck Pub
$$ • 1696 Chain Bridge Rd., McLean, Va. • (703) 356-8000

Set on 40 acres of historic farmland (complete with a duck pond) along Route 123, in the shadows of downtown McLean, Evans Farm Inn has been a longtime family favorite, particularly for holiday brunches and dinners. Featuring traditional American cuisine, the specialties include prime rib, Virginia's own Smithfield ham and other regional fare. Gourmets may be disappointed by the ho-hum cooking here, but the place undeniably has atmosphere and kids love it. The adjacent Sitting Duck Pub is fashioned after a

British pub and features Tudor tables, dartboards, copper pitchers and a roaring fireplace in winter. Lunch and dinner are served daily.

Fedora Cafe
$$ • 8521 Leesburg Pike, Vienna, Va.
• (703) 556-0100

Fedora Cafe is one of those casual, lively eateries that serves food ranging from burgers to full-course meals with an Italian accent, but it's a bit of a standout in the category. It's not that the menu selections are any more imaginative than the norm, but they take extra care with the preparation and ingredients. Exceptional for a bistro that boasts a great happy-hour crowd, as well as a busy weekend bar scene. Fedora Cafe is probably not worth a special trip, but if you're shopping in Tysons Corner, it's a good stop. Fedora Care is open for dinner nightly and Sunday brunch.

Fish Market
$$ • 105 King St., Alexandria, Va.
• (703) 836-5676

Like hundreds of other Old Town buildings, the one that houses the ever-popular Fish Market has a storied past, a onetime focal point of the Colonial-era seafaring trade when Alexandria was a port city and market of widespread importance. The city still buzzes here in the lower King Street area, but these days it's centered around the flourishing restaurant and small-retail business. Fish Market consists of several rooms, including a packed raw bar and a balcony overlooking the heavy pedestrian traffic on King Street. Waiting in line here is not at all uncommon, especially on weekends, so plan accordingly. The raw bar is stocked with spicy shrimp, oysters on the half shell, and all manner of fresh seafood. The restaurant proper offers lots of fried specialties, often accompanied by that southern favorite, hush puppies. Chowders, too, are thick and hearty here. You can get more low-calorie fare, but it somehow doesn't seem to match the raucous, checkered tablecloth ambiance. The Fish Market is open for lunch and dinner daily.

Hard Times Cafe
$ • 3028 Wilson Blvd., Arlington, Va.
• (703) 528-2233

$ • 1404 King St., Alexandria, Va.
• (703) 683-5340
$ • 394 Elden St., Herndon, Va.
• (703) 318-8941

Chili in one of a dozen incarnations is the best reason to go to Hard Times Chili. But there's nothing wrong with that reason, is there? This is down-home joint, dark and loud, lots of fun for a casual — very casual — evening or a quick bite. No one will frown if you wipe your bowl clean with a chunk of their yummy cornbread. They are open for lunch and dinner daily.

Heart in Hand
$$$ • 7145 Main St., Clifton, Va.
• (703) 830-4111

A favorite of former First Lady Nancy Reagan, romantic Heart in Hand specializes in American cuisine with a southern touch. The bread basket at the beginning of the meal may be the highlight, but soups are hearty and good, and the restaurant features great homemade desserts. You can't help but get sentimental and warm all over as you're served in this historic farmhouse in the quaint one-stoplight community of Clifton, the heart of Fairfax County's affluent horse country. Heart in Hand is open for lunch Monday through Saturday, dinner nightly and Sunday brunch.

Hermitage Inn
$$$ • 7134 Main St., Clifton, Va.
• (703) 266-1623

Just across the street from the village of Clifton's other top restaurant, Heart in Hand, Hermitage Inn offers romance that's more Continental than country. Housed in a white, two-story former hotel once visited by Presidents Grant and Hayes, Hermitage Inn features a wide verandah and second-story balcony, along with a beautifully landscaped patio garden just right for warm summer evenings. Inside, you'll find a plantation-style dining room cooled by softly whirring ceiling fans and French doors, and warmed by flattering pastel decor and fireplaces. In winter, you may prefer to dine instead in the pub-like wine bar/restaurant on the first floor, complete with its own wood-burning fireplace.

The food here is a mixture of New American and French, with a number of daily specials. Salads, even the most basic, are creative and tasty. There are some interesting game specials from time to time that are worth a try, but the real treat here is the wine list, which offers a large number of selections by the glass as well as some unusual bottles. Enjoy soaking in the atmosphere and leave renewed by the peaceful, romantic setting. They are open for lunch and dinner Tuesday through Saturday, Sunday brunch and are closed Monday.

J.R.'s Stockyards Inn
$ • 8130 Watson St., McLean, Va.
(Tysons Corner) • (703) 893-3390

There's Morton's of Chicago across the street and then there's J.R.'s, the budget alternative. At this casual, kid-friendly restaurant, the beef is all fresh from the family-owned packing plant, and it's aged and cut in-house. Try their fresh seafood, chicken, lamb chops, barbecue or gourmet salads. Nothing fancy here, just good food and lots of it. They are at Tysons Corner, and open for lunch weekdays and dinner nightly.

Kenny's Bar-B-Que
$ • 3060 Duke St., Alexandria, Va.
• (703) 823-3330

You wouldn't expect to find such a tasty barbecue joint in such an obscure place, but there Kenny's sits, wedged between an auto-repair place and a doughnut shop. It's not the easiest place to spot, but make the effort to slow down and find it. Grab a chair in the dinky, sparse and often drafty dining area and enjoy the tangy and cooked-to-perfection pork, beef and chicken barbecue sandwiches and platters. And don't forget the side orders such as corn bread, beans, cole slaw and chunky French fries, which are good enough to be main courses. They are open for lunch and dinner Monday through Saturday.

Market Street Bar & Grill
$$$ • 1800 Presidents St., Reston, Va.
• (703) 709-6262

The Hyatt Regency looms tall above Reston's impressive Town Center, which makes it easy to find your way to the hotel's first-rate restaurant, the Market Street Bar & Grill. Accented by an open grill and colorful paintings, the contemporary wood-floored dining area serves remarkably good pasta, seafood selections and soups. Visible through the curved wall of windows is an inviting terrace where meals are also served.

The chef here is creative, and at suburban prices, this place can be a bargain. Not to say that it's inexpensive. It's just that some of the menu items would cost far more downtown. Try the appetizer of lobster salad or Japanese-style sushi rolls. A lot of the seafood dishes have Asian accents that the chef executes with finesse. If you prefer American cooking, the veal chop is a thick, juicy one, often topped with gourmet mushrooms. In fact, the meat dishes here are all high quality, and vegetable accompaniments can be as tempting as the main course. Desserts here are a treat: creme brulée in interesting flavors, fruit cobblers or tarts, and sinful chocolate cakes.

At Market Street, there's always a unique twist on the old standards. They are open for lunch Monday through Saturday, dinner nightly and Sunday brunch. Also, you can enjoy live jazz there on Friday and Saturday nights.

Morton's of Chicago
$$$$ • 8075 Gallows Rd., Vienna, Va.
(Tysons Corner) • (703) 883-0800

Here's one of the exceptions to our no-national-chains pledge made at the beginning of this chapter. We didn't list Morton's location in D.C. because there are so many superb steakhouses in the District, but if you want this kind of quality in northern Virginia, there's only Morton's. It's a big-night-on-the-town kind of place without the commute and parking hassles. If this legendary steakhouse can't satisfy that hankering for prime dry-aged beef, you might as well buy some cattle and a do-it-yourself guidebook. The menu is presented with drama by the waiter who brings the cuts of meat to your table on a trolley. Along for the ride is a live lobster just waiting for someone to claim it and soak it in butter. As with other Washington area steakhouses, the vegetable accompaniments and salads (all à la carte) are served in portions generous enough to satisfy a sumo wrestler. Our favorite here is the Delmonico or, for bigger appetites, the porterhouse. But other meats and seafood are also top-drawer. For dessert, Morton's soufflés are always popular, but they must be ordered with the meal, and by the time you've made your way through the entrée, you may regret the extra course. If you want to try the D.C. location, it's at 3251 Prospect Street NW, (202) 342-6258. Here, at Tysons Corner, they are open for lunch weekdays and dinner nightly.

The Palm Court
$$$$ • Westfield's Conference Resort, 14750 Conference Center Dr., Chantilly, Va. • (703) 818-3522

Housed in the magnificent Georgian-style mansion that is the heart of the Westfield's conference center and hotel, The Palm Court is worth the drive into western Fairfax. Before you sit down to eat, enjoy the rolling, manicured lawns and the building's extravagant antique furnishings and custom-made Oriental carpets. Expect dining at its most formal, with live piano music, lavish place settings and tableside preparation. This is a place that keeps up with all the culinary trends while offering a reassuring selection of Continental and American favorites, including Caesar salad, lobster bisque, rack of lamb, duck and a bevy of sinful desserts.

There are some surprises on the menu, too. On one recent outing, we tasted a combination of bear and boar. The bear was delicious and tender, and the boar was as gamey as you would expect, but interesting nevertheless. A top drawer restaurant in the suburbs is a rare treat. Westfield's is open for lunch and dinner Monday through Saturday, and Sunday brunch.

Phillips Seafood Grill
$$$ • 8330 Boone Blvd., Vienna, Va. • (703) 442-0400

This is the seventh of the popular Phillips seafood restaurant family, but it's the first of its kind in a new concept for the chain: a fashionable bar and grill in contrast to the traditional family seafood house that has become the Phillips trademark. Surely the upscale Tysons Corner location had something to do with the change, but it's a hit just the same and little wonder why more are planned. Tucked in an office park at Va. Routes 7 and 123, the 300-seat restaurant dishes out filling

tossed salads, seafood, fish, beef and pasta entrées and dramatic desserts, all with an emphasis on freshness and creativity. A seat in the main dining room affords a view of the display kitchen and its wood-burning grills. There's outdoor seating in the summer and a raw bar and happy hour specials all the time; private dining rooms are available. They are open for lunch weekdays, dinner nightly and Sunday brunch.

Portner's
$$ • 109 S. Saint Asaph St., Alexandria, Va. • (703) 683-1776

While it may seem hard to distinguish among some of Old Town's numerous dining spots in beautiful old brick buildings, there's just something about the Portner's that helps it stand out. There are four dining areas, each appealing in its own way. The brick garden patio behind a wrought iron gate is prime seating in summer; the pub with its dark wood booths and old-fashioned bar is great for a quick bite or an evening of socializing; lunch or Sunday brunch is cheery in the sun-filled atrium; and for dinner, the upstairs dining room decorated with grand bronze lamps, polished wood and etched glass, is a setting of festive elegance. As for the food, it's perfectly good and filling American fare ranging from steaks to grilled fish to tasty pasta standards. Desserts are extravagant concoctions and definitely worth saving room for. But Sunday brunch may be where Portner's really shines, from the thick French toast, to the eggs Sardou. Portner's is open for lunch Monday through Saturday, dinner nightly and Sunday brunch.

Red, Hot & Blue
$ • 1600 Wilson Blvd., Arlington, Va.
• (703) 276-7427
$ • 208 Elden St., Herndon, Va.
• (703) 318-7427
$ • 4150 Chain Bridge Rd., Fairfax, Va.
• (703) 218-6989

Barbecue fan? You won't find better than Red, Hot & Blue. By now a Washington institution, this crowded joint in Arlington serves succulent ribs, pulled pork and chicken, and brisket. The ribs are served wet (with sauce) or dry (rubbed with spices, no sauce). Sauces and seasonings are perched on each table so you can customize your order. There are other locations in the Metro area (see Maryland listings), but we think the original one in Arlington is best. They are open for lunch and dinner daily.

Tuscarora Mill

$$ • 203 Harrison St., Leesburg, Va.
• (703) 771-9300

Tuscarora Mill is one of Leesburg's best-loved dining spots. Soaring beamed ceilings, dark wood, and old farm tools let you know you're in horse country. This casual spot is great for thick sandwiches, burgers, fries and other well-executed American dishes. The desserts of the mile-high, fudgy ilk, are the highlight. You wouldn't make a special trip to Leesburg to eat here, but the town is crammed full of history, boutiques and antique shops, so go exploring before or after your meal. Tuscarora Mill is open for lunch and dinner nightly.

Union Street Public House

$$ • 121 S. Union St., Alexandria, Va.
• (703) 548-1785

Union Street is one of the area's most popular neighborhood saloons and restaurants. Choose a lively and often-crowded bar scene downstairs, quieter dining upstairs, or something in between in the sometimes overlooked back-room oyster bar. An array of huge dinner salads and sandwiches grace the menu, along with the usual saloon fare like buffalo wings, fritters, pastas, burgers and some grilled meats. Highlighted here are a dozen or so draft beers including the house exclusive — the rich and delicious Virginia Native. They are open for lunch and dinner daily and Sunday brunch.

Warehouse Bar and Grill

$$ • 214 King St., Alexandria, Va.
• (703) 683-6868

This pleasant restaurant bills itself as New Orleans-style and offers Louisiana specialties, but the decor is casual, understated classic American, with the exception of the nice gallery on the second floor overlooking the space below. The place has a fun atmosphere, a hopping bar scene, and is a great place to drop in if you're in the neighborhood. Snag a window table to take in the interesting sights along King Street. They are open for lunch Monday through Saturday, dinner nightly, Saturday breakfast and Sunday brunch.

Italian

Generous George's Positive Pizza and Pasta

$ • 3006 Duke St., Alexandria, Va.
• (703) 370-4303
$ • 7031 Little River Tnpk., Annandale, Va. • (703) 941-9600
$ • 6131 Backlick Rd., Springfield, Va.
• (703) 451-7111

It's an odd name indeed, but the gigantic portions of superb pizza and pretty good pasta are nothing to laugh at. You'll be too busy chewing, swallowing and smiling in between. The pizza's the whole point of coming here, and at least one member of your party should order it. The toppings are all fresh and high-quality. This is no run-of-the-mill sausage! The quirky, eclectic decor — a true mishmash of the odd, the colorful and the bizarre — and a fun family atmosphere, for kids in particular, makes Generous George's a hit every time. One visit and you'll understand why people gladly sweat the lines on weekends. They are open for lunch and dinner daily.

Geranio

$$ • 722 King St., Alexandria, Va.
• (703) 548-0088

Year after year, this Old Town restaurant stays fresh. The atmosphere bursts with good-fellowship and vitality, and the decor is cheerful, particularly on cold winter nights when the fire roars. Geranio feels like the authentic Italian trattoria that it is — rustic floors of tile or hardwood, ceramic art on the walls, jolly waiters — only the pink tablecloths and simple, pretty flowers add a touch of formality. The menu lists more than a dozen pastas available for either the first course or as entrées. One of the best is rigatoni à la Jay Coupe, a Geranio invention that pairs sprightly tomato sauce with hot peppers and olives. The stuffed pastas are also great.

Surprisingly for a restaurant this modest, the seafood dishes are very good as well, especially any of the fish prepared with lemon and capers, or the prawns. Appetizers are the Italian standards, ranging from asparagus vinaigrette (or hollandaise) to antipasti. Everything is satisfying and simply prepared. Especially tasty is the olive oil served with the bread — it's full of fragrant herbs. Desserts aren't the strong point here but, again, they're competent. Instead, top off your meal with a cup of espresso. They are open for lunch weekdays and dinner nightly.

Il Cigno
$$$ • 1617 Washington Plaza, Reston, Va. • (703) 471-0121

The food here is less special than the setting, which is worth the trip if dining alfresco is what you have in mind. There's plenty of outdoor seating overlooking Reston's beautiful Lake Anne. If that weren't enough, Il Cigno's neighboring cafés, in a fan-shaped row, lend an air of festivity to the scene. This pedestrian square (actually, it's a circle) seems very European and escapist on a warm evening. There are often musicians playing at one end, and the neighborhood's residents come out in full force to enjoy a lakeside promenade or casual dining by the water. In summer, there are good appetizers that feature fresh produce, but the menu is pretty much like any other Italian restaurant. It's the setting that's extraordinary and you're sure to leave with a feeling of well-being. Il Cigno is open for lunch weekdays, dinner nightly and is closed Sunday in winter.

Paolo's
$$ • 1898 Market St., Reston, Va. • (703) 333-7353

Paolo's Reston branch is inviting, with its outdoor tables in the town square, its café-style seating just outside the front doors, and the curved, sunny room within. There's also a bar that hops on weekends, complete with loud music and attractive guys and gals out on the town.

As soon as you're seated, you'll be served Paolo's signature breadsticks, soft and warm, along with a zesty green-olive tapenade. The main courses feature lots of pastas, some quite imaginative, along with meat that's mostly grilled and infused with light sauces. Balsamic vinaigrette plays a big role in the cooking here, and that's just great as far as we're concerned. Pizzas cooked in wood-burning ovens are a house specialty, and the crusts are smoky, thin and delicious, just as you'd expect. You can make a meal of Paolo's salads— which range from steak over greens to grilled chicken with Greek-style accompaniments — and you'll always be offered fresh grated parmesan as a garnish. Paolo's serves lunch and dinner daily and Sunday brunch.

Il Radicchio
$ • 1801 Clarendon Blvd., Arlington, Va. • (703) 276-2627

Another offshoot of a downtown location, Il Radicchio is a bargain-priced eatery that still manages to seem trendy. The concept here is simple. Order an all-you-can-eat bowl of spaghetti and pair it with one of a dozen or so sauces offered. There's variety enough to satisfy anyone, from those who prefer simple pesto to those who think spaghetti ain't spaghetti unless it has tomato sauce. You won't find the haute cuisine of Roberto Donna's downtown flagship, Galileo (see the D.C. listings), but then you won't pay the prices he charges there either. At Il Radicchio, Donna caters to a whole different crowd: families, busy worker bees in need of a quick meal and young up-and-comers who want lots to eat and don't want to pay a lot. The pizzas are good too. Il Radicchio serves lunch Monday through Saturday and dinner nightly.

Tivoli Restaurant
$$$ • 1700 N. Moore St., Rosslyn, Va. • (703) 524-8900

It's a tribute to Tivoli's quality that it has managed to endure for two decades hidden away in this Rosslyn high-rise. Perhaps it helps to have a bakery and carry-out service of the same name on the ground floor — advertisement for the good things to come upstairs. This handsome dining room, rendered even more inviting by the wraparound windows and the strategically placed mirrors, is one of the more formal restaurants in the Virginia suburbs. It's a good place to take clients or a first date. Tivoli bills itself as a northern Italian restaurant, and you'll find many dishes napped in the rich sauces of that region. There are risottos and stuffed pastas, as well as old standards of the fettucine Alfredo ilk. You'll also find some Continental classics that you don't often see anymore, like veal Oscar. This is a place to linger and enjoy your meal, an elegant, leisurely experience at prices that are surprisingly reasonable. They serve lunch weekdays, dinner Monday through Saturday and are closed Sunday.

French

Café Rochambeau
$$ • 310 Commerce St., Occoquan, Va.
• (703) 494-1165

The tiny village of Occoquan draws people from the Washington area who want to step back to a more serene time, a small town atmosphere enhanced by a river view. At the northern end of Prince William County on Route 123, Occoquan attracts thousands each year with its craft shows and antique shops — and hungry shoppers have to eat. There's no more inviting spot on a summer evening than the wide, flower-filled verandah of Café Rochambeau. In a country-style white Victorian, the place positively exudes old-time romance. Inside, there are wooden floors and simple, country-style decorations — nothing cutesy. The food is good country French and the menu sticks to a few standards: a beef dish, a couple of fish preparations, chicken and often veal or lamb. The food is always tasty, but stick to the grilled dishes if you don't really like sauces. For dessert, the lemon silk pie is outstanding by any measure. They are open for lunch daily and closed for dinner on Monday.

La Bergerie
$$$ • 218 N. Lee St., Alexandria, Va.
• (703) 683-1007

La Bergerie is an old classic that always pleases. After two decades, you might expect it to fade or get sloppy, but the food here is always a delicious surprise. The origins are Basque, that region between Spain and France that produces food rich with garlic, tomatoes, bell peppers and seafood. There are also the elegant French standards like sole in creamy sauce or coq au vin. All this is served in a setting that is both cozy and formal. The walls are brick, lending warmth, but as in the best restaurants, the tables are generous and well-spaced and there are leather banquettes scattered about the dining room. Service is very proper and traditional, and some of the waiters are of the European breed that make a lifelong career in elite restaurants, taking great pride in their professions, as they should. End your meal with one of La Bergerie's desserts — many of which are made in-house. The tarts are particularly good. They serve lunch and dinner Monday through Saturday, and are closed Sunday.

La Cote d'Or Café
$$$ • 6876 Lee Hwy., Arlington, Va.
• (703) 538-3033

This place is a jewel in the rough, with the "rough" being its location right off Route 66, next to a garage. It's not a dangerous neighborhood, but it doesn't give a clue as to the lavishly romantic setting that awaits you inside. Striking arrangements of roses, pretty table settings and intimate lighting all add up to a downtown atmosphere — at downtown prices — right in the Virginia suburbs. The food lives up to the surroundings, as befits highly esteemed Washington chef, Raymond Campet, who decided to set up shop in Virginia.

There are all sorts of elegant classics featuring game, duck, and high-quality beef. The daily specials are particularly good, but often pricier than the regular menu. The dishes are expertly sauced, such as the game meats with savory berry glazes or the seafood with buttery garlic accents. Desserts, even the simple berries in sabayon sauce, can be a real treat. This place is consistently rated among the best in Washington by several critics and, on Wednesdays, there's the bonus of live piano music in the bar area. They serve lunch and dinner daily.

L'Auberge Chez François
$$$ • 332 Springvale Rd., Great Falls,
Va. • (703) 759-3800

Accessible only by a twisting two-lane road

— one of many in woodsy, fashionable and oh-so-affluent Great Falls — L'Auberge Chez Francois continues to reap awards and praise as the years go by, and never seems to falter in its appeal. There's an unmistakable country inn warmth and romance that permeates the soul. The French cuisine here hails from Alsace, that province along the German border that specializes in game and richly sauced vegetables. The wait staff is dressed in keeping with the theme: dirndl skirts, colorful vests and the whole bit. Menu selections are endless, and are all accompanied by garlic bread, salad, after-dinner sweets and a slew of side-dishes. Stick with traditional Alsation fare — duck, pork or anything in puff pastry — and you can't go wrong. Desserts are equally representative of the region, with lots of fruit tarts and soufflés that are definitely worth a try. Reservations for weekends should be made a month in advance (unless you want to wait till the last minute and hope for a cancellation), but it's worth the wait. L'Auberge Chez François is the kind of place you anticipate with a smile. They are open for dinner Tuesday through Sunday and are closed Monday.

Le Gaulois

$$ • 1106 King St. Alexandria, Va. • (703) 739-9494

The minute you walk through the door and onto the hardwood floors at Le Gaulois, you feel as though you've found refuge from the city bustle in a country French auberge — no easy feat for a streetside restaurant. Friendly, quiet and accommodating to a new degree, Le Gaulois serves creative and very reliable French-influenced cuisine at reasonable prices. The menu changes here with the seasons and, as you'd expect, winter entrées are hearty offerings in warm sauces infused with wine and garlic. Summer is the time to try seafood poached or grilled, and then spiked with zesty herbs. If you're seeking authentic French peasant fare, try the organ meats. Not many places offer such a wide selection. Accompaniments can range from crisp, buttery veggies to those homey parsleyed potatoes. This is country French cooking at its best, with prices that don't break the bank. Le Gaulois is open for lunch and dinner Monday through Saturday, and is closed Sunday.

Le Refuge

$$ • 127 N. Washington St., Alexandria, Va. • (703) 548-4661

If Le Gaulois is peaceful, then Le Refuge is the exact opposite. It's a wild place where you may feel as though you're dining in your neighbor's lap. It makes for lots of conversations and laughter between tables though, and you'll have a good time. The food here is typical brasserie fare, with good, solid cooking that is quick and inexpensive. Veggie accompaniments are French classics like calorie-laden Lyonnaise potatoes (deliciously sinful!) or green beans swimming in butter. You really can't go wrong here when the bill is so very reasonable. Le Refuge is open for lunch and dinner Monday through Saturday and is closed on Sunday.

Asian

Bee-won Secret Garden

$ • 6678 Arlington Blvd., Falls Church, Va. • (703) 533-1004

We dare you to try and find this restaurant in any other guide, since it is truly a secret in this area. Tucked into a strip mall, this is not a place you'd wander into by accident. Once inside, the decor is pleasant but simple, with a sushi bar, a scattering of booths, a long table in the center and smaller tables against the wall — all in light wood. The reason to come here is the sparkling fresh sushi as well as Korean and Japanese cooked dishes, all at rock-bottom prices.

The fresh fish tank at the entrance is not just for show. There is an Asian custom that many Westerners find abhorrent — that of serving whole fish that are still alive. Vital organs are separated from the meat, but left intact enough so the fish lives as it is eaten, assuring the ultimate in freshness. This is definitely not for everyone, but some Asians consider it a delicacy and, at Secret Garden, you can have it. As you might imagine, this is a restaurant that caters to a great many Asians, so if it's authenticity you want, this is the place. They are open for lunch and dinner daily.

Busara

$$ • 8142 Watson St., McLean, Va. • (703) 356-2288

Fans of the downtown Busara, with its

wild murals and ultramodern seating, have quickly made a hit of the Tysons Corner shopping center branch of this innovative Thai restaurant. On the menu are all the traditional Thai favorites like curries, pad thai or larb gai, but there are also some imaginative fusion dishes. For lunch or dinner, try one of the meal-sized salads, or make a meal of the dough-wrapped appetizers that range from shrimp to chicken to veggies. If you order curry or one of the other sauced dishes, specify how hot you want it to be, or use the chili-pepper scale on the menu as a guide. It's especially nice to sit in the outdoor garden on a fine day. Busara serves lunch and dinner daily.

Duangrat's
$$ • 5878 Leesburg Pk., Falls Church, Va. • (703) 820-5775

New Thai restaurants spring up all the time in Metro Washington, but Duangrat's continues to shine. Maybe it's the gracious, almost formal decor, with its rosy tablecloths, flowers and generously upholstered chairs; then again, it's probably the food as much as anything. There are always interesting daily specials — try the spicy soft-shell crab if it's available — and the menu is as long and varied as in any Thai restaurant, with a few extra soups and stews thrown in. Compare the standard Thai dishes here to those in other restaurants, and you'll see why Duangrat's is so popular. Batters are always light and fresh, peanut sauce is never cloying, and the crab stuffed chicken wings are head-and-shoulders above anyone's in town. They serve lunch and dinner daily.

Hee Been
$$ • 6231 Little River Tnpk., Alexandria, Va. • (703) 941-3737

This is where northern Virginia's large Korean community comes to celebrate special occasions, and you'll understand why once you've experienced Hee Been. Korean barbecues are always fun, grilled at the table and accompanied by a dozen condiments. The difference at Hee Been is that nothing is done by rote, and no one is rushed. Let the waiter be your guide as to what's good. You're sure to have an adventure. If language is a barrier

and you want to venture beyond barbecues, try the soups — some as thick as stews, others broth-like and delicate. Whatever you choose, don't miss the short ribs, which are a star here. Hee Been is open for lunch and dinner daily.

Matuba
$ • 2915 Columbia Pk., Arlington, Va. • (703) 521-2811

Matuba is open for lunch weekdays and dinner nightly. Please see the Maryland listing.

Nam Viet
$ • 1127 N. Hudson St., Arlington, Va. • (703) 522-7110

The name may be turned around, but we've figured it's for a reason: that's exactly what you'll be inclined to do after your first dining experience at Nam Viet. Go back again. And soon. The food is as consistently good as the atmosphere is relaxing and unpretentious, and the prices reasonable. Don't miss the bon dun, the great selection of soups, or the skewered meats grilled with fragrant herbs. You can enjoy your meal outside in warm weather, but the indoor dining room is several steps above the utilitarian atmosphere found in some of the other low-cost neighborhood restaurants. Nam Viet is open for lunch and dinner daily.

Peking Gourmet Inn
$$ • 6029-6033 Leesburg Pk., Falls Church, Va. • (703) 671-8088

This used to be a favorite of President Bush, and it still has plenty of good things to offer on the menu, but the Peking duck remains the standard against which to measure all others — crispy on the outside, lean on the inside, and carved at tableside. The appetizers are very good, too, especially the dumplings, the sesame shrimp toast and the hot and sweet cabbage. Peking Gourmet Inn takes pride in growing its own leeks and garlic sprouts, and they are featured in several main courses, but the meats can sometimes be flabby — it's often hit-or-miss here. Still, the place has kept its prices low enough so that mistakes won't spoil your evening and, if you choose right, you'll love your meal. Be sure to reserve dinner here. Despite the endless array of dining rooms, it's always crowded and there's always a line. That should tell you something right there. They serve lunch and dinner nightly.

Pho 75

$ • 1711 Wilson Blvd., Arlington, Va.
• (703) 525-7355

You don't choose this Vietnamese restaurant for the atmosphere. It's basic, very basic. And you don't go for variety. The only thing you can order, appropriately enough, is pho. But you can bet the pho's darned good here. In case you haven't tried it, pho is a soup based on beef broth and studded with wonderfully aromatic Asian spices like lemon grass, coriander and anise. But lest you think you'll leave hungry, imagine a soup so thick with noodles, meat and veggies that it easily makes a meal. If you want to spice it up even more, there's a variety of condiments that comes with each order, as well as bottles of sauce on the tables. Pricewise, the whole thing just barely breaks into the double digits, so it's an unbeatable bargain. Pho 75 is open for lunch and dinner nightly.

Tachibana

$$$ • 6755 Lowell Ave., McLean, Va.
• (703) 847-1771

Tachibana, in upscale McLean, is a low-key, western-style dining room curved around a sushi bar. Although there are many Japanese specialties to be had, the point is the sushi, which is well-executed, perfectly fresh and often displaying a variety not found elsewhere in the suburbs. Try any of the sushi chef's specials and you won't be disappointed. Unlike many Asian restaurants, the service here is unhurried, and the plush carpeting and upholstered chairs lend themselves to long, quiet conversations. You can also sit at the surprisingly roomy sushi bar and watch the master at work. Tachibana is open for lunch weekdays, dinner Monday through Saturday, and is closed Sunday.

Tara Thai

$$$ • 226 Maple Ave., Vienna, Va.
• (703) 255-2467

The decor here makes a statement. It looks like an aquarium: deep blues and greens, very moody, very pretty. There's also a touch of Africa in the zebra-striped banquettes. It's all very young, fun and vibrant. The food is vibrant, too, bursting with chilis, lemon grass, lime and cilantro. A standout is the shrimp — big, juicy and cooked just right. If you like whole fish, this is the place to have it. It is smothered in all those tongue-teasing spices and, even after you're full, you can't stop picking at it, the flavor's so memorable; in fact, all the seafood is good here, befitting the aquarium theme. After dinner, Tara Thai pays tribute to America's endless sweet tooth by offering a variety of unusual desserts. Most feature tropical fruits and flavorings, and all are delectable, though some may not suit western palates. Tara Thai is open for lunch Monday through Saturday and dinner nightly.

Woo Lae Oak River House

$$ • 1500 S. Joyce St., Arlington, Va.
• (703) 521-3706

This is a great stop if you happen to be shopping at Pentagon City, but Woo Lae Oak alone is also worth a trip. Step inside this long, crowded room and you'll know from the fragrant smoke that there's a whole lot of grilling going on. Korean-style barbecue is a favorite here, and the sushi is a good way to start the meal. It's served on ice and portions are generous. This eatery has a long menu featuring many noodle dishes and soups, so ask your waitress for recommendations or watch what the Koreans around you are ordering. They serve lunch and dinner daily.

Young Chow

$ • 420 S. 23rd St., Crystal City, Va.
• (703) 892-2566

This is a great place to kill some time during a long layover at very-nearby National Air-

---

INSIDERS' TIP

If you have Kennedy Center tickets for a Sunday matinee, try brunch right there at the Roof Terrace Restaurant. It's a lavish affair that includes a tour of the kitchen.

port. Young Chow is a mere five minutes away (even less with a little luck), barely a block off Jefferson Davis Highway, but whether you're a local or a visitor, you can depend on tasty Chinese food of the Szechuan, Hunan and Cantonese varieties. Of course, being in a veritable mecca of corporate and government offices, Young Chow's takeout business is substantial. They are open for lunch and dinner nightly.

Tex-Mex/Hispanic

Anita's

$ • 9278 Old Keene Mill Rd., Burke, Va.
• (703) 455-3466
$ • 13921 Lee Jackson Hwy., Chantilly, Va. • (703) 378-1717
$ • 701 Elden St., Herndon, Va.
• (703) 481-1441
$ • 10880 Lee Hwy., Fairfax, Va.
• (703) 385-2965
$ • 521 Maple Ave. E., Vienna, Va.
• (703) 255-1001
$ • 147 Maple Ave. W., Vienna, Va.
• (703) 938-0888

Vienna was the original home of this popular local chain of "New Mexico"-style Mexican food outlets, but the town couldn't keep Anita's to itself for long. Soon, other suburban communities began to experience what they were missing. While the fare may not satisfy Tex-Mex aficionados used to the zestier, eye-watering concoctions, it is nevertheless consistently good and inexpensive, the service is efficient and the setting is relaxed and inviting. You can't help but overdo it on the homemade chips and salsa before the entrées arrive, but be sure to leave room for the sweet, puffy sopaipillas that beg to be topped with honey. They serve lunch and dinner nightly.

La Cantinita's Havana Café

$$ • 3100 Clarendon Blvd., Arlington, Va.
• (703) 524-3611

This sleeper has finally received the notice it deserves from Washington food critics and, as a result, seems to have taken off. You'll find authentic Cuban cuisine here, quite different from Tex-Mex, but containing many of the same spices. The roast pork is especially good, robust and zinged with a combination of hearty seasonings. If you want something lighter, try the red snapper served with an addictive vinegar-based sauce that'll make your tongue do the cha-cha. Havana Café is also a step-up from Washington's Tex-Mex restaurants in terms of decor. It's a light, airy space evocative of the islands — very pretty — serving lunch weekdays and dinner nightly.

El Pollo Rico

$ • 2917 N. Washington Blvd., Arlington, Va. • (703) 522-3220

This modest, Peruvian-owned café is among the best of the area's bargain rotisserie chicken restaurants. El Pollo Rico (The Rich Chicken — go figure) does a brisk carry-out business, but you can also sit at one of the handful of small tables scattered around the simple room. The menu is limited, and the only real reason to come is the house specialty: marinated, charcoal-fired rotisserie chicken that's perfectly flavored and practically melts in your mouth. With it, you can have fries, empanadas or tamales. El Pollo Rico serves lunch and dinner nightly. They do not accept credit cards.

Rio Grande Café

$$ • 4301 N. Fairfax Dr., Arlington, Va.
• (703) 528-3131
$$ • 1827 Library St., Reston, Va.
• (703) 904-0703

Please see Maryland listing.

Santa Fe East

$$ • 110 S. Pitt St., Alexandria, Va.
• (703) 548-6900

This Old Town Alexandria restaurant couldn't be more inviting, with its white-washed walls, French doors, old bricks and beamed ceilings. Inside, it looks like an *Architectural Digest* photo shoot of a Santa Fe hacienda, though it is actually a historic, Federal-style town house dating from colonial times. The food is a departure from the normal Tex-Mex fare. This is creative southwestern. That means white chili, roasted pork and chicken, and complex sauces over good fish. Try one of the dishes that is slow-cooked, like the chilis. In keeping with the sophisticated surroundings, the wine list is what you'd expect of an upscale restaurant and, except in the bar area, the tables are set with linens and placed far enough apart for privacy. If you want southwestern cuisine that's a bit creative, in a setting a bit more formal than the norm, Santa Fe East is the answer. They are open for lunch and dinner daily.

South Austin Grill
$ • 801 King St., Alexandria, Va.
• (703) 684-8969
Austin Grill Springfield
$ • 8430 Old Keene Mill Rd., Springfield, Va. • (703) 644-3111

This Old Town Alexandria Tex-Mex spot is always jumping, and there's a reason why. The bar downstairs is crammed with attractive 20- and 30-somethings and the margaritas are good and plenty. Upstairs, there's almost always a wait for a table. Those in the know appreciate the authenticity of Austin Grill. To be won over requires a mere sample of any of the expertly prepared and presented enchiladas, fajitas, burritos, chili and even the zesty appetizers. Wash it all down with something frosty, sit back and enjoy the sights and sounds. You'll surely understand why this restaurant is a hit. They are open for lunch and dinner nightly, and serve Saturday and Sunday brunch.

Sweetwater Tavern
$$ • 14250 Sweetwater Ln., Centreville, Va. • (703) 449-1100
$$ • 3066 Gatehouse Plaza, Falls Church, Va. • (703) 645-8100

The same team who dreamed up such popular eateries as the Carlyle Grand Café and Best Buns Bread Company have ventured into Southwestern cuisine with Sweetwater Tavern. As usual, these owners know how to do it right, with high quality, imaginative variations on the old standards. The decor glows with rich wood and leather, amber lighting and Indian rugs. Wrought-iron chandeliers feature Western scenes, as do the etched glass dividers on the booths. There's a highly rated microbrewery on premises, not to mention the spicy, smoky dishes such as ribs, quesadillas with poblanos, black bean chili with smoked chicken, and grilled smoked salmon. Desserts are big and mouth-watering. Don't even try to resist the chocolate waffle filled with the richest of chocolate ganache — that's pure chocolate, butter and cream to you and me. Sweetwater Tavern is open for lunch and dinner nightly and Sunday brunch.

Tortilla Factory
$ • 648 Elden St., Herndon, Va.
• (703) 471-1156

Other parts of the region will hopefully have a Tortilla Factory to call their own some day, but until then, it's worth a trip to this small town near Dulles Airport. Tacos, fajitas, enchiladas, burritos, nachos, salsa — the Tortilla Factory prepares them all in the zesty Sonoran tradition— and the results are memorable. Plus, you get a ton for the money in this casual, friendly setting. Let the branching out of the Tortilla Factory begin! They serve lunch and dinner daily, and also host live folk music — sometimes by renowned acts — on Tuesdays.

Middle Eastern/ Indian/Afghan

Bombay Bistro
$$ • 3570 Chain Bridge Rd., Fairfax, Va.
• (703) 359-5810

You could come to Bombay Bistro every day for a month and never exhaust the menu possibilities. This is superb and very serious Indian cuisine, with some prepared in a tandoor oven, some curried and some grilled over charcoal. The main courses are so filling that there is always some left over. The solution? Bring a large group, split the main courses and sample the appetizers and those wonderful, smoky Indian breads (which you do have to order — they aren't free). The standouts among the main courses are the lamb dishes. Lamb nilgiri khorma is an irresistible type of curry served with green masala alive with fresh coriander. Whole fish is enhanced by a marinade that features ginger, garlic and yogurt. Tandoori specialties can sometimes be a bit dry, but they're so tasty that you can almost overlook the flaw. This is a casual, fairly nondescript place, but there are some low tables in a back nook that are very romantic, and the food makes every meal seem special. Lunch and dinner are served daily.

Connaught Place

$$ • 10425 North St., Fairfax, Va.
• (703) 352-5959

This tiny Indian restaurant is tucked into a group of storefronts between a parking lot and a house in the City of Fairfax. But it's worth the trouble of finding it. The curries, Indian breads and appetizers are served with style and attention to detail — you'll never be rushed here. The cooking can be as good as at its Fairfax neighbor, Bombay Bistro. The menu contains all the Indian standards, but the execution and personal warmth make all the difference here. Ask your waiter to guide you, and you'll be treated to intricate descriptions that answer your every question. Lunch and dinner are served daily.

Kabul Caravan Colonial Shopping Center

$$ • 1725 Wilson Blvd., Arlington, Va.
• (703) 522-8394

You wouldn't know this intriguing room was hidden behind the rather depressing facade of the shopping center outside, but venture in and you'll enter a world of jewel tones, rich textiles and, best of all, earthy cuisine evocative of a caravan across the rugged mountains of Afghanistan. Afghan cuisine, earthy and pungent, is similar to Indian and draws on many of the same spices; however, there are subtle differences that should make for an unusual taste experience. The stews are a bit sweeter and there are more tomato-based sauces. Kabul Caravan offers a fixed price tasting menu that provides a good introduction to Afghan cooking. You'll find a lot of lamb dishes, seasoned yogurt and noodles stuffed with mint, meat and vegetables. Pumpkin plays a big role in Afghan cuisine, too, either stuffed in noodles, sautéed or stewed. They are open for lunch weekdays and dinner nightly.

Nizam's

$$ • 523 Maple Ave. W., Vienna, Va.
• (703) 938-8948

You'll find plenty of people who will argue that Nizam's is the region's best Turkish restaurant. Small and attractive as a jewel box, Nizam's is famous for its house special, doner kebab. Slices of lamb are marinated in cumin, oil and other exotic spices, then stacked on a rotisserie spit and slow-roasted. The result is

fragrant, crusty, juicy slices of meat served with pita bread and yogurt seasoned in the Middle Eastern style. The problem is, if you want doner kebab, you have to call ahead and ensure that it is being served that day. Since it's such a major project, Nizam's usually prepares it only twice a week. In any event, you'll do fine with the regular menu, which features such delicacies as marinated lamb in a variety of styles, beef tenderloin, stuffed grape leaves and assorted eggplant preparations. Nizam's is open for lunch Tuesday through Friday, dinner Tuesday through Sunday, and closed Monday.

Pasha Café

$$ • 2109 Pollard St., Arlington, Va.
• (703) 528-2126

The cuisine here harks from Egypt and is very similar to other Middle Eastern cuisine, so expect the usual array of delicious appetizers like hummus, tabbouleh and baba ghanouj. The fun here is in mixing and matching dishes, and the menu gives you ample opportunity to do so, suggesting various combinations that provide a taste of just about everything. Meals are filling and delicious, though somewhat oversalted. Try the kofte, kebabs or, on the lighter side, lemony chicken. The waiters, many of whom are Egyptian, are warm, hospitable and happy to guide you. One problem: waits for a table can be long, and the line crowds into the front end of the one-room dining area. Ask for a table away from the door and arrive early or late to avoid a long spell of standing. They serve lunch Monday through Saturday, and dinner nightly.

Suburban Maryland

American/Continental

Bethesda Crab House

$ • 4958 Bethesda Ave., Bethesda, Md.
• (301) 652-3382

They offer famed Chesapeake Bay crabs, yes, but Bethesda Crab House is also a popular late-night dining option; they are open 'til midnight seven days a week. If you order the crabs, you'll be given a tableful along with the implements to crack 'em open, so wear washable duds. Virtually any of the seafood selections are winners here, though, so don't think you've got to stick with the crabs — but then again, when in Maryland . . .

Capitol City Brewing Company
$$ • 7735 Old Georgetown Rd., Bethesda, Md. • (301) 652-2282

This offshoot of the popular downtown location was an immediate hit in Bethesda. You can get a sampling of four of the house's brews to start, and then venture into some fine pub food, including incendiary chili, sausage sandwiches, burgers and quesadillas. Portions are predictably large and the cooking is better than at a lot of such places. Desserts are huge and gooey, and are guaranteed to satisfy any sweet tooth. An original touch, instead of a bread basket, is a generous serving of soft pretzels with mustard. They offer lunch and dinner daily.

Clyde's of Chevy Chase
$$ • 76 Wisconsin Cir., Chevy Chase, Md. • (301) 951-9600

We've told you about Clyde's in D.C. and Clyde's in Virginia, so why gild the lily by going on about the Chevy Chase location? Well, you've gotta see it to believe it. This is as much an entertainment center as a restaurant. There's a model train that circles overhead and the theme is carried through in the booths, which are replicas of Orient Express parlor cars. This place must've cost a fortune to build, with its cushy leather seats and top-quality woodwork, but Clyde's can afford it. The Chevy Chase location is a hit, as are the other branches. The food here is good and varied, but a special treat is the vegetarian platter, offering all sorts of gems, like asparagus, at a very reasonable price; otherwise, as at the other Clyde's locations, you do best when you stick to pub fare — steak, salads and sinful desserts — all particularly festive in a setting like this. They serve lunch Monday through Saturday, dinner nightly and Sunday brunch.

Crisfield's
$$$ • 8012 Georgia Ave., Silver Spring, Md. • (301) 589-1306
8606 Colesville Rd., Silver Spring, Md. • (301) 588-1572

Crisfield's used to be one of those seafood places so basic and utilitarian in decor that you knew the food had to shine — especially at these downtown prices. Well, it's lost some of its luster, but if your namesake is the tiny Maryland community that claims to be the crab capital of the solar system, you'd better serve some world-class crabs. And Crisfield's still does. Maybe that's why it's still going strong after nearly 50 years in business. If you're in the neighborhood, there's no better place for crab and crab dishes, but it's not worth a trip. Crisfield's serves lunch weekdays and dinner nightly.

Louisiana Express Company
$ • 4921 Bethesda Ave., Bethesda, Md. • (301) 652-6945

No, you haven't been transported back to "Lew-zee-ann-uh." It just seems that way at Louisiana Express Company, where authentic Cajun treats — crawfish, po' boys, jambalaya, softshell crab sandwiches, the works — are served up in a down-home atmosphere. Stop by early for a full breakfast, or on Sunday for a knockout brunch. They serve lunch Monday through Saturday, dinner nightly and Sunday brunch.

Normandie Farm
$$$ • 10701 Falls Rd., Potomac, Md. • (301) 983-8838

You're not far away at Normandie Farm. It just feels that way. This Potomac landmark has lost nothing through the years; you can still count on delicious American cuisine in a gracious setting reminiscent of a country inn. Every meal begins with a basket of puffy, hot popovers — heavenly! The menu goes on to include some rich, old-fashioned specials. Last time we looked, they were still doing beef Wellington — not for those watching their weight. Over the years, the cuisine has become more sophisticated and there are Continental touches on the menu, particularly among the seafood dishes. This is still the place to come for traditional holiday meals. Normandie Farm is open for lunch and dinner Tuesday through Saturday, Sunday brunch and is closed Monday.

O'Brien's Pit Barbecue
$ • 387 E. Gude Dr., Rockville, Md. • (301) 340-8596

Casual and inexpensive, O'Brien's has endured for years as a popular stop for some of the tastiest Texas-style barbecue around. There is other, newer, competition, but O'Brien's holds its own with favorites like chili dogs, pork spareribs, and beef brisket. Side orders like beans and rice and spicy onion rings have plenty of pizzazz, too. They are open for lunch and dinner nightly.

Old Angler's Inn
$$$$ • 10801 MacArthur Blvd., Potomac, Md. • (301) 299-9097 or 365-2425

Old Angler's Inn sits snugly in the woods across the lane from the C&O Canal towpath. It looks like an enchanted cottage from a fairy tale, with its half-timbered accents and stone walk. Cozy up next to the roaring fireplace in fall and winter, or enjoy patio dining by a fountain in spring and summer. Back inside, the spiral staircase leads from a sitting area featuring big, soft couches, to an intimate, albeit bustling dining room where the mood continues to captivate. The prices at Old Angler's Inn may give you a little pre-dinner heartburn — this is a "jackets required" kind of place — but then again, when you consider the setting, service and wonderful menu selections such as rack of lamb, venison, quail and rabbit, the financial bite seems somehow less painful. Seafood is treated with respect, carefully herbed and never overcooked. Seared tuna and several other dishes feature Asian spices that show the chef's range of skill with any number of cooking styles. If you just can't decide what looks best, let the chef choose for you with his nightly tasting menu. Sated, you can relax into one of those down-filled couches and enjoy an after-dinner digestif. They serve lunch and dinner Tuesday through Saturday, Sunday brunch and are closed Monday.

Red, Hot & Blue
$ • 16809 Crabbs Branch Way, Gaithersburg, Md. • (301) 948-7333
$ • 677 Main St. Laurel, Md.
• (301) 953-1943

Please see the Virginia listing.

Shelly's Wood Roast
$ • 1699 Rockville Pk., Rockville, Md.
• (301) 984-3300

This may be one of the most striking budget restaurants you'll ever see, and it's in an area (Rockville) short on atmospheric spots,

so it's a welcome addition. It looks like a Colorado ski lodge, and the interior is decorated with peeled log beams, antler chandeliers and hundreds of small branches placed side by side to create wall covering. It is gorgeous. The food is fine, filling, and a bargain. A basket of big, hot popovers is brought to the table right after your order is taken, and meals come with soup or salad. There are some interesting main courses, including a Cornish game hen and brisket, and servings are generous. Desserts are the kind of extravaganzas you'd expect, and generous enough for three! Lunch and dinner are served daily.

Silver Diner
$ • 11806 Rockville Pk., Rockville, Md.
• (301) 770-2832
$ • 14550 Baltimore Ave., Laurel, Md.
• (301) 470-6080

This is a recent Washington-based chain that looks like an old-time diner. The silver bullet sits at the edge of a busy Rockville shopping center, and is almost always crowded. Breakfasts and desserts are tops here, with the rest being pretty standard stuff. In keeping with the diner theme, there's meatloaf and mashed potatoes, burgers and shakes, and humongous sandwiches. Waffles and French toast are great here and can be had at any time of the day. The 2 AM closing time makes Silver Diner a favorite stop for night owls. There are six in Virginia: 3200 Wilson Boulevard, Arlington, Virginia, (703) 812-8600; 14375 Smoketown Road, Dale City, Virginia, (703) 491-7376; 12250 Fair Lakes Parkway, Fairfax, Virginia, (703) 359-5999; 8101 Fletcher Avenue, McLean, Virginia, (703) 821-5666; 8150 Porter Road, Merrifield, Virginia, (703) 204-0812; or 11951 Killingsworth Avenue, Reston, Virginia, (703) 742-0805. Silver Diner is open for breakfast, lunch and dinner daily.

Tex-Mex/Hispanic

Andalucia
$$$ • 12300 Wilkins Ave., Rockville, Md.
• (301) 770-1880
$$$ • 9431 Elm St., Bethesda, Md.
• (301) 907-0052

Rockville has a Spanish star in

Andalucia, which serves consistently good food (emphasizing the gastronomic delights of southern Spain) with the grace and flair of a matador. This place, with its wonderful guitar music in the evenings, isn't nearly as informal as the other restaurants in the Latin American category. Don't overindulge in the good and garlicky appetizers — you have to save room for such specialties as paella and zarzuela. Don't overdo it on those tasty entrées either; the desserts — especially the cakes — are a delightful way to top it all off. They are open for lunch weekdays and dinner nightly.

Cottonwood Cafe
$$ • 4844 Cordell Ave., Bethesda, Md.
• (301) 656-4844

Cottonwood Cafe showcases cuisine that is truly indigenous to the American Southwest. It has a style and taste all its own. The secret: traditional herbs and spices combined with an open-grill preparation. It may not be much of a secret, but it helps Cottonwood Cafe stand out in a crowd. The menu here ventures far beyond the normal southwestern fare we've come to expect in Metro area restaurants. You can find beef tenderloin, pasta, duck and shrimp, all prepared with a spicy twist. The setting and the service are more sophisticated than the competition. They are open for lunch Monday through Saturday and dinner nightly.

El Caribe of Bethesda
$$ • 8130 Wisconsin Ave., Bethesda, Md.
• (301) 656-0888

Latin American and Caribbean cuisine is the focus at this award-winning restaurant and bar. One of the first Latin American/Caribbean restaurants to open in the Washington area, El Caribe is also one of the decades-long survivors in a market that comes and goes. The decor is pleasant and upscale, with greenery, bright tiles, and a general tropical ambiance. In general, seafood here, particularly fish, is handled well, often spiced with bell peppers, onions and garlic. As in many Latin American restaurants, the plantains and beans-and-rice are always delicious, and you could make a meal of them. They serve lunch and dinner nightly.

Rio Grande Cafe
$$ • 4919 Fairmont Ave., Bethesda, Md.
• (301) 656-2981

It used to be that an hour-long wait was standard for a table at Rio Grande Café. Some of the furor has died down, perhaps eased by the two Virginia locations, but this casual eatery remains popular. One of the highlights here is the tortilla machine, which produces warm, fresh . . . you guessed it . . . tortillas to accompany the fajitas and other Tex-Mex fare. You'll find the usual tacos, enchiladas, burritos, plus a few unexpected items like frog legs and quail. This place is loud, busy and frenetic, so it might not be the place for an intimate evening. They are open for lunch Monday through Saturday, dinner nightly and Sunday brunch.

Terramar
$$ • 7800 Wisconsin Ave., Bethesda, Md.
• (301) 654-0888

You don't hear a lot about Terramar and that's surprising, because it's a find. The setting couldn't be more charming — an indoor courtyard paved with colorful tile and dotted with plants. The cuisine here is Central American, which means lots of plantain-based dishes and accents. If you've never tasted that starchy relative of the banana, this is the place to try it. You can have plantains fried as a side dish or stuffed with melt-in-your-mouth pork. If you're in the mood to graze, try the tapas: calamari, empanadas, tamales and guacamole, plus some dishes that you've probably never heard of. Main courses come with some great side dishes, including red beans and rice that are out of the ordinary. For the entrées, any of the marinated, grilled meats are a good choice. Terramar serves dinner Monday through Saturday.

French

La Ferme
$$$ • 7101 Brookville Rd., Chevy Chase, Md. • (301) 986-5255

La Ferme is nestled into a wealthy residential section of Montgomery County, one of the few commercial enterprises in the neighborhood, but it's hardly a drop-in kind of place. There's something both fresh and luxurious about the country French decor — you couldn't ask for a more inviting setting. As befits a restaurant in this cosmopolitan and very upscale area, the food is excellent. Cuts of meat are well-trimmed for the utmost in tenderness and taste. Veal is often pallid elsewhere but at La Ferme, it shines. Seafood classics like Dover sole are done right here, but you can also find more modern, simply grilled fish. Restaurants that serve Châteaubriand aren't exactly rare in the Washington area, but they aren't common either. La Ferme does it and does it well. This is the kind of spot that's lovely for a special occasion, or for an escapist lunch on a lazy, summer day. Lunch is served weekdays, dinner Tuesday through Sunday, and they are closed Monday.

La Miche

**$$$ • 7905 Norfolk Ave., Bethesda, Md.
• (301) 986-0707**

Think of dried flowers, lively prints and baskets, and you've pictured La Miche. This French charmer, near the National Institutes of Health, has stayed ahead of the competition for two decades by sticking to the basics of French cooking, like lobster bisque, cream sauces, puff pastries and meats redolent with garlic. You probably won't find anything unfamiliar on this menu — just calories-be-damned French cooking that takes you back to the old days. La Miche is open for lunch Tuesday through Friday, dinner nightly and is closed on Sundays in August.

Le Vieux Logis

**$$$ • 7925 Old Georgetown Rd.,
Bethesda, Md. • (301) 652-6816**

Even in restaurant-packed Bethesda, Le Vieux Logis makes you do a double take. That's because it looks like a slice of Alsace with its half-timbered facade and flower-filled window boxes. Flowers are everywhere, and what a nice greeting! Inside, there are other reminders of Alsace in the cooking, which has a somewhat German accent; for example, many of the meat dishes are paired with sauces that contain fruit or mustard. Mushrooms are used liberally in both appetizers and main courses. Try the mushroom soup, a creamy concoction with a haunting flavor. Veal, too, is paired with mushrooms and cream sauce. If seafood's your fancy, you'll find several dishes infused with citrus. They are lighter than the meat dishes

and also very good. This is interesting, unusual French cuisine, and you won't find a more pleasant setting. They serve dinner nightly.

Jean-Michel

**$$$ • 10223 Old Georgetown Rd.,
Bethesda, Md. • (301) 564-4910**

This restaurant may be located in a shopping center, but it's a very classy one and this is a classy restaurant. Step through the door and you'll think you're in one of those chic Paris eateries that tourists never find. The crowd is well-heeled, the room is alive with conversation and the lighting is flattering and rosy. Owner Jean-Michel has been a presence in Washington for decades, and he once reigned supreme in one of those downtown French restaurants that bit the dust with the three-martini lunch. He now offers cuisine on a slightly more modest scale, but you won't feel shortchanged. Try any of the beef or seafood dishes here — they're especially good. They serve lunch weekdays and dinner nightly.

Italian

Cesco

**$$ • 4871 Cordell Ave., Bethesda, Md.
• (301) 654-8333**

There's no more agreeable patio on Bethesda's restaurant row than that at Cesco, and the interior decor is just as inviting, with wonderful arches and plenty of windows. The menu here departs a bit from the Italian standards — there are some interesting ingredients and presentations; for example, the salad of endive and parmesan cheese is a work of art with large shavings of pungent cheese decorating a sculpture of greenery. The bruschetta appetizer has a tomato-based topping, which is normal, but is also punctuated with broccoli rabe and cannellini beans. If it's meat you're craving, try the sinful filet of beef with eggplant and tomato in a gorgonzola cheese sauce. Cesco is open for lunch weekdays, dinner Monday through Saturday and is closed Sunday.

C.J. Ferrari's

**$ • 143111 Baltimore Ave., Laurel, Md.
• (301) 725-1771**

There's nothing fancy about this bargain-priced eatery in Prince George's County, but surprising care is taken with several dishes. Anything tomato-based is a good bet here — the sauce is springy and flavorful. Try one of the seafood dishes, like scallops in a delicious wine sauce, zinged with a bit of mustard. You'll want to sop up that extra sauce with a slice of the restaurant's crusty bread. What put Ferrari's on the map though is the white pizza, a garlicky, cheesy version that puts others to shame. For dessert, try the homemade ice cream. They are open for lunch Tuesday through Friday, dinner Tuesday through Sunday and are closed Monday.

Fratelli

$ • 5820 Landover Rd., Cheverly, Md. • (301) 209-9006

You don't expect to find style like this in Cheverly, and you especially don't expect it at these low prices. While Fratelli's isn't worth a special foray into Prince George's County, it's a nice place to stop if you're already there. This isn't gourmet Italian, but rather good hearty cooking. Don't miss the bargain-priced antipasto, which contains all manner of seafood from clams to shrimp. Pizzas here are a safe bet when it comes to choosing a main course — there's no scrimping on the cheese here. Or, if you don't want finger food, try one of the pastas in red sauce. Fratelli is open for lunch Monday through Saturday, dinner nightly and Sunday brunch.

Il Pizzico

$ • 15209 Frederick Rd., Rockville, Md. • (301) 309-0610

In the world of restaurants, high quality at low prices seems to be oxymoronic more often than it is true; but not at the cozy and family-like Il Pizzico, where affordable and delicious Italian cuisine is the benchmark of success and praise. While the menu is not expansive, you can hardly go wrong, especially with the veal, fish and pasta selections. Ask about the daily specials, the wine list and, lest we forget, the desserts. Il Pizzico is open for lunch weekdays Monday through Saturday, and is closed Sunday.

Il Ritrovo

$$ • 4838 Rugby Ave., Bethesda, Md. • (301) 986-1447

This restaurant isn't strictly Italian — the rep-

ertoire borrows from the entire Mediterranean — but there's enough Italian on the menu for it to qualify in this category. There are risottos and pastas, but you'll also find North African dishes, such as couscous. Appetizers seem predominantly Italian, ranging from fried calamari to Portobello mushrooms (which aren't really Italian, but are usually prepared as such). The decor, too, could be Italian, but it could be Greek with its whitewashed walls. Desserts? Again, the influences vary. A real surprise are the crepes suzette — a classic French sweet that seemingly bears no relation to the rest of the menu, but is well executed. Hmmm . . . it's a conundrum. They are open for lunch weekdays and dinner nightly.

Pines of Rome

$ • 4709 Hampton Ln., Bethesda, Md. • (301) 657-8775

Pines of Rome has stuck to its guns through cooking fads from nouvelle to northern Italian to fusion. Never has it deviated from the old Italian-American standard: pasta with heavy, red sauce served on checkered tablecloths. Sure, there's a white pizza that's pretty good, and a robust spaghetti carbonara, but that's about as adventurous as you want to get here. This is a place to bring kids when you want to eat cheaply, quickly and plenty. They are open for lunch and dinner nightly.

That's Amore

$$ • 15201 Shady Grove Rd., Rockville, Md. • (301) 670-9666

You'd better pack an appetite when you go to That's Amore. Even then, one dish may be enough to serve your entire party. For cheap eats, the food here is very good, and the atmosphere is raucous and friendly, with lots of families. The cooking is heavy on the garlic, tomato sauce and cheese — nothing subtle about this place. The menu contains all the Italian standards like eggplant and veal parmigiana, but the underlying ingredients hardly matter when the toppings are so robust. Try anything that features lemon-butter sauce and you'll probably be happy. The meal-sized salads are stocked with lots of goodies like olives, onions and tomatoes. If you want to sample everything from soup to nuts, bring your extended family and share, or you'll never get through it. They are open for lunch Monday through Saturday and dinner nightly.

Tragara

**$$$ • 4935 Cordell Ave., Bethesda, Md.
• (301) 951-4935**

This may be the most extravagant — and the most formal — Italian restaurant in the Maryland suburbs, and it's one of the prettiest, with two levels, generous floral arrangements and light, bright decor. The food is mostly northern Italian, which means rich white sauces, grilled meats and a delicate hand with seasoning. You may end up spending more here than you think you should, but if you're looking for a special occasion Italian restaurant in Maryland, nothing comes close in terms of overall atmosphere and cuisine. Tragara is open for lunch weekdays and dinner nightly.

Middle Eastern/Indian

Bacchus

**$$ • 7945 Norfolk Ave., Bethesda, Md.
• (301) 657-1722**

Bacchus is open for lunch weekdays and dinner nightly. Please see their listing in the D.C. section.

Bombay Bistro

$$ • 98 W. Montgomery Ave., Rockville, Md. • (301) 762-8798

Bombay Bistro is open for lunch and dinner nightly. Please see their listing in the Virginia section.

Swagat

$ • 2063 University Blvd., East Adelphi, Md. • (301) 434-2247

There aren't a whole lot of restaurants to choose from in Adelphi — unless you're interested in fast food — so this quirky little Indian eatery is a stand-out. Why quirky? Well, for one it serves no alcohol. It's also vegetarian, which isn't unusual for an Indian restaurant. In fact, it's very good vegetarian, and you may not even miss the meat. Try any of the filled pastries as an appetizer. The veg-

etables and spices inside are tangy and the fried dough satisfying. The curries are hot and flavorful. If you can't decide, and the whole menu seems unfamiliar, try the buffet, always available at lunch and brunch, and often available at dinner. Swagat is open for lunch Monday through Saturday, dinner nightly and Sunday brunch.

Asian

Benjarong

**$ • 855C Rockville Pk., Rockville, Md.
• (301) 340-8897**

This Thai restaurant in a Rockville shopping center is unexpectedly elegant. The decor is pastel and cheery with linen covered tables set comfortably apart to allow for private conversation. There are almost one hundred items on this menu: ten soups, fifteen appetizers and the rest as main courses. Spices here are combined masterfully, and you really can't go wrong no matter what you order. Shrimp is presented in almost a dozen ways, as are whole fish, squid and soft-shell crab. Pork and beef play a lesser role, but there are several interesting duck dishes, including a shredded duck appetizer with lemon grass, pepper, onion and chili. If you want incendiary spicing, you'll have to ask, since dishes have been toned down a bit for western palates. They serve lunch and dinner nightly.

Good Fortune

$ • 2646 University Blvd. W., Wheaton, Md. • (301) 929-8818

Good Fortune has earned a name for itself in the local world of Cantonese cuisine. It's so affordable that it's almost too good to be true. An exhaustive menu may require more time than usual to peruse, but if you lack the patience, you can't go wrong with any of the selections featuring lobster, duck and fish, or the interesting casserole creations and spectacular stuffed mushrooms. Good Fortune is open for lunch and dinner nightly.

Hunan Pearl

$ • 12137 Darnestown Rd., Gaithersburg, Md. • (301) 330-8118

This is one of those neighborhood places that consistently wins high marks from the

Photo: Courtesy of Maryland Office of Tourism Development

Washington's proximity to the Chesapeake Bay gives restaurants and markets the advantage of providing fresh seafood like the Maryland blue crab.

community, but isn't that well-known farther afield. You'll find consistently good Chinese fare at this location, convenient to Interstate 270 commuters exhausted from the long trek to D.C. As crowded a field as it is, Hunan Pearl manages to distance itself just a bit from some of the formidable suburban competition. They serve lunch and dinner daily.

Mama Wok and Teriyaki
$ • 595 Hungerford Dr., Rockville, Md.
• (301) 309-6642

If nothing else, you gotta love the name. This restaurant — which features Chinese and Japanese cuisine — has more to offer than that, however. If you're not squeamish, there's live seafood prepared to your liking, and the selection's not limited to fish, as in many other restaurants. According to the season, you're likely to find oyster, clams, crab or shrimp. Even if you don't want to meet your meal before you eat it, the other seafood items are sparkling fresh, and simple preparations show them to good advantage. The decor here is as plain as could be, but when there's such fresh seafood to be had at rock-bottom prices, who cares about atmosphere? They are open for lunch and dinner daily.

Matuba
$ • 4918 Cordell Ave., Bethesda, Md.
• (301) 652-7449

For top-notch Japanese cuisine at bargain prices, Matuba can certainly dish it out. Budget sushi is almost an oxymoron, but not at Matuba, which offers sushi and sashimi in a large variety of combinations. Sushi rolls are a special treat, executed with flair. At Matuba, you can afford sushi as a first course and go on to sample tempting cooked seafood as a second course — the soft-shell crab for example. When in Arlington, Virginia, stop in for a bite at 2915 Columbia Pike, (703) 521-2811. Matuba is open for lunch weekdays and dinner nightly.

Oodles Noodles
$ • 4907 Cordell Ave., Bethesda, Md.
• (301) 986-8833

The downtown branch of Oodles Noodles often has a long line at lunch, but the Bethesda location is a bit less frenetic, albeit popular. This stylish fusion eatery features a decor with lots of sunshine and gleaming surfaces. It looks upscale, so the decidedly scaled down prices are a surprise. Japanese, Malaysian, Thai and Chinese cuisine get equal time here, with appetizers ranging from satays to Japanese dumplings stuffed with meat and served with sesame soy sauce. There are only three soups on the appetizer menu, one Chinese, two Thai, and all are good. Glance at the extensive list of entrées and you'll find other soup selections worthy of a meal. They're really bowls crammed with goodies, then spooned over with aromatic broth. The heat quotient of the chilis here will be altered to your liking. Oodles Noodles offers lots of adventure for very little money. Try the downtown location at 1120 19th Street NW, (202) 293-3138. They serve lunch Monday through Saturday and dinner nightly.

Sabang
$ • 2504 Ennalls Ave., Wheaton, Md.
• (301) 942-7859, (301) 942-7874

If you enjoy Thai, Vietnamese or virtually any other Asian cuisine, you'll like Indonesian. The trouble is in finding a restaurant that serves it. There's a lovely one downtown (see Washington listing for Sarinah), but in the suburbs you needn't look any further than Wheaton's Sabang for inexpensive, interesting creations in this unique gastronomic genre. Like the downtown Sarinah, Sabang is an exceptionally pretty and festive space — maybe it's the Indonesian aesthetic of jewel-like colors, handmade textiles and intricately carved furniture. In mundane Wheaton, this place is an oasis. As for the cooking, Indonesian is so unfamiliar to most Westerners that it's not a bad idea to order the rijstaffel, an amalgam of dishes that allows you to sample a broad range. If that doesn't appeal, try the satays, skewered meats with dipping sauce of peanuts and chilis. If you're still confused, ask your server; the staff here is warm, helpful and eager to share this cuisine with you. They serve lunch and dinner daily.

Sam Woo
$$ • 1054 Rockville Pk., Rockville, Md.
• (301) 424-0495

Sam Woo's selections are among the area's best in Korean cuisine (grilled at your table if you'd like), and you'll know it at once when you walk in and see all the Korean diners there.

There's a broad selection of main-course soups and casseroles, many that are sure to please seafood lovers — or choose from an extensive selection of Japanese entrées including chicken teriyaki, sushi and tempura. Try the weekday buffet for a truly different kind of lunch break. They are open for lunch Monday through Saturday and dinner nightly.

Seven Seas Chinese Restaurant
$$ • 1776 E. Jefferson St., Rockville, Md.
• (301) 770-5020

This restaurant is well-known in the Washington area for its seafood, and you know it's fresh from the minute you walk in and spot the large fish tank full of ocean delicacies. Seven Seas serves both traditional Chinese and Japanese fare, including dim sum and sushi. This small, storefront restaurant has also branched out even more into calorie-conscious offerings, both vegetarian and with meat. Seven Seas is open for lunch and dinner daily.

Sunny Garden
$ • 1302 E. Gude Dr., Rockville, Md.
• (301) 762-7477

Taiwanese food seems a likely candidate for that hard-to-find restaurant category, but one visit to Sunny Garden and you'll wonder why. In fact, you'll probably find more familiar items than you expect, since Taiwanese cooking incorporates some of the Chinese-American style so familiar to so many people. Seafood and vegetable specialties, in particular, help make Sunny Garden a bright spot on the list. They are open for lunch and dinner daily.

Suporn
$ • 2302 Price Ave., Wheaton, Md.
• (301) 946-7613

You've probably gathered by now that Wheaton and Rockville are meccas for Asian restaurants, and there are many Thai offerings among them. Suporn's is a bargain-priced eatery that offers some interesting dishes and

INSIDERS' TIP

If you're dining in Georgetown on a Friday or Saturday, be aware of the weekend parking restrictions or you could get towed. Either pick a restaurant with valet parking or find a pay lot.

a great deal of range. Start with one of Suporn's many salads, some flavored with lime, cilantro, anise, chilis, peanuts, or in most cases, a combination of several harmonious seasonings. Go on to hot, spicy soup or skip to a main course that features noodles, curries or stir fry. The prices here are so low, you can try it all. Suporn is open for lunch Tuesday through Saturday, dinner Tuesday through Sunday and is closed Monday.

Tako Grill
$$ • 7756 Wisconsin Ave., Bethesda, Md.
• (301) 652-7030

As the name implies, Tako Grill ventures beyond its considerable sushi menu to feature an equally wide array of grilled foods. There are grilled meats, seafood and a surprising variety of vegetables, many so exotic that they're not found elsewhere in Washington — certainly not grilled. At one time, fans would stand in line to eat here, since the restaurant accepts no reservations, but Tako Grill was recently expanded, so the wait shouldn't be as long. Try going on a weeknight just to be sure. They are open for lunch weekdays and dinner nightly.

Tara Thai
$$ • 4828 Bethesda Ave., Bethesda, Md.
• (301) 657-0488

The Maryland suburbs around Washington have lots of good, basic Asian restaurants, but here's one with glamour. For more on Tara Thai, please see their Virginia listing. They serve lunch Monday through Saturday, and dinner nightly.

Taste of Saigon
$$ • 410 Hungerford Dr., Rockville, Md.
• (301) 424-7222

This light, pretty Vietnamese restaurant is always crowded despite its hard-to-find location in the middle of a Rockville parking lot. The prices are good — which accounts for some of its popularity — but with so many reasonably priced Asian restaurants in Rockville, that's not all there is to it. There's the fashionable contemporary dining room with plenty of light and cheery linens on the tables, the outdoor patio with stylish umbrellas and there's the food. Try the whole fish bathed in spices and scallions, intriguing soups crammed with noodles and meat, and stir fries bursting with fresh veggies. They serve lunch and dinner daily.

After-hours diversions
in Metro Washington
include a little bit
of everything.

Nightlife

In a place where shuffling papers and climbing corporate ladders are forms of recreation, and starched shirts and leather pumps are considered de rigueur fashions, nightlife may not seem like a top priority for many people. Believe it or not, even stressed-out, career-minded Washingtonians know how to have a good time away from the office, embracing the work hard/play hard philosophy with ample gusto.

While the nightlife here is plentiful and diverse, don't expect a heavy dose of Los Angeles-style glitz or New York-style up-'til-dawn decadence. Instead, like the dining scene, after-hours diversions in Metro Washington include a little bit of everything, from cutting-edge music halls and stand-up comedy venues, to funky watering holes, sports saloons, yuppified fern bars and high-energy dance clubs.

First, here are a few things to keep in mind before venturing out for an evening on the town. As a general rule, the District offers the widest variety of nightlife, but you can almost always expect to pay a bit more for such things as drinks, cover charges and live entertainment. Case in point: Single beers approaching the $4 mark are common, especially at some of the city's tonier clubs — and if they don't get you at the bar, there's a good chance you paid for it at the door. Sometimes, you may get nailed at both places, but then, no one ever recommended bar-hopping as a way to save money.

Suburban establishments are generally a bit less expensive, but in some cases they lag well behind their urban counterparts in the character and atmosphere departments. Whether you live in the Virginia exurbs or far-flung Maryland counties, chances are your nightlife will occur in one of three places: Montgomery County, Maryland, Washington, D.C. or the northern Virginia suburbs immediately surrounding Washington — that is, Arlington or Fairfax counties and the city of Old Town Alexandria. Accordingly, we've used only three geographical divisions in the listing below: Washington, D.C., Northern Virginia and Maryland.

"Last call for alcohol," as the saying goes, is typically around 2 AM in the city, and 1 to 1:30 AM in the 'burbs. Some of the downtown haunts may not finish shooing people out the door until 3 or 4 AM, but alcohol cannot be legally served after 3 AM in the District.

Incredibly, soft drinks aren't always that much cheaper than booze at many bars and clubs in Metro Washington, although they certainly should be in this age of heightened awareness about the lunacy of drinking and driving. Some places do, however, occasionally offer free, unlimited nonalcoholic beverages to the designated driver in a group, so it pays (in more ways than one) to inquire. The drinking age, by the way, is 21 in Washington, D.C., Maryland and Virginia for beer, wine and liquor. Even those who are well past the legal age but blessed with youthful looks shouldn't be surprised if they're asked for identification.

The scourge of underage drinking and the increasingly tough penalties levied against those who serve minors have convinced many business owners — grocery, convenience and liquor store operators included — to be extra cautious about who's buying. So take the request to see your driver's license as a compliment, not an insult. On your drive home, don't be surprised if you encounter roadblocks where police check for drunk drivers — it's a common practice on weekends in the Metro Washington area.

For weekly updates on what's happening on the local nightlife scene, we highly recommend the "Weekend" and "Washington Weekend" sections of *The Washington Post* and *The Washington Times*, respectively. Both supplements include expansive listings of clubs, shows, special events and other pertinent information. *The Post* publishes its guide on Friday, and *The Times*'s on Thursday, a strategy that the paper says helps you get a jump on planning those blessed two days of freedom. It makes sense. We know some people who start thinking about the upcoming weekend on Monday.

As with the dining section, this is far from an exhaustive roundup of Metro Washington night spots, and again we've tried to emphasize the local spots. Entries bearing an asterisk (*) beside their name are also covered in the Restaurants chapter, so please refer to that section for more details.

Washington, D.C.

Live Music and Dancing

Badlands
1413 22nd St. NW, Washington, D.C.
• **(202) 296-0505**

Badlands is one of the gay dance clubs that newcomers to Washington will hear of first, along with Tracks. That's because it's always crowded and always rocking. There's a little something for everyone, from a music video room to pool tables. The crowd is fairly young, in shape and attractive. There are often theme nights ranging from country/western to karaoke. The club is open every night, with a weekend cover charge of $5.

The Ballroom
1015 Half St. SE, Washington, D.C.
• **(202) 554-1500**

The Ballroom is a newer version of The Bayou (see the following listing), but the same company, Cellar Door Productions, stages the shows. On occasion, The Ballroom draws international rock stars like David Bowie, along with lesser-known groups like Kevorkian Death Cycle. The crowd is young and hip, and not afraid to venture into this iffy part of town, home to a number of clubs where anything goes.

Their schedule is determined by show times. Tickets are $5 to $15.

The Bayou
3135 K St. NW, Washington, D.C.
• **(202) 333-2897**

One of the city's most venerable nightlife establishments sits across from the waterfront beneath the Whitehurst Freeway at the foot of Wisconsin Avenue. With its time-worn brick facade and modest neon sign, The Bayou is a live-music institution if there ever was one in Washington. This unpretentious, 500-seat nightclub features top-name national rock bands as well as plenty of local talent, including comedy acts. For the more popular shows, buy your ticket in advance. Their schedule is determined by show times. Tickets are $5 to $15.

Black Cat
1831 14th St. NW, Washington, D.C.
• **(202) 667-7960**

This eclectic nightclub ranges from swing music to alternative rock, depending on which night you go. On swing music nights, you'll find people sipping champagne and smoking cigars. On rock nights, it's a whole different crowd — a very young one, with lots of black jeans in evidence. To keep up with what's going on here, you'll need to call for the weekly schedule. They are open nightly, and tickets are $3 to $15.

Blues Alley
1073 Wisconsin Ave. NW, Washington, D.C. • **(202) 337-4141**

You could easily miss the aptly named Blues Alley, as it's hidden in a Georgetown alley, halfway between K and M streets off Wisconsin Avenue. For decades, this intimate supper club has been the city's top spot for the best in local and national jazz and blues acts, including the likes of Tony Bennett, Wynton Marsalis and Charlie Byrd. Reservations are a must, especially on weekends and when top talent is on the bill. Blues Alley is open nightly, and tickets are $16 to $27.50.

Bukom Café
2442 18th St. NW, Washington, D.C.
• (202) 265-4600

Washington has a large community that hails from Africa and many of its members can be found at this hot spot in Adams Morgan when the place rocks with live reggae music from Wednesday to Saturday. The atmosphere starts out relaxed, but picks up as the band plays on and the night progresses. Dress is casual as could be. They are closed Monday. There is no cover charge.

Café Lautrec
2431 18th St. NW, Washington, D.C.
• (202) 265-6436

You can dine on French bistro fare at this snug Adams Morgan eatery, or just listen to the music, which changes nightly. Most evenings feature a jazz trio, but occasionally there's a dancer instead, so you might want to check the schedule. They are open nightly, and charge a $6 minimum per person.

Chief Ike's Mambo Room
1725 Columbia Rd. NW, Washington, D.C. • (202) 332-2211

This funky Adams Morgan night club draws a casual crowd ranging in ages from 20-something to around 40. On weekends there's some very hip live music. Bands vary from reggae to rock. If you don't like the music here, you can wander down the street to any number of other locales for live tunes. They are open nightly, with a weekend cover charge of $3 to $5.

Chelsea's
1055 Thomas Jefferson St. NW, Washington, D.C. • (202) 298-8222

If salsa music makes you sizzle, check out Chelsea's after ten o'clock on weekends, when it changes from a comedy club to a hot dance spot featuring wonderful live Latin rhythms. The patrons of this Georgetown institution are mostly Latino with a scattering of Anglos who dare to brave the dance floor thronged with merengue experts. You can dress to the nines here if you like, or come in khakis. Jeans are definitely out of place though. Chelsea's is open nightly, except on Tuesday. The cover charge is $10.

Coco Loco*
810 7th St. NW, Washington, D.C.
• (202) 289-4386

A great Latin restaurant, Coco Loco is transformed into a wild nightclub when the clock strikes eleven. There's live entertainment on Saturdays, which segues into dancing on one of two floors: one is for Latin music, and one is for "international," which basically means updated disco with a Euro-beat and a smattering of American favorites. If you're rusty — or a neophyte — Wednesdays are Latin dance-lesson night. They are open Monday through Saturday, with cover charges of $5 on Wednesday and $10 Thursday through Saturday.

Dubliner Pub
520 N. Capitol St. NW, Washington, D.C.
• (202) 737-3773

For a taste of the Emerald Isle without stepping on a plane, head for this pub, which is popular with Capitol Hill staff. The Dubliner is in the Phoenix Park Hotel, reported to be the nation's only Irish-owned hotel, and considered by many to be the region's most authentic Irish pub and dining experience. While Irish cuisine may be beside the point, Irish folk music appeals to many, and is featured here nightly. They are open nightly, with no cover charge.

The Fireplace
2161 P St. NW, Washington, D.C.
• (202) 293-1293

The Fireplace has been around for decades, first as a bar and lounge for all sorts, now as a bar and lounge for a mostly gay crowd. The salient feature of this place is, in fact, the fireplace visible at the corner of the building (it looks like an outdoor fireplace at first) on P and 22nd streets. Inside, you'll find a very dark series of rooms and a couple of bars on two stories. The clientele here is definitely on the prowl, so if you're looking for a place to meet new people, this may be it. You'll find a mix of neighborhood locals and tourists from nearby hotels, along with a somewhat raffish element. The Fireplace is open nightly, with no cover charge.

Irish Times
14 F St. NW, Washington, D.C.
• (202) 543-5433

This low-key pub features live Irish music Thursday through Saturday. Entertainment is mostly of the acoustic guitar variety and the crowd is an easy mix of downtown suits, chinos and blue-jeans. Irish Times is open nightly, with no cover charge.

Kramerbooks & Afterwords Café
1517 Connecticut Ave. NW, Washington, D.C. • (202) 232-6777

Here's a fun twist: a bookstore with live music from Wednesday to Saturday. Long before Borders and the other big chains came along and tried it, this Dupont Circle mainstay dreamed up the idea of teaming these two great forms of entertainment. Expect a laid-back approach with lots of acoustic guitar and folk music — nothing too intrusive. The café serves three meals a day, and has great coffee and desserts. They are open nightly, with no cover charge.

Melrose*
24th and M Sts. NW, Washington, D.C. • (202) 789-4242

There aren't too many places in Washington for adults who prefer the fox trot to freestyle flailing. Melrose, with its Saturday evening band music in an elegant setting at the Park Hyatt Hotel, fills the gap. This is a pricey restaurant, and drinks here don't come cheap, but the room is glamorous with marble, plush banquettes and extravagant flower arrangements. It's a dressy place, and

a great way to top off a special evening. Melrose is open nightly, with no cover charge.

9:30 Club
815 V St. NW, Washington, D.C.
• (202) 393-0930

If alternative rock is your thing, you won't want to miss the 9:30 Club. The crowd here is young and pierced, and the atmosphere is dark and intense. Cutting-edge bands play here, and sport names like Death in Vegas, Voodoo Glow Skulls and Sneaker Pimps. They are open nightly, and ticket prices range from $1 to $30, depending on the show.

Pier 7
650 Water St. SW, Washington, D.C.
• (202) 554-2500

Pier 7, at the Channel Inn Hotel, is a pleasant waterfront restaurant. Here you can enjoy live music and dancing with the baby-boomer-and-up crowd. Dress is conservative, ranging from business suits to sportswear — this is a white tablecloth kind of place. Plenty of tourists make the stop here, since the riverside restaurants bring them in by the busload. Pier 7 is open nightly, with no cover charge.

The Nest
1401 Pennsylvania Ave. NW, Washington, D.C. • (202) 637-7440

This elegant room at the Willard Inter-Continental Hotel will make you think of martinis and Dorothy Parker, and on weekends, there's the special treat of live jazz by top-notch performers. The Willard is one the town's most historic and glamorous hotels, so The Nest is as cushy and classy as you might imagine. The crowd is well-dressed, with men usually sporting suits and ties. The Nest is open nightly, with a cover charge of $7.50 to $16.

Nightclubs

The Brickskeller
1523 22nd St. NW, Washington, D.C.
• (202) 293-1885

On the fringes of Georgetown, The Brickskeller remains the city's consummate beer-lover's nirvana, offering more than 700 brands from around the world. It's handy for washing down fare like pizza, sandwiches and buffalo burgers. Be sure to check out the un- believable beer-can collection lining the walls. They are open nightly, with no cover charge.

Childe Harold's Step Childe
1610 20th St. NW, Washington, D.C.
• **(202) 483-6700**

This popular pub in a Dupont Circle town house turns its third floor into a DJ-driven dance hall on Friday and Saturday. The crowd is casual, and of all ages. This is a drop-in kind of place, rather than an event, and the downstairs restaurant is a neighborhood spot for burgers and a wide selection of brews. They are open nightly, with no cover charge.

Club Zei
1415 Zei Alley NW, Washington, D.C.
• **(202) 842-2445**

Just off Eye Street, between 14th and 15th streets NW, the glamorous crowd at Club Zei ranges from fat cats — who head straight for the members-only room on the third level — to the young and hip who jam the dance floor below. The music is very loud and hi-tech, with lots of Euro-sound thrown in. There are video screens, of course, and house dancers, along with a roving band of cigarette girls. They are open Thursday through Saturday, with a cover charge of $5 on Thursdays and $10 on the weekends.

Cobalt
1639 R St. NW, Washington, D.C.
• **(202) 232-6969**

This is an upscale kind of place with a large gay clientele, as befits the Dupont Circle location. But the fun can be wild as the evening progresses and the DJ really gets going. The bar area and dance floor are on two different levels, so there's conversational space as well as party space. They are open nightly, with no cover charge.

Coco Loco*
810 7th St. NW, Washington, D.C.
• **(202) 289-4386**

Coco Loco is open Monday through Sat- urday, and closed Sunday. The cover charge

is $5 on Wednesday and $10 Thursday through Saturday. Please see the listing un- der Live Music.

Ozone Le Club Industriel
1214 18th St. NW, Washington, D.C.
• **(202) 293-0303**

This multimedia fantasy isn't just a gay club; each night there's a different theme and many of the young, hip patrons are straight. However, its being near Dupont Circle means that there's a significant gay clientele and Sat- urdays are "Girl World" nights — in other words, lesbians. They are closed Sunday, with a cover charge of $3 to $9.

Polly Esther's
605 12th St. NW, Washington, D.C.
• **(202) 737-1970**

There's nothing else quite like this place in D.C. Note the last four digits of the phone number — not to mention the club's name — and you'll have a hint as to Polly Esther's theme. Yes, it's a retro-70s disco, complete with a Saturday Night Fever dance. Not your favorite decade? Okay, step up to the Culture Club (remember Boy George?), another room featuring dance music and memorabilia from the '80s. This place is a scream — be sure to wear your platforms and white polyester three- piece suit for the best effect. They are open Wednesday through Saturday, with a cover charge of $6 on Thursday and Friday, and $8 on Saturday.

Samantha's
1823 L St. NW, Washington, D.C.
• **(202) 223-1823**

This meet-and-greet place is smack dab in the middle of the office complexes that house many of the town's top law, accounting, and public relations firms. Accordingly, the crowd is mostly young and not-so-young profession- als, and the big night is Friday, starting with happy hour. The atmosphere is pub-like, with lots of dark wood and small tables. Samantha's is open nightly, with no cover charge.

Spy Club
805 15th St. NW, Washington, D.C.
• **(202) 289-1779**

Just three blocks from the White House,

this club draws an upscale clientele of young politicos with ages ranging from the late 20s to about 40. There are two dance floors with varying musical themes. Retro, salsa, hip-hop, Euro, and 90s popular tunes are all featured regularly. It's not unusual for people to dress up here, and for the room to be filled with plenty of attractive people. You'll see lots of pearls and velvet headbands, and as the evening progresses, a somewhat wilder crowd. They are open Thursday through Saturday, with a cover charge of $5.

Third Edition
1218 Wisconsin Ave. NW, Washington, D.C. • (202) 333-3700

Nightclubs come and go in Washington, but the Third Edition in Georgetown has managed to pack 'em in for over two decades. Maybe it's the Wisconsin Avenue location right near the busy M Street intersection, or maybe it's the glass doors, thrown open to let the music out and the crowd in. Whatever the reason, Third Edition draws a fairly well-groomed crowd of mostly 20- and 30-somethings, including lots of students from nearby Georgetown University. They are open nightly, with a cover charge of $5 on Friday and Saturday.

Trumpets
1603 17th St. NW, Washington, DC • (202) 232-4141

Trumpets is an upscale sort of gay bar, in part because it contains a restaurant that has been praised by *Washington Post* food guru Phyllis Richman, in part because of its central location in Dupont Circle. It draws a smattering of straight gourmands as well as gay ones, so it's not just a meet-and-greet sort of place. It's a bright, pretty stop for a drink, and quiet compared to clubs where the main attraction is loud music and a variety of dance floors. The crowd here is mostly professionial, clean-cut and well-dressed.

Sports Bars

Buffalo Billiards
1330 19th St. NW, Washington, D.C. • (202) 331-7665

Cowboys would feel right at home here

with the pinto-printed upholstery, peeled log chairs and, of course, a southwestern menu of bar munchies and a few more substantial dishes. As the name implies, this is primarily a pool hall. There are the requisite music and TVs, of course, and a singles bar atmosphere. They are open nightly, with no cover charge.

Champions-The American Sports Bar
1206 Wisconsin Ave. NW, Washington, D.C. • (202) 965-4005

Tucked at the end of a short alleyway in Georgetown, near the famed intersection of Wisconsin and M Street, Champions, as its name implies, is a true sports bar. Expect the usual saloon beverages and chow in this sports junkie's paradise, crammed with memorabilia, souvenirs, photos, posters and the like. This is a great place to watch the hometown Redskins, Bullets (now the Wizards) and Capitals, or any televised sporting event for that matter. At night and on the weekends, dancing is de rigueur as a DJ spins popular tunes for the 20s and early 30s set. Big crowds are standard. They are open nightly, with no cover charge.

Fanatics
1520 K St. NW, Washington, D.C. • (202) 638-6800

This new sports bar advertises itself as having plenty of babes, beers and billiards. All three are probably true, since it is connected to Archibald's — a strip joint that's been around since 1969. For those whose idea of entertainment involves spectator sports of a different kind, however, there are 30 TVs, seven satellites, five pool tables and darts. One oddity: this place sits on the edge of Washington's red-light district and evening restrictions against left and right turns, depending on where you're coming from, are strictly enforced to curtail soliciting. Observe traffic and parking rules carefully or you could be hit with a hefty fine. They are open nightly, with no cover charge.

The Rock Sports Bar and Restaurant
717 6th St. NW, Washington, D.C. • (202) 842-ROCK

The neighborhood is undergoing gentrification, and The Rock has played no small part in drawing people to the area after dark. Near the new MCI Center, this sports bar features an eye-popping 27 televisions, a billiards room, a dance floor with DJ music and a rooftop Tiki Bar. There is something for everyone at this rowdy, yet upscale spot. Dress ranges from casual to business attire and the crowd is a mix of yuppies, preppies, and young singles on the prowl. They are open nightly, with no cover charge.

Piano Music

Kinkead's*
2000 Pennsylvania Ave. NW, Washington, D.C. • (202) 296-7700

Upstairs is one of Washington's best restaurants; downstairs is a spacious, woodsy bar with a piano player six nights a week. Despite the proximity to George Washington University, this is a crowd of adult professionals. Yet it's a casual scene, rarely jam-packed, and quiet enough for conversation. Drop in after dinner in the restaurant or when you're in the neighborhood. They are closed Monday night, with no cover charge.

Mr. Smith's of Georgetown*
3104 M St. NW, Washington, D.C. • (202) 337-0697

This may be Washington's most popular piano bar — it's certainly the oldest. It's also a piano bar in the traditional sense, with everyone gathering 'round the player and chiming in. The lights are low, the drinks include every fancy concoction imaginable (and some that aren't), and the crowd is convivial. You'll fit right in, no matter where you come from or what you're wearing. They are open nightly, with no cover charge.

The Pullman Bar
1914 Connecticut Ave. NW, Washington, D.C. • (202) 797-2000

Washington's top pianists play Gershwin, Berlin and Porter on Monday through Saturday nights at this sophisticated night spot. Peter Robinson, the Monday to Wednesday pianist, has been dubbed, "the Bobby Short of Washington," by some reviewers. The Pullman Bar is in the Sofitel Hotel, which is part of

a French hotel chain, so expect a cosmopolitan crowd of well-dressed travelers. They are open nightly, with no cover charge.

West End Café*
One Washington Circle NW, Washington, D.C. • (202) 293-4989

This marvelous, but casual eatery features an intimate lounge with piano players good enough to impress the many performers who drop by after their gigs at the nearby Kennedy Center. It's great for a post-theater nightcap, but you may need reservations on weekends. The room is decorated in cool neutrals and the seating is in comfortable banquettes, a small bar or at linen-covered tables. They are open nightly, with no cover charge.

Cigar Bars

Butlers, The Cigar Bar
1000 H St. NW, Washington, D.C. • (202) 582-1234

This glitzy Art Deco bar, in the Grand Hyatt Hotel, is the place to go for cigars and martinis when you're in the neighborhood of the Washington Convention Center. (The state-of-the-art ventilation system keeps the room from reeking.) The crowd is well-heeled business travelers and Washington business types from the surrounding office buildings. They are open nightly, with no cover charge.

Chi-Cha Lounge
1624 U St. NW, Washington, D.C. • (202) 234-8400

This ever-so-hip place is in D.C.'s hottest new club district. The crowd is mostly young and Euro — and just about everyone is smoking something, whether it be cigarettes, cigars or even, on certain nights, a hookah. On Sundays, there's a jazz quartet to add to the cool (attitude, not temperature), dark atmosphere. They are open nightly, with no cover charge.

Off the Record
16th and H Sts. NW, Washington, D.C. • (202) 942-7599

The Hay-Adams is one of Washington's most historic and luxurious hotels — they

Georgetown is a vibrant hub of nightclubs, specialty shops, boutiques and restored homes.

know how to do things right here. Off The Record, with its low-lit, men's club atmosphere, offers not only cigars, but a generous selection of single-malt scotch, champagnes and wines by the glass. Many are hard-to-find labels and can cost as much as $20. The Hay-Adams is right across Lafayette Square from the White House and the patrons here look like the kind of successful folk who may have come from an appointment at 1600 Pennsylvania Avenue. Thursdays through Saturdays you can enjoy entertainment by cabaret singer Vicki Ford. They are open nightly, with no cover charge.

Ozio Martini & Cigar Lounge
1835 K St. NW, Washington, D.C.
• (202) 822-6000

Ozio's may be the hippest of the town's cigar bars and it was one of the first. It's a very dark lounge with booths and tables placed around a small dance floor. The place starts to rock after midnight, when a mix of Euro-types and K Street expense-account executives crowd the dance floor. There's a wide selection of gin and vodka martinis, including a couple of original Ozio recipes. The waiter will bring the humidor to your table, and the cigar smoke will be sucked into special ashtrays in the center. They are open Monday

through Saturday, with a two-drink minimum on Friday and Saturday.

Comedy Clubs

Chelsea's
1055 Jefferson St. NW, Washington, D.C.
• (202) 298-8222

We've told you that Chelsea's is a dance club, but on weekends the first few hours of the evening are devoted to the comedy of The Capitol Steps. This ensemble of comedians from Washington spoofs politics through musical satire. They've become so popular that they've appeared at the White House several times, as well as on national television. Performances are on Friday and Saturday. Dinner and the show cost $50, while the show and a $10 bar credit cost $33.50.

The Improv
1140 Connecticut Ave. NW, Washington, D.C. • (202) 296-7008

This club — yes, we admit, it's part of a national chain — brings top acts to Washington in a convenient mid-town location. You can have dinner if you attend the 8:30 show, or wait for the 10:30 performance on weekends and dine at one of the great restaurants nearby. Acts here are often comedians you've seen on TV, and you'll recognize most of the names. They are open Tuesday through Saturday, and tickets are $12 to $15.

Northern Virginia

Alexandria's Old Town area is Northern Virginia's answer to Georgetown. That ought to give you an idea of the richness of the nightlife in this charming and beautiful area. As with Georgetown, a sidewalk stroll along the narrow, sometimes cobblestone streets will reveal a world unto itself. The hub of Old Town's nocturnal activity is located on the river side (east) of Washington Street, also known as the George Washington Memorial Parkway, especially lower King Street and the surrounding few blocks.

Not all of Virginia's nightlife is in Old Town, though. There are also pockets of activity in Rosslyn and just ten minutes further west in Clarendon. People who are serious about nightlife still head into D.C., but the suburbs have enough to keep you occupied for at least a few evenings on the town. Because of the more limited offerings, we haven't created as many categories as for downtown Washington, D.C. For example, piano lounges are not a category in and of themselves, but are rather listed under live music. One category you'll find here that's missing from D.C. is dinner theaters — we haven't found any in Washington D.C., whereas northern Virginia has a couple. As we mentioned in the introduction, we have not broken down Northern Virginia by county for two reasons: the first is that distances are insignificant for the most part, and the second is that nightlife is limited enough that any further breakdown would result in some categories having only one listing — or perhaps none. That isn't to say that fun can't be found in the 'burbs, though. Just read on if you want proof.

Live Music and Dancing

America Restaurant
Intersection of Virginia Hwys. 7 and 123, McLean, Va. • (703) 847-6610

On Friday nights, America features the 16-piece Tom Cunningham Orchestra, one of the most popular big bands in the Washington area. They play all the swing classics: Glen Miller, Benny Goodman, Tommy Dorsey and on and on from 9 PM to midnight. On Thursday nights from 10 PM to 1 AM, Orquesta Melao provides the music for Salsa-Merengue Night. The cover charge is $7. Since this spot is located right in Tysons Corner Center, the clientele varies from drop-ins to jitterbug wannabes dressed for the occasion. They are open nightly, with a cover charge of $10.

Baron's Sheraton Premiere
8661 Leesburg Pk., Vienna, Va.
• (703) 448-1234

The Sheraton Premiere, at Tysons Corner, is one of the nicer properties managed by this chain, and Baron's restaurant is just as upscale. Unlike many hotel eateries, this is a jacket-and-tie sort of place, though you'll see people more casually dressed. There's piano entertainment Monday to Saturday to enjoy with your meal. They are open nightly, with no cover charge.

The Birchmere
3901 Mount Vernon Ave., Alexandria, Va.
• (703) 549-5919

In an area known as Arlandria (Arlington/Alexandria border), this has become one of the top national venues for bluegrass, zydeco, country, folk, pop and blues performers, all in a down-to-earth, casual setting. Standing-room-only crowds are not uncommon. The schedule is determined by show times, and tickets are $10 to $18.50.

Blackie's House of Beef
6710 Commerce St., Springfield, Va.
• (703) 971-4200

There's live country music here on Tuesday through Saturday nights, and a giant dance floor to go with it. The bands are top-notch and many already have recording contracts. If you've never ventured into the fun, down-to-earth world of line dancing, there are lessons several nights a week. In keeping with the theme, most of the crowd wears cowboy boots, jeans and Stetsons. No matter what your age, you'll fit in here as long as you're a country music lover. They are open nightly, with a cover charge of $2 to $5.

Cowboy Café South
2421 Columbia Pk., Arlington, Va.
• **(703) 486-3467**

Country and western is king at Cowboy Café, and on weekends, there's live music. You'll find a lot of military personnel here from nearby Fort Myers, along with young singles, but as with most country music venues, fans of all ages come to line dance and two-step. They are open nightly, with no cover charge.

Fat Tuesday's
10673 Braddock Rd., Fairfax, Va.
• **(703) 385-8660**

Near George Mason University, Fat Tuesday's is another major force in live rock and R&B music on Wednesday to Sunday nights. This is a much smaller setting than some of the concert halls listed in this category, and it couldn't be more casual. The crowd is a mix of blue collar workers and students. Take pitchers of beer, hot music, a dark, noisy bar and a location at University Mall and you get the idea of what kind of atmosphere to expect at Fat Tuesday's any day of the week. They are open nightly, with a cover charge of $3 to $5 Wednesday through Sunday.

Fish Market*
105 King St., Alexandria, Va.
• **(703) 836-5676**

This Old Town spot always seems to be full of jolly people ready to party, and the ragtime piano player adds to the mood. You can dine on seafood while you enjoy the old-time saloon atmosphere, the humor and the cheerful music. They are open nightly, with no cover charge.

Hero's
9412 Main St., Manassas, Va.
• **(703) 330-1534**

Manassas is a sleepy little town, but there are several clubs and eateries on Main Street. What's notable about Hero's is the live music Thursday to Saturday. You'll find mostly jazz trios or quartets in this laid-back spot. Given the small-town location, it is as casual as you'd expect and the night tends to end early, even if the official business hours are standard for Virginia. They are open nightly, with a $2 to $4 cover charge on weekends.

Ireland's Own
132 N. Royal St., Alexandria, Va.
• **(703) 549-4535**

Fans of live Irish-themed acoustic music, Irish food and Irish drink can get their fill at Ireland's Own in Old Town Alexandria. St. Patrick's Day, in particular, is an occasion at this bar. This is a casual, neighborhood place, comfortable for people of any age. They are open nightly, with a $2 cover charge on weekends.

Jaxx
6355 Rolling Rd., Springfield, Va.
• **(703) 569-5940**

You wouldn't expect to find a progressive rock concert hall in suburban Virginia, especially conservative Springfield, but Jaxx is just such a place. Patrons are young college students, grunge wannabes and others in that general age group. On occasion, former big names like Johnny Winter and Eddie Money appear. Showtimes determine openings, with cover charges from $5 to $18.

Lobby Lounge
1700 Tysons Blvd., McLean, Va.
• **(703) 506-4300**

The Ritz-Carlton, at Tysons Corner, is a showplace of antiques, art and Oriental rugs, and the Lobby Lounge is as lovely a refuge as the rest of the hotel. Tables are spaced for intimacy and the piano music is low-key but high-quality. The pianist here has a range from gospel to classic, but the playing is never intrusive. They are open nightly, with no cover charge.

Murphy's of Alexandria
713 King St., Alexandria, Va.
• **(703) 462-7171**

As if it weren't cozy enough to have an intimate sweaters-and-jeans type place along the

---

INSIDERS' TIP

The newest hot strip for Washington nightclubs is U St. NW, in Adams Morgan. They seem to spring up monthly here.

cobbled walks of Old Town, this place also features a wood-burning fireplace and Irish music nightly. Like Ireland's Own, listed above, this is a hot spot on St. Patrick's day after the parade. They are open nightly, with no cover charge.

Tiffany Tavern
1116 King St., Alexandria, Va.
• (703) 836-8844

This cozy spot at the west end of Old Town isn't very well known outside the neighborhood, but it's usually crowded, thanks to the intimate space. Music is sophisticated: a bit of jazz, a couple of solo singers and some small ensembles. It varies nightly. Dress down or dress up as you please. There is no cover charge, and they are closed on Sundays.

219 Basin St. Lounge
219 King St., Alexandria, Va.
• (703) 549-1141

For a more formal setting than some of those listed previously, 219 Basin St. Lounge in Old Town offers live jazz and Louisiana cuisine one floor below the 219 restaurant. The decor here is particularly inviting, featuring a brick courtyard and wall accents, a dark, sophisticated lounge and a restaurant upstairs furnished in New Orleans-style French reproductions. They are open in the evenings Tuesday through Saturday, and Sunday afternoon. The cover charge is $5 on Friday and Saturday.

Whitey's
2761 N. Washington Blvd., Arlington, Va.
• (703) 525-9825

Arcade games, live music and a casual setting — it all comes together at Whitey's, an Arlington neighborhood watering hole that oozes with character. The hole-in-the-wall, sports-themed charm of suburbia was never better represented than here. Live rock 'n' roll and R&B help keep the place jumping on Tuesday through Saturday nights. They are open nightly, with a cover charge of $2.

Meet and Greet

You won't find live music at these places except on special occasions. However, you may find dancing and, if so, we've indicated it; otherwise, the point is to check out the crowd, have a few drinks and maybe even strike up a conversation with a stranger.

Bardo Rodeo
2000 Wilson Blvd., Arlington, Va.
• (703) 527-9399

A fairly recent entrant in college-age night spots is Bardo Rodeo, which claims to be the largest brewpub on the continent. Just look for the old Plymouth sticking through the front window. The car isn't just for looks, though; it houses the CD jukebox. Take one glimpse at this offbeat decorating idea and you'll realize this place doesn't take itself too seriously. Housed in a former Oldsmobile dealership, Bardo is garage-rock informal, from the 100-plus selections of beer on tap (including microbreweries, imports and even some stuff made on the premises), to the spraypainted wall decorations, the progressive music, the T-shirt-and-jeans casualness and the hip crowd. There's also a decidedly politically correct air to the place, with the visible recycling efforts and the vegetarian menu choices. They are open nightly, with no cover charge.

Bullfeathers
112 King St., Alexandria, Va.
• (703) 836-8088

One of the most popular nightspots for singles in particular, Bullfeathers is tucked away from streetview save for its sidewalk canopy, so look for the distinctive maroon awning that announces its presence to passersby. Although some windows would help temper the cave-like ambiance, Bullfeathers has long been a preference of Old Town barhoppers in a wide range of age and dress. To the right of the bar is a large dining area with food ranging from burgers to swordfish. If you want to avoid the lines on Friday and Saturday nights, you can have a bite earlier in the evening, and then drift over to the bar. Bullfeathers is open nightly, with no cover charge.

Chadwicks*
203 S. Strand St., Alexandria, Va.
• (703) 836-4442

Chadwicks is as inviting as the Georgetown

original, with bars upstairs and down. On weekends, 20- and 30-somethings pack the place. Beer is the drink of choice and the dress is khakis to business suits. They are open nightly, with no cover charge.

Champion Billiards
2620 S. Shirlington Rd., Arlington, Va.
• **(703) 521-3800**

Pool halls have caught on in the Washington area, and one of the places that's been around longest is Champion Billiards. This is a very casual place where enjoying a few games, drinking beer and listening to the CD jukebox make for a welcome alternative to the traditional night out. Non-pool shooters in particular will appreciate the video arcade. They are open nightly, with no cover charge.

Clyde's*
8332 Leesburg Pk., Vienna, Va.
• **(703) 734-1901**
11905 Market St., Reston, Va.
• **(703) 787-6601**

Whether you choose the location in Reston Town Center or the one in Tysons Corner, Clyde's is a hopping place for the check 'em out crowd. Tysons is more upscale, with the peak action on weeknights for after-business 30-plus patrons. The decor is extravagant art nouveau and business suits are the norm — it's a prosperous-looking bunch here. Reston, which runs a more family-oriented eatery, also has a handsome, lively bar, but expect chinos rather than custom-made suits, and leggings rather than dresses. Clyde's is open nightly, with no cover charge.

Deja Vu
6710 Commerce St., Springfield, Va.
• **(703) 971-4200**

A popular night spot in Springfield, Deja Vu is perhaps the biggest singles bar/dance club anywhere in the county. It is attached to Blackie's, the country/western dance hall, and the two clubs share a large lobby. Deja Vu, however, features a musical range of old-time disco, top 40,

Motown, and rock. The crowd is young and casual, and you'll be asked for ID at the door. They are open nightly, with a cover charge of $2 to $4.

Fast Eddie's Billiards Cafe
9687 Lee Hwy., Fairfax, Va.
• **(703) 385-7529**

This is a fun hybrid of pool hall, bar and restaurant. It's hard not to have a good time here, even if shooting pool isn't your thing. If it is, there are plenty of tables, but you can almost always count on a wait during prime time on Friday and Saturday nights. Also expect efficient, cheerful service, tasty chow and a better singles atmosphere than one might expect; it's best to go in a small group to make it easier to meet the attractive group shooting a round at the next table. Fast Eddie's is also in Springfield (yes, in yet another shopping center) at 7255 Commerce Street, (703) 912-7529. They are open nightly, with no cover charge.

JD's American Bar and Grill
20921 Davenport Dr., Sterling, Va.
• **(703) 444-2853**

The business corridor near Dulles airport has spawned a number of bars and singles clubs, and this one is among the most popular. You wouldn't make a special trip here, but these relatively new spots answer the needs of the surrounding community. JD's, like most of the rest, caters to young professionals with a busy bar and occasional live music. It's been around for a while and is well-known, so you can count on a good crowd that includes many regulars. They are open nightly, with no cover charge.

Joe Theismann's
5912 Leesburg Pk., Baileys Crossroads, Va. • **(703) 379-7777**
1800 Diagonal Rd., Alexandria, Va.
• **(703) 739-0777**

This restaurant and bar, named after the former Redskins' quarterback and current football announcer, offers great sports viewing and

---

INSIDERS' TIP

Bars in Adams Morgan are generally younger, funkier and more casual than those near mid-town office buildings.

karaoke. On Friday nights, expect a dark, clubby scene for the over-30 set. Dress ranges from casual to business suits. The Old Town location attracts a clientele that's a bit more affluent than the original restaurant in Baileys Crossroads. They are open nightly, with no cover charge.

P.J. Skidoos
9908 Lee Hwy., Fairfax City, Va.
• **(703) 591-4515**

This restaurant and bar has become something of a contemporary disco when it comes to music and the dance aura. It boasts a busy club scene and rates as a prime spot for singles — professionals and students — in their 20s and 30s, not to mention anyone with a hankering for hearty munchies. There's sometimes a decent live rock band on Saturday nights. They are open nightly, with no cover charge.

Portner's*
109 S. Saint Asaph St., Alexandria, Va.
• **(703) 683-1776**

Portner's is popular with a 30-plus group that flocks here for lively happy hours, a gorgeous setting and an ambiance that's conducive to — surprise! — the lost art of carrying on a conversation. This also doubles as a sports bar on days when the Redskins are playing. Forget conversation then: the TVs above the bar become the focal point. They are open nightly, with no cover charge.

Rocket Grill
1319 King St., Alexandria, Va.
• **(703) 739-2274**

Rocket Grill has been transformed into a club for young singles. There are karaoke nights along with dancing to DJ music. The Old Town Alexandria crowd is pretty tame — kids you wouldn't mind bringing home to Mom — and the age range is 20s to 30s, with the dress as anything you please. You won't find nearly as much grunge here as in downtown spots, however. They are open nightly, with no cover charge.

Studebaker's
8028 Leesburg Pk., Vienna, Va.
• **(703) 356-9333**

This dance club is at Tysons Corner. Please see our Maryland listing for more information.

Sweetwater Tavern*
14250 Sweetwater Ln., Centreville, Va.
• **(703) 449-1100**
3066 Gatehouse Plaza, Falls Church, Va.
• **(703) 645-8100**

Neither Centreville nor Falls Church are hot spots for nightlife, so Sweetwater Tavern — a new restaurant and brew pub — is a welcome addition in both locations. The restaurant features very good southwestern cuisine and sinful desserts, while the bar attracts singles and couples alike, not to mention folks who want to watch sports in a convivial atmosphere. You'll find a handsome, Wyoming-style ambiance with big wrought-iron chandeliers, vaulted ceilings, and all manner of Wild West art. These are casual, suburban places, so dress down. They are open nightly, with no cover charge.

Union Street Public House*
121 S. Union St., Alexandria, Va.
• **(703) 548-1785**

This has long been one of Old Town's most popular singles spots, and there seems to be no end in sight for the accolades. Crowded? Yes. But the wait that's not unusual during prime time is worth it, if only for the spirited bar ambiance, the extensive and offbeat beer selections and the friendly help. If the front bar is too much, try the often-overlooked oyster bar in back. It's smaller and less lively, but the beer is just as good and it's easier to find a seat or a quiet corner. They are open nightly, with no cover charge.

Dinner Theater/
Comedy Clubs

Fun Factory
3112 Mount Vernon Ave., Alexandria, Va.
• **(703) 684-5212**

This funky neighborhood northwest of Old Town is in the process of gentrification, which means several restaurants have opened here in recent years. Now comes a comedy club that also serves food. This neighborhood is transitioning from blue collar, so the atmosphere couldn't be more easygoing. Acts aren't world-famous, and laughs vary, but the club is surrounded by interesting restaurants — many ethnic — so even if you choose to eat elsewhere, you can park and make a fun evening of it. Performances are Thursday to Saturday, with an $11 cover charge.

Headliners Holiday Inn
2460 Eisenhower Ave., Alexandria, Va.
• (703) 379-4242

This middle-of-the-road hotel in a middle-of-the-road area has found a niche for itself by bringing in comedy acts. Since there are few comedy clubs in the area, it manages to do fairly well, and the casual clientele is indeed lively and ready to laugh. Performances are Friday and Saturday, with a $10 cover charge. There is also a Headliners at the Holiday Inn in Bethesda, 8120 Wisconsin Avenue, Bethesda, Maryland, (301) 942-4242.

Lazy Susan Dinner Theater
U.S. Hwy. 1 at Furnace Rd., Woodbridge, Va. • (703) 550-7384

Lazy Susan has been around forever and it remains a popular destination for residents of Northern Virginia who enjoy musicals. Dinner and the show together make for a nice evening. They are open nightly, except on Monday. Tickets are $30.95, except on Saturdays, when they cost $32.95.

West End Theater
4615 Duke St., Alexandria, Va.
• (703) 370-2500

Some of the plays here, mostly musicals, are very well-reviewed by Washington critics, and the location at the west end of Alexandria means that you can venture into Old Town after the show to make a night of it. Besides evening performances, there are Sunday and Wednesday lunch matinees. They are open nightly, except on Monday. Tickets range from $29 to $35. See the Kidstuff chapter for information about shows for children.

Suburban Maryland

The Maryland suburbs don't possess quaint pedestrian areas like Georgetown in Washington, D.C., or Old Town Alexandria in Virginia; as a result, there are fewer clubs. But that doesn't mean you can't find nightlife. There are essentially two hubs of nighttime activity in the Maryland suburbs, each radically different from the other. For affluent Montgomery County, Bethesda and Rockville have grown into a sprawling "downtown" of sorts, so it's not surprising that this urban-style suburban core offers its share of nighttime diversions. This is a viable alternative to the trek into Washington, and even residents of other Maryland counties come to Montgomery for the selection of nightlife and restaurants. A little further from Washington is College Park, the home of the 35,000-student University of Maryland. Here, too, the nightlife rocks, with partying students filling the bars along Interstate Route 1, also known as Baltimore Avenue. We've also mentioned some notable places outside both hubs.

Live Music and Dancing

Bethesda Marriott
5151 Pooks Hill Rd., Bethesda, Md.
• (301) 897-9400

This is a sprawling hotel that draws lots of conventioneers. It's also one of the few in the Maryland suburbs to consistently offer live piano music. The crowd here is mature, and the dress is casual to business suits. This isn't a raucous piano bar, but rather a spot for conversation and easygoing entertainment. There's also a dance spot in the hotel which can be lively when the hotel is full. They are open nightly, except on Sunday. There is no cover charge.

Flanagan's Irish Pub
7637 Old Georgetown Rd., Bethesda, Md.
• (301) 986-1007

Flanagan's features acoustic and folk music in a comfy pub setting. Food isn't bad here either, and the dress is casual, so it's a great stop for a lazy weekend evening or a bite after work. They are open nightly, with no cover charge.

Olde Town Tavern
227 E. Diamond Ave., Gaithersburg, Md.
• (301) 948-4200

Upon its opening in early 1994, Olde Towne Tavern was lauded by one local critic as " . . . the prettiest and least self-consciously trendy brewpub in the region." That may be so, but we'll just call it cool. Perhaps it's the location in the Belt Building (circa 1891) in the heart of historic Old Gaithersburg, the open-air balcony, or the three levels and the attractive marble tabletops. Then again, it could be the huge selection of microbrews, the good ol' American menu (seafood, steaks, sandwiches) or the mix of live music (blues and rock). Well, we can't decide, but we just like the place and welcome its addition to the Maryland nightlife scene. They are open nightly, with a $3 cover charge on Friday and Saturday.

Twist & Shout
4800 Auburn Ave., Bethesda, Md.
• (301) 652-3383

Grammy Award winning country singer Mary Chapin-Carpenter made this spot famous in her hit song "Twist & Shout." The place still rocks with bayou music: zydeco, rockabilly, Cajun rock 'n roll, blues and a few hybrids. It's a big dance/concert hall with lots of room to boogie and a no-frills crowd ready for fun. The schedule is determined by show times, with a cover charge of $7 to $10.

Meet and Greet

Dave and Buster's
White Flint Shopping Center, 11301
Rockville Pk., Rockville, Md.
• (301) 230-5151

Dave and Buster's is a multimedia, multi-sensation event. It's almost too much to absorb in one visit. There's an 11 screen video wall in the Players Bar, a mystery theater with audience participation on weekends, virtual reality, billiards and all manner of games. There are families and singles and date-night couples. There are weekday lunches until 5 PM, dinners until late into the night, giant servings, giant drinks . . . and the list goes on. Dress is casual, though the

neighborhood is one of the most upscale in the country, so you don't have to worry about being overdressed if you've just come from work. They are open nightly, with no cover charge.

The Hangar Club
6410 Old Branch Ave., Camp Springs,
Md. • (301) 449-6970

How do you categorize a place like this? We haven't included strip joints for male clients, so why The Hangar Club, which features male strippers on Wednesday to Saturday nights? Well, it's the only club we know in the area that caters almost exclusively to straight women, so it's unique. Its decency level, as some might put it, is a notch above many of the clubs for men featuring female dancers — here they don't take quite everything off, but it's indeed enough to send the female patrons into a tizzy. Dancing and gawking — and plenty of high-pitched screaming — are the norm here.

This cavernous establishment hosts hundreds of bachelorette parties and girls-night-out get-togethers each year. More than 30 brands of beer help keep the whistles wet. If you're a woman, however, be warned: They feature exotic female dancers Sunday through Tuesday. They are open nightly, with a cover charge of $8 to $15.

Hollywood Contemporary Ballroom
2126 Industrial Pkwy., Silver Spring, Md.
• (301) 622-5494

Dancing is the point here. It's a 6,800-square-foot, floating maple dance floor, where ballroom lessons (rumba, swing, tango, fox trot) are offered each night for an hour until the dancing-in-earnest takes over. The group is old, young and everything in between — people who love to dance and those who want to learn. There are also special nights just for singles. Dress is mostly casual, but don't be surprised if a couple in formal wear float by. They are open Wednesday through Sunday, with a cover charge of $10.

INSIDERS' TIP

Although last call in Washington dance clubs is usually 2:30 AM on weekends, most places don't pick up speed until at least 11 PM.

The Adams Morgan neighborhood is a bustling area of restaurants, bars, nightclubs and an array of shops and boutiques.

94th Aero Squadron
5240 Calvert Rd., College Park, Md.
- **(301) 699-9400**

This dance club's intriguing aviation/military theme — a nod to the nearby College Park Airport, which is the nation's oldest in continuous operation — includes a prop plane outside and a World War I ambulance inside. A mix of white-collar patrons and, of course, plenty of students from the nearby University of Maryland help keep the place hopping. There is no cover charge, and they are closed on Sunday.

Studebaker's
1750 Rockville Pk., Rockville, Md.
- **(301) 881-7340**

This dance club has a different theme party every night, including ladies' night, retro-night and cigar and martini night. Sometimes there's a jazz quartet or other live music, but it's mostly DJ dance tunes. The crowd spans a wide age range. Expect to see after-work professionals and, on weekends, a hopping singles scene, mostly for those 25 and older. The dress code here is described by management as "dress to impress." It's not too formal, but men must wear collared shirts and sneakers must be in like-new condition. They are closed on Sunday and Monday, with a cover charge of $1 to $4.

The Yacht Club
8111 Woodmont Ave., Bethesda, Md.
- **(301) 654-2396**

Washington impresario Tommy Curtis has been a presence in the nightlife scene since the 1970s, and he's launched many projects, some of which haven't lasted. With the Yacht Club, though, he's got a hit. This is a singles club for the over-30 crowd, a dress-up kinda place (jacket required), except on one of the countless theme nights. Every once in a while there's live music — often dating from the '60s — but it's mostly DJ-driven dance tunes. Curtis brags about the number of matchmaking successes he's had, and some of those couples supposedly still drop in here for old time's sake, but this is very definitely a strut-your-stuff atmosphere for those still looking. They are open Tuesday through Saturday, with some special events on Sunday. The cover charge is $3 to $5.

Dinner Theaters

Blair Mansion Restaurant
7711 Eastern Ave., Silver Spring, Md.
- **(301) 588-1689**

This restaurant, which for years was a special occasion family place, fell out of style a few years back, but it caught a second wind when the management dreamed up the Blair Mansion Mysteries. These shows will never see Broadway, but they should appeal to the whole family with lots of laughs and audience fun. Ticket prices include full dinner, tip, tax and even hors d'oeuvres. Tickets are $41.95.

Burn Brae Dinner Theater
3811 Blackburn Ln., Burtonsville, Md.
- **(410) 792-0290**

This spot in the exurbs of Maryland has long been a destination for Metro Washingtonians wanting something different from the usual dinner-and-a-movie. It's a bit of a haul from downtown, but the shows here are well-run. You'll find musical standards like *A Chorus Line* and *Singin' in the Rain* featuring a solid cast. The schedule of dinner at 6, show at 8 (or similar scheduling for matinees) ensures that there's enough time to clear the tables and eliminate cutlery noise. Ticket prices include the works. They are open nightly except Monday. Tickets are $28.95 on weekdays, and $29.95 on Friday and Saturday.

No matter where you stay, the area's comprehensive public transportation system (especially Metrorail and Metrobus) does an excellent job linking hotels with business and tourist areas.

Accommodations

Finding a room at the inn isn't a difficult task in Metro Washington. Hotels, motels, and special extended-stay lodgings are almost as common a sight in the nation's capital as lawyers and lobbyists . . . well, almost.

All kidding aside, the lodging industry is a big, big business here. Hotels and motels are the single largest contributor to the region's approximately $4 billion tourism industry. All told, there are about 50,000 hotel and motel rooms in the metro area, ranging from the ultra luxurious to the merely functional.

As a general rule of thumb, hotels in the suburbs, even close-in areas, are priced less than D.C. properties. That's not always the case, but it's pretty safe to say you can find a slew of real values out there as long as you don't mind being a bit off the beaten path. No matter where you stay, the area's comprehensive public transportation system (especially Metrorail and Metrobus) does an excellent job linking hotels with business and tourist areas. You'll discover that many hotels also offer their own shuttle and limousine services to destinations around the area.

Another rule of thumb is that the Washington tourism industry reaches its peak in spring and fall. Occupancy rates are at their highest during these months, and so too are room prices. Planning ahead is never a bad idea.

No matter what time of year, Metro Washington hotels do the bulk of their business Monday through Thursday, courtesy of the business traveler. Many hotels cut their rates on weekends, sometimes as much as 50 to 60 percent. With that in mind, always feel free to negotiate for the best deal and always inquire about weekend, off-season, holiday, corporate and family rates.

The best source we know to keep you informed of the latest seasonal rate discounts and other special hotel package programs is the Washington, D.C. Convention and Visitors Association, (202) 789-7000. When in town, also be sure to stop by the new White House Visitors Center (formerly the Washington Visitor Information Center) in the Commerce Department building at 15th and E streets NW. Operated by the National Park Service, it's yet another great source of free information.

We've divided this chapter into several categories, beginning with a section on extended-stay accommodations. For those of you who plan to house hunt in the area, or who might be on a short-term work assignment, or just simply need a place to call home for a while, the extended-stay section is intended to give you an overview of some of the region's best options. Almost all the choices here include properties that have kitchenettes, many with separate living areas as well.

We follow with a section called "Full-Service Hotels." This is intended for tourists, newcomers and longtime residents alike who are looking for, or need to recommend, interesting, practical and/or memorable places to spend a night in Metro Washington.

If you look hard enough, you'll find that the District, Northern Virginia and Suburban Maryland all have more than their share of hotel bargains — some you might even call steals. To help you along, we've listed some of our favorite values in the "On a Budget" section. Believe us, no one appreciates a bargain more than writers.

A short section on hostels and university inns lists some of the unsung and nontraditional accommodations found only in Washington, D.C.

While the following lists are by no means exhaustive, we feel they represent some of the best and most viable choices available in each category.

Price-Code Key

To give you an idea of what to expect price-wise, we've provided the following scale as a very general guide. It is based on the average cost for double occupancy, during peak season.

$	$80 or less
$$	$80 to $125
$$$	$125 to $150
$$$$	More than $150

All hotels listed accept most major credit cards. Virtually every establishment listed also extends some kind of weekend or off-season rate.

Extended-Stay Hotels and Inns

Washington, D.C.

Best Western New Hampshire Suites Hotel

$$$ • 1121 New Hampshire Ave. NW, Washington, D.C. • (202) 457-0565

This newly renovated property offers 76 suites with kitchenettes, complimentary continental breakfasts and valet parking. Bring along the jogging shoes and shorts, for you're only a hop and a skip from Rock Creek Park and its miles and miles of gorgeous wooded trails and running paths.

Capitol Hill Suites

$$$ • 200 C St. SE, Washington, D.C. • (202) 543-6000, (800) 424-9165

You can stay a night, a week, a month or a year at this flexible, all-suite property just a short walk from the Capitol, the Library of Congress, the Supreme Court, Metro and other "Hill" destinations. All 152 suites have kitchens. It's a popular extended-stay choice among government and private sector workers with ties to Capitol Hill. To accommodate that clientele, the hotel offers complimentary continental breakfast and newspaper, valet parking and lunch or dinner delivery from area restaurants.

Carlyle Suites Hotel

$$$ • 1731 New Hampshire Ave. NW, Washington, D.C. • (202) 234-3200, (800) 964-5377

This art deco, all-suite hotel in the trendy Dupont Circle area offers rooms with fully equipped kitchens, a health-club, a coin-operated laundry and free parking. From here, you're just a two-block walk from the Dupont Circle Metro station and tons of galleries, restaurants, boutiques and bars. Pets are accepted.

Corporate Suites of Washington

$$$ • 3636 16th St. NW, Washington, D.C. • (202) 483-0100

Corporate Suites — which bills itself as "Washington's largest provider of temporary housing" — specializes in month-to-month leases. Furnished studio apartments start at less than $700 a month. It's not a bad deal, especially if you need to be in the District and close to everything.

Embassy Square, A Summerfield Suites Hotel

$$$$ • 2000 N St. NW, Washington, D.C. • (202) 659-9000, (800) 424-2999

This 266-room facility offers suites, efficiencies, and even 2-bedroom, 2-bath apartments. Popular with relocating families and executives on short-term assignments, Embassy Square Suites sits in the heart of the down-

town business district, about equal distance from the White House and Georgetown. Each suite comes with a kitchenette, and guests are given free reign of an off-premise health club as well as an onsite swimming pool. There's a free continental breakfast and same-day valet service to boot.

Embassy Suites Hotel Downtown
$$$$ • 1250 22nd St. NW, Washington, D.C. • (202) 857-3388

This West End addition to the national chain boasts two-room suites with separate living rooms (including queen-sized sofa beds) and bedrooms. Standard in each suite are two color TVs, two phones with voicemail, data-port hookup, a kitchenette, iron and hairdryer. The upscale 318-suite property is close to everything: downtown, Dupont Circle, Foggy Bottom and Georgetown. Guests receive complimentary cooked-to-order breakfasts and there's room service available from the Italian restaurant onsite. Both a swimming pool and health club are on the grounds. This is an especially popular place with families.

Georgetown Suites
$$$ • 1000 29th St. NW, Washington, D.C. • (202) 298-1600

A former Marriott, this is an ideal choice for extended stays that require you to be in or near Georgetown. All rooms have full kitchens with dishwashers and microwaves. Irons and hair dryers are also supplied. The 76-room apartment-like setting is frequented by corporate managers and government employees on short-term assignment. The surrounding Washington Harbour complex is a stunning waterfront development that also houses restaurants, gift shops, boutiques and the like.

Hotel Anthony
$$ • 1823 L St. NW, Washington, D.C. • (202) 223-4320

Somewhat of a sleeper (no pun intended), the Hotel Anthony shouldn't be overlooked.

This moderately priced, all-suite hotel is in the middle of downtown, only five blocks from the White House and convenient to monuments, museums and Metro. Kid-friendly, all suites have VCRs, and there's a large stock of children's movies for the asking.

One Washington Circle

$$$ • 1 Washington Cir. NW, Washington, D.C. • (202) 872-1680

All 151 units here include kitchens and some feature balconies. Just across the circle is George Washington University and Foggy Bottom Metro. Also in walking distance are the Kennedy Center, Georgetown, Dupont Circle and parts of downtown. This property is often frequented by performers from the Kennedy Center who drop into the onsite West End Café and piano lounge (see chapters on restaurants and nightlife).

The River Inn

$$$ • 924 25th St. NW, Washington, D.C. • (202) 337-7600

It's not on the Potomac, but the river's not too far away. Nor is most of Georgetown and all of Foggy Bottom. All 128 units in this former apartment house are suites, each with a full kitchen. It's a nice place to unwind after an evening at the Kennedy Center, just a couple of blocks away.

St. James Suites

$$$ • 950 24th St. NW, Washington, D.C. • (202) 457-0500

The St. James is an upscale all-suite property that can be checked into for a night, a month or longer. It's near 24th and K streets, just off Washington Circle and near Foggy Bottom Metro and George Washington University. Georgetown and Dupont Circle are also close. Full kitchens, marble baths, robes, computer outlets, voicemail, a concierge and a health club are among the numerous amenities. Not only do they serve a complimentary breakfast, but also complimentary hors d'oeuvres. On nice days, you can also enjoy the outdoor pool and sun deck.

Savoy Suites Georgetown

$$$$ • 2505 Wisconsin Ave. NW, Washington, D.C. • (202) 337-9700

This 148-suite hotel is in earshot of the inspiring Washington National Cathedral and is largely insulated from the hustle and congestion of closer-in lodgings. Many suites have in-room Jacuzzis and full kitchens, and you can request fridges and microwaves. There's also a swimming pool, coin-operated laundry, Metro shuttle and onsite parking.

The State Plaza Hotel

$$$$ • 2117 E St. NW, Washington, D.C. • (202) 861-8200

Don't let the harried urban setting fool you. The State Plaza Hotel, across from the State Department in Foggy Bottom, is a quiet, self-contained world unto itself. The former apartment building now houses 215 spacious suites featuring separate kitchens and dining rooms, same-day valet, shoeshine, safety deposit boxes, garage parking and fitness center. The hotel is often frequented by government employees, especially State Department types, on short-term assignments.

The Watergate Hotel

$$$$ • 2650 Virginia Ave. NW, Washington, D.C. • (202) 965-2300

The Watergate complex will forever be known best as the site of the infamous "break-in" that ultimately ended the political career of President Richard M. Nixon. There's nothing suspicious about the hotel, however, one of the most luxurious in the District. Gracing the banks of the Potomac River, adjacent to the Kennedy Center, the Watergate has full kitchens, personal valet service, complimentary limousine service, a swimming pool and a health spa. There are 232 rooms, of which 85 are suites and 60 are junior suites. It's pricey, yes, but the experience is one that's quintessentially Washington.

Northern Virginia

Alexandria

Alexandria Lodgings

$ • 10 Sunset Dr., Alexandria, Va. • (703) 683-9924

This small inn-like property (two rooms and three suites) is on the western edge of Old Town, two blocks from the King Street Metro station. You're a few minutes' walk from any destination in the city's fascinating historic district, including some of its finest restaurants and shops. Guests can expect full kitchens and free onsite parking, which, as you'll soon discover, is at a premium in Old Town. Washers and dryers are also available, a nice touch for extended-stay guests.

The Executive Club Suites
$$-$$$ • 610 Bashford Ln., Alexandria, Va. • (703) 739-2582, (800) 535-CLUB

This upscale all-suite property is at the north end of Old Town, and is only a couple of minutes' drive to National Airport. Various options are available, but the best values are with extended stays. The rooms are handsome, featuring 19th century reproductions, rich jewel tones and the kind of comfortable furniture you might find in a very nice home. What's more, you have a separate living room, kitchen and master bedroom, just like a true apartment. Other amenities include free continental breakfast, evening reception, health club with sauna, shuttle service and outdoor pool.

Sheraton Suites Alexandria
$$$ • 801 N. Asaph St., Alexandria, Va. • (703) 836-4700

One of the newest hotels in Old Town, the Sheraton (once a Marriott) commands a superb location and amenities galore. Each newly renovated suite has a wet bar, refrigerator, coffee maker, iron and ironing board, two remote-control TVs, a VCR in the bedroom, two telephones with call waiting, a pool and a health club. As icing on the cake, you're a 10-minute walk away from lower King Street, the nerve center of Old Town, and maybe a five-minute drive from National Airport.

Arlington

The Executive Club Suites
108 S. Courthouse Rd., Arlington, Va.
$$-$$$ • (703) 522-2582, (800) 535-CLUB
1730 Arlington Blvd., Rosslyn, Va.
$$-$$$ • (703) 525-2582

Please see the Alexandria listing.

The Virginian
$$ • 1500 Arlington Blvd., Arlington, Va. • (703) 522-9600

Specializing in month-to-month suites, The low-cost Virginian offers hotel convenience and basic comfort. The Rosslyn location is close to Metro, Georgetown and most of Arlington and Alexandria. Guests receive Metro shuttle service, maid service, cable TV, free utilities and parking, and access to an onsite swimming pool, fitness center and saunas.

Fairfax County

Marriott Suites/ Washington Dulles
$$$ • 13101 Worldgate Dr., Herndon, Va. • (703) 709-0400

A turnkey home base for house-hunters in Fairfax and Loudoun counties, Marriott Suites/Washington Dulles is, as the name suggests, close to the airport but also within a few minutes' drive of some of the most desirable suburban neighborhoods in Northern Virginia. Besides all the perks you'd expect from this national chain, the hotel is adjacent to Worldgate Athletic Club, one of the nation's largest, and close to Reston Town Center, one of suburban Virginia's most complete shopping, dining and nightlife districts.

Embassy Suites/Tysons Corner
$$$ • 8517 Leesburg Pk., Vienna, Va. • (703) 883-0707

A Tysons Corner location — about halfway between Washington and Dulles Airport — makes this 232-suite property convenient to most points in Northern Virginia. Suites come with refrigerators and minibars and guests can help themselves to a free breakfast. There's also complimentary shuttle service, a fitness center and indoor pool. The hotel is close to one of the world's largest office and shopping complexes, and just a few minutes' drive from Wolf Trap, the nation's only national park for the performing arts.

Residence Inn By Marriott/Dulles
$$ • 315 Elden St., Herndon, Va. • (703) 435-0044

Short- and long-term stays are made easy at this all-suite Marriott property about five miles east of Dulles Airport in the town of Herndon. One- and two-bedroom suites come with fire-

Photo: Courtesy of the Washington, DC Convention and Visitors Association

This Victorian house was the residence of African-American statesman, orator and abolitionist, Frederick Douglass.

places. There's also free parking, shuttle service to Dulles and a pool and fitness area.

Suburban Maryland

Montgomery County

Marriott Suites Bethesda
$$$ • 6711 Democracy Blvd., Bethesda, Md. • (301) 897-5600

House hunters in Montgomery County and upper Northwest Washington would do well to consider Marriott Suites Bethesda as a temporary command center. It's near the intersection of the Beltway and I-270, Marriott Corporation's world headquarters and IBM. There's free parking, a swimming pool, health club, restaurant and all the other amenities you'd expect from this service-oriented national chain.

Prince George's County

Comfort Inn & Suites College Park
$$ • 9020 Baltimore Blvd., College Park, Md. • (301) 441-8110

The newly renovated hotel offers normal rooms as well as 33 suites. It's convenient both for parents of University of Maryland stu-

dents as well as travelers who need access to Baltimore/Washington Airport, 25 miles away. Suites offer fridges, in-room coffeemakers and complimentary breakfast with newspaper. You'll also find a coin-operated laundry, health club and outdoor pool.

Full-Service Hotels

Washington, D.C.

ANA Hotel
$$$$ • 2401 M St. NW, Washington, D.C. • (202) 429-2400

Owned by the Japanese airline All Nippon Airways (which happens to have nonstop service between Tokyo and Dulles Airport), this grand 415-room hotel is known for its outstanding service. The lobby is a plush, airy hall of marble, plants and Oriental rugs, and the guest rooms mirror the decor. The real highlight here though is the 14,000-square-foot fitness center, popular with big bucks Washingtonians and visiting celebrities. You can also get your exercise with a jog through nearby Rock Creek Park. Georgetown's dining and shopping are a five-minute walk away.

The Canterbury

$$$$ • 1733 N St. NW, Washington, D.C.
• (202) 393-3000, (800)-424-2950

The quiet setting of the Canterbury, just a few strides from the bustle of Dupont Circle, is one of the most picturesque streets in Washington, lined with elegant, ivy-covered townhouses. All 99 units are spacious suites furnished with Georgian reproductions and luxurious, muted fabrics. The present-day building is on the site of what once was the home of President Theodore Roosevelt. This hotel has an exclusive, European-style atmosphere and a lot of nice extras, like phones in the bathroom and good makeup and shaving mirrors.

Capital Hilton Hotel

$$$$ • 16th and K Sts. NW, Washington, D.C. • (202) 393-1000

The 12-story, 543-room Capital Hilton is a short walk to most points downtown and just two blocks north of the White House. A massive renovation a few years ago resulted in new guest rooms with multiline phones and voicemail, business amenities on the top four floors and a new health club. Not surprisingly, the hotel handles a large convention and tourist trade. Fran O'Brien's Steak House, in the hotel, is a hopping bar and restaurant, but more meet-and-greet than gourmet.

The Carlton

$$$$ • 923 16th St. NW, Washington, D.C. • (202) 638-2626

A 193-room luxury hotel just two blocks from the White House, The Carlton is a member of ITT Sheraton's distinguished Luxury Collection. Built in 1926 — and beneficiary of a $27 million renovation that restored it to its original grandeur — it was designed to resemble an Italian Renaissance palace, as evidenced by its gilded ceilings, magnificent lobby and elegantly appointed guestrooms and suites. Its array of amenities including a 24-hour health club, 24-hour room service and concierge, exemplary service and convenient location have established it as a consistent headquarters for the business, political and social elite. The latest jewel in its crown is the restaurant Lespinasse, an off-

shoot of the famous New York eatery of the same name.

Channel Inn Hotel

$$ • 650 Water St. SW, Washington, D.C. • (202) 554-2400

This basic 100-room hotel is perched right on the Southwest waterfront, with beautiful views of East Potomac Park and nearby marinas. You're also a short walk to the venerable Arena Stage Theater, the National Mall and the Smithsonian museums. Free parking is available at the hotel, as well as indoor and outdoor pools. This is also the home of the Pier 7 restaurant (see nightlife chapter), which features dining and dancing.

Dupont Plaza Hotel

$$ • 1500 New Hampshire Ave. NW, Washington, D.C. • (202) 483-6000

The unpretentious Dupont Plaza is right across the street from the Dupont Circle Metro station, close to some of the city's best art galleries, book stores, boutiques and restaurants. The 314 businesslike rooms come with refrigerators and wet bars. There's a restaurant and gift shop on the premises, as well as free parking. This hotel caters to a lot of international groups. Pets are welcome.

Embassy Row Hilton

$$$$ • 2015 Massachusetts Ave. NW, Washington, D.C. • (202) 265-1600

Location, location, location is the theme here. In the city's embassy district, near Dupont Circle, the Embassy Row handles a large, well-heeled international clientele, including newcomers shopping for more permanent residences. A massive renovation should be complete by the time we go to press, sprucing up this already-nice hotel. The rooftop bar and pool is a great warm-weather hangout. There's also a health club on the premises.

Four Seasons Hotel

$$$$ • 2800 Pennsylvania Ave. NW, Washington, D.C. • (202) 342-0444

Like so many of Washington's premium hotels, the Four Seasons is often frequented by the rich and famous. Rock stars are a common sight here, and a few years ago Donald Trump and Marla Maples staged a much-publicized brouhaha in the lobby. Despite the occasional weirdness, the Four Seasons is all class — as evidenced by its rare AAA Five Diamond rating. Guests of this Georgetown gem can expect some of the best service in Washington, an outstanding concierge, a top-rated restaurant (Seasons) and a premiere fitness center. The piano lounge is a hot spot for cocktails among the Washington business elite.

The Georgetown Inn

$$$$ • 1310 Wisconsin Ave. NW,
Washington, D.C. • (202) 333-8900,
(800) 424-2979

If it's Georgetown you want, the Georgetown Inn is the place to be. Right in the nerve center of Washington's most popular nightlife district (the daylife ain't bad either), this intimate 96-unit inn offers complimentary coffee and *The Washington Post* every morning, overnight shoe shines, turndown service and a secretarial staff. Valet parking is available, an added plus in parking-scarce Georgetown.

The Grand Hyatt Washington

$$$ • 1000 H St. NW, Washington, D.C.
• (202) 582-1234

The Grand Hyatt covers all the bases. It sits across the street from the Convention Center and a half block from bustling Metro Center. Within a short walk are Pennsylvania Avenue and the White House, the National Theater, the Shops at National Place (a shopping mall) and the Smithsonian museums. This gigantic 900-room property is built around a 7,000-square-foot lagoon with an island baby grand piano. Camp Hyatt facilities accommodate children, and of course there's a swimming pool and health club. Extra perks include a kosher kitchen and a video checkout service.

The Hay-Adams Hotel

$$$$ • 1 Lafayette Sq. NW, Washington,
D.C. • (202) 638-6600, (800) 424-5054

One of our personal favorites, this ultra-luxurious, ultra-historic property overlooks Lafayette Park and the White House to the south. Diplomats, statesmen and the who's who of the Washington elite, including former presidents and presidents-elect, bunk and dine at the Hay-Adams regularly. This is the ultimate insiders' hotel but always accommodating to all. Valet parking, a full-time concierge, nightly turndown service and butler service are just some of the amenities. Some rooms come with kitchenettes.

The Henley Park Hotel

$$$$ • 926 Massachusetts Ave. NW,
Washington, D.C. • (202) 638-5200,
(800) 222-8474

Although little more than 10 years old, the Henley Park has emerged as one of the city's leading European-style hotels. This decorative 96-room property (formerly an apartment building) is less than two blocks from the Convention Center and near Union Station, Capitol Hill and the National Mall. Guests are treated to express check-ins, minibars, complimentary limousine service, overnight shoe shines and health club privileges. A classy British atmosphere pervades.

Holiday Inn Capitol at the Smithsonian

$$$$ • 550 C St. SW, Washington, D.C.
• (202) 479-4000

A colleague visiting from South Dakota summed this place up best: "It's nothing super fancy, but it's a location you can't beat — right up close to the [National] Air and Space Museum." Indeed, the Holiday Inn Capitol knows its market. Tour groups take advantage of the takeout deli and moderate prices, considering the location. Kids pack the pool in summer. Not even Fido or Puff will be turned away here.

Hotel Lombardy

$$$ • 2019 I St. NW, Washington, D.C.
• (202) 828-2600

An inn-like hotel for those who want to be near everything, the Hotel Lombardy has 125 functional rooms with kitchenettes and minibars, free newspapers, VCRs, children's movies and turndown service. Walk to the White House, West End, Foggy Bottom, downtown and the National Mall. The Hotel Lombardy is an excellent value, when you consider its location.

Hotel Sofitel Washington

$$$$ • 1914 Connecticut Ave. NW,
Washington, D.C. • (202) 797-2000,
(800)-424-2464

The Sofitel boasts, and rightly so, a full-service business center and meeting rooms.

All 143 units are suites, all with honor bars, and some with kitchenettes. There's a health club on the premises as well as a restaurant and piano lounge (see nightlife chapter). The hotel, which was renovated several years ago, has public rooms that are very impressive, guest rooms that are comfortable and geared to the business traveler, and a location that is equally accessible to Dupont Circle and downtown.

Hotel Washington

$$$$ • 15th and Pennsylvania Ave. NW, Washington, D.C. • (202) 638-5900, (800)-424-9540

One of the city's oldest hotels, the Hotel Washington sits across the street from the Treasury Department and around the corner from the White House. It is registered with the National Trust for Historic Preservation. You might find tour groups here; accordingly, ask about discounted room prices. The hotel's Roof Terrace lounge is and always has been, bar none, the best public place in the city to watch fireworks on July 4th or any of the annual parades along Pennsylvania Avenue. All 350 rooms have been renovated, and the hotel includes a fitness center with saunas.

Howard Johnson Plaza & Suites of Washington, DC - A Taj Hotel

$$$ • 1430 Rhode Island Ave. NW, Washington, D.C. • (202) 462-7777

This convenient midtown hotel is popular with tour groups, thanks to its convenient location near a Metro subway station and just five blocks north of the White House. The neighborhood here is gracious by day, but borders a red-light district by night, so cab it when you go out to dinner. Still, the amenities of this 184-room property are impressive, including walk-in kitchens, in-room safes, coin-operated laundry, underground valet parking and outdoor rooftop pool.

Hyatt Regency Washington On Capitol Hill

$$$ • 400 New Jersey Ave. NW, Washington, D.C. • (202) 737-1234

The Capitol Hill edition of this international chain comes with everything you'd expect: valet parking, video checkout service, a game room and children's suite, a beauty salon, swimming pool and health club. The massive 865-room property is a block from the Capitol and two blocks from Union Station. The rooms are standard Hyatt, which means all the business-related amenities, but nothing too fancy. As you can imagine — given its size and location — the hotel commands a huge convention and tourist business.

The Jefferson Hotel

$$$$ • 1200 16th St. NW, Washington, D.C. • (202) 347-2200

A small and gracious hotel refuge amid the hustle of downtown, the Jefferson is popular with the old money elite who from time-to-time join the roster of presidential appointees. Many have taken apartments here and it's no wonder, considering the understated, elegant surroundings. Each room offers complimentary bathrobes, hair dryers, one-hour pressing, multiline phones, minibars and VCRs, CD and cassette players, and 24-hour concierge. Swimming pool and health club privileges are available at the nearby University Club. Pets are accepted.

JW Marriott

$$$ • 1331 Pennsylvania Ave. NW, Washington, D.C. • (202) 393-2000

Part of downtown Washington's renaissance of the 1980s, this entry boasts more than 800 rooms as well as a passageway to The Shops at National Place. Just steps from the White House and the National Mall, the Marriott is big with conventions, tourists and business travelers. There's a huge, marbled, multilevel lobby and lots of meeting and eating places. Not only are there a swimming pool and health club on the premises, but all the business amenities imaginable, including a copy center, video messaging and video check out.

Loews L'Enfant Plaza Hotel

$$$$ • 480 L'Enfant Plaza SW, Washington, D.C. • (202) 484-1000

The Loews L'Enfant is a pleasant, airy hotel near the pulse of bureaucratic Washington. Its best feature, though, is its location directly above a Metro subway station. Within a short walk are the offices of NASA, the Department of Housing and Urban Development, the Transportation and Agriculture departments and the Federal Aviation Administration. Expect to find all the amenities for business and pleasure at this 370-room property, including a swimming pool and health club. All rooms come with VCRs, minibars, stocked refrigerators, three phones, in-room safes and a TV/radio in the bathroom. Some also have kitchens. Pets are allowed.

The Luxury Collection Washington, D.C.
$$$$ • 2100 Massachusetts Ave. NW, Washington, D.C. • (202) 293-2100

This Embassy Row landmark — once known as the Fairfax Hotel, and until recently the Ritz-Carlton — is opulence personified. Here you can lounge in your complimentary terry robe after a hot bath in a marble tub. Newspapers are delivered to your door, and shoe shine and limousine services are available. Some rooms come with kitchenettes. As might be expected, it is popular with CEOs and guests of Washington officialdom. The Jockey Club restaurant is typically rife with stars of industry, government and the entertainment world (see the Restaurant chapter).

The Madison Hotel
$$$$ • 15th and M Sts. NW, Washington, D.C. • (202) 862-1600

Elegant is the only way to describe this downtown institution featuring 375 rooms appointed with French and Asian antiques acquired by renowned collector and hotelier Marshall B. Coyne. This hotel is consistently rated in national travel magazines as a top choice of business executives. To give you an idea, it's where David Rockefeller stays when he comes to Washington. Guests should expect refrigerators and stocked bars in each room, as well as indoor valet parking and all the business amenities. What's more, it's convenient to everything in federal and corporate Washington.

The Mayflower
$$$$ • 1127 Connecticut Ave. NW, Washington, D.C. • (202) 347-3000

This much-revered Stouffer hotel is a Connecticut Avenue landmark, a place to see and be seen, and a Washington institution. The Mayflower's lobby takes up an entire block,

and the property has two good restaurants and a lounge. Some of the rooms in this 800-unit-plus hotel have kitchenettes. The White House is only four blocks away, and just outside the bank of brass-and-glass doors is one of Washington's nicest shopping and restaurant districts.

The Morrison-Clark Inn
$$$ • 11th St. and Massachusetts Ave. NW, Washington, D.C. • (202) 898-1200, (800) 322-7898

This inn would be a $$$$ property were it almost anywhere else in the city. However, as luxurious as it is, it is in a neighborhood undergoing gentrification, at the eastern edge of downtown near the Convention Center. Occupying one of the oldest buildings in Washington, the Morrison-Clark features authentic Victorian decor with all the modern amenities, including computer ports, and all the old-fashioned luxuries like complimentary newspaper and shoeshine. The restaurant here is renowned for its fine American cuisine.

Normandy Inn
$$ • 2118 Wyoming Ave. NW, Washington, D.C. • (202) 483-1350, (800) 424-3729

The 75-room Normandy, in upper Northwest, is lodged between Rock Creek Park and Dupont Circle. This is an intimate, European-style inn in a residential neighborhood that includes a slew of embassies. Underground parking is available, as are onsite limousine and car-rental services. Rooms have fridges and coffeemakers, as well as valet service and a continental breakfast. Pets are accepted.

Park Hyatt Washington
$$$$ • 24th and M Sts. NW, Washington, D.C. • (202) 789-1234

Another in a long list of competitive West End hotels, the Park Hyatt is one of the most elegant in the Hyatt chain, a truly deluxe hotel. Three blocks from Georgetown, it features a wonderful restaurant and sidewalk café (see the Restaurant chapter). In the rooms, you'll find the usual Hyatt amenities plus some four-star touches, including multiline phones, minibars and complimentary fresh fruit in all rooms. There's also a

swimming pool and a health club on the premises, as well as a beauty salon.

Phoenix Park Hotel

$$$$ • 520 N. Capitol St. NW,
Washington, D.C. • (202) 638-6900

For a touch of the Emerald Isle right here in Washington, check into the Phoenix Park, America's only Irish-owned hotel. More of an inn than a hotel, it has 90 luxurious rooms and is two blocks from the Capitol and a block from Union Station and Metro. The hotel's Dubliner Pub is widely regarded as one of the best Irish bars in Metro Washington (see the Nightlife chapter).

Radisson Barcelo Hotel

$$$$ • 2121 P St. NW, Washington, D.C.
• (202) 293-3100

This 300-room property is close to both Georgetown and Dupont Circle, right in the middle of a row of wonderful restaurants and cafés, including the hotel's own Gabriel (see the Restaurant chapter). The rooms are nicely appointed, in line with the Radisson standard,

and there's a business center, sauna, swimming pool and health club. Nearby Rock Creek Park beckons joggers, strollers and romantics.

Renaissance Washington, D.C. Hotel

$$$$ • 999 9th St. NW, Washington, D.C.
• (202) 898-9000

Rapidly becoming one of the District's premiere convention and trade show sites, the Renaissance is across from the Convention Center, about halfway between the White House and Capitol Hill. Twenty-five retail shops, a fitness center, food court, post office, hair salon, and indoor pool complement the 880 rooms. In each room, expect all the business amenities related to computers and telephones. There's valet parking and a convenient Metro subway station. Pets are allowed.

Sheraton Washington

$$$$ • 2660 Woodley Rd. NW,
Washington, D.C. • (202) 328-2000

At 1,350 rooms, this is Washington's largest hotel, a sprawling behemoth of brick, white columns, French doors, endless corridors and room-sized chandeliers. The setting is a grand expanse of parkland at the edge of Rock Creek. The National Zoo is three blocks to the north. This hotel, which offers all sorts of convention and tourist services, includes a post office, pool, health club, shoe shine stand and hair salon. Rooms come with Starbucks coffee/tea service, voicemail, video check out and every other amenity imaginable for the comfort of the business traveler. Pets are allowed.

Westin City Center Hotel
$$$$ • 1400 M St. NW, Washington, D.C. • (202) 429-1700

We tainted locals still know this best as the former Vista International Hotel, the place where D.C. Mayor Marion Barry got busted — and videotaped, no less — for using crack cocaine. (After serving time in prison, he was, remarkably, reelected in 1994, succeeding Sharon Pratt Kelly, the woman who succeeded him four years prior.) That's not to knock the Westin, however. This is a fine, centrally located hotel that offers guests three telephones in every room and voicemail, as well as minibars, refrigerators and all the other business amenities. It's an impressive sight, too, with its 14-story glass atrium draped in greenery. There's a fitness room, restaurant and lounge.

The Westin Hotel
$$$$ • 2350 M St. NW, Washington, D.C. • (202) 429-0100, (800) 848-0016

This hotel has had several names, but it has remained a grand hotel throughout the years. The 263 newly renovated rooms feature marble bathrooms, minibars and all sorts of luxurious toiletries. All the premium services are here, too, as well as a swimming pool and health club. If you really want to splurge, try one of the eight suites with wood burning fireplaces and Jacuzzis. Wedged between downtown and Georgetown, the Grand is also close

to Rock Creek Park, George Washington University and the Foggy Bottom Metro.

The Willard Inter-Continental
$$$$ • 1401 Pennsylvania Ave. NW, Washington, D.C. • (202) 628-9100

Along with the Hay-Adams, the Four Seasons and a select few other properties, the Willard is among the creme de la creme of Washington hotels. Ironically, this stunning historical landmark almost fell victim to the wrecking ball before it was renovated and reopened in grand fashion in 1986. The 340 rooms and suites are as plush as you'd expect, with lots of mirrors, marble and good reproduction furniture. Within a one or two minute walk are the White House, the Treasury Department, the National Theater, the Department of Commerce and the National Mall. The hotel has two elegant lounges, a cafe and a formal restaurant, the Willard Room (see Restaurants chapter).

Wyndham Bristol
$$$ • 2430 Pennsylvania Ave. NW, Washington, D.C. • (202) 955-6400, 800-WYNDHAM

Service is key at this classic West End hotel that's just a few strides away from Georgetown. The 239-room Wyndham offers valet parking, complimentary newspapers, a shoe shine service and rooms with hair dryers and coffee machines. Classic English and contemporary decor accentuates an already classy atmosphere of this discreet, European-style hotel.

Northern Virginia

Fairfax County

McLean Hilton at Tysons Corner
$$$$ • 7920 Jones Branch Dr., McLean, Va. • (703) 847-5000

Another Tysons Corner landmark, the 458-room McLean Hilton features a glass domed

---

INSIDERS' TIP

Book hotels early if you intend to come during the first week of April when the cherry blossoms bloom. This is peak tourist season.

atrium and a splashy lobby filled with marble, brass and live plants. The rooms here are ordinary contemporary-style Hilton, but the 43 concierge-level Tower rooms offer some extras like in-room faxes and coffeemakers plus complimentary continental breakfast and evening hors d'oeuvres. There's an extensive health club, an indoor pool, minibars in each room, bathroom phones as well as all the amenities business travelers expect. You'll find a restaurant, bar and drug store on the premises, and you're close to shopping, movie theaters and still more shopping at the two nearby mega malls that are the retail focal point of Tysons Corner.

Ritz-Carlton Tysons Corner
$$$$ • 1700 Tysons Blvd., McLean, Va.
• (703) 506-4300

As they are so apt to do with many of their newer properties, the folks behind the Ritz-Carlton chain like to make sure their monied customers have easy access to fashionable shopping areas. In this case, it's the attached and oh-so-exclusive Galleria at Tysons II (Saks Fifth Avenue, Neiman-Marcus, et al.), in the heart of Fairfax County's mecca of consumerism, Tysons Corner. As for the hotel itself, it's typical Ritz-Carlton fancy to the nth degree: Expect the usual grand decor, attentive service and fine dining, as well as indoor pool and health club.

Its location is on one of the highest points in the area — all the better for a great view of some D.C. landmarks on a clear day, since there isn't much in the way of scenery in the immediate area, unless you count high-rise office buildings, stores and a patchwork of busy roads. The 399 rooms feature classic English antique reproductions, marble bathrooms, safes, minibars, and all the toiletries and business amenities. In addition, there's a business center on premises, as well as a choice of free self-parking or valet parking, and complimentary transportation within a three-mile radius. If you want to be closer to downtown D.C., check into the Ritz-Carlton Pentagon City, attached to the shopping mall of the same name and offering the same amenities, 1250 South Hayes Street, Arlington, (703) 415-5060.

Sheraton Premiere at Tysons Corner
$$$$ • 8661 Leesburg Pk., Vienna, Va.
• (703) 448-1234

One of Northern Virginia's most luxurious hotels, and one of the nicest in the Sheraton chain, the towering Sheraton Premiere (you can't miss the glass tower at Route 7 and the Toll Road; it's one of the tallest buildings in Tysons Corner) extends to guests such perks as lighted tennis courts, golf privileges, a fitness center, indoor and outdoor pools, free parking, an onsite airline ticket office, health club, racquetball courts, and free transportation to nearby Dulles Airport. Tysons Corner, a city in itself, is close to I-66 and the Beltway. There are also restaurants and lounges on premises (see the Nightlife chapter).

Washington Dulles Airport Marriott
$$$ • 333 W. Service Rd., Chantilly, Va.
• (703) 471-9500

Talk about the Marriott advantage: This is the only hotel on the grounds of Washington Dulles International Airport. A large pond and acres of wooded landscaping almost defy the location of this 368-room hotel, though. There's an indoor/outdoor pool, tennis courts, fitness center and free parking. The terminal is a two-minute drive away, and complimentary shuttle-bus service is provided. Business travelers will appreciate the video checkout.

Westfields by Marriott
$$$$ • 14750 Conference Center Dr., Chantilly, Va. • (703) 818-0300

You'd never know this 335-room hotel was part of a chain, and indeed Marriott only became involved a couple of years ago. Westfields' stately Georgian facade and 1,100 manicured acres give the impression of an old established Virginia resort. The lavish, service-driven facility, however, is the product of the boom days of the 1980s. It exudes elegance, from its state-of-the-art conference rooms to its outstanding restaurant and ornate guest rooms decorated in marble, country prints, and rich carpets. Dulles Airport is seven miles to the north along Route 28. The hotel is also about equal distance from U.S. 50 and I-66. This is an ideal venue for a corporate retreat, large or small, a wedding reception or any other special occasion. Don't miss dinner at the exquisite Palm Court (see the Restaurant chapter). Rooms feature three multiline phones and refrigerators. There's a tourist desk, pro shops, a business center, free valet parking, an indoor heated pool, outdoor pool, healthclub, tennis courts, an on-call physician and nearby championship golf.

Alexandria

Holiday Inn Select Old Town Alexandria

$$ • 480 King St., Alexandria, Va.
• (703) 549-6080

A tourist mecca, especially on weekends, the 227-room Old Town Holiday Inn offers one of the best locations in Alexandria's famed historic district. From here, you're right across the street from the town square, the site of a colorful street market held every Saturday morning, and a short walk from galleries, shops, bars, restaurants and the Potomac waterfront. This recently renovated property is one of the top hotels in the Holiday Inn chain. Colonial-themed guest rooms offer speakerphones with computer-modem capability and voicemail, safes, and coffeemakers. As you would expect, there's video checkout and a business center, indoor parking, indoor pool and exercise room. There's also free transportation to National Airport and Metro subway stops.

Morrison House

$$$$ • 116 S. Alfred St., Alexandria, Va.
• (703) 838-8000, (800) 367-0800

This elegant 18th century-style mansion in the center of Old Town is one of the region's, indeed the nation's, most-celebrated inns. Each of the 45 rooms is individually decorated with Federal-period antiques and chandeliers, and several rooms come with fireplaces and four-poster canopy beds. The inn's cozy restaurant and lounge enhance an already intensely romantic atmosphere. Morrison House is the perfect urban getaway and the site of many honeymoons.

Radisson Plaza Hotel at Mark Center

$$$ • 5000 Seminary Rd., Alexandria, Va.
• (703) 845-1010

From I-395, you can't possibly miss the Radisson Plaza, a tower of concrete and glass that emerges from the surrounding woodlands like a futuristic sentinel. The 500-room hotel, big with convention and conference folks, is surrounded by a manmade lake and about 80 acres of woods — a nice buffer from the traffic and congestion of Alexandria's West End. The property comes with an indoor/outdoor swimming pool, health club and free parking. There's complimentary transportation to National Airport, ten minutes away.

Arlington County

Hyatt Regency Crystal City

$$$$ • 2799 Jefferson Davis Hwy., Arlington, Va. • (703) 418-1234

Crystal City, a conglomeration of office buildings, fast-food restaurants, high-rise condos and big hotels, isn't going to win any awards for aesthetics, but it sure is convenient. Same can be said for the Hyatt Regency here, a 700-unit hotel that offers a health club, an outdoor swimming pool and a lounge and rooftop restaurant with a view of D.C. Guests receive complimentary shuttle service to National Airport or Metro, barely three minutes away. Crystal City is also close to the Pentagon, downtown D.C. and Old Town Alexandria.

Key Bridge Marriott

$$$$ • 1401 Lee Hwy., Arlington, Va.
• (703) 524-6400

About as close to Washington as you're going to get in Virginia, the 585-room Key Bridge Marriott is a short walk (or shorter jog) across its graceful namesake span from Georgetown and just two blocks from the Rosslyn Metro. The hotel's riverside location affords spectacular views of the Potomac and the District beyond. There's free onsite parking, an indoor/outdoor pool and health club. Each morning, guests are treated to complimentary coffee and newspapers. Rooms have all the usual business amenities.

Ritz-Carlton Pentagon City

$$$$ • 1250 S. Hayes St., Arlington, Va.
• (703) 415-5000

See preceding description under Ritz-Carlton Tysons Corner.

Sheraton National
$$$ • Columbia Pike and Washington Blvd., Arlington, Va. • (703) 521-1900

This 444-room hotel is just a mile from the Pentagon and less than a 10-minute drive from National Airport. Don't expect anything stylish — rather it's a functional meeting place for those with business at the Pentagon or downtown D.C. There's an onsite fitness center and pool, as well as a complimentary shuttle to nearby National Airport, Pentagon City shopping mall and Metro. You'll also find a rooftop restaurant and lounge, neither particularly distinctive, an indoor pool and health club.

Loudoun County

Lansdowne Conference Resort
$$$$ • 44050 Woodridge Pkwy., Leesburg, Va. • (703) 729-4071, (800) 541-4801

In a resort-like setting north of Dulles Airport, Lansdowne attracts a growing share of meetings and conventions, especially among international firms. Luxurious rooms are complemented by an attentive staff, state-of-the-art meetings technology, a world-class golf course and a fitness center and spa. Lansdowne is part of Loudoun County's burgeoning Route 7 corridor, one of the region's fastest-growing commercial districts. You don't have to leave the premises for anything, and the fine restaurant is a special treat.

Suburban Maryland

Montgomery County

Bethesda Marriott
$$$$ • 5151 Pooks Hill Rd., Bethesda, Md. • (301) 897-9400

This 407-room property is high atop a hill near the Capitol Beltway, the National Institutes of Health and White Flint shopping mall. It's a sprawling place with all manner of eateries, an indoor/outdoor pool, tennis courts and exercise room. There's also free parking and a shuttle to the Metro.

Holiday Inn Bethesda
$$ • 8120 Wisconsin Ave., Bethesda, Md. • (301) 652-2000

It's hard to get closer to the Bethesda Naval Hospital and the National Institutes of Health than this hotel, a Wisconsin Avenue landmark for almost two decades. You're about equal distance from the Beltway and the District line. The main distinction of this hotel, however, is The Yacht Club, a singles spot for those 30 and older (see the Nightlife chapter).

Hyatt Regency Bethesda
$$$ • 7400 Wisconsin Ave., Bethesda, Md. • (301) 657-1234

This bustling hotel in the heart of Bethesda's business district is atop a Metro subway station, so it couldn't be more convenient. Both Washington and the surrounding suburbs are just a few Metro stops away. Rooms come with all the business amenities now standard at most Hyatts, including video checkout, voicemail, minibars, and a striking atrium-style lobby full of shops and services. The shopping malls at White Flint and Mazza Gallerie are only a couple of subway stops away.

Prince George's County

Greenbelt Marriott Hotel
$$$ • 6400 Ivy Lane, Greenbelt, Md. • (301) 441-3700

This is probably one of the nicest full service hotels near the University of Maryland and NASA Goddard Space Flight Center. There are 283 standard rooms in this hotel as well as a concierge level and extended stay accommodations. You'll find a restaurant, lounge, free parking, indoor and outdoor pools, a health club and tennis courts.

Ramada Conference & Exhibition Center
$$ • 8500 Annapolis Rd., New Carrollton, Md. • (301) 459-6700

This small hotel near the USAirways Arena has been newly renovated to answer every possible need of the business traveler. Rooms feature kitchenettes with fridges, computer outlets, free shoeshine and newspaper. On premises, you can avail yourself of a business center that provides fax and copy services. There's a complimentary shuttle within a 10-mile radius and an onsite car rental service, gift shop, restaurant and lounge. The 38 rooms are functional and convenient.

On a Budget

Washington, D.C.

Allen Lee Hotel
$ • 2224 F St. NW, Washington, D.C. • (202) 331-1224, (800) 462-0186

Rooms at the Allen Lee in Foggy Bottom can start as low as $58 for a double with a bathroom down the hall, which partly explains why it does a brisk business with students and young international tourists. The very basic 85-room hotel is right on the beaten path — close to Metro and six blocks from the White House, the Kennedy Center and the Lincoln Memorial. It is ideal for tourists not dependent on a car.

Days Inn Uptown Connecticut Ave.
$$ • 4400 Connecticut Ave. NW, Washington, D.C. • (202) 244-5600

In the city but away from the masses, this 155-room edition of the national chain comes with free onsite parking, in-room safe, and voicemail. It's in upper Northwest D.C., a safe and exclusive neighborhood, and is made even more convenient by the presence of the Van Ness/UDC Metro two blocks away. Also close by are American University, the National Zoo, Rock Creek Park and the restaurants and shops of Tenleytown and Cleveland Park.

Hotel Harrington
$ • 11th and E Sts. NW, Washington, D.C. • (202) 628-8140, (800) 424-8532

The no-frills Harrington is for the budget-conscious who want to be in the thick of it. It's a half-block away from Pennsylvania Avenue, about equal distance from the White House and the Capitol. There's onsite parking for $6.50 a day, a restaurant, bar, barber shop and laundry room. Pets are welcome. The Harrington has always done a strong business with Europeans. More Americans should follow their lead.

Red Roof Inn Downtown DC
$ • 500 H St. NW, Washington, D.C. • (202) 289-5959

Anyone who's ever stayed in a Red Roof Inn knows what to expect from this spot. The neighborhood is neither the most scenic nor the most convenient, but the hotel is less than two blocks from the Metro and MCI Arena, four blocks to the Washington Convention Center, and seven blocks to Capitol Hill. There's a restaurant, exercise room and guest laundry on premises.

Windsor Inn
$$ • 1842 16th St. NW, Washington, D.C. • (202) 667-0300, (800) 423-9111

This is called an inn, but with 45 rooms, it's a bit large to fit into that category — more like a small hotel really. The rooms are pleasant and neat, but not luxurious. The location, though a bit off the beaten path from midtown and the sights, is convenient enough to Metro. On a nice day, you can walk the 12 blocks to the White House — a pleasant stroll past some handsome buildings. Your room comes with complimentary continental breakfast and evening sherry.

Windsor Park Hotel
$$ • 2116 Kalorama Rd. NW, Washington, D.C. • (202) 483-7700

The Windsor Park in Washington's exclusive Kalorama neighborhood is another great European-style bargain. Close to the bustle of Adams Morgan and the shopping of Dupont Circle, the inn-like setting is perfect for families with young children. All 43 simple rooms come with a small refrigerator, complimentary continental breakfast and newspaper.

Northern Virginia

Alexandria

Towers Hotel

$ • 420 N. Van Dorn St., Alexandria, Va.
• (703) 370-1000

If it's important to be near shopping malls and right off the interstate but not too far from D.C., then the Towers should fit the bill. The 186-suite hotel in Alexandria's West End is within striking distance of I-395, one of the region's busiest arteries, and Landmark Shopping Center, one of the region's busiest malls. D.C. is just 9 miles up the road, while Old Town is but 5 miles east. The area is a fast-food mecca, but you can take solace in that all suites here come with kitchens. This place could use a renovation, but you can't beat it for the price.

Arlington

Econo Lodge

$$ • 6800 Lee Hwy., Arlington, Va.
• (703) 538-5300, (800) 78-LODGE

Don't let the name rule out this property for you. This location of the popular national budget motel chain has consistently been rated as one of the best Econo Lodges in the country. Why else would inner-Beltway politicians and dignitaries and celebrities like Shirley Maclaine choose to stay over here? The location couldn't be better. The 47-room lodge is at the junction of I-66 and Lee Highway, the first interchange you'll come to when entering Washington from Dulles airport. It also puts you in proximity to the amazing French cuisine of La Cote d'Or Café (see Restaurants) and within about eight minutes of the E. Falls Church metro station. About half the rooms are nonsmoking, and several are handicapped-accessible.

Howard Johnson Plaza Hotel National Airport

$$$$ • 2650 Jefferson Davis Hwy., Arlington, Va. • (703) 684-7200, (703) 684-7200

If you haven't been to HoJos recently, get ready for a surprise. The chain's gone upscale, at least in the D.C. area, and they're aiming for the high-end corporate customer. This hotel in Crystal City has been totally overhauled and the service staff trained well. In a corridor of concrete, glass and steel, the hotel is close to National Airport, the Pentagon, Arlington National Cemetery, the Fashion Centre at Pentagon City, Crystal City Underground (shopping) and finally, ten minutes to the south, Old Town Alexandria. Service is key and guests should expect complimentary shuttle service to the airport and Metro, as well as laundry and valet service, voicemail, a health club, pool and free parking. Pets are welcome.

Quality Hotel Arlington

$ • 1200 N. Courthouse Rd., Arlington, Va. • (703) 524-4000, (800) 228-5151

A huge but pleasant hotel in an urban setting, the Quality Arlington (not to be confused with Quality Inns) is a real bargain — a nice, clean modern facility that won't break the bank. Its location can't be beat either — near the Court House Metro, which means shops, restaurants, a movie theater, and all kinds of family amusement options. What's more, a complimentary shuttle will take you there. A bit further is the Rosslyn business district and Georgetown. At the Quality Hotel, you'll find amenities like in-room coffee, free local calls, a sauna, coin-operated laundry, in-room Nintendo, a huge outdoor pool, health club and free parking. Suites have full kitchens. The place is crawling with families during the spring and summer months, testament no doubt to its budget prices and ease.

Quality Inn Iwo Jima

$ • 1501 Arlington Blvd., Arlington, Va. • (703) 524-5000

Popular with tourists, this 141-room edition of the national chain is within an easy walk of Arlington Cemetery, the Iwo Jima Memorial, the National Mall and even Georgetown. Rosslyn Metro is three blocks away. The hotel, though a bit worn, offers low prices as well as free parking, free local phone calls, in-room coffeemaker, laundry facilities and an indoor/outdoor pool, but this is an older property and you should expect only the basics insofar as rooms are concerned — nothing fancy here.

Travelodge Cherry Blossom Motel
$ • 3030 Columbia Pk., Arlington, Va.
• (703) 521-5570

For the basics the Travelodge Cherry Blossom Motel is hard to beat, especially for families and solo travelers on a budget. Prices start at $66 a night, and besides a place to sleep you get complimentary coffee, juice and doughnuts in the lobby from 6 to 10:30 AM daily, use of a fitness center and washer and dryer facilities, free onsite parking and free local phone calls. Adding to its convenient Arlington location (a great base for D.C. sightseeing), there's a Metro station less than 2 miles away. You'll have to do without a swimming pool, but with this much bang for your buck, you probably won't even miss it.

Suburban Maryland

Bethesda

American Inn of Bethesda
$$ • 8130 Wisconsin Ave., Bethesda, Md.
• (301) 656-9300

Much closer to the District than the Park Inn, the American Inn is in the middle of downtown Bethesda, about a 10-minute walk from the Bethesda Metro and only a couple of minutes' drive from NIH. This very basic property is slowly undergoing a step-by-step renovation, so ask for one of the newer rooms if that's important to you. This will always be a simple property, nothing fancy, but a great location not far from Bethesda's famed restaurant row. Guests of the American can get microwave ovens upon request, and there's a pool to cool off in.

Park Inn International
$$ • 11410 Rockville Pk., Bethesda, Md.
• (301) 881-5200

It's not exactly the most scenic place around (this is the land of strip centers and fast-food restaurants), but then again you're not paying for the view. This 154-room motel in North Bethesda just underwent a $5 mil-

lion renovation. It is clean, safe and close to White Flint Mall, the epitome of suburban shopping malls. What's more, it offers an hourly shuttle service to the National Institutes of Health, so don't be surprised if you see a lot of doctors and scientists running around.

Silver Spring

Days Inn Silver Spring
$ • 8040 13th St., Silver Spring, Md.
• (301) 588-4400

Again, it's nothing fancy but this Days Inn is near much of upper Northwest D.C. and close-in areas of Montgomery County. Walter Reed Army Hospital is a mile to the south, and Takoma Park, to the immediate east, has some interesting Bohemian-tinged shops, restaurants and nightclubs.

Holiday Inn Silver Spring Plaza
$$ • 8777 Georgia Ave., Silver Spring, Md. • (301) 589-0800

An easy walk to the Silver Spring Metro and the District line, this Holiday Inn sits in the center of one of Suburban Maryland's oldest and most established neighborhoods. The 231-room hotel's been here a long time, but it was gutted in 1996 and totally renovated. It's a great base for house hunters in Silver Spring or neighboring Takoma Park. Downtown Washington is a good 20-minute drive by way of 16th Street.

Hostels/University Inns

Georgetown University Conference Center
$$ • Hoya Station NW, Washington, D.C.
• (202) 687-3200

The nation's oldest Catholic university — alma mater of President Clinton — is the obvious main attraction of this on-campus hotel. Mostly frequented by guests of the university and seminar participants, the conference center offers some rooms with kitchenettes plus a swimming pool and health club. All of the Georgetown neighborhood is within a few minutes' walk, and the business district of Rosslyn (Virginia) looms just across Key Bridge. Don't worry about nonstop college parties keeping you up at night; the hotel is at the far-north end of campus, in a relatively quiet residential area.

The Howard Inn
$ • 2225 Georgia Ave. NW, Washington, D.C. • (202) 462-5400

Howard University, one of the nation's premiere historically black colleges, is host to this affordable 147-room hotel. Some rooms have kitchens, and there's free onsite parking for all. From here, you're within a 10-minute drive to downtown and Capitol Hill. While security is tight on campus, some of the neighborhoods surrounding Howard have been plagued by violent crime.

The International Guest House
$ • 1441 Kennedy St. NW, Washington, D.C. • (202) 726-5808

The International Guest House is a nonprofit facility maintained by the Mennonite Church to provide clean, inexpensive lodging for international visitors in a homey atmosphere. Indeed, the large brick home with its wraparound porch is in a pleasant residential area off 16th Street Northwest, across the street from Rock Creek Park. Breakfast is served family style at 8 AM, with guests and staff eating together. There is a large living room for lounging and reading, and a television is in the basement. Single guests are asked to share a room with another person. Another restriction that might cramp your style is the 11 PM curfew, after which the house is closed. However, for the rock-bottom rates of $25 per person per night, you can hardly find a more reasonable bargain in a nice, safe area.

The University Inn Hotel
$ • 2134 G. St. NW, Washington, D.C. • (202) 342-8020

On the campus of George Washington University, this small hotel (83 rooms) is just four blocks from the White House, in earshot of the Foggy Bottom Metro, and just a leisurely stroll from the Kennedy Center and the east end of Georgetown. Guests receive complimentary continental breakfast and a morning newspaper. Pets are accepted.

Washington International American Youth Hostel
$ • 1009 11th St. NW, Washington, D.C. • (202) 737-2333

A clean, safe alternative for young travelers on a budget, this 250-bed dorm-style hostel is one block north of the Washington Convention Center — not the greatest neighborhood, but one undergoing a renaissance. There's a large common area for meeting other travelers (lots of Europeans here) plus a huge kitchen for groups, and a coin-operated laundry. Free movies and tours are available and, as you can imagine, security is very tight.

Linking to The Chains

Many of the hotels listed in this chapter belong to national chains. For your convenience, we've listed their toll-free telephone numbers below.

Best Western	(800) 762-3777
Comfort Inn	(800) 228-5150
Days Inn	(800) 952-3060
Econo Lodge	(800) 558-6877
Embassy Suites	(800) 362-2779
Hilton	(800) HOTELS-1
Holiday Inn	(800) HOLIDAY
Howard Johnson	(800) 654-2000
Hyatt	(800) 233-1324
Marriott	(800) 228-9290
Radisson	(800) 333-3333
Ritz-Carlton	(800) 241-3333
Sheraton	(800) 468-9090
Travelodge	(800) 578-7878

These intimate bed and breakfasts usually provide all the amenities of home — and then some — but some may purposefully eschew modern-day intrusions.

Bed and Breakfasts & Country Inns

Whether you're a newcomer or a Washington area resident, inns and bed and breakfasts are an escape from the rush of everyday life. They provide a more intimate alternative to large, busy hotels and may sometimes, but not always, be less expensive. A recent trend among stressed urbanites has been to book a long weekend at one of these hideaways, even if it's ten minutes from home! It's cheaper than an out-of-town trip, takes less time, and yet it's so hassle-free that the sense of relaxation can be every bit as profound.

Given the historical nature of Metro Washington — and the number of large homes, former embassies and other spacious structures — it's surprising there aren't more bed and breakfasts in the area. Maybe it's because Washington and the surrounding suburbs host so many tours, school groups and conventions that the majority of accommodations are in big, full-service hotels. Whatever the reason, the immediate Metro area doesn't offer the selection of bed and breakfasts that you'll find in the surrounding countryside of Maryland and Virginia. If you don't mind driving a greater distance or if you're looking to get out of the area for a weekend hideaway, check the Daytrips chapter for further recommendations.

That said, the bed and breakfasts that do exist are often magnificent. Some are housed in historic buildings, others in stately Federal-style townhomes and most are furnished in grand style. Rooms are individually decorated and varied, with some offering luxuries like two-person Jacuzzis, down comforters and fireplaces.

Bed and breakfasts, as the name implies, generally include a full breakfast for two in the room tariff, though a few restrict themselves to continental breakfasts. Some also serve afternoon tea or evening hors d'oeuvres. Inns, on the other hand, may charge extra for all meals.

You'll see in the listings below that many area bed and breakfasts are represented by agencies that match the guest with the right accommodation — often a lovely room in someone's private residence. Your host may be the homeowner, and if both parties are willing to mingle, you'll have a chance for an intimate look at the lives of Washingtonians. These locals are also a good source of information on neighborhood restaurants, entertainment, shopping and the latest museum exhibits. They're pleased to share their knowledge and will often help you make arrangements, just like a concierge in a big hotel would. The charm of smaller hostelries is, of course, the personal touch.

These intimate bed and breakfasts usually provide all the amenities of home — and then some — or they may purposefully eschew such modern-day intrusions as in-room phones, VCRs and televisions. If you require the modern conveniences, be sure to ask whether they're provided when you make your reservation.

www.insiders.com

See this and many other **Insiders' Guide®** destinations online — in their entirety.

Visit us today!

One final note: inns and bed and breakfasts usually require a deposit to hold a reservation and they often have strict cancellation policies requiring plenty of advance notice. You can't blame them — they're small businesses and every room counts.

Price-Code Key

The price code is based on average room cost per night based on double occupancy.

$	Less than $80
$$	$80 to $125
$$$	$125 to $150
$$$$	Over $150

Washington, D.C.

Bed and Breakfast League/ Sweet Dreams & Toast

$-$$$ • P.O. Box 9490, Washington, D.C. 20016 • (202) 363-7767

This is a reservation service specializing in bed and breakfasts in Washington's historic districts. All guest houses have easy access to public transportation and offer onsite parking. Some rooms offer kitchenettes.

Bed 'N' Breakfast Accommodations Ltd. of Washington, D.C.

$-$$$$ • P.O. Box 12011, Washington, D.C. 20005 • (202) 328-3510

From budget to luxury offerings, Bed 'N' Breakfast Accommodations, Ltd. will connect you with an array of private-home lodgings and inns. Some apartments are even available for family groups and extended-stay

guests. There are many historic properties with antiques and gardens, and two with pools. Continental breakfast is included.

The Dupont At The Circle

$$ • 1606 19th St. NW, Washington, D.C.
• (202) 332-5251

Just a block from the bustle of Dupont Circle, this upscale Victorian charmer sits on a tree-lined residential street just steps from a Metro subway stop. The six nonsmoking rooms are all different, but some features include fireplaces, high ceilings, and marble bathrooms with Jacuzzis. Also available are rooms or suites with cable TV, fax machines, VCRs and kitchenettes. There's complimentary continental breakfast and newspaper as well as parking.

Kalorama Guest House at Kalorama Park

$ • 1854 Mintwood Pl. NW, Washington, D.C. • (202) 667-6369

In the lively Adams Morgan neighborhood, just a block from the restaurant district, this elegant 33-room inn (12 with private bath) is furnished in Victorian antiques. Once inside, expect peace and quiet. There are no TVs or phones in rooms. Complimentary continental breakfast and afternoon aperitifs are served in the parlor and garden.

Kalorama Guest House at Woodley Park

$ • 2700 Cathedral Ave. NW, Washington, D.C. • (202) 328-0860

This Victorian townhouse (two connected, actually) is in Northwest, in the gorgeous Woodley Park neighborhood. It's close to Washington National Cathedral and the National Zoo. Metro is three blocks away. This place is similar in atmosphere and amenities to the Kalorama in Kalorama Park.

Swiss Inn

$ • 1204 Massachusetts Ave. NW, Washington, D.C. • (202) 371-1816

Each of the six suites in this classy Euro-style inn comes with individual climate con-

Photo: Courtesy of Clifton – The Country Inn

Bed and breakfasts can return you to a bygone era.

Photo: Courtesy of the Virginia Division of Tourism

Nearby bed and breakfasts offer guests an escape from the fast pace of Washington.

trol, remote-control TV, private bath, phone and kitchenette. You're just four blocks from the Convention Center and a leisurely walk to the White House and the National Mall.

Northern Virginia

Alexandria

The Little House
$ · 719 Gibbon St., Alexandria, Va.
· (703) 548-9654

It's the smallest house in Old Town and maybe anywhere. We doubt if this historic Federal-era, two-story townhome is more than six feet wide. It was originally built as a doll house for the daughter of the owner of the adjoining property. Now it serves as one of the most interesting — and undoubtedly the coziest — guest homes in all of Metro D.C. The Little House comes with a kitchen, living area and upstairs bedroom. All of Old Town is at your fingertips.

Fairfax County

Bailiwick Inn
$$$ · 4023 Chain Bridge Rd., Fairfax, Va.
· (703) 691-2266

This early 19th-century brick townhouse is wedged in the center of Fairfax City's charming

INSIDERS' TIP

If you drive, be sure to ask about parking at in-town bed and breakfasts. Many are in residential areas with limited parking.

but often overlooked historic district, just across Route 123 from the old courthouse. The Bailiwick has 14 guests rooms, each named for one of the founding fathers, all with feather beds and some with whirlpools and fireplaces. George Mason University and its beautiful Center for the Arts is right up the road, and the Vienna Metro station is less than 10 minutes away.

Prince William County

Sunrise Hill Farm Bed & Breakfast
$ • 5513 Sudley Rd., Manassas, Va.
• (703) 754-8309

Civil War buffs, naturalists and horse-lovers will fall for this cozy bed and breakfast inside the Manassas National Battlefield Park, just 30 miles west of Washington, D.C. Hiking and horseback-riding trails abound at the park, and Sunrise Hill will even board your horse. Manassas's historic district, home to the much-acclaimed Manassas Museum, is also nearby. See our Civil War chapter for information on these historic sites.

Loudoun County

The Laurel Brigade Inn
$ • 20 W. Market St., Leesburg, Va.
• (703) 777-1010

Rooms here start at $50 a night, making this old colonial stone inn one of the better bed and breakfast bargains around. Guests can choose from five tastefully appointed rooms. The house restaurant specializes in Virginia country dining and is reasonably priced.

The Norris House Inn
$-$$$ • 108 Loudoun St. SW, Leesburg, Va. • (703) 777-1806

Right in the middle of Leesburg's historic district, The Norris House Inn (built in 1760) has guest rooms with canopied beds, antiques galore and fireplaces. It's a nice spot for a romantic night away but also conducive to small meetings and family celebrations. Guests have full use of the stately dining room, parlor, library, sun room and a rambling veranda overlooking beautiful gardens. Washington is less than an hour away.

Metro Washington is no place for shopaholics to try and kick the habit.

Shopping

For many residents of Metro Washington, shopping is more than just a necessity of life or, as some might declare, a "necessary evil." Rather, it's an avocation, even a consuming passion that, at least for those with more modest standards of living, seems to pose a regular threat to checkbook and credit-card balances, not to mention the stability of a few marriages. Some people have even elevated shopping to a sort of art form, and around here, the inspiration for a masterpiece is never far away.

To put it in another perspective: Metro Washington is no place for shopaholics to try and kick the habit. The temptations are far too great, whether the consumer is a free-spending millionaire, a penny-pinching college student, or someone in between. Whatever the object of desire, there's sure to be a place in Metro Washington to buy it, from mega-malls, outlet malls and neighborhood shopping centers, to department stores, tony designer boutiques, discount retailers, bulk-buy membership warehouses and antique havens.

Opportunities for priming the economic pump are numerous, and the locals do their part. Per-household retail sales ring up to an estimated $23,000 here, 15 percent above the national average and about $2,000 over the household average for the nine other top markets in the United States. Among the nation's top-10 markets, Metro Washington places near the top in total retail sales (furniture, home furnishings and appliances). The region also ranks in the top 10 nationally in sales at general-merchandise and drug stores, automotive dealers, restaurants, food stores and apparel and accessory stores.

The conspicuous-consumption 1980s certainly were in full swing in the nation's capital. Between 1980 and 1990, retail sales in the Standard Metropolitan Statistical Area doubled to some $31 billion annually! Northern Virginia topped the area with $14 billion, Suburban Maryland was second with $13.5 billion and the District third with $3.8 billion. With an after-tax income base of more than $60,000, area households spent an average of $24,000, or 40 percent of buying income, in the retail marketplace. Based on customer volume, the most popular shopping destinations in the region include the F Street corridor of downtown Washington, Tysons Corner Center and Fair Oaks Mall in Fairfax County, Potomac Mills outlet center in Prince William County, Montgomery Mall in Bethesda and Landmark Center in Alexandria. More on these and other places to follow.

No matter what the spending patterns of this affluent region say, saving money will always be in vogue. After all, how do you think so many of the rich stay that way? Fortunately, Metro Washington is right in step with the rest of the nation when it comes to offering places where brand-name, first-quality goods can be had at rock-bottom prices. Stores that are especially popular with bargain seekers include membership warehouses such as Price Club, and apparel outlets like Marshall's, TJ Maxx, Ross and Today's Man. Most of these stores have locations throughout the region.

One of the most audible salvos in the fierce discount wars was fired just a few years ago by Total Beverage, an innovative concept in retailing that offers terrific prices on beer, wine, soft drinks, bottled water and most any other liquid meant for public consumption — except hard liquor. In Virginia, unlike Washington, the hard stuff is sold only in state-run ABC (Alcoholic Beverage Control) stores.

Beyond grocery items, dollar-stretching Metro Washington shoppers who really do their homework — especially when it comes to purchasing big-ticket items — often turn to *Washington Consumers Checkbook* for objective product reviews and the inside scoop on where locally to find items at the best prices. Think of WCC as a kind of local version of that renowned bible of buying, *Consumer Reports*. The magazine is available by subscription and can also be found at many area bookstores and newsstands. Call (202) 347-7283 for more information.

In this chapter we offer something of a shopping tour of Metro Washington, spotlighting the major malls and other retail meccas by area, then compiling a list of more specialized stores by merchandise category. In no way do we claim to cover all the bases here.

A final note before we begin this potentially budget-busting journey into consumer nirvana: While the mega-malls and other shopping hubs of Metro Washington are indeed vital and deserve all the business they can get, remember the small merchants in your particular community when deciding where to spend those hard-earned dollars. Many of them were hit particularly hard during the economic downturn of the early 1990s and rely heavily on faithful local patrons to keep them afloat. For some items, these places can be just as competitive — and often far more convenient — than their larger rivals. While it wasn't feasible to try and assemble a substantive list of such businesses for inclusion in this chapter, we at least wanted to make a pitch for supporting them whenever possible and to urge shoppers to spread some of the wealth around.

www.insiders.com

See this and many other **Insiders' Guide®** destinations online — in their entirety.

Visit us today!

Malls and Prime Shopping Districts

Metro Washington

Washington, D.C. has a glamorous mall in almost every corner of the town, from Chevy Chase to Northeast. They're thriving places, attracting both tourists and city residents. We'd be remiss, however, if we didn't also mention several strips of prime shopping that don't classify as malls, since they aren't housed under one roof.

For example, Connecticut Avenue from Dupont Circle south to Pennsylvania Avenue, Northwest, and the blocks surrounding it, are a delightful mix of boutiques, salons, bookstores and very pricey designer shops, such as Burberry of London. Further east, one of Washington's largest department stores, Hecht's, takes up a city block at 12th and G Streets, NW. It is surrounded by plenty of smaller stores and restaurants, as well as being convenient to Metro Center metrorail station. Of course, Georgetown's Wisconsin Avenue and M Streets, Northwest, serve as the hub for dozens of boutiques, antique shops, bookstores, art galleries, restaurants and jewelry stores stretching north to New Mexico Avenue, south to K Street, east to 28th Street and west to 34th Street. Visitors often compare Georgetown to Greenwich Village and the place is a party, day or night. Don't miss an excursion here.

Besides the great districts we've described, Washington's malls are destinations in and of themselves. Here are some of the biggest and best.

Chevy Chase Pavilion
5345 Wisconsin Ave. NW, Washington, D.C. • (202) 686-5335

A lot of people think this mall, and its neighbor across the street — Mazza Gallerie — are in Maryland, but they're right over the line. And they're top of the line, too. The Pavilion houses the exclusive day spa and beauty salon, Georgette Klinger, as well as a number of artsy — and pricey — boutiques for men's and women's clothing, housewares, gourmet foods, and shoes. There's also The Limited, Honey Baked Ham, and the usual food court.

Georgetown Park
Wisconsin Ave. and M St. NW, Washington, D.C. • (202) 298-5577

There is no question that this is downtown's (as opposed to Chevy Chase, D.C.) most posh and complete mall. It's right in the heart of Georgetown and features three beautifully decorated and landscaped floors. It is so very lavish that much of the public is likely to be intimidated, which means it is rarely crowded, even at Christmas. Despite that, you'll find a lot of standard mall stores here — albeit upscale ones — like Ann Taylor and Caché and J. Crew. There are also exclusive designer boutiques like Alfred Sung and Ralph Lauren's Polo Shop. For youngsters, there's an FAO Schwartz superstore. Among the more interesting smaller shops to arrive recently are Artist's Proof, featuring autographed celebrity memorabilia, and Anatolia, which specializes in Turkish crafts and antiques. If you get hungry, you can stop at one of a half-dozen or so restaurants discreetly tucked away on the bottom floor, or pop next door for a quick bite at gourmet grocery, café and carry-out Dean & DeLuca.

Mazza Gallerie
5300 Wisconsin Ave., NW, Washington, D.C. • (202) 686-9515

This glass- and-marble structure is home to two national heavy hitters in retailing: Neiman Marcus and Filene's Basement. Aside from the big two, there are almost 50 other posh stores and boutiques here — including a fabulous jewelry store, Pampillonia, Godiva Chocolates and Laura Ashley Home.

Old Post Office Pavilion
Pennsylvania Ave. and 12th St. NW, Washington, D.C. • (202) 289-4224

If it's souvenirs or Washington memorabilia you want, this is the place to be. Rescued from demolition in the 1970s and later transformed into a shining star of the city's retail and tourism sectors, this is a don't-miss destination for shoppers, combining history, the second-highest vantage point in the city (take the glass elevator up to the 315-foot clock/bell tower), and of course dozens of shops and restaurants, including a spectacular food court.

The Shops at National Place
1331 Pennsylvania Ave. NW, Washington, D.C. • (202) 783-9090

This mall adjacent to the massive J.W. Marriott Hotel and the National Press Building is bustling with more than 90 shops, including some fascinating independent boutiques, mostly featuring women's clothing and jewelry. You'll also find such well-known mall staples as The Sharper Image, Banana Republic, The Limited and Victoria's Secret. There's a big food court that, at noon, is crowded with office workers.

Union Station
Massachusetts Ave. and First St. NE, Washington, D.C. • (202) 371-9441

Housed in the glorious 1907 Beaux Arts train station, the mall here features national chain clothing boutiques, a bookstore, a record store, a nine-screen cinema, and a food court — more than 100 shops in all. A separate section, the East Hall, offers a variety of jewelry and craft stalls, many selling unique ethnic merchandise. There is also a large selection of souvenirs and memorabilia. Stores of particular note include the U.S. Mint Shop (specializing in unique coin-themed items), The Great Train Store (a trove of railroad memorabilia), Political Americana (American political collectibles galore) and Made In America (brass and pewter Washington-themed desk accessories, patriotic gifts, jewelry and apparel). Despite its additional role as a shopping hub, Union Station chugs on as a working railroad station too, accommodating not only Metrorail but several commuter lines and Amtrak. While the station operates around the clock and the restaurants and theaters stay open fairly late, the stores operate regular mall retail hours. (So much for that 3 AM credit-card fix.)

Northern Virginia

The most varied and interesting shopping district in northern Virginia isn't even a mall — it's Old Town Alexandria. Begin at the easternmost end of King Street and work your way up — the array of stores is endless. There are antique shops, clothing boutiques for kids and adults, book stores and art galleries, craft shops, gourmet food emporiums and, when you get hungry, all manner of restaurants (see chapter on restaurants). The flagship of the area, though, is the Torpedo Factory Art Center and the adjacent minimall, at the intersection of Union and King. Local artists feature their work in side-by-side shops, all housed under one roof. Photographers, potters, jewelers, sculptors and painters are all showcased at the Torpedo Factory. See our Arts chapter for more information.

Other shops in Old Town with a charm all their own include Hats in the Belfry (112 King Street), specializing in funky and fun cranial creations; America (118 King Street), where flags, pins, patches, books and other items from all 50 states are sold with patriotic pride; the Pineapple Brass Shop (132 King Street), for authentic colonial reproduction brass pieces by Virginia metal crafters as well as handcarved duck decoys; Santa Fe Country (1218 King Street), whose treasure trove of American Southwest pottery, jewelry and food-stuffs is enough to make natives of Arizona and New Mexico homesick; and the Winterthur Museum Shop (207 King Street), an exten-sion of the Winterthur Museum in Delaware that features elegant American decorative-art houseware reproductions from 1640 to 1860.

In the northwestern part of the county, Reston Town Center (off Reston Parkway be-tween the Dulles Toll Road and Baron Cameron Avenue) is a hit with its striking architecture, pedestrian-friendly layout, and numerous pub-lic gathering spots. Some 70 shops — mostly specialty retailers such as The Gap and Ba-nana Republic — line the broad avenues. The food scene includes outdoor cafés like Clyde's and Paolo's (see the Restaurants chapter). There's also office space, a residential section (condo-mania), a public outdoor skating rink (see the Parks and Recreation chapter), an 11-screen cinema and, overlooking it all, the gor-geous Hyatt Regency Reston Town Center.

Not far from Reston is the Loudoun County line, and you won't find a mega-mall once you cross the border, but that probably suits many people just fine in this quiet area. The small towns and villages are still indeed alive with their own brand of retail activity.

Historic downtown Leesburg (intersection of Virginia Highways 7 and 15) offers more than 100 merchants, primarily specialty retail-ers stretching along Market and King streets. Leesburg's enchanting Market Station (cor-ner of Loudoun and Harrison streets) serves another 20 or so shops while, to the east, more than 250 stores are found in the Highway 7 corridor up to the Fairfax County line. This stretch includes the communities of Ashburn, Sterling, and Sterling Park.

Virginia's Prince William County offers two fun and funky shopping districts. Old Town Manassas (Virginia Highway 29, 7.5 miles off Interstate 66 in the city's downtown area), fea-tures nearly two dozen merchants. It could be that none of the stores are worth a special trip, but the old-fashioned town is charming, and if you happen to be in the area, it's worth a stroll. Also in Prince William County is the historic riverfront community of Occoquan (just off Interstate 95, about 10 miles south of the Capi-tal Beltway, but also accessible from the ex-treme southern end of Virginia Highway 123), with 120 merchants in a charming Victorian setting.

Aside from these half-dozen fun areas, malls are where most people shop in North-ern Virginia — and there are some doozies here. So without further ado, here's the scoop.

Ballston Common
4238 Wilson Blvd. at N. Glebe Rd., Arlington, Va. • (703) 243-8088

Just a one-block walk from the Ballston Metro station (Orange Line) at Fairfax Drive and N. Stuart Street, the mall features 100 spe-cialty stores on four floors, with a food court on the ground level. Hecht's and JC Penney are the anchors, but shops such as The Artist's Proof, with antique and other captivating pho-tographs, and A.J. Champions, featuring col-lectible sports memorabilia, help give Ballston its real appeal. Guys (and gals) take note: For great prices on top-quality dressy menswear, don't miss the Britches of Georgetowne store here, which serves as a consolidation outlet for the entire chain and thus offers some un-beatable bargains.

Crystal City Shops
U.S. Hwy. 1 between 15th and 23rd Sts., Arlington, Va. • (703) 922-4636

In the concrete and steel maze known as Crystal City, just off Jefferson Davis Highway (Route 1), are The Underground (on Crystal Drive, between 15th and 18th streets) and The Plaza Shops (corner of Crystal Drive and 23rd Street), two fascinating subterranean shopping experiences linked by a climate-controlled walkway. There are more than 125 stores, a movie theater, food court and numerous other restaurants. Specialty stores include Geppi's

Comic World and The Invention Store. Since these stores are covered by high-rise apartment and office buildings, they're hard to find, so it's good they're connected to Metrorail's Crystal City station (Blue and Yellow lines) at 18th Street and Jefferson Davis Highway.

Fair Oaks Mall
Intersection of U.S. Hwy. 50 and I-66, Fairfax, Va. • (703) 359-8300

This mega-mall of more than 200 stores makes a special effort to reach out to families, often using its center atrium for displays meant to appeal to kids, such as the animal-themed Christmas scenes, or for special events featuring children. Anchor stores are Lord & Taylor, Hecht's, Sears and JCPenney. Specialty retailers include Pacific Sunwear (teen fashions), Papyrus (gifts and stationery), Another Universe (science fiction and comics) and Virginia Peddler (country-style gifts and home items from the Old Dominion). There are also, of course, tons of dining options, including several casual, full-service, sit-down restaurants, as well as a freestanding cinema complex.

Fairfax Square
8045-75 Leesburg Pk., Vienna, Va. • (703) 827-0228

This classy shopping area sprouted from what used to be a big parking lot fronting Route 7 across from Tysons Corner mega-mall. It does a formidable Rodeo Drive impersonation with the likes of such ultra-upscale tenants as Tiffany & Co., Gucci, Louis Vuitton, Hermès and Fendi. There's also a multi-screen movie theater, and a Morton's of Chicago steakhouse and Chili's restaurant branch are adjacent.

Fairfax Town Center
Intersection of U.S. Hwy. 50 and West Ox Rd., Fairfax, Va.

A virtual next-door neighbor to Fair Oaks is one of the region's newest shopping experiences, Fairfax Town Center, which opened in late 1994. Gone are the days of unsightly strip shopping centers; make way for beautiful creations like this, where several dozen stores compete for attention in a snappy, well-designed, but oh-so-suburban setting. Major draws here include Tower Records, Bed Bath and Beyond, Zany Brainy (a children's educational superstore) and a United Artists movie theater.

Fashion Centre at Pentagon City
1100 S. Hayes St., Arlington, Va. • (703) 415-2400

Arlington County's premier retail showcase, Pentagon City, as it's customarily called, is one of the area's most exciting and dynamic shopping showplaces, a visual wonderland complete with towering skylights, palm trees, a sunlit food court, six-screen cinema and 130 stores spread over four levels. Anchor tenants are Macy's and Nordstrom; specialty shops include The Nature Company, Victoria's Secret, Bath & Body Works, The Disney Store, San Francisco Music Box Company, Britches of Georgetowne and Britches Great Outdoors. If all that walking and buying has left you too pooped to drive home, the snazzy Ritz-Carlton Hotel is right next door; in fact, it's joined to the mall and has its own entrance right off the promenade; however, you'd better have plenty of cash or credit left over if you plan on getting a room for the night.

Landmark Center
5801 Duke St. at I-395, Alexandria, Va. • (703) 941-2582

Alexandria's only enclosed shopping mall is Landmark Center, which some residents of neighboring Fairfax County happily call their own as well. Landmark underwent an extensive renovation, expansion and general marketing makeover several years ago that has done wonders for aesthetics and business. The "new" two-level Landmark offers a wealth of (free) covered and surface parking and some 150 stores and restaurants (but no movie theaters), including anchor tenants Hecht's and Sears.

Springfield Mall Regional Shopping Center
Intersection of Franconia and Loisdale Rds., Springfield, Va. • (703) 971-3000

This mall has local bragging rights when it comes to sheer size: close to 300 stores, including Macy's and JCPenney, since its extensive renovation and expansion a few years back. For a place this size, there's a dearth of restaurants. Aside from the ground level food court, there's only a Ruby Tuesday and a Bennigan's. Some of the most recent — and most interesting — additions to the retail lineup include Ultrazone (a virtual reality game room), a carousel and play area, World Artisan (crafts from around the globe), The One 800 Store (merchandise from TV shopping networks) and African Corner (African-inspired merchandise). Due to its convenient southeastern Fairfax location, just a few hundred yards off I-95 near the I-395 interchange, Springfield Mall is popular with District residents as well as shoppers from points south including Woodbridge, Fredericksburg and the large military community in Quantico.

Conveniently, just across Frontier Drive (by Macy's) from the mall is a mini shopping center that opened in late 1994. It's anchored by Best Buy, one of the growing number of retailers offering rock-bottom prices on major appliances and consumer electronics (TVs, stereo, VCRs and the like). Be sure to check out the superb prices on CDs and tapes, too. Best Buy has become a living nightmare for veteran retailers of the same genre such as Circuit City, which is being given a major run for its money (and customers). There are also a couple of restaurants and several other stores in the center including a PetSmart superstore (complete with veterinary and grooming services) for Fido, Fluffy and all the rest of our four-legged friends. You'll also find Upton's department store just across the road, and new retail player, Kohl's, just minutes away.

Tysons Corner Center and Tysons Galleria
Intersection of Virginia Hwys. 123 and 7, Vienna, Va. • (703) 827-7700, (703) 893-9400

Tysons Corner and Tysons Galleria (also known as Tysons II), are the shining jewels in Fairfax County's economic crown. Shoppers from throughout the region flock to Tysons Corner Center and its nearly 250 stores including Nordstrom, Bloomingdale's, Lord & Taylor, Hecht's, Brooks Brothers and Eddie Bauer. The requisite restaurants and movie theaters add to its appeal. Tysons is one of the area's oldest shopping malls (opened in the early 1970s), but you wouldn't know it. Like so many of its peers, Tysons experienced a rebirth during the mid 1980s with a major renovation and expansion that dramatically enhanced its look and customer-friendliness. Among the most welcome changes were the addition of parking decks and the conversion of underground truck tunnels into rows of specialty shops.

As if "Tysons I" wasn't enough, there's The Galleria at Tysons II (2001 International Drive), just across Chain Bridge Road (Route 123) from Tysons Corner Center and adjacent to the Ritz-Carlton Hotel. This 123-store showplace is upscale to the nth degree, with Macy's, Saks Fifth Avenue, Neiman Marcus and other posh retailers strutting their stuff. Recent additions include an FAO Schwartz superstore, Lapin (children's apparel), Lesac (French clothing and accessories) and the cleverly named maternity-clothing retailer, A Pea in the Pod. Even many of the food joints are upper crust, with Legal Seafoods an especially good bet.

If these two malls don't hold your interest, cross Highway 7 and you'll discover a series of strip malls housing car dealers, restaurants, hotels, specialty stores and large chain outlets such as Tower Records, Borders Book Shop, Sports Authority, Marshall's, Toys 'R' Us and CompUSA.

Suburban Maryland

Maryland's got malls all right, but it also has some of the priciest shopping streets around, and we'd like to touch on them before you immerse yourself in the under-one-roof experience.

Chevy Chase, Maryland — the name is synonymous with money and power. As befits such a location, you'll find some of the most glamorous retailers around here. At 5555 Wisconsin Avenue, in an area known as Friendship Heights, Saks Fifth Avenue has stood sentinel for more than three decades. This huge, stately store has almost all the cachet of the original on New York's Fifth Avenue, and its very presence has served as a catalyst for dozens of other exclusive shops to locate nearby.

Across Wisconsin Avenue, you'll find the kind of women's shops where dresses are brought out from the back for you to try on, and service is always the utmost in personal courtesy. Saks-Jandel, 5510 Wisconsin Avenue, is a Washington retailer known worldwide as a premier furrier and designer boutique. Wander south from there, or cross the street, and you'll be immersed in yet more glamour, culminating in D.C.'s Mazza Gallerie and Chevy Chase Pavilion (see this chapter's listings), just across the state line, and only two blocks away.

Drive north from Chevy Chase on Wisconsin Avenue, and you'll hit Bethesda. No matter which way you look, you'll see blocks and blocks of stores, stores, stores. There are stores that sell furniture, Oriental rugs, furs, art, clothing, shoes, toys, books and anything else you can dream up. This shopper's paradise goes on for approximately two square miles, culminating at Wilson Boulevard to the west, and Cordell Avenue to the north.

No matter how great a shopping district is, on a blowy, winter day or a sticky, summer day, a mall can be a refuge. Here are some of the biggest and best in the metro area's Maryland.

Beltway Plaza Regional Mall
1835 University Blvd., Hyattsville, Md.
• (301) 422-3300

Serving nearby University of Maryland and Prince George's County, this mall features stores like Sports Authority, Jeepers! For Kids, Caldor and, as an added convenience, the area's largest Giant Food grocery. In all, there are more than 125 fashion and specialty stores as well as 14 movie theaters and a food court.

Lakeforest Mall
701 Russell Ave., Gaithersburg, Md.
• (301) 840-5840

In northern Montgomery County, sprawl-

ing Lakeforest Mall offers anchor stores such as Hecht's, Sears and JCPenney, plus a whopping 160 other stores, five theaters and more than a dozen restaurants. Specialty stores are along the lines of The Gap and The Limited.

Landover Mall
Brightseat Rd. and Hamlin St., Landover, Md. • (301) 341-3200

This is by far the biggest mall in Prince George's County, offering more than 160 stores and specialty shops. The big department stores here are Hecht's and Sears. For kids, there's also a Virtual Reality game store, six movie theaters, and lots of fast food eateries.

Montgomery Mall
7101 Democracy Blvd., Bethesda, Md. • (301) 469-6000

More than 200 shops guarantee that a full day is needed to explore this marble, brass and glass mall in wealthy Montgomery County. There's Nordstrom, Sears, JCPenney, Hecht's, just to name the anchor stores. All the usual boutiques like Ann Taylor and The Limited are here, too, along with a movie theater and trendy mall restaurants like California Pizza Kitchen. Some not-so-usual boutiques include the African Art Gallery, which specializes in statues and crafts; Ancient Echoes, with wind chimes, aromatherapy, and New Age books and music; and Bebe, a trendy women's boutique.

Wheaton Plaza Shopping Center
11160 Viers Mill Rd., Wheaton, Md. • (301) 946-3200

This mall, once a bit down-at-the-heels, has been revamped in recent years and has gotten to be quite snazzy. It's in a solidly middle class area, though, so stores don't feature the type of upscale merchandise you see in other Montgomery County malls — and that may be all to the good, depending on your budget. There are 120 stores here, including Hecht's, a Washington department store that's pricier than Sears, but less so than Nordstrom. Indeed, Sears and JCPenney are two of Wheaton Plaza's other anchor stores, along with 120 smaller places, restaurants and cinemas.

White Flint Mall
11301 Rockville Pk., North Bethesda, Md. • (301) 468-5777

Montgomery Mall may be upscale, but White Flint is more so. The biggest stores here are Bloomingdale's and Lord & Taylor, but there's also a giant Borders Books & Music as well as the new trendy adult amusement center/restaurant known as Dave & Buster's (see the Nightlife chapter). Tucked away in the mall's nooks and crannies are some pricey independent boutiques offering avant-garde merchandise. For example, check out Aram for cocktail dresses.

Outlet Malls

They literally bring 'em in by the busloads at outlet malls, particularly the nation's largest, Potomac Mills near Woodbridge, Virginia. Since people are willing to drive long distances to visit these places, and since there aren't too many of them in Metro Washington, we haven't broken them down by geographic region, but have rather listed them alphabetically. If outlet shopping is your passion, you may want to pick up a copy of *The Outlet Shopper: A Guide to Factory Outlet Shopping in Pennsylvania, Maryland, Virginia and the District of Columbia*, by Carolyn Vogel Benson. It's published locally by The Washington Book Trading Co., P.O. Box 1676, Arlington, Virginia 22210, (703) 525-6873.

You'll notice that we've included a few destinations several hours from Washington. That's because a lot of Washingtonians make a day trip of visiting these places, and we thought it only fair to tell you about them. Within an hour of Washington, you'll find the following two:

City Place Mall
8661 Colesville Rd., Silver Spring, Md. • (301) 589-1091

City Place (Colesville Road and Fenton Street) is an outlet-shopper's paradise with five levels of off-price shopping. Among the stores you'll find here are Nordstroms Rack, Marshalls, Ross, 9 West (shoes), Fashion Warehouse (women's apparel for as little as $10), Delana's Fashions (women's apparel) and Metro Tunes (specializing in go-go music tapes). There's also a food court and a 10-theater cinema.

Potomac Mills Outlet Mall
2700 Potomac Mills Cir., near Woodbridge, Va. • (703) 643-1054

It says something about the power of shopping when the No. 1 tourist destination in history- and scenery-rich Virginia is an outlet mall, namely Potomac Mills.

Just 15 miles south of Washington off I-95 (you can't miss the signs), Potomac Mills more than lives up to its billing as a paradise for shoppers, especially those with a penchant for savings. The 220 or so off-price and outlet stores include IKEA, Waccamaw Pottery, Nordstrom Rack, Saks Fifth Avenue Outlet, Escada, Guess, Royal Doulton, Mikasa, Nike, Ray-Ban, Eddie Bauer, Guess, American Tourister, Calvin Klein, Levi's and Laura Ashley. Since colossal isn't quite big enough, new tenants keep arriving. Among the latest to make the scene are Bally of Switzerland (shoes and other fine leather goods), Boston Trader (outdoor wear), Panasonic and Tecnics (electronics) and Applause (Sesame Street and Disney goods). Kids and parents alike will love the famous "ball room" at IKEA, where little ones can romp amidst colorful rubber balls to their heart's delight under adult supervision while Mom and Dad stroll the labyrinth of aisles. In case you hadn't guessed, there's a food court and three sit-down restaurants. The mall has also spawned dozens of stores in the acres of pavement surrounding it.

Distant Outlet Malls

If you're willing to travel two hours or so for your bargains — say to outlet meccas in Reading, Pennsylvania or Martinsburg, West Virginia — your choices broaden, and you'll find acres of malls clustered together.

Blue Ridge Outlet Center
315 W. Stephen St., Martinsburg, W. Va. • (800) 445-3993

Book Warehouse, Corning, Jones New York, Leather Loft, Lenox, London Fog, 9 West and Toy Liquidators are just some of the stores at this sprawling outlet that covers everything from lingerie to housewares.

Massaponax Outlet Center
5132 S. Point Pkwy., Fredericksburg, Va. • (540) 891-8676

This smaller outlet center boasts some uncommon stores. If you're a smoker, head for the Virginia Factory Cigarette Outlet. Women seeking larger-sized clothing will appreciate Size Unlimited, which features clothing up to size 32. There's also Hat Barn, Bass Shoes, Libbey Glass, Springmaid, Paper Factory (party goods and stationery) and Rack Room shoes.

The Reading Outlet Center
801 N. Ninth St., Reading, Pa. • (610) 373-5495

The Reading Outlet Center claims to be the first outlet mall in the United States, and it serves as the hub in a town full of off-price malls for which Reading has become famous up and down the east coast. The Reading Outlet center began as a trading post in the 19th century, and then served as a hosiery mill. In the 1960s, it was transformed into an outlet center for several textile manufacturers who sold overruns and imperfects to their employees at bargain prices. A few years later, the mall opened to the public and it was such a hit that . . . well, the rest is history as the number of outlet malls across America will testify. Today, the Reading Center features upscale stores like Laura Ashley, Tommy Hilfiger, J. Crew and Pier 1 Imports. Nearby are a cluster of other similar malls, including Reading Station at Sixth and Spring streets, (610) 478-7000.

Tanger Factory Outlet Center
Foxcraft Ave. and W. King St., Martinsburg, W. Va. • (800) 727-6885

There are only nine stores at this small outlet strip mall, but they include some well-known names: American Tourister, Bass Shoes, Eagle's Eye (women's apparel), Geoffrey Beene, Reebok, Oshkosh B'Gosh, Liz Claiborne, Oneida and Van Heusen.

Bookstores

We thought it appropriate to offer a handy guide to some of the area's best bookstores — those places with such a wealth of resources (including maps, out-of-town newspapers and local see-and-do/history guides) that they're invaluable to newcomers. Visit them often enough and you've made friends with some of the most helpful and knowledgeable people around. Remember, too, that Washington's many museums and universities feature gift and book shops worth exploring, and we've listed a couple of noteworthy ones in the book-store category as well as our category later in the chapter on museum shops.

Of course, you've heard of the large chains — and they're wonderful in terms of size and variety of stock. In Washington, Maryland and Virginia, you'll find numerous branches, mostly in malls, of superstores like B. Dalton Book-seller, Barnes & Noble, Borders, Brentano's, Super Crown (and Crown) Books, Tower Books, Doubleday Book Shop, Waldenbooks and Rand McNally Map & Travel Store. Most of these places have cushy reading chairs, coffee shops and plenty of special events — they're great places to while away a lazy after-noon. There is probably one near you whether you're in Washington, Maryland or Virginia, so consult the phone directory. Also, if you happen to be in either National or Dulles air-ports, check out the wide selection at Ben-jamin Books, a national chain that has up-graded the standards for airport bookstores.

Aside from the excellent chains mentioned above, Washington is also blessed with a wealth of fine independent bookstores, many of which offer similarly inviting atmospheres. Check them out. The following are among those we especially enjoy.

Washington, D.C.

Atticus Books & Music
1508 U St. NW, Washington, D.C.
• (202) 667-8148
This is an antiquarian bookstore featuring out-of-print and used volumes, and extensive specialty sections, such as gay and lesbian studies and African-American writing. They also have a good selection of comics, music and poetry. Weekly fiction readings are a highlight.

Bridge Street Books
2814 Pennsylvania Ave. NW,
Washington, D.C. • (202) 965-5200
This intimate bookstore at the edge of Georgetown specializes in esoteric subjects like religion, Judaica, philosophy, political sci-ence and cultural theory.

Chapters
1512 K Street NW, Washington, D.C.
• (202) 347-5495
Chapters, an independent book store, has a good general selection of popular fiction, literature and political tomes. Conveniently lo-cated in the downtown office corridor along K Street, Chapters also has a small gift section, as well as books on tape.

Cleveland Park Book Shop
3416 Wisconsin Avenue NW,
Washington, D.C. • (202) 363-1112
On upper Wisconsin Avenue, this friendly neighborhood spot features all kinds of high-brow specialty volumes as well as picture books on travel and gardening. Like most indepen-dents, they're happy to order what you can't find on the shelves. Definitely part of the sur-rounding community, this store draws custom-ers with regular author signings as well as con-veniences like shipping, wrapping, and book accessories.

Franz Bader Bookstore
1911 Eye St. NW, Washington, D.C.
• (202) 337-5440
If it's a gorgeous picture book you're after, this is the place. Franz Bader specializes in

---

INSIDERS' TIP

While shopping in Old Town Alexandria, you should know that one of the best places to grab a quick bite of lunch is Deli on the Strand, on S. Union Street. You can't go wrong with the delicious selection of sandwiches served on fresh-baked mini loaves of bread. On nice days, be sure to enjoy your feast by the banks of the Potomac River — just a short stroll away.

books on the visual arts — design, graphics, photography and architecture — and most of their selections are breathtaking. Even if you don't buy, this place is worth a look for the sheer beauty of the photographs you'll see.

Glover Books & Music

2319 Wisconsin Ave. NW, Washington, D.C. • (202) 338-8100

Not only does this store have a wide selection of popular books for adults and children, but it also features sheet music, videos, computer software, and tickets for shows and sports events — it's a great all-around stop conveniently located in the cozy Glover Park neighborhood of upper Georgetown.

Health Source Bookstore

1404 K St. NW, Washington, D.C. • (202) 789-7303

Anything to do with mainstream or alternative medicine, you'll find at Health Source. There are books on nutrition (including cook books), parenting, pregnancy, psychology, self-help, nursing, diet and exercise. There's a huge selection of reference guides as well.

International Language Center

1753 Connecticut Ave. NW, Washington, D.C. • (202) 332-2894

If you're a foreign tourist in Washington, you may want to stop in here for books, magazines, videos and newspapers in more than 100 languages. If you're an American going abroad, drop by to get a feel for the culture you'll be visiting.

Kramerbooks & Afterwords

1517 Connecticut Ave. NW, Washington, D.C. • (202) 232-7481

This Washington mainstay is crowded day and night, thanks to its great, full service restaurant and outdoor café, and its central location at the hub of Dupont Circle activity. Political books and big bios are always featured in the window, as well as tomes on economics, philosophy, religion and gay/lesbian studies. The selection here is large enough to include plenty of beach reading and guides to everything under the sun.

The Map Store

1636 I St. NW, Washington, D.C. • (202) 628-2608

This little shop has been around for a quarter of a century, and continues to be a popular browsing spot for those who love to travel. Not only does the shop carry every kind of map imaginable, but it also features a nice selection of travel books, including narratives and guides.

Olsson's Books & Records

1239 Wisconsin Ave. NW, Washington, D.C. • (202) 338-9544
1307 19th St. NW, Washington, D.C. • (202) 785-1133
1200 F St. NW, Washington, D.C. • (202) 347-3686
418 7th St. NW, Washington, D.C. • (202) 638-7610

In the heart of Georgetown, as well as in other convenient spots, this popular shop is one of the largest independents in the Washington Metro area, with more than 100,000 titles in stock. You're bound to find what you're looking for in both the music and book departments. There is a very large cookbook section, as well as plenty on subjects ranging from the military to psychology and self-help. If a suburban location is more convenient, check out their store in Bethesda, Maryland, 7647 Old Georgetown Road, (301) 652-3336, or in Old Town Alexandria, Virginia, 106 S. Union Street, (703) 684-0077.

Parks and History Association Bookstore

126 Raleigh St. SE, Washington, D.C. • (202) 472-3083, (800) 990-PARK

This is the store for all manner of Washingtoniana memorabilia, as well as books on natural and environmental history. There are hardbacks, paperbacks and books for kids, as well as videos, maps and posters.

Politics & Prose Bookstore & Coffeehouse

5015 Connecticut Ave. NW, Washington, D.C. • (202) 364-1919

This bookstore is very highly thought of by Washington's intelligentsia, thanks to the personal touch of the owners and their savvy blend of the latest and most popular books, as well as the obscure. Washington authors always

Potomac Mills is Virginia's No. 1 tourist attraction.

get the spotlight here, and there are frequent readings, coffees and signings by local and national celebrities.

Reiter's Scientific and Professional Books
2021 K St. NW, Washington, D.C.
• (202) 223-3327
Reiter's claims to have more than 60,000 scientific and technical books, including tomes on computers, math, physics, engineering, medicine, nursing, business and psychology. They'll also make a special effort to hunt down anything not in stock.

Reprint Bookshop
455 L'Enfant Plaza SW, Washington, D.C.
• (202) 554-5070
Ignore the name, which originates from the fact that the shop only sold paperbacks when it opened 40 years ago (and paperbacks are, of course, reprints of hardcover books). Now, the store sells all kinds of popular fiction, nonfiction, literature and, naturally, paperbacks. Specialties include African-American literature as well as computer guides.

Second Story Books
2000 P St. NW, Washington, D.C.
• (202) 659-8884
Another Dupont Circle institution — the store's been here for 20 years — Second Story

features old and rare books, first editions, fine bound volumes, or those that are just plain used. If you're looking for something unique or just hard-to-find, try this shop. If a branch in Maryland is more convenient, drop in at 12160 Parklawn Drive, Rockville, (301) 770-0477, or 4836 Bethesda Avenue, Bethesda, (301) 656-0170.

Trover Shop
221 Pennsylvania Ave. SE, Washington, D.C. • (202) 543-8006
1250 Eye St. NW, Washington, D.C.
• (202) 659-8138
This independent has been around for 40 years, and continues to be popular with busy Capitol Hill office workers as well as the lobbyists, lawyers and White House types who frequent the midtown location. Right near the Library of Congress, the Pennsylvania Avenue shop specializes in political science, though there is plenty of lunch-hour escape reading to be found, too.

Northern Virginia

The Book Chase
102 W. Washington St., Middleburg, Va.
• (540) 687-6874, (800) 373-7323
This small bookstore makes a nice browsing break from the shopping in Middleburg's

antique district. You'll find guidebooks, as well as popular fiction, magazines, and volumes on local interest.

George Mason University Bookstore
Student Union Building 2, 4400 University Dr., Fairfax, Va.
• **(703) 993-2665**

There aren't many bookstores in this residential section of Fairfax, so the university bookstore is a blessing — a well-stocked emporium that also carries all manner of accessories and stationery. Not only will you find textbooks, but also popular and classic fiction, as well as nonfiction.

Olsson's Books & Records
106 S. Union St., Alexandria, Va.
• **(703) 684-0077**

To learn more about this Old Town location overlooking the Potomac River, please see the Washington, D.C. listing.

The Pentagon Bookstore
6917 Pentagon Concourse, Arlington, Va.
• **(703) 486-2665**

If you want to visit this bookstore in the sprawling Pentagon, you have to call when you arrive and be escorted in, which is an experience in and of itself. Once inside, you'll find all manner of books on history and the military, as well as more general subjects such as psychology, self-help, religion and careers. There's also the usual selection of paperbacks and best sellers.

Scribner's Bookstore
The Fashion Centre at Pentagon City, Arlington, Va. • **(703) 415-2005**

If the name sounds familiar, it's because Scribner's is indeed part of a national chain (which also owns Barnes & Noble), but it is the only Scribner's in the Washington area, so

we thought it worth a mention. This is a general bookstore conveniently located in one of the area's most popular shopping malls.

Suburban Maryland

Fort Washington Park Visitor Center Bookstore
13551 Fort Washington Rd., Ft. Washington, Md. • **(301) 763-4600**

This bookstore, on the grounds of the national park of the same name, features historical volumes, local guides and gifts.

Maryland Book Exchange
4500 College Ave., College Park, Md.
• **(301) 927-2510**

University of Maryland is one of the largest in the nation, with some 40,000 students, so it makes sense that this bookstore would be equally comprehensive. There are more than 100,000 volumes here and 90,000 titles — that's right, we haven't mistakenly added any zeroes. Of course there are text and reference books, as well as fiction and nonfiction best sellers, used books and all manner of accessories.

Mystery Bookshop Bethesda
7700 Old Georgetown Rd., Bethesda, Md.
• **(301) 657-2665**

This fun spot has a motto, "So many mysteries . . . so little time." As the name states, it specializes in murder mysteries, mostly new, some used. You'll find about 20,000 titles here, which is a lot considering that the very largest general independents have about 100,000 titles on all subjects.

Olsson's Books & Records
7647 Old Georgetown Road, Bethesda, Md. • **(301) 652-3336**

Please see the Washington, D.C. listing.

INSIDERS' TIP

If you live in Virginia but think you might save a few bucks by stocking up on distilled spirits at independently operated liquor stores in the District or Maryland, be aware that there are limits on the amount of alcohol that can be purchased for transport across state lines. It's a good idea to first check with local authorities to see what the law allows.

Second Story Books

12160 Parklawn Drive, Rockville, Md.
• (301) 770-0477
4836 Bethesda Avenue, Bethesda, Md.
• (301) 656-0170

Please see the Washington, D.C. listing.

Travel Books & Language Center

4931 Cordell Ave., Bethesda, Md.
• (301) 951-8533

This good-sized shop is crammed with books on every facet of travel. There are narratives, first-person accounts, coffee-table books, adventure stories, guides, foreign-language dictionaries and primers, maps, and books on travel-related industries. If you're going to an exotic location, you'll find a guide here. There are also useful books on medical care in foreign countries, travel careers and sports-oriented travel.

Metro-Area Newsstands

A special note should be made of the following stores which do a good job of specializing in those hard-to-find newspapers and magazines, including those in foreign languages.

Book-N-Card

8110 Arlington Blvd., Falls Church, Va.
• (703) 560-6999

This convenient shop in the Yorktowne Center, at the intersection of Interstate Highway 50 (Arlington Boulevard) and Gallows Road, stocks some 5,000 magazine titles — all English language — and a number of mid-Atlantic daily newspapers.

Glover Books & Music

2319 Wisconsin Ave. NW, Washington, D.C. • (202) 338-8100

See the listing under Washington, D.C. bookstores.

International Language Center

1753 Connecticut Ave. NW, Washington, D.C. • (202) 332-2894

See the listing under Washington, D.C. bookstores.

The Newsroom

1753 Connecticut Ave. NW, Washington, D.C. • (202) 332-1489

This spot features newspapers from most major U.S. cities as well as periodicals from all over the world. It's Dupont Circle location draws a colorful mix of browsers — and the management tolerates lengthy browsing.

News World

1001 Connecticut Ave. NW, Washington, D.C. • (202) 872-0190

Like The Newsroom above, this store features thousands of titles — magazines and newspapers from around the world.

Old Towne News

721 King St., Alexandria, Va.
• (703) 739-9024

This spot, conveniently located amidst the boutiques and restaurants of Old Town Alexandria, carries a wide variety of international newspapers and international magazines, as well as a large stock of those published in the United States.

Sully Plaza News

13916 Lee-Jackson Hwy., Chantilly, Va.
• (703) 263-9190

This newsstand offers an extensive selection of U.S.-published magazines and several daily newspapers from the mid-Atlantic and northeastern parts of the country.

Secondhand Stores

Outlet malls may offer bargains, but if you want something even more economical — or more offbeat — you may want to check out the area's numerous secondhand shops, many of which offer great bargains in designer clothing. Some of the more upscale include:

Classic Vintage Company, Inc.

3194 Bladensburg Rd. NE, Washington, D.C. • (202) 397-7121

This used clothing store buys and sells clothes from the '50s through the '80s.

Encore Resale Dress Shop

3715 Macomb St. NW, Washington, D.C.
• (202) 966-8122

On a genteel Cleveland Park side street, Encore has access to Washington's old money and their castoffs. The designer clothes and furs here can be great bargains, classics that often look like they came from Paris.

Once Is Not Enough
4830 MacArthur Blvd. NW, Washington, D.C. • (202) 337-3072

Socialites from ritzy Foxhall bring their once-used gowns and designer suits here for resale. There are some real bargains, including barely worn Tahari, Calvin Klein, Christian Lacroix and . . . well, the list goes on and on.

Second Chance
7702 Woodmont Ave., Bethesda, Md. • (301) 652-6606

Only top-quality, contemporary designer clothes and accessories are featured at Second Chance. You'll find a room packed with glamorous evening wear, funky, fashionable shoes, furs, sportswear and all manner of jewelry, purses, belts and scarves.

Second Hand Rose
1516 Wisconsin Ave., NW, Washington, D.C. • (202) 337-3378

If vintage clothing is your thing, check out this boutique, which features not only modern items, but also those lace-and-feather confections from yesteryear.

Secondi
1702 Connecticut Ave. NW, Washington, D.C. • (202) 667-1122

High style consignment clothing for men and women is offered in this small boutique, tucked away two blocks north of Dupont Circle. Donna Karan, Coach and Banana Republic are some of the designers you'll most frequently find here.

Secondhand Furniture

Consignment Galleries
3226 Wisconsin Ave. NW, Washington, D.C. • (202) 364-8995

This shop displays quality furniture and accessories in a charming showroom that gives you a good idea of how the other half lives. The nice thing is, you can have a piece of the good life for less-than-new prices.

Even if you're only looking for something small, this place is worth a stop. You'll find French and Italian crockery, oil paintings, whimsical lamps, Oriental screens . . . just about any style and period you can imagine.

Cordell Collection Furniture
4911 Cordell Ave., Bethesda, Md. • (301) 907-3324

In the heart of Bethesda, you'd expect to find the best in used furniture, and this shop delivers. There are antiques, reproductions and collectibles artfully blended to inspire the imagination. Prices are not cheap, but some of the pieces are in the category of "they just don't make 'em like that any more."

Upscale Resale
1456 Duke St., Alexandria, Va.
• (703) 683-3333
8100 Lee Hwy., Falls Church, Va.
• (703) 698-8100

Maybe it's the catchy name, but this has become one of the premier shops in Metro Washington for high quality secondhand furniture. This store is picky about what it carries, and its showroom is attractive and classy. There are a lot of wealthy people in Washington, and it looks like some of them have left their discards here on consignment — maybe the remainder have picked up a few pieces here?

Antique Districts, Auctions and Flea Markets

Washingtonians have an insatiable appetite for antique paintings, furniture and bric-a-brac, as demonstrated by the numerous districts and shops specializing in such merchandise. Maybe it's because there are so many historic buildings and neighborhoods in the region, or maybe it's the conservative colonial architecture of even the newest homes. Whatever the reason, there are antique emporiums for the most serious of collectors as well as those who just like to dabble.

Auctions, too, are popular here, and you

can find some real bargains if you know what you're doing. Beware: you may be seized by bidding fever and pay more than you should. If you go to an auction, carefully examine the item you wish to bid on in advance.

Antique shops often buy from the same auctions you attend, then mark up the items by as much as 100 percent, a necessity when you consider that they must pay rent, salaries, insurance and all the other incidentals associated with owning a business. Still, antique shops are a good place to get an education on quality and construction. Many are sleepy little stores where the proprietors are happy to share their knowledge. Owners realize that a browser today may be a paying customer tomorrow, so don't be shy about asking questions.

Flea markets, of which there are several in the Washington area, are a bit of a hybrid between antique stores and plain old thrift shops. If you don't mind sifting through a lot of junk, you can find some nice pieces, but don't expect to discover a Van Gogh in that stack of dusty paintings propped in the corner. Owners are savvy.

If variety is what you're after, you'll want to stroll through one of Washington's several antique districts. One of the foremost is Georgetown in Washington, D.C., which has stores on every block offering serious furniture and accessories like grandfather clocks, 19th-century paintings and sterling. These are the shops that furnish those mansions hidden along the side streets, so expect to fork over serious bucks.

If your budget is more restrained, you might venture to Howard Avenue in Kensington, Maryland. This is one of the foremost antique districts in the mid-Atlantic, with store after store featuring genuine antiques, reproductions, lighting and other accessories. It's serious, but not as rarefied as Georgetown. On the streets branching out from Howard, you'll discover furniture makers and restoration experts who provide value for the money. Nothing here is cheap, but the quality is good.

The cobbled streets of Old Town Alexandria in Virginia will lead you to dozens of antique shops. King Street from the west end of town to the river offers stores that stock everything from genuine Persian rugs (pre-embargo antiques), to French, English and American period furniture. The streets that intersect King (Washington, Asaph, Royal), as well as those parallel to it (Cameron, Prince), likewise offer many specialty antique stores with merchandise such as chandeliers, mirrors, tableware and art. Quality varies widely from store to store, and the search here could easily occupy several days, depending on how long you linger at each shop.

Along the western stretches of U.S. Highway 50 in Virginia, hunt country delights are the name of the game in the Middleburg Historic Shopping District. The tiny burg offers a fair number of stores for its size, many along Washington and Madison streets. Middleburg's antique specialties run the gamut from hunt prints and accessories to period furniture and jewelry. Be sure to check out the Middleburg Antiques Center (105 West Washington Street) for fine estate items, rugs, lamps and silver.

So . . . ready to explore? It'll take you a long time to cover all Metro Washington has to offer, so you better get started!

Alexandria House of Antiques
124 South West St., Alexandria, Va.
• (703) 836-3912

At this conglomeration of 20 dealers under one roof, you'll find items ranging from Civil War memorabilia to Audubon art, sterling, collectibles, crystal, jewelry and furniture.

Chevy Chase Antique Center
5215 Wisconsin Ave., NW, Washington, D.C. • (202) 364-4600

This is a high class collection of over 75 dealers offering fine porcelain; 18th through 20th century furniture, paintings and accessories; objets d'art, Middle- and Far-Eastern antiquities and estate jewelry. This is where you'll also find specialists in every aspect of antique restoration and repair.

Laws Auction & Antiques
7209 Centreville Rd., Manassas, Va.
• (703) 631-0590

Auctions take place several days a week here, and a lot of the merchandise is junk — which the owners unabashedly admit during the proceedings. There are also some bargains to be had though, particularly when there's a catalogue auction. At such times, you may discover some fine early 20th-century and 19th-century furniture and decorative items. More often, you'll find decent reproductions and lots of rococo, European-style furniture. Across the gravel drive from the auction gallery is an antiques mall, with shops ranging from serious purveyors of 19th-century furniture to those selling cutesy country-style pieces.

Old Market Antiques
442 S. Washington St., Falls Church, Va.
• **(703) 241-1722**
There are more than 30 shops in this 10,000-square-foot space offering furniture from Mission- to European-style. You'll also find antique tools, trunks and textiles.

Sloan's Auction Galleries
4920 Wyaconda Rd., Rockville, Md.
• **(301) 468-4911**
Sloan's offers everything from nice reproductions to serious furniture, paintings and jewelry. The serious stuff is featured at multiday catalogue auctions with plenty of advance notice and several days set aside for previewing. Less valuable items are sold every Thursday in what Sloan's terms "attic" auctions. This business is family-owned and highly respected, though no Washington auctioneers are considered to be on a par with New York's Sotheby's or Christie's.

Thieves Market
8101 Richmond Hwy., Alexandria, Va.
• **(703) 360-4200**
This huge, dusty warehouse on raffish Richmond Highway has been around for more than 40 years, and every Washingtonian who collects antiques knows about it. It's only open on weekends, and you have to sift through a lot of merchandise to find something truly worthwhile, but it's fun to poke around among the old paintings, rugs, furniture, coins, china and other bric-a-brac.

Washington Antiques Center
6708 Wisconsin Ave., Bethesda, Md.
• **(301) 654-3798**
Bethesda is an upscale place and the 20 shops collected here are likewise upscale. You'll discover fine art, period furniture and decorative objects fit for estates from Georgetown to Potomac.

Adam Weschler & Son Fine Art Auctioneers and Appraisers
909 E St. NW, Washington, D.C.
• **(202) 628-1281**
Since 1890, Weschler's has been a premier spot for those interested in fine antique furniture, jewelry, paintings and decorative items — hardly any schlock here. There are auctions every Tuesday as well as special catalogue events. This is a highly reputable house offering some very nice pieces, but the people who shop here — including dealers — usually know what they're doing, so bargains may be snapped up from under your nose if you're an amateur.

Furniture and Home Decorating

With so many people moving in and out of the D.C. area all the time, it's no wonder that furniture stores here thrive. There are stores to fit every budget — sprawling furniture warehouses to high-style designer shops.

Of course, every mall has a Pottery Barn or Crate & Barrel, both great stores for picking up smart home accents at a reasonable price. If you've lived in the United States within the last five years, you know all about these places, so we won't waste space on descriptions. Instead, we'll try to give you an overview of stores particular to the region, hit the highlights, and get you started. By no means is this a comprehensive list, and for more ideas, consult your telephone directory, the home section in Thursday's *Washington Post*, the ads in *Washingtonian* magazine, and the regional advertising pages in *Architectural Digest*. Note that our list is alphabetical rather than geographical. If you're like us, borders don't matter in your quest for just the right piece!

Danker Furniture
120 Halpine Rd., Rockville, Md.
• **(301) 881-6010**
10670 Lee Hwy., Fairfax, Va.
• **(703) 691-4333**
This place is as swank as a large furniture store gets. Pieces are high-style and high-qual-

One of the nation's most extensive historic districts, Old Town Alexandria combines specialty shops, boutiques, restaurants and nightclubs with 18th-century cobblestone streets and architecture.

Photo: Courtesy of Virginia Department of Economic Development

ity, ranging from Chippendale to ultra-contemporary. The showroom is beautifully decorated — inspiring, in fact, and designers on the premises will help you envision what the pieces will look like in your own home. In 20 years, they've never steered us wrong.

Levitz Furniture Corp.
4949 Allentown Rd., Camp Springs, Md.
• **(301) 899-7000**
Rockville Pk. and Randolph Rd., Rockville, Md. • **(301) 881-7950**
2950 Gallows Rd., Falls Church, Va.
• **(703) 560-1130**
50 Orchard Rd., Glen Burnie, Md.
• **(410) 636-5400**

Levitz Furniture Warehouse was the first such showroom in the Washington area, and it made a hit with its vast selection and semi-self-serve atmosphere — you can take your pieces home at the time of purchase in many cases. The furniture is reasonable to the point of being inexpensive. It looks good, it's cheap and it's quick.

The Loft Bed Store
3622 King St., Alexandria, Va.
• **(703) 379-7299**
605 Hungerford Dr., Rockville, Md.
• **(301) 340-0998**
14080-E Sullyfield Cir., Chantilly, Va.
• **(703) 803-7785**
14980 Farm Creek Dr., Woodbridge, Va.
• **(703) 494-3999**

Are you short on space? Consider drop-down, fold-out furniture. The Loft Bed Store are cabinetmakers primarily, and they can construct a multipurpose piece to fit the tiniest studio apartment. There are entertainment units, dressers, bookcases, Murphy, trundle and platform beds — or you can have it all combined in one wall system. The pieces are solid hardwood and don't come cheap, but they're built to last.

Marlo Furniture Warehouse & Showroom
901 7th St. NW, Washington, D.C.
• **(202) 842-0100**

INSIDERS' TIP

Look to Metrorail to get to and from many of your favorite shopping destinations, particularly during rush hour, the busy Christmas season and when nasty winter weather hits.

7801 Marlboro Pk., Forestville, Md.
• (301) 735-2000
13450 Baltimore Ave., Laurel, Md.
• (301) 419-3400
5650 General Washington Dr.,
Alexandria, Va. • (703) 941-0800
725 Rockville Pike, Rockville, Md.
• (301) 738-9000

You won't be in Washington a day before you see or hear ads for Marlo. This store seems to be open around the clock, seven days a week, and is always pushing a special sale. It's no wonder — there's room after room of merchandise here, and it's gotta be moved! There are some good bargains to be had in styles ranging from colonial to contemporary.

Mastercraft Interiors

1428 Rockville Pk., Rockville, Md.
• (301) 770-0400
615 N. Washington St., Alexandria, Va.
• (703) 684-1776
10390 Lee Hwy., Fairfax, Va.
• (703) 273-7800

If Williamsburg colonial is your style, then you'll be in hog heaven at Mastercraft. This is good quality furniture — silky mahogany, fluffy down, solid brass — and it's not cheap, but there are some great sales where you can pick up bargains.

Mission Possible

5516 Connecticut Ave. NW, Washington, D.C. • (202) 363-6897

Original period Mission arts and crafts furniture and accessories are the specialty of this store. A lot of the pieces are built and finished by hand in, of course, solid woods. It's pricey, but high-quality.

Persnickety

Wildwood Shopping Center, 10305 Old Georgetown Rd., Bethesda, Md.
• (301) 530-8805
Tysons Corner Center, Intersection of Virginia Hwys. 123 and 7, McLean, Va.
• (703) 760-8996
Fair Oaks Mall, I-66 at West Ox Rd., Fairfax, Va. • (703) 352-1495

This genteel little shop stocks furniture and fabrics that seem meant for a lady's boudoir or a sun room. There are sunny French pro-vincial-style flowers and stripes by Pierre Deux, Nina Campbell and Colefax & Fowler, to name just a few. They're meant to be draped over the cushy sofas, ottomans and easy chairs that decorate the store. You'll also find whimsical lamps and four poster beds of decorative wrought iron and brass.

Saah Unfinished Furniture

2330 Columbia Pk., Arlington, Va.
• (703) 920-1500
5641 General Washington Dr.,
Springfield, Va. • (703) 256-4315
14802 Jefferson Davis Hwy.,
Woodbridge, Va. • (703) 494-4167
811 Hungerford Dr., Rockville, Md.
• (301) 424-6911

If you're a do-it-yourselfer, then Saah may have just what you want. You'll find unfinished armoires, hutches, shelves, entertainment centers, tables and chairs in pine, oak, aspen and birch. Prices are reasonable, value is good and you'll have the satisfaction of seeing your handiwork every day.

Sofas By Design Fast

7305 Arlington Blvd., Falls Church, Va.
• (703) 698-7632

The name is misleading, since this shop sells much more than sofas. There are stylish lamps, tables and all sorts of eye-catching accent pieces. There are also sofas . . . and they are made relatively fast, for custom design. You pick the frame and fabric — there are hundreds to choose from — and in four to six weeks, you have your merchandise. Of course, the pieces in the showroom are delivered much more quickly. What's more, the quality down and wood here cost less than you would expect.

Theodore's

2233 Wisconsin Ave. NW, Washington, D.C. • (202) 333-2300

For 30 years, Theodore's has been at the vanguard of Washington's contemporary furniture scene. No fake colonial stuff here: just sleek, eclectic, innovative pieces that you won't find just anywhere. Its location in upper Georgetown makes it a popular spot for trendies in the surrounding neighborhood, but people are also willing to travel to this one-of-a-kind shop.

Urban Country
7801 Woodmont Ave., Bethesda, Md.
- **(301) 654-0500**

This eclectic design studio features top-quality furniture that's a blend of antique, ethnic and a touch of contemporary. Here, they strive for an entire design concept rather than simply a sofa or a dining room table, so you'll find wall, window and floor treatments, as well as decorators to help you pull it all together.

Museum Shops

Any overview of shopping in our Nation's Capital has to include a mention of the city's great museum and gallery shops, particularly those at any of the Smithsonian's vast collection of properties. These places aren't just for tourists. Locals love them as well, especially for gifts that are hard to find anywhere else, including books, jewelry, china, framing-quality posters and prints, and assorted novelties.

Bureau of Engraving and Printing
14th St. and Independence Ave. SW, Washington, D.C. • (202) 874-3019

Buy sheets of uncut $1 and $2 bills, always fun for the kids to see.

Decatur House
748 Jackson Pl. NW, Washington, D.C.
- **(202) 842-0920**

This museum on Lafayette Square, across from the White House, sells reproduction home accessories of the 18th and 19th centuries.

Fredericksburg National Military Park Bookstore
Chancellorsville National Military Park Bookstore, 1011 Lafayette Blvd., Fredericksburg, Va. • (540) 373-6122

At these national historic sites, you'll find must-see bookstores on local history, particularly (as the name implies) military history. There are also videos and other accessories of interest to Civil and Revolutionary War buffs.

Hillwood Museum
4155 Linnean Ave. NW, Washington, D.C.
- **(202) 686-8500**

This former residence of Marjorie Merriweather Post (the cereal heiress), features a large collection of French and Russian decorative arts, and reproductions are on sale in the gift shop. You'll remember your visit with the Fabergé-style egg pendants and other items relating to the permanent collection. The museum is being remodeled and should re-open in the year 2000.

Hirshhorn Museum
950 Independence Ave. NW, Washington, D.C. • (202) 357-1300

The Hirshhorn Museum features modern art, and the jewelry in the gift shop reflects it. It's quirky and interesting, especially the earrings, which are not the kind of merchandise you'll find in a shopping mall.

Kennedy Center
Rock Creek Pkwy and New Hampshire Ave. NW, Washington, D.C.
- **(202) 467-4600**

For a range of gifts with music, dance, theater or opera themes, there's no better place in Washington than the Kennedy Center.

Manassas National Battlefield Park Bookstore
6511 Sudley Rd., Manassas, Va.
- **(703) 754-7107**

The battlefield here draws tourists from around the nation, and when you're through visiting, you'll want to stop at the small bookstore, which specializes in historical memorabilia and tomes.

Mount Vernon Inn Gift Shop
George Washington Memorial Pkwy., Alexandria, Va. • (703) 780-0011

The gift shop at George Washington's estate has reproductions of his key to the Bastille, Martha Washington's cookbook, china and silver, as well as toys and souvenirs. Particularly nice as mementos are the Christmas ornaments.

National Air and Space Museum
6th St. and Independence Ave. SW, Washington, D.C. • (202) 357-1300

Kids love the stuff here, from the freeze-dried ice cream like the astronauts eat, to the kites and other flight-related objects. There are also books and videos for the aspiring pilots and astronauts on your gift list.

National Archives Museum Store
7th St. and Constitution Ave. NW, Washington, D.C. • (202) 501-5000

Here you'll find great replicas of the Declaration of Independence, the U.S. Constitution and the Bill of Rights, along with posters and postcards. These make wonderful learning tools and souvenirs for kids. What's more, there are games, gifts, greeting cards, books, clothing and crafts.

National Gallery of Art
600 Constitution Avenue NW, Washington, D.C. • (202) 737-4215

In the basement of the National Gallery is a vast collection of inexpensive prints and postcards of masterpieces that are suitable for framing. You'll also find stationery, jewelry, scarves and glorious picture books.

National Geographic Society
17th and M Sts. NW, Washington, D.C. • (202) 857-7000

For superb wall maps, globes, books and educational children's toys, the National Geographic Society can't be beat.

National Museum of African Art
950 Independence Ave. SW, Washington, D.C. • (202) 357-2700

Every home could benefit from a few eclectic accents, and you'll find just the right touch of ethnic artistry here. There are textiles, dolls, crafts and jewelry from Africa — you're sure to get compliments on these exotic items.

Navy Museum
901 M St. SE, Washington, D.C. • (202) 433-4882

Kids love the hands-on nature of this museum, with its uniforms, medals, guns and ship parts. The shop stocks small souvenirs and elegant gifts relating to the U.S. Navy, Coast Guard, Marine Corps and Merchant Marines.

Smithsonian Institution Retail Headquarters
600 Maryland Ave. SW, Washington, D.C. • (202) 287-3563

Every Smithsonian museum has a superb shop and bookstore, but the above address and phone number are a hotline to retail operations, should you wish for an overview or a specific item. Each museum sells items pertaining to its own exhibits, as well as more general items of interest to tourists in Washington, and then there are the wearables: pretty scarves, earrings, ties and shawls. Desktop accessories galore abound, from stationery and pens to paperweights. Some of the specialized items you'll find, depending on which museum you're visiting, include polished minerals and common gems, items on space exploration, zoological models, and crafts of African or Native American origin, just to name a few.

Washington National Cathedral
Wisconsin and Massachusetts Aves. NW, Washington, D.C. • (202) 537-5766

The shop here stocks unusual Gothic and Medieval products such as stuffed gargoyles, colorful window decorations and stained-glass-patterned scarves. If you're home decorating, pick up one of the dramatic tapestries, or Gothic stone garden accessories.

Beauty Spas and Salons

Beauty products are easy to find — any department store or salon has them. If you're like most people, you stick to certain brands and you know where to find them. What about beauty services? If you're looking for sessions that can last anywhere from an hour to a day, and which may include manicures, waxing, facials and massage, you'll need a day spa — a wonderful place to unwind from Washington's frenetic pace. Here are some of the top names in the Washington area, and most serve both men and women:

Elizabeth Arden
5225 Wisconsin Ave. NW, Washington, D.C. • (202) 362-9890

Remember those 1940s movies where women would sit in a steam box with their cold-cream slathered faces poking out? Chances are, they were in Elizabeth Arden, who started the whole day spa concept decades ago. Well, the Washington salon is still going strong, though a lot of competition has come along in the interim. Maybe it's because of that same competition that this salon, once so pricey, is now relatively reasonable. Facials are $65 to $110, whereas many other places start around $100. You can also buy all-day packages starting at $255 that include some combination of haircare, manicure, pedicure, body wraps and massage .

Georgette Klinger
5345 Wisconsin Ave. NW, Chevy Chase Pavilion, Washington, D.C.
• (202) 686-8880

The Hungarian-born Klinger founded her first salon in New York, and was an immediate hit with all manner of celebrities. She has since brought her skincare methods and products to Washington, where the salon is equally successful. Whatever beauty treatment you can imagine, you can find at Klinger. On your first visit, you'll be asked to fill out a skincare questionnaire, much as you would in a dermatologist's office. The questionnaire becomes part of your "chart," which is kept on file for future reference.

The atmosphere at Klinger is soothing, feminine (though there are male clients, too), and ultra-clean. The specialty here is facials, some of which last more than an hour and involve the use of aromatic herbs or fruit acids. There are also manicures, pedicures and haircuts and cosmetic makeovers available. Ask about packages, and you'll save some money, but expect to pay $76 for a 60-minute facial. Never mind . . . you'll leave with a glow.

Jacques Dessange
5410 Wisconsin Ave., Chevy Chase, Md.
• (301) 913-9373

This full service salon has it all, and you don't even need to venture into downtown. Facials start at $60, and body wraps are $105. You can also have a haircut, makeover, manicure, pedicure, waxing and massage. The atmosphere is energetic, trendy and upscale.

Lillian Laurance Ltd.
2000 M St. NW, Washington, D.C.
• (202) 872-0606

Lillian Laurance was a day spa before the term was invented. It's always been on the cutting edge of beauty treatment and continues to be so, offering facials, massage, body wraps, mud packs, body polishing, waxing, and nonsurgical face-lifts. Facials begin at $70 for a 90-minute treatment, and massages are $70 for an hour. It's a pleasant refuge, conveniently located in the lower level of a midtown office building — very discreet, da-a-ahrling.

Petra's Skin Spa
3915 Old Lee Hwy., Suite 21A, Fairfax, Va. • (703) 385-6800

This sweetly scented hideaway in the heart of Fairfax stays on the cutting edge of all beauty developments. There are therapies for every problem: toning facials that stimulate with light electrical pulses, fruit-acid facials to exfoliate, aromatherapy massages, hydradermie peels to clean and oxygenate the skin and anti-stress treatments. None of it comes cheaply, but you save a bit when compared to downtown salons. Facials run from $55 to $98, and a 2½-hour massage, beauty treatment, facial combo is $143. The atmosphere is both intimate and elegant, with a stylish sitting area, and spotless therapy rooms.

s/p/alon
1605 17th St. NW, Washington, D.C.
• (202) 462-9000

This trendy day spa and salon offers massages, haircutting and coloring, facials, alphahydroxy treatments, makeup, manicures, pedicures and body- and eye-firming treatments. You can also shoot the works and go for a package. Facials start at $42 for 30 minutes and go to $79 for 90 minutes. Massages are $60 an hour.

The Washington Institute for Skin Care
2311 M St. NW, Washington, D.C.
• (202) 785-8855

If we could go anywhere in the world for a facial, this would be the place. Its decor is hushed, spare and elegant, not frilly or trendy like many day spas — maybe because it's associated with a doctor's office — but the sterile atmosphere is very reassuring. Facials cost plenty here, from $100 on up, but you can get glycolic peels, extractions and acid treatments with complete assurance that the job will be done right and your skin won't be damaged. Waxing and makeup are also available, as well as a wide assortment of skincare products only available in doctors' offices.

Hair Salons

Following is a list of Washington salons most often mentioned in national beauty magazines. They serve both men and women.

Daniel's Salon
1831 M St. NW, Washington, D.C.
• **(202) 296-4856**
In a handsome townhouse, Daniel's is three stories packed with beauty services. It's always bustling with patrons of both sexes, generally up-and-coming executives from the surrounding office district.

La Coupe
1775 K St. NW, Washington, D.C.
• **(202) 775-1934**
Near the White House, La Coupe bustles with a young, business-oriented clientele and a slew of Eurostyle hairdressers.

Okyo Beauty Salon
2903 M St. NW, Washington, D.C.
• **(202) 342-2675**
This bright, spare-looking loft attracts all sorts of Washington celebs. It's acclaimed for fine cuts and coloring, as well as long waits for appointments. Call well in advance.

PR & Partners
805 King St., Alexandria, Va.
• **(703) 683-6600**
6701 Lowell Ave., McLean, Va.
• **(703) 734-9680**
7710 Woodmont Ave., Bethesda, Md.
• **(301) 657-4488**
This suburban mini-chain is notable for

being the only salon outside the city recommended by *Washingtonian* magazine. Strategically located in the most upscale suburban neighborhoods, the clientele reflects that.

Roche Salon
3050 K St. NW, Washington Harbour Plaza, Washington, D.C.
• **(202) 775-0775**
This salon is a fantasyland, complete with paintwork to simulate blue skies and brightly colored cabanas (changing rooms) that make you think of a day at the beach. Don't let the whimsy fool you though: cuts and color are taken seriously here, and the salon is regularly named in national magazines as one of Washington's best. What's more, they won't try to chop off your long hair or give you an unsuitable, hard-to-manage style.

Salon Jean Paul
4820 Yuma St., Washington, D.C.
• **(202) 966-4600**
This has been a favorite of the Washington establishment for many years. In upper northwest, Salon Jean Paul attracted a number of patrons from the affluent residential area surrounding it.

Sylvain Melloul Salon
3034 M St. NW, Washington, D.C.
• **(202) 965-4421**
1901 K St. NW, Washington, D.C.
• **(202) 862-9888**
7101 Democracy Blvd., Bethesda, Md.
• **(301) 469-7090**
11936 Market St., Reston, Va.
• **(703) 481-1835**
This local chain just keeps on expanding — a tribute to its personality. The shops are trendy, upbeat and convenient.

Unique Stores

Some stores just don't fit into any category,

INSIDERS' TIP

Count on Sunny's Surplus stores (three D.C. locations) for great bargains on clothing, equipment and accessories for hikers, campers, hunters, anglers and other outdoor enthusiasts.

or if they do, they're the only ones in it. The stores listed below either offer more of their specialty than anyone in Metro Washington, or they offer obscure merchandise.

Ademas
816 N. Fairfax St., Alexandria, Va.
• **(703) 549-7806**

If you like unique flooring, head for this Old Town designer showroom, where you can choose from handmade tile, marble, granite, terra cotta and limestone. You'll be amazed at the variety of colors, textures and patterns.

The Artisans
6828 Old Dominion Dr., McLean, Va.
• **(703) 506-0518**

The artistry of American craftspeople is featured at this shop in high-toned McLean. You'll find wearable art, gifts, housewares and jewelry — all of it unique. Full-length coats feature abstract landscapes, candlesticks are sculptures containing glass and semiprecious stones and brooches are striking enough to make a memorable outfit of any little black dress. Not everything here is costly, though. You can buy hand-printed T-shirts for as little as $30, and beaded denim jackets for $125.

Backstage
2101 P St. NW, Washington, D.C.
• **(202) 775-1488**

This boutique in the heart of Dupont Circle will actually make your costume to order, if you wish, or you can choose from the large selection of ready-made disguises. There are also all kinds of accessories, including wigs, masks, makeup and dancewear.

The Brass Knob
2311 18th St. NW, Washington, D.C.
• **(202) 332-3370**

You've selected the perfect furniture, wall coverings and draperies for your new house, but how do you pull it all together? It's the details that count, and The Brass Knob can provide them. The store carries a wide variety of antique lighting fixtures, stained and beveled glass, doorknobs and hardware. You'll also love the architectural accents here, such as fireplace mantels, porcelain sinks, tiles, ornamental ironwork and carved stone.

Christmas Attic
125 S. Union St., Alexandria, Va.
• **(703) 548-2829**
107 N. Fairfax St., Alexandria, Va.
• **(703) 548-4267**

These two Old Town shops are magical. They are decorated year round with Christmas trees jam-packed with gorgeous ornaments. Trees have themes ranging from Victorian lace to gold-and-glass, musical instruments and toys. The stores smell like Christmas, thanks to bushels of apples at the door and strategically placed potpourri. Baskets of ornaments enchant with their variety and intricacy of design. Here, you'll always feel in the Christmas spirit — even in midsummer.

The Counter Spy Shop
1027 Connecticut Ave. NW, Washington, D.C. • **(202) 887-1717**

Are you sure your conversations are private? Find out with a bug-buster from The Counter Spy Shop. The store has all sorts of gadgets for the aspiring 007. There are night-vision goggles, a parabolic mike that claims to pick up sound from miles away, the so-called Truth Phone, which is meant to act as a lie detector by measuring voice stress, and many more secret agent items.

Distinctive Bookbinding and Stationery
1150 Connecticut Ave. NW, Washington, D.C. • **(202) 466-4866**

This shop will take you back to an era when people prided themselves on the quality of their stationery and penmanship, on the leather-bound volumes in their libraries. You'll find exotic Florentine writing paper of the highest quality here, as well as all sorts of writing accessories, including scented ink. If you already own some worn first editions, this is the place to have them rebound and restored.

Fahrney's
1430 G St., NW, Washington, D.C.
• **(703) 628-9525**

There are other stores in Washington that sell fine pens and pencils, but Fahrney's is an institution. Appropriately located near the National Press Building, this small shop has been around since 1929, and the service is just as

Photo: Courtesy of the Fairfax Economic Development Authority

The Washington, D.C., area is known for its outstanding shopping.

personal today as it was then. It specializes in writing instruments from Montblanc, Parker, Cross, Sheaffer, Waterman and Pelikan.

The Gamekeeper
Fashion Centre at Pentagon City, 1100 S. Hayes St., Arlington, Va.
• (703) 415-5110
Tysons Corner Center, 1961 Chain Bridge Rd., McLean, Va.
• (703) 821-5468

It's a store full of board games for adults and children, including games you never heard of, as well as the standards like Scrabble and Monopoly. There are also dartboards, playing cards, and chess and checker sets.

Mark Keshishian and Sons Oriental Rugs
4505 Stanford St., Chevy Chase, Md.
• (301) 951-8880

Sometimes it seems as though there's an Oriental rug dealer on every corner in Washington and the surrounding 'burbs. Many of them are excellent, but Keshishian is widely considered the cream of the crop when it comes to appraising, variety of merchandise and restoration. The store carries antiques of the first quality, as well as more contemporary pieces. The staff is friendly, knowledgeable and, most importantly, willing to share information.

Modigliani
Georgetown Park, 3222 M St. NW, Washington, D.C. • (202) 337-1390

There are lingerie shops galore in every Washington area mall — the national chains are well represented here. Modigliani, however, is in a class by itself when it comes to quality and selection. This quiet, elegant boutique specializes in top-of-the-line European dainties by La Perla, Nina Ricci, Lejaby and others. They also carry hard-to-find sizes.

Music Box Center
918 F St. NW, Washington, D.C.
• (202) 783-9399

Choose from more than 1,500 music boxes, both antique and modern, and then personalize your choice with one of more than 500 melodies. You'll be amazed at the cunning shapes and sizes of these pretty boxes.

Palais Royal
1125 King St., Alexandria, Va.
• (703) 549-6660
10231 Old Georgetown Rd., Bethesda, Md. • (301) 897-5009
6651A Old Dominion Dr., McLean, Va.
• (703) 356-3085

For the best in French linens for the bed, bath and table, head straight for this classy emporium. The high thread count in their sheets will make you think you're sleeping on silk, but it's cool crisp linen and cotton instead. The table displays are inspiring, but bring your gold card.

Park Place
2251 Wisconsin Ave. NW, Washington, D.C. • (202) 342-6294

You won't believe the selection of garden furniture, fixtures and accessories here. There are classic styles in teak, wicker and metal; ornaments like lampposts, massive flower pots, and stained-glass panels. There are even interior lamps in the Tiffany style. Whether you have an estate or a tiny kitchen garden, you're sure to find the whimsical or dramatic touch you need here.

The Surrey
10107 River Rd., Potomac, Md.
• (301) 365-1250

Potomac is traditional horse country, and this high-toned shop caters to those wealthy enough to belong to that set. You'll find all manner of riding clothes and equipment, including leather jackets and pants, boots, riding crops and cold weather gear.

Tennis Factory
2500 Wilson Blvd., Ste. 1000, Arlington, Va. • (703) 522-2700

Tennis players will be agog at the selection of women's, men's and children's clothing, shoes and rackets here. There's every brand imaginable and trained staff to help with your decisions. Still not sure? There are demo racquets for rent. They'll also restring your own racquet overnight.

Tiny Jewel Box
1147 Connecticut Ave. NW, Washington, D.C. • (202) 393-2747

Yes, there are dozens of jewelry stores in

Metro Washington, and every mall seems to have at least three, but the Tiny Jewel Box is special. There's modern designer jewelry, of course, like David Yurman and Silvio Hidalgo; but the real attraction here is the area's largest collection of antique and estate jewelry. You can find Art Nouveau brooches, rings and earrings for as little as $200, but you can also spend tens of thousands of dollars for some of the shop's diamond and platinum pieces.

Veneman Music & Sound

12401 Twinbrook Pkwy., Rockville, Md.
• (301) 231-6100
8319 Amherst Ave., Springfield, Va.
• (703) 451-8970

A look in the yellow pages will show you lots of stores specializing in musical instruments and sheet music, but Veneman has been around longer than most, and it is highly respected in the Washington area. The store buys and sells used instruments, does all sorts of repairs and, of course, carries a wide selection of new instruments and accessories.

Washington Golf Centers

1722 Eye St. NW, Washington, D.C.
• (202) 728-0088
2625 Shirlington Rd., Arlington, Va.
• (703) 979-7888
9811 Washingtonian Blvd., Gaithersburg, Md. • (301) 948-7888

These super showrooms are filled with thousands of the latest proline clubs, bags, shoes, balls, apparel and accessories. Because of the volume sold, the Washington Golf Center can offer considerable discounts when compared to smaller pro shops, but don't expect the same kind of personalized service.

Yes Natural Gourmet

3425 Connecticut Ave., NW, Washington, D.C. • (202) 363-1559
1825 Columbia Rd., Washington, D.C.
• (202) 462-5150

A lot of mainstream grocery chains have jumped on the organic food/herb/vitamin bandwagon, and they do a wonderful job. A look at the telephone directory will reveal dozens of listings for health food stores, but we have to takes our hats off to one of the most long-lived and consistent in the Washington area, Yes Natural Gourmet. Its two locations prove its success — many health food boutiques fade away after a couple of years. Yes sells organic produce and groceries, diet products, bulk food and herbs, vitamins and bodycare items. There's also a deli and juice bar.

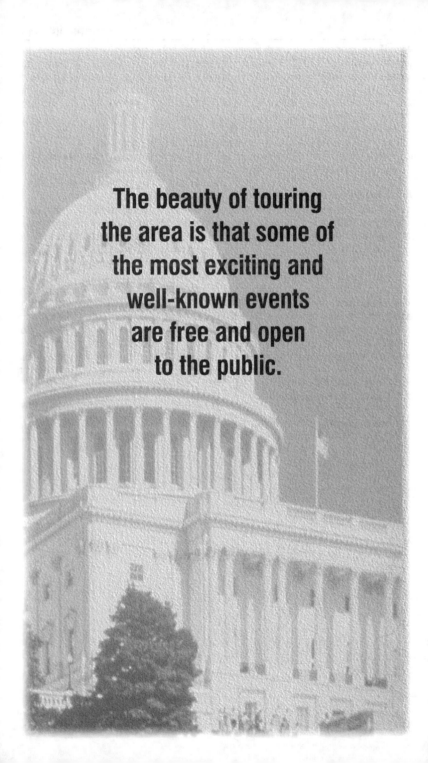

The beauty of touring
the area is that some of
the most exciting and
well-known events
are free and open
to the public.

Annual Events

How many times have you seen photos of the president emerging from the massive portals of the Washington National Cathedral, surrounded by Secret Service and Cabinet officials? Imagine attending Christmas Eve services in that same house of worship, surrounded by the very newsmakers you've glimpsed on CNN. If that doesn't sound like your cup of tea, rest assured that in Washington, you'll have plenty to do and see. Year-round you'll find parades, festivals and ceremonies, many of which you may have seen on television — like the annual lighting of the national Christmas tree.

Many who come to Washington plan their trips around special celebrations and exhibitions. From the exuberance of the Chinese New Year to the ceremonial splendor of the Marine Color Guard on parade, Washington visitors and residents can choose from an endless variety of fascinating, amusing distractions. The beauty of touring the area is that some of the most exciting and well-known events are free and open to the public.

Here you'll find a month-by-month calendar of events in the Washington Metro area. In the monthly categories you'll find geographic subdivisions: Washington, D.C., Maryland and Virginia. Most events are free, but 1997 adult admission fees are shown for those that aren't. Please note that for the most part we have not included dates and times because they so often change from year to year. Instead, you'll find contact numbers for people and organizations who can provide a wealth of information.

January

Washington, D.C.

Chinese New Year Parade
H St. NW, between 5th and 8th Sts., Washington, D.C. • (202) 724-4091
The Lunar New Year is a time to close accounts, pay debts, clean house, honor ancestors, prepare exotic foods and thank the gods for a prosperous year. The residents of Washington's Chinatown do it all in style, with traditional firecrackers, drums and colorful dragon dancers that make their way through the streets flanked typically by more than 10,000 onlookers.

Martin Luther King Jr.'s Birthday Observance
23rd St. and Independence Ave., Lincoln Memorial, Washington, D.C.
• (202) 619-7222
Local choirs, guest speakers and a military color guard salute the memory of the influential civil rights leader at the site where, on a sweltering summer afternoon in 1963, he led one of the largest public demonstrations ever held in Washington. King delivered his famous "I Have a Dream" speech from the memorial steps.

Northern Virginia

Robert E. Lee's Birthday Celebration
Arlington National Cemetery, Memorial Dr., Arlington, Va. • (703) 557-0613

In tribute to one of Virginia's and the South's greatest military heroes, the doors of Lee's cherished Arlington House open wide for an afternoon of 19th-century music, samples of Civil War-era food and displays of restoration work.

www.insiders.com

See this and many other Insiders' Guide® destinations online — in their entirety.

Visit us today!

Suburban Maryland

Annapolis Heritage Antique Show
Medford National Guard Armory, Hudson St., Annapolis, Md. • (410) 222-1919

This giant of an antiques show — 7,700 square feet of exhibit space — is set most appropriately in a city that's one of the nation's premiere antique meccas. You'll find dealers from all over the United States showing wares as varied as 19th-century French furniture to Shaker, Chinese export and American country styles. You'll also find, appropriately enough (Annapolis is a yachting capital), marine artifacts and maps, and a myriad of other decorative items such as porcelains, Oriental rugs and paintings. The show runs for three days and opens with a preview party for serious private collectors, charging a $35 admission fee that allows you into the following day's shows. The show benefits The London Town Foundation, which supports historic preservation, research and interpretation in Maryland. Admission is to the Annapolis Heritage Antique Show is $6.

February

Washington, D.C.

Abraham Lincoln's Birthday
Lincoln Memorial, 23rd St. and Independence Ave. NW, Washington, D.C. • (202) 619-7222

A wreath-laying ceremony and reading of the Gettysburg Address are highlights of the 16th president's birthday celebration on February 12, at his namesake memorial. The site is inspiring with its view of the Reflecting Pool, the Washington Monument and the U.S. Capitol. Inside, the 19-foot marble statue is set against inscriptions of Lincoln's second inaugural address and the Gettysburg Address.

International Tourist Guild Day
Old Post Office Pavilion, Pennsylvania Ave. and 12th St. NW, Washington, D.C. • (202) 298-1474 select #4

Meet at Old Post Office Pavilion on Pennsylvania Avenue and 12th streets NW. Admission is $1. This one-day-only event is sponsored by The Guild of Professional Tour Guides of Washington, D.C. and features a professionally narrated four-hour tour to the U.S. Capitol and memorials. Drive by the White House, Washington Monument, Smithsonian Museums, Washington National Cathedral and Embassy Row. They do not take reservations or sell advance tickets. Call for dates and times.

Washington Boat Show
Washington Convention Center, 900 9th St. NW, Washington, D.C. • (202) 789-1600

Surrounded by rivers, and with the Chesapeake Bay just a short drive away,

Drama on Parade: Silent Drill at Sunset

The Marines move in such crisp and perfect unison that they almost look like robots. The hush of the audience is absolute. Faces are rapt, awestricken at the finesse of the Silent Drill Platoon. In the setting sun, the bayonets fixed atop the M-1 rifles gleam like mirrors. The platoon stands erect and still — not a muscle seems to twitch.

Despite the heat of the summer evening, they are in full dress: white gloves, white caps and slacks, and the famous navy jackets. Above the scene towers the U.S. Marine Corps War Memorial, the famous bronze sculpture that captures the moment in World War II when U.S. Marines raised the flag on the Japanese island of Iwo Jima. It's a perfect backdrop for the dramatic demonstration that takes place at sunset on the green lawn below. The Marines hold the sunset parades here, each Tuesday evening in summer, in tribute to the men who fought at Iwo Jima, as homage to those whose "uncommon valor was a common virtue." (The base of the sculpture bears the quotation in gold lettering.)

The parade begins with the Marines marching onto the green from an area behind the memorial. First come the Battle Colors, the Official Colors of the Corps. The streamers and silver bands that grace the Colors represent every battle, campaign and expedition the Corps has participated in since its founding more than two centuries ago. The Color Sergeant has the responsibility of carrying the National Colors, and by virtue of that billet is considered the senior sergeant in the Marine Corps; then, clad in red jackets and white slacks, the U.S. Marines' Drum and Bugle Corps, known as "The Commandant's Own," parade to a series of toe-tapping marches and popular tunes. Their choreography is intricate, and the marching patterns are fascinating to watch.

The climax of the evening is unquestionably the Silent Drill Platoon, a corps of elite

— continued on next page

Photo: Courtesy of McGehee & Associates

The marching platoons emerge from behind the U.S. Marine Corps War Memorial in Arlington, Virginia, to take their places for the Tuesday evening Sunset Parade.

military showmen. They stand on the field alone, their bearing ramrod straight, their positioning accurate to a hair's breadth. Their silent exercise begins, a breathtaking drill punctuated only by the sound of the rifles thumping into their owners' gloved hands. The Rifle Inspector, who stands facing his 24-person team, issues no verbal commands. The rifles twirl, change hands and come to rest in a ruler-straight row pointing at the evening sky. Onlookers gasp with each twirl of the bayonets — risky maneuvers that miss the marines by only centimeters.

Each member of the platoon has spent six weeks training for 12 to 14 grueling hours a day. Training doesn't end there. New members must practice for six months before they are permitted to perform before the public. The goal is to spin the rifle and march without looking at the weapon. The group makes it look effortless, but around fifty percent of the Marines recruited for the Silent Drill Team fail to graduate to the ranks. Mistakes during the parades are seldom seen, although if one does occur, it is then up to the Marine to save face with another dazzling maneuver.

The highlight of the eleven-minute drill is the moment when the Rifle Inspector comes to a stop before a single member of the team. The Marine throws his rifle, spinning it into the air. The Rifle Inspector catches it with one hand, and there is the sharp report of metal as it hits. It's a strong, authoritative sound. Not a breath is heard from the audience as the two Marines exchange the rifle, tossing it, spinning it, twisting it in different patterns and directions. When it is over, the audience exhales in relief that there were no mishaps, and then erupts in giddy applause.

The Tuesday evening Sunset Parades have been a summer tradition in Washington since 1956. They are free and no reservations are required, since there is only lawn seating. Those who plan ahead, however, can make reservations to attend the somewhat more elaborate Friday Evening Parades, held at the Marine Barracks in Washington, D.C. The Friday Evening Parades are 15 minutes longer than the Sunset Parades and searchlights add to the drama. More Marines also participate, including Private First Class Chesty XI, a brindle and white-colored pedigreed English bulldog who serves as the official mascot of the Marine Barracks of Washington, D.C.

During the closing ceremony, the Marines march away and the searchlights are extinguished as a lone bugler comes out and plays Taps.

For information on parking, reservations and transportation, contact the Marine barracks at (202) 433-6060.

Photo: Courtesy of McGehee & Associates

Marines in the Silent Drill Platoon spin their M-1 rifles with fixed bayonets as they pass stationary members of the unit during a ceremony at Marine Barracks, Washington, D.C.

Metro Washington is boat-crazed. This five-day event has become a tremendous draw in a town where people have the money to spend on grown-up toys. It showcases next year's models of hundreds of boats from dinghies to motor yachts. If you're a serious buyer, you can often snag great buys at the show. Flash your wallet and representatives from the big boatmakers will be ready to negotiate. If you're not in that league, you can still purchase nautical accessories and pick up brochures from yacht charter companies. Admission is $12.

Northern Virginia

George Washington's Birthday Parade
Wilkes and St. Asaph Sts., Old Town Alexandria, Va. • (703) 838-4200

Old Town plays host to the nation's largest birthday parade, honoring a native son and America's first president. The cobbled streets of Old Town, flanked by 18th- and 19th-century historical buildings, including private residences, make a perfect backdrop for the celebration. The route begins in a beautiful residential section of town, and ends at Gadsby's Tavern, a nationally designated historical building dating from the 18th century. It is now a restaurant with costumed servers and 18-century–style minstrels. Make sure to bundle up because it can be cold and windy in February.

Mount Vernon Open House
Mount Vernon Estate, George Washington Memorial Pkwy., Alexandria, Va. • (703) 780-2000

After the parade in Old Town, head south to George Washington's lovely estate on the Potomac for an afternoon of period costumes, music and food. Admission is free of charge on this special day which includes a performance on the bowling green by the U.S. Army Old Guard Fife and Drum Corps and the Commander-in-Chief's Guard. A tour of the house is worth the wait, and "George Washington" will be on the grounds all day to receive your birthday wishes.

March

Washington, D.C.

Washington Flower & Garden Show
Washington Convention Center, 900 9th St. NW, Washington, D.C.
• (703) 823-7960

An extravaganza of color and scent featuring gardening experts, landscape designers and, of course, masses of flowers and plants. This four-day show features almost 200 exhibitors in a space larger than two acres. Over half of that space is filled with gardens that have been forced into bloom — breathtaking gardens that can include waterfalls and bridges, magnificent statuary and dramatic trees. A retail area includes greenhouses, books, plants, flower arranging accessories and garden antiques. Admission is $8.

D.C. Spring Antiques Fair
The D.C. Armory, 2001 E. Capitol St. SE
• (301) 738-1966 prior to show,
(202) 547-9215 during show

The area's most popular antique show, this 5-day display features almost 200 dealers from the United States, England, France and Canada. You'll find an eye-popping array of collectibles from delicate sterling, porcelains, Oriental rugs and fine furniture. Browsers are welcome, but it's also a good place to connect with dealers in far-flung areas who will be more than happy to ship you their wares as well as notifications of their latest finds. Admission is $5.

National Cherry Blossom Festival
Various parks and downtown locations, Washington, D.C. • (202) 619-7222

Perhaps Washington's most visible fete, the National Cherry Blossom Festival honors the extraordinary blooming of the city's 6,000 Japanese cherry trees — surely one of the most beautiful sights in America. The capstone event is the Cherry Blossom Festival Parade (usually the first Saturday in April), but scores of related parties and ceremonies begin the last week of March. The trees bloom anywhere from late March to early April, depending on

Mother Nature. A word to the wise: If at all possible, take Metrorail into Washington and walk to the Tidal Basin. It's a short jaunt from most stops downtown, and you'll save yourself the agony of trying to find a parking space.

St. Patrick's Day Parade
7th to 17th Sts. and Constitution Ave. NW, Washington, D.C. • (301) 879-1717

Salute the Irish and sport the green in style during this always-festive downtown parade that features traditional dancers, bagpipers and floats galore. The parade, which lasts about three hours, has been a major Washington event for 29 years, spilling over into the bars and eateries that flank the parade route. High school bands from around the country join in, as well as bands from Ireland. It's not nearly as big as the one in New York, but it manages to clog traffic for most of the day, so take the Metro.

Smithsonian Kite Festival
15th St. and Constitution Ave. NW, Washington, D.C. • (202) 357-2700

Cherry blossoms excepted, nothing signals the dawn of spring quite like the sight of colorful kites dipping and soaring next to the Washington Monument. Kite makers and flyers of all ages compete for prizes and trophies.

Northern Virginia

St. Patrick's Day Parade
King and West Sts., Old Town Alexandria, Va. • (703) 838-4200

Usually held a day or two before the D.C. parade, Old Town's festivities extend beyond the parade route and into the city's extremely popular Irish pubs, such as Murphy's and Ireland's Own.

Woodlawn Plantation Annual Needlework Exhibition
George Washington Memorial Pkwy. and U.S. Hwy.1, Alexandria, Va.
• (703) 780-4000

Needlework crafts from the 18th century to the present day are on display at this lovely plantation, about 3 miles east of the Mount Vernon estate. The exhibition includes works by amateur and professional stitchers, as well

as celebrities like Barbara Bush. Admission is $6.

Suburban Maryland

Annual Quilt Show
Bowie City Hall, 2614 Kenhill Dr., Bowie, Md. • (301) 925-8300

Heirloom and contemporary quilts are showcased in this popular Prince George's County show. Admission is $4.

April

Washington, D.C.

Design for Living/Washington's Home Show
Washington Convention Center, 900 9th St. NW, Washington, D.C.
• (301) 261-2180, (410) 268-8890

"Design for Living" is the area's largest and longest running residential design and home products show; however, there's more than just furniture and home design examples and ideas at this event, held twice yearly. Along with gourmet cooking demonstrations and seminars, you can participate in a wine tasting that features local and regional wineries. Admission is $8.

Washington International Film Festival
Theaters and reception halls, Washington, D.C. • (202) 724-5613

The Clintons aren't the only ones with Hollywood connections. All of Washington is the focus of the cinematic world during this two-week festival of international and American film. Washington is one of the top U.S. movie markets and one of the most filmed cities in the world. Admission is $7 for screenings, and $15 to $50 for special events.

Shakespeare's Birthday Celebration
Folger Shakespeare Library, 201 E. Capitol St. SE, Washington, D.C.
• (202) 544-4600

The Capitol Hill building is an attraction

in itself, with its replica of Shakespeare's Globe Theatre, but during the birthday celebration, the library also offers music, theater, children's events, food and special exhibits.

Smithsonian's Washington Craft Show
National Building Museum, 401 F St. NW, Washington, D.C. • (202) 357-2700

Some 100 juried exhibitors show their crafts at this wildly popular event, which features fiber, ceramics, glass, jewelry, leather, metal, paper, textiles and wood. Admission is $10.

White House Easter Egg Roll
The White House (Southeast Gate), E. Executive Ave. NW, Washington, D.C. • (202) 456-2200

Children ages 3 through 6, accompanied by adults, gather on the White House South Lawn for the annual Easter Egg Roll. This is easily the best opportunity in town for youngsters — and for that matter, parents — to play at the president's house. Similar festivities for older children take place on the Ellipse, located just across E Street from the executive mansion.

White House Spring Garden and House Tours
The White House, 1600 Pennsylvania Ave., Washington, D.C. • (202) 456-2200

The spectacular gardens of the presidential home are open to the public during these annual tours (usually for two days during the second week of the month). Highlights include the Jacqueline Kennedy Rose Gardens and the spectacular West Lawn Gardens.

Northern Virginia

Easter Sunrise Service
Arlington National Cemetery, Memorial Dr., Arlington, Va. • (703) 607-8052

The cemetery's Memorial Amphitheatre, an inspiring setting, awaits early-morning worshipers. A changing roster of prominent Washington ministers officiate, along with a moving, dignified tribute by the Army's Old Guard.

Historic Garden Week in Virginia
Statewide • (804) 644-7776

The finest in Virginia homes and gardens are spotlighted during this week-long festival. Our favorites include the gardens at such area plantations as Mount Vernon, Gunston Hall and Oatlands. Call to find out more about tours in northern Virginia. The admission fee is $10 to $20.

Suburban Maryland

Annapolis Waterfront Festival
Annapolis Yacht Basin, Compromise and Main Sts., Annapolis, Md. • (410) 268-8828

The capital city honors its maritime heritage during this three-day festival, which features handicrafts from around the nation. All work must be done by exhibitors themselves from handmade materials. The exhibit comprises one block at the foot of Main Street and a tented area adjacent to the City Dock, which is flanked by Compromise Street. You'll find wearable art, paintings, carvings and all manner of decorative items.

Give a Day for the Chesapeake Bay
Statewide • (410) 974-5300

Marylanders statewide have plenty of opportunities to help beautify the Chesapeake Bay, which is America's largest estuary and the Free State's most treasured natural resource. Local activities include tree plantings, stream cleanups and trash removals.

May

Washington, D.C.

"The Commandant's Own"
U.S. Marine Corps Barracks, 8th and I Sts. SE, Washington, D.C. • (202) 433-6060

Reservations are recommended, but admission is free to these extraordinary weekly parades, beginning in May and running through August. Here is your chance to see the elite of the United States military in a 75-

minute performance of music and precision marching. The evening parade begins with a concert by "The President's Own" United States Marine Band. After the concert, "The Commandant's Own" United States Drum and Bugle Corps and the Marine Corps Silent Drill Platoon perform.

Reservations must be made in writing and requested at least three weeks in advance. Address requests to the Adjutant, Marine Barracks, 8th and I streets SE, Washington, D.C. 20390-5000. The request should include the name of the party (either group or individual), the number of guests, a complete return address, and a point of contact with a telephone number.

Georgetown Garden Tour
Various locations, Washington, D.C.
• (202) 333-4953

The private gardens of this famous neighborhood are on display, with proceeds benefiting the Georgetown Children's House. You'll be surprised at the extensive landscapes hidden behind Georgetown's walled courtyards and gardens. Some go an impossibly long way — you'd never guess it from the outside. Guided and self-guided tours are available. Admission is $15.

Gross National Parade
M and 18th Sts. NW, Washington, D.C.
• (202) 686-3215

Washington pokes fun at itself and its offbeat traditions during this annual parade that draws upward of 100,000 spectators. You'll see "lawyers" or "executives" dressed in business suits, toting whatever comical items or signs satirize the political controversy of the day. Political celebrity look-alikes are walking caricatures of those whom they portray. No serious bands or pageantry in this parade! The festival benefits the Police Boys and Girls Clubs of Washington.

Goodwill Embassy Tour
Starting spot determined each year
• (202) 636-4225, ext. 1628

An event held each spring, the embassy tour benefits Davis Memorial Goodwill Industries. It's a grand opportunity to view places you would otherwise be unlikely to see, complete with art, furniture, architecture and decor representing the best of their respective nations. You will see some priceless items and catch a glimpse into the way the world's most rarefied society lives. Tour tickets include shuttle-bus transportation. Reservations are required. Admission is $25 in advance, and $30 on the day of tour.

Memorial Day Ceremonies
Vietnam Veterans Memorial, Constitution Ave. and Henry Bacon Dr. NW, Washington, D.C. • (202) 619-7222

Speeches, military bands and a keynote address are the centerpieces of this solemn event. Directories help you find names on the walls, and you can request a name rubbing.

Memorial Day Weekend Concert
West Lawn of the Capitol, Capitol Hill, Washington, D.C. • (202) 619-7222

As a kickoff to the summer tourist season, this popular concert features the globally acclaimed National Symphony Orchestra in an unforgettable setting under the stars.

"The President's Own" U.S. Marine Chamber Orchestra Concert Series
National Academy of Sciences, 2101 Constitution Ave. NW, Washington, D.C. • (202) 433-4011

The free Sunday concerts, held all month, are rare opportunities for the public to enjoy the orchestra which frequently performs at state dinners and diplomatic receptions. These are talented professional musicians, and Washingtonians normally crowd the hall, so come early.

Washington National Cathedral Flower Mart
Massachusetts and Wisconsin Aves. NW, Washington, D.C. • (202) 537-6200

Each year, the mart's theme is a salute to a different country featuring flower booths, entertainment and decorating demonstrations.

Northern Virginia

"The Commandant's Own"
Iwo Jima Memorial, U.S. Hwy. 50 at Arlington National Cemetery, Arlington, Va. • (202) 433-4173

Beneath the shadows of the dramatic Ma-

Photo: Courtesy of Becki Swinehart

The Virginia Gold Cup race is run every spring and fall.

rine Corps War Memorial, commonly known as the Iwo Jima Memorial, you'll be awed by the precision and discipline of the Marine Corps Silent Drill Platoon, stirred by the patriotic music of the Drum and Bugle Corps. These concerts will rivet you, and your children will remain fascinated for the entire hour. The site itself offers an inspiring view of the nation's capital and the Potomac River in the setting sun. Bring a picnic dinner and blanket — there's plenty of space on the lawn. See this event weekly, May through August.

Memorial Day Ceremonies
Arlington National Cemetery, Memorial Dr., Arlington, Va. • (202) 475-0856

Wreath-layings at the John F. Kennedy grave site and the Tomb of the Unknowns are part of the ceremonies that wind down with a service at the Memorial Amphitheatre. The president usually delivers the keynote address.

The Virginia Gold Cup
5089 Old Tavern Rd., The Plains, Va. • (540) 253-5001

Usually held the same day as the Kentucky Derby, this premier steeplechase of Virginia and the international community has blossomed into one of the largest sporting and social events in Metro Washington. Held at Great Meadow, riders compete for a $40,000 purse which, if they win the Gold Cup's counterpart in England, grows to $200,000. Great Meadow is in the heart of the state's gorgeous hunt country, about an hour west of Washington in Fauquier County. Admission is $40 per car in advance, and $50 at the gate.

Suburban Maryland

Andrews Air Force Base Open House
Andrews Air Force Base, Camp Springs, Md. • (301) 981-4511

This airshow is an impressive display of American military and technological might. You'll see all those bombers and fighter planes you read about in the news, as well as precision formation flying by the crack Air Force Thunderbirds. As is often the case with sites and events in Metro Washington, you need to be early to avoid traffic.

Chesapeake Bay Bridge Walk
Chesapeake Bay Bridge, Annapolis, Md. • (410) 288-8405

Here's your opportunity to take in the magnificent vistas of the Chesapeake Bay, but at a leisurely pace several hundred feet above the water. The 4.3-mile jaunt, enjoyed by thousands of all ages and shapes, goes from east to west and occupies an entire span of the twin-span Bay Bridge. For those who are truly in shape and looking for a different way to cross the bay, an organized run precedes the official walk. Whatever the mode of transport, buses take participants to the bridge from a staging area in the stadium parking lot at the Naval Academy in nearby Annapolis.

Kemper Open Pro-Am Golf Tournament
TPC at Avenel, 10000 Oaklyn Drv., Potomac, Md. • (301) 469-3737

The Pro-Am classic features some of the brightest stars on the PGA Tour plus a handful of local celebrities. Former Redskins quarterback Mark Rypien made the rigorous final cut several years ago but met his match against the likes of Greg Norman and John Daly. Admission is $25 to $290, depending on the number of days covered.

June

Washington, D.C.

Carnival Extravaganza
Emery Park, Georgia and Missouri Aves. NW, Washington, D.C. • (202) 726-2204

Washington has a large Caribbean population, and the carnival is reminiscent of Brazilian celebrations, though on a smaller scale. Participants wear elaborate costumes with sequins and peacock-like feather headpieces.

Children's Festival
Carter Barron Amphitheatre, 16th St. and Colorado Ave. NW, Washington, D.C. • (202) 619-7222

Sponsored by the Capital Children's Museum and the National Park Service, this all-day festi-

val includes live music, performing arts and a host of interactive programs. Admission is $10.

Dupont-Kalorama Museum Walk Day
Various locations on Dupont Cir., Washington, D.C. • (202) 667-0441

D.C.'s most famous arts district extends a gracious welcome through house tours, craft demonstrations and concerts on the first Saturday in June. A shuttle service is provided.

Festival of American Folklife
National Mall, between Independence and Constitution Aves., Washington, D.C. • (202) 357-2700

The rich cultural and folklife heritage of the Americas is played out on the National Mall in the form of lectures, concerts, working villages and hands-on exhibits. You'll see performances and exhibits from obscure societies you may not have known existed, as well as the more familiar ones, like Cajun or Navajo Nation. The festival runs through the 4th of July and attracts upward of 1 million people.

Marine Band's Summer Concert Series
The U.S. Capitol and the Sylvan Theater at the Washington Monument, 15th St. and Constitution Ave. NW, Washington, D.C. • (202) 433-4011

Concerts are held once a week through August. Check for days and times. These are concerts only, as distinct from the parades/concerts/military drills held at Iwo Jima and the Marine Barracks from May to August (see pertinent listings under the month of May).

Northern Virginia

Antique Car Show
Sully Plantation, Va. Rt. 28 (Sully Rd.), Chantilly, Va. • (703) 437-1794

A car-lover's fantasyland unfolds at this his-

INSIDERS' TIP

While attending summer outdoor concerts, consider applying bug spray to keep the gnats and mosquitoes away. They can be fierce!

toric plantation in western Fairfax County, in the shadows of Washington Dulles International Airport. You'll find almost 400 cars, ranging from the era of the Model-T to 1954. Admission is $6.

Fairfax Fair
Fairfax County Government Center Grounds, Government Center Pkwy., Fairfax, Va. • (703) 324-3247

This is not exactly a country fair, but then again, Fairfax County hasn't been rural for quite some time. Instead of livestock and produce, you'll get your fill of government service information and community programs. There's also plenty of music, games and rides along the midway for the kids and the young at heart. Admission is $7.

Red Cross Waterfront Festival
Oronoco Bay Park, base of Oronoco St. at the waterfront, Old Town Alexandria, Va. • (703) 549-8300

One of Alexandria's top summer events, the Red Cross Waterfront Festival brings in a weekend full of music (including some top-name rock, country, folk and reggae acts), ethnic foods, arts and crafts, fireworks, tall ships and, alas, a 10K run to work off all the calories. Admission is $5 to $8.

July

Washington, D.C.

Annual Soap Box Derby
Begins at Constitution Avenue NW, between Delaware and Louisiana Aves. • (301) 670-1110

It takes an Act of Congress each year to close the easternmost section of Constitution Avenue for this race, and each year Congress passes a joint resolution enabling the event — which proves that politicians aren't all sourpusses. Approximately 50 children from ages 9 to 16 participate in the "Gravity Grand Prix" as it's sometimes called, racing a course from Constitution and Delaware avenues NW, to Louisiana Avenue, NW. The route runs between the Russell Senate Office Building and

the U.S. Capitol, and the event lasts all day. The kids build their own cars, some from kits and some not, and many have even recruited local businesses as sponsors. Participants take this 50-year plus tradition seriously, and put a lot of effort into their entries, but the event couldn't be more fun.

Bastille Day
12th St. and Pennsylvania Ave. NW, Washington, D.C. • (202) 347-6848

Washington has a large French-speaking community, plus many French restaurant fans, so this Gallic Independence Day celebration on July 14 draws plenty of participants. Enjoy live entertainment and watch waiters bearing trays race to the Capitol and back.

Latin-American Festival
Adams Morgan, (Columbia Rd. NW) and the National Mall, Washington, D.C. • (202) 724-4091

Latin American music, dance, art, food and theater are the focus of a two-day heritage festival that takes place in the eclectic Adams Morgan neighborhood and on the grounds of the Washington Monument.

National Independence Day Celebration
The National Mall, between Independence and Constitution Aves. NW, Washington, D.C. • (202) 619-7222

Washington fittingly plays host to the nation's largest 4th of July party, with a parade down Constitution Avenue, colonial military maneuvers, concerts at the Sylvan Theatre next to the Washington Monument and an evening performance by the National Symphony Orchestra on the west steps of the Capitol. The day ends with a spectacular 45-minute fireworks exhibit that has been known to draw more than a million onlookers — on both sides of the river.

Northern Virginia

Vienna's Fourth of July Celebration
Waters Field, Cherry and Center Sts., Vienna, Va. • (703) 255-6300

One of suburban Washington's oldest July 4th celebrations, Vienna presents a viable small-town alternative to the pressing crowds and traffic associated with the downtown D.C. festivities. There's music and also some surprisingly good fireworks.

Virginia Scottish Games
Episcopal High School, 3901 W. Braddock Rd., Alexandria, Va.
• **(703) 838-4200**

Northern Virginia (Alexandria in particular) shows off its proud Scottish heritage at this weekend fete, which features Highland dancing, bagpiping, fiddling and traditional athletic events. Scottish foods, crafts and genealogy exhibits are also an integral part of the popular festival. Admission is $10 to $15.

Suburban Maryland

Rotary Crab Feast
U.S. Navy-Marine Corps Stadium, Farragut Rd., Annapolis, Md.
• **(410) 841-2841**

Lovers of Maryland's prized crustacean should bring a hefty appetite to the world's largest crab feast, held for over 50 years. More than 185,000 gallons of crab soup and 325 bushels of Maryland blue crabs are consumed at this spicy event, which benefits the Annapolis Rotary Club. Admission is $30.

August

Washington, D.C.

Georgia Avenue Day
Georgia and Eastern Aves. NW, Washington, D.C. • **(202) 723-5166**

Georgia Avenue, D.C.'s longest business corridor, comes alive with a parade, carnival rides, live music and a wealth of festive foods. It's an ethnic mix here, with traditions from Africa, the Caribbean and the American South.

U.S. Army Band's "1812 Overture"
Sylvan Theatre, adjacent to the Washington Monument, Washington, D.C. • **(202) 426-6841**

Guaranteed to get the patriotic juices flow-

ing, the "1812" gets a dose of firepower from the Salute Gun Platoon of the 3rd U.S. Infantry.

Northern Virginia

Arlington County Fair
Thomas Jefferson Center, 3501 S. 2nd St., Arlington, Va. • **(703) 358-6400**

Arlington's urban multicultural heritage is the reason for this four-day fair typically held the third week of the month. Craftsmen and exhibits are indoors, while food vendors are outside.

Civil War Living History Day
Fort Ward Museum and Park, 4301 W. Braddock Rd., Alexandria, Va.
• **(703) 838-4848**

Fort Ward was one of several Union fortifications that encircled Washington during the Civil War. This living history reenacts Union and Confederate camp life, complete with artillery drills. See our Civil War Sites chapter for more on this park.

Suburban Maryland

Kunte Kinte Heritage Commemoration and Festival
St. John's College, 60 College Ave., Annapolis, Md. • **(410) 349-0338**

Made into a household name with the airing of TV's 1977 landmark miniseries *Roots*, Kunte Kinte was brought into the harsh New World at the Port of Annapolis. The festival honors his legacy and the rich traditions of generations of succeeding African Americans. There are educational programs for both children and adults, as well as African-American crafts exhibits and demonstrations. Food vendors represent many ethnic backgrounds, and entertainment ranges from gospel singers to calypso. Admission is $5.

Maryland Renaissance Festival
Crownsville Rd., off Md. Hwy. 450 E., Crownsville, Md. • **(410) 266-7304**

The Free State slips into a medieval state of mind during this well-attended festival usually held the last weekend of August and extending into October. Jousting events, jugglers, and medieval foods and crafts are just some of the many delights awaiting visitors at this 20-acre "village" located in the heart of suburban Crownsville. Admission is $12.95.

Montgomery County Agricultural Fair
Montgomery County Fairgrounds, Exit 10-11 off I-270, Gaithersburg, Md. • (301) 926-3100

There's still plenty of rural character in this highly urbanized county, as evidenced by the size and popularity of this old-fashioned country fair. You'll find livestock judging, amusement park rides, games of chance, concerts and plenty of food concessions. Admission is $5.

September

Washington, D.C.

Adams Morgan Day
Columbia Rd. and Florida Ave. NW, Washington, D.C. • (202) 724-4091

This giant ethnic festival, a salute to Adams Morgan's multicultural character, is a hot ticket with the city's young and hip crowd. Expect to hear great music — reggae, jazz, R&B and salsa — and be tempted by some of the city's best international cuisine.

Ambassadors' Ball and Benefit
Grand Hyatt Hotel, 1000 H St. NW, Washington, D.C. • (202) 296-5363

One of Washington's premier dress-up events, and the kickoff to the Washington social season, the Ambassadors' Ball benefits the National Multiple Sclerosis Society. Chairwomen for the event invariably include the wives of national politicians. For a few hundred bucks, you too may attend — and it's all for charity. Admission $300.

Hispanic Designers Gala Fashion Show and Benefit
1000 Thomas Jefferson St. NW, Washington, D.C. • (202) 337-9636

This splashy event draws top Hispanic entertainers and politicians. Proceeds are used for scholarships for young Hispanic designers. Admission is $350.

Kalorama House and Embassy Tour
Kalorama Neighborhood, Woodrow Wilson House, 2340 S St. NW, Washington, D.C. • (202) 387-4062

Historic Kalorama is still one of D.C.'s most exclusive and interesting neighborhoods. Homes and gardens in this area are lavish and beautifully maintained. You begin at the Woodrow Wilson House, a museum property of the National Trust for Historic Preservation. Admission is $18 in advance, and $20 on the day of the tour.

Kennedy Center Open House,
John F. Kennedy Center for the Performing Arts, 2700 F St. NW, Washington, D.C. • (202) 467-4600

Stroll the towering red-carpeted halls of Washington's premier performing arts center, and then enjoy the free concerts and performances at this annual open house.

Labor Day Weekend Concert
West Lawn of the Capitol, Capitol Hill, Washington, D.C. • (202) 619-7222

The National Symphony Orchestra officially closes Washington's summer tourist season with a rousing selection of classical and patriotic arrangements. This event is packed, so plan to come early, maybe with a blanket and a picnic, and take public transportation or you'll be caught in the mother of all traffic jams.

National Frisbee Championships
Washington Monument grounds, 15th St. and Constitution Ave. NW, Washington, D.C. • (800) 786-9240

This annual contest featuring disk-catching canines never fails to make the evening news. The dogs are amazing, and you'll wonder how the owners trained them to make some of those catches. Dogs are judged on showmanship, leaping agility and execution.

Rock Creek Park Day
Nature Center, Rock Creek Park, 5200 Glover Rd. NW, Washington, D.C. • (202) 426-6829

The nature center is headquarters for a

slate of environmental, recreational and historical programs during this day-long tribute to one of the world's largest and most beautiful urban parks. Each year, Rock Creek Park Day commemorates the founding of the park — the year 2000 will be its 110th birthday. There's cake and a raffle, and a program in the nature center's planetarium.

Washington International Antiquarian Book Fair
Washington Convention Center, 900 9th St. NW, Washington, D.C.
• (202) 789-1600

Dealers from the U.S. and Europe exhibit and sell rare books, including first editions, manuscripts, prints, autographs and maps. There are often special exhibits by the Library of Congress, as well as seminars and demonstrations on a variety of topics. Admission is $10.

Washington Post Super Sale and Gala
Locations vary, Washington, D.C.
• (202) 334-4263

The Super Sale is a star-studded event whose main draw is a ballroom full of bargain-priced clothes from top fashion designers. Supermodels and high society mix at the pre-sale gala the night before, an event always covered in *The Washington Post* and usually in *Vogue* or *Town and Country*. Tickets to both events sell out quickly, in part because the organizers include some of Washington's most high-powered women, like society doyenne Katharine Graham, the chairwoman of *The Washington Post*.

Proceeds are donated to the Nina Hyde Center for Breast Cancer Research at Georgetown University Hospital. (The center is named for the longtime fashion editor of *The Post*.) Admission is $15 for the sale, and $200 for the gala. Reservations are required.

Northern Virginia

Historic Homes Tour of Old Town Alexandria
Meet at the Athenaeum, 210 Prince St., Alexandria, Va. • (703) 548-0035

Much of Old Town dates from the 18th century, but this is a chance to see homes still used as private residences. The tour is a one-day-only event benefiting the Alexandria Hospital. Admission is $15.

International Children's Festival
Wolf Trap Farm Park for the Performing Arts, 1624 Trap Rd., Vienna, Va.
• (703) 255-1900

At America's only national park for the performing arts, kids take center stage for a three-day outdoor festival celebrating the global arts. Sponsored by the Arts Council of Fairfax County, the popular event features a variety of performances and educational workshops presented by groups from the local area, throughout the U.S. and around the world. Most of the performance groups are largely made up of children. Admission is $10.

Occoquan Fall Craft Show
Mill, Union, Washington and Commerce Sts., Old Town Occoquan, Va.
• (703) 491-4045

More than 300 juried artisans, representing 30 states, exhibit their wares in front of some 100,000 shoppers in this tidy and historic waterfront community. This weekend fair just might be the largest craft show on the East Coast.

Oktoberfest
Reston Town Center, Market St.
Reston, Va. • (703) 787-6601

More than 20,000 people usually attend this four-day beer, polka and sauerbraten festival in lively Reston Town Center. This is a big, open area where you can let the kids run, and there's plenty to amuse them, from balloons to dancers and musicians.

Old Town Chili Cook-Off
Oronoco Bay Park., Oronoco St. at the waterfront, Old Town Alexandria, Va.
• (202) 244-7900

This annual event featuring chili and other comestibles from local restaurants is to benefit the National Kidney Foundation of the National Capital area. It's held at the edge of the Potomac River in Old Town Alexandria, near many shops and restaurants of the charming historic district. Admission is $5.

Photo: Courtesy of the Virginia Division of Tourism

Colorful bagpipe bands are a major feature of Alexandria's Scottish Christmas Walk.

Vienna Harvest Festival

Vienna Community Center, 120 Cherry St. SE, Vienna, Va. • (703) 281-1333

Dancing, carnival rides, live music and the Taste of Vienna are all wrapped into this two-day festival. Crafts and baked goods are for sale in the indoor center, but on a crisp fall day, there's also much to do outside.

Suburban Maryland

Maryland Seafood Festival

Sandy Point State Park, U.S. Hwy. 50 at the Chesapeake Bay Bridge, Annapolis, Md. • (410) 268-7682

The bounty of the Chesapeake Bay is baked, steamed, grilled, broiled, sautéed, and fried at this waterside park, next to the western end of the towering Bay Bridge. Admission is $8.

Prince George's County Fair

Prince George's Equestrian Center, U.S. Hwy. 4, Upper Marlboro, Md. • (301) 952-7900

Like neighboring Montgomery County, urbanized Prince George's still holds on to its rural origins. The county was once a major producer of tobacco, and vestiges of that tradition can still be seen in areas far beyond the Beltway. Admission is $5.

Prince George's Community College Blue Bird Blues Festival

Prince George's Community College, 301 Largo Rd., Largo, Md. • (301) 322-0853

It's a blues festival, but there are also children's activities, food and crafts. The one-day event features a half-dozen or so local bands.

October

Washington, D.C.

Annual Lombardi Gala
Various locations throughout
Washington, D.C. • (202) 687-1067

All proceeds from this benefit go to the Lombardi Cancer Center at Georgetown University Medical Center. The Lombardi Center is one of only 26 centers in the nation designated as a comprehensive cancer center by the U.S. National Cancer Institute, a part of the National Institutes of Health. The gala features a dinner and a silent auction of many high-ticket items. Admission is $250.

Fall D.C. Antiques Fair
D.C. Armory, 2001 E. Capitol St. SE,
Washington, D.C. • (301) 738-1966
before show, (202) 547-9215 during
show

Nearly 200 dealers travel from 20 states to display their Canadian and European heirlooms at this popular show. For more information, see the D.C. Spring Antiques Fair listing, in this chapter. Admission is $5.

Taste of D.C. Festival
Freedom Plaza, Pennsylvania Ave.,
between 9th and 14th Sts. NW,
Washington, D.C.
• (202) 724-4091

Washington's top restaurants lay it on the line in this public tasting, which also includes live entertainment, arts and crafts exhibits and games for the kids. Proceeds go to various charities. Admission is free, but food samples start at $4.

Theodore Roosevelt's Birthday Celebration
Theodore Roosevelt Island, George
Washington Memorial Pkwy., Arlington,
Va. • (703) 285-2598

The scenic urban wilderness sanctuary of Roosevelt Island plays host to this birthday party honoring the nation's first environmental president. Hike along trails in this 88-acre preserve, and view the 17-foot bronze statue of Roosevelt; then, stop and chat with the Roosevelt look-alike who plays the former president for the day. There's even birthday cake!

Northern Virginia

Marine Corps Marathon
Iwo Jima Memorial, U.S. Hwy. 50 at
Arlington National Cemetery, Arlington,
Va.• (703) 784-2225

Thousands of world-class runners snake through the downtown streets and parks in what has become one of the nation's most prestigious marathons. While most of the action takes place in Washington, the race begins and ends at the Iwo Jima Memorial in Arlington. Registration is $35 for runners.

Vienna Halloween Parade
Branch and Maple Aves., Vienna, Va.
• (703) 255-6300

Vienna claims the region's oldest (since the 1940s) and largest (several thousand strong) Halloween Parade, which wends its way along a stretch of the town's main thoroughfare.

Waterford Homes Tour and Crafts Show
I-662 to High St., Waterford, Va.
• (540) 882-3018

About 50 years ago a group of Waterford residents had the foresight to set up a preservation foundation in Loudoun County to save this picturesque National Historic Landmark village from suburbia. The annual homes tour and crafts fair, which features over 100 juried artisans, benefits ongoing restoration and preservation efforts. Admission is $10 in advance, and $12 on the day of the event.

Suburban Maryland

Taste of Bethesda
Fairmont, Norfolk and St. Elmo Sts.
Bethesda, Md. • (301) 215-6660

Tens of thousands flock to this food and music festival showcasing over 40 prime res-

Cherry trees line the Tidal Basin in front of the Jefferson Memorial.

taurants from Bethesda. Admission is free, and food samples start at $5.

U.S. Sailboat Show/U.S. Power Boat Show
Annapolis City Dock, Dock St. Annapolis, Md. • (410) 268-8828

Held on consecutive weekends, with the sailors going first, these are the largest in-water boat shows in the nation. With many boats and nautical products from the world's leading manufacturers, Annapolis turns into a festival for the water-loving set. Admission is $12 for general admission, and $25 for VIP opening day.

Washington International Horse Show
USAirways Arena, 1 Harry S. Truman Dr., Landover, Md. • (301) 840-0281

Equestrian teams from the United States and Europe compete in a week of events, with plenty of sideline shows for laypeople and kids. There are competitions in dressage and jumping, and exhibition events. Admission ranges from $18 to $42, depending on dates and seat locations.

November

Northern Virginia

Alexandria Antiques Show
Best Western Old Colony Inn, 615 First St., Old Town Alexandria, Va. • (703) 838-4200

You guessed it — more antiques and crafts from the heirloom gold mine of the mid-Atlantic. The furniture here is often quite formal, in keeping with the Old Town setting, with lots of oil paintings and European pieces. Admission is $8.

Veterans Day Ceremonies
Vietnam Veterans Memorial, Constitution Ave. and Henry Bacon Dr. NW; Arlington National Cemetery, Memorial Dr., Arlington, Va. • (202) 619-7222

Both solemn and celebratory, the ceremonies attract thousands of veterans, mili-

tary VIPs, general spectators and, often, the commander-in-chief of the armed forces (a.k.a. the president).

Suburban Maryland

Capital Cat Fanciers Cat Show
Montgomery County Fairgrounds, Exit 10-11 off I-270, Gaithersburg, Md. • (301) 926-0746

For fans of felines, this is the cat's meow with two days of pawing and purring from prized cats. Admission is $5.

Sugarloaf's Autumn Crafts Festival
Montgomery County Fairgrounds, Exit 10 or 11 off I-270, Gaithersburg, Md. • (301) 926-3100

This is it, the granddaddy of all Metro D.C. craft shows, featuring 425 juried artisans. It'll take you two hours just to walk the grounds, let alone browse and shop. Admission is $6.

December

Washington, D.C.

The Annual Capital Area Auto Show
Washington Convention Center, 900 9th St. NW, Washington, D.C. • (202) 371-4200

Each year, this massive exhibition introduces car buffs to next year's models as well as wildly imaginative concept cars that may one day come to market in modified form. There are often autograph signings by Washington celebrities, live radio broadcasts and, of course, those glamorous human models in their glittering outfits.

National Christmas Tree Lighting/ Pageant of Peace
The Ellipse, behind the White House, between 15th and 17th Sts. NW, Washington, D.C. • (202) 619-7222

The president lights the giant National Christmas Tree and officially kicks off the Christmas season. From early December to

New Year's Day, the Ellipse is the site of nightly choral concerts, a nativity scene, live reindeer, a burning yule log and lighted Christmas trees from each of the nation's states and territories.

Washington National Cathedral Christmas Celebration and Services
Washington National Cathedral, Massachusetts and Wisconsin Aves. NW, Washington, D.C. • (202) 537-6200

The Christmas Eve service here, at Washington's answer to the great cathedrals of Europe, is simply breathtaking; however, passes are required and you should write for them in November if you expect to snag one of the 3,400 seats available for either the 6 PM or 10 PM service on Christmas Eve. At the earlier service, the cathedral's 24-person girls' choir performs; the later service features 40 singers of the men's and boys' choir.

Up to six tickets per person may be requested by sending a self-addressed stamped envelope to: Christmas (the year), Washington National Cathedral, Massachusetts and Wisconsin Aves. NW, Washington, D.C. 20016. Be sure to include your own name, address and a daytime phone number with your request. Also specify which service you would like to attend. On Christmas Day, there are three services at 9 AM, noon and 4 PM, and none require passes. The 9 AM is televised and features a choir, while the two later services have only organ music and hymns.

Northern Virginia

Alexandria Scottish Christmas Walk
Campagna Center, 418 S. Washington St., Alexandria, Va. • (703) 549-0111

A gathering of the clans — bagpipes and all — takes over the streets and alleys of Old Town for one of the holiday season's most festive events. Adjunct activities include a designer tour of homes (admission $20) and a Christmas marketplace of decorations and ornaments at the Campagna Center (no admission fee).

Suburban Maryland

Christmas Lights Parade
Annapolis City Dock, Dock St., Annapolis, Md. • (410) 267-8986

Annapolitans decorate their yachts with Christmas lights for this highly visual, and often chilly, evening on the Chesapeake Bay.

Festival of Lights
Washington Mormon Temple Visitors' Center, 9900 Stoneybrook Dr., Kensington, Md. • (301) 587-0144

Tens of thousands of lights adorn the grounds of this Oz-like temple looming above the Capital Beltway. Inside the Visitors' Center are Christmas trees bearing decorations from around the world. The temple itself is open only to those of the Mormon faith. See the Worship chapter for more information.

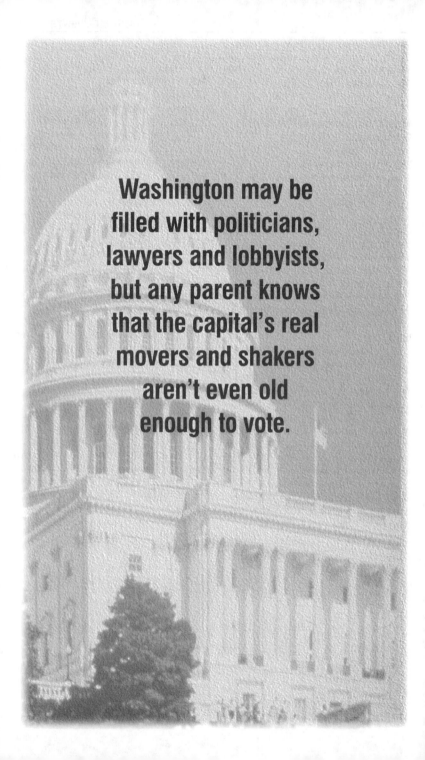

Washington may be
filled with politicians,
lawyers and lobbyists,
but any parent knows
that the capital's real
movers and shakers
aren't even old
enough to vote.

Kidstuff

Washington may be filled with politicians, lawyers and lobbyists, but any parent knows that the capital's real movers and shakers aren't even old enough to vote. Endlessly energetic and inquisitive, kids are always ready to leap into action, while moms and dads scramble to arrange outings that are safe, educational and — most of all — fun. In this chapter, you'll find dozens of destinations that prove surefire hits with kids of all ages.

What are you waiting for? Round up the family and head out for an adventure.

Family Friendly Museums

Your kids just want to have fun; you want them to learn too. They can do both at these great museums, where hands-on activities and special family programs make visits entertaining and enlightening. And here's a bonus: Many have free admission, so you needn't feel obligated to stay for hours if the little ones get fidgety. Be sure to check our Attractions and Arts chapters for more information on many of these and other museums and galleries.

Washington, D.C.

The Smithsonian Institution

The Smithsonian museums are gradually adding more and more interactive exhibits and special activities with kid-appeal. Start at the Castle to collect information and make your Smithsonian plan.

See our Attractions chapter for hours and more information. Also see Arts and Annual Events for information.

The Smithsonian Information Center
1000 Jefferson Dr. SW, Washington, D.C. • (202) 357-2700

Before you visit, call or stop by the Smithsonian Information Center (a.k.a. the Castle) at the listed address, and ask for "10 Tips for Visiting Smithsonian Museums with Children" and "The Smithsonian Quiz for Children." See our Arts, Attractions, Annual Events and Education chapters for more information about the museums listed here and other Smithsonian museums and programs.

Hirshhorn Museum and Sculpture Garden
7th St. and Independence Ave. SW, Washington, D.C. • (202) 357-2700

You may need to caution your kids not to touch the assorted pieces in the outdoor Sculpture Garden, which looks a lot like a funky playground. Children can do lots of looking, however, and they'll see and learn plenty of interesting things about modern art by using the museum's wonderful "Family Guide," available free of charge at the information desk. The eye-catching folder contains 12 colorful "artcards," each of which features a picture of an art work, information about the artist, observations about the piece and at least one activity.

Look for kid-pleasers like Alexander Calder's fish mobile, Andy Warhol's *Marilyn Monroe's Lips* and Joan Miró's sculpture, *Lunar Bird*. The museum hosts free, monthly "Young at Art" family programs, featuring hands-on activities for children ages 6 to 9 accompanied by adults. Call (202) 357-1618, extension 116, for reservations, which are required. Also see our Arts chapter for more information.

National Air and Space Museum
6th and Independence Sts. SW, Washington, D.C. • (202) 357-2700

Voted Best Museum for Children by the readers of *Washington Families* newspaper, this most popular Smithsonian museum awes kids as soon as they walk in and spy all the hanging aircraft. They can experience firsthand the principles of flight by visiting the interactive "How Things Fly" gallery, where they can work the controls on a real plane and perform numerous experiments. Related activity sheets describe additional fun to try at home.

Elsewhere in the museum, kids enjoy walking through a space lab and touching a moon rock. If you visit before November, look for "Star Wars: The Magic of Myth," a must-see for young fans of the sci-fi trilogy; call the Stars Wars Exhibition Hotline at (202) 786-2122 for up-to-date information. The museum offers free highlights tours, which can be tailored toward children, daily at 10:15 AM and 1 PM. Check the daily schedule for IMAX theater and planetarium shows, which require tickets. Call the public affairs office at (202) 357-1552 to obtain a calendar of events.

National Museum of African Art
950 Independence Ave. SW, Washington, D.C. • (202) 357-2700

Kids like looking at sculptures that dance and clap at the push of a button, colorful masks and patterned clothing. The museum regularly offers drop-in, family-oriented events such as storytelling and the "Let's Read About Africa" reading program. Kids' activity sheets related to special exhibits sometimes are available at the information desk.

National Museum of American Art
8th and G Sts. NW, Washington, D.C. • (202) 357-2700

Children enjoy many of the museum's folk-art pieces, especially giraffe and tiger sculptures made from bottle caps, a quilt created with buttons, Hispanic wood carvings, the fiberglass Mexican cowboy sculpture on the museum's front steps and *The Throne of the Third Heaven*, James Hampton's room-size

sculpture, which kids can study to find such familiar items as hubcaps, light bulbs and jelly jars. The second-floor gallery includes several paintings and sculptures featuring children.

Art Stop!, a free parent/child program held one Saturday each month from 10:30 AM to noon, features a tour and related hands-on activity. Call (202) 357-4511 for a schedule or to make the required reservations. The museum also sponsors Family Day in the spring and fall.

National Museum of American History
14th St. and Constitution Ave. NW, Washington, D.C. • (202) 357-2700

Kids getting restless from too much looking and not enough touching? Head for one of the museum's two hands-on rooms, open to visitors "from ages 5 to 105" but especially geared toward youngsters, who must be accompanied by adults. In the Hands On History Room on the second floor, children can pedal a high-wheeled bicycle, try on old-fashioned clothing, rummage through a peddler's pack and decorate a paper pot with Indian symbols, among other activities. All subjects relate to museum exhibits. The center is open free of charge Tuesday through Sunday, noon to 3 PM. Tickets, available at the door, may be required on weekends and during other busy times.

Part of the "Science in American Life" exhibition in the first floor's west wing, the Hands On Science Center lets children 5 and older try such experiments as testing food additives, unraveling DNA genes, measuring with lasers and determining their sunglasses' UV ratings. Hours are 10 AM to 5:30 PM daily, and tickets may be required during busy periods.

Elsewhere in the museum, children like to scan bar codes at the interactive "Information

---

INSIDERS' TIP

Take a break from the Mall museums and go for a spin on the circa 1940s Allan Herschell carousel on the Mall in front of the Arts and Industries Building at 900 Jefferson Drive SW. The ride operates daily, weather permitting, 10 AM to 5:30 PM.

Age" exhibition, and discover what modern things are made of in "A Material World." Kids also enjoy looking at the collection of First Ladies' gowns, the Bradford Doll House and familiar pop-culture items such as Fonzie's leather jacket and Mr. Rogers' sweater. Visit the Victorian-style Palm Court ice cream parlor on the first floor for a light meal or treat. The large gift shop carries interesting children's books and toys.

National Museum of Natural History
10th St. and Constitution Ave. NW, Washington, D.C. • (202) 357-2700

Kids love this museum from the moment they walk in and spot the rotunda's giant elephant. From there, head for the dinosaur exhibit or the taxidermy displays, sort of like a still-life zoo. The Discovery Room, also on the first floor, features hands-on activities for all ages using a variety of items like quartz, seashells and native crafts from the museum's collections. Hours are 10:30 AM to 3:30 PM daily during the summer; regular hours are Tuesday through Friday, noon to 2:30 PM, and Saturday and Sunday, 10:30 AM to 3:30 PM. Obtain free passes at the door. Upstairs, the No. 1 kid-pleasing attraction is the O. Orkin Insect Zoo, filled with live creepy crawlies. Look for bugs and their relatives, such as hissing cockroaches and centipedes, and don't miss the tarantula feedings, weekdays (except Monday) at 10:30 and 11:30 AM and 1:30 PM and weekends at 11:30 AM and 12:30 and 1:30 PM.

National Postal Museum
2 Massachusetts Ave. NE, Washington, D.C. • (202) 357-2700

Visit the information desk for "A Self-Guided Tour for Very Young Visitors," a brochure highlighting exhibition elements children appreciate. Older kids can search for answers to true-or-false questions in the "Check It Out!" pamphlet. The museum's many kid-pleasing exhibits include a "wooded" trail that simulates a colonial mail route, a stage coach in which sitting is permitted, interactive computer games, a puzzle-like stamp collection and a railway mail car to explore. Children also like to look at Owney, a postal dog who collected

more than 1,000 dog tags during his travels aboard mail trains. "What's in the Mail For You?" includes several entertaining holographic characters who explain the history of mail-order before visitors take a computerized survey to obtain personalized mail, delivered at the exhibit's end. Computer kiosks in the lobby create postcards that can be mailed from the museum.

Freer Gallery of Art
Jefferson Dr. and 12th St. SW, Washington, D.C. • (202) 357-2700
Arthur M. Sackler Gallery
1050 Independence Ave. SW, Washington, D.C. • (202) 357-2700

Visit the information desks at these two connected museums of Asian art to obtain a variety of free children's activity sheets on such subjects as Japanese screens, scrolls, Hindu gods and gallery terminology. The museum gift shops carry *The Princess and the Peacocks*, a children's book about the Freer's ornate Peacock Room, designed by James McNeill Whistler. The popular ImaginAsia program, for youngsters ages 6 through 12 and their parents, features a different theme each month. Sessions take place Saturdays from 10 AM to 12:30 PM March through June and September and October, and 10 AM to 12:30 PM Mondays and Wednesdays in July and August.

Other Kid-Friendly Museums in Washington

Capital Children's Museum
800 3rd St. NE, Washington, D.C. • (202) 675-4120

Here's your itinerary: Drink hot chocolate in Mexico, create a colorful kite in Thailand, play games in Japan, hide in a prehistoric cave and pal around with Bugs Bunny. You don't need a passport to do these and lots of other cool hands-on activities at the Capital Children's Museum, which adheres to the motto "Where learning is an adventure." One of the oldest and largest children's museums in the country, CCM features 40,000 square feet of exhibits on three floors. The circa 1873 former convent's exterior looks rather dreary to first-time visitors, who are quickly reassured when they spot the entrance courtyard's giant Cootie and whimsical sculpture garden made from recycled odds and ends. Inside, kids often travel first to Mexico, the museum's original and most popular exhibit, which includes a festive marketplace with a fountain and props for shopping. Volunteers show you how to grind chocolate and make crafts like tissue-paper flowers. Preschoolers especially enjoy the sandy "beach" in the Yucatan room, which also features a pyramid to climb. (Go inside to visit a tiny secret room!)

In another favorite exhibit, "Animation: The World of Chuck Jones," amazed kids co-star in cartoons with Loony Tunes characters, thanks to a magical blue wall. Visitors can create designs for experiments using early animation techniques, and discover the instruments behind cartoon sound effects.

Other interactive highlights include: the lavishly decorated "From the Hands of Thailand"; a communications hall with an old-fashioned printing press; a computer room; a city scene with an "underground" crawl space; giant soap bubbles; a puppet play room; face games; a music machine; a maze; and a Japanese Tatami room, one of the newest exhibits. The museum holds frequent story times, workshops and guest appearances by authors and entertainers. Two birthday party rooms feature undersea and circus themes.

Visit the museum daily, 10 AM to 6 PM. (It's closed on New Year's Day, Thanksgiving and Christmas.) Admission is $6 per person, $4 for seniors and free for children younger than age 2. Admission is half-price on Sundays before noon. A one-year family membership costs $50 and includes unlimited visits.

Discovery Creek Children's Museum of Washington
4954 MacArthur Blvd. NW, Washington, D.C. • (202) 364-3111

Set in a former one-room schoolhouse, this unique, program-based museum serves as a hands-on science, natural- history and art-learning lab for families and school groups. Visitors participate in workshops related to themed exhibits that change twice a year. Transformed into a living rainforest last spring, the museum held such activities as Tagua Nut Treasures and Canopy Critters. Children visit-

ing during the coral reef exhibit made their own coral creations.

Program hours vary, but the museum is generally open to the public for several workshop sessions on weekends only. Most activities are geared toward children ages 3 to 10 and cost $6 per child for museum members, and $8 for nonmembers. A one-year family membership is $50 and includes members-only programs, a subscription tot he programming newsletter and discounts. The museum is slated to open an additional site this spring at Glen Echo Park, a unique national park that's described later in this chapter.

Corcoran Gallery of Art
17th St. and New York Ave. NW, Washington, D.C. • (202) 639-1700

The city's oldest private art gallery is small enough not to overwhelm youngsters, who enjoy its large landscape paintings and works featuring children and animals. Visit the information desk for a free brochure, "Musing for Myths," a scavenger hunt for pictures with mythological themes, geared toward kids ages 6 to 12.

The museum's free, ongoing "Sunday Traditions" program, held at 2:30 on some Sunday afternoons, features performances, workshops and storytelling designed for families with children 4 and older. Call (202) 639-1725 for a schedule of upcoming events or to make required reservations. Occasional daylong, drop-in Family Day celebrations include workshops, storytelling and other activities built around a theme such as Artists of Our Town. See our Arts chapter for a complete description.

DAR Museum
1776 D St. NW, Washington, D.C. • (202) 879-3254

Docents lead guided tours, tailored to visitors' ages and interests, of the museum's period rooms, weekdays from 10 AM to 2:30 PM and Sundays from 1 to 4:30 PM. Children especially enjoy the "Touch of Independence" area, where they can play with a genuine 19th-century, hand-painted Noah's Ark; roll a hoop with a stick; and enjoy a tea party with dolls, using a miniature Blue Willow china set. Nearby, the New Hampshire Toy Attic contains a display of numerous antique toys, dolls and games. Other period rooms feature musical instruments, tea-party settings and children's furniture that appeal to kids.

Call the museum for information about children's programs, such as the popular, free Colonial Adventure for ages 5 to 7, offered by reservation the first and third Sundays of each month from 1:30 to 2:30 PM and 3 to 4 PM. The museum holds a one-week quilt camp for kids ages 9 to 12 during July. See our Attractions chapter for more.

National Aquarium
Commerce Department Building, 14th St. between Constitution and Pennsylvania Aves. NW, Washington, D.C.
• **(202) 482-2825**

Children have an easy time seeing exhibits at the nation's oldest aquarium, which is much smaller and less crowded than the better-known and unrelated National Aquarium in Baltimore. A Touch Tank features horseshoe and hermit crabs, starfish and pencil urchins, all of which may be handled by little hands. Look for the electric eel, which emits an audible charge, and the alligator exhibit. Kids also enjoy watching shark feedings Saturday, Monday and Wednesday at 2 PM, and piranha feedings Sunday, Tuesday and Thursday at 2 PM. The annual summer Shark Day includes hands-on activities and costumed characters.

The aquarium is open 9 AM to 5 PM daily, except Christmas. Admission is $2 for adults and 75¢ for children ages 2 to 10.

National Building Museum
401 F St. NW, Washington, D.C.
• **(202) 272-2448**

Kids love to roam the open space in the museum's great hall and touch tactile models of Washington monuments in the "Washington: Symbol and City" exhibit.

Three free children's activity booklets, available at the front desk, feature such topics as patterns, building history, architectural terms and museum treasure hunts. Visit on Saturday at 2:30 PM to learn how to build arches and trusses during a hands-on demonstration suitable for ages 5 and older. Call for a schedule, costs and registration information regarding the museum's monthly family programs. See Attractions for additional information.

National Gallery of Art
4th St. and Constitution Ave. NW, Washington, D.C. • **(202) 737-4215**

Kids will be less intimidated by this awe-inspiring, free museum's large scale if you start your family outing in the Micro Gallery in the West Building Art Information Room. Here, visitors can have fun using the touch-screen computer monitors to view art works featuring their favorite animals or other subjects and learn more about the artists. Design a personalized tour, featuring a printed map showing the locations of works your children want to see.

Art Information Desks, centrally located on both levels of the West Building and on the East Building's ground level, feature free fliers describing self-guided family tours. Among children's favorite works in the West Building are Sir Peter Paul Rubens' *Daniel in the Lions' Den*, John Singleton Copley's *Watson and the Shark* and Gilbert Stuart's presidential portraits. In the East Building, children like the untitled red Alexander Calder mobile and Jackson Pollock's splattered *Lavender Mist*. Call (202) 789-3030 for a schedule of family programs held in conjunction with special exhibits.

The museum shops sell three family guides ($2.50 each) containing activities geared toward kids preschool-age and older: *West Building Highlights*, *Portraits and Personalities* and *Shapes and Patterns*. The shops also carry a 112-page *National Gallery of Art Activity Book* ($16.95), a 44-page *My Journey Through Art: Create Your Own Masterpieces* ($6.95) and the *National Gallery of Art Great Paintings Coloring Book* ($12.95), as well as an abundance of postcards, perfect for creating a museum scavenger hunt.

Bringing a baby or toddler? Free strollers for museum use are available at every entrance in both buildings. Hungry kids enjoy visiting the Cafe/Buffet to eat a snack or meal while they watch a mesmerizing waterfall outside a large window. See the Arts chapter for more information.

National Geographic Society's Explorers Hall
17th and M Sts. NW, Washington, D.C.
• **(202) 857-7588**

"Geographica: The World at Your Fingertips" features numerous kid-pleasing hands-on exhibits, including video touch-screens exploring assorted topics, a simulated tornado and a black-box aquarium containing lifelike images of different fish for children to "catch." An interactive amphitheater, Earth Station One, features an 11-foot globe and simulated space flight. The free museum also holds family-oriented special events twice a month. See the Attractions chapter for more details.

National Museum of Women in the Arts
1250 New York Ave., Washington, D.C.
• **(202) 783-5000**

Visit the information desk for a free "Art Ventures" booklet that includes activities related to kid-pleasing works such as Lilly Martin Spencer's realistic painting *The Artist and Her Family at a Fourth of July Picnic*, Frida Baranek's untitled abstract wire sculpture and Gabriele Munter's landscape *Staffelsee in Autumn*. Call (202) 783-7370 for recorded information about upcoming events, including family programs held monthly on Sunday from 2 to 4 PM. See the Arts chapter for more information.

The Navy Museum
Building 76, Washington Navy Yard, 9th and M Sts. SE, Washington, D.C.
• **(202) 433-2651**

Ships ahoy! Kids may not care much about the U.S. Naval history presented here, but they love to climb aboard the hulking antiaircraft guns, pretend to be an astronaut in a space capsule and imagine how oceanographers work in an underwater research vessel. Young visitors enjoy other hands-on activities, such as the popular submarine room, where children can pretend to steer a sub and operate assorted buttons and toggle switches on genuine instrument panels. Two periscopes offer a revolving view of the Navy Yard outside. Kids also like to drive their parents crazy by repeatedly sounding the Klaxon, a diving alarm that blares an ear-piercing "WhaOOOOOga!" throughout the museum.

Call (202) 433-4882, preferably with three weeks' notice, to arrange a free, themed family or group tour. In "Ships to the Sea," children create their own ship models after looking at the museum's collections. Another tour, "Hats Off," looks at different styles of sailor hats and concludes with a hat-making session. Visitors

also can take self-guided scavenger hunts using brochures obtained at the information desk. See Attractions for more information about Navy Yard hours and attractions.

Washington Dolls' House and Toy Museum
5236 44th St. NW, Washington, D.C.
• **(202) 244-0024**

Although it lacks hands-on activities, this sweet little museum charms all ages with its thoroughly researched displays of 19th-century dolls, dolls' houses, toys and games from the collection of founder and director Flora Gill Jacobs. Kids especially enjoy the turn-of-the-century Mexican mansion and seasonal displays such as a revolving musical Christmas tree surrounded by toys in their original boxes. Birthday parties in the Edwardian Tea Room include a demonstration of antique windup toys. Look in the gift shop for Jacobs' children's books, *The Toy Shop Mystery* and *The Doll House Mystery*, both featuring objects from the museum's collection. See Attractions for a complete description.

Northern Virginia

The Newseum
1101 Wilson Blvd., Arlington, Va.
• **(703) 284-3544, (888) NEWSEUM**

Extra! Extra! School-age children who enjoy reading and current events will love the hands-on exhibits at this new museum devoted to the history of news making and reporting. In the Interactive Newsroom, visitors can try sportscasting from a realistic sound-booth, appear on a national magazine cover, hone reporting skills through a computer game, read "on-air" news from a TelePrompTer and participate in an editorial meeting. Visit the Information Desk for children's guides and activity sheets. See Attractions for a complete description.

Suburban Maryland

Imagine That! Discovery Museums for Children
Congressional Plaza, 1616 E. Jefferson St., Rockville, Md. • **(301) 468-2101**

With a maze of more than 20 themed activ-

Recreation centers throughout Metro Washington sponsor Little League ball teams.

ity areas, the 16,000-square-foot Imagine That! is a museum disguised as an indoor play center where children can play "Let's Pretend" to their hearts' content. Kids gravitate to the transportation area, where they can climb aboard a real fire truck, pilot an airplane, become a race-car driver or sit in the "monster" truck and talk on the phone to a friend at the TV news station, pirate ship, grocery store or Victorian house. In the medical room, children can tour an ambulance, lay in a dentist's chair and try to maneuver a wheelchair up a small incline. A dance studio features tutus, ballet and tap shoes and an instructional video; and a music room includes a drum set and other percussive instruments, an electronic keyboard and a piano with a window to its inside. A computer room, Sand Castle, play area and arts and crafts station also prove highly popular.

Readers of Washington Families newspaper voted Imagine That! the best place to hold a birthday party. The museum holds frequent special activities related to a weekly theme, collects money for a different children's charity each month and hosts a monthly Volunteer Day during which children save $1 on admission when they donate a jar of peanut butter or jelly and help make sandwiches for a soup kitchen.

Hours are Sunday through Thursday, 10 AM to 6 PM, and Friday and Saturday, 10 AM to 8 PM. Admission is $7.99 for children ages 18 months to 12 years, $2 for adults and teens. A "late rate" admission of $6 for children, free for adults with a paying child, is valid Monday through Thursday from 3 to 6 PM, Friday and Saturday from 6 to 8 PM and Sunday from 4 to 6 PM.

NASA Goddard Space Flight Center Visitors Center
Soil Conservation Rd., Greenbelt, Md.
• **(301) 286-8981**

Kids interested in space and rocketry will enjoy the museum's interactive exhibits pertaining to Goddard's involvement in the space program. Visitors can build and launch a space satellite via a computer game, and sit in a Gemini space capsule that includes an audio recording simulating liftoff in a Titan rocket. Model rocket enthusiasts hold launches the first and third Sundays of each month at 1 PM. See Attractions for more information.

National Capital Trolley Museum
1313 Bonifant Rd., Wheaton, Md.
• **(301) 384-6088**

All aboard for an old-fashioned trolley ride! Most kids probably won't be too interested in the museum's collection of streetcar memorabilia, but they'll enjoy riding an American trolley, European tram or Washington street car along the museum's demonstration railway that runs through Northwest Branch Park. Along with exhibits, the Visitors Center features a model streetcar layout and museum shop. Birthday rides are available for groups of 20 or more. See Attractions for a complete description.

National Wildlife Visitor Center
10901 Scarlet Tanager Loop, Laurel, Md.
• (301) 497-5760

Budding naturalists will have fun pushing buttons and playing with interactive videos in exhibits that focus on global environmental problems, habitats, endangered species and life cycles. A guided electric tram tour travels through the woods and around the lake of the surrounding Patuxent Research Refuge (described further in our Attractions chapter), operated by the U.S. Fish and Wildlife Service. Tram tickets are $2 for teens and adults, $1 for seniors 55 and older and children 12 and younger.

Old MacDonald Had a Farm . . .

And on that farm he had animals, gardens and a lot of fun for kids. Leave the bustling city and suburbs behind and head for a close-at-hand yet more pastoral experience at one of the following historic sites or working, pick-your-own produce farms.

Farm Museums and Plantations

Northern Virginia

Claude Moore Colonial Farm at Turkey Run
6310 Georgetown Pk., McLean, Va.
• (703) 442-7557

Your kids will think they've stepped back in time as they watch a poor farm family of 1771 work their land, tend to their livestock and perform their chores at this living-history site. The authentic-looking re-enactors, often including children, are happy to answer curious, modern-day visitors' questions. Youngsters enjoy looking at the farm animals and participating in special events like harvest time and periodic 18th-century market fairs. Be prepared for a lot of walking. Admission is $2 for adults and teens, $1 for seniors and children ages 3 to 12; tots 2 and younger get in free. Hours are 10 AM to 4:30 PM Wednesday through Sunday, early April through mid-December. The farm is closed during bad weather and on Thanksgiving.

Historic Sully
Va. Rt. 28, across from Washington Dulles International Airport, Chantilly, Va. • (703) 437-1794

Young visitors to this restored 1794 plantation home of Northern Virginia's first congressman enjoy year-round family-oriented weekend programs on such topics as Toys and Games of Yesteryear, Quill Pen Writing and Ice Cream Making. During the summer, Sully offers a variety of hands-on educational programs for children ages 8 to 12. See the summer issue of *Parktakes*, a guide to Fairfax County parks, for details. To obtain a copy, call (703) 324-8588. Admission to the site is $4 for adults, $3 for students 16 and older and $2 for children and seniors. Hours are 11 AM to 4 PM daily, except Tuesdays.

Kidwell Farm at Frying Pan Park
2709 West Ox Rd., Herndon, Va.
• (703) 437-9101

Children love visiting this small, working model of a 1930s family farm, which features a barnyard full of pigs, goats, dairy cows, sheep, draft horses, chickens and peacocks, and many baby animals in the spring. It's also home to the official Presidential Turkey, which arrives after its traditional Thanksgiving pardon. Special programs include fall hayrides, blacksmithing demonstrations every other Sunday and occasional "Putting the Animals to Bed" story times for children. Events are free or require a nominal charge. Call (703) 324-8588 for a schedule. Daily farm hours are 10 AM to 6 PM. Admission is free.

Mount Vernon
Southern end of the George Washington Memorial Pkwy., Mt. Vernon, Va.
• (703) 780-2000

George Washington's historic estate and

gardens are becoming increasingly kid-friendly, with year-round interactive programs. Throughout the summer, children can visit the Hands-On History Tent to learn how to harness a mule, play Colonial games, try on period clothing and make wooden buckets, among other activities. They also can measure themselves next to a life-size likeness of the first president. Year round, kids can visit the "George Washington: Pioneer Farmer" exhibit, which features, March through November, hands-on activities such as fence-building, corn cracking and fishnet making. Youngsters especially like looking at the farm animals, including such rare breeds as Ossabaw hogs and Hogg Island sheep. Even a visit to the mansion becomes fun for kids when they follow the "Treasure Map of Mount Vernon," a puzzle-filled souvenir brochure available free of charge at the main gate. Admission is $8 for folks 12 and older, $7.50 for seniors 62 and older and $4 for children ages 6 through 11.

Suburban Maryland

National Colonial Farm of the Accokeek Foundation
3400 Bryan Point Rd., Accokeek, Md.
• **(301) 283-2113**

Mount Vernon's neighbor directly across the Potomac River, this colonial tobacco farm, part of the National Park Service, features many barnyard animals such as cows, sheep, geese, chickens and roosters. Look for babies in the spring. Weekend tours feature rotating demonstrations. Call for information about upcoming special programs such as Children's Day and seasonal celebrations. Admission is $2 for adults, 50¢ for children younger than 12 , with a maximum of $5 per family. Hours are Friday through Sunday and Tuesday through Thursday from 10 AM to 5 PM, but are subject to seasonal changes.

Oxon Hill Farm
6411 Oxon Hill R., Oxon Hill, Md.
• **(301) 839-1177**

This turn-of-the-century working farm, owned by the National Park Service, offers daily hands-on events for children, who enjoy seeing the many barnyard animals. Kids can help milk a cow, feed chickens and gather

eggs. Call for more information about these and special weekend events. Admission is free. The farm is open daily, 8 AM to 4:30 PM.

Farm-fresh Fun

Visit these farms in October for special children's activities. Some also feature pick-your-own crops in spring and summer.

Northern Virginia

Chantilly Farms Inc.
19270 James Monroe Hwy. (Va. Rt. 15), 1.25 miles south of Leesburg, Va.
• **(703) 777-4831**

Kids have a blast during the annual Pumpkinland, held throughout October. Visitors participate in such activities as pumpkin picking, face painting, hayrides through an Enchanted Witch's Forest, a hay-filled schoolbus and an 8-acre pumpkin-shaped corn maze. The farm is open from 9 AM to 6 PM Monday through Friday; 10 AM to 7 PM on Saturdays and Sundays in October. General admission is $6.50, $3.25 for seniors, and free for tots younger than age 2.

Cox Farms
15621 Braddock Rd., Centreville, Va.
• **(703) 830-4121**

The annual fall festival, throughout October, features tractor-drawn hayrides, tunnels, climbable hay bales, a 72-foot slide, hay swings, a corn maze, face painting and live entertainment on weekends, along with cider, apples and pumpkins for visitors. The hours are 10 AM to 6 PM (or dark) daily in October. The entry fee for Fall Festival activities is $6.50 on weekends and Columbus Day, $4 on weekdays, with no fee for tots younger than age 2.

Suburban Maryland

Butlers Orchard
22200 Davis Mill Rd., Germantown, Md.
• **(301) 972-3299**

Butlers holds one of the area's most popular pumpkin festivals on weekends during October. Kids love to go for rides in a hay wagon and Cinderella's fiberglass mouse-pulled pumpkin coach, feed billy goats and other farm animals, jump in a hayloft, navigate a tunnel and straw maze and look at the many characters who populate Pumpkin Land. The orchard is open 10 AM to 5:30 PM Tuesday through Sunday, with the festival held from 10 AM to 5 PM Saturdays and Sundays. Admission is $4 per person, and free for tots younger than age 2.

Cherry Hill Farm
12300 Gallahan Rd., near Oxon Hill, Md.
• (301) 292-1928

Weekend Halloween tours feature a hayride to the pumpkin patch, a pumpkin to carve, apples to eat and visits to a petting zoo, slides, tunnels, a maze and a Fun Barn filled with illusions, animated figures and Halloween scenes. Visitors of all ages enjoy looking at scarecrow characters displayed along the hayride path, sampling cider and helping make apple butter the old-fashioned way — in a big copper pot over an open flame. Don't leave without treating the kids, and yourself, to homemade cider doughnuts or apple-pie flavored ice cream.

The market is open from 8:30 AM to 6:30 PM, Monday through Saturday, 7 AM to 5 PM Sundays; Halloween tours and apple-picking run 9 AM to dusk daily. Weekend admission is $5 per person. Weekday admission is $4 per person.

Darrow Berry Farm
Bell Station Rd., Glenn Dale, Md.
• (301) 390-6191, (301) 390-6611

Storybook characters decorate Pumpkin Land during October, when kids also can take hayrides to the pick-your-own pumpkin patch, visit a haunted house, ride a pony, get their faces painted and watch cow-milking and apple butter-making demonstrations. The farm is open 10 AM to 6 PM Saturdays and Sundays, beginning the second Saturday in October. Most activities are free or require a small admission fee.

Rainy-day Activities

Actually, you needn't wait for a rainy day to visit these children's stores and craft places, big and small, all of which offer indoor fun through story times, creative activities and other special events.

Books and Toys

Barnes & Noble Booksellers
3040 M St. NW, Washington, D.C.
• (202) 965-9880
6201 Arlington Blvd., Falls Church, Va.
• (703) 536-0774
1851 Fountain Dr., Reston, Va.
• (703) 437-9490
4801 Bethesda Ave., Bethesda, Md.
• (301) 986-1761

Free story hours, young adult book clubs, interactive music and movement classes and craft sessions take place regularly in the children's departments of most stores in this large chain. Costumed characters and well-known authors also make occasional appearances. Visit to obtain a monthly events calendar.

Borders Books & Music
18th and L Sts. NW, Washington, D.C.
• (202) 466-4999
1201 S. Hayes St., Arlington, Va.
• (703) 418-0166
5871 Crossroads Center Way, Baileys Crossroads, Va. • (703) 998-0404
11054 Lee Highway, Fairfax, Va.
• (703) 359-8420
8311 Leesburg Pk., Vienna, Va.
• (703) 556-7766
11301 Rockville Pk., Kensington, Md.
• (301) 816-1067
534 N. Frederick Ave., Gaithersburg, Md.
• (301) 921-0990

These nationally known bookstores carry

INSIDERS' TIP

The *Capital Kids and Teens Book* is loaded with discount coupons for kid-pleasing attractions, classes, special events, restaurants and stores. Use just a couple of coupons and you'll recoup the $15 cost. The book sells as a fund-raiser for local schools. Call (301) 365-9898 to find out how to obtain a copy.

a large selection of children's volumes, and each features at least one weekly free story time for preschoolers. On Saturday, many of the stores hold free special events such as craft workshops, book signings by children's authors, puppet shows, storytelling and visits from costumed characters like Curious George and the Cat in the Hat. Times vary at individual stores; stop by for a schedule.

Zany Brainy

3513 S. Jefferson St., Baileys Crossroads, Va. • (703) 998-1203
2890 Prince William Pkwy., Woodbridge, Va. • (703) 680-9870
9490 Main St., Fairfax, Va.
• (703) 323-3658
12180 W. Ox Rd., Fairfax, Va.
• (703) 691-1896
46262 Cranston Way, Sterling, Va.
• (703) 404-8850
6575 Frontier Dr., Springfield, Va.
• (703) 719-9585
11870 Spectrum Ctr., Reston, Va.
• (703) 318-1875
1631 Rockville Pk., Rockville, Md.
• (301) 984-0112

Kids are never bored when they visit these big, bright educational toy stores, which feature a different free, drop-in event every day. Preschoolers enjoy story times and character photo days, and older kids have fun making crafts or trying out new games and building sets. Nationally known authors and illustrators sometimes drop by to sign books, and popular recording artists occasionally perform miniconcerts. Children like to push kid-size carts alongside their parents through the various departments — including music and books at a 10 percent discount — and watch ongoing videos or play with sample toys. Pick up a monthly calendar to keep track of what's scheduled.

Washington, D.C.

Cheshire Cat Book Store

5512 Connecticut Ave. NW, Washington, D.C. • (202) 244-3956

From mid-August to late September, families flock to the 20-year-old store to gaze in wonder at live monarch butterflies emerging by the dozens in the front window. The shop builds workshops around the annual tradition, and children enjoy gently holding the butterflies and releasing them outside as their wings dry. Throughout the year, the store hosts many appearances by nationally known authors and holds a variety of special events, most of which are free. Kids, and occasional sleepy parents, like to visit the "Rabbit Hole" cubby, a small play area stocked with books, pillows and stuffed animals. Hours are Monday through Saturday 10 AM to 6 PM and Sunday 1 to 5 PM. Call the store for a newsletter, published four times a year.

Northern Virginia

A Likely Story

1555 King St., Alexandria, Va.
• (703) 836-2498

In its 14th year, this independent children's bookstore in Old Town features seasonal activities, monthly costumed character appearances and eight to 10 author visits annually. The shop holds story times twice a week. A drop-in program Tuesday at 11 AM offers songs and finger plays for infants to age 3. Reservations are requested for programs held Saturday at 11 AM, usually with themed crafts for ages 3 to 6. The store also holds events for parents and teachers. While grown-ups browse, kids can visit the store's hermit crabs or hang out in a play space stocked with toys. Hours are 10 AM to 6 PM Monday through Saturday and 1 to 5 PM Sunday. Call for a newsletter, published five times a year.

Aladdin's Lamp Children's Books & Other Treasures

126 W. Broad St., Falls Church, Va.
• (703) 241-8281

Run by a children's librarian, Aladdin's Lamp is another of the area's few remaining independent, family-owned children's bookstores. The shop hosts frequent special programs, most of which are free. Reservations are recommended for story hours, usually held Wednesdays and Saturdays at 11 AM for ages 2½ to 6. Workshops for older children often feature authors or community volunteers who share special talents and feature such topics as origami, sports and American Girls. The

The D.C. Mini-Guide to Kids' Dining

"I'm tired! I'm thirsty! I'm *hungry*!"

What parent doesn't dread these words, especially when they're pronounced by a whining child in the middle of a sight-seeing expedition? Here's your challenge: Find a restaurant — now! — with kid- and adult-pleasing food, fast and friendly service, reasonable

prices and some diversion to keep your youngster entertained until the meal arrives.

Such a task can prove difficult even when you're close to home, let alone touring a new city. Fortunately, Washington and its surrounding suburbs offer countless options for family dining, from neighborhood eateries to familiar chains. Follow our tips and recommendations and you'll find that eating out with kids can be fun — really!

• Build mealtimes into your itinerary, and try to find out in advance if kids' meals or favorite à la carte items are available at whatever attraction you're visiting. With planning, you won't be caught off guard by a hungry child in the middle of touring a museum that doesn't have a restaurant.

• Eat at "off" times to avoid unsettling crowds. You'll find restaurants in popular tourist areas packed to the gills during the noon hour and between 6:30 and 8:30 PM. Eat a late lunch or early dinner and you'll have a much shorter wait for your food.

• Find out if a restaurant features free or discounted children's meals during certain times. Many chains in the Washington area offer great specials during the week to entice families to dine on otherwise slow nights.

• To reduce the waiting time, especially when a restaurant is crowded, order the kids' meals or an appetizer such as soup as soon as you're seated. A cup of ice and a spoon also help stave off boredom for a while.

• Traveling with an infant or toddler? Avoid restaurants with few or no high chairs and booster seats, as such establishments generally aren't used to accommodating young

— continued on next page

Photo: Courtesy of Mary Jane Solomon

Children can make their own pizza at Generous George's Positive Pizza & Pasta Place.

children. Find out if the women's and men's rooms have changing tables, and ask whether the dining area or restroom offers a discreet place to nurse a baby. Many restaurants with salad bars allow toddlers to eat for free, a welcome option for parents whose children like to nosh on cheese, crackers and fresh fruit or sliced vegetables.

• Carry a small backpack with a few emergency snack items like crackers, cereal bars and packets of juice-fortified gummy treats. Also include some small games or toys, as well as a pad of paper and pen or pencil for each child. Elementary-age youngsters can hone their reading and writing skills by copying everyone's orders from the menu. Or, have your youngster draw or write about someplace you've just visited. You can also use your waiting time to write postcards to mail to friends or to your child as a unique way of recording the trip.

• As soon as you enter an eatery, locate the restrooms. Some kids enjoy visiting restaurant bathrooms just to check them out.

• Have realistic expectations. Don't count on a child to tolerate sitting for more than 45 minutes.

• Ask for a souvenir menu or placemat, inexpensive collectibles that prove easy to display or store. You might wish to circle and label each family member's meal.

The following restaurants are favorites of Metro Washington families, who appreciate their dependable service and kid-pleasing food. Note that, contrary to our usual policy, we do include some chains here because of their special features for kids. In general, expect to pay $2.50 to $5 for a child's meal featuring a burger or chicken fingers, fries and drink.

Washington, D.C.

National Gallery of Art
4th St. and Constitution Ave. NW, Washington, D.C. • (202) 737-4215

If you're visiting museums on the National Mall, the cafe/buffet in the gallery's Concourse is a good bet for a quick bite. We've watched one of the world's pickiest little eaters polish off a meal of favorite à la carte items like fresh fruits and french fries. Lines at the various self-service stations — salads, sandwiches, hot meals, desserts, etc. — usually move quickly. Look for a seat near the huge window with a view of a mesmerizing waterfall outside.

Planet Hollywood
1101 Pennsylvania Ave. NW, Washington, D.C. • (202) 783-7827

Movie buffs of all ages have a blast checking out the museum-like displays of costumes and other film memorabilia, not to mention watching previews on television. The food is standard fare, but folks who dine here visit more for the atmosphere than the menu.

Union Station
50 Massachusetts Ave. NE, Washington, D.C. • (202) 371-9441

This bustling, beautifully refurbished train station also holds a shopping mall and numerous restaurants, including a huge food court with a wide selection of kid favorites. If you prefer a full-service restaurant, visit America Restaurant, (202) 682-9555, which offers great views of the U.S. Capitol upstairs. Downstairs, children can color on white butcher paper table coverings. The menu of more than 200 à la carte items, about $3 and up, features state specialties such as Maryland crabcakes and Virginia chicken pot pie. Kids like such dishes as plain spaghetti, macaroni and cheese and miniature hamburgers. The National Postal Museum, with many hands-on exhibits, is right across the street, and the Capital Children's Museum is a few blocks away.

— continued on next page

Northern Virginia

Bad Habits Grille
5444 Columbia Pk., Arlington, Va. • (703) 998-5808

Dining here with your family might actually become a good habit: Children 10 and younger eat free from the kids' menu — with entrees normally priced at $2.50 each — from 5 to 8 PM Sunday through Thursday. Your server also supplies complimentary kiddie appetizers such as crackers, fruit and carrot sticks. Youngsters still fidgety while waiting for their meals? They can play with toys or fill the time with a coloring book and crayons.

Calvert Grill
3106 Mt. Vernon Ave., Alexandria, Va. • (703) 836-8425

When restaurant owners also happen to be parents of twins, a kid-friendly atmosphere just comes naturally. Young visitors enjoy playing with toys kept on hand and coloring on white paper that covers tables and walls.

Generous George's Positive Pizza & Pasta Place
3006 Duke St., Alexandria, Va. • (703) 370-4303
7031 Little River Tnpk., Annandale, Va. • (703) 941-9600
6131 Backlick Rd., Springfield, Va. • (703) 451-7111

George doesn't call himself generous for nothing: The portions are huge at these funky pizza parlors, which specialize in pasta served atop pizza crust. (Prepare to ask for "doggy" boxes!) Kids enjoy more than the food, however. The colorful decor includes ceiling tiles splashed with paint squiggles and hung with rocking toys; old-fashioned Formica-topped tables; and, best of all, replica carousel animals upon which children can sit with adult supervision. The kids' menu includes make-your-own pizzas, available when the restaurant's not too busy. Family-oriented promotions include such events as clown/magician performances.

IKEA Washington
2700 Potomac Mills Cir., Potomac Mills, Woodbridge, Va. • (703) 643-2687

The restaurant in this huge, popular Swedish furniture and housewares store features a brightly decorated children's dining area, kids' bag lunches and baby food for the littlest gourmets. The store also offers a free supervised ballroom and play area, where youngsters can romp while parents shop.

Paradiso Ristorante
6124 Franconia Rd., Franconia, Va. • (703) 922-6222

Can't get a babysitter? This restaurant just down the street from Springfield Mall is your dream come true: Kids ages 3 to 10 eat at plastic picnic tables, color and watch the latest videos in a children's dining area while their parents enjoy a quiet meal in an adjacent room, 5 to 10 PM daily. A waitress/babysitter supervises the youngsters, and parents keep an eye on things from a picture window that's a mirror on the kids' side. Children's meals, which include ice cream, are $4.99. We recommend you call ahead for reservations.

Rainforest Cafe
Tysons Corner Center, 1961 Chain Bridge Rd., McLean, Va. • (703) 821-0247

Voted the 1997 Best Restaurant for Families by readers of Washington Families newspaper, this so-called "Wild Place to Shop and Eat" captivates kids from the

— continued on next page

moment they catch the live parrot show out front. Don't expect things to quiet down once you're inside: The dining areas feature animatronic gorillas who periodically holler and beat their chests, elephants who screech and raise their trunks and realistic lightning, among other special effects and sounds that create a tropical atmosphere. A favorite destination for birthday celebrations, the restaurant offers a kids' menu with such fun selections as dinosaur-shaped chicken nuggets and Chocolate Banshee Screamer Sundaes. Don't miss the talking tree, real aquarium and assorted surprises in the gift shop.

Suburban Maryland

B.J. Pumpernickel's
18169 Town Center Dr., Olney, Md. • (301) 924-1400
Kids eat free at dinner, Monday through Wednesday, at this deli-diner. While the youngsters pick a meal, including a drink and cookie, from the Kids' Korner selections, you'll have to make up your mind over which of more than 300 items to choose from the regular menu.

Bugaboo Creek Steak House
15710 Shady Grove Rd., Gaithersburg, Md. • (301) 548-9200
6820 Commerce St., Springfield, Va. • (703) 451-3300
Built to resemble rustic Canadian mountain lodges, these entertaining restaurants feature a talking fir tree, buffalo and moose, as well as other animatronic animals. The kids' menu includes space for a child to draw a picture that can be entered in the chain's periodic art contest. Winners appear on future menus. Come here for a birthday and a moose puppet may join the staff in singing a rousing celebratory song.

Franklins General Store and Delicatessen
5121 Baltimore Ave., Rt. 1, Hyattsville, Md. • (301) 927-2740
Kids love eating at the New York-style deli, which offers 99-cent children's meals, and shopping in the newfangled, old-fashioned store, set in a building that used to house Hyattsville Hardware. The store's original fixtures, such as nail bins and wooden boxes, now hold such items as candy, toys and cooking gadgets.

Geppeto Restaurant of Bethesda
10257 Old Georgetown Rd., Bethesda, Md. • (301) 493-9230
If your children like puppets, they'll enjoy looking at the glass cases that display marionettes from *Pinocchio* and other classic tales. The coloring menu placemat features a *Pinocchio* scene from a rug hanging in the restaurant.

Stained Glass Pub Too
3333 Olney Sandy Springs Rd., Olney, Md. • (301) 774-3778
This friendly neighborhood eatery features a clown performance from 5:30 to 7:30 PM Fridays. Kids often get balloon animals, and can order from a children's menu.

Multiple Locations
We also recommend the following chains, with multiple locations throughout the metro area.

— continued on next page

Black-eyed Pea Restaurant

Children love the baskets of hot, fresh rolls, and the variety of items on the coloring placemat menu. Many locations offer "kids eat free" promotions on weekdays.

Clyde's

This popular local chain specializes in fresh, seasonal dishes. Kids enjoy the Busy Bag, which contains an activity booklet, crayons and toy.

Fuddruckers

Families flock to these burger restaurants Monday through Thursday nights, when kids 12 and younger eat free. Youngsters enjoy free cookies, balloons, entertainers, game rooms and play/reading areas.

Shoney's

These family restaurants often offer Kids' Night promotions, including free or discounted meals, balloons, lollipops and visits from a costumed Shoney Bear.

Silver Diner

Resembling old-fashioned diners, complete with at-the-table jukeboxes, these friendly eateries feature kids' meals served in cardboard replicas of classic cars.

store also carries a large selection of unusual Baltic amber jewelry made by the owner's family. Hours are Monday, Wednesday, Friday and Saturday, 10 AM to 6 PM; and Tuesday and Thursday, 10 AM to 8 PM. Ask for a newsletter describing special events.

Imagination Station
4524 Lee Hwy., Arlington, Va.
• (703) 522-2047

This neighborhood children's bookstore holds a drop-in story hour for youngsters 3 and older Saturdays at 10:30 AM. Other events include book signings and parties with costumed characters. The store carries a large selection of foreign-language books. Hours are Monday through Friday, 10 AM to 7 PM; Saturday, 10 AM to 6 PM; and Sunday, 11 AM to 4 PM. Call for a quarterly newsletter. Visit the neighboring, affiliated Kinder Haus Toys, with two floors of playthings and clothing at 4510 Lee Highway, (703) 527-5929, open 10 AM to 7 PM Monday through Friday, 10 AM to 6 PM Saturday and 10 to 4 PM Sunday.

Once Upon a Time
120 Church St. NE, Vienna, Va.
• (703) 255-3285

A realistic tree and beautiful displays of collectible dolls, miniatures and stuffed animals charm visitors at this 16-year-old toy store, which hosts at least one creative special event a month. Children attending Madeline Day in the spring meet the popular book character and sample French pastries. Breyer horse collectors celebrate their shared interest with a party featuring carrots, apples and sugar cubes. A summer reading program culminates in a store visit from a popular literary character. A newsletter, published three or four times annually, details upcoming programs. The store is open Monday through Saturday from 10 AM to 5 PM, and, October through May, Sunday from noon to 5 PM. Stop by after taking in a children's concert at Wolf Trap Farm Park (see the subsequent "There's No Business Like Show Business" section as well as our Arts chapter).

Why Not?
200 King St., Alexandria, Va.
• (703) 548-4420

Kids "ooh" and "aah" over the whimsically detailed plush animal scenes in the window of this charming corner store, right in the heart of historic Old Town Alexandria. Inside, you'll find two floors of specialty clothing, books and toys, including many display models for children to try throughout the shop and in an enclosed "playpen" area for toddlers. Hours vary seasonally, but usually are from 10 AM to 5:30 PM Monday, 10 AM to 9 PM Tuesday through Saturday and noon to 5 PM Sunday.

Suburban Maryland

Bookoo Books for Kids
4945 Elm St., Bethesda, Md.
• (301) 652-2794

This small, independent children's bookstore hosts a weekly story time for ages 1½ and older Wednesdays at 10 AM. Reservations are recommended. The shop also holds such special events as American Girl craft parties and character appearances, and specializes in storybook-themed birthday parties. While parents shop, kids can play with beanbags, puzzles and tea sets. Hours are Monday through Wednesday, Friday and Saturday, 10 AM to 6 PM; Thursday, 10 AM to 7 PM; and Sunday, noon to 5 PM. Call for a newsletter.

Whirligigs & Whimsies
Wildwood Shopping Center, 10213 Old Georgetown Rd., Bethesda, Md.
• (301) 897-4940

American Girl Days, costumed character appearances and book signings by well-known children's authors are among the free special events that take place at least once a month at this speciality toy store. Although the shop doesn't publish a newsletter, its mailing-list customers receive advance notification of activities. A pleasant stop after a visit to nearby Cabin John Regional Park (see the listing later in this chapter), the store is open Monday through Wednesday, Friday and Saturday from 10 AM to 6 PM and Thursday from 10 AM to 7 PM.

Pottery Painting

Creativity is the name of the game at the following studios, the latest rage in drop-in craft places and ideal outings for kids who like to say, "I made it myself." Choose a white-clay figurine or serving piece, pick your colors and start painting; the studio staff does the cleanup, glazing and firing. Studio fees include unlimited paint, use of supplies and glazing and kiln firing. The bisque item(s) you pick to

paint cost extra — usually anywhere from $3 to $45. All supplies are nontoxic, and most clear glazes are lead-free. Birthday party packages are available at all locations.

Made By You
3413 Connecticut Ave. NW, Washington, D.C. • (202) 363-9590
1826 Wisconsin Ave., Washington, D.C.
• (202) 337-3180
2319 Wilson Blvd., Arlington, Va.
• (703) 841-3533
4923 Elm St., Bethesda, Md.
• (301) 654-3206

Hours vary at the different locations. A discounted Kids Club project is featured every weekday. Call ahead for details. The studio fee is $7 for the first hour and $1.50 for each additional 15 minutes. Ask about daily specials. Reservations are recommended on weekends.

Northern Virginia

The Mud Factory
The Village at Shirlington, 2772 S. Arlington Mill Dr., Arlington, Va.
• (703) 998-6880

Hours are Tuesday through Thursday, 11 AM to 8 PM; Friday and Saturday, 11 AM to 10 PM; and Sunday, noon to 6 PM. The studio fee is $7 per hour, $1.75 for each additional 15 minutes.

Paint Your Own Pottery
10417 Main St., Fairfax, Va.
• (703) 218-2881

Hours are Monday through Friday, 10 AM to 6 PM; Saturday, 10 AM to 5 PM; and Sunday, noon to 5 PM. The studio fee is $7 for the first hour, $1 for each additional 10 minutes. Ask about specials, such as half-price kids' days.

Paint 'N Place
Springfield Mall, 6500 Franconia Rd., Springfield, Va. • (703) 719-9732

Hours are 10 AM to 9:30 PM Monday through Saturday and noon to 5 PM Sunday. The studio fee is $6 per hour. A monthly calendar features special discounts on most days.

Educational Crafts

Cathedral Medieval Workshop
**Washington National Cathedral,
Massachusetts and Wisconsin Aves. NW,
Washington, D.C. • (202) 537-2934**

The Cathedral Medieval Workshop's seven hands-on stations give families a close-up look at the creative process behind the magnificent gothic building's art and architecture. Designed for children 5 and older accompanied by adults, the activity center lets visitors create gargoyles from self-drying clay, carve limestone with a mallet and chisel, design a Gothic bookmark, hammer copper on an anvil, make a crayon rubbing of a brass engraving, construct arches with blocks and a wooden frame and piece together stained glass.

As you leave the workshop, pick up pamphlets featuring cathedral-related family activities, from puzzles to scavenger hunts. Kids who enjoy Disney's *The Hunchback of Notre Dame* especially like *Eight Great Gargoyles — A Self-Guided Tour for the Young at Heart*, featuring some of the most popular of the 107 gargoyles and countless grotesques that adorn the building's exterior.

The workshop, in the northwest crypt, is open to the public year round on Saturday from 10 AM to 2 PM, and Monday through Friday, 1 to 4 PM, in July and August. The admission fee of $3 per person includes a ball of clay and paper for the bookmark and brass rubbing. (See the Attractions, Annual Events and Worship chapters for other activities.)

Amusements

When the kids need to let off some steam, visit one of these amusement places for nothing but fun and games. Unless otherwise noted, prices vary widely according to the type of activity, age of participant and time of day. Hours also vary seasonally. Your best bet is to call ahead with specifics on your visit. See our Parks and Recreation chapter for more ideas.

Sportrock Climbing Centers
**5308 Eisenhower Ave., Alexandria, Va.
• (703) 212-7625**

**14708 Southlawn Ln., Rockville, Md.
• (301) 762-5111**

Kids — and grown-ups too — literally climb the walls at these indoor recreation centers, where the walls resemble rocky surfaces just waiting to be scaled. Check out Kids' Nite on Friday from 6:30 to 8:30 PM, when children ages 6 to 14 get vertical with help from experienced instructors. The cost is $17.50 per child, $28 for two siblings and $37 for three siblings. Call for information about regular hours and rates, summer camps and classes.

Northern Virginia

Centreville Mini Golf & Games
**6206 Multiplex Dr., Centreville, Va.
• (703) 502-7888**

If you're not already on vacation, you may feel like you are when you play the 18-hole, resort-style miniature golf course, landscaped to resemble a lush, natural setting complete with waterfalls. Ready for something completely different? Head inside for a game of Laser Storm, a futuristic tag game using laser beams and accented by special lighting effects. Active kids 10 and younger can climb all over a three-story indoor playground, while less adventurous family members try their skills at arcade games that offer redemption tickets.

Champions Go-Kart Raceway and Family Fun Park
**13585 Minnieville Rd., Woodbridge, Va.
• (703) 730-3866**

Go, Speed Racer, go! Kids who are at least 8 years old and 4½ feet tall can zoom at 11 to 22 mph along a Grand Prix Go-Kart track with 22 hairpin turns. (Younger children can ride alongside Mom or Dad in a double Kart.) Bolder drivers — at least 12 years old and 5 feet tall — can steer 8-horsepower NASKARTS around a 440-foot oval slick track. All vehicles are equipped with seat belts and roll bars and regulated so young speed demons can't go too fast.

Ready to get wet? The 5,000-square-foot bumper boat pond features a fountain just waiting to soak anyone whose motorized floating craft veers too close to the center. The 11-

acre amusement facility offers other options for those who prefer to stay dry. An 18-hole miniature golf course includes real sand traps, and batting cages let sluggers swing at slow-pitch softballs or four speeds of baseballs. An arcade contains more than 80 games and a coupon redemption center.

Putter's Paradise
Sterling Plaza, 22330 Sterling Blvd. N., Sterling, Va. • (703) 430-1200

An erupting volcano, singing alligator and life-size gorilla, zebra and tiger highlight this 18-hole miniature golf course. The indoor setting makes it playable even in the lousiest weather, and surprise sound effects on several holes add to the tropical jungle ambiance. The snack bar specializes in pizza, and the arcade features video-game classics. The cost for golf is $6 to play all day, $4 per game for adults, $3 per game for ages 4 through 17 and $1 for tots 3 and younger accompanied by an adult.

Suburban Maryland

Adventure World
13710 Central Ave., Largo, Md. • (301) 249-1500

Kids needn't fret over being too little for this theme/water park's thrill rides: A Day at the Circus features 15 rides and a live show especially for children. They can soar in Aerial Elephants and hot-air balloons, twirl on the carousel, take to the tracks on a miniature circus train and get aggressive in bumper boats and cars. When they've worked up a good sweat, take them to Crocodile Cal's Outback Beach House, a five-story, interactive play area with more than 100 water-powered attractions, including a barrel that dumps 1,000 gallons of water on unsuspecting passersby every few minutes. Still not wet enough? Play on the slides and submarine in the 10,000-square-foot Kids' Cove pool. (See our Recreation chapter for more about Adventure World.)

Jeepers
6042 Greenbelt Rd., Greenbelt, Md. • (301) 982-2444
700 Hungerford Dr., Rockville, Md. • (301) 309-2525

What's faster than a rolling grape? How about a flying banana? Banana Squadron is one ride you'll find at these indoor amusement parks, which also feature kid-size roller coasters, bumper cars and a few other jungle-themed, moving attractions. Rambunctious youngsters enjoy climbing about the maze-like playground's many tunnels and chutes and playing arcade games for coupons to redeem for prizes.

Sportland America
Rio at Washington Ctr., 9811 Washingtonian Blvd., Gaithersburg, Md. • (301) 840-8404

This spacious, indoor-games center is abuzz with activity and lots of choices for energetic children. Visitors can roller skate, shoot holes-in-one at miniature golf, scale the Gladiatior wall, ride bumper cars, take cuts in the batting cages, and climb around in a soft play area. Kids can collect prize tickets playing numerous arcade games. Sportland is in a complex that includes cinemas, restaurants and shops, and is near an attractive lake and pathway which make for a pleasant walk from the neighboring Gaithersburg Marriott Washingtonian Center.

There's No Business Like Show Business

Watching plays, puppet shows and other live performances stimulates children's powers of imagination and promotes a love of the arts. We've selected a few of our favorites places to see entertaining, high-quality productions for families. Check out the Arts chapter for additional ideas.

Washington, D.C.

Discovery Theater
Smithsonian Institution's Arts and Industries Building, 900 Jefferson Dr. SW, Washington, D.C. • (202) 357-2700

Now in its 18th year, this theater puts on 16 shows a year, including five or six original works written or directed by local actors. Popular field trips for local schoolchildren, the performances include puppet shows, dance, plays and storytelling by various artists, many of whom are nationally known. Shows take place weekdays at 10 and 11:30 AM and Saturdays at 11:30 AM and 1 PM, September through July. Admission is $5 per person, and reservations are recommended. Call (202) 357-1500 for information about upcoming programs.

John F. Kennedy Center for the Performing Arts
2700 F St. NW, Washington, D.C.
• (202) 467-4600

Think you can't afford to take the whole family to a show at this internationally renowned showcase for the performing arts? Check out the free programs offered on the Millennium Stage. The series features something different every night, including children's performers. The center also features plays and concerts for kids throughout the year. Recent Kennedy Center Youth and Family Programs, presented in the Theatre Lab, have included such favorite tales as *The Best Christmas Pageant Ever* and *Tales of a Fourth Grade Nothing*. The Washington Chamber Symphony holds an annual series of educational Concerts for Young People, this year featuring such themes as The Mighty Strings and Beethoven's "Symphony No. 5." The symphony's Family Series includes a traditional Holiday Sing-a-Long so popular it sells out four months in advance. The center also holds Broadway-caliber musicals such as *The King and I* and Disney's *Beauty and the Beast*; tickets are pricey, but worth considering for a special occasion. See our Arts chapter for more about the Kennedy Center's programs.

Northern Virginia

Wolf Trap Farm Park
1551 Trap Rd., Vienna, Va.
• (703) 255-1860

The National Park Service's venue for the performing arts features many kids' shows, including those of the 27-year-old Children's Theatre-in-the-Woods outdoor summer concert series. Call (703) 255-1827 in early June for a schedule of puppet shows, plays, songs, stories, dancing and clowning. Reservations for the free series fill up quickly. The park's annual

summer concert series in the open-air Filene Center often includes children's performers like Raffi and Sharon, Lois and Bram. Kids' shows also take place during the fall and winter in the Barns of Wolf Trap just down the road. The park's International Children's Festival, held annually during a September weekend (see our Annual Events chapter) features an eclectic array of young performers from around the world. Kids can also create a variety of beautiful craft projects in a hands-on tent staffed by adult volunteers. Call (703) 642-0862 for more details. Admission is charged. See our Arts chapter for additional information.

West End Children's Theatre
Children's Theatre at the West End Dinner Theatre, 4615 Duke St., Alexandria, Va. • (703) 370-2500

Look around the audience here on a Saturday afternoon and you're liable to see dozens of little girls in pretty party dresses. The children's matinees, featuring musicals like Winnie the Pooh and Cinderella, make this a popular birthday celebration spot, where kids can celebrate right at their tables after shows end. Most performances take place at 2 PM on Saturday. Tickets cost $6 per person and $5 per person for groups of ten or greater. No meals are served, but snacks and beverages are available before the show and during intermission. See our Nightlife chapter for information about the theater's evening dinner shows.

Suburban Maryland

Adventure Theatre
Glen Echo Park, 7300 MacArthur Blvd., Glen Echo, Md. • (301) 320-5331

Headquartered in a former amusement-park penny arcade, Adventure Theatre is the oldest continuous children's theater in the Washington area. Semiprofessional actors annually perform eight shows, many of which are based upon classic stories for young people and recommended for ages 4 to 12. Among this season's scheduled offerings are *The Further Adventures of Maide Marian* and *The Adventures of a Bear Called Paddington*. The audience sits on carpeted steps to watch the performances, which take place Saturdays and Sundays at 1:30 and 3:30 PM. Tickets are $5 a person regardless of age. After the show, kids enjoy meeting the performers, who are more than happy to sign autographs. (See the subsequent Puppet Co. Playhouse and Glen Echo Park entries for related information.)

Now This! Kids!
Blair Mansion Inn, 7711 Eastern Ave., Silver Spring, Md. • (202) 364-8292

If you missed the debut performances of *The Ugly Princess and the Mean Carrot* and *The Duck Who Burped*, you won't get another chance to see the shows. They're among the one-time-only titles presented by Now This! Kids!, the area's only totally improvised musical theater company for kids. Using suggestions from children in the audience, the wacky adult troupe creates on-the-spot songs, comic sketches and fairy tales. The company received the International Special Events Society's award for best entertainment and WRC-TV Channel 4's nod for Best Bet for Children's Entertainment.

The troupe, which also performs improvisationally for adults, works its magic on young audiences ages 5 to 12 each Saturday at 1:30 PM during a luncheon theater that attracts a lot of birthday parties. (Performers make up an original song about each birthday child.) Ticket prices vary, and reservations are requested.

The Puppet Co. Playhouse
Glen Echo Park, 7300 MacArthur Blvd., Glen Echo, Md. • (301) 320-6668

A hop, skip and a jump from the neighboring Adventure Theatre (see previous entry), the Puppet Co.'s claim to fame is its status as the only East Coast theater between Atlanta and New York that performs only puppet shows.

The three-person company creates their own marionettes and other puppet styles for year-round shows, featuring both original stories and new takes on classic fairy tales like *Jack and the Beanstalk* and *Little Red Riding Hood*. The company's popular annual production of *The Nutcracker* includes stunning special effects.

Children sit on the carpeted floor, and adults squeeze in behind the kids and on the sides, where they won't block the little ones' view. Warning: Some toddlers and preschoolers may become frightened by the realistic witch and giant puppets used in many shows. Afterward, kids can meet the puppeteers and say hello to a marionette or two.

Shows are performed Wednesday through Friday at 10 and 11:30 AM, and Saturday and Sunday at 11:30 and 1 PM. Reservations are recommended.

The Green Grass Grows All Around

When the weather's great and your children get tired of their own backyard, head for the park. We've selected a sampling of family favorites, filled with such dependable kid-pleasers as playgrounds, pools, merry-go-rounds and nature centers. Be sure and check the Parks and Recreation chapter for more information about these and other locations your family might enjoy.

Washington, D.C.

National Zoological Park
3001 Connecticut Ave. NW, Washington, D.C. • (202) 673-4800

With its 5 miles of winding, sloping pathways, the zoo proves a great destination for burning off energy. Time your visit to see a kid-pleasing animal demonstration, such as

---

INSIDERS' TIP

Many area parks house nature centers that feature hands-on exhibits and children's programs that describe local natural history, plants and wildlife. Call the nearest parks and recreation department for a nearby location. See the Parks and Recreation chapter for phone numbers.

the Giant Panda feeding at 11 AM and elephant training at 11:30 AM. Rent an Audio Safari Tour package for a self-guided narrated tour that includes a children's activity booklet. School-age youngsters in particular enjoy hands-on attractions in the popular Amazonia, Reptile Discovery Center and Invertebrate Exhibit, which features a Pollinarium filled with butterflies and hummingbirds.

The Friends of the National Zoo membership program holds numerous children's programs, including camps and family overnights and camp-outs.

See the Attractions chapter for more details about zoo hours and features.

Rock Creek Park
3545 Williamsburg Ln. NW, Washington, D.C. • (202) 426-6834

This huge, popular urban park holds a gallery, historic mill and planetarium and nature center, all of which feature programs for children. The Rock Creek Gallery holds a children's art festival in June and a summer art camp. At Pierce Mill, (202) 426-6908, kids can visit an activity table to grind corn and make a model of the mill. Free story times take place twice monthly. The Rock Creek Nature Center, open 9 AM to 6 PM daily, features hands-on activities and special events for kids. Call (202) 426-6829 for information about programs there and at the Planetarium. See the Parks and Recreation chapter for more about this park.

Northern Virginia

SplashDown Waterpark
7500 Ben Lomond Dr., Manassas, Va.
• (703) 361-4451

This 11-acre park, a popular family destination on sticky summer days, is highlighted by a pool with many special features. Visitors can cool off in the 770-foot Lazy River and slip down a boat slide and two 70-foot-tall water slides. A kids' area features four water slides. Children also enjoy getting splashed by "raindrops" and "bubblers." Umbrellas and pavilions offer much-needed shade. The park is open Memorial Day weekend through Labor Day. Hours vary while school is still in session, but June 18 through September 7 in 1998 the park is open 11 AM to 7:30 PM Sunday through Thursday, and 11 AM to 9 PM Friday and Saturday. Admission is $11.50 for people taller than 48 inches, $8.50 for visitors shorter than 48 inches and free for children 1 year old and younger.

Burke Lake Park
7315 Ox Rd., Fairfax Station, Va.
• (703) 323-6600

A favorite of Fairfax County families, this park features numerous kid-pleasing attractions, including a carousel, a *C.P. Huntington* train ride that goes through a tunnel and woods, and an ice cream parlor for snacks or birthday parties. Youngsters also love to ride the pontoon tour boat on the lake and feed bread to the many ducks and Canada geese that flock around the marina. The park hosts a children's festival in the spring, nature camps and Saturday morning kids' concerts during the summer and a Ghost Train Ride near Halloween. The park is open 7 AM to dark daily. Call for times and prices of the rides, which operate throughout the summer and during some weekends in the spring and fall. See Parks and Recreation for more information.

Colvin Run Mill Historic Site
10017 Colvin Run Rd., Great Falls, Va.
• (703) 759-2771

Grab some homemade ice cream at Thelma's country store just down the road, then stroll the grounds around this working, water-powered gristmill. No reservations are needed for the educational puppet show for preschoolers, held at 1 PM every Thursday. Admission is $3 for kids, free for accompanying grown-ups. Afterward, children get to feed crushed grain to the resident millpond ducks. On many Sundays throughout the summer, the Northern Virginia Woodcarvers offer free carving lessons to kids and adults. The site frequently holds special events on weekends, including child-only holiday shopping in the old-fashioned General Store that sells candies, toys and fun gifts. The site is open daily, 11 AM to 5 PM, except Tuesdays. Mill tours, offered on the hour from 11 AM to 4 PM, cost $4 for adults, $3 for any students 16 and older and $2 for children and seniors.

Lake Fairfax Park
1400 Lake Fairfax Dr., Reston, Va.
• **(703) 471-5414**

The park's newest attraction, the Western-themed Water Mine Family Swimmin' Hole, features several slides, bubblers, water cannons and shallow play areas for young children. The park itself is an all-round kid-pleaser, offering rides on a miniature train, carousel and sight-seeing pontoon boat for nominal fees. Call for admission prices and hours, which vary seasonally. See the Parks and Recreation chapter for more information.

Meadowlark Gardens Regional Park
9750 Meadowlark Gardens Ct., Vienna, Va. • **(703) 255-3631**

Here's a favorite spot for stroller-pushing parents, who get their day's exercise navigating more than 2 miles of winding walkways around landscaped gardens and three small lakes that attract ducks and geese. Kids have fun getting sprayed by a fountain, crossing stepping stones over shallow water and watching the waterfowl and fish from a wooden gazebo overlooking Lake Caroline. Although no food is permitted in the park, you can munch in the air-conditioned visitors center snack room. Youngsters also like browsing the toys and nature-related items in the gift shop. Call for hours, which vary seasonally. See the Parks and Recreation chapter for more information.

Reston Animal Park
1228 Hunter Mill Rd., Vienna, Va.
• **(703) 759-3637**

Kids adore this little petting farm, where such animals as goats and potbellied pigs roam free. Daily programs include elephant painting and aerobics demonstrations, live animal shows and feedings. Weekend programs feature topics like The Living Rainforest. For extra fees, visitors can ride an elephant or pony. Hours and admission costs vary seasonally; call for information.

River Farm
7931 E. Boulevard Dr., Alexandria, Va.
• **(703) 768-5700**

Kids love visiting the children's gardens on the grounds of the American Horticultural Society's headquarters, just down the road from George Washington's home, Mount Vernon (see previous entry). Among the interactive, themed plots are the crawl-through Bat Cave, a Little House on the Prairie garden filled with wildflowers, an Alphabet Garden featuring plants starting with each letter, and Beau Beau's Garden, featuring a yellow-brick road leading to a fort-like bridge that crosses a dry riverbed containing fun discoveries. Bring a picnic to enjoy as you gaze out at the Potomac River. Except for occasional weekend events, the gardens are open weekdays only from 8:30 AM to 5 PM.

Suburban Maryland

Cabin John Regional Park
7400 Tuckerman Ln., Rockville, Md.
• **(301) 469-7835**

An old-fashioned miniature train takes visitors on a 1.3-mile wooded ride that passes the large, inviting playground. Play equipment includes a complex Action Playground for school-age children plus slides, swing and storybook-themed climbing equipment for preschoolers. Children enjoy looking for scampering chipmunks, in plentiful supply through-

INSIDERS' TIP

Enjoy Loudoun County's beautiful rural scenery during the annual Spring Farm Tour and Fall Farm Color Tour of the Loudoun Valleys. Kid-pleasing highlights include hayrides, berry and pumpkin picking, straw mazes, pony rides, face painting and lots of live animals such as llamas, peacocks, burros and all the standard barnyard favorites. For free brochures, including directions to and descriptions of each location, call the Loudoun Tourism Council at (800) 752-6118.

The National Museum of Natural History contains more than 81 million items documenting humankind and the natural environment.

out the park. Cabin John Station, where the train boards, doubles as a garage, and kids like to watch the big metal doors roll shut after the day's last ride. The station also houses a snack bar. A nearby waste container features a talking pig that "eats" litter. See the Parks and Recreation chapter for more information.

Glen Echo Park
MacArthur Blvd. at Goldsboro Rd., Glen Echo, Md. • (301) 492-6663

The sound of the antique Dentzel carousel's Wurlitzer band organ beckons visitors before they even catch sight of the prancing ponies, ostriches and rabbits. This enchanting park, a former trolley-line amusement park now operated by the National Park Service, is full of quirky fun, from the resident artists' studios in grass-covered yurts to the Spanish ballroom that hosts Big Band and folk dancing every week. It's a nice spot for birthday parties after a show at the Puppet Co.

or Adventure Theatre (see the previous "Show Business" section). Just watch out for the yellow jackets! The annual free Children's Chautauqua Day, usually in September, features entertainers and a variety of hands-on art projects. The carousel, with rides for 50¢, operates Wednesday and Thursday from 10 AM to 2 PM and Saturday and Sunday from noon to 6 PM, May through September. Other attractions are open all year. See the Arts chapter for more information.

Robert M. Watkins Regional Park
301 Watkins Park Dr., Upper Marlboro, Md. • (301) 249-9220

Eenie, meenie, minie, moe: With so many choices, kids may have a hard time deciding what to do first. Stop at the Lottsford-Largo Train Station for tickets to take a ride on the *C.P. Huntington*, a miniature version of the antique locomotive. Grab a treat at the snack bar, then go for a spin on the antique carousel. Visit Old Maryland Farm to look at live barnyard animals, play miniature golf or stop by the nature center. This park is also listed in the Parks and Recreation chapter.

Summit Hall Farm Park
502 S. Frederick Ave., Gaithersburg, Md.
• (301) 258-6350

Gaithersburg residents flock to this pool and its special features, like 250-foot water slides, a frog slide, water fountains and a seal that spouts water. The surrounding grounds offer a playground with a ball pit and climbing equipment, a sand volleyball court, concession stand, miniature golf course and five-hole "kiddie" course. Costs and hours vary, so please call ahead.

Our city has produced
more than its fair share
of cultural luminaries,
especially in the areas
of stage, screen
and studio.

The Arts

A rich and diverse arts scene is flourishing in Metro Washington, from repertory theaters and burgeoning artists' colonies to the esteemed National Symphony Orchestra and National Gallery of Art, not to mention such renowned venues as The John F. Kennedy Center for the Performing Arts and Wolf Trap Farm Park, the nation's only national park for the performing arts.

Washington, D.C. offers more museums and public galleries than any other North American city. Visitors come from all over the globe to view the National Gallery's many treasures and once-in-a-lifetime retrospectives. While the National Gallery alone would be enough to secure our city's reputation as a visual arts center, Washington is also home to such esteemed galleries as the Smithsonian Institution's art museums, the Corcoran, the Phillips Collection and the National Museum of Women in the Arts.

Up-and-coming artists can be found in galleries in such areas as Dupont Circle and Georgetown in D.C., and Old Town Alexandria in Virginia. In the performing arts, Washington surpasses both New York and Los Angeles in per capita public performances. Our city has produced more than its fair share of cultural luminaries, especially in the areas of stage, screen and studio. Among those with ties to the area, whether by birth or stints working or attending school here, are actors Warren Beatty and big sister Shirley MacLaine, Goldie Hawn, Robert Prosky and Helen Hayes, for whom Washington's equivalent of the Tony Award is named; singers Pearl Bailey, Toni Braxton, Mary Chapin Carpenter and Roberta Flack; opera stars Placido Domingo and Beverly Sills; jazz legends Duke Ellington and Ella Fitzgerald; guitar virtuosos Roy Buchanan and Danny Gatton; and rock 'n' roll icon Jim Morrison.

No one will ever question the fact that the Washington area moves to a different beat.

That includes the literal interpretation. Anchored by the aforementioned Kennedy Center and Wolf Trap, Metro Washington knows no music unfamiliar to its discerning ears. Live-music aficionados new to the Washington area should find nary a dull moment here. Each week, you can bet you'll uncover at least one major concert that fits your taste or mood, whether it be rock, country, opera, classical, bluegrass, R&B, rap, world beat or folk.

If all the world's a stage, and if Washington is indeed the nerve center of the globe, then it stands to reason that the Nation's Capital should have a relatively unparalleled theater scene. The truth is, we don't have the equivalent of the Great White Way here. If you want too see the biggest, brightest and best in American theater and dance, New York's Broadway is only 220 miles away. Broadway touches Washington, however, whether by national touring productions of shows like *Cats* and *The Phantom of the Opera* or pre-New York stagings of the newest play by Neil Simon or a musical like *How to Succeed in Business Without Really Trying*.

Metro Washington is one of the most filmed communities in the world, and the city enjoys increasingly close ties to Hollywood. It only seems logical that film stars including John Lithgow, Susan Sarandon and Jon Voight cut their theatrical teeth at Washington's own Catholic University, whose drama department is among the finest in the nation.

Hollywood has taken a liking to Metro Washington. Not only does the entertainment industry supposedly have a friend in the White House these days, but it also enjoys robust box office support here. The Washington area is one of the largest film markets in the nation, rivaling Los Angeles, New York and Chicago.

This city of monuments and magnificent vistas is also one of the most-filmed locations in the world. Chances are you won't live here long before you spot a movie crew in

Georgetown, Capitol Hill, Old Town Alexandria, Annapolis or along the National Mall. In the past few years, such blockbuster hits as *No Way Out*, *JFK*, *A Few Good Men*, *In the Line of Fire*, *Patriot Games* and *The Pelican Brief* have used Metro Washington as a backdrop.

In this chapter, you'll find an overview of Metro Washington's performing arts, galleries and movie houses. You'll also want to check out our Nightlife chapter for the lowdown on Washington's club scene, where you'll find a wide range of entertainment. Other cultural institutions, like museums, are profiled in our Attractions chapter.

Performing Arts

Washington, D.C.

DAR Constitution Hall
1776 D St. NW, Washington, D.C.
• **(202) 628-4780**

Near the White House and next to the DAR National Headquarters and Museum, this concert hall hosts a variety of musical performances, from classical to pop, including such acts as the Washington Symphony Orchestra; the United States Air Force, Army and Navy bands; and Earth, Wind and Fire. It's been said that Vladimir Horowitz, the legendary pianist, preferred to perform in this classy and surprisingly intimate atmosphere. Avoid parking hassles by taking Metro to Farragut West. See our Attractions and Kidstuff chapters for information about the neighboring DAR Museum.

Ford's Theatre
511 10th St. NW, Washington, D.C.
• **(202) 347-4833**

Walk into this theater where John Wilkes Booth assassinated President Abraham Lincoln on April 14, 1865, and you'll view a room that looks eerily the same as it did on that ill-fated night. The painstaking restoration includes the Presidential Box, adorned with patriotic bunting, gold drapes and a portrait of George Washington. Nobody's allowed to sit in Lincoln's seat. Many people want to though, desiring to tempt fate, according to John Rogers, receptionist at Ford's.

Today, Ford's remains an active and immensely popular theater, a tribute to Lincoln's love for the performing arts. The 699-seat theater each year stages four or five musical revues and plays that otherwise might not find a national showcase, and that Lincoln most likely would enjoy. Annual events include a presidential gala and the holiday staging of Dickens' *A Christmas Carol*. Satirist Mark Russell usually performs during inaugural week. Ford's does not offer parking, but two public lots are within a block. The nearest Metrorail stops are Metro Center and Archives-Navy Memorial. For information on touring the theater and its museum, call the National Park Service, (202) 426-6924, and see our Civil War chapter.

George Washington University's Lisner Auditorium
730 21st St. NW, Washington, D.C.
• **(202) 994-1500**

Students aren't the only listeners who flock to Lisner's eclectic lineup, from university concerts, plays and ballets to international acts like Ondekoza: Demon Drummers of Japan and popular performers like the Pat Metheny Group. The 56-year-old concert hall boasts 1,490 seats which offer good views but not a lot of leg room. Look for the whimsical hippopotamus statue out front. If you're driving, you may be lucky enough to find on-street parking. Otherwise, opt for a nearby garage or take Metrorail's Orange or Blue Line to Foggy Bottom-GWU.

The John F. Kennedy Center for the Performing Arts
New Hampshire Ave. at Rock Creek Pkwy., Washington, D.C.
• **(202) 467-4600**

Sitting majestically along the Potomac just south of Georgetown, this "living memorial" to the nation's 34th president proves even more impressive inside, where the grand foyers alone, like the flag-laden Hall of Nations, are worth a trip. This unique arts center offers much more than beautiful hallways, though.

Topping the list is the center's newly renovated, 2,500-seat Concert Hall, which reopened in October of 1997 to rave reviews on its improved acoustics and ground-breaking, accessible accommodations for disabled patrons. Among the $13 million worth of innovations are onstage boxes and lower-priced chorister seats onstage behind the musicians; an adjustable, multi-panelled stage canopy to enhance sound; seats with swing-away arms, and specially designed ramps for easy wheelchair access; and elegant decor features like the Israeli Room on the Box Tier and the Chinese Lounge on the Second Tier.

The world-renowned National Symphony Orchestra, (202) 416-8100, directed by Leonard Slatkin, performs here from October through April. The 1997-98 season includes works by Beethoven, Mozart and Baroque, Russian and Caribbean composers. Tickets range in price from $12 to $58. Consider a subscription if you plan to attend concerts frequently and want to be assured of the best seats.

The 2,318-seat Opera House hosts Broadway productions such as the 1997-98 season's *Smokey Joe's Cafe* and *Dreamgirls*, as well as several national and international dance troupes. The Eisenhower Theater also showcases large-scale productions, while smaller shows, like the long-running *Shear Madness*, a comic whodunit, are accommodated in the Terrace Theater and Theater Lab.

The Kennedy Center is home to the Washington Opera, (202) 416-7800, with popular tenor Placido Domingo as its artistic director. The center hosts numerous events sponsored by the 32-year-old Washington Performing Arts Society, (202) 833-9800, which brings a diverse array of international acts to performance sites throughout Metro Washington. The Washington Ballet, (202) 362-3606, presents shows here in the fall, winter and spring. The company, founded by Artistic Director Mary Day, also performs The Nutcracker annually at the Warner Theatre and George Mason University's Center for the Arts.

In 1997, the center launched a new "Performing Arts for Everyone" initiative, the highlight of which is daily free concerts at 6 PM on the Millennium Stage. You don't even need a ticket!

To get a close-up look at the center's many outstanding features, take a free, guided, hourlong tour, offered by the Friends of the Kennedy Center from 10 AM to 1 PM daily. You don't need reservations, but you can call (202) 416-8340, TTY (202) 416-8524 for more details. The center boasts three restaurants, the Roof Terrace for elegant dinners, Hors D' Oeuverie for light refreshments and Encore Cafe for casual dining. Visit the two gift shops, open from 10 AM to 9 PM, for a variety of performing arts-related merchandise.

The center offers three levels of underground parking, priced at $8, but it tends to fill up rather quickly. Your best bet is to park at the nearby Columbia Plaza Garage, 2400 Virginia Avenue NW. You also can take Metro to the Foggy Bottom-George Washington University station and catch the Kennedy Center Show Shuttle, which operates 9:45 AM to midnight Monday through Saturday, and from noon to midnight on Sundays and holidays.

Don't miss visiting the center during December, when it's all decked out for the holiday season. In 1997, designer Christopher Radko actually "gift-wrapped" the building's exterior with 10-foot-wide red ribbon! You'll also find some of the Kennedy Center's most popular programs, like the annual free Messiah Sing-Along (tickets are distributed early in the month — and they go fast!), the Paul Hill Chorale's Christmas Candlelight Concerts and the Oratorio Society of Washington's Music for Christmas. December also marks the annual gala for recipients of the Kennedy Center Honors, awarded in 1997 to Lauren Bacall, Bob Dylan, Charlton Heston, Jessye Norman and Edward Villella. See our Kidstuff chapter for information about children's shows at the Kennedy Center.

MCI Center
601 F St. NW, Washington, D.C.
• (202) 432-SEAT

One of the city's most heralded new additions, the spacious athletic arena also hosts concerts by the likes of Barry Manilow, Billy

The Torpedo Factory, a refurbished 1918 torpedo-shell plant, now houses a thriving arts colony.

Joel and Alan Jackson. See our Spectator Sports chapter for a Close-up and complete information on the center and the teams that play here.

The National Theatre
1321 Pennsylvania Ave. NW, Washington, D.C. • (202) 628-6161, (800) 447-7400 for ticket charges

The National, the city's oldest theater, has been bringing stage entertainment to Washingtonians since 1835; in fact, every president since then, with the exception of Dwight Eisenhower (and we're not sure why), has attended a show here at "The Theatre of Presidents." The National gives the impression of a Broadway theater. Whether you're sitting in the orchestra, mezzanine or balcony of the 1,676-seat theater, you'll enjoy first-rate acoustics and elegant details like crystal chandeliers.

The National's forte is booking the big musicals such as *Bring in 'Da Noise, Bring in 'Da Funk*, *Rent*, *Chicago* and the perennial favorite, *Cats*. The schedule for 1998 includes the national touring company premiere of *Ragtime* April 14 through June 14. The theater has played host to several world premieres, including *Showboat* in the 1920s, and, more recently, *Crazy for You* and *Whistle Down the Wind*.

The theater also hosts three entertainment series in its second-floor Helen Hayes Gallery. Admission is free, on a first-come, first-serve basis. Send a self-addressed, stamped envelope for a schedule. Saturday Morning at the National features family shows at 9:30 and 11 AM, generally during the fall and mid-January through mid-April. Monday Night at the National showcases various performers at 6 and 7:30 PM. Weekly film screenings highlight the Summer Cinema series.

Arrange a tour, given for groups of 10 or more, by calling (202) 783-3370. You'll view a slide show about the National's history (the theater was rebuilt five times after devastating fires in the 1800s), get a behind-the-scenes look at the theater and even learn about resident friendly, opening-night ghost John McCullough, an actor reportedly murdered by a fellow performer in the basement.

Warner Theater
13th and E Sts. NW, Washington, D.C. • (202) 783-4000

A former vaudeville and movie palace, the beautifully restored, gilt- and chandelier-accented Warner now specializes in concerts and

Broadway productions. Recent shows include Singin' in the Rain, Peter Pan and A Tuna Christmas, and the 1998 schedule features Unforgettable: The Music of Nat King Cole and Cirque Ingenieux. The theater seats 1,850 people. Ticket prices vary according to the event.

Suburban Virginia

George Mason University's Center for the Arts
Va. Rt. 123 and Braddock Rd., Fairfax, Va. • (703) 993-8888

Touted as the "Kennedy Center of Northern Virginia," this showcase for local as well as nationally known acts opened with much fanfare in 1988. If offers a pleasant alternative for folks who'd rather avoid D.C.'s traffic and parking hassles. The center continues to attract prominent artists such as, during the 1997-98 season, Nancy Wilson, the Miami City Ballet, Mark Morris Dance Group, The Academy of St. Martin in the Fields, Virginia Opera, pianist Andras Schiff and violinist Joshua Bell. Tickets are available by subscription or individually, with prices varying according to the performance.

The resident theatrical company, Theater of the First Amendment, performs critically acclaimed contemporary works, including world premieres like Anna Theresa Cascio's Crystal. The 41-year-old Fairfax Symphony, (703) 642-7200, Virginia's answer to The National Symphony, performs here with such guest artists as Jean-Pierre Rampal. The center also offers film series, with tickets priced at just $5, at its Cinema at the Johnson Center. Inexpensive parking is available at an adjacent parking deck, which connects to the center via a pedestrian bridge.

Patriot Center at George Mason University
4400 University Dr., Fairfax, Va. • (703) 993-3000

This 12-year-old, 10,000-seat arena hosts a variety of events in addition to the men's and women's Patriots' home basketball games. The center's annual concert slate features 25 shows, mostly by nationally known popular and country performers like Sarah

McLachlan. Family programs like Walt Disney's World on Ice and Sesame Street Live take place several times a year. See our Spectator Sports chapter for more on the center's sporting events.

Suburban Maryland

Publick Playhouse
5445 Landover Rd., Cheverly, Md. • (301) 277-1710

This entertainment showcase specializes in family concerts and plays by visiting performers and drama troupes, including local community theater. Tickets vary in price according to the event, and discount subscriptions are available.

Strathmore Hall Arts Center
10701 Rockville Pk., Rockville, Md. • (301) 530-0540

In 1997 this beautiful, circa 1902 mansion underwent a 14-month, $3.2-million renovation and expansion. Originally a well-to-do private residence, Strathmore Hall now serves as an elegant setting for concerts, visual arts and literary readings. The Music in the Mansion series, running September through May, features esteemed classical ensembles, instrumental soloists, vocalists and folk groups. Tickets start at $18 for adults, $16 for seniors age 60 and older and $7 for children age 18 and younger. Subscriptions offer a discount.

The center also presents monthly concerts by professional musicians in the Friday Morning Music Club. The second-floor Gudelsky Gallery Suite and first-floor Invitational Gallery, hallways and stairway host free, changing exhibits of visual art. Strathmore promotes the literary arts through its Friends of the Library lunchtime lecture series, $15 each or $55 for a four-event series. The Strathmore Library features more than 500 works by Montgomery County residents, as well as a collection of children's books on the arts. It's open from noon to 3 PM Saturdays. Among the center's other programs are Afternoon Tea at 1 PM Tuesdays and Wednesdays, with instrumental performances in the Dorothy M. and Maurice C. Shapiro Music Room, at $10 per person; and Art After Hours, featuring performances in the cafe beginning at 9 PM Wednesdays. The galleries and gift shop are open from 10 AM to 4 PM Mondays, Tuesdays, Thursdays and Fridays, from 10 AM to 9 PM on Wednesdays and from 10 AM to 3 PM on Saturdays.

USAirways Arena
1 N. Harry Truman Dr., Landover, Md.
• (301) 350-3400

The cavernous, 19,000-seat arena, with surprisingly good acoustics, is where some of the largest rock, country and pop music acts of the day perform. See our Spectator Sports chapter for more on the sporting events held at this facility, conveniently right off the Beltway in Prince George's County.

Outdoor Stages

Washington, D.C.

Carter Barron Amphitheatre In Rock Creek Park
4850 Colorado Ave. NW, Washington, D.C. • (202) 619-7222, (202) 426-6837 during summer

In beautiful Rock Creek Park, this popular outdoor stage sponsors an annual summer musical festival, including many top names in jazz, soul and R&B, Saturday and Sunday nights. The theater seats 3,700. Annual free events include performances of a Shakespearean work by the Shakespeare Theatre, the D.C. Blues Festival and National Symphony Orchestra concerts. Note that tickets for paid concerts are nonrefundable, rain or shine. Plenty of free parking is available.

RFK Stadium
2400 E. Capitol St. SE, Washington, D.C. • (202) 547-9077

Due east of the Capitol, this 56,000-seat former home of the Washington Redskins football team also is used for those monolithic rock concerts and festivals that seem synonymous with summertime. Acoustically, well, it's a football stadium, but as a host for the often excessive pageantry of rock 'n' roll, RFK plays the role rather well.

Sylvan Theatre
The National Mall, Washington, D.C. • (202) 426-6839

With the Washington Monument looming in the background, this outdoor theater stages a number of military, big band and pop concerts during warm-weather months.

Northern Virginia

Nissan Pavilion at Stone Ridge
7800 Cellar Door Dr., Bristow, Va. • (703) 754-6400

The state-of-the-art, 25,000-seat amphitheater made its debut in June 1995, presenting Metro Washington music fans with yet another attractive warm-weather venue for rock, pop and country music concerts. It's three times the size of the more prominent Wolf Trap Farm Park (see the following listing) and features two 30-by-40-foot video screens, the largest in any U.S. amphitheater. It also offers a separate sound system just for the lawn. Concerts feature such performers as Jimmy Buffet, James Taylor, Dave Matthews and Blues Traveler.

The annual Capital Jazz Festival, held in early June, is a veritable who's who of contemporary jazz artists. Ticket prices range from free (for radio-sponsored festivals and occasional National Symphony shows) to $50. Children 12 and younger are admitted free to some shows, like James Taylor and Aretha Franklin. Give yourself plenty of time to travel, as traffic on Interstate 66 frequently backs up. Your best bet is to call the pavilion for alternative directions.

INSIDERS' TIP

Many area community centers boast resident theater companies whose performances prove highly entertaining, yet easy on the budget.

Wolf Trap Farm Park
1551 Trap Rd., Vienna, Va.
• **(703) 255-1860**

This beautiful National Park Service facility, with its open-air Filene Center wooden pavilion and lawn seating, brings to the Virginia suburbs some of the world's leading musical entertainers during the spring and summer. The park's annual summer concert series is virtually free of musical boundaries. The Moody Blues may perform on a Friday night, followed by a Saturday afternoon Cajun music festival, a Sunday journey through Lake Wobegon with Garrison Keillor and a Monday evening with Peter, Paul and Mary.

Concertgoers often tote elegant picnics, turning the lawn into a patchwork quilt of blankets and baskets. Ticket prices vary, starting at about $14 for some lawn seats. Note that everyone, regardless of age, must have a ticket to enter. Also, be forewarned that rarely does rain drown out a concert: If you have lawn seats during a downpour, prepare to get soaked.

A smaller indoor concert hall just down the road, the intimate Barns of Wolf Trap, (703) 938-2404, is used primarily as a fall-and-winter showplace for folk and acoustic musicians. See our Kidstuff chapter for information about children's programs at Wolf Trap.

Suburban Maryland

Merriweather Post Pavilion
10475 Little Patuxent Pkwy., Columbia, Md. • **(301) 596-0660**

In the Howard County planned community of Columbia, a short drive from Montgomery County, Merriweather is Maryland's answer to Wolf Trap. While not as polished as its Virginia cousin, this was still one of the pioneer outdoor music halls in the United States, and its summer rock and pop concert series (harder-edged than Wolf Trap's) attracts huge crowds from the Washington-Baltimore corridor. The summer lineup features from 20 to 65 shows and generally includes such acts as Jimmy Buffet, the Beach Boys, Chicago, the Moody Blues and James Taylor.

Theater

Washington, D.C.

Arena Stage
1101 6th St. SW, Washington, D.C.
• **(202) 488-3300**

Across the street from the Southwest waterfront, the nationally recognized and critically acclaimed Arena Stage presents a mix of classical and contemporary shows, including the provocative works of David Mamet and August Wilson and even occasional musicals like *Sunday in the Park with George*. The three-theater complex has proven to be a hotbed for emerging talent and previously untried productions, and boasts more than 50 Helen Hayes awards for its efforts. It's also the first theater outside of New York City to receive a Tony Award for Theatrical Excellence, awarded in 1976. The theater recently hired a new artistic director, Molly D. Smith, to succeed Douglas C. Wager, who steps down in July.

Among 1998 productions are Jon Klein's *Dimly Perceived Threats to the System*, Moss Hart's and George S. Kaufman's *You Can't Take It With You* and Syl Jones's *Black No More*. Tickets, available by subscription, range in price singly from $26 to $45. The theater seats 800 in its Fichlandler theater in the round, and 500 in the Kreeger. A third stage, the Old Vat, features works by visiting troupes. Free, on-street parking usually is easy to find in the neighborhood. Disabled patrons can park in the theater's lot.

Folger Shakespeare Library's Elizabethan Theatre
201 E. Capitol St. NW, Washington, D.C.
• **(202) 544-4600**

Fans of the master British playwright will want to venture over to Capitol Hill to the Folger, where you can see innovative productions of the Bard's plays and other works presented by visiting troupes. The intimate wooden theater, modeled after a true Shakespearean stage, seats 250 people.

Theater is just the tip of the arts iceburg here, however. The library itself, open only by appointment to scholars, features the largest collections of early editions of Shakespeare. The public can visit the reading rooms annually during Shakespeare's Birthday Open House in April. The Folger holds rotating gallery exhibits on period topics such as old-fashioned remedies. The PEN/Faulkner Novel Reading Series features nominees for the nation's largest juried fiction award, and a poetry series includes poets of national fame. The library also sponsors family programs on such topics as "Exploring Shakespeare's Plays." The Folger Consort Group, meanwhile, presents a slate of concerts of medieval, renaissance and baroque music.

Public tours take place at 1 PM on Saturdays, and tours of the Elizabethan Herbal Knot Garden take place at 10 and 11 AM every third Saturday from April through October. Shakespeare etc., the library's gift shop, sells Folger editions of Shakespeare's plays and other merchandise related to the Bard. The building is open from 10 AM to 4 PM Monday through Saturday, and is closed on federal holidays. On-street parking is available, and the nearest Metro stations are Capitol South and Union Station.

GALA! Hispanic Theatre
1625 Park Rd. NW, Washington, D.C.
- **(202) 234-7174**

The city's only Spanish-language theater offers both classic and contemporary plays by Spanish and Latin American playwrights, including some premieres. Hugo Medrano is the artistic director.

No habla español? Not to worry: You can hear a simultaneous English translation through a headset. Tickets cost $18 to $20, with discounts available for seniors, children and groups of 10 or more. The theater also sometimes features community nights, with greatly reduced ticket prices. On-site parking is free.

The Shakespeare Theatre
450 7th St. NW, Washington, D.C.
- **(202) 393-2700**

Buy your tickets early for productions of this critically acclaimed theater company, which specializes in Shakespearean and other classic drama by the likes of Ibsen and Williams. The company performs five main-stage

plays annually, under the direction of Michael Kahn. Shows like the recent production of *Othello*, featuring Patrick Stewart in the title role, sell out quickly, with just $10 standing-room-only seats available at the last minute. (SRO tickets are available one hour before sold-out shows for cash only, with a limit of two per person.) Regular tickets, if you're lucky enough to get them, range in price from $13.50 to $49.50.

In a revitalized section of downtown near the National Gallery of Art, the 449-seat theater is home to Washington's resident Shakespeare company. It's housed at the Lansburgh, a former department store building that is a longtime Washington icon. Parking is available on-site for $8 in a garage accessible from 8th Street. The nearest Metro Stations are Gallery Place-Chinatown and Archives-Navy Memorial. The theater also presents two weeks of free performances of a Shakespearean play each June at Carter Barron Amphitheatre in Rock Creek Park.

Source Theatre Company
1835 14th St. NW, Washington, D.C.
- **(202) 462-1073**

This innovative, 21-year-old theater company is known for its stagings of new plays and musicals and reinterpretations of classics like The Cherry Orchard. Joe Banno is artistic director. The 101-seat theater's month-long, midsummer Washington Theatre Festival showcases 70 full-length plays and one-acts written primarily by local playwrights.

The Aftershocks Series features alternative plays, staged late at night. Tickets are $20 to $25 for main stage productions, $8 to $15 for festival performances and $12 for Aftershocks shows. Parking is available for $3 at an attended lot at 1914 14th Street. If you prefer to take Metro, the U Street/Cardozo station is a block and a half away.

The Studio Theatre
1333 P St. NW, Washington, D.C.
- **(202) 332-3300**

This 20-year-old regional theater strives to combine quality and affordability in its broad range of productions. With slightly fewer than 200 seats, it offers an intimate setting for plays like *Hair*, *Love! Valour! Compassion!* and *Old*

Wicked Songs. Joy Zinoman is artistic director of the theater, which produces five to six plays annually on its main stage. Ticket prices range from $19.50 to $34.50. Attended parking is $4 — with no change available — at a lot on P Street between 14th and 15th streets. The nearest Metrorail station is Dupont Circle.

Woolly Mammoth Theatre
1401 Church St. NW, Washington, D.C.
• (202) 393-3939

This cutting-edge theater specializes in world and national premieres, including 1998 offerings such as Regina Porter's *Man, Woman, Dinosaur* and *Dead Funny* by Terry Johnson. Howard Shawlwitz is artistic director. Tickets generally cost from $24.75 to $32, but each show also features two "pay what you can" previews. The theater also offers community arts programs, such as acting classes, at $225 for eight weeks. Free, attended parking is available.

Northern Virginia

Signature Theatre
3806 S. Four Mile Run Dr., Arlington, Va.
• (703) 820-9771, (703) 218-6500
box office

This 8-year-old company performs in an intimate, 136-seat black-box theater, a mere six-minute drive from the Kennedy Center. Signature, under the artistic direction of Eric D. Schaeffer, is highly regarded for its productions of Sondheim shows and other musical theater revivals, as well as new plays. It has garnered 18 Helen Hayes Awards and 57 nominations, and twice been reviewed by *The New York Times*. The company performs three musicals and two plays annually. The 1998 season includes the American premiere of a new musical, *The Fix*, and a production of Sondheim's *A Little Night Music*. Single-show tickets are $18 to $25, but nonsubscribers often find that performances sell out early. Free, on-street parking is available.

The company also holds *STAGES*, a series of free public readings of new plays at 7 PM on most Mondays. Signature also offers a drama education program for high-school students.

Suburban Maryland

Olney Theatre Center for the Arts
2001 Olney-Sandy Spring Rd., Olney, Md. • (301) 924-3400

Suburban Maryland's best-known playhouse, this converted bar in the Montgomery County countryside is a staple for quality summer theater, with productions like William Nicholson's Broadway hit, *Shadowlands*.

Round House Theatre
12210 Bushey Dr., Silver Spring, Md.
• (301) 933-1644

Celebrating its 20th anniversary season, this Montgomery County repertory company specializes in contemporary works and new translations of classics such as *Uncle Vanya*. The 218-seat theater presents four to six shows annually, under the artistic direction of Jerry Whiddon, and in 1998 will close out its season with a new production of *Godspell*, the first show performed by the company when it started. Tickets range in price from $20 to $27, and some performances feature last-minute, $6 "student rush" tickets. The theater also conducts classes for adults and children and participates in a school outreach program. Free, on-site parking is available.

Visual Arts

Major Galleries and Museums
Washington, D.C.

The Corcoran Gallery of Art
500 17th St. NW, Washington, D.C.
• (202) 639-1700

Of all the fine arts showcases that the nation's capital has to offer, the Corcoran ranks as the largest and oldest private gallery. It boasts an amazing selection of American paintings and sculpture and a smaller assortment of European pieces. It also hosts numerous special solo and group exhibitions, featuring a wide array of works by local, national and international artists. Some shows feature students of the *Corcoran School of Art*, the city's sole professional school of art and design.

Among special exhibitions scheduled for 1998 are *Rhapsodies in Black: Art of the Harlem Renaissance*; *ArtSites 98*, a biennial exhibition of contemporary art held at the Corcoran and 11 regional art centers; and *45th Biennial: The Corcoran Collects*, including works by such artists as Eakins, Hopper, Homer and Cassatt.

The gallery also hosts frequent concerts, lectures and family programs (see the Kidstuff chapter). Visit the gift shop and café, which features a popular brunch on Sundays. The Corcoran is open from 10 AM to 5 PM Friday through Monday and Wednesday, and 10 AM to 9 PM on Thursday. Admission by recommended donation is $3 for adults, $1 for students and seniors and $5 per family. The nearest Metro stations are Farragut West (17th Street Exit) and Farragut North (K Street Exit).

Freer Gallery of Art
Jefferson Dr. at 12th St. SW,
Washington, D.C. • (202) 357-2700,
(202) 357-1729 TDD

An extensive renovation several years ago did wonders for the Freer Gallery of Art, which showcases a world-renowned collection of Asian works such as Chinese paintings, Japanese screens and Egyptian glass, and 19th- and early 20th-century American art by painters such as John Singer Sargent and James McNeill Whistler. The granite and marble building, one of the Smithsonian Institution's museums on the National Mall, opened in 1923. The undisputed highlight is Whistler's gorgeous Peacock Room, a lavish dining room designed by the artist for Frederick R. Leyland during the 19th Century.

Many first-time visitors to the Freer find that it isn't long before they're wanting to make a return trip. The museum regularly hosts special events like concerts and films; pick up a schedule or call Dial-a-Museum, (202) 357-2020 for information about upcoming programs here and at other Smithsonian museums. Tours of special exhibitions usually take place at 11:30 AM daily, while highlights tours begin at 12:30 PM. Museum hours are 10 AM to 5:30 PM daily except December 25. Admission is free. Your best bet is to take Metro to the Smithsonian station, practically right outside the museum's door. See the Kidstuff chapter for information about family programs.

Hirshhorn Museum and Sculpture Garden
7th St. and Independence Ave. SW,
Washington, D.C. • (202) 357-2700

This striking doughnut-shaped building is yet another hard-to-miss Smithsonian landmark abutting the National Mall. The Hirshhorn, established in 1974, specializes in modern art, including 19th- and 20th-century paintings and sculpture by such greats as de Kooning, Pollock and Rothko. Adjoining and just to the north, the idyllic Sunken Sculpture Garden features works by Matisse and Rodin. Like all Smithsonian museums, the Hirshhorn features special programs such as film screenings and lectures. Call Dial-a-Museum at (202) 357-2020. Hours are 10 AM to 5:30 PM daily except December 25. The museum is a short walk from the Smithsonian Metro stop. Our Kidstuff chapter describes family activities here.

National Gallery of Art
4th St. and Constitution Ave. NW,
Washington, D.C. • (202) 737-4215

What are your plans for fall of 1998? Washington's most anticipated art exhibition of the year is slated to open here on October 4, and if you're a Vincent Van Gogh aficionado, you won't want to miss it. *Van Gogh's Van Goghs: Masterpieces From the Van Gogh Museum* will feature 70 paintings by the Dutch artist, on display for three months. As with major exhibitions in the past, this one will require free, timed passes for admission. Expect crowds, especially on weekends. Of course, the show is just icing on the cake, an added bonus at a gallery which permanently houses many of the world's best-loved masterpieces.

Actually two buildings, the National Gallery of Art is one of the world's preeminent cultural attractions, housing a collection vast and rich enough to command repeated visits. Created in 1937 by a joint resolution of Congress, the gallery grew from the bequest of prominent financier Andrew Mellon and opened in 1941. You'll not find a better cultural bargain anywhere: Admission is free, except for occasional moderate fees to popular special exhibitions.

The gallery's magnitude and diversity of exhibits can make a visit daunting, especially for the first-time tourist. We recommend starting at the Micro Gallery, conveniently located off the West Building's main entrance off the National Mall. Here, you can preview more than 1,700 works on an interactive computer screen and design a personalized tour, complete with a map, of art you'd especially like to see. You can search for works categorized according to artists, subjects or time periods, and learn more about the artists' backgrounds.

The original West Building features some of the best in American and European paintings, sculpture and graphic arts from the 13th through 19th centuries. Here, you'll find works by Botticelli, Raphael and Rembrandt, and the only da Vinci painting on exhibit outside Europe. The popular Impressionism collection includes famous works by Renoir, Monet, Manet, Cassatt, Pissaro and others. You'll also see well-known American works like Gilbert Stuart's presidential portraits. The East Building, designed by I.M. Pei and completed in 1978, showcases modern art, including a giant Calder mobile. The east wing also hosts many of the museum's major exhibitions, such as recent shows featuring retrospectives of works by Vermeer, La Tour, Picasso, Whistler, Escher and American landscape artist Thomas Moran.

The two buildings are connected by a dramatic fountain- and skylight-enhanced underground, automated walkway. Here you'll also find the informal Concourse Buffet and a great gift shop featuring beautiful books and postcards and reasonably priced, framing-quality prints. Another gift shop, featuring an even more extensive selection of prints and postcards, is on the West Building's ground floor. Other dining options include the Garden Café in the West Building, the Cascade Espresso Bar on the Concourse and the Terrace Café in the East Building. Call (202) 347-9401 for restaurant information, and (202) 842-6466 for gift-shop details.

The museum holds numerous special programs, most of which are free of charge. Obtain information by calling (202) 737-4215, or request a free monthly calendar of events by calling (202) 842-6360. A Sunday evening concert series, (202) 842-6941, features free performances by the National Gallery Orchestra at 7 PM on most Sundays, October through June. Arrive at the West Garden Court as early as 6 PM; admission is first-come, first-served. The East Building Auditorium offers free screenings of art films on weekends and some weekdays. Admission is on a first-come, first-served basis. Call (202) 842-6799 for a schedule. See our Kidstuff chapter for a description of family-oriented features.

Enhance your visit with a free, guided tour. Meet in the Rotunda to learn about the West Building's collection at 11:30 AM and 3:30 PM Monday through Friday, 10:30 AM and 12:30 PM Saturday, and 12:30, 2:30 and 4:30 PM Sunday. The East Building Collection tours start at the art information desk at 10:30 AM and 1:30 PM Monday through Friday, and 11:30 AM, 1:30 PM and 3:30 PM Saturday and Sunday. Tours of the American Collection start at 2:30 PM Monday through Saturday in the Rotunda, and tours describing the museum's 19th-century French paintings begin at 12:30 PM Monday through Friday in the Rotunda. You can rent audiotours in the Rotunda, at $4 for adults, and $3.50 for seniors and students.

The National Gallery is open from 10 AM to 5 PM Monday through Saturday, and 11 AM to 6 PM Sunday. Take Metro to the Judiciary Square, Archives or Smithsonian stations.

National Museum of African Art
950 Independence Ave. SW, Washington, D.C. • (202) 357-2700

This is a fascinating highlight on any Smithsonian tour if only for one reason: It's the one national museum dedicated solely to the collection, study and exhibition of the art and culture of Africa. Established in 1987, it's also one of the Smithsonian's newest and most modern-looking museums. Permanent exhibitions feature *Images of Power and Identity*; aesthetic, everyday African objects such as chairs, snuff containers and drinking horns; and treasures from the ancient cities of Benin and Kerma. Among scheduled shows for 1998 are *Olowe of Ise: A Yoruba Sculptor for Kings*, March 15 through September 7; and *African Design and the Furniture of Pierre Legrain*, August 16 through November 29. Visit the museum's gift shop for hard-to-find art objects and books. The museum is open from 10 AM to 5:30 PM daily, except on December 25. It's close to the Smithsonian Metro station. See Kidstuff for information on family activities.

National Museum of American Art and National Portrait Gallery
8th and G Sts. NW, Washington, D.C.
• (202) 357-2700

The National Museum of American Art's permanent collection of more than 37,000 works, including paintings, sculptures, folk art and photographs, offers a rich panorama of the nation's artistic heritage, from colonial times to the 20th century. The Portrait Gallery features likenesses of individuals who have made significant contributions to the development of the nation, including each president. Both museums have restaurants and gift shops, and are open from 10 AM to 5:30 PM daily, except on December 25. If you're walking from the National Mall, you'll arrive in about 15 minutes. If you're taking Metro, exit at the Archive-Navy Memorial or Gallery Place-Chinatown stations. Our Kidstuff chapter describes kid-pleasing features.

National Museum of Women in the Arts
1250 New York Ave. NW, Washington, D.C. • (202) 783-5000

The works of women artists, including O'Keefe, Cassatt and Le Brun — spanning four centuries — are showcased in this first museum in the world dedicated to women artists. Special shows slated for 1998 will feature works with a travel theme, sculptures by Nancy du Pont Reynolds, 16th-century paintings by Lavinia Fontana and other women artists of Bologna, and photographs by Sarah Charlesworth. The museum marked its 10th anniversary in 1997. In what could be the answer to a trivia question, the collection is housed, ironically enough, in a former Masonic temple. The museum boasts frequent education programs, a library and research center (by appointment only), a quarterly magazine called *Women in the Arts*, a café and a gift shop. Metro Center is the closest Metro stop.

Hours are from 10 AM to 5 PM Monday through Saturday, and noon to 5 PM Sunday.

It's closed January 1, Thanksgiving and December 25. Admission by suggested contribution is $3 for adults, and $2 for seniors, students and children. You'll find additional information in Kidstuff.

Phillips Collection
1600 21st St. NW, Washington, D.C.
• (202) 387-0961

In the shadows of Embassy Row, the former home of Duncan Phillips features a diverse collection of masterpieces of French Impressionism, Post-Impressionism and modern art. In 1997, the museum held an enormously popular Impressionism on the Seine exhibition, built around Renoir's *The Luncheon of the Boating Party*, the Phillips' best-known work from its permanent collection.

Be sure to inquire about the museum's wonderful free Sunday concerts, gallery talks and tours. The museum has a small eatery and a gift shop. Admission is $6.50 for the general public, $3.25 for seniors and students, free for ages younger than 18 and is voluntary on the weekends. The Thursday evening admission, $5 from 5 to 8 PM, features a musical performance. The museum is open 10 AM to 5 PM Tuesday, Wednesday, Friday and Saturday; 10 AM to 8:30 PM Thursday; and noon to 5 PM Sunday. The Dupont Circle Metro stop is just a block away.

Renwick Gallery
Pennsylvania Ave. and 17th St. NW, Washington, D.C. • (202) 357-2700

Leave the outside world and step into the late 19th century. The Renwick Gallery, a Smithsonian museum established in 1972, is a showcase of American design, crafts and contemporary arts. The Grand Salon and the Octagon Room boast period furnishings and decorations from the 1860s and '70s. The building itself dates to 1859 and is the original site of the Corcoran Gallery of Art. (See our Civil War chapter for more on the building's historical significance.) The museum, which has a gift shop, is open from 10 AM to 5:30 PM daily, except on December 25. It's near the Farragut West Metro station.

Arthur M. Sackler Gallery
1050 Independence Ave. SW,
Washington, D.C. • (202) 357-2700

Distinctively international, the Sackler Gallery features a permanent collection of masterpieces of Asian and Near Eastern art that spans from the beginning of civilization to the present. Works include jades, bronzes, lacquerware, sculpture, paintings and furniture. Many of the exhibits are on loan from various sources, while nearly 1,000 are gifts from museum namesake Dr. Arthur M. Sackler. This Smithsonian museum, which opened in 1987, connects underground with the neighboring Freer. The museum also houses a comprehensive research library and hosts numerous public programs. Admission is free, and it's open from 10 AM to 5:30 PM daily, except December 25. The museum is close to the Smithsonian Metro station. See the Kidstuff chapter for details on family programs.

The Textile Museum
2320 S St. NW, Washington, D.C.
• (202) 667-0441

This small, elegant museum houses renowned collections of textile art, including rare oriental carpets. Visitors can explore hands-on activities in an interactive gallery. The museum also offers frequent lectures and monthly family programs. Suggested admission is $5 per person. Hours are from 10 AM to 5 PM Monday through Saturday, and from 1 to 5 PM Sunday.

The Gallery Scene

Metro D.C.'s flourishing arts community and gallery scene sometimes get overlooked due to some of the region's more internationally visible art treasures we've described. Here's a sampling of galleries from the area's most prominent art districts.

Washington, D.C.

Galleries of Dupont Circle
(202) 232-3610

Call this information line for details about upcoming programs at the 21 diverse galleries in Washington's Gallery District. The first Friday evening of each month, the galleries stay open late, from 6 to 8 PM, to mark new exhibition openings. Several galleries host free, informal, 15-minute artists' talks on the second Saturday afternoon of each month. All galleries are in walking distance of the Dupont Circle Metrorail stop.

Foundry Gallery
9 Hillyer Ct. NW, Washington, D.C.
• (202) 387-0203

One of the Dupont galleries, this 26-year-old artist's cooperative features abstract and experimental contemporary art. It's open from 11 AM to 5 PM Tuesday through Saturday, and from 1 to 5 PM on Sunday.

Galerie Lareuse
2820 Pennsylvania Ave. NW,
Washington, D.C. • (202) 333-5704

The inspiring works of such 20th-century masters as Chagall, Matisse, Picasso and Renoir highlight the collection of this Georgetown gallery. It's open from 11 AM to 6 PM Tuesday through Saturday, and by appointment on Sundays.

Gallery Affrica
2010 R St. NW, Washington, D.C.
• (202) 745-7272

This 19-year-old Dupont Circle Gallery showcases the beadwork, masks, textile and pottery of Africa.

Touchstone Gallery
406 7th St. NW, Washington, D.C.
• (202) 347-2787

This 30-artist cooperative gallery each month features two single-artist shows of contemporary, modern work. The 22-year-old gallery also occasionally hosts invitational shows featuring international artists. Hours are from 11 AM to 5 PM Wednesday through Friday, and from noon to 6 PM Saturday and Sunday. The gallery is part of the Pennsylvania Quarter District, between the White House and Capitol Hill.

Troyer Fitzpatrick Lassman Gallery
1710 Connecticut Ave. NW, Washington,
D.C. • (202) 328-7189

This 15-year-old Dupont Circle gallery features new works by Washington and national painters, sculptors and photographers. The business also offers art consulting for local law firms and corporations. Hours are from 11 AM to 5 PM Wednesday through Saturday and by appointment.

Veerhoff Galleries
Canal Square, 1054 31st St. NW, Washington, D.C. • (202) 338-6456

Established in 1871, Veerhoff is the oldest commercial gallery in the city, and one of the oldest family-run businesses, now operated by the original owner's great-granddaughter, Margaret Veerhoff. It specializes in realistic oils and pastels and original graphics, and also carries many antique prints. New shows open the third Friday of each month. The gallery is one of nine at picturesque Canal Square in Georgetown. Hours are 11 AM to 6 PM Tuesday through Saturday. Customer parking is available in the retail center's basement.

Very Special Arts Gallery
1300 Connecticut Ave. NW, Washington, D.C. • (202) 628-0800

This "very special" gallery near Dupont Circle displays some wonderful works by artists with disabilities. It's open from 10 AM to 6 PM Monday through Friday, and 11 AM to 5 PM Sunday.

Northern Virginia

Arlington Arts Center
3550 Wilson Blvd., Arlington, Va. • (703) 524-1494

This gallery, in a renovated schoolhouse, showcases ambitious works of regional artists. The building also contains studio space for up to eight artists. Hours are from 11 AM to 5 PM Tuesday through Friday, and from 1 to 5 PM Saturday and Sunday.

First Friday Gallery Walk Downtown
Downtown Leesburg, Va. • (800) 752-6118

The Loudoun Tourism Council and Town of Leesburg sponsor this ongoing event, held from 6 to 8:30 PM the first Friday of each month except January. Visit several galleries in historic downtown Leesburg for show openings, wine and hors d'oeuvres, book signings and live music. Pick up a map at the Tourism Council Office, 108-D South Street SE, Leesburg, Virginia.

The Greater Reston Arts Center Inc. (GRACE)
11911 Freedom Dr., Reston, Va. • (703) 471-9242

In Reston Town Center, the lively downtown hub of one of the nation's first planned communities, this gallery features changing exhibitions of contemporary works. It sponsors an annual summer arts festival and sells unique artistic holiday gifts each December. Hours are from 11 AM to 5 PM Tuesday through Saturday.

McLean Project for the Arts
McLean Community Center, 1234 Ingleside Ave., McLean, Va. • (703) 790-0123

MPA presents themed exhibitions of works by regional and international artists in its Emerson Gallery. The nonprofit organization also sponsors community classes for adults and children, and special events such as lectures and tours. The gallery is open from noon to 4 PM Monday through Saturday.

Torpedo Factory Art Center
105 N. Union St., Alexandria, Va. • (703) 838-4565

If you enjoy watching artists at work, you'll love visiting this nationally known attraction in historic Old Town Alexandria. Once a waterfront munitions factory, the massive building now houses studio and gallery spaces for more than 160 professional artists, including painters, sculptors, glass makers, jewelry makers and potters. The view of the Potomac and bustling harbor provides an added bonus as you observe and chat with artists. Most work is for sale, including bargains like pottery seconds.

The Art League, (703) 683-1780, a local arts organization headquartered here, offers classes for children and adults. The Art League gallery holds juried exhibitions and sells a wide variety of affordable original works by regional artists. The building also houses Alexandria Archaeology, Room 327, (703) 838-4399, where visitors can look at museum exhibits on the city's history and watch archaeologists at work in the laboratory. The organization also offers hands-on courses. The museum is open to the public from 10 AM to 3 PM Tuesday through Thursday, from 10 AM to 5 PM Friday and Saturday and from 1 to 5 PM on Sunday.

Admission to the Torpedo Factory is free. The building is open from 10 AM to 5 PM daily, although individual studio hours vary. The building is closed on New Year's Day, Easter, July Fourth, Thanksgiving and Christmas.

Suburban Maryland

Glass Gallery
4720 Hampden Ln., Bethesda, Md.
• (301) 657-3478

As its name implies, the gallery focuses on blown-glass works and multimedia forms of glass sculpture. It's open from 11 AM to 5 PM Wednesday through Saturday.

Glen Echo Park
7300 MacArthur Blvd., Glen Echo, Md.
• (301) 492-6282

"Unique" describes in a nutshell this National Park Service arts site, which began as a National Chautauqua Assembly in 1891, evolved into an amusement park and now promotes visual and performing arts. You can watch artists work in their studios inside yurts, funky little huts topped with rounded, grass-covered roofs. Other studios fill space in buildings that once served as game arcades, rides and concessions. You'll also find resident artists' and instructors' works exhibited in the Gallery and Bookshop in the Stone Tower, one of the site's original buildings.

Hours are from noon to 5 PM Tuesday through Sunday, and closed Mondays and holidays. The annual Labor Day Art Show, now in its 28th year, fills the park's 65-year-old Spanish Ballroom with a variety of works by local artists. The park also hosts music festivals, such as WAMU-FM's Pickin' in the Glen, a bluegrass event. Pick up a free quarterly catalog for information about special events as well as scheduled art, music and dance workshops and classes for adults and children. To learn more about the park's history, watch the 60-minute "Glen Echo on the Potomac" at 2 PM on Saturday, or take a ranger-conducted tour at 2 PM on Sunday. Plenty of free parking is available. See our Kidstuff chapter for information about the park's antique carousel and children's theaters, and check out Parks and Recreation for details on dances held in the restored ballroom.

At the Cinema

If you're a film buff, you'll want to check out the following events and theaters. Also, contact the city's major art museums, described earlier in this chapter, for information about their film series.

Washington, D.C.

American Film Institute and the AFI Theatre
John F. Kennedy Center, Hall of States
• (202) 785-4600

The prestigious AFI, which also publishes a magazine for members, draws heavily from film buffs and purists who regard cinema as a high art form. Each year, more than 600 movies, from the silent years and early talkies to the Golden Age and avant-garde eras, are screened at the 224-seat theater, which doubles as home to special film revivals, festivals and premier showings.

Cineplex Odeon Avalon
5612 Connecticut Ave. NW, Washington, D.C. • (202) 966-2600

This two-screen refurbished movie theater in upper Northwest is a great spot to catch some of the most important films of the day. The theater is not wheelchair accessible. The Friendship Heights Metro station is about a 15-minute walk.

INSIDERS' TIP

Washington's suburbs are rich with community orchestras and bands, most of which perform concert series in auditoriums at community centers and high schools.

Cineplex Odeon Uptown Theatre
3426 Connecticut Ave. NW, Washington, D.C. • (202) 966-5400

Don't let the boxlike, drab facade fool you. Inside, this theater offers what you'd expect from the heyday of Hollywood: velvet-backed seats, an ornate and towering proscenium, a plush reception area and a huge screen. It's easily the area's best film-watching venue. Tickets are $7.75 for adults, $4.75 for children younger than age 11 and adults age 62 and older. Before 6 PM, admission is $4.75 for all ages. The theater is a quick walk from the Cleveland Park Metro station.

Cineplex Odeon Wisconsin Avenue Cinemas
4000 Wisconsin Ave. NW, Washington, D.C. • (202) 244-0880

This six-screen complex, built in the late '80s, offers cutting-edge sound and screen technology, as well as a palatial interior that reminds you that movie-going can still be a memorable event. Validated garage parking costs $1. The theater is six blocks from the Tenleytown Metro station.

Washington International Film Festival
D.C. Commission on the Arts and Humanities, 415 12th St. NW, Ste. 803, Washington, D.C. • (202) 724-5613

This two-week celebration of American and international film, from the alternative to the mainstream, takes place in late April to early May. The city becomes the focus of the movie world, with scores of screenings, seminars and receptions held throughout town.

Washington Jewish Film Festival: An Exhibition of International Cinema
16th and Q Sts. NW, Washington, D.C. • (202) 518-9400

This week-long, December event in the District of Columbia Jewish Community Center's Cecile Goldman Theater includes feature and short films, as well as documentaries, plus talks with filmmakers and scholars. Tickets cost $5.50.

Northern Virginia

Arlington Cinema 'n' Drafthouse
2903 Columbia Pk., Arlington, Va. • (703) 486-2345

At this popular moviehouse/restaurant, you can sit at a table munching nachos, pizza and Buffalo wings and throwing back a beer or two, while watching second-run films on a big screen. Admission is $3.50 to $3.99, depending on the time of the show. Special features include midnight flicks and big-screen Redskins games.

Suburban Maryland

Bethesda Theatre Cafe
7719 Wisconsin Ave., Bethesda, Md. • (301) 656-3337

Like its Arlington counterpart, this theater/cafe serves food, desserts and drinks at tables while patrons watch a second-run show on a large screen. Admission runs from $1.50 to $4.50. The theater also features big-screen Redskins games, weekend family matinees and nonsmoking screenings on Sundays, Tuesdays, during matinees and at the first show on Friday. Take Metrorail to the Bethesda station; the theater is just two blocks north.

Literary Arts

Suburban Maryland

The Writer's Center
4508 Walsh St., Bethesda, Md. • (301) 654-8664

This 2,200-member nonprofit organization for people in the literary and graphic arts fields

INSIDERS' TIP

See inexpensive screenings of art films and cinema classics at local colleges and universities.

sponsors poetry, fiction and play readings by local and nationally known writers. The center also hosts workshops and events like the annual Mid-Atlantic Small Press Conference and Book Fair, offers a book gallery of literary magazines and works by local authors, gives technical assistance and publishes a newsletter for members. Most events are open to the public; members receive admission discounts. Membership is $30 annually for individuals, $20 for students and $45 for families.

A Word About Tickets

The most convenient way to get tickets to Washington area shows is over the phone via TicketMaster, (202) 432-7328; Telecharge, (800) 233-3123; or ProTix, (703) 218-6500. Unfortunately, with any of these services, expect to fork over a surcharge of a few dollars. You can always buy at the box office, but sometimes finding same-day tickets, especially during the tourist season and for big shows, can be tricky. Your best bet is to reserve seats as far in advance as possible.

If you're like us, though, and place a pre-mium on discount tickets, then head over to Ticketplace, (202) 842-5387, on the ground floor of the Old Post Office Pavilion, 1100 Pennsylvania Avenue NW, Washington, D.C., right across from the Federal Triangle Metro Station. (Take Metro if you want to avoid parking hassles!) Here you can find reduced-rate tickets for day-of-performance shows only; the cost is typically half the regular price plus a service charge of 10 percent of the full ticket price. There are no advance purchases, with the exception of a few Sunday performance tickets available on Saturday, and all transactions are made by cash, travelers checks or debit cards. The outlet is open from 11 AM to 6 PM Tuesday through Saturday, and closed Sunday and Monday, Thanksgiving, Christmas and New Year's Day. You never know exactly what you'll find available, but sometimes that's part of the fun! If you're a student, senior or enlisted military employee, you may not have to venture to Ticketplace for half-price tickets. Inquire at the box office or ticket charge service about availability. Some theaters also offer last-minute "student rush" and "standing room only" tickets.

We'll fill you in on some of the region's most popular attractions, from monuments and museums to famous historic sites.

Attractions

You'll never, ever be lacking for something to do in Metro Washington. Just when you think you've seen it all, a new monument opens or the Smithsonian Institution hosts a special exhibit. In this chapter, we fill you in on some of the region's most popular attractions, from monuments and museums to famous historic sites. At the end, we've included information on some of the leading commercial tour operators as well as the numerous convention and visitors bureaus and tourism offices that serve the Washington area.

Please be aware that you'll also find some important attractions in other chapters. Washington's major art museums, such as the National Gallery, are described in our Arts Chapter. Our Kidstuff chapter details the family-oriented exhibits and programs at many museums listed here. We have also listed cross references where applicable.

Washington, D.C.

Monuments

Franklin Delano Roosevelt Memorial
West Potomac Park, 1850 W. Basin Dr. SW, Washington, D.C. • (202) 426-6841

Dedicated in May of 1997, this tribute to FDR's presidency is notable for being the city's first completely wheelchair-accessible monument. It's also been the subject of mild controversy, with some critics expressing disappointment that the statue of the seated president fails to depict him in his own wheelchair. It does, however, include his little terrier, Fala. Another statue represents First Lady Eleanor Roosevelt.

On 7 acres near the Jefferson Memorial, the monument features four outdoor "galleries" representing each term of FDR's presidency. Gardens, pools and fountains accent the pathway that connects the different sections; in fact, visitors found the water so inviting on hot summer days that park police issued an order banning people from splashing in the fountains! The site is staffed from 8 AM to midnight daily, except on December 25. Admission is free.

Korean War Veterans Memorial
Independence Ave. NW, Washington, D.C. • (202) 426-6841

The Korean War Veterans Memorial is one of the city's newest memorials, dedicated in 1995. This startling tribute to the 1.5 million U.S. men and women who served during the Korean War features a stainless-steel patrol of 19 lifesize statues, designed by World War II veteran Frank Gaylord. Depicting members of the four branches of the armed forces, the scattered sculptures face a black granite wall that's etched with photographic images of actual American service men and women. The site, featuring a circular Pool of Remembrance and grove of trees, is near the Lincoln Memorial Reflecting Pool. Hours are 8 AM to midnight daily except December 25. Admission is free.

Lincoln Memorial
On 23rd St. and Independence Ave. NW, Washington, D.C. • (202) 426-6895

The somber, seated War President looks past the stairs that have served as a site for many public demonstrations and across the vast Reflecting Pool shimmering with the images of the Washington Monument and the Capitol building 2 miles away. An equally captivating vista is the one in the opposite direction, straight across Memorial Bridge and up to Arlington House on the hill overlooking Arlington National Cemetery.

Completed in 1922 and modeled after the Parthenon in Athens, the memorial, designed by architect Henry Bacon, includes walls that are inscribed with the Gettysburg Address and Lincoln's Second Inaugural Address. Daniel Chester French's 19-by-19-foot marble statue has eyes that really do seem to follow you as you walk past, gazing up at the serious face. The free site, staffed by National Park Service rangers from 8 AM to midnight daily except Christmas, includes a bookstore on the lower level.

The National Law Enforcement Officers Memorial
605 E St. NW, Washington, D.C. • (202) 737-3400

The National Law Enforcement Officers Memorial features a tree-lined pathway leading past a granite wall displaying the names of fallen officers. The list, tragically, is expansive, with more than 14,000 names, including the first police officer ever killed in the line of duty, back in 1794. The memorial, open 24 hours daily, is at Judiciary Square, between E and F streets and 4th and 5th streets NW. A visitors' center features exhibits relating to many of the slain officers. It also houses a gift shop. Hours are from 9 AM to 5 PM Monday through Friday, 10 AM to 5 PM Saturday and noon to 5 PM Sunday and holidays, except New Year's Day, Thanksgiving and Christmas. Admission is free.

Theodore Roosevelt Memorial
Roosevelt Island in the Potomac River, Washington, D.C. • (703) 285-2598

This obscure, enchanting monument to America's environmental president is set amid a densely wooded island in the middle of the Potomac River between the Roosevelt and Key bridges, accessible only from the northbound George Washington Memorial Parkway in Virginia. Besides a giant statue of the gregarious 25th president, the island is laced with more than 3 miles of trails — perfect for jogging or a leisurely walk. Its marshy shoreline offers excellent views of the Washington and Northern Virginia skylines. Open from sunrise until dark, Roosevelt Island is accessible only from the Virginia side via a footbridge. A bicycle/pe-

destrian bridge spanning the G.W. Parkway near the north end of the parking lot offers an easy connection to Rosslyn, Key Bridge and, just beyond, Georgetown. Admission is free.

Thomas Jefferson Memorial
Southern end of 15th St. SW, Washington, D.C. • (202) 426-6821

Breathtaking any time, but especially at night, the Jefferson Memorial has an undeniable aura, sensed by locals and tourists alike. Inspired during our first visit to the city, our touring high-school youth group huddled on the memorial's moonlit front steps and harmonized on "Let There Be Peace on Earth."

This awesome memorial, built in the style of Jefferson's Rotunda at the University of Virginia and dedicated in 1943 on Jefferson's 200th birthday, was designed by the same architectural firm that blueprinted the National Gallery of Art. Marble walls inscribed with Thomas Jefferson's writings surround the 19-foot bronze likeness of our third president. Created by Rudolph Evans, the statue crowns a 6-foot pedestal. Looking from the memorial across the Tidal Basin affords an unforgettable illuminated view of downtown Washington. Add blossoming cherry trees and a warm, sunny spring day and you're talking tingles up and down the spine.

The memorial is open 24 hours a day, staffed from 8 AM to midnight daily, except on December 25. You can purchase Jefferson-related books and other items in the bookstore on the lower level and in the gift shop upstairs near the rotunda. Admission is free.

U.S. Navy Memorial and Naval Heritage Center
8th St. and Pennsylvania Ave. NW, Washington, D.C. • (202) 737-2300

This interesting memorial at Market Square, open 24 hours, features the largest map of the world, inlaid in granite on the plaza. Keeping sentry is the "Lone Sailor," a beautiful Stanley Bleifeld sculpture, and nearby are two walls holding 22 bronze sculpture panels, a representation of American naval history and a salute to those who have served or will serve in the Navy. Fountains and pools further accent the plaza. Inside the adjacent Naval Heritage Center, guests can view "At Sea," a riveting account of life on a naval carrier, shown at 11 AM and 1 and 3 PM. Tickets, available at the box office at 701 Pennsylvania Avenue, are $3.75 for adults, $3 for seniors and students 18 and younger and free for active duty and active reserve military personnel. The center, which also features interactive videos, a log room and a gift shop, is open 10 AM to 4 PM Tuesday through Saturday. Admission is free.

Vietnam Veterans Memorial
23rd St. and Constitution Ave. NW, Washington, D.C. • (202) 634-1568

Just a short walk from the Reflecting Pool and the Lincoln Memorial, the Vietnam Veterans Memorial, or simply "The Wall," has become one of the most-visited monuments in the city since its controversial opening in 1982, attracting more than 1.7 million people annually. Built with private funds, the structure — designed by a young architecture student named Maya Ying Lin — is composed of simple black granite panels embedded in the earth and etched (in chronological order) with the names of the more than 58,000 Americans who perished in the war. A few steps away are a pair of amazingly lifelike bronze sculptures depicting servicemen and women in wartime action scenes. The Wall is often the site of some of the most moving personal tributes ever witnessed at a very public place. It's staffed from 8 AM to midnight daily, except on Christmas. Admission is free.

Washington Monument
15th St. NW, Washington, D.C. • (202) 426-6840

This 555-foot signature landmark of the Nation's Capital is hard to miss, even for newcomers. If you visit during the next couple of years, however, be prepared for a temporary new look resembling a Christo art project: The scaffolded structure will be shrouded in clear, blue fabric as workers repair worn spots on the exterior. The monumental renovation began with interior improvements in January of 1998. Until that work is finished, most likely by early summer, the inside is closed to visitors. The monument will be open during the outside renovation, which is expected to continue until 2000.

Certainly one of the most photographed icons anywhere, the simple marble obelisk — the tallest masonry structure in the world — contains nearly 200 memorial stones from all 50 states and numerous countries and organizations. A 70-second elevator ride to the 500-foot level rewards one with an unsurpassed view of Washington and environs. Expect a substantial wait in line anytime you go, but crowds probably will be heaviest when the monument reopens, in mid-May at the earliest. Call ahead so you won't be disappointed.

Admission is free. Hours are from 9 AM to 5 PM September through March, and 8 AM to midnight April through August. The site is closed December 25. See our Civil War chapter for more on the monument's history.

Federal Sites

Bureau of Engraving and Printing
14th and C Sts. SW, Washington, D.C. • (202) 874-2330

Few people ever get closer to so much money than they do at the Bureau of Engraving and Printing, which boasts a newly renovated gallery from which to watch currency being printed. A 35-minute guided tour, one of the most popular in Washington, offers visitors a look at the fascinating process involved in the production of U.S. currency as well as stamps. Tours begin every 10 minutes, from 9

INSIDERS' TIP

Contact your Congressional representative's office to request Congressional passes and tickets for special tours of the White House, Supreme Court, Federal Bureau of Investigations and Bureau of Engraving and Printing. They're in limited supply, and you must ask for them at least three months in advance.

AM to 2 PM Monday through Friday except federal holidays. They also take place from 5 to 6:30 PM from June through August.

Tickets, required during the peak tourism period from March through August, are free but available only on a first-come, first-served basis. The ticket booth on the building's 15th Street side opens at 8 AM for daytime ticket distribution, and at 1:45 for summer extended hours tickets. Tours end in the Visitor Center, open from 8:30 AM to 3:30 PM, where you can purchase fun souvenirs like pens filled with shredded currency.

Congressional Cemetery
1801 E St. SE, Washington, D.C.
• (202) 543-0539

This cemetery on the Anacostia River in Southeast is a final resting place for members of Congress. Today, more than 60 senators and representatives are buried here, as are scores of interesting American personalities, such as John Philip Sousa and J. Edgar Hoover. At Congressional, you can also view the grave of Vice President Elbridge Gerry of Massachusetts, the man who gave us the term "gerrymander," a reference to voting district alterations that give one political party an unfair advantage and often result in oddly shaped jurisdictions. Admission is free.

Department of State
22nd and C Sts. NW, Washington, D.C.
• (202) 647-3241

This massive agency, responsible for creating and carrying out U.S. foreign policy, is partly accessible to the general public: Free tours are offered of the eighth-floor diplomatic reception areas at 9:30 and 10:30 AM and 2:45 PM Monday through Friday, except federal holidays. The tour is not recommended for children unless they're over the age of 12, and strollers are not permitted. Call to make required reservations. Written materials about the many interesting aspects of the department are available by calling the Public Information Division at (202) 647-6575.

Department of the Interior Museum
1849 C St. NW, Washington, D.C.
• (202) 208-4743

This museum features exhibits of surveying equipment, maps, historical documents, natural history and American Indian cultures. It's free, and open from 8 AM to 5 PM Monday through Friday, except on federal holidays.

Department of the Treasury
1500 Pennsylvania Ave. NW,
Washington, D.C. • (202) 622-0896,
(202) 622-0692 TDD

This National Historic Landmark opens for guided public tours on Saturday mornings. Highlights of the 90-minute walk through the lovely building, which dates to 1836, include the elegant suite used by Abraham Lincoln's treasury secretary, Salmon P. Chase; the marble Cash Room used for Ulysses S. Grant's inaugural reception (note the 1,500-pound chandelier); and a Burglar Proof Vault from 1864. The free tours begin at 10, 10:20, 10:40 and 11 AM. You must make a reservation and provide your name and date of birth by noon on Friday, and on arrival, you must present a photo ID. Enter through the Appointment Center on 15th Street between F and G streets NW. Parking may be scarce, so take Metro to Metro Center or McPherson Square.

Federal Bureau of Investigation
10th St. and Pennsylvania Ave. NW,
Washington, D.C. • (202) 324-3447

A tour of the J. Edgar Hoover Building is as intriguing as the man himself. The free, one-hour excursion through America's top law-enforcement agency offers an inside look at crime-fighting techniques and crime laboratories, a peek at photos of the FBI's Ten Most Wanted Fugitives, and a thrilling live firearms demonstration, viewed safely from behind glass. Like so many of the city's other popular tours, early arrival is recommended. Tours are offered from 8:45 AM to 4:15 PM Monday through Friday.

Library of Congress
Independence Ave. at 1st St. SE,
Washington, D.C. • (202) 707-5458

Another one of Thomas Jefferson's legacies to Washington, his personal collection was the seed stock for what would become the largest library in the world, totaling some 84 million items in 470 languages. The volumes are rivaled only by the magnificence of the Italian Renaissance structure that houses

The Janet Annenberg Hooker Hall of Geology, Gems and Minerals

Dazzling: That's the word that immediately comes to mind when you visit the Janet Annenberg Hooker Hall of Geology, Gems and Minerals at the Smithsonian Institution's National Museum of Natural History. After a two-year, $13-million renovation, the 20,000-square-foot hall opened in September of 1997 with new, well-

lit displays of old favorites like the Hope Diamond as well as recent acquisitions. Many specimens underwent cleaning and repair.

Hooker, for whom the hall is named, died in 1997, just a few weeks after the new exhibit opened. She contributed $5 million to the privately funded project and also donated Cartier-designed yellow starburst diamonds and, several years ago, the Hooker Emerald, a jaw-dropping 75.47-carat stone surrounded by 20 baguette diamonds in a platinum setting.

The exhibit begins in the Harry Winston Gallery, named for the jeweler who in 1958 donated what would become the Smithsonian Institution's most popular attraction: the Hope Diamond. The flawless blue gem takes center-stage here, rotating inside a

— continued on next page

The Hope Diamond is from the National Gem Collection.

Photo: Courtesy of Dane Penland, Smithsonian Institution, National Museum of Natural History, Washington, D.C.

circular display vault while surrounding onlookers marvel at the illuminated 45.52-stone's clarity. Written displays tell all about the Hope Diamond's intriguing history. Also in this room, you'll find such large natural treasures as a 1,300-pound slab of quartz, a sheet of nearly pure copper and a natural sandstone formation that looks like abstract art.

If you enjoy window-shopping at elegant jewelry shops, you'll love the National Gem Collection. An amazing array of treasures glistens from illuminated display cases. The one-of-a-kind, Art Deco-style Clagett Bracelet features an exotic hunt scene, painstakingly created of 626 diamonds, 73 emeralds, 48 sapphires and 20 rubies. Nearby, you may be temporarily blinded by flashes of light emanating from the 22,892.5-carat American Golden Topaz. Among the collection's royal jewels, Marie Antoinette's pear-shaped diamond earrings create tiny rainbow-hued points of light throughout the case. Empress Marie-Louise's crown, a wedding gift from husband Napoleon I, contains — count 'em — more than 1,000 diamonds. An empress can never have too many diamonds, though: Celebrating the birth of the couple's first son, Napoleon presented his wife with a necklace bearing 172 of the glittering stones, weighing more than 263 carats!

The gem collection — which also includes numerous rubies, sapphires, emeralds and aquamarines in various sizes and cuts — by itself would impress most visitors. It's followed by the equally awesome Minerals and Gems Gallery. Here, you'll see cases filled with more colors, shapes and sizes of natural formations than you'd dream possible. (It's a great place to take kids for a visual scavenger hunt!) The Mineral Rainbow display showcases such samples as florescent blue azurite, purple quartz, avocado pyromophile, coral crocoite, lemon yellow sulphur and red rhodochrosite.

Elsewhere in the room, look for wulfenite that resembles a pile of peanut brittle, and precariously piled iron pyrite cubes that look like a carefully cut and stacked sculpture.

After mingling with the minerals, check out the mine gallery, where you can walk through a simulated mine and see what stones look like underground. The new hall also includes a gallery devoted to plate tectonics, the scientific concept that explains such phenomena as earthquakes and volcanos. Here, you can create your own earthquakes and touch a 3.96-billion-year-old rock, the world's oldest. You'll end your tour in the Moon, Meteorites and Solar System Gallery, where you can look at moon rocks and stardust.

The hall also includes computer programs, films and interactive exhibits. A Rocks Gallery, scheduled to open in 1998, contains hands-on displays. Like most Smithsonian exhibitions, the gems and minerals hall is free. You can, however, enhance your visit with an audio tour, available for $4.25 rent at the iGo Interactive AudioTour Desk in the museum's Rotunda.

them. The library's Thomas Jefferson Building reopened in May of 1997, sporting a new Visitors Center and 90-seat theater where you can watch a new film about the library.

Among the other highlights are a large gift shop, a performing arts gallery and special rooms that display some of the library's important collections. Take a free guided tour at 11:30 AM, 1 PM, 2:30 PM and 4 PM, Monday through Saturday. Call TTY (202) 707-6362 in advance to arrange for sign-language inter-

pretation, available at 2:30 PM Monday and 11:30 AM Friday. Visitors should enter the Carriage entrance at 1st Street and go to the information desk, where tours start.

National Aquarium
Commerce Department Bldg., 14th St. between Constitution and Pennsylvania Aves. NW, Washington, D.C.
- **(202) 482-2825**

Not to be confused with the centerpiece of

Baltimore's Inner Harbor that shares the same name, this is the nation's oldest aquarium (originally established in 1873) yet is one of the city's lesser-known attractions, due in part, perhaps, to its basement location. Some 70 tanks house more than 1,000 aquatic creatures including alligators, sea turtles and denizens of the Touch Tank, a favorite with children that offers a thrilling hands-on experience with underwater life. Be sure to check on times for the popular shark and piranha feedings. See our Kidstuff chapter for a complete description.

National Archives
Constitution Ave. between 7th and 9th Sts. NW, Washington, D.C.
• (202) 501-5000

The three most important documents in America — the Declaration of Independence, the Constitution and the Bill of Rights — all make their home in a special display case in the rotunda of this well-guarded building. To keep the precious parchment out of harm's way, the case is lowered 20 feet each evening into a special bombproof, fireproof vault. In the rotunda, you'll also see the 1297 Magna Carta, and an exhibit of American Originals, important historical documents. For a totally different experience, trace your family history in the cavernous Research Room, or simply take advantage of one of the free lectures, films or other exhibits.

For a free schedule of public events, write to the National Archives Public Affairs Office, Room G6, Washington, D.C. 20408. The building is open 10 AM to 5:30 PM daily after Labor Day through March 31, from 10 AM to 9 PM April 1 through Labor Day. It's closed December 25. Free 90-minute tours, by reservation only, (202) 501-5205, take place at 10:15 AM and 1:15 PM Monday through Friday. The nearest Metro stop is Archives/Navy Memorial.

Organization of American States
17th St. and Constitution Ave. NW, Washington, D.C. • (202) 458-3000

The incredible art and culture of Latin America unfolds at this impressive compound, which is across from the Ellipse. The building has a monumental entrance hall and huge Palladian windows. While in the vicinity, be sure to walk across Virginia Avenue and take a look at the striking statue of Símon Bolívar, the liberator of much of South America. The building is open to the public from 9 AM to 5 PM Monday through Friday, except on federal holidays. Admission is free.

Pavilion at the Old Post Office
Pennsylvania Ave. at 12th St. NW, Washington, D.C. • (202) 289-4224

This landmark soaring above America's Main Street was built in 1899 as the nation's postal headquarters. Set to be demolished in 1934, it was saved by concerned citizens and has since been masterfully renovated into one of the city's premier shopping, dining and entertainment attractions and site of an annual New Year's Eve gala. Ride the glass elevator up to the tower's 12th-floor observation deck for a dramatic view. The Pavilion is open from 10 AM to 7 PM Monday through Saturday, noon to 6 PM Sunday. Admission is free.

Supreme Court of the United States
1st St. and Maryland Ave. NE, Washington, D.C. • (202) 479-3211

The weightiest legal decisions in the land are handed down behind the imposing columned facade of this renowned building. While their work is of paramount importance, the nine justices don't deliberate for a full calendar year, going into session only between October and June. Orders and opinions are typically handed down on Mondays, an exciting time to visit. When the nation's highest court is not in session, free lectures are given on weekdays every hour on the half hour from 9:30 AM to 3:30 PM. When court is in session, line up early on the Front Plaza for limited seating. The building, open from 9 AM to 4:30 PM weekdays except holidays, also has exhibits, a film, a gift shop and food. Union Station and Capitol South are the nearest Metro stations.

United States Capitol
East End of the Mall on Capitol Hill, Washington, D.C. • (202) 225-6827

Perhaps the strongest competitor to the Washington Monument in terms of worldwide recognition, the Capitol looms majestically over the city as its tallest building, something that will never change, thanks to the farsighted vision of early planners of the federal district. Tours of the great halls and the magnificent Central Rotunda of this regal edifice are a highlight of any visit to the Hill. Guided tours take place from 9 AM to 3:45 PM Monday through Saturday; wait in line on the east front staircase. Following your tour, you can visit the House and Senate chambers. The building is open daily, from 9 AM to 4:30 PM, and you're welcome to meander through on your own. For a peek at Congress in action, obtain a pass through the office of your representative or senator. You don't need a pass to visit the House and Senate galleries when Congress isn't in session.

U.S. Department of Agriculture
12th St. and Jefferson Dr. SW, Washington, D.C. • (202) 720-5505

Trace America's agrarian roots at the Department of Agriculture Visitors Information Center, located in the Administration Building. Exhibits and displays change regularly. This monolithic agency is housed in one of the largest structures in Washington, just a short walk from the National Mall. In Room 103A, the center is open from 9 AM to 4:30 PM Monday through Friday, except holidays. Admission is free.

U.S. Information Agency
330 Independence Ave. SW, Washington, D.C. • (202) 619-3919

The American propaganda machine comes alive on the *Voice of America* tour at the U.S.I.A. The free tour is offered at 10:30 AM and 1:30 and 2:30 PM, Monday through Friday, except on holidays. It tells the story of how the VOA's shortwave radio systems and television programs, magazines and books are used to gain support abroad for American policies. Call in advance for a reservation.

The Washington Post
1150 15th St. NW, Washington, D.C. • (202) 334-7969

Well, *The Post* isn't a federal institution, but it's an important bureaucracy nonetheless. To get the inside scoop on how the news is gathered, disseminated, printed and distributed, take a tour of this bastion of American journalism. Free guided tours, offered every hour except noon, from 10 AM to 3 PM on Mondays (except for federal holidays), are open to adults and children at the fifth-grade level and above. Make reservations in advance.

The White House
1600 Pennsylvania Ave. NW, Washington, D.C. • (202) 456-7041

Known as the "President's Palace" in its early days, this masterpiece of Federal architecture each year hosts scores of dignitaries, entertainers and other luminaries, not to mention more than 1 million curious tourists. Burned by the British during the War of 1812, the White House has been home to every president and his family except George Washington. Despite the rash of security-threatening incidents at or near the White House in recent years, no other residence of a head of state remains as accessible as this place, where seven of the 132 rooms are part of a self-conducted free public tour offered Tuesday through Saturday, from 10 AM to noon.

You'll need to pick up a timed ticket, available beginning at 7:30 AM on the day of your tour, at the White House Visitor Center, southeast corner of 15th and E streets, (800) 717-1450. To obtain a free VIP pass that's good for a guided tour, offered from 8:15 to 9 AM Tuesday through Saturday, contact the office of your representative or senator. The Visitor Center, open from 7:30 AM to 4 PM daily, features a video presentation and exhibits about the White House. There's also a sales area. See our Annual Events chapter for details about the Easter Egg Roll and Spring Garden tours.

INSIDERS' TIP

Become a Smithsonian Resident Associate to enjoy benefits like a subscription to *Smithsonian* magazine, discounts on museum shop purchases and free events just for members. Annual membership is $45 for individuals. Call (202) 357-3030.

Directly south of the White House grounds is an expanse of parkland known as the Ellipse, the site of the annual Pageant of Peace holiday celebration (see our Annual Events chapter). One of the Ellipse's little-known features is the Settlers' Memorial, a granite marker located near 15th Street. Here you will find inscribed the names of the 18 landowners whose corn and tobacco farms ultimately became the land that is today's Washington, D.C.

Museums and Galleries

The Smithsonian Institution — On the National Mall

Arthur M. Sackler Gallery
1050 Independence Ave. SW,
Washington, D.C. • (202) 357-2700
The Sackler features a permanent collection of Asian and Near Eastern masterpieces. See our Arts chapter for a complete description. Our Kidstuff chapter describes family programs.

Arts and Industries Building
900 Jefferson Dr. SW, Washington, D.C.
• (202) 357-2700
You'll feel as though you've stepped back in time when you enter this building, next to the Castle. This unique collection of Victorian Americana is a re-creation of the 1876 Philadelphia Centennial Exposition. Attractions include working steam engines and other machines and a 51-foot model of the war sloop Antietam. The gift shop carries items related to the old-fashioned theme. The museum is open from 10 AM to 5:30 daily, except December 25. Admission is free. See Kidstuff for information about the museum's Discovery Theater.

The Castle
1000 Jefferson Dr. SW, Washington, D.C.
• (202) 357-2700
Take one look at its imposing reddish-brown, Norman-Gothic exterior and you'll know how this building got its name. The Castle has been a fixture on the Mall since 1855 and now almost seems out of place in the company of some of the more modern architecture. But what a story it has to tell. This is the original building of the Smithsonian Institution that now encompasses 14 museums and the National Zoo, in Washington, D.C., making it the largest museum complex in the world and an unparalleled national treasure. An ideal place for newcomers to begin exploring the Smithsonian collection, the Castle houses the high-tech Visitors Information Center as well as the crypt of James Smithson, the Englishman whose donations led to the birth of the institution that bears his name. It's free, and open daily except Christmas, from 10 AM to 5:30 PM.

Freer Gallery of Art
Jefferson Dr. at 12th St. SW,
Washington, D.C. • (202) 357-2700
This impressive gallery features an important collection of Asian and 19th- and early 20th-century American art. See our Arts chapter for a thorough description, and Kidstuff for information about children's activities.

Hirshhorn Museum and Sculpture Garden
7th St. and Independence Ave. SW,
Washington, D.C. • (202) 357-2700
Visit this gallery to view works by many of the great 19th- and 20-century artists. See our Arts chapter for a complete description, and Kidstuff for details about family programs.

National Air and Space Museum
6th St. and Jefferson Dr. SW,
Washington, D.C. • (202) 357-2700
Humankind's insatiable fascination with flight is dramatically underscored by the National Air and Space Museum's status as the most-visited museum in the world. Its more than two dozen galleries — including the magnificent glass-walled lobby where dozens of aircraft hang in suspended animation — showcase the evolution of aviation and space technology.

The collection features history-making planes flown by the Wright brothers and Charles Lindbergh, the Apollo 11 command module, a space station, and the wiry "flying fuel tank" that was flown on a record-breaking nonstop flight around the world. Since the museum no longer has room to accept

Every president except George Washington has lived in the
Palladian-influenced White House.

large items for display, an annex has been approved for a site on the grounds of Washington Dulles International Airport, where several large aircraft wait in storage.

If you visit before October 31, 1998, don't miss the super popular *Star Wars: The Magic of Myth* exhibition, featuring more than 250 original props, costumes, creatures and other items from the Star Wars trilogy. The show requires free, timed passes, available at area ticket outlets or at the museum on the day of your visit.

The museum features two restaurants, the full-service Wright Place restaurant and the cafeteria-style Flight Line. Free highlights tours take place at 10:15 and 1 PM. Special tours can be arranged by calling the Educational Services Tour Office at (202) 357-1400. Check the museum's daily events schedule for times of the awesome IMAX and planetarium shows, which require tickets. The museum is open from 10 AM to 5:30 PM daily, except on December 25. Admission is free.

National Museum of African Art
950 Independence Ave. SW, Washington, D.C. • (202) 357-2700

This unique museum dedicated to African culture and art features permanent exhibits and rotating shows. See our Arts and Kidstuff chapters for more information.

National Museum of American History
14th St. and Constitution Ave. NW, Washington, D.C. • (202) 357-2700

Visitors of all ages love the exhibits of American culture, politics and technology, brought to life at this ever-popular National Museum of American History. From White House dishes to an original Model T, from Archie Bunker's armchair to Mr. Rogers' sweater and the M*A*S*H gang's stage props, the exhibits are as varied and interesting as history itself. The interactive Information Age exhibit is among the most popular, as is the extensively renovated display of the First Ladies' gowns. The museum features intriguing

INSIDERS' TIP

Legend has it that Washington planner Pierre L'Enfant hated Chief Justice John Jay with such a passion, he intentionally left out the letter J in his layout of alphabetically designated streets.

temporary exhibits, such as a 1997 show revolving around The Family Car. Take a break in the old-fashioned ice-cream parlor downstairs, and be sure to visit the large museum shop, filled with fascinating books, recordings, toys and unique gift items. (Our Kidstuff chapter describes features geared toward children.) The museum is open from 10 AM to 5:30 daily, except December 25. Admission is free.

National Museum of Natural History
10th St. and Constitution Ave. NW, Washington, D.C. • (202) 357-2700

You'll know you've arrived at the National Museum of Natural History when you look up and see the colossal stuffed elephant in the rotunda — and it only gets more intriguing from there. This treasure house contains more than 81 million items documenting humankind and the natural environment.

Prepare to be dazzled as you enter the new Janet Annenberg Hooker Hall of Geology, Gems and Minerals: It's filled with some of the most impressive jewelry most people will ever lay eyes on, as well as an enormous collection of natural gems and minerals (see the "Close-up" in this chapter.)

Among the museum's other highlights: dinosaur skeletons (an even bigger hit with youngsters thanks to Barney-mania and the gargantuan success of Steven Spielberg's dino flicks), displays of early man, a live coral reef and a lifesize, hanging whale model.

The museum's immensely popular insect zoo underwent a dramatic metamorphosis that culminated in a grand reopening in late 1994 as the O. Orkin Insect Zoo. It's named after — that's right — the founder of Orkin Pest Control (Otto Orkin to be precise), perhaps the most familiar of all monikers in the bug-bagging business. It's not a simple case of product recognition that inspired the Smithsonian to attach the Orkin name to one of its museums, however; the Atlanta-based company contributed a half-million dollars (and a bevy of unwitting exhibit residents?) to modernize the place. It was money well spent; in fact, once here, you may have a hard time getting the kids to leave.

Besides the fascinating historical aspects that mom and dad will appreciate — such as

the evolution of insects millions of years ago — and the amazing collection of winged and crawling critters, the zoo includes a 14-foot model of an African termite mound that children can crawl through, a live beehive (behind glass, thankfully), a Southwest desert diorama and a rain forest exhibit complete with live giant cockroaches and leaf-cutter ants. (See our Kidstuff chapter for more kid-pleasing attractions here.)

Recorded audio tours, narrated by Meryl Streep, are available for a small fee. Guided highlights tours are offered daily at 10:30 AM and 1:30 PM, and Friday at 10:30 AM. Be sure to visit the beautiful new gift shops on the lower level. The museum's Naturalist Center, a hands-on study facility, is temporarily at 741 Miller Drive, Leesburg, Virginia, (703) 779-9712. The museum is open from 10 AM to 5:30 daily, except December 25. Admission is free.

The Smithsonian Institution — Off the National Mall

Anacostia Museum and Center for African American History and Culture
1901 Fort Pl. SE, Washington, D.C.
• (202) 357-2700, (202) 357-1729 TDD

At the small Anacostia Museum, you'll find two intriguing changing cultural and historical exhibits focusing on regional and national topics. For example, *Man Made: African-American Men and Quilting Traditions*, on display through June 30, 1998, showcases approximately 40 pieces created by African American men. After a recent renovation, the museum now is handicapped accessible and boasts a new archival space. You'll find a gift shop, but no restaurant here. (Bring food to eat in the picnic area.) Call in advance to arrange a free museum tour or guided walk on the quarter-mile George Washington Carver Trail. The museum also hosts free public programs. Hours are daily from 10 AM to 5 PM. Admission is free. Some free parking is available, and the nearest Metro station is Anacostia.

The affiliated Center for African American History and Culture is in the Arts and Industries Building at 900 Jefferson St. SW on the National Mall (see the Arts and Industries entry in this chapter). It also features changing exhibits related to African-American culture.

National Museum of American Art and National Portrait Gallery
8th and G Sts. NW, Washington, D.C.
• (202) 357-2700

The National Museum of American Art's permanent collection features paintings, sculptures and photographs from colonial to modern times. See our Arts chapter for a complete description, and Kidstuff for children's activities.

National Postal Museum
2 Massachusetts Ave. NW, Washington, D.C. • (202) 357-2700

The newest museum in the vast Smithsonian collection, the National Postal Museum opened in July 1993 with great fanfare. Especially excited were philatelists, who queued up for several hours just to get one of the special first-day-of-issue commemorative stamps. The museum documents the founding and development of the modern postal system and features interactive displays and the largest stamp collection in the world, including all U.S.-issue stamps since 1847. The museum is open from 10 AM to 5:30 daily, except December 25. Admission is free. See Kidstuff for more on the museum's many child-friendly exhibits.

National Zoological Park
3000 block of Connecticut Ave. NW, Washington, D.C. • (202) 357-2700

Nearly 5,000 animals — including the rare giant panda — call the National Zoo home. Of special interest are the ape house, the big cats and the reptile collection, but be sure to leave time for a stroll through a re-created rain forest in the popular Amazonia exhibit, one of the newest additions to the zoo. Some of the wild animals on display aren't the only scarce items around here; ditto for parking spaces. Do yourself a huge favor and take Metrorail to the Woodley Park/Zoo station (on the Red Line). From there it's a pleasant 10-minute walk up the street. Visit early in the morning to avoid crowds: The grounds are open from 8 AM to 6 PM daily mid-October through mid-April, and 8 AM to 8 PM the rest of the year. Most animal

buildings are open from 9 AM to 4:30 PM year-round. Call to schedule guided tours. Friends of the National Zoo (FONZ) offers numerous special programs in the visitors center, during and after zoo hours. Visit the gift shop for a variety of animal-related souvenirs. Admission is free. See Kidstuff for additional information.

Renwick Gallery
Pennsylvania Ave. and 17th St. NW, Washington, D.C. • (202) 357-2700

This off-the-Mall gallery showcases American design, crafts and contemporary arts. See our Arts chapter for a complete description.

Other Museums and Galleries

B'nai B'rith Klutznick National Jewish Museum
1640 Rhode Island Ave. NW, Washington, D.C. • (202) 857-6583

The permanent collection of this 51-year-old museum features items spanning 4,000 years of Jewish culture and history. Highlights include correspondence between George Washington and the sexton of a Rhode Island synagogue, a Torah cover marking the Finzi-Contini wedding, ancient bowls, 17th-century candlesticks, unique menorahs and ritual objects. The museum also showcases several changing exhibitions annually. A recently refurbished gift shop sells a variety of Judaic merchandise. Museum hours are from 10 AM to 5 PM Sunday through Friday. The museum is closed on federal and major Jewish holidays. Admission is free. The nearest Metro stop is Farragut North.

Capital Children's Museum
800 3rd St. NE, Washington, D.C. • (202) 543-8600

Not as well-known as it should be, the Capital Children's Museum is nirvana for the kids and a nice change of pace for mom and dad. This is a place that should be a big hit with virtually any young one. Learning is made fun with hands-on exhibits, interactive displays and a special emphasis on world cultures. See our Kidstuff chapter for a full description.

DAR Museum
1776 D St. NW, Washington, D.C.
• **(202) 879-3241**

This museum of the Daughters of the American Revolution features state-named period rooms, decorated with lovely furnishings, china settings and other accent pieces. Tell your docent if there's a certain room you wish to visit during your tour. The museum is open from 8:30 AM to 4 PM Monday through Friday and 1 to 5 PM Sunday, with guided tours of the period rooms given from 10 AM to 2:30 PM weekdays and 1 to 4:30 PM Sundays. Admission is free.

Ford's Theatre
511 10th St. NW, Washington, D.C.
• **(202) 426-6924, (202) 347-4833**
box office

Forever memorialized as the place where President Lincoln was shot by John Wilkes Booth, Ford's still is very much a working year-round professional theater. See our Arts and Civil War chapters for complete details about the theater and its museum.

Frederick Douglass National Historic Site
1411 W St. SE, Washington, D.C.
• **(202) 426-5960**

Cedar Hill, the beautifully restored Victorian home of former slave Frederick Douglass, is the centerpiece of this slice of tranquility near the banks of the Anacostia River. A Visitors Center features a 30-minute film and numerous exhibits on the life of the famed abolitionist, editor, orator and advisor to Lincoln. Take a half-hour tour and stop by the bookstore with volumes on black history. Hours are 9 AM to 4 PM daily except New Year's Day, Thanksgiving and Christmas. The site stays open until 5 PM mid-April through mid-October. Admission is $3 for the general public, $1.50 for seniors and free for children younger than age 6. Also see our Civil War chapter.

National Building Museum
401 F St. NW, Washington, D.C.
• **(202) 272-2448**

Created by an act of Congress in 1980, this is the only national museum of its kind, offering a variety of exhibits and programs about building aspects from architecture to urban planning. Housed in the beautiful 1887 structure originally occupied by the Pension Bureau, the museum is known for its spectacular 316-by-116-foot Great Hall, a frequent site of presidential inaugural balls. Its 75-foot-high Corinthian columns are among the world's tallest indoor pillars. The museum's permanent exhibitions include *Washington: Symbol and City*, a must-see for anyone interested in the stories behind the capital's monuments and famous buildings. Changing exhibitions focus on such topics as engineering and home improvement.

The museum boasts an interesting gift shop and a Courtyard Cafe featuring light meals and snacks from 10 AM to 3 PM Monday through Saturday. Free, guided tours, which start next to the fountain in the Great Hall, take place at 12:30 PM weekdays; 12:30, 1:30 and 2:30 PM Saturdays; and 12:30 and 1:30 PM Sundays. Other free programs include films, concerts, lectures and family activities (See our Kidstuff chapter). Museum admission also is free. Hours are 10 AM to 4 PM Monday through Saturday, and noon to 4 PM Sunday.

The museum stays open until 5 PM June through August, and is closed on Thanksgiving, December 25 and January 1. Taking Metro couldn't be more convenient: Walk out of the Judiciary Square station and you're right there!

National Gallery of Art
4th St. and Constitution Ave. NW, Washington, D.C. • **(202) 737-4215**

Housing one of the world's greatest art collections, the National Gallery is another of Washington's amazing free attractions. For a complete description, see our Arts and Kidstuff chapters.

National Geographic Society
17th and M Sts. NW, Washington, D.C.
• **(202) 857-7588**

At the headquarters of this venerable institution, you'll find Explorers Hall, a geography and map lover's paradise. Exhibits, ranging from earth science and cultural geography to environmental and social issues, change regularly and never fail to fascinate. Like so many wonderful attractions in Washington, admission is free. It's open from 9 AM to 5 PM Monday through Saturday and holidays except Christmas, 10 AM to 5 PM Sundays. See the Kidstuff chapter for more information.

National Museum of Women in the Arts
1250 New York Ave. NW, Washington, D.C. • (202) 783-5000

This is the world's first museum devoted entirely to works by women artists. You'll find a thorough description in our Arts chapter.

The Navy Museum
Building 76, Washington Navy Yard, 9th and M Sts. SE, Washington, D.C. • (202) 433-2651

Housed in the former Naval Gun Factory, this museum offers a fascinating look at United States Naval history from the American Revolution to the present day. Among the more than 5,000 artifacts on display are gunmounts, full-size equipment models, decorations and awards, uniforms and artwork. Explore exhibits about such topics as polar exploration (including Admiral Richard E. Byrd's Antarctic hut), World War II, space travel and undersea study.

A favorite rainy-day destination for families, the museum features hands-on activities, plenty of space for active kids and a gift shop with fun souvenirs (see our Kidstuff and Shopping chapters). Don't miss the Washington Navy Yard's neighboring attractions, including the decommissioned destroyer Barry (DD-933), the first marine railway and a gate designed by Benjamin Latrobe. Museum hours are 9 AM to 4 PM (5 PM Memorial Day through Labor Day) Monday through Friday, 10 AM to 5 PM weekends and holidays except Thanksgiving, December 24 and 25 and January 1. Call in advance to schedule a tour. Admission is free. Parking is free and generally plentiful. Eastern Market is the closest Metro station.

The Octagon
1799 New York Ave. NW, Washington, D.C. • (202) 638-3221

History and architecture buffs alike will find plenty of interesting features at this National Historic Landmark, the country's oldest architecture museum. Designed by William Thornton, first architect of the U.S. Capitol, the building served as James and Dolley Madison's temporary home after the British burned the President's House during the War of 1812. In fact, Madison signed the war-ending Treaty of Ghent at the Octagon. A five-year, $5 million restoration which ended in 1996 included repainting rooms in true period hues.

A gift shop is set to open late spring or early summer of 1998 in the adjacent ice house, and the enclosed garden will feature a vending cart and seating for outdoor dining. Visitors can view furnished period rooms, as well as architecture- and design-related exhibitions which rotate twice a year. The American Architectural Foundation operates the museum, which is open from 10 AM to 4 PM Tuesday through Sunday. Tours are available upon request. Admission is $3 for adults, and $1.50 for students and seniors. Please note that the building isn't elevator-equipped, and therefore is not completely wheelchair accessible. You should be able to find on-street parking. Taking Metro to Farragut North or Farragut West will require you to walk a few blocks.

Phillips Collection
1600 21st St. NW, Washington, D.C. • (202) 387-0961

Renoir's beloved *The Luncheon of the Boating Party* highlights the permanent collection at this intimate art museum. Read more about it in our Arts chapter.

Sewall-Belmont House
144 Constitution Ave. NE, Washington, D.C. • (202) 546-1210

Almost lost amid the grandeur of Capitol Hill, this 18th-century building now houses the headquarters of the National Woman's Party and contains mementos of the equality movement, including writings and heirlooms belonging to Susan B. Anthony and Alice Paul, the woman who penned the Equal Rights Amendment. The mansion was once the abode of Albert Gallatin, the treasury secretary who masterminded the finances of the $15 million Louisiana Purchase in 1803.

The building also houses the country's first feminist library. Docent-led tours, which include a half-hour film about the suffragist movement, take place at 11 AM, noon and 1 PM on weekdays, and at noon and 1, 2 and 3 PM Saturday. The tours last approximately an hour and are recommended for ages 8 and older. Visit the gift shop for history books, women's crafts and unique souvenirs like replica jail door pins. Museum hours are 10 AM to 3 PM Tuesday through Friday, noon to 4 PM Saturday. Admission is free, but donations are accepted.

The Textile Museum
2320 S St. NW, Washington, D.C.
• (202) 667-0441

You'll be amazed at the intricate handwork exhibited in this museum's collection of Oriental carpets and other important textiles. See our Arts chapter for a description.

United States Holocaust Memorial Museum
100 Raoul Wallenberg Pl. SW
Washington, D.C. • (202) 488-0400

As compelling as it is disturbing, the U.S. Holocaust Memorial Museum — another recent addition to the city's cultural roster — documents the horrors of the Holocaust through photographs, film, interactive exhibits and incredible artifacts. Built with private funds and opened in the spring of 1993, the museum occupies a two-acre parcel right next to the Bureau of Engraving and Printing, just off the National Mall. The five-story building, between 14th and 15th streets, is itself a fascinating architectural statement and tribute to the victims. Due to the graphic nature of some displays, the tour is not recommended for children younger than 11. The museum also houses resource and research facilities and a theater and auditorium for special programs. Grab a light meal in the dairy café. The Museum Shop features books and other Holocaust-related items.

Visitors must obtain tickets to tour the museum's permanent exhibition; they're free, albeit not always easy to come by. Pick them up at the 14th Street entrance, beginning at 10 AM, the day of your visit or obtain them in advance through PROTIX, (800) 400-9373. The museum is open from 10 AM to 5:30 PM daily.

Washington Dolls' House & Toy Museum
5236 44th St. NW, Washington, D.C.
• (202) 244-0024

This little gem is as popular with adults as it is with children. As you view the exhibits, a tiny world unfolds, tracing the development of homes and home life from around the globe — all from a miniature perspective. Enjoy the amazing collection of antique dollhouses, dolls, toys and games. Top it off with a trip through the museum's toy shop. If the visit is part of a birthday celebration, the little ones can feast in a special ice-cream parlor. Best bet is to book early for parties. The museum is open from 10 AM to 5 PM Tuesday through Saturday, and from noon to 5 PM on Sunday. It's closed on Mondays, New Year's Day, Thanksgiving and Christmas. Admission is $3 for adults, and $1 for children. See our Kidstuff chapter for more on youngsters' favorites here.

Neighborhoods

Embassy Row
Along Massachusetts Ave. NW,
Washington, D.C.

Nearly 50 of the city's approximately 150 embassies are clustered along this two-mile stretch of prime real estate, hence the designation Embassy Row. From the grand and ornate to the simple but elegant, the homes make for a wonderful walking tour, especially in the spring and fall. Look (very closely in some cases) for the flag and coat of arms that designate each diplomatic mission. From an architectural perspective, some of the more noteworthy embassies include those of Brazil, Japan, Britain, Austria, Pakistan and Turkey. See our International Washington chapter for more information.

Georgetown
M St. and Wisconsin Ave. NW,
Washington, D.C. • (202) 789-7000

A thriving tobacco port and completely independent Maryland community when Washington was established as the Nation's Capital in the late 1700s, Georgetown is the city's oldest and best-known neighborhood and one that's synonymous with wealth, power and prestige. Locals and out-of-towners alike come here to stroll the narrow, cobblestone streets, view the elegant homes and sample the incredible array of nightclubs, bars, art galleries, restaurants, funky shops and elegant boutiques. Keep an eye out for that precipitous set of steps made famous in a memorable but gruesome scene from *The Exorcist*, the classic devil flick starring Linda Blair.

The nerve center of Georgetown is at M Street and Wisconsin Avenue NW, through the years the spillover site of some spirited post-Super Bowl, New Year's Eve and Halloween celebrations. Besides those steps we mentioned, prime attractions in this part of town include venerable and beautiful Georgetown University (whose graduates include President Clinton), described in our Education chapter; and C&O Canal National Historic Park, described in our Parks and Recreation chapter. Amid the noisy drama of M Street lies the Old Stone House, 3051 M Street NW, (202) 426-6851, built in 1766 and believed to be the oldest building in the District.

Step into the backyard and you'll enter another world. A quiet garden, maintained by the National Park Service, overflows with seasonal plants, exotic butterflies and birds. It's a great place for a brown-bag lunch. When you're finished, take a tour of the historic house which many parapsychologists claim is one of the most haunted buildings in Washington. It's open 9:30 AM to 5 PM daily except January 1 and December 25. Admission is free. You'll also find Dumbarton Oaks, at 1703 32nd Street NW, (202) 339-6400, the aristocratic former home of Mr. and Mrs. Robert Woods Bliss. Now owned by Harvard University, the 16-acre property features a museum with pre-Columbian and Byzantine collections, open 2 to 5 PM Tuesday through Sunday, with free admission; and beautifully landscaped gardens, accessible from an R Street entrance, open 2 to 6 PM April through October and 2 to 5 PM November through March, with $5 admission for adults, and $3 for children and seniors. Call the docents' office at (202) 339-6409 for information about tours.

You'll have to wait a couple of years if you're interested in seeing the priceless collection of Fabergé eggs at Hillwood Museum and Gardens, 4155 Linnean Avenue NW, (202) 686-8500. This former home of cereal heiress Marjorie Merriweather Post is closed for extensive renovation until spring of 2000. Call for information about Hillwood's music, lecture and travel programs, continuing at other locations.

Religious Sites

See our Worship chapter for more information about these and other historic places of worship.

The Basilica of the National Shrine of the Immaculate Conception
4th St. and Michigan Ave. NE, Washington, D.C. • (202) 526-8300

With a lofty bell tower, ornately carved entryway and vibrantly decorated dome, the country's largest Roman Catholic church takes your breath away even before you go inside. Enter you must, however, to see the many treasures of this Byzantine-Romanesque house of worship. Guided tours take visitors throughout the building to see stained-glass art, mosaics and sculptures, most of which honor Mary, the Mother of Jesus. Highlights include more than 50 chapels, each designed to express a unique vision of Mary; the world's largest mosaic portrait of Jesus, the Byzantine Christ in Majesty; and pillars of different types of marble, symbolizing the universality of the church.

The building is open from 7 AM to 6 PM daily November through March, and from 7 AM to 7 PM daily, April through October. Free, guided tours, which last 30 minutes to an hour, take place from 9 to 11 AM and from 1 to 3 PM Monday through Saturday, and 1:30 to 4 PM Sunday. Call in advance to arrange group tours. You can also pick up a brochure for a self-guided tour. The church frequently holds carillon and organ recitals and other concerts, as well as regular services. Visit the gift shop for a variety of Catholic-oriented merchandise. A cafeteria offers breakfast and lunch. Free, on-site parking is available. The nearest Metro stop is Brookland-CUA.

This red brick "Castle" on the National Mall was the first of the great Smithsonian museums. Built in 1846, it now houses administrative offices and an information center.

Franciscan Monastery
14th and Quincy Sts. NE, Washington, D.C. • (202) 526-6800

Guided tours, lasting about 45 minutes, include a look at full-scale replicas of Holy Land shrines such as the Roman Catacombs. This is a beautiful, peaceful enclave that many Washingtonians know nothing about. Free tours take place on the hour except at noon from 9 AM to 4 PM Monday through Saturday, and from 1 to 4 PM Sundays.

Washington National Cathedral
Massachusetts and Wisconsin Aves. NW, Washington, D.C. • (202) 537-6200

This magnificent Gothic stone church took 83 years to build, and it's filled with unique and stunning art. The cathedral offers a wide assortment of tours on a regular basis. Your best bet is to take a general highlights tour to receive a 30- to 45-minute overview of the building's features, like its more than 200 stained-glass windows, including a Space Window, an abstract tribute to the Apollo 11 mission that contains a moon rock.

Regular tours, beginning at the West Entrance doors, take place from 10 AM to 3:15 PM Monday through Saturday, and from 12:45 to 2:45 PM on Sundays. No tours are given on Palm Sunday, Easter, Thanksgiving and Christmas. The suggested donation for most tours is $2 for adults, and $1 for children. The cathedral offers specialized tours and programs like "Tour and Tea." Call for times and costs. See our Kidstuff and Annual Events chapters for more information about cathedral programs and special events.

Northern Virginia

Museums and Other Attractions

Alexandria Black History Resource Center
638 N. Alfred St., Alexandria, Va. • (703) 838-4356

For an introduction to the city's rich African-American heritage, stop by this center, where exhibits help convey the significance of historical figures and events, while a library next door offers a wealth of information. It's open from 10 AM to 4 PM Tuesday through Saturday. Admission is free.

Arlington National Cemetery
Memorial Dr., Arlington • (703) 692-0931

With its sea of white headstones spread across 612 wooded, hilly acres overlooking the capital city, Arlington National Cemetery is perhaps the most famous burial site in the world, and one of Washington's most popular tourist attractions. This is the final resting place for more than 250,000 American military personnel who served in conflicts from the Revolutionary War to the present. Among the many famous graves are those of President John F. Kennedy and his brother Robert; President William Howard Taft; 12 astronauts, including Mercury's Virgil "Gus" Grissom and those aboard the Space Shuttle Challenger; and prizefighter Joe Louis.

It's also the site of the new Women in Military Service Memorial, the country's first national memorial honoring all women who have served their country in the armed services. Dedicated in October of 1997, the memorial at the cemetery's main gateway includes a hall of honor, a 196-seat theater, exhibit space and computerized details and photos about registered servicewomen.

Also on the cemetery grounds is the Tomb of the Unknowns, where crowds gather to view the somber Changing of the Guard every hour on the hour from October 1 through March 31 and every half-hour during the daytime hours, and hourly at night from April 1 through September 30. (The tomb has made recent headlines with a controversy over whether the "unknown" bones of a Vietnam soldier buried there actually belong to Air Force First Lieutenant Michael J. Blassie. At press time, Pentagon officials were trying to decide whether the remains could be exhumed so that Blassie's family would know for certain the fate of the soldier, whose plane was shot down in 1972.)

Majestic Arlington House, Robert E. Lee's former home, sits high on a hill facing the Lincoln Memorial. Arlington House is also where Pierre Charles L'Enfant, the French architect who drafted the original plans for Washington, is buried. See our Civil War chapter for information about Civil War-related sights.

Continuous 30-minute Tourmobile tours

run daily (except on Christmas) from 8:30 AM to 6:30 PM April through September, and from 8:30 AM to 4:30 PM October through March. Tours depart from the Arlington Cemetery Visitors Center, where you'll also find exhibits and a gift shop. Admission to the cemetery is free. Tourmobile tickets cost $4, and $2 for children ages 3 to 11.

Carlyle House
121 N. Fairfax St., Alexandria, Va.
• (703) 549-2997

One of the first houses built in Alexandria, this nearly 250-year-old replica of a Scottish manor home was the residence of John Carlyle and his wife Sara Fairfax. Among other uses, the house served in 1755 as the headquarters of General Braddock, leader of the British forces during the French and Indian War. We recommend you take a guided tour of the home and its terraced garden. Hours are from 10 AM to 4:30 PM Tuesday through Saturday, and noon to 4:30 PM on Sunday. Tours begin every half-hour. Admission is $4 for adults, $2 for ages 11 to 17 and free for ages 10 and younger.

Colvin Run Mill Historic Site
10017 Colvin Run Rd., Great Falls, Va.
• (703) 759-2771

Visit this working, water-powered 19th-century gristmill on the weekend and you'll often find special events like Civil War encampments, ice-cream making, woodcarving lessons and outdoor concerts. Stop by the general store for old-fashioned candy, handmade crafts and fun gift items, as well as a display of old tins, bottles and utensils. The site is open daily from 11 AM to 5 PM, except Tuesdays. Mill tours, offered on the hour from 11 AM to 4 PM, cost $4 for adults, $3 for students ages 16 and up and $2 for children and seniors. See our Kidstuff chapter for information about programs for youngsters.

Gadsby's Tavern Museum
134 N. Royal St., Alexandria, Va.
• (703) 838-4242

The social nerve center of Colonial Alexandria, Gadsby's is noted as "the finest tavern built in the colonies." Gadsby's was the site of numerous balls, meetings and political functions. Among the luminaries who unwound here were the Marquis de Lafayette, John Paul Jones, Aaron Burr, George Mason, Francis Scott Key, Henry Clay and, of course, George Washington. The tavern — now functioning as a museum — has been restored to its Colonial condition and is open for tours. The 200-year-old George Washington Birthnight Banquet and Ball is still held here every year and is one of the most prestigious social events in Virginia.

Other special events include dance classes, costumed reenactments, teas for girls and their dolls and Colonial-themed summer camps. The museum is open from 11 AM to 4 PM Tuesday through Saturday and from 1 to 4 PM Sunday October 1 through March 1; from 10 AM to 5 PM Tuesday through Saturday and from 1 to 5 PM Sunday April 1 through September 30. It's closed on Mondays and major holidays, and occasionally during private rentals. Admission is $4 for adults, $2 for students ages 11 to 17 and free for children ages 10 and younger accompanied by a paying adult. Stop by the adjacent Gadsby's Tavern Restaurant, 138 N. Royal Street, (703) 548-1288, for a Colonial bite to eat, served by costumed waiters.

George Washington Masonic National Memorial
101 Callahan Dr., Alexandria, Va.
• (703) 683-2007

Beltway travelers passing Alexandria can't miss this tall granite tower, standing majestically atop a hill just outside of Old Town. Modeled after the ancient lighthouse in Alexandria, Egypt, the familiar landmark was erected by Freemasons throughout the nation to honor their fraternal brother, who served as Worshipful Master of the Alexandria-Washington Lodge No. 22 in 1788 and 1789. (Ironically, the very hill upon which the monument sits could have held the U.S. Capitol, but Washington vetoed the site!)

Visitors see several of Washington's personal and family possessions, as well as portraits and Masonic relics. Among the artifacts displayed in the Replica Lodge Room are the clock that Washington's doctor stopped the moment Washington died and the little silver trowel which Washington used to lay the cornerstone of the U.S. Capitol. A Mason-led tower tour is the only way for visitors to view the nine-story memorial's upper levels, which house more Washington-related displays, Masonic organizations' exhibits, a Masonic library and a top-floor observation deck. Children especially enjoy the detailed mechanical model of an Imperial Shrine Parade, complete with tinier renditions of those unique tiny Shriners' cars.

The memorial is open from 9 AM to 5 PM daily except New Year's Day, Thanksgiving and Christmas. Visitors can take guided 45-minute tours of the tower and observation deck on the half-hour during the morning and on the hour during the afternoon. Note that the building is only partially handicapped-accessible, and eating, drinking and smoking are prohibited inside. Parking is free and plentiful, and the King Street Metro station is a short walk. Admission is free, but you're welcome to make a donation.

Gunston Hall Plantation
10709 Gunston Rd., Lorton, Va.
• (703) 550-9220

This southeastern Fairfax County landmark was built in 1755 by George Mason, a framer of the Constitution and the father of the Bill of Rights whose namesake university is also in Fairfax. With its 18th-century furnishings, formal gardens and exhibits, Gunston Hall serves as a landmark connection with the region's colonial past. The home is more than just a museum or monument, though. It's also a favorite spot for small meetings, parties and receptions. Request a schedule of annual events, featuring such seasonal favorites as a kites celebration in March and Christmas programs in December. The plantation is open 9:30 AM to 5 PM daily, except New Year's Day, Thanksgiving and Christmas. Home tours begin every half-hour. Admission is $5, $4 for seniors older than age 60 and $1.50 for children ages 6 to 18.

Iwo Jima Statue
U.S. Hwy. 50 at Arlington National Cemetery, Arlington, Va.
• (202) 433-4173

Officially known as the U.S. Marine Corps War Memorial, this is the largest bronze statue in the world and depicts the raising of the American flag on Mount Suribachi during World War II. Presented to the nation by members and friends of the Marine Corps, the statue was created by Felix de Weldon based on the famous photograph by Joe Rosenthal. Nearby, the Netherlands Carillon was a thank-you gift from the Dutch people for America's aid during World War II. In season, a gorgeous field of tulips lies at the base of the bell tower. At night, the statue is illuminated, and it's an awesome sight, indeed.

The Lyceum
201 S. Washington St., Alexandria, Va.
• (703) 838-4994

Alexandria's History Museum showcases a permanent collection of city-related artifacts, including locally produced furniture and housewares. Changing exhibits focus on various cultural and historical topics. The museum also hosts special events in its lecture hall. Visit the gift shop for local souvenirs. The Lyceum is open from 10 AM to 5 PM Monday through Saturday, from 1 to 5 PM Sunday. It's closed on Thanksgiving, December 25 and January 1. Admission is free.

Mount Vernon
Southern end of the G.W. Memorial
Pkwy., Alexandria, Va. • (703) 780-2000

One look at the view from the green expanse of lawn and it's easy to see why George Washington chose this site for his gracious riverside plantation that has become America's most-visited historic house. Washington's final resting place, Mount Vernon offers a wealth of information about the life of the man as well as the turbulent colonial period. Present-day archaeological digs on the site continue to tell us more. Mount Vernon is easily one of the most popular tourist attractions — especially among foreign guests — in all of Metro Washington.

After touring the mansion, sit a spell on the long, white-columned porch, where you can take in the most glorious view of the Potomac. Garden enthusiasts will enjoy walking through the estate's many authentic gardens and looking at original trees from Washington's day. The wonderful new *George Washington: Pioneer Farmer* exhibit features a round, 16-sided barn, farm animals and fields of crops, between the mansion and the Potomac Wharf. Open year-round, the site offers hands-on activities March through November. Mount Vernon features special events throughout the year, including a wreath-laying ceremony for Washington's birthday and candlelight tours during December.

Mount Vernon is open from 8 AM to 5 PM April through August; 9 AM to 5 PM during March, September and October; and 9 AM to 4 PM November through February. Admission is $8 for adults, $7.50 for seniors ages 62 and older, with identification, and $4 for children ages 6 through 11. Annual passes and group discounts are available. Visit Mount Vernon's gift shop for colonial-themed merchandise. Visitors can dine at the colonial Mount Vernon Inn or a snack bar at the visitors center.

The Newseum
1101 Wilson Blvd., Arlington, Va.
• (703) 284-3544, (888) NEWSEUM

It's only fitting that a city always in the headlines should house the world's only museum devoted to the news. This sleek, $42 million facility, funded by the Freedom Forum, features changing exhibits, as well as hands-on activities for all ages. You can view historic front pages and newscasts, learn how editors make decisions and meet working journalists. Visit the Newseum store for newsworthy souvenirs. At the News Café, you can surf the Net while you nosh on snacks. Like so many entertaining and educational Metro Washington museums, this one offers free admission. It's open from 10 AM to 5 PM Wednesday through Sunday except New Year's Day, Thanksgiving and Christmas. See our Kidstuff chapter for more about the hands-on exhibits.

Oatlands Plantation
On Va. Rt. 15 near Leesburg, Va.
• (703) 777-3174

About 6 miles south of Leesburg, in Loudoun County, this classic revival home built in 1803 is one of the state's foremost historic plantations. The grounds and architecture are accented by 4 acres of formal terraced English gardens. Oatlands is the site of various events and gatherings throughout the year, including annual plays and a needlework exhibition. It's open from late March through December from 10 AM to 4:30 PM Monday through Saturday, and from 1 to 4:30 PM Sundays.

The Pentagon
Arlington, Va. • (703) 695-1776

With 17½ miles of corridors housing more than 23,000 Defense Department employees, the Pentagon remains the largest single-structure office building in the world. A 90-minute public tour of this Arlington facility helps scale down the monolith to a more human dimension. Guided tours include the history of the Pentagon's construction that began in the early 1940s, an exhibit of military art and a walk through the Hall of Heroes, where the names of those who have received the Congressional Medal of Honor are listed. The free tours leave every half-hour from 9:30 AM to 3:30 PM Monday through Friday, except on holidays.

Potomac Mills
2700 Potomac Mills Cir.,
Prince William, Va.• (703) 643-1770,
(800) VA-MILLS

Forget the Civil War sites, historic homes, national parks, even Colonial Williamsburg. Incredibly, Potomac Mills, 15 miles south of the Capital Beltway (follow signs from I-95 near Woodbridge) is Virginia's No. 1 tourist attraction. For shopaholics and bargain seekers in general, the allure is obvious: hundreds of stores, including numerous upscale retailers, offering superb prices on clothing, household goods, appliances and all manner of other merchandise. It ranks as one of the world's largest outlet malls. When hunger pangs strike, you can choose from more than 20 international eateries. See our Shopping chapter for more on this mall.

Ramsay House Visitors Center
221 King St., Alexandria, Va.
• (703) 838-4200

Visit this historic house to peek into the life of William Ramsay, the town overseer, census-taker, postmaster and member of the committee of safety. Ramsay was a close friend of George Washington and it is said that the president spent the last night before his inaugura-

tion at Ramsay House. You'll also find numerous free pamphlets about local tourist sites, restaurants and lodgings.

Stabler-Leadbeater Apothecary Shop
105 S. Fairfax St., Alexandria, Va.
• (703) 836-3713

From 1792 to 1933, this early pharmacy dispensed medicine to Alexandrians, including loyal customers James Monroe, Robert E. Lee and George Washington's family. When it closed, it was the second-oldest apothecary shop in the United States and the oldest in Virginia. Today, the shop is a museum exhibiting an array of Colonial medical implements and patent medicines. It also contains the most comprehensive collection of apothecary jars in the nation.

It's open from 10 AM to 4 PM Monday through Saturday, and 1 to 5 PM Sunday. January through March, the museum is closed on Wednesdays. Admission is $2.50 for adults, $2 for ages 11 to 17 and free for ages 10 and younger.

Woodlawn Plantation and Frank Lloyd Wright's Pope-Leighey House
9000 Richmond Hwy., Alexandria, Va.
• (703) 780-4000

Another of southern Fairfax County's architectural icons, Woodlawn Plantation was the Georgian estate home of Nellie Custis Lewis, granddaughter of George and Martha Washington. The richly appointed mansion, a virtual neighbor of Mount Vernon, was designed by William Thornton, architect of the U.S. Capitol. Our favorite time to visit is during March, when hundreds of handstitched entries in the annual needlework exhibition decorate the rooms. Browse in the gift shop downstairs, and, only during March from 11:30 AM to 2 PM, enjoy lunch in the Woodlawn Pub.

The spacious grounds also feature the Pope-Leighey House, designed by Frank Lloyd Wright in 1939. Hours are 10 AM to 4 PM daily during March, 10 AM to 4 PM Monday through Saturday and noon to 4 PM Sunday April through December. Admission to one house is $6 for adults and $4 for students in kindergarten through 12th grade and seniors ages 65 and older. Admission to both houses is $10 for adults, and $7 for students and seniors.

Suburban Maryland

Museums and Other Attractions

Beall-Dawson House and the Stonestreet Medical Museum
103 W. Montgomery Ave., Rockville, Md.
• (301) 762-1492

This authentically restored brick house, dating to 1815 and furnished in the Federal style, is the headquarters of the Montgomery County Historical Society. The adjacent museum offers fascinating insight into early surgical practices and medical treatments. Hours are from noon to 4 PM Tuesday through Saturday, and the first Sunday of the month. Admission is $3 for the general public, and $2 for seniors and students older than age 13.

Chesapeake Bay Bridge
Md. Rt. 50, Anne Arundel/Queen Anne's counties, Md. • (410) 288-8405

Officially the William Preston Lane, Jr. Memorial Bridge, the Bay Bridge, as it's affectionately known, connects Metro Washington with the rural charms of Maryland's Eastern Shore and the Atlantic Coast resorts of the Delmarva Peninsula. The approximately 4-mile twin spans offer a spectacular view of the world's largest estuary. Motorists pay a $2.50 toll before heading eastbound.

Garber Preservation, Restoration and Storage Facility
3904 Old Silver Hill Rd., Suitland, Md.
• (202) 357-1400

Surprisingly, few fans of the National Air and Space Museum — the most-visited museum in the world — know about this hidden gem in Prince George's County. That's unfortunate, because this facility, essentially the aeronautical restoration shop for the Smithsonian Institution, houses more aircraft than Air and Space. Inside the multibuilding installation, visitors can get up close and personal with actual restoration projects, a British Hawker Hurricane 11C employed in World War II's Battle of Britain and a Nieuport 28, a French-built airplane flown by American pilots during World War I. You can also see several astronautical artifacts, such as the nose cone from a Jupiter launch vehicle that carried monkeys into space. To take a guided tour, you must make a reservation, recommended at least three weeks in advance.

Tours take place at 10 AM on weekdays and at 10 AM and 1 PM Saturday and Sunday. Take heed of these caveats: Tours last three hours and are not recommended for children younger than age 14. The site has no restrooms or water fountains, and many buildings lack heating and air conditioning.

Maryland State House
State Cir., Annapolis, Md.
• (410) 974-3400

The beautiful Maryland State House is yet another reason to visit the historic sailing mecca of Annapolis. The focal point of Maryland's government, this is the nation's oldest state house in continuous legislative use. It even served as capitol of the United States for several months in 1783-84 and is the place where George Washington resigned his commission as commander of the Continental Army and where the Treaty of Paris was ratified, ending the Revolutionary War. Be sure not to miss the great exhibits depicting Annapolis during Colonial times. The visitor center is open from 9 AM to 5 PM Monday through Friday, and from 10 AM to 4 PM on Saturday and Sunday. Free 25-minute tours take place at 11 AM and 3 PM daily.

NASA Goddard Space Flight Center Visitors Center
Soil Conservation Rd., Greenbelt, Md.
• (301) 286-8981

If space flight sends you into orbit, visit this museum to learn about the history of American rocketry, from its humble beginnings on Robert Goddard's Massachusetts farm in 1926 to the current research involving the

Hubble Space Telescope. The center is open from 9 AM to 4 PM daily. Call for tour information. Parking and admission are free. See our Kidstuff chapter for information about hands-on activities and model rocketry programs.

National Capital Trolley Museum
1313 Bonifant Rd., Wheaton, Md.
• **(301) 384-6352**

This underappreciated regional attraction features demonstrations and displays of antique electric streetcars from the U.S. and Europe. There's also an interesting audiovisual show. See Kidstuff for information about the trolley rides here. The museum is open from noon to 5 PM Saturday and Sunday Jan. 2 through Nov. 30; from 11 AM to 3 PM Wednesdays during July and August; and additional hours in December during the annual Holly Trolleyfest. It's closed December 24, 25 and 3, and January 1. Admission is free, but trolley rides cost $2.50 for adults, and $2 for children ages 2 through 17.

National Institutes of Health
Bldg. 10, 9000 Rockville Pk., Bethesda, Md. • **(301) 496-1776**

NIH is where doctors, scientists and technicians wage war against some of society's most devastating illnesses and disorders including cancer, AIDS, heart disease, diabetes, arthritis and Alzheimer's disease. This sprawling federal research complex — a branch of the U.S. Department of Health and Human Services — is perhaps the nation's preeminent medical resource.

NIH's National Library of Medicine, (301) 496-6308, is the largest medical library in the world and features a reading room and a department specializing in historic and rare books. The NIH Visitor Information Center offers a slide show, films and a "working" lab. Free tours of the grounds are available for walk-in visitors at 11 AM on Monday, Wednesday and Friday; special-interest tours can also be arranged. The Visitor Information Center is open from 8:30 PM to 4 PM.

National Wildlife Visitor Center
Patuxent Research Refuge, Md. Rt. 197, Laurel, Md. • **(301) 497-5772**

There's a wildlife research facility amid the din of Metro Washington? Indeed. This agency of the U.S. Department of the Interior conducts vital investigations involving a variety of endangered species. It's open from 10 AM to 5:30 PM daily, except December 25. Admission is free. Guided tram tours through the woods are $2, $1 for seniors older than age 55 and children younger than age 12. See Kidstuff for more information.

U.S. Naval Academy
Bordered by King George St. and the Severn River, Annapolis, Md.
• **(410) 263-6933**

It's hard not to get a lump in your throat and feel exceedingly patriotic when you set foot on the gorgeous grounds of this National Historic Site where naval officers have been trained since 1845. The academy chapel dominates the scene; below the building lies the crypt of John Paul Jones. Other campus highlights include a museum featuring models, swords and paintings; Bancroft Hall, where the Brigade Noon Formation takes place; numerous monuments dedicated to naval heroes and battles; and Navy-Marine Corps Memorial Stadium. Tours of the academy are available at 10 and 11 AM and 1 and 2:30 PM Monday through Saturday, and 12:30, 1:30 and 2:30 PM on Sunday. Admission is $5.50 for adults, $4.50 for seniors ages 62 and older, $3.50 for 1st through 12th-graders and free for preschoolers. Tours start inside Gate 1.

Tour Operators

It takes a while to find your way around any new place, so until you get your bearings straight, what better way to get an overview of all the top attractions than to take a professionally guided tour? It's not just something visitors do, ya know.

The following companies provide regular, scheduled sightseeing excursions for the general public:

All About Town
519 6th St. NW, Washington, D.C.
• **(202) 393-3696**

Air-conditioned motor coaches transport visitors to monuments, museums and government and historic sites. Choose from a variety of packages, including Washington by twilight.

Bike the Sights
3417 Quesada St. NW, Washington, D.C.
• (202) 966-8662

For a more leisurely way to see Washington, you might consider a bicycle tour of the C&O Canal, Mount Vernon and other sights in and near the city.

Capitol River Cruises
Washington Harbour, 3050 K St. NW at 31st St., Washington, D.C.
• (301) 460-7447, (800) 405-5511

The 91-person Nightingale II, a riverboat originally built for Mackinac Island, takes passengers on 50-minute, narrated cruises along the Potomac River from Georgetown to Ronald Reagan Washington National Airport and back.

D.C. Ducks
2640 Reed St. NE, Washington, D.C.
• (202) 832-9800

Ride in the area's only amphibious touring vehicles — part bus, part boat, they must be seen to be believed.

Doorways to Old Virginia
P.O. Box 20485, Alexandria, VA 22320
• (703) 548-0100

Guides attired in Colonial costumes, created by company owner Stella Michals, lead Footsteps of George Washington walking tours of historic Alexandria daily from late March through early November. A candlelit Ghosts and Graveyard walking tour, recommended for ages 7 and older and offered on weekends, chronicles documented eerie happenings. Group tours are available by appointment. Tours last approximately one hour.

Gray Line Inc.
Gray Line Terminal, Union Station, 50 Massachusetts Ave. NE, Washington, D.C. • (202) 289-1995

Guided Walking Tours of Washington
9009 Paddock Ln., Potomac, Md.
• (301) 294-9514

Local historian Anthony Pitch leads two-hour walking tours of the Adams-Morgan district and Georgetown on Sundays from mid-March through mid-December and by appointment. The guide specializes in "anecdotal history," focusing on homes of famous Washingtonians past and present.

Liberty Helicopter Tours & Charters
1724 S. Capitol St. SE, Washington, D.C.
• (800) 927-9279, (202) 484-8484

These pilot-narrated tours provide great views from a different perspective.

Odyssey Cruises
Gangplank Marina, 600 Water St. SW, Washington, D.C. • (202) 486-6000

This long, sleek ship is low enough to pass under the 14th Street Bridge, so you get to travel the Potomac River from Georgetown to Old Town Alexandria. Savor an elegant meal and dance to live music as you view the passing sights from the glass-atrium dining rooms, or enjoy the fresh air as you take a walk around the quarter-mile deck.

Old Town Experience
P.O. Box 19898, Alexandria, VA 22320
• (703) 836-0694

Carolyn Cooper, a 25-year local resident, leads walking tours of Alexandria's historic district.

Old Town Trolley Tours of Washington
2640 Reed St. SE, Washington, D.C.
• (202) 832-9800

A lively, old-fashioned trolley with gold lettering will be a big hit with the kids.

Potomac Party Cruises, Inc.
Zero Prince St., Alexandria, Va.
• (703) 683-6076

The Dandy offers popular lunch, brunch and dinner and dancing cruises along the Potomac, from Old Town Alexandria to Georgetown and back. The riverboat is climate-controlled for year-round tours.

Potomac Riverboat Company
Alexandria City Marina, King and Union Sts., Old Town Alexandria, Va.
• (703) 548-9000

The Matthew Hayes riverboat offers 90-

minute narrated excursions on the Potomac between Alexandria and Georgetown. A 50-minute cruise takes passengers to Mount Vernon, where they can explore George Washington's home before reboarding for the return trip. To learn more about historic Alexandria, take the 40-minute narrated Admiral Tilp cruise along the waterfront area.

Scandal Tours of Washington
1602 South Springwood Dr., Silver Spring, Md. • (888) 436-3886, (301) 587-4291

Take a humorous look at landmarks involved in Washington scandals, such as Gary Hart's townhouse and the Watergate.

Shore Shot
Washington Harbour, 31st and K Sts., Washington, D.C. • (202) 554-6500

Breeze past the Washington sights while cruising the Potomac aboard a 53-foot speedboat. The 45-minute, narrated tours travel between Georgetown to Boiling Air Force Base.

Spirit Cruises
Pier 4, 6th and Water Sts. SW, Washington, D.C. • (202) 554-8000

This ship seats 600 people and travels to Alexandria.

Tour D.C.
1912 Glen Ross Rd., Silver Spring, Md. • (301) 588-8999

Two-hour walking tours of lower Georgetown feature interesting historical highlights. See our Civil War chapter for more information.

Tourmobile Sightseeing
1000 Ohio Dr. SW, Washington, D.C. • (202) 554-5100

Free all-day reboarding is offered by this service, which is the only one authorized by the U.S. National Park Service to board and discharge people on the National Mall and in Arlington National Cemetery.

Convention and Tourist Bureaus/ Tourist Information

Contact the following agencies to receive free, comprehensive packets of travel and tourism information.

Washington, D.C.
Washington, D.C. Convention and Visitors Association, 1212 New York Avenue NE, Washington, DC 20005, (202) 789-7000.

Northern Virginia
Virginia Division of Tourism, 901 E. Byrd Street, 19th Floor, Richmond, Virginia 23219, (804) 786-2051; Local office: 1629 K Street NW, Washington, D.C. 20006, (202) 659-5523

Alexandria Convention and Visitors Bureau, 221 King Street, Alexandria, Virginia, 22314, (703) 838-4200

Arlington Convention & Visitors Service, 735 S. 18th Street, Arlington, Virginia 22202, (703) 358-5720

Suburban Maryland
Maryland Office of Tourist Development, 217 E. Redwood Street, Baltimore, Maryland 21202, (410) 767-3400

Annapolis & Anne Arundel County Conference and Visitors Bureau, 26 West Street, Annapolis, Maryland 21401, (410) 280-0445

Montgomery County Conference & Visitors Bureau, 12900 Middlebrook Road, Suite 1400, Germantown, Maryland 20874, (301) 428-9702

Prince George's County Conference & Visitors Bureau, 9200 Basil Court, Suite 101, Largo, Maryland 20774, (301) 925-8300

The war forever
changed the complexion
of this once sleepy
Southern town.

Civil War Sites

Undeniably the most tragic event in our country's history, the Civil War claimed more than 620,000 American lives and shattered the lives of millions of soldiers and families.

For four harsh years, the Washington area stood at the epicenter of this tragedy. Even before April 12, 1861, when Confederates fired the first shots on Fort Sumter, South Carolina, the tense capital city found itself in a most precarious location — 60 miles south of the Mason-Dixon Line and just 100 miles north of Richmond, the Confederate capital. Across the Potomac River in Virginia, the Stars and Bars flew defiantly from homes and shops within eyesight of Union soldiers. Surrounding Washington on the eastern side of the river lay Maryland, the powerful border state whose loyalties shifted from town to town, and often from house to house.

Even residents of the capital city grappled with the loyalty issue. Not surprisingly, many fled to join the Confederate cause, while thousands of other Southern sympathizers remained at home, many taking part in clandestine operations under the nose of the Federal military complex.

The war forever changed the complexion of this once sleepy Southern town. Temporary shelters, office buildings, camps, hospitals and supply depots cropped up throughout the city. Each day, hundreds of new residents flocked to the District. Housing was scarce, crime soared, slums grew up in the shadows of the Capitol and the White House, and public services were virtually nonexistent. Tiber Creek, a marshy tributary now covered by Constitution Avenue, was an open sewer. The unsanitary conditions led to a typhoid epidemic that killed thousands of residents, including the young son of President Abraham Lincoln.

Ironically, for much of the war, Washington was a slave-holding city. Only six months before the Emancipation Proclamation became law did the District ban slavery.

If conditions were tough in Washington, then they were simply tortuous in the surrounding countryside of Virginia and Maryland. At the Battle of First Manassas in July 1861, 35,000 Union soldiers under the command of Gen. Irvin McDowell met a Rebel force of 32,000 troops. It was supposed to be an easy Northern victory: so easy that hundreds of Washingtonians rode out to the site 30 miles west of the city to witness the festivities. First Manassas turned out to be anything but a Northern cakewalk. The Confederate army, bolstered by the brave showing of Gen. Thomas Jackson (who earned the nickname "Stonewall" here) crushed the Union advance. By day's end, nearly 900 young men lay dead on the fields of Matthews Hill, Henry Hill and Chinn Ridge. Ten hours of fierce fighting ended any notion that the war would be settled quickly.

First Manassas sent a shockwave through Washington, which erected forts and gun batteries at a frantic pace, encircling the anxious city that many grew to believe could be overrun by Gen. Robert E. Lee (a native to the area) and his adept Southern army.

Indeed, the South did come close to striking the Union nerve center. At Fort Stevens, in the present-day Rock Creek Park, Confederate Gen. Jubal Early led his troops into the District's northern fringes on a balmy July evening in 1864. President Lincoln was among the many spectators who witnessed the attack that the Union eventually repelled.

The Civil War ultimately devastated neighboring Virginia. In Fredericksburg and surrounding Spotsylvania County, just 50 miles south of Washington, four major battles (Fredericksburg, Chancellorsville, The Wilderness and Spotsylvania Court House) raged between 1862 and 1864. Over a patch of land no larger than 500 square miles, some 100,000 Union and Confederate soldiers died — nearly twice the casualties of the Vietnam War. Tens of thousands more casualties would be claimed in the hundreds of skirmishes and battles, including the bloody Battle of Second Manassas (3,300 killed), that took place within a 60-mile radius of Washington; in fact, more American lives were lost on Virginia's Civil War battlefields than in all other American wars combined.

The single most violent day of the war took place near the rural Maryland hamlet of Sharpsburg, less than 70 miles northwest of the District. Here, on Sept. 17, 1862, at the Battle of Antietam, more than 12,000 Federal troops and 10,000 Confederates were killed in some of the most gruesome hand-to-hand combat ever witnessed. Never in our history have more Americans been killed in one day.

The point here is not to be macabre or sensational in describing these events, most of which took place at historic sites easily accessible to modern-day Washington — rather, it is to help put into perspective the full tragedy of the war, which sometimes is lost amid the crowds and commercialization that inevitably seize the region's battlefields and shrines during the tourist season.

The rest of this chapter is designed to offer a brief look at some of Metro Washington's fascinating Civil War sites. If you're a Civil War buff, you can look forward to a plethora of outings. If you're simply interested in learning a little more about The War Between the States, you'll find the Washington area an excellent instructor.

Those wishing to read more in-depth analyses of the Civil War in Washington, should pick up a copy of The Insiders' Guide® to the Civil War in the Eastern Theater, by Michael P. Gleason, as well as Richard M. Lee's fascinating book, Mr. Lincoln's City.

If you're a Civil War purist, you may want to join one of the area's many roundtable groups or battle re-enactment troupes, clubs that meet regularly at locations around Metro Washington. For more information, contact any of the national battlefield parks mentioned.

Washington, D.C.

African American Civil War Memorial
10th and U Sts. NW, Washington, D.C.
• (202) 667-2667

Slated to open July 18, 1998, this memorial honors the 185,000 African-American soldiers who fought in Union troops during the Civil War. The memorial is set in the city's historic Shaw neighborhood, named for Robert Gould Shaw, the white colonel who led his 54th Massachusetts Volunteer Infantry in the ill-fated attack on Confederate soldiers depicted in the acclaimed film Glory. The Shaw community nearly became the site of a similar memorial in 1888, but Civil War veteran George Washington Williams' proposal failed to garner House support. The new monument, located outside Metro's Shaw-Howard University station on the Green Line, features a sculpture by Kentucky artist Ed Hamilton, as well as two curved granite walls bearing the names of the men who fought in the United States Colored Troops. A Family Heritage/Visitors' Center in Garnet-Patterson Middle School just across U Street offers exhibits and genealogical information.

Albert Pike Statue
3rd and D Sts. NW, Washington, D.C.

One of the most peculiar and controversial statues in Washington, this memorial supposedly was erected to honor the man who headed the Scottish Rite of Freemasonry (the Masons)

www.insiders.com
See this and many other Insiders' Guide® destinations online — in their entirety.
Visit us today!

INSIDERS' TIP

The Virginia Civil War Trails project features detailed driving maps of historic sites, museums and other tourist attractions throughout the state. Call (888) CIVIL WAR to obtain free brochures.

during the mid- to late-19th century. Little is actually known about Albert Pike, however, other than his role with the Masons and a career that dabbled in poetry, newspaper publishing and adventuring. It was later learned that Pike served as a general in the Confederate Army.

Consequently, this statue is the only such outdoor fixture in D.C. that honors a rebel military officer. In recent years, protests have called for its removal, but based on precedent, the likelihood of that ever happening is slim.

Blair House
165 Pennsylvania Ave. NW,
Washington, D.C.

This venerable mansion has served as a guest house for visiting heads of state and other dignitaries since the administration of Franklin D. Roosevelt. Here, Robert E. Lee received the offer to command the Union Army. As we all know, the troubled Virginian turned down the invitation extended by Francis P. Blair, a trusted Lincoln advisor. Four days later, Lee swore allegiance to his beloved Old Dominion and the rest is history. The building is not open to the public.

Mathew Brady's Photo Studio Site
627 Pennsylvania Ave. NW,
Washington, D.C.

The upper floors of this Pennsylvania Avenue office building once housed the gallery and studio of the nation's most celebrated Civil War photojournalist, Mathew Brady (note the single 't' in his first name, which is often seen spelled the traditional, albeit incorrect, way). Brady's haunting photographs have done more to unlock the mysteries and nuances of the tragic war than have all subsequent volumes of written documentation. His studio was frequented by the great and near-great of official Washington, including one of Brady's biggest admirers, President Lincoln. The site is not open to the public.

Ford's Theatre National Historic Site and The Petersen House
511 10th St. NW, Washington, D.C.
• (202) 426-6924

The night of April 14, 1865, forever changed the face of America. At 8:30 PM, the Lincolns and their guests, Maj. Henry Reed Rathbone

and Clara Harris, arrived at Ford's Theatre to see a performance of the critically acclaimed comedy Our American Cousin. Less than two hours later, Confederate activist and former actor John Wilkes Booth entered the presidential box, shot Lincoln and stabbed Rathbone during a struggle as Booth tried to leave. As Booth escaped the city, the president, already brain-dead, was carried across the street to the Petersen House, where the official pronouncement of death came at 7:22 the next morning.

Today, Ford's Theatre, a national historic site, is largely restored to the way it looked the night of the assassination. It is still a performing theater, with plays scheduled throughout the year. (See our Arts chapter.) A must-stop here is the lower-level museum exhibiting Lincoln memorabilia, featuring some 3,000 items, such as the 44-caliber Deringer Booth used to shoot the president. The exhibit includes information about the conspirators tried for the assassination and details about all 12 of the president's funerals. Visit the museum's book store if you want to read up on the president. At Petersen House (516 10th Street) you can view the room where the president died. The free site generally is open daily from 9 AM to 5 PM, and is closed on Christmas day. Call ahead though, because the site also closes during matinees, rehearsals and special occasions.

Fort Dupont Park
Minnesota Ave. and Randle Cir. SE,
Washington, D.C. • (202) 426-7723

Located in the hills of Anacostia, Fort Dupont was one of 68 Union forts and 93 gun batteries that formed a ring around the city. It guarded the vital 11th Street Bridge that linked the southeast neighborhood with the Federal district of Washington. Although it never saw battle, the fort served as an important sanctuary for runaway slaves, many of whom joined D.C.'s growing community of contrabands. The guns and barracks are gone, but the fort's earthworks can still be found in the 376-acre namesake park that is run by the National Park Service. The park is open Monday through Friday from 8 AM to 4 PM. It's also the site of summer concerts which are generally held on Saturdays from 7 to 11 PM. Other park features include an ice-skating rink, basketball and tennis courts, sports fields, picnic areas, community gardens and environmental education and seasonal programs. Admission is free.

Frederick Douglass National Historic Site
1411 W St. SE, Washington, D.C.
• (202) 426-5960

Former slave Frederick Douglass became a famed abolitionist, editor, orator and advisor to Abraham Lincoln. Douglass's home, Cedar Hill, contains a vast collection of personal items and artifacts from this turbulent period in American history. Visitors can expect a 17-minute film followed by an engaging 30-minute tour. Cedar Hill, a national historic site, is located in the southeast neighborhood of Anacostia. It affords a stunning view of downtown to the north. The site is open daily April through September from 9 AM to 5 PM; October through March from 9 AM to 4 PM; and closed New Year's Day, Thanksgiving and Christmas. Admission is $3 per person, $1.50 for seniors ages 62 and older and free for children younger than age 7. Reservations are required for groups of 10 or more people.

Ulysses S. Grant Memorial
1st St. NW, Washington, D.C.
• (202) 426-6841

Sculptor Henry Shrady's memorial to the tireless Union general is one of the most striking images in the District. It's modeled after a sketch made of Grant by a young soldier from Massachusetts during the aftermath of battle at Virginia's Spotsylvania Court House. The general sits atop his warhorse, Cincinnati, and his penetrating eyes seem to survey the vastness of the National Mall that unfolds to the west. The adjacent bronzed images of cavalry troops in action are some of the most moving combat sculptures ever crafted. The memorial is in front of the Capitol Reflecting Pool.

Joe Hooker's Division Site
Below Pennsylvania Ave., between 9th and 15th Sts. NW, Washington, D.C.

Washington's most notorious red-light district cropped up during the Civil War, in an area wedged between Pennsylvania Avenue

and the National Mall. Houses of ill-repute sprung up to cater to the growing masses of troops and administrators who were flooding the Northern capital. Along with the soldiers and bordellos came swarms of gamblers, thieves, pimps and other unsavory characters. As legend has it, Gen. Joseph Hooker, a one-time commander of the Army of the Potomac, was responsible for rounding up the city's growing legion of prostitutes (some estimates ran as high as 15,000) and confining them to this area that became known as Hooker's Division. Legend also has it that this is where the slang name for prostitutes originated. The once lively district is now the site of the sterile and staid Federal Triangle, a sprawl of government offices and facilities that includes the Internal Revenue Service.

Lincoln Memorial
The National Mall at 23rd St. NW, Washington, D.C. • (202) 426-6841, (202) 426-6895

The awesome marble shrine to perhaps the nation's greatest president is loaded with symbolism, from the wall-carved inscription of the Gettysburg Address to the 36 Doric columns representing the reunion of the 36 states at the time of Lincoln's death. Perhaps the most poignant symbol associated with the monument, however, is the nearby Arlington Memorial Bridge. The stately bridge connects the Lincoln Memorial with Arlington House, Robert E. Lee's plantation home that overlooks the monument from the Virginia side of the Potomac River. The symbol suggests not only the healing of the nation but a common linkage between two great Americans. Admission is free to the memorial, which is open 24 hours. See our Attractions chapter for tour information.

The Old Capitol Prison Site
1st and E. Capitol Sts. NE, Washington, D.C.

When the original Capitol was burned by the British in the Battle of 1812, a temporary building was constructed across the street. The interim structure was used for a variety of purposes but was probably most famous as a prison for Southern spies and sympathizers, as well as your garden variety of criminals (both

Civil War re-enactments are popular throughout Virginia.

Yanks and Rebs), rogues, drunks, con artists and other suspected misfits.

In 1865, the prison was the site of the hanging of Confederate Capt. Henry Wirz, commander of the Andersonville Prison in Georgia, where more than 13,000 Federal troops died of disease and hunger. The Old Capitol was demolished in 1867. The Old Capitol Prison site is the present-day U.S. Supreme Court, open to the public from 9 AM to 4:30 PM Monday through Friday. See our Attractions chapter for tour information.

Old Corcoran Art Gallery
17th St. and Pennsylvania Ave. NW, Washington, D.C. • (202) 357-1300

During the first three years of the war, the Old Corcoran Art Gallery (now the Renwick Gallery) was the Union's largest supply depot in Washington, dispensing tens of thousands of uniforms, tents and equipment to soldiers fighting in the Virginia countryside. Gen. Montgomery C. Meigs, director of transportation and supply, used the building as his headquarters during the last year of the war. The gallery is open daily except Christmas, 10 AM to 5:30 PM. Admission is free. See our Arts chapter for more information about the Renwick and the current Corcoran Gallery.

The Rock Creek Park Forts
Rock Creek Park, 5000 Glover Rd. NW, Washington, D.C. • (202) 282-1063

In and around Rock Creek Park, Washington's huge and surprisingly pristine urban forest, one can roam the grounds of a handful of strategic Civil War forts that guarded Washington from the Confederates. Fort Stevens, just to the east of the park at 13th Street and Piney Branch Road, is where Gen. Jubal Early's spirited Southern forces squared off against an aggressive Union line in July of 1864. Among the battle's many spectators was President Lincoln, who only after much pleading from a Union commander reluctantly retreated to safer ground. It was the first and only battle the president ever witnessed.

Fort Reno, at Belt Road and Chesapeake Street, no longer remains, but you can check out its key vantage point as the highest spot in the District, more than 400 feet above sea level. Fort DeRussey, meanwhile, sits right off a bike path at Oregon Avenue and Military Road, in the heart of Rock Creek. To the west of the park, at Western Avenue and River Road, is Fort Bayard, now a popular picnicking site. The park is open daily during daylight hours. Admission is free. Check out our Parks and Recreation and Kidstuff chapters for more details about Rock Creek Park features.

Sherman Monument
15th St. and Pennsylvania Ave. NW, Washington, D.C.

Between the Treasury Department and the Ellipse is a small park area that contains the mounted statue of Gen. William T. Sherman, the Union commander who almost single-handedly destroyed the Deep South. A fierce soldier, Sherman was also a compassionate man who had sincere sympathies for the South. In fact, many of the radical Republicans in the U.S. Senate thought he was too sympathetic, and Sherman later found himself ostracized from the inner circles of power after the war.

TOUR D.C.
1912 Glen Ross Rd., Silver Spring, Md.
• (301) 588-8999

Although no Civil War battles took place in Georgetown, the city nonetheless stood in the thick of the conflict, as citizens expressed divided loyalties and Union soldiers took over schools, hospitals and churches. Enthusiastic guide Mary Kay Ricks' two-hour walking tours of lower Georgetown feature many Civil War-related sights and stories — the current Gap site once served as a jail for Union Army deserters, for instance — as well as highlights from other historical periods. Tours, arranged by appointment and also offered frequently at 10:30 AM on Saturdays, cost $15 per person. Ricks recommends the tours, which cover about 2 miles, for ages older than 10. Ricks also offers a 90-minute tour of N Street for $12. Call in advance for the latest schedule and to make reservations. See our Attractions chapter for other tours of D.C. and vicinity.

The United States Capitol
Capitol Hill, 1st St. between
Independence and Constitution Aves.,
Washington, D.C. • (202) 225-6827

Probably the most visible and accessible building in America, the Capitol is a required stop for anyone visiting or living in Metro D.C. Next time you're in these hallowed halls, consider that during the Civil War the Capitol was used for a variety of functions, including a fort, barracks and hospital for Union troops. Perhaps its most unusual function was as a bakery. Believe it or not, during the early months of the war, some 60,000 loaves of bread were baked each day in cellars under the West Wing. The bread was distributed to hungry soldiers stationed at the nearby forts that protected Washington. The building is open daily from 9 AM to 4:30 PM, and admission is free. See our Attractions chapter for tour information.

U.S. Patent Office Site
8th and F Sts. NW, Washington, D.C.
• (202) 357-1300

Today, the former U.S. Patent Office houses two of the city's greatest cultural treasures: the National Museum of American Art and the National Portrait Gallery. During the war, besides being a place where inventions were inspected, the building served as temporary barracks and as an Army hospital. Lincoln held his second inaugural ball here on March 5, 1865, barely a month before the war's end. See our Arts chapter for more about the gallery.

Washington Arsenal Site
4th and P Sts. SW, Washington, D.C.

The Washington Arsenal, the largest such Federal installment of the Civil War, also served as the nearest rail and water shipping point for ammunition headed to the battle fronts in Virginia. Two days after the assassination of President Lincoln, the conspirators who aided John Wilkes Booth were brought to the arsenal's prison and tried. On July 7, 1865, the four condemned, including Mary Surratt, were hanged here and buried in the adjacent prison yard. Four years later, the bodies were released to their respective families. This is now the site of Fort McNair.

Washington Monument
Constitution Ave. and 15th St. NW,
Washington, D.C. • (202) 426-6841

Like just about everything else in Washington, the city's most visible landmark was greatly impacted by the Civil War. Work on the monument, which had begun in 1848, came to an abrupt halt during the war. At that time, it stood only 156 feet high, or less than a third of its completed height (555 feet). One can readily see the point where work stopped on the memorial; the masonry patterns of the last two-thirds of the obelisk are different from the original section. Interestingly, former Confederate prisoners were employed to help build the final stretches of the monument, which opened to the public in 1888. The monument is open daily except Christmas, from 9 AM to 5 PM September through March, and 8 AM to midnight April through August. Please note that this schedule is subject to change in 1998 because of a major renovation. Admission is free. See our Attractions chapter for more information.

The White House
1600 Pennsylvania Ave. NW,
Washington, D.C. • (202) 456-7041

America's most famous home wasn't all that majestic in the years leading up to and during the Civil War. In fact, just two years before the outbreak of the war, sewage from the White House was still being emptied directly onto the Ellipse (known in those days as the White Lot), the marshy park immediately to the south. Nearby, at the bottom of 17th Street, stood the city dump near a polluted, disease-ridden canal. You may remember that Lincoln's son, Willie, died of typhoid fever and the president himself came down with small pox — all no doubt due to the unhealthy surroundings. The White House is open for tours 10 AM to noon, Tuesday through Saturday. Admission is free. See our Attractions chapter for more details.

Willard's Hotel
1401 Pennsylvania Ave. NW,
Washington, D.C. • (202) 628-9100

Perhaps the grandest of Washington's grand hotels, Willard's (today known as Willard Inter-Continental Hotel) was the undisputed social center of the nation's capital during the Civil War. Both Lincoln and Grant slept here during their first nights in the city, and Julia Ward Howe, while staying here, penned "The Battle Hymn of the Republic," the spiritual anthem of the North. Ironically, John Wilkes Booth frequented the hotel during the weeks prior to the Lincoln assassination. See our Accommodations chapter for more about this hotel.

Northern Virginia

Alexandria

Boyhood Home of Robert E. Lee
607 Oronoco St., Alexandria, Va.
• (703) 548-8454

Like George Washington, Robert E. Lee was born on Virginia's Northern Neck, a vast plantation region bounded by the Potomac and Rappahannock rivers and the Chesapeake Bay. Like the first president, Lee would ultimately move north to Alexandria, a bustling port city that was becoming one of the East Coast's leading trade and shipping centers. Lee's father, the Revolutionary war hero "Light Horse Harry" Lee, brought his family to the house in 1812. Young Robert spent 10 years in the large Federal-period home on Oronoco Street in Old Town.

Among the home's many distinguished guests was Gen. Marquis de Lafayette, the Frenchman who fought side by side with the elder Lee and Washington during the Revolutionary War. (The museum reenacts his visit each October.) The home was also the site of the 1804 marriage of George Washington Parke Custis (Martha Washington's grandson) and Mary Lee Fitzhugh, which the museum stages each July. Robert E. Lee married their daughter, Mary Anna Randolph Custis, at Arlington House. The museum is open from 10 AM to 4 PM Monday through Saturday, and from 1 to 4 PM Sunday. The museum is open by appointment only December 15 through January 31, and it's closed Easter, Thanksgiving and for some special events. Admission is $4 for adults and $2 for students through age 17. The museum celebrates Lee's birthday each January and holds candlelight tours in December.

INSIDERS' TIP

A Guidebook to Virginia's Historical Markers, published for the Virginia Historic Landmarks Commission, contains descriptions of markers throughout the state. Look for it at local libraries.

Confederate Statue
**S. Washington and Prince Sts.,
Alexandria, Va. • (703) 838-4554**

At the busy intersection of South Washington and Prince streets stands Alexandria's memorial to its fallen Confederate comrades. The statue is simple enough: a single soldier standing upright and gazing steadfastly toward the south. Several years ago the statue, which stands in the middle of the street, accidentally was knocked over by a speeding motorist, an act that set off a minor controversy. Some folks in the community claimed it was a traffic hazard, an insensitive one at that, and should be removed permanently. A legion of powerful city elders sensed an underhanded Yankee plot to rid Alexandria of part of its history. Johnny Reb was mended and placed back in his original position, a striking reminder that the passions of the Civil War still run deep.

Fort Ward Museum and Historic Site
**4301 W. Braddock Rd., Alexandria, Va.
• (703) 838-4848**

Named after the first Union officer to be killed in the Civil War, Fort Ward was one of dozens of Union fortifications that suddenly popped up following the North's embarrassing defeat at the Battle of First Manassas, just 30 miles to the west. Armed with 36 guns, it was the fifth-largest fort surrounding the nation's capital.

Today, visitors can see much of the same structure as it appeared more than 100 years ago. A self-guided walking tour takes about 45 minutes. The Fort Ward Museum contains an impressive collection of Civil War artifacts and photographs. Each August, the park holds its annual Civil War Living History Day, one of the region's better period reenactment events. The grounds of the 45-acre park are open 9 AM to sunset daily, and the museum is open 9 AM to 5 PM Tuesday through Saturday, noon to 5 PM Sunday. It's closed Thanksgiving, Christmas and New Year's Day. Admission is free. Guided tours can be arranged, at least a month in advance, for groups of 10 or more people. Tour admission is free for city residents and $1 per person for other visitors.

Lloyd House
**220 N. Washington St., Alexandria, Va.
• (703) 838-4577**

This public-library branch specializes in Virginia and Alexandria history and Virginia genealogy. Its Civil War collection includes the War of the Rebellion Official Record in books and on CD, books about Confederate Virginia and photographs of Union-occupied Alexandria. The house, dating to 1797, belonged to John Lloyd, whose wife, Ann, was Robert E. Lee's first cousin. Lee visited their home before and after the war. The library is open Monday through Friday 9 AM to 5 PM and is closed Sunday.

Arlington County

Arlington House/Arlington National Cemetery
**Memorial Dr., Arlington, Va.
• (703) 692-0931**

Perched on a bluff overlooking the Potomac River, Arlington House once was the home of Robert E. Lee. When Lee left to command the Confederate forces, the Georgian-style mansion and its several thousand acres of surrounding property were seized by Federal troops and became the headquarters for the Army of the Potomac. Three Union forts were built on the land, and casualties (both Northern and Southern) from local battles were buried here beginning in June 1864.

Today, the area is known as Arlington National Cemetery and is one of the most visited burial grounds in the world. The house, also known as the Robert E. Lee Memorial, is completely restored and furnished with Lee family heirlooms. From the front steps of the mansion, one can experience perhaps the most spectacular views of Washington.

Civil War buffs should look for the following points of interest: the heavily symbolic, $75,000 Confederate Memorial, designed by a Confederate soldier and commissioned by the Daughters of the Confederacy; Memorial Amphitheater, near the site of a Freedman's village where 1,100 freed slaves lived after the war; Section 27, where 3,800 former slaves known as "Contrabands" are buried; and the equestrian statue honoring Major General

Philip Kearny, killed during Fairfax County's only recorded Civil War battle (see Marr Monument listing).

The cemetery is open daily from 8 AM to 5 PM, October through March, and from 8 AM to 7 PM, April through September. Admission is free. See our Attractions chapter for more information about tours and highlights of this popular tourist site.

The Civil War Trust
2101 Wilson Blvd., Ste. 1120, Arlington, Va. • (703) 516-4944

As most Civil War buffs know, many battlefields remain sites of potential destruction, this time in the form of encroaching development. The Civil War Trust, a nonprofit organization, works to preserve these hallowed grounds, including sites in Maryland and Virginia. The trust also sponsors tours, and its Civil War Discovery Trail includes more than 420 museums, battlefields, cemeteries, historic houses and other sites in 24 states. Membership is $25 annually.

Fairfax City and County

Fairfax City Cemetery
10561 Main St., Fairfax, Va.
• (703) 385-8414

A gray granite obelisk marks the graves of 200 unknown soldiers of the Confederacy, including 96 Fairfax County Civil War fatalities. Nearby, a monument close to Fair Oaks Shopping Center on Route 50 honors two Union officers, Major General Philip Kearny and General Isaac Stevens, killed during the Battle of Ox Hill, the only documented Civil War battle fought in Fairfax County, on that site.

Fairfax County Public Library - Virginia Room
Fairfax City Regional Library, 3915 Chain Bridge Rd., Fairfax, Va. • (703) 246-2123

The Virginia Room contains a variety of resources for people interested in the Civil War and other Virginia history, including local and church histories, building files, maps and newspapers. Hours are 10 AM to 9 PM Monday through Thursday, 10 AM to 6 PM Friday, 10 AM to 5 PM Saturday and noon to 6 PM Sunday. Admission is free.

Fairfax Museum and Visitors Center
10209 Main St., Fairfax, Va.
• (703) 385-8414, (800) 545-7950

Visit the museum to pick up a "Courting History" brochure, detailing a self-guided walking tour of historic Old Town Fairfax that includes six Civil War-related sites: the Ford Building, Moore House, Dr. William Gunnell House, Fairfax Court House, Joshua Gunnell House and Marr Monument. The museum itself chronicles local history, including Civil War events. A new exhibit slated for a May 16 opening features a Civil War encampment. Visitors also can obtain numerous free pamphlets on area attractions. Hours are from 9 AM to 5 PM daily. Admission is free.

Fort Marcy Park
Accessible only from northbound lanes of George Washington Memorial Pkwy. near McLean, Va. (follow signs)

Fort Marcy, or what remains of it, sits atop Virginia's Prospect Hill, about a mile west of Chain Bridge. The Union earthwork defense compound acted as a buffer for both Chain Bridge, which spans across the Potomac into northwest Washington, and the vital Chesapeake and Ohio Canal, the main supply link for the wartime capital. During the war, the fort, named for Gen. George McClellan's father-in-law, held 18 guns, including a 10-inch mortar, two 24-pound mortars and 15 smaller cannons. Today, visitors can view the fort's remaining earthworks and take in dramatic vistas from the grounds, which sit 275 feet above the Potomac.

A morbidly ironic footnote to the history of a place associated with guns and violence: Fort Marcy assumed an unwanted notoriety with the 1993 death of Vincent Foster, a Clinton administration official whose body was found here following an apparent suicide. The park is open to the public during daylight hours, and admission is free.

Marr Monument
4000 Chain Bridge Rd., Fairfax, Va.
• (703) 385-8414

On the lawn of the Old Fairfax Courthouse, at the intersection of Routes 123 (Chain Bridge Road) and 236, is a stone monument built in 1904 in memory of Capt. John Quincy Marr,

Photo: Courtesy of the Richmond Times-Dispatch

Robert E. Lee (1870) and Stonewall Jackson (1851)
led Southern forces in the Civil War.

the first Confederate officer killed in the Civil War. Marr was in command of the Warrenton Rifles when, on the night of June 1, 1861, he was killed in a skirmish in Fairfax City with Company B of the Union Second Cavalry. Like all Confederate cannons, those flanking this monument face north.

Loudoun County

Ball's Bluff Regional Park
Ball's Bluff Rd., Off Rt. 15, just north of Leesburg, Va. • (703) 729-0596

The viciously fought Battle of Ball's Bluff (October 21, 1861), won by the South, was an event of significant national importance because it raised serious questions in the U.S. Congress as to how the Civil War should be conducted. The Union suffered heavy casualties, a result of a series of strategic blunders. Shortly after the battle, Congress established the Joint Committee on the Conduct of the War, an organization charged with reviewing all military procedures and other leadership issues that became politicized through war. The 168-site includes a 3/4-mile loop trail and the second smallest national cemetery, in which 54 Union soldiers are buried. It is open to the public during daylight hours. Admission

is free. The site does not have restrooms or a park office.

John S. Mosby Heritage Area Driving Tour
John S. Mosby Heritage Area, P.O. Box 1178, Middleburg, VA 20118
• (540) 687-6681

This self-guided driving tour begins at Mt. Zion Church in Aldie, (703) 777-0343, where Confederate officer John Singleton Mosby met with his guerrilla cavalry unit, Mosby's Rangers. The building also served as a Union hospital. The tour continues along scenic Route 50 to Paris, where Mosby's Rangers spent a lot of time on the property that now is Sky Meadows State Park, (540) 592-3556. Free brochures and $17 "Prelude to Gettysburg" audiotapes are available through the organization or at local visitors' centers.

Loudoun Museum
16 Loudoun St. SW, Leesburg, Va.
• (703) 777-7427

Featuring exhibits detailing county life from prehistoric Indian times to the present, this museum includes Civil War-related artifacts. Stop here to pick up brochures about self-guided walking tours of Leeburg's quaint historic district and the county's Town of Middleburg, both of which include buildings with Civil War significance.

"A Perfect Sneering Nest of Rebels: Leesburg in the Civil War," a guided walking tour designed by an award-winning local history teacher, leads visitors to sites relating to key events in the town's Civil War involvement. The tours generally take place Friday nights and Saturday and Sunday afternoons, spring through mid-fall. Admission is $5 for adults and $3 for children younger than age 12. Call for times and dates.

Thomas Balch Library
208 W. Market St., Leesburg, Va.
• (703) 779-1328

Operated by the town of Leesburg, this local history and genealogy library houses a Civil War collection. Hours are Monday from 10 AM to 5 PM, Tuesday from 10 AM to 8 PM, Wednesday from 2 to 8 PM, Thursday and Friday from 11 AM to 5 PM and Saturday from 11 AM to 4 PM.

The Village of Waterford
Waterford Foundation Inc., 2nd and Main Sts., Waterford, Va. • (540) 882-3018

This tiny and immaculate hunt country village on Route 662, about 15 minutes northwest of Leesburg, traces its roots to its 1733 founding by Amos Janney, a Quaker who had emigrated from Pennsylvania. By the time of the Civil War, the strongly abolitionist residents supported the Union — not surprisingly a very unpopular stance in Virginia. During the war, the village suffered Union harassment because of its location and Confederate harassment because of its Quaker-influenced abolitionist beliefs. As a result of the Confederate backlash, Samuel Means, a resident miller, abandoned his Quaker principles to form the Independent Loudoun Rangers, the only organized troops in Virginia to fight for the Union.

The village's historical organization, the Waterford Foundation, Inc., keeps office hours from 9 AM to 5 PM Monday through Friday in the Corner Store. Stop by for brochures, books and posters. See our Annual Events chapter for information about the renowned Waterford Homes Tour and Crafts Show.

Prince William County

Confederate Cemetery
Center St., Old Town Manassas, Va.

Two years after the South's surrender at Appomattox, Confederate veteran W.S. Fewell donated one acre of land in the center of Manassas for a cemetery. A year later, more than 250 Southern soldiers had been reinterred there. The focal point of the cemetery is a red sandstone monument that is capped by a bronze statue titled "At Rest."

Manassas Museum
9101 Prince William St., Manassas, Va.
• (703) 368-1873

The Manassas Museum (not affiliated with the battlefield park) reopened in 1992 in a modern and spacious building in downtown Manassas. It interprets the history and material culture of the community and the surrounding Northern Virginia Piedmont region. On display here is an array of prehistoric tools, Civil War weapons and uniforms, railroad artifacts, Victorian costumes, quilts and photos that collectively tell the story of this historic part of the Old Dominion. Of special interest is a pair of video programs that describe the settlement of the Manassas area and the legacy of the Civil War. Above all, the museum helps one understand why two of the most important battles of the war were fought in this otherwise peaceful community.

Annual special events include commemoration of the museum's February anniversary, a Civil War weekend in the summer, a summer concert series and a Christmas Open House. The museum is open from 10 AM to 5 PM Tuesday through Sunday, and is closed Monday except on federal holidays. It's closed New Year's Day, Thanksgiving and Christmas Eve and Day. Admission is $2.50 for adults, $1.50 for children ages 6 through 17 and seniors ages 60 and older. There is no charge for children younger than age 6. Admission for groups of 10 or more is $1.50 per person. On Tuesdays, individual admission is free. Visitors can shop in the museum store without paying admission.

Manassas National Battlefield Park

6511 Sudley Rd., Manassas, Va.
• (703) 754-1861, (703) 361-1339
visitors center

Just 30 miles west of the Nation's Capital, Manassas National Battlefield Park looks much the same as it did in 1861. Several square miles of Virginia countryside have been preserved as a memorial to the two landmark Civil War battles that took place here — fighting that claimed more than 4,000 lives and left 30,000 wounded. In recent years, developers have had their eyes on parcels of land abutting the park. In one of the more inane proposals, a prominent builder nearly won approval to construct a shopping mall within eyesight of these hallowed grounds. Fortunately, preservationists had more clout on Capitol Hill than did the developers. Consequently, at least for now, Manassas remains remarkably untouched given its proximity to suburbia.

The beauty of the battlefield goes beyond the rich history and graceful monuments. With more than 5,000 acres, Manassas is a park in every sense of the word, with miles of horse and hiking trails, interpretive roadside tour markers and picnic areas. The Stone House, a former tavern and way station, opens for tours during the summer. At the Visitors' Center, an electric map presentation and a small museum help tell the story of the two great battles.

Park rangers can provide brochures outlining some of the more interesting walking and driving tours. The Visitors' Center is open from 8:30 AM to 5 PM during the winter, and until 6 PM in the summer; grounds are open daily during daylight hours. Admission, good for three days, is $2 per person for ages 17 and older, and free for visitors younger than age 17. No trip to the area should be considered complete without a stop at the Manassas Museum in the neighboring city's Old Town district, about a 10-minute drive from the battlefield (see the previous listing).

Suburban Maryland

Montgomery County

Cabin John Aqueduct Bridge

Off the Clara Barton Pkwy. in Cabin John, Md.

There's only one place in the nation where the names of both President Lincoln and Confederate President Jefferson Davis appear together. They're inscribed on a plaque on the Cabin John Aqueduct in Suburban Maryland. The aqueduct, the longest stone arch bridge in the world, was commissioned in the 1850s when Franklin Pierce was president and Jefferson Davis was secretary of war. It was designed to transport water from the Great Falls of the Potomac to Washington. A commemorative marker was placed on the bridge abutment upon completion. When the Civil War broke out, someone discovered Davis's name and it was quickly removed. Years later, under the presidency of Theodore Roosevelt, a new plaque was installed that included the Confederate hero. The bridge and the plaque remain to this day.

Clara Barton National Historic Site

5801 Oxford Rd., Glen Echo, Md.
• (301) 492-6245

Known as the "angel of the battlefield," Clara Barton was one of few women allowed behind the lines by the Union Army. She tended to the thousands of wounded at Antietam, the bloodiest day in American history. She also proved instrumental in helping locate and identify the graves of more than 22,000 Civil War soldiers scattered throughout eastern and southern theaters. Barton perhaps is best known, however, as the founder of the American Red Cross. This house, now a fascinating museum, was originally built as a warehouse for Red Cross

---

INSIDERS' TIP

The 17.5-mile Bull-Run Occoquan Trail takes hikers and horseback riders through woodlands that include the remains of Civil War fortifications. Contact the Northern Virginia Regional Park Authority at (703) 352-5900 for a map.

supplies. After Barton made it her permanent home in 1897, the house grew to 36 rooms and now is considered an important landmark in Victorian design. The site is open daily from 10 AM to 5 PM. House tours begin every hour on the hour, from 10 AM to 4 PM. Admission is free. The site is part of Glen Echo Park, which is described in our Arts, Kidstuff and Parks and Recreation chapters.

White's Ferry
24801 White's Ferry Rd., Dickerson, Md.
• (301) 349-5200

White's Ferry on the Potomac River is the site where Confederate Gen. Jubal Early led 13,000 troops across the river into Maryland in July 1864. Early and his troops would eventually make their way into the present-day Rock Creek Park, thus becoming the only Rebel forces to ever come in striking distance of the nation's capital. This also is the site where Robert E. Lee earlier crossed the river en route to his first large-scale invasion of the North. Today, at White's Ferry, you can load your car onto the cable-guided Jubal Early ferry and cross the river into Virginia. It is the only ferry boat still operating on the Potomac and is accessible from both the Maryland and Virginia shores. Docks are 6 miles west of Poolesville on Route 107, and 4 miles north of Leesburg, Virginia, off Route 15. The ferry operates daily from 5 AM to 11 PM. Admission for cars is $3 one way, and $5 round trip; admission for pedestrians is 50¢ each way. The boat leaves approximately every 12 minutes, ferrying up to 24 cars across an undeveloped, scenic area of the Potomac between Dickerson and Leesburg. The Maryland side boasts a picnic area, convenience store, canoe and boat rentals and the C&O Canal.

Prince George's County

Fort Washington Park
13551 Fort Washington Rd., Fort Washington, Md. • (301) 763-4600

Gorgeous views of the Potomac and the District in the distance await visitors to the 341-acre park on the Potomac River. Origi-nally built to guard Washington from the British during the Battle of 1812, this impressive and fully restored masonry fort was the southern lookout for Union troops during the Civil War. In January 1861, manned by just 40 Marines, it was the sole fort protecting the capital. The park offers artillery and firearms demonstrations, generally one Sunday per month, April through November. Visitors can take guided tours at 2, 3 and 4 PM Saturday and Sunday. Admission is $4 per vehicle and $2 per pedestrian. The grounds are open from 8 AM to dark daily, and the Visitors Center, which includes a film, exhibit area and bookstore, is open from 9 AM to 5 PM.

The Surratt House Museum
9118 Brandywine Rd., Clinton, Md.
• (301) 868-1121

This unassuming tavern and post office also served as the home of Mary Surratt, who was charged as a conspirator in the Lincoln assassination. On the day Lincoln was shot, Surratt supposedly left a package behind at the tavern. It contained field glasses for the fleeing John Wilkes Booth. She also had hidden guns there. As a result of her involvement, Mary Surratt was hanged along with three other conspirators, thus becoming the first woman ever to be executed by the federal government.

The Visitors' Center includes an electric map display of Booth's escape route, exhibits, a gift shop, research library and special events. The museum is open March 1 through mid-December, Thursday and Friday from 11 AM to 3 PM; and Saturday and Sunday from noon to 4 PM. The last tours begin a half-hour before closing. The museum also opens briefly in February to display its collection of 100 19th-Century Valentines. Admission is $3 for adults, and $2 for seniors ages 55 and older, $1 for children ages 5 to 18 and free for children younger than age 5. Christmas candlelight tours take place in mid-December. The museum sponsors 12-hour, $45 per person bus tours of Booth's escape route during the spring and fall. Call in mid-January to be put on the spring waiting list, and mid-June for the fall waiting list.

Re-enactors fight a Civil War battle.

Charles County

Dr. Samuel A. Mudd
House Museum
Dr. Samuel Mudd Rd., off Poplar Hill Rd.
near Waldorf, Md. • (301) 934-8464

After shooting President Lincoln, John Wilkes Booth escaped from the scene by jumping from the president's box and onto the stage at Ford's Theatre. In the process, he badly fractured his leg, and this is where the story of Dr. Samuel Mudd comes in. On their escape route through Southern Maryland, a disguised Booth and his accomplice, David Herold, made a stop at the country doctor's farmhouse. Mudd, supposedly not knowing the identity of the assassins, set Booth's leg and even tried to arrange for a carriage for the two men's journey. (Booth and Herold ultimately left on horseback.)

Despite his alleged innocence, Mudd was convicted by a military court of aiding and harboring an escaping fugitive. He was sent to Ft. Jefferson Prison near Key West, Fla., only to be pardoned later by President Andrew Johnson. While in prison, Dr. Mudd was called on to treat fellow prisoners during an outbreak of yellow fever. After being discharged for his humanitarian efforts, Mudd returned to his Maryland home and became a noted national expert on treating the fever.

Today, the Mudd home is a fully restored historic site, complete with period furniture — most of which actually belongs to the Mudd family — and mementos that detail the doctor's struggle to establish his innocence. Louise Mudd Arehart, the youngest of the doctor's 33 grandchildren, founded and still oversees the museum. The museum is open from early April through the weekend before Thanksgiving; Saturday and Sunday from noon to 4 PM; and Wednesday from 11 AM to 3 PM. Admission is $3 for adults, and $1 for children younger than age 18.

Frederick County

Barbara Fritchie House and Museum
154 W. Patrick St., Frederick, Md.
• (301) 698-0630

Forever immortalized in the John Greenleaf Whittier poem bearing her name, Barbara Fritchie was a staunch Union supporter who lived in Frederick, a town of split loyalties during the war. As legend has it, Fritchie proudly flew the Stars and Stripes from her upstairs window as Gen. Stonewall Jackson and his Confederate troops marched in and captured the sleepy Maryland village. Jackson, noting the flag, confronted the 96-year-old patriot about her loyalties. The unfazed Fritchie shouted to the general: "Shoot if you must, this old gray head, but spare your country's flag." Jackson, struck by the woman's determination and bravery, proclaimed: "Who touches a hair on your gray head dies like a dog."

The house, part of Frederick's large historic district, is filled with Fritchie heirlooms, including a poet's corner dedicated to Whittier's tribute. The museum is open from April to October 1, Sunday from 1 to 4 PM and Monday, Thursday, Friday and Saturday from 10 to 4 PM. It's open weekends only during October and November, and is closed from December through March except during Frederick's annual Christmas Candlelight Tour. Admission is $2 for adults, $1.50 for seniors older than age 55 and children ages 5 to 12, and free for children younger than age 5. Groups of 10 or more people are admitted for $1.50 per person.

Monocacy National Battlefield
Off Md. Rt. 355 near Frederick, Md.
• (301) 662-3515

Here, Gen. Lew Wallace's Union forces suffered defeat by the Rebs under Gen. Jubal Early, who later went on to attack Washington, D.C., at Fort Stevens. Wallace is probably best remembered as the author who penned *Ben Hur*, and most military strategists would claim that he was a better writer than a commander. Like Manassas, Antietam and virtually every Civil War battlefield in the nation, Monocacy is under relentless pressure from developers determined to turn the surrounding countryside into condominiums and shopping centers.

Visitors can watch an 8½-minute, electric-map presentation, complete with lights and sound effects, and use a touch-screen computer to learn intriguing tidbits about local social history of the period. The site also features a half-mile loop trail. Monocacy is open daily from 8 AM to 4:30 PM Memorial Day through Labor Day, and Wednesday through Sunday from 8 AM to 4:30 PM the rest of the year. Admission is free.

National Museum of Civil War Medicine
48 E. Patrick St., Frederick, Md.
• (301) 695-1864

Situated in a circa-1832 building used as an embalming station after Antietam, this growing museum features five vignettes that depict the recruiting process, a surgeon's tent, a field hospital, a fixed-bed hospital and a parlor area. The exhibits include such unusual items as a real Civil War ambulance and a unique type of holding coffin used to transport bodies home via train. At least twice a month, the museum hosts living history presentations. It's also the starting point to Civil War walking tours, Saturday and Sunday mid-April through the first weekend in December. Tour admission is $4.50 for adults; $3.50 for seniors age 61 and older, college students and military personnel with ID, and children ages 10 to 16; and free for children younger than age 10.

The museum is open Monday through Saturday from 10 AM to 5 PM, and Sunday from 11 AM to 5 PM, except from mid-November to mid-March, when it closes at 4 PM. Museum admission is $2.50 for adults; $2 for seniors age 61 and older and military personnel and college students with ID; $1 for children ages 10 to 16; and free for children younger than age 10. Don't miss the gift shop, with such items as unique clothespin dolls and tin leech boxes for storing rubber leeches. The museum will remain open during a major renovation, scheduled to start late in 1998.

In keeping with its international presence and status as the Nation's Capital, Washington sometimes plays host to worldwide or national events.

Spectator Sports

Just because government and politics tend to dominate the very character of Metro Washington and outsiders' perceptions of it, don't underestimate the importance of leisure activities — spectator sports especially — to residents. In fact, there's probably a clear and perfectly understandable link between the awesome presence of the governmental/political establishment and the fervor with which we embrace our sporting diversions.

You'll find every level of competition here, from outstanding high school and college action to professional teams representing a variety of sports. In keeping with its international presence and status as the Nation's Capital, Washington sometimes plays host to worldwide or national events.

In September 1997, tennis enthusiasts cheered Michael Chang and Pete Sampras to victory over Aussies Mark Philippoussis and Patrick Rafter in the Davis Cup semifinals, played at William H.G. Fitzgerald Tennis Center in Washington, D.C.'s Rock Creek Park. (The Americans lost in the finals in Sweden — oh, well!) The city became the center of the golf universe in 1997, when TPC at Avenel in Potomac, Maryland, served as the site of the prestigious U.S. Open.

In 1996, the summer Olympics arrived at RFK Stadium, where more than 58,000 soccer fans watched Portugal beat the United States. RFK also is one of seven sites expected to host games in the 1999 Women's World Cup soccer tournament.

Washingtonians, by and large, hold a special place in their collective heart for one sport and one team in particular. For at least six months a year, the sports scene focuses intensely on our beloved Washington Redskins, proud member of the NFL's finest division, the NFC East. In a bittersweet turn of events in 1997, the team's new Jack Kent Cooke Stadium opened — just 160 days after its 84-year-old namesake died of a heart attack. The

Redskins won the stadium opener, beating the Cardinals 19-13 in overtime.

Despite a disappointing 1997 season — 8 wins, 7 losses and 1 tie — the team enjoys an almost divine status among its faithful fans. After all, the Redskins have been in Washington for more than 60 years and boast a solid winning tradition fueled by three Super Bowl victories (all under the reign of inimitable former coach Joe Gibbs) in five appearances. Getting a ticket to a home game, however, is another matter altogether. We'll include more on this later.

Non-fans, don't despair. You'll soon discover that an ideal time to go grocery shopping or roam the malls is during a Redskins game, when a large part of the local population is at home glued to the TV.

Before becoming further immersed in Redskins mania (see, we're as vulnerable as anyone around here), we should also mention Metro Washington's representatives in the National Basketball Association, the Washington Wizards (formerly the Bullets), and the National Hockey League, the Capitals. Conveniently, they both have the same home, the sparkling new MCI Center (see our "Close-up" for a complete profile). Here you also can watch the popular Georgetown University Hoyas basketball team and, starting in summer 1998, the Washington Mystics, a brand new WNBA team. Soccer fans are finding plenty of ways to get their kicks. In October 1997, two-year-old D.C. United won its second straight Major League Soccer championship before a capacity crowd at RFK Stadium. The city also boasts an indoor soccer team, the Washington Warthogs, a favorite with kids.

Incredibly, the Nation's Capital has been without a Major League Baseball team since 1971, when the Senators moved out for a second and final time, heading southwest to become the Texas Rangers. Years before, the original version of the Senators left and turned up in Minnesota as the Twins; an expansion version of the Senators played in the interim. Attempts to gain a team for the District or even Northern Virginia, either through league expansion (in which, just a few years ago, Colorado reached new heights with the Rockies and Florida reeled in the Marlins) or perhaps the relocation of an existing club, have proven fruitless. Organized efforts to that end will likely persist in one form or another. Fortunately, baseball junkies can get their fix with the 1997 American League Eastern Division champions, the Baltimore Orioles, whose home field, the spectacular Oriole Park at Camden Yards, sits barely an hour up the road and just blocks from the city's famous Inner Harbor.

Devotees of the diamond will also be happy to know that minor league baseball has a strong presence in Metro Washington, with the Prince William Cannons, Bowie Bay Sox, Frederick Keys and Hagerstown Suns all within a short drive.

Intercollegiate athletics are a big part of the sports scene as well, and the region's many colleges and universities afford plenty of opportunities for the spectator. Schools with the most prominent athletic programs include the University of Maryland, Georgetown University, the United States Naval Academy, George Washington University, Howard University and George Mason University. Meanwhile, Johns Hopkins University, just up the road in Baltimore, is a perennial lacrosse powerhouse; and to the south in Charlottesville, the University of Virginia wields a big stick in lacrosse, as well as soccer, basketball and football.

You also can live out your sports fantasies with a variety of other events, including horse and auto racing, golf and tennis, to name a few. So, having discarded the stodgy, white-collar, work-reigns-supreme label that seems permanently affixed to Washingtonians, let's take a closer look at an abundant sporting roster. The following provides an overview of spectator sports in Metro Washington; general recreational pursuits are covered in our Parks and Recreation chapter.

Baseball

Major League

Baltimore Orioles
Oriole Park at Camden Yards, 333 W. Camden St., Baltimore, Md.
• (202) 432-7328 or (703) 573-7328 for tickets, (410) 685-9800 for information

Unable to root, root, root for a home team, many Washingtonians get their baseball fix by supporting the Baltimore Orioles. In fact, an estimated 28 to 30 percent of the home crowds travel from the Washington suburbs, and they're rewarded with some of the finest baseball in the majors. In 1997, the O's finished at the top of their division with a 98-64 record, having remained in first throughout the entire season. Second Baseman Roberto Alomar finished second in the league in individual batting averages with .333, and only New York topped Baltimore in American League pitching. The team also boasted the league's largest attendance, with 3.7 million people.

A league championship just wasn't meant to be — at least not in 1997. The Orioles ousted the Seattle Mariners in the first round of playoffs, only to face the Cleveland Indians, ready to settle the score after being knocked out of the playoffs by Baltimore in 1996. The Tribe shocked the O's by winning the bizarre, yet exciting, best-of-seven series 4-2, with the final 1-0, 11-inning victory celebrated in Baltimore in front of a stunned and highly disappointed crowd. More bad news came shortly after the sports media named Davey Johnson American League manager of the year: Orioles owner Peter Angelos engaged in a public feud with Johnson, who eventually submitted his letter of resignation. Despite 1997's disappointments, 1998 holds a lot of promise. Fans look forward to watching the team's beloved shortstop-turned-third baseman, Cal "Iron Man" Ripken Jr., add to his 2,478 Major League record streak of consecutive games. Popular center fielder Brady Anderson decided to stay

Inside Washington's New MCI Center

The National Museum of Natural History may boast the city's most amazing collection of jewels and minerals, but Washington's biggest gem, in the eyes of many residents, is the dazzling MCI Center.

Close-up

The $200 million, 1,000,000-square-foot, 20,000-seat sports and entertainment arena debuted December 2, 1997, to all-round kudos from the fans who watched the Washington Wizards handily defeat the Seattle SuperSonics. City officials and media covering the grand opening expressed amazement at how smoothly everything went. The massive, brightly lit building indeed seems poised to fulfill hopes for a downtown revitalization, especially now that the city's crime rate appears to be on a welcome decline.

The center beckons visitors in several ways. For starters, many folks find the new arena's location — at 7th and F streets NW, just a hop, skip and jump from the Gallery Place Chinatown Metro station — much more convenient than USAirways Arena in Landover, Maryland, which requires most people to hit the Beltway, frequently during evening rush hour. Now, those who have jobs in the city can walk or take a brief ride to a game after work, while suburbanites need drive only as far as their closest Metro station.

Here are more reasons to check it out:

• Sports — The arena's biggest stars, the NBA Washington Wizards, boast a new identity to go with their new home. Owner Abe Pollin (who, by the way, also owns the NHL Capitals and the center itself), felt that the longtime Bullets moniker held a negative, violence-oriented connotation. He chose Wizards as a replacement name, and while the team isn't exactly magical yet, it has conjured up a lot of home court victories in the new arena. If you miss any action on the floor, you can look up at one of the four 12-by-16-foot screens on the 15-ton, video scoreboard cube that hangs from the center of the ceiling. It's the biggest of its kind!

— continued on next page

Photo: Courtesy of Mary Jane Solomon

The NBA's Washington Wizards, shown in action against Cleveland, play in the new MCI Center.

Hoops fans also are excited about the city's newest team, the Women's National Basketball League's Washington Mystics, set to debut July 11. One of two expansion teams joining the WNBA as it starts its second season, the Mystics will play 30 games, through mid-August. Off to a promising start, the team landed American Basketball League guard and MVP Nikki McCray as its first player. And don't forget the Georgetown Hoyas, one of the country's preeminent college teams.

The basketball playing surface dismantles to reveal a permanent ice hockey rink underneath, used by the Capitals. The NHL team is overdue: Perhaps a new coach and winning attitude will turn the team around in 1998.

• Concerts — Barry Manilow presented MCI's inaugural musical event, followed a month later by country singer Alan Jackson. Billy Joel is due in early spring of 1998. These visiting superstars get their own special dressing area, a four-room suite with a sauna/steam room, which you can see during a tour of the center (more on that later).

• Special events — The smooth ice glowed in various pastel hues, coordinating with spangled costumes worn by top skaters like Kristi Yamaguchi and Kurt Browning during the Equal World Professional Skating Championship in December.

The annual competition, previously held at USAirways Arena, was the first of several MCI special events, such as professional wrestling, Disney on Ice's "Beauty and the Beast" and the Ringling Brothers and Barnum & Bailey Circus.

• MCI National Sports Gallery — This unique interactive museum gives fans a chance to be a part of the action in baseball, basketball, football, golf, hockey, skiing, soccer and sportscasting. At nine Attraction Zones, you can participate in virtual games with stars like Chris Webber and Ken Griffey Jr., and, from a sportscaster's booth, call the plays for historic sports moments. Visitors also experience the multimedia *A Nation of Sports-Lovers* exhibit and view historic memorabilia like the basketball Wilt Chamberlain used to score his 25,000th point.

The gallery also houses the American Sportscasters Association Hall of Fame, featuring such famous voices as Red Barber and Harry Caray. Admission to the gallery, including credits to try out each Attraction Zone, is $9.50 for adults, $7.50 for kids 12 years and younger. Admission to the gallery alone is $5.50 for adults, $3.50 for kids 12 and younger. Hours generally are 10 to 10 Monday through Saturday, 10 to 6 on Sundays without events, 10 to 10 on Sundays with events. Call (202) 661-5133 for information.

• Tours — Get a behind-the-scenes look at the center during a one-hour tour that includes, as mentioned earlier, a look at the "Presidential Suite" star dressing room. You'll also see a Discovery Channel film about the Nation's Capital, the teams' locker rooms, the television control room, a luxury suite (these cost $100,000 to $175,000 annually, so they're usually inaccessible to most of us) and everyone's favorite ice-smoothing machine, the Zamboni.

Tours take place hourly, from 10 AM to 4 PM daily, starting at the box office in the F Street lobby. Admission is $7.50 for adults and $5 for children ages 12 and younger. Call (301) 350-1500 for tour information.

• Food — Want to watch the Wizards work out? The three-floor Velocity Grill restaurant overlooks the team's practice court. The sports-themed restaurant, at F and 6th streets, also features sports and entertainment videos, more than 100 beer taps and hand-held, electronic ordering and payment gizmos. Entrees start at around $10, and kids' meals are available for around $3 to $4.45. Hours are from 11:30 AM to midnight daily. Call (202) 347-7780 for more information.

The center also houses 24 concession stands, with traditional stadium items as well as Chinese food, grilled sandwiches and desserts. Many are open during nonevent,

— continued on next page

main concourse hours, from 9 AM to 4 PM Monday through Friday. Be prepared for the prices: We paid $4 for a soft pretzel and $3 for a soda!

•MCI arena Net Stations — Seventeen multimedia kiosks in the arena's main and upper concourses and sports gallery let visitors play trivia games, create digital postcards and access sports and tourism information.

• Shopping — The interactive Discovery Channel Store: Destination Washington, D.C., features international merchandise in a unique setting that includes three themed levels: beneath the earth's surface, animal habitats and world cultures, and outer space. The store includes discovery-related exhibits.

Customers at Modell's Sporting Goods can watch games on 12 television monitors while they shop. The store sells licensed home team merchandise and other apparel.

• Miscellaneous features — The center — built in compliance with the Americans and Disabilities Act — features 175 to 204 seats accessible for wheelchair-bound patrons and their companions. Call (301) 350-3400, extension 1370. Other services for the disabled include Braille signs and menus, TTY phones, 12 elevators, assisted listening devices and lowered counters.

The building boasts 24 restrooms, with extra toilets in the women's rooms. Three restrooms are designed for family use. Your best bet, as we mentioned above, is to take Metro to the center. The adjacent stop, Gallery Place-Chinatown, is on the Red, Yellow and Green lines. If taking the Metro from the suburbs, give yourself at least an hour: Crowds can be heavy, and trains slower, before big events. If you choose to drive, you'll find 7,000 parking spaces in lots and garages within a 10-minute walk. The center's own 500 spaces, accessible on 6th Street between F and G streets, are open to the public only during the day and nonevent weekend hours. Taxi stands for center visitors are at the corner of 5th and F streets and 8th and F streets. Concerned about safety? The center is equipped with a police command post, complete with two holding cells!

The arena's marketing center is at 325 7th Street NW, Washington, D.C., (202) 624-9732. You can also call the MCI Center information line at (202) 628-3200.

with the team, and Mike Mussina will continue as the ace of the pitching staff.

Going to see an O's game is much easier and more enjoyable than it used to be for Metro Washingtonians. Oriole Park at Camden Yards is a good half-hour closer than Memorial Stadium, the team's home for 38 years, and sits in a wonderful attraction-filled area easily accessed by rail, bus and automobile.

From Northern Virginia, Suburban Maryland and the District, just take the Baltimore/Washington Parkway north into Baltimore and the stadium is right there looming in front of you as you near the downtown area. It's a straight shot and the route is well-marked. You can also take I-95 into Baltimore, which feeds into where the Parkway hits the city, but this route is a bit longer and subject to more traffic hassles. Want to ride the train? Just take Metrorail to Union Station where you pick up a MARC

(Maryland's passenger railroad system) train to the Baltimore station literally right next to the stadium; the trip takes about 45 minutes.

Camden Yards seats about 48,000 people, a perfect size for baseball, and offers a great view from virtually every seat. Modern yet old-fashioned in an architectural sense, this is no boilerplate concrete doughnut of a stadium. It's truly a ballpark designed for the way baseball was meant to be played, with the city skyline as a backdrop. You'll see no artificial turf, no dome and no annoying pillars disrupting the sight lines, but you will find plenty of wonderful food and drink and a particularly friendly atmosphere. (The seating areas are smoke-free, by the way; smoking is permitted only on the concourse.) From a fan's perspective, you couldn't ask for more except maybe another World Series title.

Even the stadium's location is interesting.

Camden Yards sits in a historic area of downtown Baltimore and masterfully incorporates the nearly 100-year-old B&O Warehouse, which looms just beyond the right field wall. Refurbished during construction of the stadium, the warehouse now houses office space for the team, along with a cafeteria, bar/lounge and the exclusive, members-only Camden Club. During the early 1900s, a piece of land that's now part of the outfield was the site of a house/watering hole called Ruth's Cafe, operated by the father of baseball's immortal George Herman "Babe" Ruth, a Baltimore native.

Capitalizing on the popularity of the O's in Metro Washington, an Orioles Baseball Store at 914 17th Street NW in the District, (202) 296-BIRD, sells team memorabilia. The store is open from 9:30 AM to 6 PM Monday through Friday, and 10 AM to 4:30 PM on Saturday.

The Orioles's 162-game, 1998 season — with 81 home games — runs March 31 through September 20, finishing up against the rival Yankees. Tickets, which went on sale in January, range in price from $7 (for standing room only) to $35, and many games sell out quickly. Bargain Nights — set for April 1, 2, 15, 16, 27 and 28 and September 15 — feature $6 tickets in the left field upper reserved and bleacher seats. Kids ages 12 and younger can join the O's Dugout Club. The $3 membership fee includes a T-shirt, membership card, keychain, poster and discounts for four pre-selected games. Call the information number above, or write to O's Dugout Club, 333 W. Camden Street, Baltimore, MD 21201.

Minor Leagues

Northern Virginia

Prince William Cannons
G. Richard Pfitzner Stadium, 7 County Complex Ct., Woodbridge, Va.
• (703) 590-2311
Think there's no such thing as a good, old-fashioned, up-close baseball game with reasonably priced admission? Head to Pfitzner Stadium to watch the Cannons, the Class A affiliate of the St. Louis Cardinals. These Minor League games provide inexpensive family entertainment and a chance to watch future big-leaguers in action: Past Cannons players include Bernie Williams, Andy Pettit, Barry Bonds and the championship Florida Marlins' Bobby Bonilla.

The Cannons play 70 games each season — running from mid-April to early September — at the 6,000-seat stadium off Davis Ford Road in Woodbridge. Carolina League opponents include the Durham Bulls, a team made famous a few years back by the hit movie *Bull Durham* that starred Kevin Costner.

Despite a so-so record — 69 wins and 70 losses in 1997 — the team often draws sellout crowds, especially on Saturday nights that feature such promotions as mini-bat and baseball cap giveaways. Fans enjoy the goofy between-innings contests, like mock sumo wrestling and dizzy-bat races. Ticket prices range from $4 to $9, with supermarket-sponsored discounts available on some weeknights. Weeknight and Saturday games begin early evening, while Sunday games are played during the afternoon. The team caters to kids, with a special smoke- and alcohol-free family seating area, a kids' club and frequent promotions. Youngsters who wait near the locker room after the game often meet players, who, unlike most Major League superstars, usually prove more than happy to sign autographs. They've even been known to supply the baseballs!

Suburban Maryland

Bowie Bay Sox
Prince George's Stadium, 4101 Northeast Crain Hwy., Bowie, Md. • (301) 805-6000
The Bay Sox, a Class AA affiliate of the Baltimore Orioles, play in the Eastern League. Like the Cannons, the Bay Sox offer fun, family entertainment. Tickets range in price from $6 to $10, with discounts available some weeknights. Children ages 12 and younger who wear their baseball or softball team jerseys get free general admission to the 10,000-plus-seat stadium. Just for kids, the stadium includes an amusement area with a carousel, jungle gym, games, face painting and concession stand with all food items priced at $1. The Junior Baysox club, $6 for youngsters ages 5 to 14, includes a T-shirt, certificate, membership card and invitation to a baseball clinic.

Frederick Keys
Harry Grove Stadium, 6201 New Design Rd., Frederick, Md. • (301) 662-0013, (301) 831-4200 Montgomery County

The Orioles' Class A affiliate, the Keys compete in the Carolina League, which includes the rival Cannons. The team had its best-ever record, 45-25, in the first half of 1997, and its worst-ever record, 24-46, in the second half. The Keys lost in the first round of the playoffs to the eventual champion Lynchburg Hillcats. Fans have watched the likes of Brady Anderson, Armando Benitez, Ben McDonald and David Segui before they were stars. Ticket prices range from $3 to $9, and some promotions, such as fireworks nights, sell out in advance. The Junior Keys Club, $6 for kids ages 12 and younger, includes a T-shirt and clinic with Keys coaches and players.

The Hagerstown Suns
Municipal Stadium, 274 E. Memorial Blvd., Hagerstown, Md. • (301) 791-6266

Visit the Suns' 68-year-old Municipal Stadium to see a piece of baseball history: This is where Willie Mays played his first professional game. An A affiliate of the Toronto Blue Jays, the Suns play in the South Atlantic League. They've boasted such future stars as Mike Mussina, Arthur Rhodes, Billy Ripken, José Mesa and Bob Milacki. Admission ranges from $3 for youths and seniors to $7 for reserved seats. The Knothole Gang kids' club, $5 annually, features a T-shirt, certificate and card entitling the bearer to 25¢ admission to certain games.

Basketball

Professional

The Washington Wizards
MCI Center, 601 F St. NW, Washington, D.C. • (202) 432-SEAT, (703) 573-SEAT

Redskins or no Redskins, for some people, basketball is the only game in town. It's easy to understand why. Metro Washington, from the public and private high schools on through the college ranks, is a veritable breeding ground for top basketball talent.

An NBA powerhouse in the late 1970s as the Bullets, the Wizards have been mired in mediocrity for some time. However, with an infusion of some superb young talent — lottery draft pick Juwan Howard, former Golden State Warrior Chris Webber (acquired in a blockbuster trade) and superb veteran Rod Strickland — it appears the cornerstones for long-term success have finally been put into place. In 1997, the Wizards made the playoffs for the first time in years. Although they lost in the first round, they refused to go without a fight. Their games against the NBA champion Chicago Bulls proved surprisingly competitive. The future indeed looks bright. Under new coach Bernie Bickerstaff, the team got off to a winning start at its new home, MCI Center, during the 1997-98 season (see the "Close-up" in this chapter).

Most Wizards' tickets are priced at $19, $32 and $40. One thing's for certain about the Wizards: They play hard and they're fun to watch, winning or not.

Collegiate

American University
Bender Arena, Washington, D.C. • (202) 885-3267 tickets, (202) 885-DUNK sports updates

The Eagles, with an 11-16 1996-97 season, play in the Colonial Athletic Conference. The women's team, coached by Jeff Thatcher, finished 18-9 in the 1996-97 season. Tickets are $6 and $10 for men's games, and $6 for women's games.

Georgetown University
MCI Center, 601 F St. NW, Washington, D.C. • (202) 432-SEAT, (703) 573-SEAT

MCI Center's other roundball tenant, Georgetown University, has earned a reputation as one of the nation's strongest programs and one that demands that athletes work as hard in the classroom as they do on the court — a rarity in major college athletics today. John Thompson, the physically imposing and highly regarded coach of the Hoyas, deserves much of the credit. Under Thompson's direction, Georgetown has won a national championship, become a regular in post-season play, and remained a force in the formidable Big East Conference.

Georgetown alumni appear on team rosters throughout the NBA. But three names, all products of the Thompson era and all dominating big men, stand out — and up: Patrick Ewing, Dikembe Mutombo and Alonzo Mourning. With Thompson at the helm, it's a safe bet that Georgetown will continue to serve as a training school for future stars of the NBA.

Tickets to Hoyas home games cost $5, $15, $22.50 and $35.

George Washington University
Smith Center, Washington, D.C.
• (202) 994-6650

Not to be excluded from Metro Washington's major college basketball lineup, George Washington University is an emerging program in its own right.

Coach Mike Jarvis, who has never had a losing season as a head coach, has engineered a dramatic turnaround at "GW" in a relatively short period of time, guiding the Colonials to a lofty position in the tough Atlantic 10 Conference and notching a fair number of major upsets along the way. GW landed a berth in the NCAA tournament following the 1997-98 regular season.

You can catch the Colonials in action at the cozy Smith Center, located in the heart of the Northwest Washington campus. Tickets are $15 and $12 for men's games, and $9 for women's.

George Mason University
Patriot Center, 4400 University Dr.,
Fairfax, Va. • (703) 993-3000

Without marquee players competing in a marquee conference, sometimes it takes a marquee coach to carry a basketball program to the next level and beyond the first round of the NCAA tournament. Such was the case at George Mason, where the well-traveled Paul Westhead — whose vast coaching history includes a stint in the NBA with the Los Angeles Lakers — installed his hyper-paced "Paul Ball" style of play that has become his trademark. It didn't take long for the Patriots' Colonial Athletic Conference foes to discover what fast-break basketball is really all about (triple-digit scores are not uncommon). Still, the Patriots finished the 1996-97 season with a disappointing 10-17 record. The 1997-98 season brought a new coach, Jim Larranga.

Women's coach Jim Lewis resigned early in the 1997-98 season to accept a new job: head coach of the WNBA Washington Mystics, a position that fulfills his longtime dream to coach professional basketball. At George Mason, he won the most games of any women's coach in the school's history. He departed with a 201-177 record. Associate Coach Debbie Taneyhill moved into the head coaching spot for the remainder of the season.

Lucky for the spectators trying to keep up with the action on the floor, George Mason's home arena in Fairfax is the comfy 10,000-seat Patriot Center, the only sports/entertainment facility of its kind in Northern Virginia. Call for ticket information. The men's team plays about 15 home games, with tickets selling for $10 each. The women's team plays approximately 12 home games, with tickets priced at $5. The arena also hosts special sporting events such as the Harlem Globetrotters, tennis and beach volleyball tournaments and gymnastics programs.

Howard University
Burr Gymnasium, 6th and Girard Sts.
NW, Washington, D.C. • (202) 806-7140

These small but powerful Mid-Eastern Athletic Conference teams have played admirably in recent years. Tickets for both men's and women's Bison games are $6 general admission, and $10 reserved.

Photo: Courtesy of the Baltimore Area Convention and Visitors Association

Oriole Park at Camden Yards, home of the Baltimore Orioles,
is easily accessed by rail, bus and automobile.

University of Maryland
Cole Field House, Campus Dr., College Park, Md. • (301) 314-7070 or (800) 462-TERP tickets, (301) 314-TERP updates

Another of the region's prominent basketball programs is the University of Maryland, which holds court at Cole Field House.

The past couple of years have seen a dramatic turnaround in Terps basketball, particularly since Maryland alumnus Gary Williams, a proven winner with other major-college programs, took over as coach. Buoyed by a strong showing in the 1994 NCAA Tournament, Maryland is again flexing its hoops muscle both nationally and within that basketball paradise known as the Atlantic Coast Conference. Their 1996-97 record was 21-11. The 1997-98 season was one of major contrasts: The Terps beat top-ranked North Carolina in overtime, 89-83, just days after a 104-72 home loss to Duke. Erratic behavior notwithstanding, Gary Williams' charges were able to snag a bid to the NCAA tournament. The women's team finished their 1996-97 season with a respectable 18-10 record. Tickets to their home games, also played at Cole, are $5 for adults, and $3 for people ages 18 and younger. Tickets to the men's games are $21.

Pro Football

Washington Redskins
Jack Kent Cooke Stadium, 1600 Raljon Rd., Landover, Md. • (301) 276-6050

Just how high a pillar do the men in burgundy and gold occupy in the community? Without even getting into the amazing depth of the news coverage, consider that home games have been sold out for more than 30 years (an NFL record) and, with thousands on the waiting list for season tickets, even with the new 80,000-seat stadium, will likely remain sold out for the foreseeable future. The lucky season ticket holders pay $40 to $60 per ticket (executive suites cost from $59,950 to $159,950). You can buy tickets through brokers, but it'll cost you a pretty penny. The good news about consistent sellouts is you never have to be concerned about home games being blacked out on local TV — an unfortunate reality in some NFL markets. Even in the midst of a years-long rebuilding program, when victories have been few and as sophomore head coach Norv Turner works to return the Redskins to their glory days, the stands continue to be filled. Fortunately, most football fans in Metro Washington aren't of the fair-weather variety. They have reason to expect big things in 1998, as management doled out blockbuster bucks to snare two blocks of granite for the defensive front: former 49er Pro Bowler Dana Stubblefield and ex-Bengal Dan Wilkinson, who was the first player selected in the NFL draft a few years back.

Another fact to frame your perspective on just how big the Redskins are in this neck of the woods: It's not unheard of for the fate of season tickets to be determined in divorce court or estate settlements. Yes, they're that coveted.

Perhaps most compelling is that in a region where people are too often divided by political party, race, gender or socioeconomic status, the Redskins have remained the one unifying force that transcends these and other barriers. It's truly a phenomenon to behold.

Trying to be one of the 80,000 fans who jam Cooke Stadium for every home game, however, is tough to do when there are no tickets for sale to the general public. A limited number are available each summer for the one or two home preseason games in August, but they usually sell out, too. So you've got to act fast. The eye-catching, contemporary new stadium, built in just 17 months, took years of planning and false starts, but overall, fans seem pleased with the results. On the plus side, the stadium offers roomier seats, highly visible scoreboards in each end zone, 38 concession stands with food ranging from traditional stadium fare to crab cakes and Mexican food, larger restrooms and, for those with the big bucks, two tiers of luxury seats. On the

down side, there's traffic, traffic, traffic! With no nearby Metrorail access, the stadium offers limited transportation options.

Ice Hockey

Washington Capitals
MCI Center, 601 F St. NW, Washington, D.C. • (202) 432-SEAT, (703) 573-SEAT

The Capitals also boast a high entertainment value. While they've had a long string of playoff appearances, the club has yet to put it all together each spring when it counts. The elusive Stanley Cup remains just that for the Caps — elusive. If you thought Washington wasn't a hockey town, think again. While no one is about to mistake the Nation's Capital for such NHL-crazed places as Montreal, Toronto, Boston or even Dallas, the Capitals have built a strong following since first taking to the ice in 1974.

Despite the absence of that coveted Stanley Cup — tough to acquire when the season ends with an early exit from the playoffs — the Caps have nevertheless developed into a consistent winner and post-season contender. Under Bryan Murray, the winningest coach in team history, the Caps posted five consecutive second-place finishes in the Patrick Division during the 1980s, topped by a first-place showing in 1988-89.

Sweeping personnel moves over the years, including some unpopular and questionable trades of star players, have yet to yield the dividends necessary to win it all. Seemingly always on the brink of greatness, the Caps have yet to achieve it. The team went into the 1997-98 season with a new coach, Ron Wilson, and new general manager, George McPhee. A playoff berth appeared likely at this writing, with sharpshooter Peter Bondra having an all-star season and "Oly the Goalie" — Olaf Kolzig — performing well in net.

Ticket prices for Capitals games are $12, $28, $35, $38, $41 and $45.

Chesapeake Icebreakers
Show Place Arena, 14900 Pennsylvania Ave., Upper Marlboro, Md.
• (301) 952-7999

The new East Coast Hockey League's

only Maryland team plays in a Prince George's County arena just off the Capital Beltway. The minor league Chesapeake Icebreakers, an AHL and NHL farm team, compete through late March, with nearly all games starting at 7:30 PM. With tickets priced at $15 for adults and $10 for kids ages 12 and younger, the games are especially popular with families.

Soccer

D.C. United
RFK Stadium, E. Capitol and 22nd Sts. SE, Washington, D.C. • (202) 547-9077

The 1994 World Cup games played in Washington and other U.S. cities were a huge success by any measure — a surprise, perhaps, to some people except diehard fans, including those among the region's diverse and substantial immigrant population. Now, soccer ("football" to the rest of the world) is beginning to catch on with the American public, in part because of the infant Major League Soccer league. Washington's MLS team couldn't have gotten off to a much better start: It won the first two MLS Cups. The champion team finished its 1997 season with a 21-11 record and wowed fans with its rapid goal scoring. The team plays at RFK Stadium, former home of the Washington Redskins.

Washington Warthogs
USAirways Arena, 1 Harry S. Truman Dr., Landover, Md. • (301) 350-3400

The Washington Warthogs, a member of the Continental Indoor Soccer League (CISL), plays at the former home of the Washington Wizards. Purists may scoff at this indoor version of the game, which is played on the carpeted floor of cavernous arenas built for basketball and hockey, but it does have its mo-

ments and makes for a unique if not fairly entertaining climate-controlled spectator sport option during the sweltering summer months. Call for schedule and ticket information.

Horsing Around

Horse-racing enthusiasts are in luck. Maryland is home to several equine venues (Virginia has approved horse betting as the latest form of gambling, but the first local tracks have yet to open; the sport is illegal in the District).

From April through August, and again from early September through November, riders saddle up for polo most every Sunday afternoon in West Potomac Park, across from the Lincoln Memorial. General admission is free.

Steeplechase events, usually held in the spring and fall in the hunt country of Metro Washington, are as much social gatherings as they are sporting spectacles. Kentucky we're not, yet the influence of the equine industry is astounding in Virginia and Maryland. Entire towns such as Middleburg, Warrenton and Keswick in Virginia, and Upper Marlboro and Potomac in Maryland, are dedicated to the care, training and competition of the sport horse. Both states are home to a large number of equine-related organizations and happenings, far too many to list. Check local newspapers, especially the weekend/calendar sections, for steeplechase dates and locations.

Here are some of the region's most popular arenas and events.

Northern Virginia

Contact the Loudoun Tourism Council, 108-D South Street SE, Leesburg, Virginia, (800) 752-6118, for a free "Welcome to Virginia Horse Country" brochure. Here are two Loudoun County highlights:

INSIDERS' TIP

If you just can't get enough of the Redskins, pick up a copy of *Redskins — A History of Washington's Team*, published by *The Washington Post*. It's chock-full of articles by *Post* sportswriters, every stat you could ever want, loads of photos and even trivia quizzes. You'll find it at area bookstores, supermarkets and pharmacies.

The Fairfax Hunt
Belmont Plantation, Va. Rt. 7, 4 miles east of Leesburg, Va. • (703) 787-6673

This annual event, usually held the third Saturday of September, features racing over hurdles and timber. Post time is 2 PM.

Morven Park Races
P.O. Box 6228, Leesburg, VA 20178 • (703) 777-2414

Spectators enjoy tailgating parties before these steeplechase races, held the second Saturday of October.

Suburban Maryland

Laurel Park
Md. Rt. 198 and Laurel Racetrack Rd., Laurel, Md. • (301) 725-0400

Live thoroughbred racing takes place Wednesdays through Sundays January through March, late June through late August and October through December. Admission is $3 for grandstand seats, and $5 for clubhouse seats. Reservations are recommended for the Turf Club Dining Room, which features televised races and a view of the track and charges a $2 seating fee. The 9-furlong track is open all year, with simulcast racing when live races aren't held. Minimum betting usually is $2. A free Pony Pals kids' club features a monthly Sunday morning stable tour, craft activity and live entertainment for children ages 2 to 12, accompanied by an adult.

Pimlico Race Course
Hayward and Winner Aves., Baltimore, Md. • (410) 542-9400

The showcase event at this historic course (dating to 1743), is, of course, the Preakness, the second jewel in Thoroughbred racing's Triple Crown, held the third Saturday in May. Tickets are hard to come by for this prestigious event, but you can watch other thoroughbred racing during April, May and most of June. Simulcast races are televised the rest of the year. Admission is $3 for grandstand seats, and $5 for clubhouse seats. Reservations are recommended for the enclosed dining room, which charges a $2 seating fee.

See the Laurel Park entry for information about kids club activities, which also take place at this course.

Rosecroft Raceway
6336 Rosecroft Dr., Fort Washington, Md. • (301) 567-4000

Just a few minutes from the Wilson Bridge, this raceway features live harness racing starting at 7:20 PM Thursday through Saturday, most of the year. Patrons also can watch simulcast thoroughbred races. Admission is $2, as are minimum bets. You also can watch the races from an enclosed dining room, which offers televisions at each table; reservations are recommended.

Show Place Arena
14900 Pennsylvania Ave., Upper Marlboro, Md. • (301) 952-7900, (301) 952-7999

This 5,800-seat, multipurpose arena often plays host to horse-riding competitions. Call for a rundown of upcoming events.

The Washington International Horse Show
USAirways Arena, 1 Harry S. Truman Dr., Landover, Md. • (301) 840-0281, (202) 432-SEAT

This annual event, held for more than a week each fall (October 18 through 25 in 1998) features some of the world's top show jumpers, hunters and dressage riders, not to mention those entertaining canine show-stealers, the racing Jack Russell terriers. This is a fun event that the whole family can enjoy. Tickets for the evening shows usually run $18 and up. Daytime event admission is $6. Tickets go on sale in mid-August, but also are available at the door.

Golf

Kemper Open
TPC at Avenel, 10000 Oaklyn Dr., Potomac, Md. • (301) 469-3737

Major professional golf tournaments don't appear very often on Washington's sports calendar, so it's understandable why so many local enthusiasts of the game mark off the days in anticipation of one event: the nationally televised Kemper Open, held in May or June at the TPC (Tournament Players Championship) at Avenel course in beautiful Potomac, Maryland. The event is set for June 1 through 7 in 1998, and features a $2 million purse.

Tickets are available to the public, but they can go fast, especially if some of golf's big names are taking part in the tourney. Justin Leonard won in 1997. Daily Grounds tickets are $25 and grounds and pavilion admission is $35, through April 15; admission at the gate is $5 higher.

Tennis

Washington Tennis Classic
William H.G. FitzGerald Tennis Center, 16th and Kennedy Sts. NW, Washington, D.C. • (202) 722-5949

Tennis anyone? If the answer is yes, then the showcase event to see is the Washington Tennis Classic, held each summer (usually in July), on the fringes of beautiful Rock Creek Park. The lineup usually features several stars of the tennis world in addition to lower-ranked players and some solid local talent. USAir Arena also hosts occasional tennis events, often for charity.

Auto Racing

Yes, we even have car racing. To take a vicarious trip around the oval and past the checkered flag, consider the following.

Hagerstown Speedway
15112 National Pk., west of Hagerstown, Md. • (301) 582-0640

Stock-car racing is featured on Sunday afternoons during spring and fall, and Saturday nights during summer late February through October. General admission is $8, with children younger than 12 admitted free. Special events like TNT Monster Trucks and World of Outlaw Sprints take place every other weekend. The track is a half-mile clay oval, semi-banked.

Old Dominion Speedway and Dragstrip
Rt. 234, Manassas, Va. • (703) 361-7753

Stock car and drag racing take place Friday and Saturday, March through September.

Watersports

It's free, it's exciting and it's a lot closer than you think. Here are some of your best bets.

Washington, D.C.

Washington Boat Show
Washington Convention Center, Washington, D.C. • (202) 789-1600

If the water is enough to put you in the mood for looking at some larger and more expensive pleasure craft, keep an eye out for this annual trade show, held each February.

Northern Virginia

Great Falls Park
Old Dominion Dr. and Georgetown Pk., Great Falls, Va. • (703) 285-2966

For a different kind of thrill, head over to this national park in the well-heeled Fairfax County community of Great Falls, and watch gutsy kayakers and occasional canoeists attempt to negotiate the wicked Great Falls of the Potomac River, just north of Washington. Definitely not for the faint of heart.

Even if you show up and don't spot any boaters, you won't have wasted a trip. The water and surrounding countryside are spectacular in themselves and worth a look any time of year. See our Parks and Recreation chapter for more on this park.

Suburban Maryland

United States Powerboat Show
City Dock, Annapolis, Md. • (410) 268-8828

The boating mecca of Annapolis lays claim to hosting the world's largest in-the-water exhibition, held in October at the City Dock.

United States Sailboat Show
City Dock, Annapolis, Md. • (410) 268-8828

Boating purists get their due as well in October with this show, also held at the City Dock.

The new Jack Kent Cooke Stadium is home for the Washington Redskins.

Running

Marine Corps Marathon
Downtown Washington, D.C., next to the National Mall • (703) 690-3431

This fall classic (usually in November) sometimes referred to as the "People's Marathon" remains accessible to everyday runners as well as serious contenders. Those who would rather watch than actually attempt to run 26 miles and 385 yards, will find abundant prime vantage points along the course, which begins and ends in Arlington but canvasses a large section of the National Mall area downtown.

Mobil 1 Invitational
George Mason University, Fairfax, Va. • (703) 993-3270

Track-and-field fans will want to mark their calendars for this annual event, held in February at George Mason University. The meet, often nationally televised, brings together some of the world's finest athletes and affords spectators an up-close (and very affordable) look at some of the most exciting but least appreciated events in all of sports.

No other American
urban area can claim as
many National Park
Service properties as
can Metro Washington.

Parks and Recreation

From small, leafy plots of land in the inner city to the giant state and regional parks found in the suburbs, our fair capital area features an abundance of lush, green spaces, beckoning both nature lovers and outdoor sports enthusiasts. With almost 90,000 protected acres, Washington, D.C. rates as one of the country's greenest metropolitan areas, according to the Greater Washington Board of Trade. No other American urban area can claim as many National Park Service properties as can Metro Washington. It's one of the many perks of being in or near the Nation's Capital.

Metro Washington also boasts scores of recreation centers offering gymnasiums, swimming pools, fitness rooms, sports leagues, classes and camps.

This chapter presents a brief survey of prominent national, state, regional and local parks in the National Capital Area and follows with information about recreation centers and other resources for leisurely pursuits. Note that when we don't list park hours, you'll find the park open from dawn until dark.

Parks

Washington, D.C.

Anacostia Park
1900 Anacostia Dr. SE, Washington, D.C.
• (202) 690-5182

One of the biggest parks operated by the city, this 750-acre park along the Anacostia River features a bird sanctuary for waterfowl, picnic areas and playgrounds, an outdoor pool, playing fields and courts and an outdoor roller-skating pavilion.

Chesapeake & Ohio Canal National Historical Park
Georgetown Visitor Center, 1057 Thomas Jefferson St. NW, Washington, D.C.
• (202) 653-5190

In the 1800s, the Chesapeake & Ohio Canal was built to link Washington with the western reaches of the Potomac River. It stretches 184 miles from Georgetown to Cumberland, Maryland, passing through 74 lift locks. In 1971, the entire length became a national park, and today the C&O Canal and Towpath is one of Washington's and Suburban Maryland's most coveted recreational retreats. In 1996, in the aftermath of one of the region's biggest ever snowstorms, floodwaters devastated much of the canal and its adjacent pathways. Volunteers pitched in to help with cleanup efforts, and by the summer of 1997, bikers and joggers once again enjoyed the tree-lined gravel pathways extending along the route. The canal itself, meanwhile, makes for gentle canoeing and kayaking.

Visitors also can take an hour-long, guided ride aboard the *Georgetown*, an authentic replica of a mule-pulled, 80-person canal boat. The schedule varies seasonally, but the boat generally runs from mid-April through mid-October. Admission is $3.50 for children and seniors, and $4 for adults. During the summer at 4 PM every other Sunday, free concerts take place on the canal, between Thomas Jefferson and 30th streets.

Kenilworth Aquatic Gardens
Intersection of Douglass St. and Anacostia Ave. NE, Washington, D.C.
• **(202) 426-6905**

Metro Washington sits amid a region of beautiful and fragile wetlands. At this lovely national park in Northeast D.C. naturalists can spend an afternoon traversing 11 acres of aquatic gardens featuring dozens of species of pond and marginal plants, such as waterlilies, lotuses and hyacinths.

Arrive first thing in the morning in the summer to get a good look at both night- and day-blooming waterlilies. More than 40 natural ponds attract water birds, frogs, turtles and kids. Take a guided tour at 9 and 11 AM and 1 PM on weekends and holidays, Memorial Day to Labor Day. Tours also may be arranged at other times, depending on staff availability. The park is open daily from 7 AM to 4 PM. The visitors' center is open from 8 AM to 4 PM.

The National Mall
900 Ohio Dr. SW, Washington, D.C.
• **(202) 426-6841**

The Park Service's domain begins with the National Mall, that vast esplanade as envisioned by the capital city's French designer, Pierre Charles L'Enfant. The three-mile expanse of green extends westward from the foot of Capitol Hill to the Lincoln Memorial and Potomac River. It contains the highest density of museums and monuments in the world. (See our Annual Events, Arts, Attractions and Kidstuff chapters for more on those.)

The Mall, as you'll probably discover, is every bit as humble as it is inspiring. It was designed to be used by the people, and used it is. Visitors love to walk their pets, jog, toss Frisbees and fly kites. Informal games of soccer, volleyball, softball and touch football are almost as common a sight here as the museums and monuments. From spring through fall, Capitol Hill staffers, among others, use the Mall for their various athletic leagues.

The Mall is also the site of some of the nation's most important public gatherings. In 1963, for instance, Dr. Martin Luther King, Jr. led one of the largest public demonstrations in U.S. history on these hallowed grounds (see our History chapter). Every four years, the East Mall, at the base of the Capitol Building, is the site of presidential inaugural swearing-in ceremonies. Whatever your political affiliation, the ceremony and the setting make for an unforgettable Washington experience.

Between the Washington Monument and Lincoln Memorial, you'll find the beautifully landscaped Constitution Gardens, just north of the long Reflecting Pool and near the Vietnam Veterans Memorial. Look for ducks, geese and other water birds swimming in the gardens' 6½-acre lake, as well as in the Reflecting Pool and the nearby Tidal Basin, around which thousands of delicate Japanese cherry trees burst into bloom each spring (see our Annual Events chapter for details about the National Cherry Blossom Festival). Look for the Tulip Library, which boasts more colors and varieties of the flower than you'd dream possible. If you'd like to take in the sights from the water, rent a pedal boat at the Tidal Basin Boat House, (202) 484-0206. They're generally available during good weather, April through October.

On the fringes of the river end of the National Mall, West Potomac Park contains the beautifully designed Franklin Delano Roosevelt Memorial, described in our Attractions chapter. East Potomac Park, south of the Tidal Basin, features picnic areas, a playground, an outdoor pool and tennis courts, a pathway for biking and exercising and an unusual statue, "The Awakening," that looks like a giant about to get up from his underground resting place. See our golf-course listings for information about the East Potomac Park Golf Course.

Rock Creek Park
3545 Williamsburg Ln. NW, Washington, D.C. • **(202) 426-6834**

The city's second most visible green space is Rock Creek Park, covering nearly 2,000 acres of rolling hills, woods, meadows and the name-

www.insiders.com

See this and many other **Insiders' Guide®** destinations online — in their entirety.

Visit us today!

sake boulder-strewn creek in the center of Northwest. President Benjamin Harrison signed the legislation creating Rock Creek Park in 1890, making it one of the nation's oldest city parks. It's also one of the world's largest urban parks, boasting plentiful amenities like its popular trails, frequented by hikers, bikers and horseback riders. Its bike trail is also part of a larger trail network, connecting the District with both Maryland and Virginia. The park also holds picnic and play areas, an equestrian center, a golf course, tennis courts, historic Pierce Mill, the Rock Creek Nature Center and Planetarium, Civil War sites and an art gallery. The Carter Barron Amphitheater hosts concerts throughout the summer. (See our Recreation listings and Kidstuff, Sports and Civil War chapters for more information on some of the most popular attractions within this urban forest.)

United States National Arboretum
3501 New York Ave. NE, Washington, D.C. • (202) 245-2726

The arboretum, a national site operated by the United States Department of Agriculture, showcases a lush variety of plants, flowers and trees. The 444-acre park bursts into an incredible blaze of color during the spring azalea and summer rhododendron seasons, prime times to plan a visit. The grounds are open from 8 AM to 5 PM, except on Christmas. Admission is free. The National Bonsai and Penjing Museum is open from 10 AM to 3:30 PM daily. The arboretum also boasts a gift shop and administrative building.

Northern Virginia

See our Civil War chapter for information about Manassas National Battlefield Park, and our Arts chapter for a description of Wolf Trap Farm Park for the Performing Arts.

Algonkian Regional Park
47001 Fairway Dr., Sterling, Va.
• (703) 450-4655

Set along the Potomac in eastern Loudoun County, this park features an outdoor pool, miniature golf, picnic tables and shelters, a nature trail, boat ramp, and boat and RV storage. The 500-acre park's riverfront cabins, available for rent year-round, offer a pleasant family camping experience. Call (703) 352-5900.

Bull Run Regional Park
7700 Bull Run Dr., Centreville, Va.
• (703) 631-0550

Not far from Manassas National Battlefield Park, Bull Run features scenic hiking trails and several acres of springtime wildflowers. A large outdoor pool includes a tropical-island-themed water slide. Visitors also enjoy trying their skills at miniature and disc golf and skeet- and trap-shooting at the Bull Run Shooting Center, (703) 830-2344, open 4 to 8 PM weekdays and 10 AM to 4:30 PM Saturdays and Sundays. The park also offers group and family camping. Call (703) 352-5900 for reservation information. The main park is open mid-March through November. Non-area residents must pay an entrance fee.

Burke Lake Park
7315 Ox Rd., Fairfax Station, Va.
• (703) 323-6600

A favorite with local fishing and boating enthusiasts, this 888-acre park features a 218-acre lake. You can rent rowboats or take a guided pontoon-boat tour of the lake, which includes an island sanctuary for waterfowl. The park also offers a campground, picnicking, play areas and more than 4 miles of hiking trails. See our Kidstuff chapter for more on the park's kid-pleasing attractions. See our Golf listings for information about the park's course.

Cameron Run Regional Park
4001 Eisenhower Ave., Alexandria, Va.
• (703) 960-0767

A favorite spot for cooling off on steamy summer days, Cameron Run is a water park with a large wave pool, three-flume water slide and water playground for youngsters. It's open Memorial Day weekend through Labor Day. Batting cages and miniature golf are open Mid-March through October.

George Washington's Grist Mill Historic State Park
VA. Rt. 235, 3 miles west of Mt. Vernon, Va. • (703) 339-7265

This interpretive historical site in Fairfax County offers tours of a reconstructed mill once used by the first president, who resided just down the road at his Mount Vernon estate.

George Washington Memorial Parkway
Turkey Run Park, McLean, Va.
• **(703) 285-2598**

In Northern Virginia, the George Washington Memorial Parkway and its adjacent Mount Vernon Trail provide spectacular riverside hiking and biking trails extending from the river banks opposite Theodore Roosevelt Island southward 18.5 miles to Mount Vernon. You'll also find boating opportunities and nature preserves, where you may spot resident waterfowl and other critters.

Great Falls Park
Old Dominion Dr. and Georgetown Pk., Great Falls, Va. • (703) 285-2966

Visit this park to view one of the most impressive natural sights in Metro Washington: the cascading Great Falls of the Potomac, plunging (in some places more than 35 feet) through a series of jagged rocks and gigantic boulders that make up Mather Gorge. The falls also can be viewed from the Maryland side of the river at the C&O National Historical Park. The park is a favorite with outdoor sports enthusiasts, from kayakers to rock climbers. The water can be as dangerous as it is beautiful, so pay attention to posted warning signs.

Stop by the park's Visitor Center, open from 10 AM to 4 PM, with longer hours during the warmer months, to see a 10-minute slide show, exhibits relating to the park's natural resources and to the Patowmack Canal, a project over which George Washington presided. Rangers lead special programs on weekends and holidays all year. The park intermittently charges admission of $4 per car, valid for three consecutive days. You can obtain an annual park pass, good for Great Falls and the C&O Canal, for $15. The park is open daily from 7 AM to dusk, except on Christmas. The gates are locked at dark.

Green Spring Gardens Park
4603 Green Spring Rd., Alexandria, Va.
• **(703) 642-5173**

This garden-filled park is a beautiful and popular spot for strolls and outdoor weddings. The historic Manor House, open noon to 4 PM Wednesday through Sunday, features a gift shop, art exhibits and special programs. See our Kidstuff chapter for information about children's programs.

Huntley Meadows Park and Visitor Center
3701 Lockheed Blvd., Hybla Valley, Va.
• **(703) 768-2525**

This 1,261-acre park draws nature lovers, who love to explore the meadows, forests and 2/3-mile boardwalk trail through the wetlands. Wildlife — from butterflies and songbirds to deer, beaver and waterfowl — abounds throughout the park, and can be watched from an observation tower. Park naturalists conduct hundreds of programs annually at the Visitor Center, which features exhibits pertaining to the area's natural resources. It's open from 9 AM to 5 PM Monday and Wednesday through Friday, and from noon to 5 PM Saturday and Sunday.

Lake Accotink Park
5660 Heming Ave., Springfield, Va.
• **(703) 569-3464**

Another popular Fairfax County park, Lake Accotink features wetlands, streams and a 77-acre lake with canoe, rowboat and pedal boat rentals, along with tour-boat rides. Visitors also can fish, play miniature golf, ride a carousel and hike trails in this 482-acre park.

Leesylvania State Park
2001 Daniel K. Ludwig Dr., Woodbridge, Va. • (703) 670-0372

This 508-acre park, off U.S. Route 1, in Prince William County offers precious access to the Potomac River, upon which visitors enjoy fishing and boating. Hiking and picnicking are also popular activities. On the National Register of Historic

---

INSIDERS' TIP

Pontoon-boat tours of several parks' lakes offer excellent opportunities to view wildlife such as herons and turtles.

Landmarks, Leesylvania sits on land once owned by Revolutionary War hero "Light Horse" Harry Lee and, later, the Fairfax family. A new visitors center with natural and historical exhibits is set to open the summer of 1998.

Mason Neck State Park
7301 High Point Rd., Lorton, Va.
• **(703) 550-0960**

This 1,800-acre park adjoins more than 2,000 acres designated as a wildlife refuge. Mason Neck is a birdwatcher's dream: Approximately 40 bald eagles nest among the towering pines and hardwoods. Observe them unseen in blinds placed along the 3.5 miles of hiking trails. With wetlands as well as fields and forests, the park proves ideal for environmental study. Visitors also enjoy picnicking, fishing, canoeing and windsurfing. The park is open 8 AM to dusk daily. Parking is $1 on weekdays, $2 on weekends.

Pohick Bay Regional Park
6501 Pohick Bay Dr., Lorton, Va.
• **(703) 339-6100**

Like neighboring Mason Neck State Park, this park in southeastern Fairfax County is home to nesting bald eagles. Water is the park's mainstay. Visitors can bring their own boats, or rent sailboats or pedal boats. The park also features an outdoor pool, miniature and disc golf, picnic areas and nature trails and bridle paths. You also can camp out here year-round at the family campground. See our Golf listings for information about the course here. Non-area residents must pay an entrance fee.

Prince William Forest Park
18100 Park Headquarters Rd., Triangle, Va. • **(703) 221-7181**

Part of the Quantico Creek watershed, Prince William Forest Park covers more than 18,500 acres of dense pine and hardwood forests and meandering creeks. The park's miles of trails beckon bikers, hikers and cross-country skiers, on those rare occasions when the region receives more than a dusting of snow. The Pine Grove Visitor Center, open from 8:30 AM to 5 PM daily, features exhibits about the area's resources and, on weekends, naturalist-led programs. The park offers plenty of tent sites for campers, as well as cabins for family camping during the summer and group camping year-round. Admission to the park, valid for three consecutive days, is $4 per car. An annual pass is $15.

Upton Hill Regional Park
6060 Wilson Blvd., Arlington, Va.
• **(703) 534-3437**

Upton Hill is known for its challenging, beautifully landscaped miniature golf course, open, along with batting cages, mid-March through October. The large outdoor pool is open Memorial Day weekend through Labor Day.

Suburban Maryland

See our Dance listing and Kidstuff and Arts chapter for information about Glen Echo Park.

Black Hill Regional Park
20930 Lake Ridge Dr., Boyds, Md.
• **(301) 972-3476**

With more than 1,850 acres, this park attracts trail lovers and fishing and boating enthusiasts. You can rent a canoe or rowboat, or ride on a guided pontoon boat, which offers tours on the hour, noon to 6 PM, on summer weekends. Admission is $2 per person. You may be lucky enough to spot beavers, muskrats, otters or other resident wildlife. The park attracts lots of waterfowl and other birds. The Visitors Center houses wildlife exhibits and is surrounded by natural gardens that attract songbirds and butterflies.

Cabin John Regional Park
7400 Tuckerman Ln., Rockville, Md.
• **(301) 469-7835**

This popular park features numerous recreational activities including indoor and outdoor tennis courts, (301) 365-2440, a year-round ice-skating rink, (301) 365-2246, handball and volleyball courts, playing fields and trails for bikers and hikers. There's also limited camping space. See our Kidstuff chapter for more on the park's child-pleasing attractions.

Great Falls Tavern, Chesapeake and Ohio Canal National Historical Park
11710 MacArthur Blvd., Potomac, Md.
• **(301) 299-2026**

The Maryland side of Great Falls and the

Photo: Courtesy of Jules Kitzen, NVRPA

Pohick Bay in southeastern Fairfax County is a
popular place to spend a summer afternoon.

C&O Canal looks remarkably similar to the way it appeared more than 100 years ago. It's a lovely park in which to bike, walk and take a narrated, hour-long canal boat ride aboard the mule-guided *Canal Clipper*, generally offered mid-April through the beginning of November. Admission is $7.50 for adults ages 15 to 61, $6 for seniors and $4 for children ages 3 to 14. Ages 2 and younger ride for free. The park's visitor center, open from 9 AM to 4:30 PM daily, features exhibits and an audiovisual presentation, as well as special programs. Park admission is the same as Great Falls' Virginia admission.

Greenbelt Park
6565 Greenbelt Rd., Greenbelt, Md.
• (301) 344-3948

Just off the Beltway in Prince George's County, this 1,100-acre park defies its highly urban setting with acres of wooded trails and special interpretive nature programs for kids. It also offers numerous campsites for tents and vehicles.

Little Bennett Regional Park
23701 Frederick Rd., Clarksburg, Md.
• (301) 972-6581

This park in upper Montgomery County is a popular site for family camping from

spring through fall, (301) 972-9222. Historic sites' remains accent the park's expansive network of hiking trails.

Louise F. Cosca Regional Park
11000 Thrift Rd., Clinton, Md.
• (301) 868-1397

This 500-acre Prince George's County park features a 15-acre lake for fishing and boating. You can rent rowboats and paddle boats. It also boasts indoor and outdoor tennis courts, (301) 868-6462, trails for hiking and horseback riding, athletic fields and a family campsite.

Robert M. Watkins Regional Park
301 Watkins Park Dr., Upper Marlboro, Md. • (301) 390-9224

Besides the many offerings for children, described in Kidstuff, this park of more than 400 acres boasts indoor and outdoor tennis courts, playing fields and camping sites, (301) 249-6900. It's a popular recreational site for Prince George's County residents.

Seneca Creek State Park
11950 Clopper Rd., Gaithersburg, Md.
• (301) 924-2127

Near Gaithersburg, this park's 6,000-plus

acres offer outstanding hiking, boating and fishing opportunities almost within eyesight of suburban housing developments. The Blue Heron pontoon boat takes visitors on naturalist-guided, one-hour tours on the 90-acre lake at 1:30 PM and 3 PM Saturday and Sunday during the summer and early fall months, at $1 per person.

Summit Hall Farm Park
502 S. Frederick Ave., Gaithersburg, Md.
• **(301) 258-6350**

Gaithersburg residents cool off at this pool with special features like 250-foot water slides, a frog slide, water fountains and a seal that spouts water. The surrounding grounds offer a playground with a ball pit and climbing equipment, a sand volleyball court, a concession stand, a miniature golf course and a five-hole "kiddie" course. Costs and hours vary.

Wheaton Regional Park
2000 Shorefield Rd., Wheaton, Md.
• **(301) 946-6396**

This Montgomery County favorite bustles with activity, particularly on weekends, when families and large groups flock to the park for some much-needed R&R. The park boasts numerous attractions for children — see our Kidstuff chapter for more on those — as well as hiking and biking trails; a 5-acre stocked lake for fishing; an ice-skating rink that's open October through March, (301) 649-2250; and sports courts and fields. You can walk or drive to the peaceful Brookside Gardens, offering 50 acres of various flowers and other plants, as well as a sparkling new visitors' center for educational programs.

Recreation

We could go on forever listing and describing the thousands of recreational opportunities available to residents throughout Metro Washington. Here's a sampling of popular resources to get you started in your leisurely pursuits. If you don't see your favorite activity listed individually here, contact your local recreation department. You'll find phone numbers in this chapter. Check our Parks listings in this chapter for camping, trails and sports court locations. Look at our Kidstuff and Senior Scene chapters for additional ideas for children and senior citizens.

Amusement Parks

Adventure World
13710 Central Ave., Largo, Md.
• **(301) 249-1500**

The closest theme park to Washington, Adventure World seems to grow in size and reputation annually. Formerly known as "Wild World," the 115-acre park still boasts a high concentration of water rides. Recent new attractions, touted by official "Spokeshero" Cal Ripkin, include Skull Island, a 10-acre, pirate-themed section featuring the uniquely terrifying Typhoon Sea Coaster. A hybrid of a roller coaster and log flume, the ride includes a backwards drop and a forward-facing 60-foot descent. Prepare to scream!

Renegade Rapids whisks riders along a simulated wild river, while Shipwreck Falls features a huge splash-inducing flume plunge. Don't miss the Tower of Doom, designed to simulate the sensation of free-falling from 15 stories at a speed of 56 mph. The park also offers three more roller coasters, the inverted, looping Mind Eraser; a wooden classic, The Wild One, featuring a 98-foot lift and 90-degree spiral helix; and The Python, a 360-degree vertical loop coaster.

INSIDERS' TIP

Keep track of upcoming hikes, runs and cycling events; recreational club activities; amateur sports leagues; and classes in such areas as diving and kayaking by checking out the "On the Move" listings in *The Washington Post*'s "Weekend" section, and by perusing these free periodicals: *Sports Focus Magazine*, 124 E. Diamond Avenue, Suite 7, Gaithersburg, Maryland, (301) 670-6717; and *Washington MetroSports Magazine*, 6733 Kenyon Drive, Alexandria, Virginia, (703) 768-6186.

Adventure World is open weekends during early May, and daily from Memorial Day weekend to Labor Day. It reopens early October through early November for the annual HallowScream, a festival with scary shows and events like haunted hay wagon and train rides geared toward all ages. Admission prices vary according to age and time of visit. See our Kidstuff chapter for a description of children's activities at Adventure World.

Ballooning

How about a birds-eye view of all that gorgeous green space we described earlier? The following FAA-certified pilots offer hot-air balloon excursions, complete with champagne and treats, at sunrise and sunset over the scenic Virginia and Maryland countrysides. Call at least a couple of weeks before the date you wish to book, and be flexible: Lousy weather or high winds can whip up before you know it, forcing a postponement. Don't forget your video camera! Your pilot will be happy to recommend a bed and breakfast, should you want to extend your getaway.

Northern Virginia

Balloons Unlimited
2946-O Chain Bridge Rd., Oakton, Va.
• **(703) 281-2300**

Owner Bob Thomas has been piloting balloons above Middleburg and the Shenandoah region for 21 years. Flights cost $150 per person and last approximately an hour. You can book your trip for any day of the week, April through mid-November. Thomas also offers ballooning classes, and sells balloons of the helium-filled variety at his Oakton store.

Suburban Maryland

Fantasy Flights
438 Girard St., #101, Gaithersburg, Md.
• **(301) 417-0000**

This 18-year-old company offers flights in a new, five-person balloon above the Sugarloaf Mountain countryside between Gaithersburg and Frederick, looking out over the Potomac toward Virginia and West Virginia. Owner/pilot Randy Danneman says that on a clear day, you can see, well, not forever, but all the way to downtown Washington. The cost is $200 per person for a 1- to 1½-hour flight. You'll also get a fancy flight certificate and a color picture of the balloon. Danneman offers flight instruction also.

Sky High Adventures
17513 Soper St., Poolesville, Md.
• **(301) 605-0500, (301) 972-7004**

Now in its 23rd year, Sky High Adventures is the oldest ballooning business in the Metro D.C. area. Trips generally cost $185 to $200 a person and travel for about an hour over upper Montgomery County. Owner/pilot Pat Michaels also offers individualized flight instruction.

Baseball

Ponce d'Leon Baseball Inc.
P.O. Box 73, Spencerville, MD 20868
• **(301) 989-0945**

Now, folks over 30 have a league of their own. About 500 adults, mostly men, play on this recreational league, with 10-game seasons played on Sundays during spring, summer and fall at fields in Montgomery and Fairfax counties. The teams don't keep standings, but players look forward to a single-elimination playoff at season's end. Registration is $125 per person per season, and a onetime uniform cost is $90.

Basketball

One On One Basketball Inc.
3811 39th St. NW, Washington, D.C.
• **(202) 244-2255**

This company offers individualized and team instruction in the fundamentals of shooting hoops, for children and adults. (Look for its Never Too Late Basketball clinics at local recreation centers.) Each class of a six- to 10-week session includes a scrimmage. The company also plans to begin an adult league. Call for a schedule of upcoming clinics and games.

Bicycling

Our biking buddies highly recommend *Chuck and Gail's Favorite Bike Rides*, a comprehensive guidebook by Chuck and Gail Helfer. It offers detailed maps and descriptions of 75 rides in the mid-Atlantic region, including 12 favorites in and around Washington. They even recommend lodgings and eateries. Look for it at bookstores and libraries.

Virginia Bicycling Federation Inc.
P.O. Box 5621, Arlington, VA 22205
• (703) 532-6101

This advocacy organization promotes bicycling safety, keeping its members informed about such issues as road and trail improvements, new riding facilities and legislation pertinent to cyclists. The bimonthly newsletter also includes information about upcoming rides and events sponsored by bicycling organizations throughout the state. Individual membership is $18 annually, and a family can join for $30 a year.

Washington Area Bicyclist Association
1819 H St. NW, Ste. 640, Washington, D.C. • (202) 872-9830

Metro Washington boasts several bicycling clubs. The best way to find out more about them, and discover which ones might be right for you, is to contact this advocacy organization, which promotes safe bicycling conditions and greater bicycle use in the Metro Washington area. The 2,200-member organization sponsors events like the National Capital Bicycle Tour and puts together newsletters and other publications. Membership is $25 per individual and $35 per family. Call to request a free copy of the *Bicycle Resource Directory*, listing clubs throughout the Washington area.

Birdwatching

Audubon Naturalist Society of the Central Atlantic States Inc.
8940 Jones Mill Rd., Chevy Chase, Md.
• (301) 652-9188

Beginning bird walks take place at Woodend, the society's headquarters and 40-acre wildlife sanctuary, at 8 AM on Saturdays from September through June. Meet at the Audubon Naturalist store entrance. Call for directions and information about other birding events. Call (301) 652-1088 to hear the Voice of the Naturalist, describing recent local bird sightings.

Fairfax Audubon Society
P.O. Box 82, Vienna, VA 22183
• (703) 256-6895

This organization sponsors frequent bird walks and educational programs, detailed in its *Potomac Flier* newsletter. Its meetings at the National Wildlife Federation, 8925 Leesburg Pk., Vienna, Virginia are free and open to the public. Society membership is $20 and includes *Audubon Magazine*.

Bowling

Nation's Capital Area Bowling Association
4710 Authority Pl., Camp Springs, Md.
• (301) 899-5978

Are you interested in joining a men's bowling league? Call for information about sanctioned leagues in your community.

Washington D.C. Area Women's Bowling Association
450 W. Broad St., Falls Church, Va.
• (703) 534-6561

Contact this association for information about sanctioned leagues in your neighborhood, details about rules or a membership application. Annual dues are $12.

Chess

U.S. Chess Center
1501 M St. NW, Washington, D.C.
• (202) 857-4922

Adults and children can take classes and participate in tournaments at this center in the heart of the city. It's open evenings, starting at 6 PM, Monday through Thursday, and weekends, noon to 6 PM. Chess enthusiasts shouldn't miss the center's free U.S. Chess Hall of Fame and Museum and gift shop.

Climbing

Adventure Schools Rock Climbing
4531 Everett St., Kensington, Md.
• **(301) 564-0941**

Before you attempt to scale those inviting formations at Great Falls and other local parks, learn from an expert. Dave Nugent gives lessons for beginners and advanced students, generally taking folks on-site for a day of hands-on education. He provides all the necessary equipment, too. A one-day course, for ages 11 and older, is $65; a two-day session is $110. Nugent also leads climbing adventures in places like West Virginia, North Carolina and New York. Sign up for a trip and you'll get preparatory lessons at no extra cost. The climbing school also offers indoor practice at its 24-foot tower with four climbable rope stations at Wakefield RECenter, 8100 Braddock Rd., Annandale, Virginia, from 4 to 9:30 PM Tuesdays and Thursdays, at $7 per person. Call for a course catalog.

Sportrock Climbing Centers
5308 Eisenhower Ave., Alexandria, Va.
• **(703) 212-7625**
14708 Southlawn Ln., Rockville, Md.
• **(301) 762-5111**

These indoor climbing facilities feature 30- and 40-foot walls with a multitude of routes. Novices can learn beginning climbing skills, and more experienced climbers can hone their techniques with indoor practice sessions. The centers are open noon to 11 PM Monday through Friday, 11 AM to 8 PM Saturday and noon to 8 PM Sunday. Daily rates are $13 for adults, $6 for ages 12 and younger. Discount passes and memberships also are available. See our Kidstuff chapter for information about children's programs here.

Dancing

Glen Echo Park
7300 MacArthur Blvd., Glen Echo, Md.
• **(301) 492-6282**

The 65-year-old Spanish Ballroom at this former amusement park turned national park still possesses the same sprung maple floor on which dancers swayed to the sounds of Big Bands led by the likes of the Dorseys and Artie Shaw. Today, you can take your pick from several dances offered on a regular basis.

Friday nights feature traditional country dances like contras, squares and mixers from 8:30 to 11:30 PM, usually at $5 a person. Two left feet? Show up an hour early, March through October, and you'll get a lesson in beginning contra dancing, included in the admission fee.

"Big Night Out" Saturdays attract as many as 500 people who relish swing dancing. Dances run from 9 PM to midnight, preceded by a beginners' workshop at 8 PM. Admission is usually $8 to $10.

During warm months, the first and third Sunday afternoons feature ballroom-style dancing from 4 PM to 6 PM, at $5 per person, preceded by waltz lessons at 3:30 PM. The second and fourth Sundays feature family events followed by international dancing from 3 PM to 5:30 PM, at $5 for adults and $4 for children, sponsored by the Folklore Society of Greater Washington. The society also holds traditional American dances on Sundays from 7:30 PM to 10:30 PM. Admission is $8.

Northern Virginia Country/Western Dance Association
P.O. Box 384, Merrifield, VA 22116
• **(703) 860-4941**

Southern Maryland Country & Western Dance Association
P.O. Box 1077, Clinton, MD 20735
• **(301) 868-5490**

Looking for a place to show off your Two Step? Contact either of these organizations, both of which sponsor workshops and dances and keep members posted on events throughout the region.

Diving

Professional Association of Diving Instructors (PADI) International
1251 E. Dyer Rd., Santa Ana, Ca.
• **(800) 729-7234**

Want to learn how to dive? PADI, the certification agency for diving instructors, will be happy to send you a list of certified diving establishments. Call the number listed.

Golfing

Our region offers numerous attractive and challenging public golf courses, many operated by local park authorities. We can't begin to list them all, but here's a representative sampling. Be sure to check our Sports chapter for information about the professional golf scene.

Washington, D.C.

East Potomac Park Golf Course and Driving Range
Hains Pt. and Ohio Dr. SW, Washington, D.C. • (202) 554-7660

How about a game of golf in the shadow of the Washington Monument? You'll aim right at the towering obelisk on the 9th hole of the par 31, 1929-yard Red Course. You'll also see the familiar landmark in the background of the 9th hole on the 18-hole regulation, par 72 Blue Course, which has a yardage of 6653 from the blue tees and 6197 from the white tees. The 9-hole regulation White Course is par 34, with a yardage of 2480. Set on National Park Service land next to the Potomac, the flat course is open year-round, generally from dawn to dusk.

Weekday greens fees are $9 for nine holes, and $15 for 18 holes; weekends and holidays, fees cost $12.25 for nine holes, and $19 for 18 holes. Power carts are available for $11.50 for 9 holes, and $18 for 18 holes. Rent a pull cart for $2.50 for 9 holes, and $3.50 for 18 holes. Rental clubs, available in half-sets, are $5.75 for nine holes, and $8.50 for 18. A double-deck, 100-station driving range is partially covered. A bucket of balls costs $3.75. The course also has a snack bar and grill, a fully stocked pro shop and, open mid-March through October, an 18-hole miniature golf course.

Langston Golf Course and Driving Range
26th and Benning Rd. NE, Washington, D.C. • (202) 397-8638

This 18-hole, par 72 course features tree-lined fairways and three holes with water. The total yardage is 6340. The facility includes a pro

shop, snack bar and driving range that's set to reopen in April after a renovation. Fees are nearly identical to those at East Potomac Park.

Rock Creek Park Golf Course
16th and Rittenhouse Sts. NW, Washington, D.C. • (202) 882-7332

Here's another of Rock Creek Park's many surprises: a hilly, wooded golf course in the middle of the city. The 18-hole, par 65 course has a yardage of 4800. Its signature hole, No. 17, features a downhill par 3 to a narrow fairway. The course has a snack bar and pro shop, but no driving range. Fees are virtually the same as those at the previously mentioned courses.

Northern Virginia

Burke Lake Golf Center
7315 Ox Rd., Fairfax Station, Va. • (703) 323-164

Adjacent to popular Burke Lake Park, this 18-hole, par 54 course with 2539 yardage boasts a pleasant, lakeside setting. It features a putting green and lighted driving range, along with a full-service clubhouse. Tee times for this and four other Fairfax County Park Authority courses can be arranged through an automated phone-in system, with a $25 annual subscription. Burke offers private and group lessons and a Junior Golf Program for youngsters ages 5 to 17.

Lansdowne Golf Club
44050 Woodbridge Pkwy., Leesburg, Va. • (703) 729-4071

This esteemed 18-hole, par 72 course, designed by Robert Trent Jones Jr., is part of the posh Lansdowne Resort in Loudoun County. The course has a yardage of 7051 and slope of 130. Fees range from $55 to $95. The resort offers a Hole-in-One package that includes golf, accommodations, breakfast and such golf amenities as a clinic and unlimited use of the driving range.

Pohick Bay Regional Park Golf Course
10301 Gunston Rd., Lorton, Va. • (703) 339-8585

One of three Northern Virginia Regional

Park Authority courses — the others are the 7015 yard Algonkian in Sterling and 6764 yard Brambleton in Ashburn — Pohick Bay takes pride in being rated by golf magazines as one of the area's most challenging courses. It features a 6405 yardage. Reserve tee times by phone or in person at 6 PM Tuesday for Friday, Saturday, Sunday and holidays.

Raspberry Falls Golf & Hunt Club
41601 Raspberry Dr., Leesburg, Va.
• **(703) 779-2555**

Gary Player designed this 18-hole, par 72 course, noted for its challenging play, abundance of bentgrass and stunning views of the surrounding Hunt Country. Yardage is 7191, with a 134 slope. Fees range from $45 to $65. You'll find the club off Route 15, just 3 miles north of Leesburg.

Reston National Golf Course
11875 Sunrise Valley Rd., Reston, Va.
• **(703) 620-9333**

This 18-hole, par 72 semiprivate course, noted for its tree-lined fairways, is the Metro Washington area's top-ranked public golf course, according to *The Washington Post* and *Washington Flyer* magazine. Yardage from the middle tee is 6506. Hole No. 10 proves most challenging, with an elevated green guarded by three bunkers. Although not required, tee times preferably are made a week in advance at this bustling course. The course has a driving range and putting and chipping greens, as well as a snack bar and pro shop. Summer fees, including carts, run $60 on weekends, and $45 Monday through Thursday.

Suburban Maryland

Needwood Golf Course
6724 Needwood Rd., Derwood, Md.
• **(301) 948-1075**

One of the Maryland Park and Planning Commission's four golf courses, Needwood is a par 70, 18- and 9-hole executive course with a yardage of 5948 from the white tee. The front is flatter than the back, and there's water on the back nine holes. Fees vary from $7 to $25, depending on the day and player's age, with discounts for ages younger than 18 and older than 60. The course includes a pro shop

with snack bar, putting green, driving range and a resident pro who gives lessons.

Trotters Glen Family Golf Center
16501 Batchellors Forest Rd., Olney, Md.
• **(301) 570-4951**

On the No. 11 hole at this 18-hole, par 72 course, a player must hit a perfect tee shot to avoid a water pond to the right and woods to the left. The course has a 6300 yardage. Amenities include a practice area, putting and chipping greens, pro shop, snack bar and golf school. Call seven days in advance to make a required tee time. Fees are $26 on weekends, and $21 during the week.

Hang Gliding

Silver Wings Inc.
6032 N. 20th St., Arlington, Va.
• **(703) 533-3244**

If you get the urge to soar like an eagle after your visit to Mason Neck State Park, consider learning how to hang glide. John Middleton, a U.S. hang gliding certified instructor, runs the area's only hang gliding school. Beginners start at Ground School, a $10, 90-minute class in which Middleton shows videos and describes the sport. He offers flight classes, complete with essential equipment, on Saturdays and Sundays, usually from around 10 AM to 5 PM or 6 PM. Students carpool to a training site, where they start on small hills. Classes are $70 each per person. Most folks need five to eight lessons before they get the "hang" of it.

Horseback Riding

Rock Creek Park Horse Center
Rock Creek Park, Washington, D.C.
• **(202) 362-0117**

Jump in the saddle at the Rock Creek Park Horse Center, in the heart of Washington's largest park. The National Park Service offers weekend and weekday guided trail rides on miles of bridle paths, riding instruction, a summer day-camp program and year-round boarding. While clip-clopping along the pathways, keep an eye out for deer. Yes, there's a herd right in the thick of Washington.

Ice Skating

Fairfax Ice Arena
3779 Pickett Rd., Fairfax, Va.
• (703) 323-1131, (703) 323-1132

U.S. Olympian Michael Weiss trains at this popular indoor skating facility, celebrating its 25th anniversary this year. Call for a schedule of public skating, offered daily at varying times. Sessions cost $4 to $6, and skate rental is $2.50. The arena offers private and group lessons for all skill levels, holds an annual competition and occasionally hosts ice shows. An in-house adult ice-hockey league plays fall/winter and spring/summer seasons. The Skating Club of Northern Virginia, an organization for competitive skaters, practices here.

Pershing Park Ice Rink
Pennsylvania Ave. and 14th St. NW,
Washington, D.C. • (202) 737-6938

Skate under the stars at this popular rink, right across the street from the elegant Willard Inter-Continental hotel and just steps from the city's theater district. For a picture-perfect holiday outing in December, hit the ice after visiting the National Christmas Tree and Pageant of Peace on the Ellipse, only a couple of blocks away. The rink is open mid-December until the ice starts to melt, usually early March. Two-hour sessions take place from 3 to 11 PM Monday through Thursday and from 9 AM to 11 PM Friday, Saturday and Sunday. Admission is $5 for adults, $4 for children, and figure-skate rental is $2.50. Parking is scarce, so you're better off taking Metro to nearby Federal Triangle or Metro Center.

Reston Ice Skating Pavilion
1818 Discovery St., Reston Town Center,
Reston, Va. • (703) 709-6300

In Reston Town Center, this elegant, glass-domed, open-sided pavilion is Northern Virginia's answer to Rockefeller Center, complete with a huge Christmas tree across the street. A visit to the rink is one of our favorite winter outings, whether we skate or just sip hot cocoa and watch those who know what they're doing. Public skating takes place usually from early November until the weather

warms up. Hours are from 11 AM to 11 PM on weekends and 11 AM to 9 PM on weekdays. A two-hour session is $5.75 for adults and $4.75 for kids. Skate rentals are $2.50, and you can rent free helmets for the little ones. You can also purchase season passes and discount books. Lessons for various skill levels take place before and after public sessions. In the summer, the pavilion hosts open-air concerts.

Orienteering

Quantico Orienteering Club
6212 Thomas Dr., Springfield, Va.
• (703) 528-INFO

This club sponsors map hikes and orienteering events for all ages and skill levels, throughout the Metro Washington and Baltimore area.

Outdoor Sports

Washington Women Outdoors Inc.
7007 Ellen Ave., Falls Church, Va.
• (301) 864-3070

This nonprofit organization offers instruction in outdoor sports, by women and for women. All skill levels are welcome to participate in such outings as hiking and backpacking, bicycling, rock climbing, canoeing and kayaking. Nonmembers are welcome, but members get discounts, as well as newsletters, use of equipment and other perks. Basic annual membership is $30.

Running

American Running and Fitness Association
4405 East-West Hwy., Ste. 405,
Bethesda, Md. • (301) 913-9517,
(800) 776-2732

With so many wonderful park trails and pleasant streets at their disposal, many Washingtonians choose running as their favorite way to exercise. This nonprofit, national association promotes the benefits of running and other aerobic exercise for fitness. Membership, $25 annually, includes a monthly newsletter, discounts on books, travel and programs; free trails maps; and other benefits. Contact the organization for a list of more than 50 running clubs in Metro Washington.

Road Runners Club of America
1150 S. Washington St., #250, Alexandria, Va. • (703) 836-0558

If you're a long-distance runner, you'll be interested in this national association of non-profit running clubs. RRCA educates runners on different facets of the sport, supports legislation that benefits runners and publishes a quarterly newsletter. Contact the national headquarters for a list of more than 25 member clubs in the Washington/Baltimore area.

Sailing

The Mariner Sailing School
Belle Haven Marina, Inc., P.O. Box 7093, Alexandria, Va. • (703) 768-0018

You'll find the biggest sailing school in the Metro Washington area just off the George Washington Memorial Parkway. Qualified sailors teach hands-on classes in adult basic sailing, youth (ages 8 to 15) basic and intermediate sailing, windsurfing, cruising and racing. The facility is an authorized American Red Cross provider, as well as a charter member of U.S. Sailing's Commercial Sailing Program. Call for class schedules and rates.

Washington Sailing Marina
1 Marina Dr., Alexandria, Va. • (703) 548-9027

The Washington Sailing Marina, about 1½ miles south of Ronald Reagan Washington National Airport, will rent you a cute little Sunfish sailboat for $10 an hour.

Soccer

Northern Virginia

Fairfax Women's Soccer Association
Fairfax County, Va. • (703) 541-6194

Players of all skill levels are welcome in this league of 700 women in three age groups: Open for age 18 and older, Master for age 30 and older and Grand Master for age 40 and older. Teams play April through June and September through November, usually 10 games per season. Most games take place Saturdays on Fairfax County soccer fields. Registration is $35 for county residents, $55 for out-of-county residents.

Sports Network
8320 Quarry Rd., Manassas, Va. • (703) 335-1555

This indoor soccer arena holds year-round leagues, mostly for adults, as well as winter youth leagues and summer camps. Volleyball and lacrosse teams also play here. Soccer team registration generally costs from $400 to $550 per session. Call for a schedule.

Virginia Coed Sports and Recreation Association
P.O. Box 3050, Merrifield, Va. 22116 • (703) 503-9821

Metro Washington's largest coed adult soccer league includes about 500 people on 24 teams that play outdoors March through November. Games take place seven nights a week in Burke, Va. Registration is $1,500 per team, $75 per individual per 12-game session, and is available on a first-come, first-serve basis. Usually, men's spots fill up more quickly than women's. Affiliated with the U.S. Soccer Federation, the league also sponsors at least two big annual tournaments that draw approximately 45 teams from the area and other states. The league also plans to develop a domestic and international trip and travel program.

Suburban Maryland

The Corner Kick
18707 N. Frederick Rd., Gaithersburg, Md. • (301) 840-5425

This indoor soccer facility, which also houses a bar and restaurant, holds year-round adult soccer leagues and kids' soccer leagues on weekends from November to April. Team registration is $495. Some local volleyball leagues also play here.

Photo: Courtesy of NVRPA

Algonkian Regional Park offers riverfront vacation cottages along the Potomac in Loudoun County.

Ultimate Frisbee

Washington Area Frisbee Club (WAFC)
1808 N. Quantico St., Arlington, Va. 22205 • (301) 588-2629

Kind of like football played with a flying disc, Ultimate Frisbee boasts quite a following in Metro Washington, judging from WAFC's 1,200-address mailing list. The club sponsors spring, summer (most popular) and fall/winter coed leagues for a range of skill levels. Serious players participate in WAFC's traveling teams, while folks looking for informal play usually can find pickup games on Saturday and Sunday afternoons at the Ellipse in D.C. Most league games take place on the National Mall, next to the Reflecting Pool. League fees are $5 to $10, and members can buy their own Frisbees for $5 each through the club. Call for more information.

Wrestling

Washington Wrestling Club
7717 Babikow Rd., Baltimore, Md. • (202) 260-8525

This 31-year-old informal club geared toward former high school and college wrestlers — although all skill levels are welcome — meets from 1 to 3 PM on Sundays in the varsity wrestling room of the American University gymnasium in Northwest Washington, D.C. Members practice four types of wrestling: collegiate, Olympic freestyle, Greco-Roman and Sombo, a Russian self-defense combination of judo and wrestling. This spring, the club hosts the national Sombo championships. They have also held self-defense classes for women. Members must belong to USA Wrestling, the national governing body for amateur wrestling. Annual membership for both organizations is $50.

INSIDERS' TIP

Some local bowling lanes offer "duckpin" bowling, featuring smaller pins, lightweight balls about the size of cannon balls and three turns per frame.

Yoga

Mid-Atlantic Yoga Association Inc.
P.O. Box 10658, Silver Spring, MD 20914
• (202) 332-9401

Take a deep breath, relax and contact MAYA to learn all about this unique way to exercise mind and body. Student membership is $22, while teachers pay an annual fee of $32. Benefits include the nonprofit corporation's quarterly newsletter, discounts on educational events and opportunities to attend yoga exchanges.

Youth Sports

Ready to become a soccer mom — or dad? Your best bet for locating a youth sports organization that's just right for your child is to call your local recreation center. (See our list in this chapter.) They frequently sponsor their own leagues, and can point you in the direction of groups in the area. Don't overlook smaller neighborhood pools and community centers, most of which offer competitive team sports and instruction.

Parks and Recreation Authorities

Many of the area's recreational opportunities can be found through national, regional and state park authorities and through community departments of parks and recreation. Here's a rundown of Metro Washington's major parks and recreation authorities and community centers. All the recreation departments and community centers listed here, unless otherwise stated, offer after-school and seniors' activities, enrichment classes, sports instruction, gymnasiums, pools, exercise programs, leagues for kids and adults and recreational excursions. Contact them to receive their latest programming guides.

Washington, D.C.

District of Columbia Department of Recreation and Parks
3149 16th St. NW, Washington, D.C.
• (202) 673-7660

The department oversees more than 70 neighborhood recreation centers, the newly renovated Anacostia Wellness/Fitness Recreation Center, seven indoor swimming pools, 57 tennis courts, three therapeutic recreation centers and many park spaces.

National Capital Parks, National Park Service
1100 Ohio Dr. SW, Washington, D.C.
• (202) 619-7222

The park service oversees more than 6,500 acres of park space in Washington, D.C., along with such landmarks as Ford's Theatre and Frederick Douglass national historic sites; Korean War Veterans, Lincoln, Thomas Jefferson, and Vietnam Veterans memorials; the Washington Monument; and the White House. Contact the number above or visit any National Park Service site for a copy of their monthly calendar of park events, "Kiosk."

Northern Virginia

Alexandria Department of Recreation, Parks and Cultural Activities
1108 Jefferson St., Alexandria, Va.
• (703) 838-4343

The department has seven recreation centers, including recently renovated Mount Vernon and Nannie J. Lee. Chinquapin Park & Recreation Center boasts a 25-meter indoor pool and diving well. The department also oversees 12 major parks, the City Marina, seasonal special events, camps and weekend nature programs at Jerome

Mt. Vernon Recreation Center offers ice-skating classes for the young and old.

"Buddie" Ford Nature Center, 5700 Sanger Avenue, (703) 838-4829.

Arlington County Department of Parks, Recreation and Community Resources
300 N. Park Dr., Arlington, Va.
• (703) 358-4747

Arlington's department oversees 12 community centers, three year-round swimming pools, two nature centers, Virginia Cooperative Extension programs, a 68,000-square-foot fitness facility and six parks with picnic pavilions.

City of Fairfax Parks and Recreation
John C. Wood Complex, 3730 Old Lee Hwy., Fairfax, Va. • (703) 385-7858

The department sponsors 14 parks, including the 48-acre Daniels Run Park and 20-acre Van Dyck Park; a network of recreational trails for bikers, walkers and runners; the City of Fairfax Band and other arts programs, includ-

INSIDERS' TIP

Call the National Park Service's Dial-A-Park, (202) 619-PARK, for recorded details about park events in the Metro Washington area.

ing free summer concerts and performances at Old Town Hall, 3999 University Drive; and seasonal celebrations. The city does not have a swimming pool.

City of Manassas Recreation and Parks
9027 Center St., Manassas, Va.
• **(703) 257-8237**

This department sponsors tours, special events and classes and oversees community gym programs at local schools.

Virginia Department of Conservation and Recreation
203 Governor St., Ste. 302, Richmond, Va. • **(804) 786-1712**

Contact the department for information about its 43 parks and natural areas.

Fairfax County Community and Recreation Services
12011 Government Center Pkwy. Ste. 1050, Fairfax, Va. • **(703) 222-4664**

Not to be confused with the county park authority, Community and Recreation Services offers a wide variety of quarterly hobby and recreational classes — everything from aerobics and art to weight training and yoga — for Fairfax City and County residents. Most activities take place after hours at schools. The program also operates seven community centers, nine teen centers, 12 senior centers, therapeutic recreation services and summer camps. The department shares its quarterly catalog with Fairfax County Public Schools' Office of Adult and Community Education.

Fairfax County Park Authority
12055 Government Center Pkwy., Ste. 927, Fairfax, Va. • **(703) 246-5700**

This massive park authority oversees more than 350 parks on more than 16,000 acres, including 11 multiple purpose parks and numerous neighborhood and community parks. Eight full-service recreation centers, 11 historical or archaeological sites, five golf courses and a county-wide farmers market program also fall under the park authority's jurisdiction.

Falls Church Recreation and Parks
223 Little Falls St., Falls Church, Va.
• **(703) 241-5077**

Based at the Falls Church Community Center, the department sponsors a variety of classes, an adult gym program, a Saturday farmer's market, bike trails, nine parks and numerous seasonal events, many of which take place at the historic Cherry Hill Farmhouse, 312 Park Avenue, (703) 241-5171. The department does not offer swimming. Its events schedule also lists offerings of the Office of Community Education, 7124 Leesburg Pike, (703) 241-7676.

Herndon Parks and Recreation
814 Ferndale Ave., Herndon, Va.
• **(703) 435-6868**

Headquartered at the Herndon Community Center, this department offers extensive aquatics classes, nature walks at Runnymede Park, a children's performance series and numerous special interest and fitness activities.

Loudoun County Department of Parks and Recreation
18 N. King St., Leesburg, Va.
• **(703) 777-0343**

The department owns or oversees more than 10 parks and 10 community centers offering a variety of programs.

Northern Virginia Regional Park Authority
5400 Ox Rd., Fairfax Station, Va.
• **(703) 352-5900**

The park authority's vast network includes 17 parks, the Bull Run-Occoquan Trail, historic Carlyle House, four regional park swimming pools, three golf courses and areas for boating and camping.

INSIDERS' TIP

Look for gorgeous plantings of seasonal flowers at National Park Service-maintained sites throughout Washington. In the spring, more than a million daffodils adorn the Potomac's west bank.

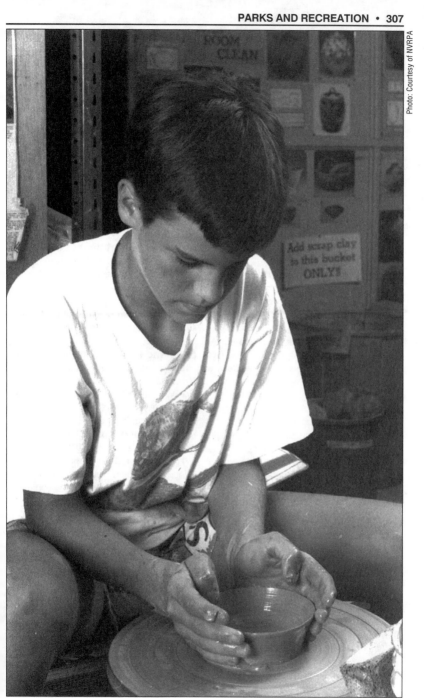

Photo: Courtesy of NVRPA

Children's classes for pottery making are available at several recreation centers.

Prince William County Park Authority
14420 Bristow Rd., Manassas, Va.
• (703) 792-7060

The park authority oversees several parks, a public golf course, community centers and the Chinn Aquatics and Fitness Center.

Reston Community Center
2310 Colts Neck Rd., Reston, Va.
• (703) 476-4500

This center serving the community in western Fairfax County includes an indoor pool, art exhibits, a game room and a theater that hosts performances by its resident theatrical troupe and nationally known performers.

Town of Leesburg Department of Parks and Recreation
50 Ida Lee Dr. NW, Leesburg, Va.
• (703) 777-1262

The department's 11 parks include the 138-acre Ida Lee Park, the site of Ida Lee Recreation Center and a diverse aquatics program. The department also sponsors numerous seasonal events.

Town of Vienna Parks and Recreation
120 Cherry St. SE, Vienna, Va.
• (703) 255-6360

Most activities take place at the community center, which includes a teen center and boasts a new outdoor bocce ball court. The department also oversees four parks, the Vienna Community Band and numerous special events. Swimming is not available.

Suburban Maryland

City of Laurel Department of Parks and Recreation
Laurel Municipal Center, 8103 Sandy Spring Rd., Laurel, Md. • (301) 725-7800

Laurel's department oversees two community centers, a golf and recreation center, an outdoor municipal pool, a senior center, playing fields and the Granville Gude Park and Lakehouse at 8300 Mulberry Street, Laurel, Maryland, (301) 490-3530.

City of Rockville Recreation and Parks
111 Maryland Ave., Rockville, Md.
• (301) 309-3340

This department oversees 51 parks and seven community centers in Montgomery County's large city of Rockville.

Greenbelt Recreation Department
25 Crescent Rd., Greenbelt, Md.
• (301) 397-2208

Greenbelt's facilities include an aquatics and fitness center, community center, youth center and recreation center, as well as parks available for community rentals.

Maryland Department of Natural Resources/State Forest and Park Service
580 Taylor Ave., E-3, Annapolis, Md.
• (410) 974-3771, (800) 830-3974

Contact the department for information about its 280,000 acres of public parks and forests.

Maryland-National Capital Park and Planning Commission
Montgomery County Department of Parks, 9500 Brunett Ave., Silver Spring, Md. • (301) 495-2525
Prince George's County Department of Parks and Recreation, 6600 Kenilworth Ave., Riverdale, Md. • (301) 699-2407

This massive department, covering all of Suburban Maryland, includes numerous parks and, in Prince George's County, community centers. You'll also find historic sites, nature centers and golf courses.

Montgomery County Department of Recreation
12210 Bushey Dr., Silver Spring, Md.
• (301) 217-6800

Contact this department for information about its nine swimming pools, more than a dozen community centers and numerous special programs such as summer camps.

Takoma Park Recreation Department
7500 Maple Ave., Takoma Park, Md.
• (301) 270-4048

Facilities include a community center, municipal gym, four parks and two playing fields. Swimming is not available.

Jewish Community Centers

These full-service community centers require membership, which is open to anyone. Many special events are open to nonmembers for a fee.

Washington, D.C.

District of Columbia Jewish Community Center
1529 16th St. NW, Washington, D.C.
• (202) 518-9400

Housed in the extensively renovated original JCC building from the 1920s, the city's modern JCC offers a wide range of programming, including an arts center, children's after-school and camp programs, an early childhood and parenting center, a library and activities for all ages. Health and fitness features include a pool, gymnasium, racquetball and squash courts, an aerobics and dance studio, steam room and exercise equipment and training.

Northern Virginia

Jewish Community Center of Northern Virginia
8900 Little River Tnpk., Fairfax, Va.
• (703) 323-0880

The center boasts an indoor pool, regula-tion-size gymnasium, fitness room, library and auditorium for entertainment and community events. The JCC hosts a variety of programs for all ages, including an early childhood program, before- and after-school care and summer camps. Many events are open to the public.

Suburban Maryland

Jewish Community Center of Greater Washington
6125 Montrose Rd., Rockville, Md.
• (301) 881-0100

The JCC's facilities include a Sports and Fitness Center with indoor and outdoor pools, exercise equipment, a steamroom, and courts for handball, racquetball, squash and basketball. Men's and women's health clubs are available for additional membership fees. JCC Programs include preschool and kindergarten, summer camps and after-school activities, classes and special events for all ages, a library and a cultural arts series.

YMCA

YMCA of Metropolitan Washington
1112 16th St. NW, 7th Fl., Washington, D.C. • (202) 232-6700

This membership association holds a variety of fitness, recreation, camp and child-care programs at its area branches, including five in Washington, D.C., five in Northern Virginia and six in Suburban Maryland. Call to find the nearest location.

Put the maps in the
glove box, check the
fuel gauge and fasten
those seatbelts. It's time
to let your imaginations
and frontiers soar.

Daytrips and Weekend Getaways

Let's not kid ourselves. Scores if not hundreds of books have been written about daytripping and weekend frolicking in and around the Nation's Capital — and for good reason. Few areas in the United States can boast of the inexhaustible array of scenic, cultural, historic and recreational attractions within an honest day's drive from an urban region as can Washington, D.C.

Our point here is not to rewrite what already has been inked. Instead, we want to take you to some of the most- and lesser-known nearby destinations — places we proudly put on our must-see itinerary for visiting families and relocating friends eager to discover the rich environs and folkways beyond the Beltway.

When we say "beyond the Beltway" what we really mean is away from the metro area but close enough to more than justify a day's outing or a weekend mini-vacation. What a palette we have to work with. From the ancient, forest-covered Blue Ridge Mountains to the tranquil majesty of the Chesapeake Bay, the world's largest and most productive estuary, to all those points in between, the storybook quality of the mid-Atlantic countryside and all that it offers is the stuff of inspiration, rejuvenation and endless repeat visits. It is part of the cultural fabric of being a Washingtonian.

We've begun this chapter at the beginning — our colonial roots in Virginia. From there, we travel to Virginia Hunt Country and the Blue Ridge, from West Virginia to Maryland, south to the Maryland antique meccas of Frederick County. We've touched on a few ski resorts, then, at the opposite end of the meteorological spectrum, the Chesapeake Bay and the Beaches, with special mention of those waterview towns Baltimore and Annapolis. Of course, from time to time, we may meander beyond our geographic parameters. After all, we couldn't, in good conscience, omit such special places as the Dolly Sods Wilderness of West Virginia or the Victorian charm of Cape May, New Jersey.

We've touched on a few suggestions for overnight stays, and you can assume that rates are per room, per night unless otherwise specified. Also, bed and breakfasts include breakfast for two in the room rates, but if other snacks or meals are included, we've noted it. Please remember that rates can and do change with time and also with the seasons.

So let's go, weekend warriors! Put the maps in the glove box, check the fuel gauge and fasten those seatbelts. It's time to let your imaginations and frontiers soar.

Colonial Roots

Before there was Washington, there were Williamsburg, Yorktown and Jamestown, Virginia's historic triangle. Wedged between the James and York rivers, arguably the Tigris-Euphrates of the South, if not the nation, **Colonial Williamsburg**, (800) HISTORY, Yorktown Battlefield, (804) 898-3400 and **Jamestown Colonial National Historical Park**, (804) 898-3400, represent, quite frankly, the best and worst of Virginia — the worst in the sense that they are obvious tourist traps and you can't help but feel a bit regretful upon seeing a McDonald's or an outlet shop within a stone's throw from some of the most hallowed ground in North America; the best in the sense that the actual historical parks are run by altruistic foundations striving for class over commercialism. It's hard not to walk out of these shrines feeling like a patriot, or at least a pioneer, and we highly recommend that you budget a full day for each locale. The drive there takes a bit more than three hours from Metro Washington, an easy shot south on Interstate 95, and then east on Interstate 64. Once in the Williamsburg area, the three towns are easily connected by way of the Colonial Parkway, a gorgeous brick road that winds its way through forests and along the banks of the James and York rivers.

Jamestown Island is the site of North America's first permanent English settlement in 1607, and in Jamestown Settlement, you can board replicas of the three ships that carried the settlers to the Virginia shores. At Jamestown's Colonial National Historical Park, you'll see thousands of items from the 1600s that have been unearthed by archeologists or preserved from the era. The equally impressive James River plantations, proud residences of three presidents and numerous statesmen, are a 40-minute drive up panoramic Virginia Route 5. These 200-year-old beauties rest gracefully on hills overlooking the James River.

It was at Berkeley Plantation, the birthplace of 9th U.S. President William Henry Harrison, that in 1619 the first official celebration of Thanksgiving occurred. Sherwood Forest Plantation was the home of John Tyler, the 10th U.S. president, and Tuckahoe Plantation was the boyhood home of Thomas Jefferson. Tuckahoe is considered by architectural historians to be the finest existing early 18th-century plantation in America.

Yorktown, due east from Jamestown on Virginia Route 31, is where the Revolutionary War ended. Important battles — including the Boston Tea Party and the British surrender at Yorktown — are depicted for tourists by actors in costume. Wherever you visit in the historic triangle, you're most likely to stay in or near Colonial Williamsburg, the area's prime attraction, and the world's largest and most extensively restored 18th century town. There are more than 500 original and reconstructed buildings in the square that comprises Colonial Williamsburg. You've seen the photos of the costumed actors who depict 18th century townspeople, replicas of old-time taverns, smithies and apothecaries. It's all great fun, especially for kids, who delight in re-enactments of times of yore.

There are scads of hotels in the area to fit every budget, but the gracious **Williamsburg Inn**, right in the center of the colonial section at 136 E. Francis Street, will transport you to a former era when waiters wore white gloves and afternoon sherry was a daily ritual. Individually designed rooms are furnished in the Regency manner and the formal public rooms overlook sweeping manicured lawns flanked by a broad terrace. All reservations for accommodations and dining can be made by dialing (800) HISTORY.

Mr. Jefferson's Country

We move forward in history to the time of Thomas Jefferson, arguably Virginia's favorite son. You won't live in Virginia, or for that matter in Maryland, a week before someone mentions Charlottesville, which is about three hours from Washington: south on I-95, then west on I-64. Charlottesville is popular for good reason: As home to Virginia's and the nation's most-celebrated Renaissance Man — Thomas Jefferson — Charlottesville is one of the most cherished sites in the region. Here you'll find **Monticello**, (804) 984-9822, Jefferson's captivating hilltop home, and the University of Virginia, one of his many intellectual and architectural achievements.

Charlottesville and surrounding Albemarle County are also about dogwood-lined country roads, hillside vineyards, funky bookstores and sophisticated galleries, museums and restaurants. At the **Boar's Head Inn**, on Virginia Highway 250 West just outside of town, you can unwind at a full-service spa and spend the night in one of its many guest rooms decorated in cozy, country English style, (800) 476-1988. Room prices are from $175 to $279.

www.insiders.com

See this and many other **Insiders' Guide®** destinations online — in their entirety.

Visit us today!

For a more intimate experience check out the renowned **Clifton-The Country Inn**, 1296 Clifton Inn Drive, Charlottesville, (888) 971-1800. Rooms are $150 to $300. At Clifton, there's a fireplace in every room, beds are four-posters or canopies and dressed with line-dried, cotton sheets. The decor consists of Jeffersonian antiques and reproductions, and no wonder: The estate belonged to Thomas Jefferson's daughter Martha. There's a well-regarded, full-service restaurant on the premises and breakfast, included in the room tariff, is a calorie-busting affair that might include waffles, quiches, omelets, fruit compote, muffins and freshly ground coffee.

Fifteen miles east of Charlottesville is the gloriously romantic **Prospect Hill Plantation Inn**, Virginia Highway 613 at Zion Crossroads, Trevilians, (800) 277-0844. Set amidst rolling hills where sheep graze and wildlife wander, Prospect Hill looks like an idyllic painting. Each room is different — some have Jacuzzis and fireplaces, others are set in cabins of their own apart from the main house — so ask for descriptions. Dinners are a leisurely affair of four or five courses preceded by cocktails in the salon. Rooms are $260 to $345, including breakfast and dinner.

Mr. Jefferson's Country is also Mr. Monroe's Country and Mr. Madison's Country. Literally just down the road from Monticello is **Ashlawn-Highland**, (804) 293-9539, James Monroe's home . . . and about 20 miles to the north, in Orange, Virginia, is **Montpelier**, (703) 672-2728, the impressive country estate of James Madison.

Farther south, off the Blue Ridge Parkway in neighboring Nelson County, is **Wintergreen Resort** off Virginia Highway 664, (800) 325-2200 (see section on skiing, this chapter). The year-round facility offers a fine golf course, and the moderate climate makes it possible at times to ski in the morning and play a round of golf in the afternoon. Accommodations range from hotel-style rooms to private rental homes with walls of windows overlooking the mountains.

The Gray Lady of the Confederacy

The capital city of Virginia, and for a time, the South, is a living, breathing memorial to the Commonwealth. History isn't just a fact of life in Richmond, it's a way of life. Getting there is easy — it's 100 miles due south of Washington on I-95.

Monument Avenue, the South's answer to Pennsylvania Avenue, immortalizes the fallen sons of the Old Dominion through huge statues, tasteful gardens and expansive greens. The newest addition is the statue of tennis legend Arthur Ashe, Jr., who was the first and only African-American man to win Wimbledon. His monument depicts him surrounded by children, holding books and his tennis racket overhead.

Monument Avenue cuts through the heart of "The Fan," one of Richmond's trendiest and most desirable residential areas, à la Georgetown in Washington, D.C. It is said to be the largest intact Victorian neighborhood in the United States, with approximately 2,000 townhouses.

The White House of the Confederacy, (804) 649-1861, and many of the original government buildings of the Confederate States of America sit within earshot of downtown and the Virginia State Capitol, yet another building designed by Thomas Jefferson. Adjacent to the White House, you'll find the Museum of the Confederacy, the world's largest collection of Confederate artifacts. One exhibit features Robert E. Lee's tent as intact as if he'd just left it. Here you will also find the **Edgar Allan Poe Museum**, (804) 648-5523, which also happens to be the oldest building in the city.

Richmond is rightfully proud of its premier museum, the **Virginia Museum of Fine Arts**, (804) 367-0844, housing one of the world's largest collections of Fabergé eggs as well as a stunning array of Asian antiquities, French Impressionists and British sporting art.

INSIDERS' TIP

During the summer months, trek to Solomons Island or any of the winding creeks and inlets around Annapolis and catch your fill of Maryland blue crabs.

A Refuge for Solitude-Seekers

Each weekend in summer, thousands of Washingtonians clog the roads to Ocean City, Rehoboth and Virginia Beach. Fun spots all, but crowded with boardwalks, condos, fast-food joints and . . . well, thousands of Washingtonians. Choose the road less traveled, though, and you'll be rewarded with miles of pristine beach, wide, fluffy dunes that go on forever — and sweet isolation. Too good to be true? Not on Assateague Island National Seashore, a wildlife refuge of breathtaking, unspoiled beauty, half in Virginia, half in Maryland.

Here you'll find the wild ponies made famous in Marguerite Henry's classic children's book, *Misty of Chincoteague*. A bike ride along the narrow asphalt road that borders the wetlands is the best way to glimpse these graceful herds. They are fairly accustomed to tourists and continue to graze as you look on, but don't get too near because they'll kick!

For a truly dramatic spectacle, station yourself in nearby Chincoteague, Virginia, on the last Wednesday of July, when the local fire department rounds up the ponies and swims them across the bay for auction the next day — to the delight of thousands of spectators. When the crowds depart, Assateague is left once more in tranquillity.

— continued on next page

Photo: Courtesy of Virginia Tourism Corporation

The lighthouse on Assateague Island has operated as a guide for the southern end of the island since it was first lighted on October 1, 1867.

On Assateague, be prepared to make your own fun. You won't find amusement parks or family-fun centers — the only facilities are a bathhouse and restrooms on the Virginia side, two campgrounds on the Maryland side. What you will find, though, are more than 300 species of birds and 44 species of mammals, such as the endangered Delmarva fox squirrel and the miniature oriental deer. Scan the water and you may be lucky enough to spot a pod of bottlenose dolphins. A stroll along the undeveloped shoreline will bring you face to face with dozens of sandpipers, pelicans and gulls. No one bothers these creatures, so they aren't overly bothered by humans.

At the southern end of the island is the picturesque red and white striped lighthouse, first lighted in 1867, and still in use today. The original light system, however, has been replaced by a modern system, but it remains on display in the lighthouse. The structure is operated by the U.S. Coast Guard and is accessible via a cleared trail through the woodlands.

You won't find hotels on Assateague, but a short drive to Chincoteague will lead you to some nice inns, as well as a dozen or so budget motels. The closest to Assateague — only about 100 yards away, in fact — is **Driftwood Motor Lodge**, (800) 553-6117, on Maddox Boulevard, right beside the bridge that connects the preserve to Chincoteauge. You'll also find bicycle rentals everywhere you turn, since that is a great way to see the area.

Assateague's two campgrounds are on the Maryland side, which takes about one hour to reach via the mainland — you can't cross over on the island in a vehicle. One campground is run by the National Park Service, (410) 641-1441, and the other is operated by the state of Maryland, (410) 641-2120. A word of advice: During the months of July and August, be prepared to battle giant mosquitoes and horse flies; however, from April through June and from September through early November, few spots can rival enchanting Assateague.

Richmonders are also fond of their numerous parks and cemeteries, some of the most elegant in the South. **Hollywood Cemetery**, (804) 648-8501, is the burial place of Presidents Monroe and Tyler, as well as Confederate President Jefferson Davis and more than 18,000 Confederate soldiers.

A premier place to stay in Richmond is the 275-room **Jefferson** at Franklin and Adams Streets, (800) 424-8014, a grand hotel in the old style, with marble columns, palace-sized Oriental carpets, and a sweeping staircase from the mezzanine to the lounge. It also contains one of Richmond's top restaurants, Lemaire, featuring French and fusion cuisine. Rooms start at $175.

For more intimate quarters, try the **Linden Row Inn**, 100 East Franklin Street, (800) 348-7424. Built in 1847, the 71-room structure is listed in the National Register of Historic Places and is located in the middle of the historic district. Rooms are $89 to $159.

For more information on Richmond, as well as hotel reservations, call (888) RICHMOND.

A Hunt Country Tapestry

Closer to Washington, in fact just 40 miles west of the bustle of Pennsylvania Avenue, is a quiet, rolling green land of Thoroughbred horses, country squires and antebellum stone mansions. This is hunt country, and you'll be hard pressed to find a more beautiful setting than the farms and fields of Loudoun and Fauquier counties.

Middleburg, the self-proclaimed "Hunt

INSIDERS' TIP

Order a lunchbox from Sutton Place Gourmet before heading out for an afternoon sail on the Chesapeake Bay.

Country Capital," retains its 18th-century charm but with new twists like gourmet bakeries, upscale restaurants and internationally celebrated antique shops. A popular lodging and dining spot here is **The Red Fox Inn and Tavern**, 2 East Washington Street, (540) 687-6301, housed in a quaint stone building in the center of town. You'll find four-poster beds, fireplaces, and a full-service restaurant serving three meals a day. Room prices start at $150.

The Middleburg Inn & Guest Suites, (800) 432-6125, at 105 West Washington Street, offers an 18th century-style atmosphere with modern amenities, including suites with kitchens. Room prices start at $130.

To the west of Middleburg lie the lovely hill country hamlets of Upperville and Paris, where warehouse-size stables and horses seem to outnumber people five to one. Just outside Paris, meanwhile, is the public's access to hunt country living, **Sky Meadows State Park**, (703) 592-3556. Once a working plantation, Sky Meadows' 1,100 acres entice weekend warriors with a maze of hiking trails, including a stretch of the Appalachian Trail. Leesburg, the largest city in the area, is steeped in Virginia history; indeed, it was named after one of the most prominent families in the Old Dominion.

During the War of 1812, when the British were on their way to burn Washington, the Federal Archives, including the Declaration of Independence and the Constitution, were hauled through town in 22 wagons on their way to safekeeping in an estate outside of town. Today, Leesburg and the surrounding villages of Hamilton, Lincoln, Waterford, Hillsboro and Purcellville are waging another successful battle for preservation, a concept near and dear to the hearts of hunt country residents who consider themselves just a few miles yet "light years" removed from Washington suburbia.

Though Leesburg is less than an hour from downtown D.C., those looking for a quick, romantic getaway might reserve a room at the **Norris House**, 108 Loudoun Street, (703) 777-1806, a beautifully restored 1806 home. The interior is reminiscent of Colonial Williamsburg, both in terms of colors used and period antiques. This bed and breakfast has five rooms,

and guests are welcomed with complimentary wine or soft drinks. Breakfast is a spread featuring fresh fruit, baked goods and a hot entrée (also see our chapter on Bed and Breakfasts and Country Inns).

Also less than an hour from Washington, but due south, is Fredericksburg, another popular daytrip. This historic town, now a hot spot for antiques, was founded in 1728 as a trade route for the tobacco grown in Virginia.

George Washington's boyhood home, **Ferry Farm**, is just across the Rappahanock River from Fredericksburg, on Virginia Highway 3 at Ferry Road in the village of Falmouth, (540) 372-4485. This is where he reportedly cut down the famed cherry tree, but it later became a major artillery base and river crossing point for Revolutionary forces in the Battle of Fredericksburg.

Fifth President James Monroe was also a Fredericksburg resident at one time — he practiced law here — and his office is now The **James Monroe Museum and Library**, (540) 899-4559. Here, you can see the desk on which he signed the Monroe Doctrine in 1823.

A popular pastime in Fredericksburg — aside from shopping — is a 75-minute trolley tour of the historic district (540) 898-0737, or, weather permitting, a tour by horse-drawn carriage, (540) 752-9379. There are also tour packages available which allow admission to multiple historic sights. For information, call the Fredericksburg Visitor Center, (800) 678-4748 or (540) 373-1776.

The Blue Ridge Mountains

Named for their pervasive blue haze, the result of a complex photochemical reaction involving trees, light and moisture, the Blue Ridge Mountains are the nation's easternmost range, running from north Georgia to southern Pennsylvania, with Virginia claiming the largest stretch.

To give you an idea of their proximity to Metro Washington, D.C., residents of western Fairfax County can see the mountains on a clear day while driving along busy Virginia Highway 28. Conversely, Skyline Drive in Shenandoah National Park got its name because in earlier times one could make out the Washington skyline from its eastern overlooks.

It's the Big Kahuna, the Grand Poo-bah of the Virginia Blue Ridge. Stretching more than 130 miles along the spine of the mountains, from Front Royal south to Waynesboro, **Shenandoah National Park**, (703) 635-4558 or (703) 999-2266 (recorded information), is a naturalist's paradise.

Each year, nearly two million people make the 90-minute pilgrimage (Interstate 66 West from Washington) to the park and its famed **Skyline Drive** to take in dramatic vistas of the Appalachians and the rolling, fertile farmland of the Shenandoah Valley and the Piedmont. Don't let the number of visitors scare you, though: The park contains more than 195,000 acres, and once you venture off of Skyline it's possible to hike, fish and camp for several days without seeing another human. The same can't be said about wildlife, however. Bobcat, deer, fox, turkey and bear, among other critters, are prevalent in these parts; in fact, the density of deer and black bears is among the highest anywhere in the United States, so if you plan to do some backcountry trekking, be sure to check in at the ranger station to get briefed on safeguarding your camp.

For a less rugged but equally woodsy experience, try one of the park's four drive-in campgrounds — Big Meadows, Lewis Mountain, Loft Mountain and Matthews Arm — or two lodges, Skyland and Big Meadows. For information on any of these destinations, call (800) 999-4714.

If bed and breakfasts are more your style, try **Steeles Tavern Manor** on Virginia Highway 11, Steeles Tavern, Virginia, (800) 743-8666. This five-room inn is a sprawling 1916 mansion on 55 acres overlooking the mountains. Coffee is brought to your door each morning prior to the candlelight breakfast served in the dining room. Rooms are in the $100 range.

Aside from the fabled Appalachian Trail, which runs the distance of the Shenandoah National Park, excellent hiking opportunities can be had on dozens of peaks that comprise the highest mountain range between the Catskills and the Smokies. We highly recommend a day-climb on venerable Old Rag Mountain (elevation 3,291 feet). A hike on the

less-strenuous but taller Hawksbill Mountain (4,049 feet) is another favorite of daytrippers, especially in late October when the park's thick, deciduous forests turn into a technicolor fantasyland.

Above all, Shenandoah is ripe with wonderful hidden nooks and crannies. Things like abandoned settlers' cabins, cascading waterfalls and virtually untouched trout streams brimming with native brookies are just some of the treasures awaiting those with a penchant to leave the beaten path.

A personal favorite is the five-mile hike to **Camp Hoover**, President Herbert Hoover's "summer White House" and austere fish camp built along the banks of the pristine Rapidan River, one of the best trout fishing rivers in the Old Dominion. Each year around August 10, Hoover's birthday, the National Park Service hosts a "Hoover Days" weekend in which the public is allowed to visit the camp and learn a bit about the president's leisure habits and the interesting guests who frequented the remote enclave. The event offers you the option of taking a bus ride down the mountain or hoofing it, trips that both begin at the park's Byrd Visitor Center, Skyline Drive, at milepost 51.

Advance information can be obtained from the Front Royal-Warren County Visitors Center, (800) 338-3576, or the Shenandoah Valley Travel Association, (540) 740-3132.

Little Washington, the Little Apple and the Caverns

Blue Ridge Mountain towns move to their own whimsical, unpretentious beat. Folks still wave to strangers, and shopkeepers are gracious even if you're just browsing. Surprises abound here, sometimes bordering on the surreal.

For instance, in tiny Washington, Virginia, on U.S. Highway 211, sits one of the most highly acclaimed restaurants and country inns in the world — **The Inn at Little Washington**, (540) 675-3800.

Well-heeled guests have been known to come from as far away as New York and Atlanta to dine on the restaurant's nouvelle French cuisine and spend a night in one of the 12 lavishly furnished rooms. Indeed, this is often a must-do for European visitors as well. On any given Sunday morning, "Little Washington," the oldest of 28 towns in the United States named for our first president, probably could claim the world's highest concentration of Jaguars and Mercedes-Benzes. You can count on dropping at least a couple of hundred bucks for dinner at the inn, and several hundred for a place to lay your head, but the food and accommodations live up to their reputations. The penthouse suites, in particular, feature living areas that look like Arabian nights fantasies — albeit tasteful. They have marble bathrooms with jetted tubs tucked into bay windows, double-headed showers as large as most normal bathrooms and loft bedrooms with balconies overlooking a panoramic mountain vista.

Just down the road is a lesser-known, but no less delectable stop called the **Bleu Rock Inn**. Owned by the proprietors of La Bergerie restaurant in Alexandria, Virginia (see our Restaurant chapter), the Bleu Rock, (540) 987-3190, offers a bucolic setting overlooking a pond and the inn's own vineyards. The five bedrooms here are homier than at The Inn at Little Washington, but they are charming and about half as expensive. On a summer night, there's nothing more romantic than dinner on the terrace as you watch the sun set. You'll enjoy memorable French cuisine with some interesting twists, then drift up to your room for the kind of restful sleep that only country nights provide. Rooms are from $109 to $195.

Other reasonably priced (rooms between $95 and $195), charming bed and breakfasts in the little Washington area include **Heritage House**, P.O. Box 90, Washington, VA 22747, (540) 675-3207, in the heart of town, a country-style abode where all the knickknacks and furnishings in the room are for sale! So if you love the decor, you can take it home with you.

Sycamore Hill House, 110 Menefee Mountain Lane, Washington, Virginia, (540) 675-3046, about one mile from little Washington atop Menefee Mountain (1,043 feet) has a more contemporary atmosphere at similar prices, with huge picture windows overlooking the Blue Ridge, cathedral ceilings (and

fans to go with them), and shining brass beds. The standout here is the 75-foot verandah and patio — a perfect spot to take in the breathtaking scenery.

Down the road from Little Washington and at the base of Shenandoah National Park lies perhaps the busiest hamlet in all of Virginia. Sperryville, the self-proclaimed "Little Apple," is an enterprising apple-farming-village-turned-gift-shop mecca that almost dares you to drive through without picking up mountain crafts, antiques or fresh-squeezed cider from places like the Sperryville Emporium or Wolf Mountain Store. For accommodations here, try **The Conyers House**, Slate Mills Road, Sperryville, Virginia, (540) 987-8025, which features a peaceful country locale and lavish breakfasts. The 1770 manor, with rates to $195, has been beautifully restored and contains such touches as beamed ceilings, Oriental rugs, stone fireplaces, and elegant country-house furnishings.

Also in the area are several vineyards where you can observe winemaking in progress, sample a bit of the product and even have lunch or dinner. Two of the better known are Meredyth Vineyards on Virginia Route 628, just south of Middleburg, (540) 687-6277, and Piedmont Vineyards on Virginia Route 626, (540) 687-5528.

Across the mountain from Sperryville, the Shenandoah Valley town of Luray is home to the much-hyped, but nevertheless fascinating Luray Caverns, (540) 743-6551. Take the tour — it's an hour long and you'll see some of the most colorful and stunning stalactites and stalagmites in the East. Among the attractions is the Great Stalacpipe Organ, a natural formation that plays haunting music.

In the same complex as the caverns is the Historic Car and Carriage Caravan, an exhibit of antique cars, carriages and coaches, some dating from the 17th century. Rudolph Valentino's 1925 Rolls Royce is even here.

Of Patsy Cline, Drive-ins and Barbecue

If the pressures of the big city start turning you a tad cynical, take a spin out to the northern Shenandoah Valley and rediscover vintage Americana. Winchester, the region's largest city, is home to dozens of historical attractions, including the western frontier command office of young General George Washington and the Civil War headquarters of Thomas "Stonewall" Jackson.

Civil War buffs may remember that Winchester changed hands at least 70 times during the war, far more than any other community. It is also in Winchester that the spirit of native daughter and country music legend Patsy Cline lives on. Cline, who gave us such heartfelt renditions of "I Fall to Pieces" and "Sweet Dreams," died in a plane crash in 1963 at age 30. She's buried at the Shenandoah Memorial Cemetery on Route 522, also known as the Patsy Cline Memorial Highway. Her mother still lives in town.

Virtually all the towns of the northern Valley are riddled with antique stores, including **Strasburg**, at the foot of Massanutten Mountain, takes the cake. Here you can find nearly 100 dealers in the downtown Strasburg Emporium, (540) 465-3711, which houses furniture from every American era, as well as intricate chandeliers, rugs, quilts, lace, old carousel horses and pottery. Top it off with a gourmet meal at the Victorian-inspired Hotel Strasburg, 201 Holliday Street, Strasburg, Virginia, (540) 465-9191, where you can also stay the night ($74 for a regular room, and $169 for a three-room suite with a Jacuzzi). For a more down-home experience, try a platter of hickory-fired ribs and chicken at Bad Water Bill's Barbecue, (540) 465-4988, which is worth the drive alone.

On the Wild Side of Front Royal

Between Strasburg and Front Royal, the heavily trafficked gateway to Shenandoah National Park, lies one of the region's truly undiscovered natural gems, the Elizabeth Furnace Recreation Area. Off of twisty Virginia Highway 678, in the heart of the sprawling George Washington National Forest, (540) 828-2591, this rugged gorge country of spiraling limestone outcroppings and the swift-moving Passage Creek is more akin to the wilds of West Virginia than to the gentle Shenandoah Valley. It also was the site of many a clandestine

military operation during the Civil War. Creekside campsites are available at the recreation area, and hikers are encouraged to make the enjoyable day-climb to the summit of Signal Knob, with its commanding views of the valley.

The Generals' City

The legacies of Stonewall Jackson and Robert E. Lee pervade their beloved Virginia, but nowhere is their presence felt more than in the scenic Shenandoah Valley town of Lexington in beautiful Rockbridge County.

Here, you can tour the only house Jackson ever owned and walk the hallowed grounds of Virginia Military Institute where he taught natural philosophy to Confederate cadets. At the **VMI Museum**, (540) 464-7334, displays include such objects as Jackson's bullet-pierced raincoat and a taxidermy of his favorite war horse, Little Sorrel. The museum added new exhibits and updated some old ones as part of a refurbishment project that was completed in the spring of 1995.

Within earshot of VMI is the impressive **Washington and Lee University and Lee Chapel**, (540) 463-8768, the still-used shrine to Jackson's confidant and the final resting place of the South's greatest hero. Don't leave Lexington without visiting the office Lee inhabited while assuming the presidency of W&L after his defeat in the Civil War. It's in virtually the same state as he left it in 1870. Buried nearby on campus is Lee's favorite mount, and maybe the most famous war horse in American history, Traveller.

There are several luxurious bed and breakfasts around Lexington, three of which are owned by a single company known as **Historic Country Inns** (rates from $95). By dialing a single phone number, (540) 463-2044, you can choose among the **Alexander-Withrow** (3 West Washington Street) or **McCampbell** (11 North Main Street) inns in the center of Lexington's historic district, or **Maple Hall**, set amidst 56 acres of meadow and forest 6 miles north of town.

Maple Hall even has a restaurant serving gourmet dinner fare. The country manor looks like it belongs on the set of *Gone With the Wind*, with its massive white columns and dra-

The restored village at Harpers Ferry National Historic Park provides a journey into days past.

matic front staircase. All three properties feature gracious, southern-style verandahs, antiques and fireplaces.

An equally quaint manor is **Fassifern**, (540) 463-1013, conveniently located on Virginia Highway 39, less than a mile from Interstate 64 (rates from $95). This cozy brick home is nestled in the trees and features a serene patio as well as beautifully manicured grounds. Inside, it feels like home, with brick fireplaces and comfy living areas that invite lounging. Breakfasts include fresh-squeezed juice, fruit, homemade baked goods and aromatic, fresh ground coffee.

A Tale of Two Mountain Resorts

Lodging is in no short supply in the Virginia upcountry; however, two of the more interesting spots to rest and recreate are **Mountain Lake Lodge**, near Blacksburg, and the queen of mountain resorts, **The Homestead in Hot Springs**. Still best known as the place where the hit movie *Dirty Dancing* was filmed, Mountain Lake Lodge (rates from $190, including dinner and breakfast for two) on Virginia Highway 700 in Blacksburg, (800) 828-

0490, sits nearly 4,200 feet up in the Allegheny Mountains of Giles County. Semi-rustic in nature, although a far cry from earthy, Mountain Lake caters to families in the summer and has developed quite an extensive package of theme weekends during the off-season including, of course, a "Dirty Dancing Weekend." It is isolated, yes, but once you get there expect a wealth of indoor and outdoor activities such as a full spa, great hiking trails, excellent fishing in the natural spring-fed pond and plenty of interpretive programs such as the one on Appalachian folk art.

Up the mountains to the north, The Homestead, Main Street, U.S. Highway 220 in Hot Springs, (800) 838-1766, is consistently rated by international travel writers as one of the world's top resorts. This plush but relaxed setting is a favorite of the corporate-retreat set (as well as of members of Congress and other segments of Washington officialdom) but also is frequented by couples and families looking to pamper themselves in the resort's five-star spa, restaurants, stables and golf courses. Golf legend Sam Snead, who grew up in the area, considers the Homestead's Cascades course one of the finest in the South. A bit on the pricey side — double occupancy during the popular month of October starts at more than

$200 a night per person, with breakfast and dinner — The Homestead nevertheless is something to be experienced if just once. Our advice is to start saving now.

Wild, Wonderful West Virginia

The Mountain State just may be the best-kept secret in the nation. Its rugged terrain and inspiring mountain vistas seem to defy its proximity to the Eastern megalopolis. Within a two-hour drive of Metro Washington one can be in country as remote and beautiful as Montana or Idaho. The state's laid-back tenor and affordability are attracting increasing numbers of tourists, but don't ever worry about being crowded out here. In the **Dolly Sods Wilderness Area**, (304) 257-4488, near Petersburg, you can walk the land of the Seneca Indians, through patches of wild orchids and blueberries and huge granite boulders that afford hikers views in excess of 100 miles.

About 20 miles south of Dolly Sods is **Seneca Rocks**, (304) 567-2827, a gray wall of ancient sandstone that juts 1,000 feet above the floor of the South Branch Valley. For the truly adventurous, take a mountain-climbing lesson through Seneca Rocks Climbing School, (304) 567-2600, Seneca Rocks Mountain Guides, (304) 567-2115, or Blackwater Outdoor Center, (304) 259-5117.

For those who want to keep their feet firmly on the ground, take a drive up to the Canaan Valley, the highest valley east of the Mississippi River. Spend a night or two in the cozy lodge at **Canaan Valley State Park**, (304) 866-4121, a woodsy retreat and conference center that boasts, and rightly so, the best fall colors in the United States.

For woodsmen who don't like to rough it, head to the super-expensive and super luxurious **Greenbrier Resort**, 300 West Main Street, White Sulphur Springs, West Virginia. The Greenbrier, (800) 624-6070, is considered even more upscale than The Homestead ($458 to $562 per couple, including breakfast and dinner) so know what you're getting into. If you can afford it, the experience is well worth the cost. It's a taste of the antebellum South, complete with a sprawling veranda, dancing and a

black-tie affair at dinner, afternoon tea, and enough activities to keep you occupied every minute of the day: horseback riding, shooting, golf, bowling, hiking and of course, taking the waters and all the related spa activities.

Closer to home and easier on the pocketbook, is Berkeley Springs, West Virginia, an area that offers something for both body and spirit. As the name implies, the area revolves around the restorative hot springs and spa, and weary Washingtonians often make the 2½-hour pilgrimage to the **Berkeley Springs Country Inn**, 207 South Washington Street, (304) 258-2210, to be pampered by facials, body scrubs, massages and, of course, soaks in the hot springs (rates from $39 to $119).

An attraction of equal allure is the scenery just outside of town. The Panorama Overlook on West Virginia Highway 9, four miles west of Berkeley Springs has been named by *National Geographic* magazine as one of America's most breathtaking vistas.

Coolfont Resort, 1777 Cold Run Valley Road, Berkeley Springs, West Virginia, (304) 258-4500, near Berkeley Springs is the spa of choice for many among the Washington stress set (rates $110 to $134 per person per night, including meals). Former Bush drug czar William Bennett kicked his cigarette habit here, and Vice President Gore has been a loyal customer for years, even once setting off a mini-panic by getting lost in the woods with Tipper. The accommodations are modest, but comfortable.

A bit further, and just as scenic, is **Cacapon State Park**, the third largest in West Virginia, (304) 258-1022. There are almost 30 miles of well-marked hiking trails — a great place to get your fix of fall color.

For a taste of true West Virginia Gothic, check in at the intimate and oh-so-isolated **Cheat Mountain Club**, West Virginia Highway 250, Durbin, West Virginia, (304) 456-4627, with rates from $80 per person, including meals. Hosts Norm and Debbie Strauss will see to it that you're fed three delicious squares a day; between meals, you can walk out the lodge's back door and catch native brook trout or swim in a natural pool on Shavers Fork Creek. Both Henry Ford and Harvey Firestone visited this rugged lodge, where it's as down-home as it gets.

A Tale of Two Rivers

The mighty Shenandoah and Potomac rivers meet in Harpers Ferry, West Virginia, site of abolitionist John Brown's raid on the U.S. Arsenal, the spark that ignited the Civil War. Now operated by the **National Park Service**, (304) 535-6298, this perfectly restored village provides an excellent journey into days past, with influences spanning not only the Civil War but the founding of the nation, including a healthy dose of period architecture and steep, narrow cobblestone streets.

Craft shops abound, as do glorious views of the Blue Ridge and the wild, crystal-clear rivers running below the hilltop city. At just over 400 feet in elevation, Harpers Ferry marks the lowest point in the state of West Virginia.

When the summer steam envelopes Washington, head north approximately 65 miles on Interstate 270 to Harpers Ferry for a day of tubing, whitewater rafting or hiking — the Appalachian Trail runs right through the town center. Trips can be arranged through **River & Trail Outfitters**, (301) 695-5177, in nearby Knoxville, Maryland.

If the hour-plus drive back to town seems much too formidable after an exhausting day shooting rapids, bunk down at one of the town's atmospheric bed and breakfasts. The circa 1800 **Ranson-Armory** bed and breakfast, 690 Washington Street, (304) 535-2142, has only two guest rooms, but each offers a private bath and a splendid view for $75 to $80 per night, including breakfast.

If you'd like something a bit more formal, head up the road to Shepherdstown, the second-oldest burgh in the state and home to the gracious **Bavarian Inn and Lodge**, (304) 876-2551, just off West Virginia Highway 480 or directly across the bridge (and state line) from Maryland Highway 34. The inn is a stone structure with a knoll-top perch above the Potomac (rates from $115 to $155, no meals). The dining room here features hearty German and game dishes. Several rooms have two-person Jacuzzis and gas fireplaces and all are furnished with American colonial reproductions, including some four-poster beds.

Shepherdstown has one of the nation's highest concentrations of 18th-century buildings, making it an ideal spot to just meander.

Be sure to duck into **O'Hurley's General Store**, (304) 876-6907, known throughout the East for its wonderful crafts, antiques and curios.

Just Across the River: The Mountains of Maryland

On the Maryland side of the Potomac from Harpers Ferry lies Washington County, home to the Civil War's Battle of Antietam, the deadliest clash of the war and one of the bloodiest days in American history. It's amazing to think anything so brutal could happen in this quiet, bucolic setting of dairies, wheat fields and vineyards.

On a more upbeat note, Washington County, the first such jurisdiction named for George, is home to four of Maryland's best state parks. At **Washington Monument State Park**, (301) 432-8065, high atop South Mountain, you can view the first monument built in the president's honor. Originally constructed by the residents of Boonsboro, Maryland, in 1827, the stone tower has been rebuilt twice since. Climb the monument's 34 steps to take in spectacular views of the Cumberland Valley.

If you plan to stay overnight in the area, book a room at **Antietam Overlook Farm**, (800) 878-4241, off Maryland Highway 34 in Keedysville, Maryland. The view from the property encompasses portions of Maryland, Virginia, West Virginia and Pennsylvania. The inn's most lavish room features a screened porch and sun deck overlooking the vista (rates from $95).

Moving south along the mountain, you'll hit **Gathland State Park**, (301) 791-4767, which includes the ruins of Gapland, the country home of Civil War and Reconstruction journalist George Alfred Townsend. Near the entrance to the park stands the imposing War Correspondents Arch, a 50-foot high structure Townsend built to honor the documentarians of the great war. Joseph Pulitzer and Thomas Edison contributed to the $5,000 building fund.

Just up the road from both Gathland and Washington Monument is **Greenbrier State**

Park, (301) 791-4767, and its sparkling spring-fed Greenbrier Lake, said to be among the clearest in the nation. Camping, fishing and hiking are popular activities here as well as across the county at **Fort Frederick State Park**, (301) 842-2155.

Nestled along the banks of the Potomac and containing a stretch of the Chesapeake & Ohio Canal, Fort Frederick was originally built as a defense outpost on the western frontier. Still standing, although in a carefully preserved state, the fort survived the French and Indian, Revolutionary and Civil wars and is now honored through a series of historical re-enactments each spring through fall.

The President's Mountain

Largely overshadowed by Shenandoah National Park, Maryland's **Catoctin Mountain Park**, (301) 663-9388, is an ideal place to beat the crowds, especially during the autumn months when its 10,000-acre forest of beech, hickory, poplar, oak and maple trees turns to brilliant shades of red, orange and gold. Catoctin is probably most famous for being home to Camp David, the woodsy presidential retreat. Don't expect the First Family to wave you on in, though. The compound is well-hidden and security, as you can imagine, is intense.

You can, however, spend the night at the park's Owens Creek Campground or in a rustic cabin at Camp Misty Mount. Catoctin's numerous trails and wild trout streams make it a great place for families and novice campers. From the park, you're also within a short drive of the history-rich towns of Gettysburg, Pennsylvania, and Frederick, Maryland.

Also, near the park entrance is the quaint railroad town of Thurmont, and immediately to the south is **Cunningham Falls State Park**, (301) 271-7574, with its gorgeous namesake waterfall.

At the northern end of this area, on U.S. Highway 15 just south of the Pennsylvania

border, is the town of Emmitsburg, whose Main Street is still lit by gas lamps today. This picturesque town, aside from its proximity to the aforementioned parks, is also an antique-lovers mecca, with its Antique Mall featuring 120 shops.

After a day of hiking or shopping, you can settle at the **Stonehurst Inn**, (301) 447-2880, where the owners pamper you with a lavish breakfast, afternoon tea, hors d'oeuvres and dessert. You hardly need to go out for dinner! The inn is located in its own little private park, pond included, at 9436 Waynesboro Road in Emmitsburg (rates $65 to $95).

Just south of town on U.S. Highway 15 is the **National Shrine of St. Elizabeth Ann Seton**, (301) 447-6606, dedicated to the first American-born saint, who lived from 1774 to 1821, and was beatified in 1963.

Maryland's Heartland

Fifteen miles south of Emmitsburg, and about one hour north of Washington via Interstate 270, in the heart of the Free State, are two of Maryland's most endearing towns, Frederick and New Market.

Both are nationally renowned antiques meccas, even more so than Emmitsburg, but they're also just great spots to unwind and enjoy the simple pleasures of graceful centuries-old buildings, perfectly manicured gardens and friendly denizens. Frederick's 33-block historic district, punctuated by towering church spires, is a must for history and architecture buffs.

At the edge of town is **Rose Hill Manor**, a 1790s mansion and estate that is now a living museum of 19th century life. Costumed guides lead you through an orchard, blacksmith shop, log cabin and the manor house itself. On the premises are also a carriage museum and farm museum where the vehicles on display are explained in depth and related to developments today. Rose Hill Manor is at 1611 North Market Street, Frederick, Maryland, (301) 694-1648.

INSIDERS' TIP

Call the Virginia Office of Tourism in downtown Washington, (202) 659-5523, to book a room at any bed and breakfast in the Commonwealth.

If you get hungry, drop in at **Cream of the Crop**, an indoor farm market on East South Street, open weekends from 9:30 AM to 5:30 PM. To learn of more interesting sights in and around Frederick, contact the **Tourism Council of Frederick County,** 19 East Church Street, Frederick, Maryland, (800) 999-3613.

New Market comes alive virtually every weekend of the year with a bazaar-like setting of antique dealers and craftspeople. It is the self-proclaimed "Antiques Capital of Maryland" and is home to more than 40 shops. You'd be able to walk the length of the village in a few minutes if you didn't need to stop so often to explore the wares for sale.

Both these towns are so close to Metro Washington that an overnight stay is unnecessary; however if you're looking for a romantic getaway, consider the **Bluebird on the Mountain** bed and breakfast, north of Frederick on Maryland Highway 550, (301) 241-4161. Set into the woods like a fairy-tale cottage, the five-room inn is a light, bright home furnished with lace and wicker. Some rooms have fireplaces and Jacuzzis.

Further south, on Maryland Highway 85, is the romantic **Inn at Buckeystown**, (301) 874-5755, in the village of the same name ($157 to over $300 per couple, depending on meal plan). The eight rooms are furnished in lavish Victorian style, including crystal chandeliers, brocade upholstery, and brass-screened fireplaces. Dinner is equally lavish, with rich Continental specialties like creamy bisques, game pâtés and homemade pastries.

If you're in the mood for something more simple, try the cute little **Strawberry Inn**, a bed and breakfast at 17 Main Street in New Market, (301) 865-3318. This five-room property is a homey whitewood building in the center of town with rooms furnished in antiques such as pineapple four-posters and Victorian settees (rates from $65).

Maryland's Last Frontier

High in the Allegheny Plateau, in the westernmost reaches of the Free State, sparkles Maryland's Deep Creek Lake. A fishing and boating dreamland (it's possible to catch walleye, bass, catfish and trout in the same day), Deep Creek also affords weekend travelers with a number of lakeside cabin, cottage and chalet rentals. **A&A Realty**, (800) 336-7303, can arrange for overnight or extended stays.

With 65 miles of shoreline, Deep Creek is best seen from the deck of a sailboat or motorboat. Rentals are available, but escalating insurance costs have made them an expensive option. Our advice is to bring your own boat or make friends with someone who has one. Honestly though, it's possible to enjoy the plentiful attractions of Garrett County without ever dipping a toe in the lake.

In nearby Oakland you can hop on the **Western Maryland Scenic Railroad**, (800) 872-4650 (TRAIN-50), or arrange for an afternoon of whitewater rafting on the Cheat and Youghiogheny (pronounced YOK-eh-gain-e) rivers. No trip to Western Maryland would be complete without a stop along the boulder-strewn banks of the aptly named Savage River, site of the 1989 World Whitewater Canoe/Kayak Championships and the 1992 U.S. Olympic Trials.

A Downhill Run

Snow? Around here? Okay, the Appalachians aren't exactly the Rockies, but you can sneak in a couple of days of passable skiing in these parts without taking the time and money for a trip out West.

In Virginia, if you're looking for full-service, hotel-style resorts, you have the option of **Wintergreen**, $155 to $195 per night, off Virginia Highway 664, (800) 325-2200. They also have some very nice condos about which you may want to inquire. The **Homestead** is another good choice, (800) 838-1766, at $207 to $235 per person per night, including breakfast and dinner. Both offer all the après-ski amenities you could wish and the restaurants are very good. You could easily spend a luxurious few days at either locale, but Wintergreen has been rated by the national ski magazines as one of the best downhill spots in the South. For daytrippers or a self-catering holiday, try the modest hills at Bryce, (703) 856-2121, or Massanutten, (800) 207-6277 (MASS).

West Virginia's **Snowshoe**, (304) 572-1000 — a sprawling complex off U.S. Highway 250 that spans several miles — and the smaller

Canaan Valley of West Virginia Highway 32, (304) 866-4121, though further from Washington (four to five hours), are popular with more experienced skiers — trails are a bit longer and more varied. Snowshoe has the extra attraction of **The Red Fox Inn**, (304) 572-1111, one of the premier restaurants in the mid-Atlantic region, a surprising find for gourmets who also like to ski. Reserve ahead if you intend to eat here during your stay — all those raves in the national foodie magazines guarantee a packed house. Snowshoe has an extensive condo and hotel complex with rates from $120; Canaan's rates begin at $88.

Just 90 minutes from Washington (off Interstate 270, right past the Maryland-Pennsylvania border), Pennsylvania's **Ski Liberty**, (717) 642-8282, and **Whitetail**, (717) 328-9400, are easy daytrip destinations. Liberty is an older ski area with a simple lodge, but Whitetail is a spiffy new day-resort whose design has won raves from national ski magazines. The trail selection at both places is limited, and even those ranked most difficult would be considered easy runs in Colorado, but they can't be beat for convenience. **Wisp Resort**, 296 Marsh Hill Road, McHenry, Maryland, (301) 387-4911, near Deep Creek Lake, is Maryland's lone downhill ski area (room rates $159).

By the Water: Beaches and Beyond the Chesapeake Bay

Legendary Baltimore journalist and social commentator H.L. Mencken once called the Chesapeake Bay a "great big protein factory" on account of the inordinate amount of fish, crabs and oysters found in its brackish waters. If Mencken were alive today he would probably amend his definition to include the number of people who regularly find sanctuary on the fabled body of water. Of course, the Bay is a different creature today than it was during Mencken's time — in some ways better, in other ways worse.

Ecologically, the Bay is being tested by humanity's heavy hand. Pollution and urban sprawl have been blamed for historically low populations of oysters and some fish. Chesapeake watermen, for centuries the life and blood of the region, are slowly dying off as real estate prices escalate and competition heats up in the global seafood industry.

To speak of the Bay and its rich traditions in the past tense would be foolish though. New conservation efforts, such as those of the Chesapeake Bay Foundation, have elevated awareness of this vital natural resource. As the Chesapeake, divided nearly equally between Maryland and Virginia, continues to attract record numbers of tourists to its pleasant shores and peaceful waterside villages, one can only hope that we will continue to find the energy and courage to save the Bay.

The Shore

You may have heard it called Delmarva Peninsula. Washingtonians know it as the Eastern Shore. To locals, it's simply "the Shore." For the uninitiated, it's the land found on the eastern side of the Chesapeake Bay Bridge.

This fertile coastal-plain peninsula contains the entire state of Delaware, a good chunk of Maryland and a sliver of Virginia, thus the name Delmarva. Bounded by the Bay and the Atlantic Ocean, the Eastern Shore is the land of proud watermen, of Canada geese and duck blinds, sprawling farms, colonial villages and what seems like more water than land.

To experience the true flavor of the Chesapeake — which inspired James Michener's novel of the same name — it's imperative to "cross the bridge." Maybe you've already seen the bumper stickers proclaiming, "There is No Intelligent Life West of the Chesapeake Bay." It's a bit parochial (and tongue-in-cheek), sure, but once you catch the spirit of the place you just might start agreeing with the notion.

After crossing the bridge — the Chesapeake Bay Bridge that is — think about getting off of U.S. Highway 50. There's nothing particularly exciting about this highway unless you're into strips of shopping centers, boat yards and liquor stores. Our advice is to take the slower-moving but scenic Maryland Highway 213 and head north to Chestertown, Maryland, on the banks of the Chester River. On the way, you'll pass through Centreville, government seat of Queen Anne's County and

The William Paca House and gardens is a popular destination in Annapolis.

site of the oldest courthouse, circa 1792, and still in use in Maryland.

Chestertown, with its 18th-century waterside Georgian mansions, is best discovered on foot, like during the Candlelight Walking Tour each September. Stroll through the grounds of Washington College, the 10th-oldest college in America and the only one to which George Washington personally granted the use of his name. For an overnight stay, consider the **White Swan Tavern** at 231 High Street, (410) 778-2300, in the heart of the historic district and a stone's throw from the Chester River (rates from $95). Guests are welcomed with a bottle of wine in their room and, in the morning, served a continental breakfast. The inn is small — only six rooms — so it's best to reserve early in summer. You'll enjoy the flower-rimmed patio and the bright antique-filled rooms.

From Chestertown, backtrack on Highway 213 and connect with U.S. Highway 50 (but just for a short 20 miles) south to Easton. Now you're in the heart of Talbot County, undeniably Maryland's most aristocratic jurisdiction. Easton is the site of the massive **Waterfowl Festival** held each November, in which the world's finest wildlife artists, woodcarvers and sculptors gather to strut their stuff along with tens of thousands of migratory Canada geese.

Easton's fabled **Tidewater Inn**, 101 East Dover Street, (410) 822-1300, accommodates sportsmen (including their hunting dogs), sailors, antique hunters and the occasional diplomat (rates from $110). Nearby, you can visit Third Haven Friends Meeting House, circa 1682, believed to be the oldest frame building dedicated to religious meetings in America.

Heading west, take a spin through St. Michael's, a waterfront hamlet that fooled the British Navy one evening during the War of 1812 when citizens placed lamplights in the tops of trees, thus giving the illusion that the village sat on a hill. The British ships fired at the tops of the trees and missed the town altogether.

You won't want to miss an outdoor crabfeast at **The Crab Claw**, (410) 745-2900, overlooking the harbor, or a walk through the **Chesapeake Maritime Museum**, (410) 745-2916, with its signature "screwpile" lighthouse, more than a century old. The place to stay in St. Michael's — if you want to splurge — is **The Inn at Perry Cabin**, 308 Watkins Lane, (410) 745-2200, owned and decorated by the husband of the late Laura Ashley (summer high-season rates from $295 to $695, including full breakfast and afternoon tea). This is a deluxe, English country-house spot overlooking the water, just the getaway for a special occasion.

From St. Michael's, you're just a few minutes' drive from Tilghman Island, a working waterman's community, and Oxford, arguably the most scenic town in Maryland. Tilghman is crab and oyster docks, colorful watermen and rusted boats. It's authentic Eastern Shore. The most colorful lodging on the island can be found at **Harrison House**, (410) 886-2121, a traditional Chesapeake fish camp that specializes in regional cuisine and hassle-free fishing trips (rates $60).

Oxford, on the other hand, is glistening million-dollar sailboats, painstakingly restored Federal-style homes and charming bed and breakfasts, like **The Robert Morris Inn** at the end of Maryland Highway 333, (410) 226-5111 (rates from $125). Head into Oxford from the north and cross the placid Tred-Avon River aboard the **Oxford-Bellevue Ferry**, (410) 745-9023, the oldest ferry still in use in the United States. The 10-minute trip is well worth the nominal fee, especially if you're into lowering the old blood pressure.

Don't leave the region without a stop down the bay in Cambridge, hometown of American hero Harriet Tubman, founder of the Underground Railroad. Tubman was born on a plantation outside of town and single-handedly made her way to freedom in the North. She ventured back into the South at least 20 times to help free hundreds of other slaves during the Civil War era.

Islands in Time

Near the geographic center of the Chesapeake Bay lie two of the most intriguing islands in the area. **Smith Island**, Maryland, (410) 425-5311, and **Tangier Island**, Virginia, (804) 787-7911, are indeed places that have defied the encroachment of modern society. Both islands, just a few square miles large, were settled by the first wave of British explorers to the Chesapeake Bay in the early 17th century (led by Captain John Smith). The descendants of the colonists, folks with names like Bradshaw, Harrison, Smith and Crosby, still work the water for crabs and oysters. Other islanders make and sell high quality crafts, such as hand-carved duck decoys.

These islands are insular, as evidenced by the fact that electricity only arrived there in the 1940s. Also, the islanders' speech even today has traces of the area's Elizabethan/Cornish roots. Residents are friendly and you may notice that those traveling in trucks and cars honk their horns and wave to greet all other vehicles and pedestrians. Visitors are greeted with good cheer to be sure, but leave your motorized vehicles and pets at home — they're banned from the islands and, anyway, bicycles are more fun and can be easily rented (see information phone numbers below). Spring is a particularly lovely time to visit, since you'll find a variety of exotic trees in bloom, including pomegranates, pears, figs and, later in the year, mimosas.

Religion has always been a very important part of island life, ever since the Methodist Church was established in the Bay islands during the late 1800s, and tourists are welcomed at local church services. If getting as far off the beaten path as possible interests you, both islands are accessible by U.S. Mail boats from Crisfield, Maryland, along the far southern edge of the Eastern Shore.

Private cruise lines also provide access in season (April to October). Contact Tangier Island Cruises in Crisfield, at (800) 863-2338. To reach Crisfield from Washington, head east on U.S. Highway, south on U.S. Highway 13, and then follow Maryland Highway 413 to Crisfield. Closer to home, you can reach Smith Island from Point Lookout, Maryland. To get there from Washington, follow U.S. Highway 301 south to Maryland Highway 235 — it will lead you right to the Point, where cruises to the islands originate aboard the *Capt. Tyler*, (410) 425-2771. For more information on charter companies and schedules, contact the Somerset County Tourism Office at (800) 521-9189.

The Humble Western Shore

In all fairness, you don't have to cross the bridge to enjoy the bounty of the Bay. While less rustic and authentic than the land to the east, Maryland's Western Shore is doing a pretty good job of balancing suburban growth while retaining some of its maritime character. If you've got angling in your blood but lack a good, solid boat to grapple the Chesapeake, drive down to Chesapeake Beach's **Rod N Reel Dock**, (410) 257-2735, and charter a captain for a day or grab a spot on a headboat. Either option will place you with appropriate tackle and bait and a knowledgeable skipper and first mate.

Typically, fishing on the Bay is best in the late spring and fall when bluefish and striped bass are biting. Summer is always good for panfish or redfish. South from Chesapeake Beach, head down Route 4 to Solomons, the picturesque sailing hamlet that boasts some of the finest seafood dining on the Bay, including The Harbor View, (410) 326-3202, and Solomons Pier, (410) 326-2424, restaurants.

Within a short drive you can visit the crucifix-shaped Middleham Chapel, circa 1748, the fossil-lined Calvert Cliffs State Park, (410) 888-1622, and historic St. Marys City, Maryland's 17th-century capital.

If you still have energy, drive down to Point Lookout State Park, (301) 872-5688, on the southernmost tip of Western Maryland, and explore the remains of Fort Lincoln, one of the largest Union-run prisons during the Civil War. The park's Civil War Museum is open weekends May through September.

Charm City

In many ways, Baltimore is the ultimate Chesapeake city. The Bay's influence is virtually everywhere, from the seafood cuisine (Ralph Waldo Emerson once dubbed the city "the gastronomic center of the universe"), to the thriving Inner Harbor area of shops, museums and hotels, to Fells Point, the rejuvenated harborfront district with eclectic pubs, galleries and Federal-style townhomes.

From Fells Point, a variety of sailing trips is available through **Schooner Nighthawk Cruises**, (410) 327-7245, including a three-hour buffet moonlight sail, a Sunday champagne brunch sail, a Sunday evening crab cruise and a two-hour midnight mystery cruise on Saturdays.

If you're not on the water or at an Orioles game at the showplace Oriole Park at Camden Yards, the next best place to be in Baltimore is the **National Aquarium**, (410) 576-3800. It offers 7,000 species of aquatic life and probably the best shark tank in the nation, from nurse sharks to great whites! Wrap the day up with an overnight's stay at the cozy **Admiral Fell Inn**, 888 South Broadway, (800) 292-4667, overlooking the harbor in Fells Point, and you'll discover why Baltimore is called "Charm City." Rates start at $165, including continental breakfast.

Chesapeake (Largely) Undiscovered

Maryland may be for crabs, but Virginia is equally tied to the history, traditions and fortunes of the Bay. There's no better starting place to explore the Old Dominion's maritime mystique than the Northern Neck, the verdant, five-county-long jut of land bounded by the Bay and the Potomac and Rappahannock rivers.

Less than a three-hour drive from Washington, the tiny Northern Neck village of Irvington has been welcoming anglers, boaters, golfers and antique collectors for generations. The centerpiece of the town has to be the opulent **Tides Inn**, 1 St. Andrews Lane, Irvington, Virginia, (804) 438-5000, a combination resort and conference facility that claims perhaps the top golf course in the state, the world-class Golden Eagle (rooms from $300 per couple, including breakfast and dinner). Overlooking Carter's Creek and the Rappahannock River, the Tides is just a half-day sail from several points along the open Bay, including the equally refined resort area of Windmill Point.

Sailors can charter a boat for the day, weekend or week at **Crockett's Landing**

INSIDERS' TIP

To appease the kids, or simply to get your quota of thrills, make a daytrip down to Paramount's King's Dominion theme park in Ashland, Virginia, just north of Richmond.

Charters, (804) 438-6559. Farther north up the Neck lies the sleepy little town of Reedville, a popular stay for bed and breakfast lodgers, many of whom come from as far away as the Carolinas and New England to soak up the quiet Chesapeake atmosphere. On Reedville's shaded Main Street, visitors can choose from the Gables, (804) 453-5209, a dramatic waterside Victorian mansion, or Morris House, a renovated early 19th-century fish-captain's house, (804) 453-7016, (rates at both from $95).

Just south of the Northern Neck is the Middle Peninsula, a region of wide-open spaces and shadowy coves; it's amazingly undiscovered given its proximity to Richmond and the Hampton Roads area. One of the more interesting sites on the peninsula is the Rappahannock River town of Urbanna, home to a number of antique stores and perhaps the world's largest oyster festival, scheduled every fall. The nearby communities of Gloucester, with its village green dating back to the early 18th century, and Gwynn, on postcard-perfect Gwynn's Island, make for interesting sidetrips through the peninsula's fragrant backroads.

The Urban Bay

Rivaling Baltimore in industrial stature is Hampton Roads, a booming metro area that includes the Virginia cities of Norfolk, Hampton, Newport News, Portsmouth, Chesapeake, Suffolk and Virginia Beach. It's a region of hyperboles, beginning with the world's biggest natural harbor, Hampton Roads, and the world's largest naval installation, based in Norfolk.

A leisurely Bay cruise is mandatory here, and one of the best is offered by the **Miss Hampton II**, (804) 722-9102, in Hampton Harbor. The skipper will bring you up close to some of the nation's most awesome military vessels, including Trident subs and aircraft carriers seemingly the size of Rhode Island. The region is also pocketed with great museums, including the world-class (fine art) Chrysler Museum, (804) 622-1211, in Norfolk; the Mariners Museum, (804) 595-0368, in Newport News; the Virginia Marine Science Museum, (804) 425-FISH, in Virginia Beach; the

Virginia Air & Space Center, (800) 296-0800, in Hampton; and the Casemate Museum, (804) 727-3971, also in Hampton.

Also, be sure to budget time to walk through prestigious Hampton University, one of the nation's first historically black colleges and easily one of the most beautiful academic settings in the Commonwealth.

Those Crazy Beaches

A cultural phenomena strikes Washington every Friday afternoon during the summer. It seems like the whole metro area has gone to the beach, at least judging from the endless snake of traffic along U.S. Highway 50 or down Interstate 95. Beachgoing in these parts isn't a solitary experience, so don't expect the ambiance of a deserted tropical island once you get there (the exception is Assateague, described in this chapter's Close-Up).

The mid-Atlantic, however, does have its share of perfectly fine beaches, each with its own distinctive personality. To beach his own, in other words. Assateague Island National Seashore, a favorite place in the sun, is 33 miles of pristine, undeveloped beachfront stretching from nearly Ocean City, Maryland, to Chincoteague, Virginia. It is much less visited than any other beach in the region and is highlighted in this chapter's "Close-Up."

Five other beaches in brief: Ocean City, Maryland, three hours from Washington, is a nice stretch of beach, but extremely commercial both on and away from the water (tacky boardwalk emporiums, strip malls, honkytonks and high-rise condos, etc.). It is, nonetheless, a huge hangout for the young and wild at heart. There are hotels, motels and rentals galore — too many to name and in every price range — so your best bet is to contact the Ocean City (or O.C.) Visitor Information line at (410) 289-2800.

To the north, Bethany Beach, Delaware, attracts a much older (late 20s through retirees) crowd than O.C. but is not nearly as developed with high-rises and commercial properties. Parking is a hassle, though; it's very restricted in residential areas, and options are few so you'll probably end up walking a bit. Still, it's a great weekend destination just for the relaxed setting and comparatively pristine beaches. Rehoboth Beach, Delaware, just north of Bethany, is something of a cross between the latter and Ocean City. Plenty of families and older singles can be found roaming Rehoboth's busy, colorful boardwalk, but there are also some very posh beach homes here, as well as upscale eateries.

Dewey Beach, Delaware, is the recognized hip place for the 20- and 30-something weekenders from Metro Washington. It has an active nightlife with lots of bustling restaurants and bars (like Mardi Gras in New Orleans, the legendary Bottle and Cork must be experienced at least once).

Finally, we have to mention Cape May, New Jersey, on the southernmost tip of the Garden State and a world apart from the urban corridor of the Northeast.

A ferry ride away from the Delaware shore by way of the Cape May-Lewes Ferry, (302) 645-6313, Cape May, New Jersey is a seaside dreamscape of Victorian homes, shops and cottages. At the turn of the century it was a gambling mecca for southern aristocrats and sea captains but today enjoys a robust tourist trade, luring visitors to such atmospheric bed and breakfasts as the elegant **Mainstay Inn** ($155, breakfast and tea included), 635 Columbia Avenue, (609) 884-8690, and the Gothic-style **Abbey**, Columbia Avenue and Gurney Street, (609) 884-4506 (rates from $115, breakfast and tea included). The entire town is listed on the National Register of Historic Places; it's one of those treasures of the mid-Atlantic that's not to be missed.

It is easy enough to find lodging at all these areas by searching the classified ads (rentals) or travel section of the Washington, D.C. newspapers. You can also contact the Delaware State Visitor Center at (302) 739-4266.

Annapolis — Boating and Bars

Maryland's state capital is a pretty town of cobbled streets, historical sights and glorious waterviews, but thanks to the United States Naval Academy and St. John's College, it's also a party capital extraordinaire. Just 45 minutes from downtown D.C., Annapolis is an easy

daytrip, and many Washingtonians make the short trek just to browse the antique shops, walk along the harbor or dine in one of the myriad restaurants that line the town's main arteries.

Summer or winter, you'll gravitate to the city dock at the foot of town. All roads seem to lead here and, as you might imagine, the horseshoe-shaped harbor is bordered by shops, bars and restaurants for every budget and age group. You will, of course, run into plenty of cadets from the Naval Academy, spiffy in their uniforms. A favorite pastime in summer is to hang out at the water's edge, admiring the yachts that moor here. The singles scene can be very active, with fancy boats replacing fancy cars.

For more serious sightseeing, don't miss the **Naval Academy**, a sprawling campus that dominates the town. There's a visitors' center in Ricketts Hall near the entrance (Gate 1 at the base of King George Street, just past the intersection with Randall Street, and overlooking the water), where you can sign up for one of four daily walking tours (adult admission $5.50). You'll learn that the academy was founded in 1845 and now trains some 4,300 cadets each year. You'll see the world's largest dormitory, Bancroft Hall, and even visit a sample room. Naval hero and Revolutionary War patriot John Paul Jones is buried in the chapel, which features stained-glass windows depicting Biblical stories of the sea. Finally, you'll be left free to browse the Academy Museum, filled with model ships and nautical artifacts. For information, call (410) 263-6933.

Maryland's State House is also open for tours. It is the oldest in the nation to remain in continuous legislative use, and many historical events have occurred here, such as the ratification of the Treaty of Paris ending the Revolutionary War (1784). It also once served as the nation's capitol building, and it is where George Washington resigned as commander-in-chief in 1783. Tours, which begin with a short video, are free and conducted daily, (410) 974-3400. The State House is in the center of State Circle, the confluence of Maryland Avenue, Francis Street, East Street and West Street.

Travel east on Maryland Avenue, then make your first left onto Prince George Street to arrive at St. John's College, a small, beautiful liberal arts campus famous for teaching the great classics. Founded in 1696, it is the third oldest college in the United States. On campus is the Liberty Tree, a tulip poplar estimated to be more than 400 years old.

Another major Annapolis attraction is **William Paca House** and adjoining gardens. The grand Georgian mansion was built by Paca, who served as governor of Annapolis from 1782 to 1785; however, you won't see his handiwork if you visit Paca House. The original was torn down in the 1960s, and only through the painstaking work of preservationists and archeologists was it able to be reconstructed. It is a remarkably accurate work, and many of the original remains have been incorporated into the building. The gardens have been as beautifully restored, and feature formal parterres, fountains, a Chinese bridge and a miniature forest. The site can be rented for weddings and other ceremonial occasions.

Close to the city dock is the **Maritime Museum**, (410) 268-5576, a small exhibit that covers the history of the city. It is housed in the 18th century Victualling Warehouse, used during the Revolutionary War to store supplies.

When you get hungry, there's plenty to choose from in Annapolis. Opposite the city dock is the Market House, a restored historical structure that used to serve as a warehouse, it now is home to all sorts of fast-food eateries. For real local, try Buddy's Crabs & Ribs at the center of Market Place near the city dock, at 100 Main Street, (410) 626-1100. This big informal warehouse overlooking the waterfront is a great place for kids. You'll get crabs by the bushel or ribs by the rack and lots of newspapers and napkins so you can plunge in with no worries about the mess.

For special occasions, try the Treaty of Paris restaurant in the historic Maryland Inn, 16 Church Circle. The menu features Continental and New American cuisine served in a formal setting. You can also stay overnight at the inn, (410) 263-2641. Annapolis has plenty of chain hotels and inns. For more information, contact the Annapolis and Anne Arundel County Conference & Visitors Bureau, 26 West Street, Annapolis, Maryland, (410) 268-8687.

State Tourism Offices

All begin with (800):

Maryland	543-1036
Virginia	934-9184
West Virginia	225-5982
Pennsylvania	847-4872

State Bed and Breakfasts

Virginia	934-9184
Maryland	736-4667 or 899-7533

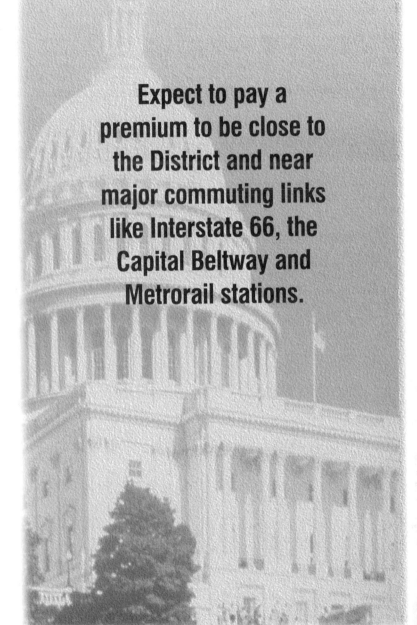

Expect to pay a premium to be close to the District and near major commuting links like Interstate 66, the Capital Beltway and Metrorail stations.

Neighborhoods and Real Estate

Finding a home — whether it's an apartment, condominium, townhome or a detached house — can be one of the most stressful activities you'll ever engage in. It's tough enough if you're already familiar with the market, but for most newcomers this isn't the case.

The Metro Washington real estate scene is one of the most intimidating anywhere, given the physical expanse of the region, its exorbitant housing costs, and the subtle but important differences (political, social, demographic) that exist among Washington, D.C., Virginia and Maryland.

This chapter doesn't promise any easy remedies for evading the house-hunting blues. Our point is simply to introduce you to the residential real estate market, the types of neighborhoods and homes available here and the major players in the home brokerage and construction industries.

The Residential Real Estate Market

There are two fundamental truths about the Metro Washington housing market. One, we will never, ever, see the kind of price appreciation that took place around here in the gold rush days of the mid '80s. In some neighborhoods, a less than auspicious rambler that was priced at $90,000 in 1980 could go as high as $130,000 in 1986 and $155,000 in 1988. Twenty-percent-plus annual appreciation was not uncommon in several areas!

Two, Metro Washington, was once thought recession-proof because of the high percent-

age of government workers with jobs that were theoretically secure. The crash of the early '90s, however, proved the assumption false. Prices for houses in the half-million dollar range — not at all uncommon in Metro Washington — crashed as much as 20 to 30 percent.

Even today, recovery is not complete in the upper brackets, but sales of new homes in the Washington area are indeed up 48 percent since the start of the decade, a year most economists call the abyss of the most recent national recession. Home values are appreciating over 5 percent a year in the mid-priced homes and the outlook for the remainder of the decade is for over 5 percent annual gains, well above the national average. To illustrate, the median price of a home sold in Metro Washington in 1995 was $156,000, while the median in 1996 was $178,459, an increase of 14 percent over a single year. The rate of sales of existing homes is up, too, with the end of 1997 reflecting the best performance since the boom years of the late 1980s — up 21 percent from the previous year, according to statistics compiled by local Realtors (some figures courtesy of Douglas G. Cofer, Long and Foster Real Estate, Burke, Virginia). Prices in Virginia are up 9 percent since 1992, and in Maryland, they're up 6 percent. The District, however, has seen no appreciation in home prices, though the rate of resales increased a whopping 57 percent in 1997 from the previous year.

To sum up, housing is still awfully expensive in the Nation's Capital, and we doubt that will ever change. The average price of a home here is $198,200; for a new home it's

$205,000. These are steep numbers when you consider the national average price of a new house is about $150,000. According to Runzheimer International, a firm that compiles such statistics, you can expect to pay $245,400 for a four-bedroom, 2½-bath, 2,000-square-foot home in Washington's suburbs.

With that said, the Washington area still commands a high home ownership rate. About 80 percent of householders own their homes, compared with 65 percent nationally. The implication is that while Metro Washington homes are expensive, many people can still afford them.

About 38 percent of owners live in detached single-family houses, while 40 percent live in townhouses and 22 percent in condominiums. For those 20 percent who don't own, the fair-market rent for a one-bedroom apartment is an estimated $750, if you take the entire Metro area into consideration. For two bedrooms expect to pay $825, and for three bedrooms $950. House rentals can range from $700 a month for a townhome in the outer suburbs to $3,500 for a plush Georgetown dwelling.

One thing to keep in mind whether you're going to buy or rent is that the pricing rationale here is similar to other large urban areas. In other words, expect to pay a premium to be close to the District and near major commuting links like Interstate 66, the Capital Beltway and Metrorail stations. Prices drop as you move outward; commute times increase. It's the age-old trade-off.

For more information on the local real estate market, licensing practices, ethics and other issues involving buying or renting a home, we suggest you call one or more of the following agencies:

Maryland Association of Realtors, (301) 261-8290

Washington Area Council of Real Estate Organizations, (202) 789-8889

District of Columbia Real Estate Commission, (202) 727-7849

Northern Virginia Association of Realtors, (703) 207-3200

Neighborhoods and Homes

Washington, D.C.

People tend to forget that Washington, beyond the monuments, is a city of neighborhoods — communities with their own dynamics, history and sense of place. Most of these enclaves are close-knit and largely self-contained. The whole effect is something akin to a patchwork of small towns, albeit connected to an urban core.

In a city tagged for its transience, it may come as a surprise that the majority of the District's neighborhoods are home to several generations of families.

As a place to live, the District offers proximity to all major employment centers, including those in Suburban Maryland and Northern Virginia. Virtually no one here commutes longer than 40 minutes to work. Washington's prized Metro mass-transit system, famed nightlife and cultural opportunities, miles of parks and forests, stately homes and shaded streets, plus its allure as the nation's capital, will always make it a desirable address.

That desirability comes with a price, however. The average price of a home in D.C. is $224,000. The median rent is $459, although rents of $800 to $1,200 are more the norm in prime neighborhoods.

The vast majority of newcomers who relocate to the District settle in Northwest, so we'll begin our neighborhood tour here.

Adams Morgan, which radiates from Columbia Road and 18th Street NW, is Washington's largest and most celebrated ethnic neighborhood. Its global-minded eateries are famous in these parts (see our dining chapter) and it's here where you'll find African clothiers next to Spanish bridal shops and Turkish shoe stores. Adams Morgan and neighboring Mount Pleasant have attracted a growing number of young professionals, including many tied to the White House and Capitol Hill who live in gentrified townhouses and large apartment buildings. A few years ago, Mount Pleasant experienced an unfortunate riot, but the tensions have cooled and the neighborhood seems determined to carry on as one of Washington's most integrated communities.

Immediately to the south of Adams Morgan is Dupont Circle, Washington's answer to Greenwich Village. Interspersed among the cafés, art galleries and boutiques are grand old brownstones and row houses. Many prominent members of the gay community, artists, young progressives and aging bohemians call Dupont home. While claiming many of the same attributes as Adams Morgan, Dupont is decidedly more established and thus housing costs tend to be higher here.

Closer to downtown, and wrapping around the campus of George Washington University, are the highly urbanized neighborhoods of Foggy Bottom and the West End. Both are apartment and condo dense, with the former consisting mostly of students and professors and the latter primarily single professionals who commute by Metro or walk to nearby offices. The neighborhoods are wedged between Georgetown to the west and downtown to the east, a consolation to the area's overall lack of restaurants and nightlife.

Downtown living is enjoying somewhat of a renaissance thanks to the continued revitalization of the Pennsylvania Avenue corridor. Several older buildings, including the historic Lansburgh, have been revamped and now house some of the most exclusive condo units in Washington.

By most measures, Washington's toniest address is still Georgetown, with its famed M Street/Wisconsin Avenue nightlife, stylish federal townhomes and secluded estates. West of Wisconsin Avenue is dominated by Georgetown University and its students; east of the avenue is markedly quieter, with bigger homes and well-heeled residents. For those with money — tiny townhouses can demand half a million dollars — and patience to bear the weekend crush of partiers, there is simply no other close-in neighborhood that can match the charm and convenience of Georgetown.

Immediately to the north, in Glover Park, a more down-to-earth atmosphere pervades. Brick townhomes and duplexes cluster around small parks and green spaces all within a short stroll of Wisconsin Avenue. Young families, Georgetown University professors, middle-aged empty nesters and longtime residents live side by side and in harmony in this civic-minded and politically progressive neighborhood.

Moving farther north puts you in the land of milk and honey. The neighborhoods of Foxhall Road, Spring Valley and Wesley Heights are the stuff of *Architectural Digest* photo shoots. The neighbors tend to be older than those who reside to the south, politically more conservative and measurably wealthier. On some streets, multi- million-dollar homes are more the rule than the exception.

To the east, in the heart of Northwest, are Cleveland Park and Woodley Park, a checkerboard of beautiful Victorian homes with wide porches, shady yards, and sprawling square footage. You'll also find along Wisconsin Avenue numerous older apartment buildings and remodeled townhouses. Easy access to Massachusetts, Wisconsin and Connecticut avenues, Metro and such attractions as the National Zoo give the neighborhoods considerable prestige with up-and-coming professionals.

In the far stretches of upper Northwest, neighborhoods like Tenleytown, American University Park, Barnaby Woods and Chevy Chase (not to be confused with neighboring Chevy Chase, Maryland) glow with a sense of Small Town America charm, complete with quiet treelined streets, beautiful spacious lawns and kids on bicycles. Along the upper western edges of Rock Creek Park, Forest Hills unfolds with palatial homes and tucked-away streets that allow maximum privacy for the rich and powerful.

East of Rock Creek, along upper 16th Street NW, Shepherd Park, Brightwood Park and Crestwood move to a relaxed suburban beat. Homes are substantially more affordable than similar dwellings to the west of the park, and 16th Street provides a mostly hassle-free link to downtown and points south.

Two Northwest neighborhoods that are rebounding from years of neglect are Shaw, which straddles 14th Street above downtown, and LeDroit Park, just to the south of Howard University. The Metro Green Line stop at Shaw/Howard University comes with the promise of further revitalization of these Victorian neighborhoods, but crime remains an ongoing problem.

In Northeast, another neighborhood on the rebound is Brookland, which houses an interesting mix of Catholic University students and professors, as well as elderly middle-class residents who live in well-kept row houses and Cape Cods. The university and its rolling, wooded campus dominate much of the neighborhood and bring a sense of respite from the clamor of the inner city.

The most sought-after address in Northeast is Capitol Hill, which also spreads into Southeast. As you might imagine, Capitol Hill teems with young congressional staffers, lobbyists and members of Congress. Huge brownstones and smaller townhomes are the mainstays but a few apartment and condo units can be found. As a rule, those areas closest to the Capitol command the highest prices and are considered the safest. The higher the street numbers, however, the likelier you are to encounter crime. Even in the most exclusive sections, crime remains more of a problem than in other Washington neighborhoods of comparable price.

In Southwest, the neighborhood of choice is the Waterfront, located north of the Anacostia River. A haven for federal employees, much of the Southwest Waterfront is within a short walk of Capitol Hill and L'Enfant Plaza, the massive government complex. The area boasts some fine restaurants, theaters and pricey townhomes. Seventies-style, high-rise condo and apartment buildings, however, make up the bulk of housing, which is typically more affordable than similar close-in units found to the north of the National Mall.

Anacostia, on the opposite side of the river, contains the District's largest concentration of public housing. This portion of Southeast continues to battle widespread poverty and violent crime, the worst in D.C.

Northern Virginia

Parts of northern Virginia, such as Rosslyn, are so close to Washington that you can walk to the city in 10 minutes or, as in the case of Arlington and Alexandria, drive there in five.

Other Virginia suburbs are so far-flung that you need close to an hour to reach the city.

Close-in suburbs are hardly distinguishable from D.C. itself. They have high-rises, choked traffic, restaurant rows, and lots of businesses. On the other hand, there are some suburbs that seem to typify the centuries-old vision of Virginia: gracious colonial manors, lush greenery, rolling meadows, white fences and horses. The remarkable thing is, even some of the suburbs within 40 minutes of the city have that Virginia Hunt Country atmosphere. A good real estate agent will help you narrow down your choices, weigh factors in your decision, such as distance, cost, schools and atmosphere. To help get you started, you may want to contact some agencies prior to your arrival. Later in this chapter, we've listed the largest ones in Metro Washington. Below, is an area-by-area overview of Washington's closest Virginia suburbs.

Alexandria

Sharing ranks with Arlington County as Northern Virginia's closest-in suburb, Alexandria has strong historical and cultural ties to the District of Columbia. Make no mistake, though: while Alexandria may be a suburb of Washington, it's a Virginia city first and foremost.

Alexandria is immersed in an almost overpowering sense of place. How can it not be with George Washington and Robert E. Lee once calling it home? The municipality is also characteristically Virginian in the way it is run — efficiently and pragmatically.

During rush hour no part of Alexandria is more than 40 minutes from Washington. Metrorail has three stations within the city limits. These are just some of the reasons why the average price of a home ($240,000) is higher than in the rest of Northern Virginia. Most newcomers' impressions of Alexandria are that it's a lot like Georgetown, but without the urban chaos. And they're right. Sort of.

Old Town, the city's most visible neighborhood, could stand double for its northern counterpart on a number of accounts. It's also pricey: townhouses start at $220,000, but you're more likely to see them up in the $350,000 to $700,000 range, especially as you progress east toward the handsomely restored Potomac waterfront. Since colonial-era homes weren't designed with the automobile in mind, on-street parking is almost always the rule here and on weekends things can get a little sticky. But Old Town is, well, Old Town, and that's the biggest selling point of all, especially among the young up-and-coming crowd that tends to migrate here.

Though some would be hard pressed to admit it, there's more to Alexandria than Old Town. Not too long ago Del Ray, which wraps around U.S. Highway 1 and Potomac Yards (a massive train switching yard), was solely a blue-collar neighborhood. Gentrification has set in and many bungalows and Cape Cods now command upward of $200,000.

Alexandria communities that most resemble suburbia are Rosemont, Seminary and Beverly Hills. Mount Vernon, to the south, has a city address of Alexandria, but is actually part of Fairfax County, so we'll cover it in that section. A lot of the homes in suburban Alexandria were built in the early 1960s on large lots; prices run from $200,000 to more than $1 million, with the greatest concentration in the $350,000 range.

Along the western edge of town are the self-contained neighborhoods of Park Fairfax and South Fairlington. The majority of housing is townhomes and apartment buildings, many of which sprang up after World War II to house federal workers. Now they're popular with single professionals and first-time buyers.

Also out in the West End is Landmark, an area of high-rise condos, apartment buildings and shopping centers located off Interstate 395. Condos start at $75,000 for a one-bedroom unit and can run upwards to $200,000 for deluxe models.

Arlington County

Arlington looks and acts a lot like a city. Its 26 square miles are a collage of satellite business districts, high-rise apartment complexes

and tucked away residential neighborhoods. The county has more Metro stations per capita than any other suburb and its population is decidedly middle-aged.

Arlington is the most urban county in Metro D.C. and it's unique in that there are no incorporated cities or towns within its borders. Like Alexandria, it was once part of the District of Columbia and many residents here are closer to downtown D.C. and Capitol Hill than are most Washingtonians. Needless to say, Arlington is a convenient and especially attractive area for single, workaholic professionals who like being less than 15 minutes from most of the area's employment centers.

The county is usually identified with its massive business/residential corridors — Crystal City, Pentagon City, Clarendon, Ballston and Rosslyn. Apartments and condos are the most plentiful housing options here, with the former ranging from $600 to $1,100 a month for one-bedroom units, and the latter commanding $75,000 to over $200,000.

The northern tier of the county is almost exclusively residential neighborhoods, some of the most stately areas in Metro Washington. Single-family homes in communities like Country Club Hills run from $250,000 for older brick colonials to one million dollars and more for estate homes.

Despite its dense nature, Arlington has set aside hundreds of acres of park land, and its riverfront bike path, which affords stunning views of Washington and the Potomac, is a source of intense civic pride.

Fairfax County

Northern Virginia's largest jurisdiction runs the gamut on the types of neighborhoods and living options available to newcomers. In Fairfax County you'll find two-story colonials on quiet cul-de-sacs, modest Cape Cods and ramblers in older neighborhoods, lakefront townhomes in new developments, California contemporaries in planned communities, giant estate homes in wooded parklike settings

INSIDERS' TIP

For a helpful resource in planning and making your move, check out *The Insiders Guide® to Relocation*.

The Carlyle House in Old Town Alexandria served as the headquarters of Gen. Braddock, leader of the British forces during the French and Indian War.

and turnkey condos in high-rise buildings. If there is a common thread that runs through this massive county, it is that it's overwhelmingly middle- to upper-class.

Fairfax is among the top five counties in the nation in median household income, at $70,000 per household (also see the Metro Washington Overview chapter) and in the top 15 in median housing values. The average price for a new house is $225,000. Apartments start at $700 a month in the newer complexes. Those are values if you're coming from the urban areas of the Northeast or parts of the West Coast but a shock if you hail from virtually any other part of the nation.

One affordable neighborhood inside the Beltway is Annandale, an area that has long been a magnet for federal workers and their families. Annandale's signature red-brick ramblers and comfortable ranch homes are priced in the $150,000 to $250,000 range. The community is one of the oldest suburbs in Northern Virginia and is centrally located next to several busy road arteries and Interstate 495.

To the north, Falls Church, an independent municipality, comes with a small-town charm and a mix of older stately Victorians and new townhouse developments. Single-family homes start at $140,000 and work their way up to more than $600,000. Virginia Highway 7 (Leesburg Pike) cuts through the center of the city, offering easy access to Washington and most of Fairfax County. The average commute time to downtown D.C. is 35 minutes.

Great Falls, located in the gorgeous bluffs that tower above the Potomac River in northern Fairfax, and extending through rolling countryside all the way to the Loudoun County line, is a community of large houses situated on expansive lots of a half-acre and more. Most of the homes here are colonial in design, and $500,000 to multimillion dollar price tags are the norm. Great Falls and neighboring McLean, a neighborhood closer to Washington, are known for their great schools, country lanes and serene, wooded surroundings. Horse farms, ponds and large wildflower meadows are not uncommon here, and you can still escape the sense of overdevelopment rampant in other parts of the Metro area. While only a 20- to 30-minute drive to D.C., the morning commutes along Chain Bridge Road (Route 123), Georgetown Pike and the George Washington Memorial Parkway can be trying at times.

Moving outside the Beltway, the fast-growing planned community of Burke attracts suburbanites looking for newer houses, plenty of parks for the kids and proximity to major shopping centers. The typical single-family home starts at approximately $200,000; townhouses run from $150,000. For all its pluses, Burke commuters face a challenge each day along Braddock and Old Keene Mill roads, or via the Fairfax County Parkway to always-congested Interstate 66. Expect a 35- to 50-minute commute into the city.

Wedged between Burke and Annandale is Springfield, another older community of modest ramblers on large lots mixed with newer and larger homes on small lots. Like Annandale, Springfield is home to thousands of government and military workers. A large stock of detached homes falls into the $125,000 to $300,000 range. Townhouses begin at around $120,000 and condominiums start at $80,000. Although only 15 miles south of Washington, Springfield's major link to the District is Interstate 95, one of the region's most congested arteries. In all fairness, however, the Virginia Department of Transportation has done miracles in recent years improving existing roads and constructing convenient new secondary roads such as the Franconia-Springfield Parkway.

The parkway (as well as Franconia Road and ever-lengthening South Van Dorn Street) has become a vital transportation link for the massive yet still-developing Kingstowne community and its much smaller and less-exclusive neighbor, Manchester Lakes — places that have become especially attractive to single professionals, the newly married and young families. Located just east of Springfield in the Franconia section of the county (which in many parts carries an Alexandria mailing address), Kingstowne and Manchester Lakes offer a selection of nice apartments, condominiums, townhouses and (in Kingstowne only) single-family homes. Some of the smaller condos in Manchester Lakes can be had for less than $100,000; expect to pay well more than $100,000, meanwhile, in either community for townhouses and closer to $200,000 and more for single-family residences.

Whatever turns the housing market takes, Kingstowne and Manchester Lakes will likely only grow in popularity thanks to their appealing character, accessibility, convenience to the District and Old Town Alexandria and prime location some two miles from the shopping mecca of Springfield Mall and the new Franconia-Springfield Metro station.

Mount Vernon, in southeastern Fairfax County, retains a sense of exclusivity because of its proximity to George Washington's venerable riverside estate and Old Town Alexandria. Detached homes on large lots are the backbone of this beautiful, verdant neighborhood located between U.S. Highway 1 and George Washington Memorial Parkway. Small side streets and country lanes lead you to manicured estates overlooking the Potomac River — many with private docks. This is a neighborhood for brisk walks on a fall day, thanks to the numerous quiet roads and bicycle paths in the area. Tucked into this affluent area are some amazing bargains — small ramblers and older homes on large lots just waiting for young families to add improvements. Traveling south on the George Washington Memorial Parkway from Old Town Alexandria, turn right on Wellington Road and take any of the side streets. You'll discover neighborhoods where children still play outside, families walk together along sleepy roads where traffic is so infrequent that no sidewalks are necessary and old, tall trees form shady canopies on even the warmest summer days.

Heading to Oakton and Vienna in the north-central part of the county, (it wasn't long ago that these two were considered Fairfax's far-western suburbs), you'll encounter an area in transition from woodsy to highly developed. Located off of I-66, just a couple miles outside the Beltway, these communities are now right in the heart of the county, a factor that bodes well with commuters, many of whom use the nearby Vienna Metro station. Oakton is mostly a maze of sprawling subdivisions — albeit with larger-than-normal lots — but some parts resemble Great Falls in both topography and opulence. Vienna, an incorporated town settled by the Scots in the early 1800s, has a more established, small-town feel. Homes in the former range from $200,000 to $800,000, while in Vienna, prices are more modest, at $180,000 to $500,000.

Farther west along I-66, the City of Fairfax, another independent municipality, boasts a fine old historic district and an ample supply of moderately-priced homes. Single-family units start at $150,000 while townhouses are available from $120,000. Fairfax is at the junction of several busy roads; commutes into Washington range from 40 to 60 minutes.

In the far western reaches of the county, the rapidly growing communities of Centreville and Chantilly attract first-time home buyers with a plentiful variety of townhomes and condominiums. Move-up buyers can purchase large colonials ($170,000 to $350,000) for 20 to 30 percent less than comparable homes closer in. Commuting times into downtown can run 45 to 75 minutes. Nearby, bordered by Virginia Highway 123 and Virginia Highway 28 are the pastoral districts of Clifton and Fairfax Station. The town of Clifton is actually a small village of white picket fences, gingerbread houses, kitchen gardens, gravel roads, and front porch swings. You can walk through this historical little town in 15 minutes — it is surrounded by estates of five or more acres that blend into the area known as Fairfax Station.

You can hardly tell the difference between the countryside bordering Clifton and Fairfax Station: both feature colonials of three to seven thousand square feet on five-acre tracts, private roads, abundant wildlife, unspoiled woods, and tranquil family neighborhoods. The northern end of Fairfax Station culminates at the edge of the aforementioned Burke — a decidedly middle-priced area, and the rolling hills give way to smaller lots and, in some developments, tract mansions. In fact, at the Burke-Fairfax Station border, the subdivisions are no different from elsewhere in suburbia. The Fairfax Station-Clifton area, further south, is a version of lavish Great Falls for a cost of 20 to 30 percent less.

Out near Washington Dulles International Airport, Herndon, an independent town, and Reston, a lake- and tree-rich planned community, are populated with young professionals and their families. Detached single-family homes ($130,000 to $500,000) are the residences of choice, but a sizable number of townhouse and condo developments offer first-time buyers $80,000 and up alternatives. Both areas are booming, and it seems that upscale malls and pedestrian shopping/entertainment complexes are added every few months. Hidden away from the traffic are wonderful recreation areas, like Reston's Lake Anne, where waterside residents have docks, pontoon boats and motorized floats. Winding along this beautiful refuge are townhouses and single family dwellings with large windows overlooking a scene right out of Monet painting — whimsical bridges, flower-lined canals, weeping willows and, at the center of it all, a glass-surfaced lake suitable for swimming, windsurfing and even fishing. Also at water's edge is a town plaza featuring a crescent of restaurants and outdoor cafés.

You'd never know that these wonderful areas are bordered by the Dulles Toll Road — heavily trafficked but nonetheless functional — and just minutes from Washington Dulles International Airport.

Prince William County

In a metropolitan area where the term "affordable housing" seems like an oxymoron, Prince William County has become a sanctuary for suburbanites seeking value and space at prices that don't raise blood pressure.

At $135,160, the county's median-price home is about 30 to 50 percent lower than those in jurisdictions to the north, explaining why more first-time buyers and homeowners in the move-up market have settled in Prince William over the last decade. Simple demographics partly tell the story of the county's widespread appeal to young families: Nearly a third of Prince William's 215,000 residents are younger than 18 and more than half are younger than 35, according to the U.S. Census Bureau (see chapter on economy).

The sprawling bedroom community is one of the fastest-growing areas in the nation. In 1980, less than 150,000 residents were spread across the county's 350 square miles. By the year 2,000, Prince William officials expect 350,000 people to call the county home.

Neighborhoods along the Interstate 95 corridor such as Lake Ridge, Woodbridge and Montclair have been the biggest gainers so far, with most single-family homes selling between $120,000 and $265,000. Townhouses start at $80,000 and seldom exceed $175,000, while condos typically start at $70,000. The next area pinpointed for growth is the western part of the county near Manassas and I-66, where large single-family homes in new subdivisions can be purchased for $170,000.

The rapid transformation from a quiet exurb to thriving suburb has come with its share of growing pains. Road congestion, while getting better, is still chronic. Prince William commuters spend more time on the road than anyone else in Metro Washington. The Virginia Railway Express, a relatively new commuter train service with several stops in Prince William, has lured some motorists off the road.

Loudoun County

The fortunes of this beautiful county 30 miles northwest of Washington are closely tied to the development of Washington Dulles International Airport.

Dulles' renaissance over the last 10 years has played out nicely for Loudoun, helping bring in new aerospace and international high-tech firms and boosting the population (see our Metro Washington Overview chapter). Most of the county's population lies in and around Leesburg and points east along Route 7. Homes in diverse communities like Sterling, Ashburn and Sugarland run between $130,000 to $300,000. The average townhouse costs $123,000.

As one moves west and south of Leesburg, the graceful county seat, you enter hunt country, a land of blue bloods and stone fences, breathtaking country estates, Kentucky Derby-winning stables and rolling vineyards. The most modest of homes in communities like Middleburg, Upperville and Bluemont will cost about $175,000 and these are easily eclipsed by the number of multi-million-dollar horse farms that crisscross the pretty countryside.

Suburban Maryland

Montgomery County

Montgomery County was the first true suburb of Washington, D.C. Virginia, after all, was across the river; to get to Montgomery all you had to do was cross Western Avenue. Manmade borders, as Marylanders will tell you, are easier to cross than physical borders.

Go up to Montgomery County today and real estate agents will be the first to remind you of this. Indeed, getting into Washington is likely to be less of a hassle from the close-in suburbs because of the absence of bridges. That said, be warned that Interstate 270, which runs north to Rockville, Gaithersburg and Frederick County, can be a commuting nightmare. In the past few years, major improvements, including new lanes and upgraded feeder roads, have resulted in a better stretch of highway, but a look at the daily traffic reports will show that the improvements have barely kept up with demand. Interstate 495, the Beltway into Montgomery County, is hardly better, though both are good, multi-laned roads.

Like Fairfax County, Montgomery County has every type of housing and neighborhood option under the sun. Like its Virginia cousin, housing doesn't come cheap, with $228,000 the average price for a home. Renters can expect to pay $750 for a newer, one-bedroom apartment and $850 for a two-bedroom unit.

The quintessential Montgomery County community has got to be Bethesda, a residential sanctuary for thousands of government officials and industry leaders. North Bethesda, convenient to the Beltway and Metro, is the denser section of town, chock full of townhouse developments and mid-rise condo units. To the south, in neighborhoods like Chevy Chase, you'll find vintage suburbia, with large Victorians and colonials situated on impeccably-manicured lots. Single-family homes range between $200,000 and $800,000. Condos start at around $100,000. Commuting time into the city seldom exceeds 30 minutes.

The equestrian set is still holding on in Suburban Maryland, and nowhere is it more evident than in posh Potomac. In some areas, subdivisions have chopped down once-magnificent farms into gaudy five-acre horse "farmettes," but the overall atmosphere remains largely pastoral. Townhouses — the few that are here — start at $220,000, while single-family abodes range from $400,000 to several million. This is where many Washington sports, media and political figures live and the name "Potomac" in your address is sure to add cachet to your image. River Road, Potomac's lovely link with the outside world, is a winding two-laner that wasn't designed for express commuting, and the moderate crowding at rush hour is testimony to that. Then again, many of the folks who live in Potomac can probably set their own schedules, which probably explains why rush hour isn't worse.

Hovering the District line east of Rock Creek Park are Silver Spring and Takoma Park, two established and quite different residential areas. Silver Spring is probably Montgomery's most ethnic community and of late its downtown corridor has witnessed a renaissance of sorts, boasting some very good international restaurants. Single-family homes start at $140,000 and are rarely more than $300,000.

Takoma Park, immediately to the south, is Metro Washington's answer to Berkeley, California, or Boulder, Colorado. Almost beyond politically correct (the entire city is designated a Nuclear Free Zone), the town, which straddles the Montgomery/Prince George's border, is a flash point of community activism. A mix of young, free spirits, middle-aged bohemians and elderly longtime residents live in older and mostly modest Cape Cods and Victorians, and the prices pretty much mirror those in Silver Spring, but the setting is more about trees and big yards than in neighboring Silver Spring (the latter has similar enclaves, however).

The village of Kensington, 8 miles north of D.C. and 1 mile north of the Beltway, defies its highly suburban location. Fewer than 2,000 people live in this half-square-mile community that is among the oldest suburbs in Metro Washington (incorporated in 1894). Many of the Victorian homes date back to the 1890s, adding a nostalgic air to the place. There are rolling hills and mature trees dotted with houses on generous lots, as well as more typical suburban streets featuring sidewalks and closely spaced homes. Parts of Kensington border Rock Creek Park's Beach Drive, and the homes along here can be in the half mil-lion dollar range. For the most part, though, houses start at $175,000 and work their way upward of $400,000.

Most of the people north of the Beltway live in or around the communities of Wheaton, Rockville and Gaithersburg. Metrorail and Georgia Avenue connect Wheaton — a middle-to lower middle class, ethnically mixed neighborhood — with Washington. In Wheaton, you'll find reasonably priced apartments (from $750 for a two-bedroom), and small, modest brick ramblers and Cape Cods, many under $200,000. The more affluent Rockville, the county seat, and Gaithersburg, its fast-growing northern neighbor, were once serene little dairy towns whose pastures are now dotted with townhomes and single-family developments. Rockville has most of the detached housing ($200,000 to $600,000) and is family oriented. Gaithersburg has a large population of young professionals and young families who tend to migrate toward moderately priced townhomes ($120,000 and up) in areas like Montgomery Village, a planned residential community.

Two northern Montgomery County communities in transition are Germantown and Damascus. Germantown is the denser of the two, with its rolling hills carpeted by new condominiums, townhouses and shopping centers. About 10 miles up Maryland Highway 27), once-sleepy Damascus is evolving into a bedroom community of first-time homeowners who are just as likely to commute to Baltimore as Washington.

Prince George's County

The average price of a home in Prince George's County is $135,900, more than 30 percent less than a comparable house next door in Montgomery County. Rents are much cheaper, too; the median is $610 for a two-bedroom apartment unit.

INSIDERS' TIP

You want to look, but don't want to hook up with a real estate agent yet? Most agents will be happy to provide you with a long, computer-generated list of homes in your price range in hopes of ultimately securing you as a client. Get a map and drive by the homes to get an idea of those you want to explore further.

Why the sizable price difference? Perception. Prince George's could use some good spin doctors. The county's reputation is as a blue-collar haven with subpar schools and too much crime. Yes, it's more working-class than Montgomery and Fairfax and yes, it's had its share of crime problems, especially in neighborhoods close to the District border. Prince George's is also the most racially integrated county in Metro Washington and its schools have made tremendous progress in recent years.

Progressive communities like College Park teem with college students, artists, writers and aging activists. University Park and Greenbelt (home of Goddard Space Center) have high concentrations of academicians, scientists and engineers, while Bowie, Mitchellville and Upper Marlboro attract white-collar professionals and families. Waterfront living gives Fort Washington's Tantallon neighborhood a distinct panache, and this is where you're likely to find some of the most expensive real estate in Prince George's, with many homes hitting the half million mark.

Several major road arteries, including U.S. Highway 50, Interstate 295, Branch Avenue and Pennsylvania Avenue, connect the county with nearby Washington, helping make commuting times here among the lowest in Metro D.C.

Property Taxes

In the District of Columbia and Virginia, homes are appraised at 100 percent of their market value. Homeowners in D.C. also get an exemption for the first $30,000 of their property's value. In Maryland, 40 percent of the house's value is taxed but at a much higher rate.

For a $200,000 home — about the average price in Metro D.C. — this is roughly what you'd pay in property taxes in the following jurisdictions: Washington, D.C., $3,080;

Northern Virginia: Alexandria, $2,140; Arlington County, $1,920; Fairfax County, $2,320; Loudoun County, $2,040; Prince William County, $2,720;

Suburban Maryland: Montgomery County, $2,480; Prince George's County $2,752.

Washington, D.C. recently enacted a tax break for owner/occupants of private residences. Called the Homestead Act, citizens may apply for a $30,000 deduction on the assessed value, then pay only $0.96 tax per $100 of assessed value, which would almost halve the above levy to $1,632.

In Maryland, there is a state transfer tax usually paid by the home buyer, but negotiable as to the buyer-seller split. That tax is 0.25 percent on residences up to $40,000, 0.50 percent on residences costing $40,000 to $70,000, and one percent on residences costlier than $70,000. If, however, the purchaser is a first-time home buyer, the seller is required by law to pay 0.25 percent of the transfer tax.

When you look at these figures it's important to keep in mind the type of property for which you're being taxed. A $200,000 home varies from being a condo in a premium Washington neighborhood to a modest townhouse in Old Town Alexandria to a spacious colonial on a large lot in Prince George's and Prince William counties.

Real Estate Companies

The scene in Metro Washington is changing daily, with two giants — Long & Foster and Weichert Realty — gobbling up most smaller firms or crowding them out of the area market. As of this writing, the following are some of the major real estate brokerage firms doing business in the entire Metro Washington area. You will find agents at each covering Washington, Maryland and Virginia. Any of these firms can provide you with good service in residential properties because all have various agents who specialize in different types of property, like undeveloped land or condos.

But how to choose one particular agent? Some suggestions include driving through the area you are interested in and seeing whose name appears on the most signs. That agent may be very busy, but he or she is likely a full-time real estate professional and a go-getter who knows your chosen area and is willing to invest time in prospective clients. If you're not sure of the area in which you'd like to live, browse through the classifieds of area newspapers — including the county papers and free tabloids found in supermarkets — to get an idea of pricing and types of houses available. Many real estate agents advertise in these publications, and they'll often tout their honors and awards (such as million dollar agent, president's club, or No. 1 agent in a given area, county or state).

Another method of finding an agent is to ask neighbors or coworkers for recommendations. Remember, once you've narrowed down your choices, get three references from former clients. Find out if their agent advertised to their satisfaction, gave them the service they required and, most important, sold their home or located a new one in a timely fashion. Ask the agent directly what he or she will do to market your property or help you find a new one. How much do they spend on advertising? Do they hold open houses? How often do they deal with the type of property you are hoping to buy or sell? What is the median price of the homes they deal with? If the agent specializes, for example, in condos and you're looking for a half-million dollar home in the exurbs, then they're probably not for you.

Finally, be sure your agent is a good source of newcomer information and services, whether you're buying or selling. If you're selling, you'll want them to put together a nice introductory package on your house and neighborhood for prospective buyers. If you're a buyer, you'll want the information yourself.

Coldwell Banker
Residential Real Estate, 465 Maple Ave. W., Vienna, Va. • (703) 281-1400

One of the most established brokerages in Metro Washington, and indeed the nation, Coldwell Banker is another billion-dollar sales producer, with 25 offices and 750 licensed agents. The company has its own referral network service, which can be of value, since the agency was ranked No. 1 in U.S. residential sales by both *Real Trends* magazine and *National Relocation and Real Estate* magazine.

Long & Foster Real Estate Inc.
11351 Random Hills Rd., Fairfax, Va. • (703) 359-1500

Long & Foster, the dominant regional player in both the residential and commercial markets, handles about $6 billion in residential sales in the mid-Atlantic area, according to

the region's Associations of Realtors, and based on Multiple Listing Service data. In 1996, it sold 24 percent of the homes in Metro Washington, far outdistancing its closest competitor, Weichert Realty, with 14 percent of market share. The firm's forte is in new-home sales, relocation and property management. It's also ubiquitous: Some 4,400 licensed agents work out of 140 offices scattered throughout the area.

Pardoe/Pardoe & Graham
2828 Pennsylvania Ave. NW, Washington, D.C. • (202) 333-6100

This firm specializes in upper end residential real estate, particularly in Georgetown, Potomac and McLean. It's not unusual for Pardoe properties to sell for well over $1 million dollars, which may explain why, although the firm is relatively small compared to others in Metro Washington, it ranks third behind giants Long & Foster and Weichert Realty in dollar amount of area residential sales.

RE/MAX Central
6707 Democracy Blvd., Bethesda, Md. • (301) 564-9681

From starter homes to mansions, RE/MAX has one of the largest listings in the market. It has dozens of offices throughout Northern Virginia, Washington and Suburban Maryland and is part of the RE/MAX International Referral Roster System. One interesting point about RE/MAX: its agents keep 100 percent of their commissions rather than splitting them with the company, as is typical at other companies. In exchange, they receive little administrative or advertising support. Does this make a RE/MAX agent work harder? It's difficult to say, but agents who agree to these terms are bound to be confident go-getters.

Weichert Realty
6410 Rockledge Dr., Bethesda, Md. • (301) 718-4111

Just a few years ago, this Maryland-based firm bought out a portion of D.C.'s Shannon and Luchs Co. and Virginia's Mount Vernon Realty (absorbing both names) and overnight became one of the largest and most powerful residential brokerage firms in Metro D.C., second behind Long & Foster. The company is

Blocks of quaint old rowhouses can be found on Prince Street in Alexandria.

particularly noted for its large inventory of luxury homes and estates.

Relocation Information

Following are some services and organizations you may wish to contact for information before you relocate.

• Employee Relocation Council: a national organization headquartered in Washington that serves corporations which are relocating their employees. It serves as a clearinghouse of ideas, options and services companies interested in discovering how other companies are handling relocations. The council publishes a related monthly magazine, *Mobility*. Call (202) 857-0857.

• The Relocation Counseling Center: a one-stop-shopping type of service that provides a multimedia guide to corporations sending employees to Washington. Among other things, newcomers get a relocation packet containing maps, tables on area taxes and settlement costs, breakdowns of neighborhoods and commuter mileage guides. It's operated by Long & Foster, one of the region's largest real estate agencies, and has several locations. Call (703) 359-1850.

• Quixsearch: A free, computerized service designed specifically for folk relocating to Metro Washington. It includes listings for apartments, single-family homes, townhomes and short-term housing. To find a location near you, call (800) 486-EASY.

• *New Homes Guide*: Washington's leading directory of new housing, and an invaluable tool for newcomers. This monthly publication includes maps, useful buying tips, community directories complete with price guidelines, and helpful mortgage charts and real estate tables. For a free copy, call (301) 588-0681.

• Operation Match: A regional home-sharing service sponsored by the Metropolitan Washington Council of Governments. This program matches singles, single parents with one child or small families to those who have space to rent in their homes and is ideal for those who wish to "test the waters" before making a long-term buying or renting decision. Call (202) 962-3716 for a recorded list of locations.

• Corporations are the main clients of Runzheimer International, which provides cost of living data on major U.S. markets; however, individuals can also obtain less extensive information for a cost of about $20. Call Runzheimer International at (800) 942-9949.

Relocation Guidelines

We're assuming, since you're reading this section, that you've already made the move to Metro Washington or are at least deep into the process. Therefore, we're not going to harp on the actual planning and moving stages. Instead, the following tips are intended for recent arrivals to the area.

• Keep family involved in all discussions: Although the biggest decisions already have been made, it is imperative that even the youngest family members continue to feel like they are part of the relocating process, that they have a say as a newcomer.

• Sever the moving ties — unpack: It sounds so simple, but you'd be amazed how many people are still living out of boxes six months, sometimes even a year, after their move. Stories abound of young Capitol Hill staffers who come to Washington, work for two years and leave without ever unpacking all their belongings. The quicker the boxes are emptied, the sooner your new place actually feels like home.

• Move into the culture: Don't drop long-held interests or traditions just because you've moved. If the kids were in Cub Scouts in St. Louis, get them in Cub Scouts here. If you were a member of a garden club in Boston, join one here. If you were into whitewater rafting in Colorado, investigate the opportunities in these parts. At the same time, explore the myriad new possibilities indigenous to the Washington area.

• Get out and see the city and the region: It's somewhat natural to hibernate after a move, given all the unpacking and home-maintenance logistics that loom. Try to budget time, even if it's just for an hour or two on weekends, to play tourist. You'll find that this will do wonders for reducing stress and, at the same time, will likely inspire a sense of pride in your new hometown.

• Drop the guilt trip about uprooting the kids: Although relocating can be traumatic for youngsters and teens, they're much more malleable than we give them credit for being. For instance, it used to be that parents were advised to wait and move during the summer, so the kids wouldn't have to be uprooted during the school year. Now, conventional wisdom has it that kids do better if they move into a new area during the school year, even if it's just a few weeks before the summer break. They'll have a chance to get a feel for their school, their teachers and classmates. When fall rolls around, many of the pent-up anxieties will have disappeared.

• Stock up on regional and local maps: Coming to grips with Metro Washington's patchwork of roads and highways can be as trying as advanced calculus. Maps are required reading here and the best in the land can be had through the ADC map company of Alexandria, Virginia.

You'll see their maps in virtually all the area's bookshops, as well as in most grocery and convenience stores. For more information, call ADC at (703) 750-0510.

• Make trial runs to place of work, school, etc.: A little planning here will greatly improve your mental health. Make the trial commutes during normal rush hours or the approximate times you'll be going to these places. Experiment with different routes and always have a contingency plan. We can't stress enough the importance of following this step.

• Subscribe immediately to a community newspaper and *The Washington Post* and/or *The Washington Times*, the region's two largest daily newspapers. We may be biased here, but there's still no better information access to Metro Washington than through the printed word. Tapping into the Fourth Estate is really the first step in becoming part of the community.

• Get involved with state societies, alumni groups, or embassy cultural-outlet programs. Homesickness is a natural consequence of relocation. Fortunately, the Washington area has a plethora of remedies. Virtually every state has a state society — a social and networking group — based in Washington. Chances are your alma mater also has an alumni chapter in Washington. If they don't, you may consider organizing one. For international newcomers, most embassies offer some type of cultural programming, whether it's through open houses, lecture series or social clubs. (See related information in the "International Washington" chapter.)

When considering a
facility, observe the
staff, the other children
and the indoor and
outdoor spaces.

Child Care

As we have mentioned at least a couple of times by now, Metro Washington is a wonderful place to live and — as many people happily discover — raise children. Few places can match the abundance of stimulating cultural, educational, historical and recreational outlets for youngsters to pursue. Here's a brief look at child care, an important consideration in an area where household budgets may only be fulfilled with two incomes.

First, here are a few words about what to expect from this chapter. Like some of the other subjects we've covered, child care is one that could easily be the sole focus of an entire book. Because Washington-area residents can choose from literally thousands of child-care options, to present a complete rundown with descriptions, services and other information is simply not possible here. Instead, we've tried to provide a primer on the subject, combining sound advice for choosing child-care facilities with a listing of agencies, nonprofit organizations and referral agencies. The experts there can answer specific questions and help parents make decisions.

Few quality-of-life issues have become as important to families in recent years as the availability of top-notch child care, something that experts agree is crucial to a child's well-being and healthy development. As with any large expenditure, especially one involving a family member, parents should carefully weigh the various options and talk with relatives, friends, neighbors and co-workers who have experience in this area.

Whether you're in search of a chain-affiliated commercial day-care center, a private in-home operation, a program associated with a school or religious institution or something tailored to the special needs of groups such as the physically challenged, the learning disabled and the non-English-speaking, you're sure to find it in the Washington area. A scan through the Yellow Pages, a community directory or a listing provided by a human-services agency will quickly confirm the wealth of choices available.

The High Cost of Care

Just as housing, groceries and other necessities tend to cost more in Metro Washington than in many parts of the nation, the same holds true for child care. Indeed it can be one of the biggest financial issues for parents with moderate incomes, particularly if they don't have in-home offices, the luxury of subsidized day-care centers at work, or nearby relatives who can help out.

Typically, according to the Fairfax County Office for Children, full-time child care for infants and toddlers costs from $115 to $185 weekly in a private home, and $143 to $180 weekly at a child-care center. Preschool-age child care ranges from $85 to $155 weekly in a private home, and $110 to $142 weekly at a center. Before- and after-school care for school-age children costs $80 to $150 a week, or $2 to $4 an hour in a private home, and $110 to $138 or $2.75 to $3.50 an hour at a center. Your best bet is to sign up as early as possible. Before- and after-school programs in particular often start taking first-come, first-serve applications in early spring before the next school year.

A growing segment of the child-care sector in Metro Washington involves in-home operations, often classified by licensing agencies as family day care homes. Their popularity is a reflection not only of the region's No. 1 national ranking in the number of working women, but also of the high cost of living here. Many people opt to set up child-care operations in their homes, providing a much-needed source of income without having to commute to faraway offices. Like other child-care facilities, private homes must be licensed, insured, inspected and otherwise held to certain standards for safety, health and sanitation. Also, those caring for more than five children (although the number may vary slightly in different jurisdictions) must obtain special permits and licenses from local and state authorities.

Parents who wish to examine licensing standards may request comprehensive booklets published by the area's licensing agencies: the D.C. Department of Consumer and Regulatory Affairs in Washington, the Virginia Department of Social Services in Virginia or the Maryland Department of Human Resources in Maryland. (State guidelines are available through local government offices, listed later in this chapter.) Regulations vary slightly among the three jurisdictions, but to receive licenses, child-care centers and homes generally must meet requirements adhering to staff-to-children ratios (as small as one caregiver to four children younger than age 2 in centers, and one caregiver to two children in family day-care settings), providing developmentally appropriate activities, following safety precautions with furnishings and equipment, administering authorized health procedures, keeping records for each child and maintaining a sanitary, smoke-free, drug-free environment.

www.insiders.com

See this and many other **Insiders' Guide®** destinations online — in their entirety.

Visit us today!

Finding the Right Option

Remember that just because a child-care facility is licensed after meeting the minimum requirements it doesn't necessarily guarantee your child a stimulating, high-quality educational experience. When considering a facility, observe the staff, the other children, and the indoor and outdoor spaces. Ask about the daily routine, nutrition, exercise, learning activities and materials, fees and payment schedules, child/staff ratio, extent of parental involvement, and numerous other factors.

Other types of child care include day-care centers, where group care is provided for children typically of ages 6 weeks to 5 years. These centers are open for full days all year, and some provide transportation. Nursery schools and preschools offer group care for the pre-school-age child, but may not be open full days or all year. Extended day-care programs, meanwhile, offer supervised settings for school-age children when school is not in session. Besides providing before- and after-school care, the programs — much to the delight of parents — often cover snow days and holidays, and some have full-day summer programs.

Nannies — private, full-time and sometimes live-in — offer another option, although it is more expensive. Local child-care agencies often have lists of individual nannies or nanny services, or at least can put you in touch with sources that do. Weekly salaries for full-time nannies range from $250 to $550, with live-out nannies earning about $50 a week more than live-in nannies. If choosing a nanny through a placement agency, parents can expect to pay a registration/application fee of $75 or more and, on hiring, a placement fee of $1,500 or more.

Parents seeking a nanny should pay attention to the type of screening — such as criminal, background and Social Security checks — required by an agency. Consider the person's experience, age, whether he or she smokes, whether the nanny has a valid driver's license and whether he or she can speak English. Families planning to hire a live-in nanny should be prepared to provide a private room and bath, preferably on a separate level, a private phone line and use of a car.

The au pair (French for "as an equal") program is perhaps the most unusual and interesting child-care option, and one that probably will continue to increase in popularity as the global society becomes further pronounced. It's little wonder that au pairs are popular in Metro Washington, with the region's strong multi-ethnic character and well-traveled populace. Au pair is an international youth exchange program organized to create cross-cultural understanding and cooperation between American families and western European young adults. Sanctioned by the United States Information Agency (USIA), the program provides a great opportunity for young people overseas to learn about American culture and family life while living in the United States, and also serves as a wonderful learning experience for the hosts. The program typically involves au pairs between the ages of 18 and 25 who come to the United States for a year and care for the host family's children. Reciprocal programs allow American youths to perform these services in Europe.

While most au pair experiences are positive for both young people and host families, it's not something for a family to enter into lightly. Veteran host families, as well as the organizations listed later in this chapter, can help steer prospective hosts in the right direction. Besides what can be a rewarding, memorable, cross-cultural experience, the au pair program can also mean cost savings for a family, compared with other types of in-home child care. Stipends average about $130 per week for 45 hours of child care, but bear in mind that host families must also be prepared to pay $200 or more for the application, $500 for tuition and $3,000 to $4,000 for program fees that cover airfare, insurance and child safety instruction.

All of these choices may seem mind-boggling, but the following resources can help you narrow down your options and zero in on the best situation for your family.

Local Government-based Child-Care Resources

For listings of the child-care centers in your area, tips on what to look for, guidelines, requirements, financial assistance and other information on any facet of child care, contact the appropriate agencies in your jurisdiction.

Washington, D.C.

D.C. Department of Consumer and Regulatory Affairs
614 H St. NW, Rm. 1035, Washington, D.C. • (202) 727-7226

This department licenses and monitors child development facilities, home- and center-based day care and foster homes.

Washington Child Development Council
2121 Decatur Pl. NW, Washington, D.C. • (202) 387-0002

Contact the council for referrals and other child-care resources.

Office of Early Childhood Development
717 14th St. NW, Ste. 730, Washington, D.C. • (202) 727-0284, (202) 310-2020 recording

This office of the Department of Human Services provides financial assistance for day care for ages 6 weeks to 14, and to age 15 for disabled children. The recorded message is available 24 hours a day, providing information about day-care provider training opportunities and parental education programs.

Northern Virginia

City of Alexandria

Child Care Information Services
2525 Mt. Vernon Ave., Alexandria, Va. • (703) 838-0750

This service of the Office for Early Childhood Development in the city's Department of Human Services registers and trains child-care providers and provides lists of licensed centers, nurseries and preschools, in-home day care, before- and after-school programs and summer camps.

Arlington County

Child and Family Services
1801 N. George Mason Dr., Arlington, Va. • (703) 358-5101

The county's child-care office licenses family day care, preschools and centers, and offers free referral lists.

Public Schools Extended Day Program
2801 Clarendon Blvd., Ste. 312, Arlington, Va. • (703) 358-6069

Contact this division for details about the supervised before- and after-school recreational program offered in elementary and middle schools.

Fairfax County

Department of Family Services Office for Children
12011 Government Center Pkwy., Fairfax, Va. • (703) 324-8100

This early childhood education agency includes the following programs, each of which has its own phone number:

Child Care Assistance Program
8th Fl. • (703) 449-8484

This office subsidizes day-care costs for low- and moderate-income families, and offers parental education.

Head Start Programs
9th Fl. • (703) 324-8290

This national program offers early childhood and parental education to low-income families.

School-Age Child Care Program
9th Fl. • (703) 449-8989

SACC provides before- and after-school and summer programs at county elementary schools.

Child Care Resource System
9th Fl. • (703) 449-9555

Parents can contact this office for lists of child-care providers throughout the county.

Employer Child Care Council
9th Fl. • (703) 324-8075

This office promotes on-the-job child care and early education.

Permits and Regulation
8th Fl. • (703) 324-8000

This division inspects and issues permits for family child-care homes.

Child Care Training Programs
8th Fl. • (703) 324-8043

Child-care providers can contact this office to enroll in training courses.

Child and Adult Care Food Program
8th Fl. • (703) 324-8019

This program provides nutrition education and food cost assistance for child-care providers.

City of Fairfax

Human Services Coordinator
10455 Armstrong St., Fairfax, Va.
• (703) 385-7894

Contact the coordinator to learn about child-care opportunities within the city.

City of Falls Church

Department of Housing and Human Services
300 Park Ave., Falls Church, Va.
• (703) 241-5005

This office provides child-care counseling and offers directories of day-care opportunities.

Office of Community Education
7124 Leesburg Pk., Falls Church, Va.
• (703) 241-7682

Contact this office for information about the before- and after-school child-care program.

Loudoun County

Department of Social Services
102 Heritage Way NE, Leesburg, Va.
• (703) 777-0353

This department provides a list of day-care providers, both facilities and individuals.

INSIDERS' TIP

Latchkey children in Washington, D.C. can call PhoneFriend, (202) 223-2244, 3 to 9 PM Monday through Friday and 1 to 5 PM Saturdays for homework assistance, reassurance or just to talk. Staffed by trained volunteers, the phone service receives more than 10,000 calls a year.

Prince William County

Department of Social Services/ Child Care Unit (Options in Child Care)
15941 Cardinal Dr., Woodbridge, Va.
• (703) 792-4300

The office handles research and referral and provider certification and training, and operates the USDA food program.

Suburban Maryland

Montgomery County

Children's Resource Center
332 W. Edmonston Dr., Rockville, Md.
• (301) 279-1260

This building houses a variety of child-care oriented programs, including the following which are at the same address.

The Arc of Montgomery County Family, Infant and Child-Care Center
Rms. C-2, 4 and 5 • (301) 279-2165

This specialized center offers care for children between the ages of 6 weeks and 5 years who have chronic medical conditions.

Child Care Connection, Inc.
Rm. B-6 • (301) 279-1773

This division of the Department of Health and Human Services offers the county's only approved child-care referral for licensed providers. It also trains prospective child-care providers.

Child Care Services
Rm. A-15 • (301) 279-1260

This Department of Health and Human Services office provides technical assistance to child-care providers, supports a citizens' advisory group and refers parents and providers to helpful services.

The Family Works
Rm. B-6 • (301) 929-2025, (301) 424-5666

This office, funded by the U.S. Department of Education, fosters learning partnerships between parents and their children's schools and child care.

Montgomery County Infant and Toddler Program
Rm. A-9 • (301) 279-1250

Parents with developmentally delayed young children can find services through this program of the Department of Health and Human Services, public schools and other agencies.

Parenting Resource Center
Rm. D-4 • (301) 279-8497, (301) 929-2025

Sponsored by Montgomery County Public Schools, this office provides resources to parents and caregivers and offers parenting and other enrichment classes.

Wintergreen Child Development Center
Rm. B-1 • (301) 424-7522

Part of the Rockville Day Care Association, this nonprofit center offers a year-round program to more than 100 children.

Montgomery County Child Care Administration
51 Monroe St., Ste. 200, Rockville, Md.
• (301) 294-0344

This division of the Department of Human Resources licenses and monitors child-care providers in Montgomery County.

Prince George's County

Child Resource Center (Locate Child Care)
9475 Lottsford Rd., Ste. 202, Largo, Md.
• (301) 772-8400

As part of the Prince George's Child Resource Center, which offers child-care information and training to parents and providers, Locate Child Care provides referrals to licensed child-care programs in the county. Information is free by phone, or $6 by mail, to cover shipping costs. The office is open 9 AM to 4 PM Monday through Thursday, and is closed Fridays and weekends. A computerized, 24-hour referral service, (900) 773-2273, costs $2 per minute. Call (301) 772-8420 for information about upcoming parent and provider training opportunities.

Helpful Organizations

Metropolitan Washington Council of Governments (COG)
777 N. Capitol St. NE, Ste. 300, Washington, D.C. • (202) 962-3200

COG, as it's often called, is an excellent source for child-care information and virtually anything else you can think of in which local governments play some sort of role. COG provides such resources as reports on the status of child care, guidelines for seeking quality child care and scholarship coordination for child-care providers. As a vast information clearinghouse, COG also refers residents to other organizations, many of which are headquartered in Metro Washington.

National Association for the Education of Young Children (NAEYC)
1834 Connecticut Ave. NW, Washington, D.C. • (202) 232-8777, (800) 424-2460

Founded in 1926, NAEYC is the country's largest organization focused on promoting quality education for children ages 8 and younger. Membership includes 400 local, state and regional affiliated organizations. The association offers educational literature and videos and a national voluntary accreditation program for early childhood centers, among many other services.

National Black Child Development Institute
1023 15th St. NW, Ste. 600, Washington, D.C. • (202) 387-1281

This nonprofit organization, founded in 1970, strives to improve the quality of life for African-American children. It provides child-care resources to parents and professionals, and offers leadership training in child care and education.

Nannies

These agencies place part-time, full-time, live-in and live-out nannies throughout the Washington metropolitan area. Unless otherwise indicated, they also provide short-term and, with at least four hours' notice, emergency or sitter referrals. For long-term placement, try to call at least a month in advance.

Extra Assistance, Inc.
1109 Spring St., Ste. 401, Silver Spring, Md. • (301) 495-9587

This agency has been placing nannies, domestic help and companions for 22 years.

Mothers' Aides Inc.
5618 Ox Rd., Fairfax Station, Va. • (703) 250-0700

Founded in 1979, this agency is a member of NAEYC, an organization described earlier in this chapter.

Nannies, Inc.
3031 Borge St., Ste. 107, Oakton, Va. • (301) 718-0100 Bethesda, (703) 255-5312 Fairfax

Washington Families newspaper voted this 9-year-old agency, founded by a single dad, the Best Nanny Service in the Washington metropolitan area. The agency places only long-term, full-service nannies.

Potomac Nannies, Ltd.
7315 Wisconsin Ave., Ste. 1300-W, Bethesda, Md. • (301) 986-0048

This agency, which opened in 1985, places only live-in and live-out nannies.

TLC Nanny Search Consultant
1000 Hertford St., Herndon, Va. • (703) 736-0594, (703) 838-8444

Tami L. Cox, a former nanny, provides customized nanny searches for individual families, who pay a consultation fee and expenses for such services as newspaper advertising, phone screening and interviewing.

White House Nannies
7200 Wisconsin Ave., Bethesda, Md.
• (301) 654-1242 for permanent,
(301) 652-8088 for temporary

This 13-year-old agency began when the owner experienced frustration during her own nanny search.

Au Pairs

For more information about au pairs, contact one of the following organizations, sanctioned by the United States Information Agency (USIA) to recruit European participants and unite them with American families.

Au Pair Homestay U.S.A., 1015 15th Street NW, Suite 750, Washington, D.C. 20005, (202) 408-5380, (800) 479-0907

Au Pair in America, 102 Greenwich Avenue, Greenwich, Connecticut 06830, (203) 869-9090, (800) 928-7247

AuPairCare, 1 Post Street, 7th Floor, San Francisco, California 94104, (415) 434-8788, (800) 428-7247

Au Pair Programme U.S.A., 6955 Union Park Center, Suite 360, Salt Lake City, Utah 84047, (801) 255-7722

EF Au Pair, EF Center Boston, 1 Education Street, Cambridge, Massachusetts 02141, (800) 333-6056

EurAupair, 250 North Pacific Coast Highway, Laguna Beach, California 92651, (800) 618-2002

InterExchange AuPair U.S.A., 161 6th Avenue, 13th Floor, New York, New York 10013, (212) 924-0446, (800) 287-2477

Education is the fabric that holds this cerebral community together.

Education

The Metro Washington area owes much of its well-respected business, political and economic development to a single driving force: education.

People here wax proudly about the outstanding educational infrastructure, and with good reason: Few metro areas can hold a candle to our high-quality and diverse public and private schools, not to mention the concentration of internationally renowned colleges, universities and research institutions. Washington boasts double the national average of college-educated adults.

Indeed, education is the fabric that holds this cerebral community together. The region relishes its reputation as the most educated community in America, and it places a premium on the learning resources available to its citizens of all ages. Moreover, many residents champion lifelong learning, and that's why you'll find the area among the nation's leaders in participation in continuing-education programs.

This chapter highlights the educational opportunities found throughout the area, beginning with the public school systems and a selection of private institutions. The final section briefly describes the area's major colleges and universities, nearly all of which offer programs for working adults.

Public Schools

The common theme here, especially in the suburbs, is rabid parental interest in quality public education. Whether they're tutoring beginning readers, assisting with computer labs or working at PTA fund-raisers, parent volunteers are helping schools create new and better programs for students. At the same time, teachers and administrators are implementing strategies to improve reading skills and test scores.

Washington, D.C.

District of Columbia Public Schools
415 12th St., Washington, D.C.
• **(202) 724-4044**

Like many of America's inner-city public school systems suffering from budget cutbacks, violence and chronic absenteeism, the District's has suffered through tough times of late. The 1997-98 academic year got off to a controversial start, when a judge ordered more than 40 schools closed for roof replacements, causing School Chief Executive Julius W. Becton Jr. to delay the opening of all D.C. public schools for three weeks. Meanwhile, school officials continue to meet with a Congressional subcommittee to devise plans for improving students' academic performance. SAT scores for 1997 dropped 10 points to a disappointing 811, the weakest in the area.

The school system is not without its bright spots, however. The District's city-wide magnet schools have always held their ground for students with special skills or artistic talents. The Ellington School of the Arts, named for esteemed native son Duke Ellington, has some of the finest dance, theater and music departments in the metro area. Senior High Academies let students specialize in such areas as culinary arts, international studies, teaching and travel and tourism. Eligible high-school students can take Advanced Placement courses.

D.C. schools enroll nearly 80,000 students. Testament to the city's international character, students represent more than 130 nations and speak at least 90 languages. Bilingual programs in Spanish and Chinese have earned the District kudos from educators around the country. Smaller groups of international students are taught English by itinerant teams of language teachers. There's even a school that teaches foreign adults English and prepares them for U.S. citizenship.

Washington, of course, is one giant learning laboratory, and the public school system has tapped into it through a motivated-students program called "School Without Walls." Former dropouts receive academic help through two "Street Academies" — schools that stress personal and career counseling as much as classroom performance. The District extends child-care services for students who are parents and offers programs in substance abuse prevention and health awareness.

Like everything else in Washington, D.C., the public schools are constantly under the national microscope, especially in terms of funding and performance. All education programs, after being approved by an elected school board and the city government, must pass the financial scrutiny of Congress and the White House. Needless to say, not all plans win approval. Budgets and, unfortunately, politics often get in the way of much-needed resources. Teachers' salaries, however, have remained competitive, ranging from $25,937 to $53,615. Student/teacher ratios average about 23-to-1.

Problems aside, the D.C. school system has the unlimited educational resources of Washington in its backyard — resources that are the envy of every school district in the nation.

Northern Virginia

Alexandria Public Schools
2000 N. Beauregard St., Alexandria, Va.
• (703) 824-6600

This small (about 10,200 students) school system boasts a large emphasis on computers in education: The multimillion-dollar, five-year Technology Initiative provides for such goals as a multimedia computer workstation in each classroom, school-wide Internet access, laptops available for student loan, video production facilities and faculty training. The program, funded through the school budget

and private partnerships, brings five schools online annually.

The district includes 12 elementary schools, two middle schools, one ninth-grade school and one senior high school. Special programs include all-day kindergarten, a gifted and talented curriculum, instruction for homebound students and comprehensive special education services for handicapped students ages 2 to 21. More than 1,000 students receive English as a Second Language education, and pupils in grades one through eight may participate in a Spanish immersion program. Volunteer tutoring services are available during and after school.

The city's lone high school, T.C. Williams, offers 20 Advanced Placement and honors courses, a vocational education program with post-secondary degree credit, an award-winning JROTC program and 12 varsity sports programs for boys and girls. T.C. students average 964 on the SAT, compared with the national average of 1,016; about 79 percent go on to some form of higher education.

Average class sizes are 20 in elementary grades, 21 in middle school and 23 in secondary grades. Alexandria's per-pupil expenditure of $9,386 is among the highest in Metro Washington. The system's Adult and Community Education Office provides adult basic education classes along with job skills and training, GED and high-school diploma programs and special interest classes. A nine-member school board meets the first and third Thursdays of the month.

Arlington County Public Schools
1426 N. Quincy St., Arlington, Va.
• (703) 358-6000

This innovative public school system ranked No. 1 in the recent Children's Environmental Index survey published by Zero Population Growth, which also named Arlington County the 11th most kid-friendly place in the country. Arlingtonians care deeply about education: 52 percent of residents age 25 and older are college graduates, and 24 percent have graduate or professional degrees.

Diversity defines Arlington County Public Schools, where the 18,500 students hail from around the world and speak more than 70 languages, from Spanish and Vietnamese to Arabic and Farsi. Although the county is Virginia's smallest geographically, it boasts the 12th largest of the state's 136 school divisions. With 30 schools and several special programs, the district caters to all segments of its varied student population. Parents may choose to send their children to a neighborhood school or to an "alternative" school offering a unique learning environment. Some examples include the Claremont Early Childhood Center for grades kindergarten through 2nd grade; Drew Model School, the county's only public Montessori program for ages 6 to 9; Science Focus School, at which kindergartners through 5th graders incorporate science into all areas of learning; Kenmore Middle School, where arts and communications technology take center stage; and H-B Woodlawn Secondary Program, in which 6th through 12th graders control much of their educational experience.

Other special programs include instruction for gifted students, English for speakers of other languages/high-intensity language training, extended day care, outreach for teenage parents, a Spanish partial-immersion program, high-school Advanced Placement and International Baccalaureate courses, summer school, special education and athletics and other extracurricular activities. Technology proves a high priority: All schools have Internet access, and the district boasts three "electronic classrooms."

The county's comprehensive Adult Education Program offers high-school equivalency studies, senior citizens' activities and an array of multicultural programs.

Arlington spends $9,305 per pupil, and the average class size is 21 students. The investment is paying off: 86 percent of Arlington high school graduates go on to college. The average SAT score is 1,044, higher than the national average. The five-member school boards meets two Thursdays a month, and meetings are shown live on Cable TV Arlington Channel 30.

Fairfax County Public Schools
10700 Page Ave., Fairfax, Va.
• (703) 246-2502

Fairfax County Public Schools, with more than 149,000 students and 10,400 teachers, is the 12th-largest school district in the United States and the largest in Virginia. Growing every year, the district now boasts 134 elementary schools, 20 middle schools, three secondary (grades 7-12) schools, 20 high schools, 24 special-services centers and 33 alternative schools. The county's 1,242 school buses handle 100,000 students every day, making the fleet one of the nation's largest.

To put its size in a more regional perspective, the county accounts for 13 percent of all Virginia students. These tremendous numbers do not equate to mediocrity or impersonalization in the classroom. More than 41 percent of the state's National Merit Scholarship Exam semifinalists come from Fairfax County Public Schools. Students averaged 1,088 on the 1997 SAT, the second-highest average score in the region.

The system, with a per-pupil cost of $7,451, features county-wide programs for students who are gifted and talented, for students with learning disabilities, and for international students who speak English as a second language. Several elementary and middle schools provide partial-immersion programs in French, German, Japanese and Spanish. Two elementary magnet schools feature arts and sciences curricula, and 51 elementaries are designated Model Technology Schools. At the high-school level, about 91 graduates go on to some form of higher education. The county's prized magnet school in Alexandria, Thomas Jefferson

INSIDERS' TIP

Registering your child for public school? Make sure you have their birth certificate, proof of residency, social security number, transfer records from previous schools, record of a recent medical examination and current immunization records.

High School for Science and Technology, consistently boasts the country's largest concentration of National Merit Scholars. Admission is competitive and open to 9th and 10th graders in the county and other participating Northern Virginia school districts. Three schools offer the academically demanding International Baccalaureate Program, which includes college-level courses. Extracurricular high-school activities include award-winning music programs and interscholastic team sports for boys and girls.

Vocational programs feature studies in business education, home economics, industrial arts and horticulture. On-site technical studies programs take place at a shopping mall, airport, hotel, construction site and car dealership. Extended-day care is offered at 117 elementary schools through the Fairfax County Office for Children. Fees are based on a sliding scale. A Head Start early childhood program is available for eligible 3- to 5-year-olds. The school system also sponsors adult education, alternative high-school programs, a school-to-work transition academy and a variety of enrichment classes for children and adults.

Administratively, the district is divided into three geographic areas, each of which is represented by a superintendent and an office staff. A 12-member elected school board meets the second and fourth Thursdays at 7:30 PM, broadcast live on Cable Channel 21. Parental involvement in the schools is high: 50,304 volunteers provided 1,122,048 hours of service during the 1995-96 school year. Parents, teachers, administrators and students regularly voice their opinions at school-board meetings and have great influence over budgets, curriculum and the establishment of new facilities and programs.

The system also has a new superintendent, Daniel A. Domenech, a Cuban immigrant who was known for his bold leadership style as a superintendent in the Long Island district. He replaces Robert R. Spillane, the 12-year school chief who, although credited with helping the county attain a national reputation for excellence, often did not see eye to eye with board members. He retired when the board refused to renew his contract.

Within the county, meanwhile, are two separate municipal school districts: one serving the City of Fairfax and one serving Falls Church. Fairfax City's system, City Hall, 10455 Armstrong Street, Fairfax, Virginia, (703) 385-7910, includes four elementaries, one middle school and one high school. The system operates under a partnership with the county and has its own superintendent and school board. Falls Church, 7124 Leesburg Pike, Falls Church, Virginia, (703) 241-7600, enrolls approximately 1,467 students in its system, widely considered one of the best in the region. The district includes only four schools: Mt. Daniel for kindergarten through 1st grade, Thomas Jefferson for 2nd through 5th grades, George Mason Middle School for 6th through 8th grades and George Mason High School for 9th through 12th grades. Highlights include the International Baccalaureate Program, special education instruction, gifted and talented services, ESL courses, extended day care and, through the Office of Community Education and the Recreation and Parks Department, adult education and enrichment classes.

Prince William County Public Schools
14800 Joplin Rd., Manassas, Va.
• (703) 791-7200

The tremendous — and often overwhelming — growth that transformed Prince William over the past 15 or so years never short-changed the county's public school system. If anything, it improved it. Eighty-seven percent of the county's high school graduates go on to college, and the average SAT score keeps rising, with 1997's at 1,019. Educational staff, half of whom hold advanced degrees, have earned numerous awards in recent years, including last year's honors of Virginia Art Educator and Elementary Counselor of the Year and Greater Washington Reading Council Reading Teacher of the Year. The district maintains eight health- and education-related partnerships, and continues to upgrade its school-wide computer technology.

In all, more than 48,000 students attend 66 public schools, where the per-pupil cost is $5,945. Prince William's curriculum earmarks specific learning objectives by grade level for each subject. The schools also offer extensive programs for gifted students in all grades, and rigorous Advanced Placement and International Baccalaureate courses for high-school students. Other special programs target pupils with disabilities, students who want to pursue vocational studies, those who speak English as a second language and adults continuing education. Several elementary schools offer before- and after-school care.

Public school policy is set by the county school board of eight members elected to four-year terms. Widely attended public meetings of the school board take place the first, second and fourth Wednesdays of each month.

Both independent cities within the county — Manassas, 9000 Tudor Lane, Manassas, Virginia, (703) 257-8800, and Manassas Park, 1 Park Center Court, Manassas, Virginia, (703) 335-8850 — have their own school systems, with enrollments of almost 6,000 and 1,630, respectively. Academically, they tend to mirror the county.

Loudoun County Public Schools
102 North St. NW, Leesburg, Va.
• **(703) 771-6427**

The rapidly growing, 23,873-student Loudoun County public school system is among the best in exurban Metro Washington. The average elementary class size is 22.5 students, and the per-pupil expenditure is approximately $6,351. The system has 28 elementary, five middle and five high schools, including a new 1,375-student high school and two 800-student elementaries. A technology center serves vocational and adult education students and an alternative education program helps middle- and high-school students who have trouble fitting in to traditional programs.

Courses are available for gifted and special-education students, and several Advanced Placement courses are available at the high-school level. Each school offers computer education, emphasizing state-of-the-art technology, and has Internet access. The 2.1 percent dropout rate is among the lowest in the state and the nation, and 87 percent of county graduates continue their formal education. SAT scores, consistent over the past two years, average 1,037. Monthly meetings of the nine-member school board are shown live on Cablevision of Loudoun's Channel 59.

Suburban Maryland

Montgomery County Public Schools
850 Hungerford Dr., Rockville, Md.
• **(301) 279-3391**

Arguably the best public school system in Metro Washington, Montgomery County boasts the area's highest SAT scores, averaging 1,092. About 53 percent of high-school students take honors courses, and 89.3 percent of county graduates go on to higher education. A whopping 85.6 of county teachers hold master's degrees or equivalents. Schools, staff and students frequently receive honors at national, state and local levels.

As in Fairfax, Montgomery's system is gigantic. More than 123,700 students attend 181 public schools, including 21 senior high schools and centers specializing in magnet programs, gifted and talented instruction, technology and research, visual arts and foreign language immersion.

The county also offers some all-day kindergarten, extended elementary programs, ESOL, instruction for disabled students, adult education and on-the-job training in business and industry. The schools' Global Access initiative is integrating up-to-the-minute technology into classrooms.

The student/faculty ratio here is 15.7-to-1, and the per-pupil cost is more than $6,700. A seven-member elected school board sets the district's policies.

Prince George's County Public Schools
Sasscer Administration Bldg., 14201 School Ln., Upper Marlboro, Md.
• **(301) 279-3391**

Prince George's County Public Schools are recognized nationally for their progressive approach to education, which has produced the most-improved schools in the Washington area.

Graduation requirements for high school students call for more credits in math and social studies and fewer in electives. University High School offers rigorous, college-prep courses like the International Baccalaureate program. The Visual and Performing Arts High

A youngster gets a helping hand netting inhabitants of Springfield's Lake Accotink.

School houses a TV and recording studio, 1,000-seat auditorium and dance studio. Through a special partnership, some dancers appear at the Kennedy Center for the Performing Arts. The county has innovative comprehensive reading initiatives, ESL instruction, classes for gifted students, a K-12 French Immersion program, schools for the learning and physically disabled, evening schools for adults, and even an educational project geared toward the needs of Native American children.

More than 121,800 students attend the county's 178 schools. Given the amount of services available, the expenditure per student, $5,650, is on the low side, suggesting a great degree of efficiency. The nine-member elected school board meets two Thursdays a month.

Private Schools

Private schools in the region range from traditional liberal arts institutions to alternative programs for gifted or learning-disabled students. Of course, the benefits of such highly personalized and specialized study come with a price tag. Generally speaking, tuition fees here can range from $1,500 to upwards of $20,000 a year, the latter being for boarding schools. A good clearinghouse for additional information on private schools in the area is the Association of Independent Schools of Greater Washington, (202) 537-1114.

Washington, D.C.

Archbishop Carroll High School
4300 Harewood Rd. NE, Washington, D.C. • (202) 529-0900

On a small campus near Catholic University, Archbishop Carroll is one of the city's leading Catholic high schools. The coed school, founded in 1951, has an enrollment of 706 students in grades 9 through 12 and is known for its rigorous academic standards, dedicated faculty and strong athletic and activities programs. Its state-of-the-art computer lab includes Internet access. All students must participate in service projects, such as volunteering at a local soup kitchen. Graduates go on to Catholic, Georgetown, the University of Virginia, the University of Maryland and other nationally competitive colleges.

Capitol Hill Day School
210 S. Carolina Ave. SE, Washington, D.C. • (202) 547-2244

Founded in 1969, this independent, coed school for 225 children in pre-kindergarten through eighth grade offers an integrated curriculum with a hands-on emphasis. Students study such specialty subjects as Spanish, French, art and music. Socially, the school encourages both self-reliance and care for others.

Georgetown Visitation Preparatory School
1524 35th St. NW, Washington, D.C. • (202) 337-3350

Next door to Georgetown University, on a 27-acre campus, Visitation has been grooming young women for higher education since 1799. About 400 students in grades 9 through 12 attend the prestigious day school, which is affiliated with the Roman Catholic Church and boasts Honors and Advanced Placement courses in English, foreign language, history, mathematics and science. A bridge program with the neighboring university enables some seniors to take courses for college credit. The school's athletic program features a variety of team sports, and students can choose from more than 30 co-curricular activities, featuring such subjects as computers, Great Books, music and Christian service. Visitation grads go on to a wide variety of colleges, including some of the top schools on the East Coast.

The Lab School of Washington
4759 Reservoir Rd. NW, Washington, D.C. • (202) 965-6600

The Lab School is designed for intelligent students with learning disabilities, who benefit from the school's four- or five-to-one student/teacher ratio. The 30-year-old, coed day school, with 285 students in grades kindergarten through 12, features an ungraded elementary curriculum that's equally divided between academic skills and a variety of arts. Students study history by participating in Academic Clubs with themes such as Knights and Ladies and Industrialists. They also have the opportunity to dig for and study ancient artifacts buried on the school grounds. Grades 7 through 12 follow a more traditional college preparatory curriculum, supplemented by arts and humanities classes in junior high.

High-school students apprentice off-campus in such places as museums and radio stations, and perform community outreach like giving birthday parties at a homeless shelter. Competitive team sports include basketball, soccer and softball. The school is set in a quiet residential area of upper Georgetown, not far from Mount Vernon College, which participates in a college preparatory program for intelligent young women with learning disabilities. The Lab School also offers career and college counseling, tutoring, clinical services and night classes for adults with learning disabilities.

Nannie Helen Burroughs School Inc.
601 50th St. NE, Washington, D.C. • (202) 398-5266

This private, coed Christian school, affiliated with the Progressive National Baptist Convention, enrolls 203 students in grades pre-kindergarten through 7th. Burroughs founded the school in 1909 with a "three B's" philosophy: bath, bible, and broom — signifying clean body, mind and environment. Among the curriculum's prominent features are cultural enrichment, hands-on math and science, formal Bible instruction, values education and computer literacy. The students take many field trips. The school offers before- and aftercare.

Sheridan School
4400 36th St. NW, Washington, D.C. • (202) 362-7900

Founded in 1927, this small, coed school for grades kindergarten through 8th, follows traditional liberal arts instruction in a family-like, values-oriented atmosphere. The 215 students, divided into one class per grade, learn through a "central subject" approach, in which a single topic such as anthropology is used to integrate the curriculum. Among program highlights are an annual science fair, visits to the school's 130-acre Mountain Campus next to Shenandoah National Park, a French trip for 7th and 8th graders and an extended-day program that includes a variety of extracurricular activities. The campus is in North Cleveland Park, a residential neighborhood not far from the Tenleytown Metro station.

St. Anselm's Abbey School
4501 South Dakota Ave. NE, Washington, D.C. • (202) 269-2350

Part of the sprawling academic complex that radiates from Catholic University, St. Anselm's is a college-prep school for 6th- through 12th-grade boys of all faiths. About 200 students attend the school, founded in 1942 and operated by the Benedictine monks of St. Anselm's Abbey. The small average student/teacher ratio of 8-to-1 pays off: A 10-year average 65 percent of the school's graduates receive National Merit recognition, and the 10-year average SAT score is 1280. One hundred percent of graduates go on to attend four-year college. The curriculum includes challenging programs in music, drama, visual arts, publications and athletics. The Brookland/CUA Metro is nearby.

St. John's College High School/ Middle School
2607 Military Rd. NW, Washington, D.C. • (202) 363-2316

Run by the De La Salle Christian Brothers, the religious order that founded the school in 1851, St. John's features a Catholic, coed college prep high school and all-boys middle school. The school is known for balancing academics with comprehensive extracurricular activities, such as an Army JROTC program and competitive league team sports. St. John's takes pride in its computer center, and each

of the 570 students has his or her own e-mail address. The 27-acre campus borders scenic Rock Creek Park.

St. Patrick's Episcopal Day School
4700 Whitehaven Pkwy. NW, Washington, D.C. • (202) 342-2805

The liberal arts are taken seriously at this traditional Episcopal day school. St. Patrick's touts progressive elementary-school programs in the arts, music, French and science.

Sidwell Friends School
3825 Wisconsin Ave. NW, Washington, D.C. • (202) 537-8100

Sidwell Friends, affiliated with the Society of Friends, was founded in 1883 and has since become one of the preeminent college-prep schools in D.C. The coed day school enrolls more than 1,050 students on its two campuses, a Bethesda location for pre-kindergarten through 4th graders, and a District site for grades 5th through 12th. The school follows a demanding liberal arts curriculum, including required studies in fine arts, foreign languages, math and science. Extracurricular activities such as interscholastic sports also play an important role in student life. Personalized community service programs are required of all graduates. First Daughter Chelsea Clinton graduated from Sidwell Friends in 1997.

Washington International School
3100 Macomb St. NW, Washington, D.C. • (202) 364-1815

It's only fitting that an international city claim a bold international college prep school. The coed school enrolls approximately 660 students, from nursery through 12th grade, and promotes diversity. The students and their families represent more than 90 countries. A globalized curriculum, including bilingual stud-

---

INSIDERS' TIP

Hoya, the name used for Georgetown University's mascot, comes from a Greek and Latin phrase, "hoya saxa," which means something like "what rocks"! Nobody's quite sure whether the term has to do with the school's stone walls or is an early cheer for the school's Stonewalls baseball club.

ies, is the bread and butter of this independent day school. All 11th- and 12th-grade students follow the challenging International Baccalaureate curriculum, and nearly all graduates continue their education.

Northern Virginia

Burgundy Farm Country Day School
3700 Burgundy Rd., Alexandria, Va.
• (703) 960-3431

Burgundy Farm, founded in 1946 and situated on a 25-acre rural campus, offers an interdisciplinary approach to its 250 coed students in pre-kindergarten through eighth grade. All classes are taught by two instructors, with strong emphasis on the liberal arts. Parents are actively involved as volunteers. Extended-day programs feature a variety of enrichment activities. The school sponsors a summer day camp and a residential camp at its Burgundy Center for Wildlife Studies in the Appalachians in West Virginia.

The Congressional Schools of Virginia
3229 Sleepy Hollow Rd., Falls Church
• (703) 533-9711

These coeducational schools, which enroll 114 infants to kindergartners and 262 students from 1st through 8th grades, promote traditional education and values. The curriculum emphasizes language arts and also includes hands-on learning in recently upgraded computer and science labs. The student/teacher ratio ranges from 16 to 2 in preschool to 22 to 1 in middle-school classes. Graduates usually continue their education at the area's most prestigious college prep schools. Physical education, art and music round out the curriculum, with many activities both during and after school taking place in a new gym and auditorium that opened last spring. Founded in 1939, the schools are nestled on a 40-acre campus that includes such outdoor activities as nature trails, playgrounds, swimming pools and an outdoor education ropes course. During the summer, the campus hosts day camps for children ages 3 to 14.

Episcopal High School in Virginia
1200 N. Quaker Ln., Alexandria, Va.
• (703) 379-6530

One of Virginia's most celebrated prep schools, Episcopal is small, personal and highly demanding of its diverse 400 students. Founded in 1839 mere minutes from the nation's capital, this coed boarding school for 9th through 12th grades follows a tradition-rich Honor System that has created an environment of openness among students and instructors. Students follow a challenging liberal arts-based curriculum that includes Advanced Placement courses. The school takes advantage of the myriad resources of the neighboring District through field trips and internships at political and cultural institutions. Many students also spend time studying abroad. The school boasts numerous athletic facilities, including a 2,800-seat stadium, seven playing fields and a six-lane, 400-meter outdoor track. Spirituality plays an important role in campus life, with students regularly attending chapel and volunteering for community service. The 130-acre, wooded campus resembles a small college, complete with historic buildings.

The Fairfax Christian School
1624 Hunter Mill Rd., Vienna, Va.
• (703) 759-5100

This coed school for kindergarten through 12th grade, founded in 1961, stresses a traditional liberal arts curriculum in a nondenominational Christian setting. Enrollment numbers around 300 students. Most 4-year-olds in the school's kindergarten learn how to read using a phonetic approach. The school offers extended care and provides transportation for most Northern Virginia students. The 28-acre, rural campus is conveniently situated between Vienna and Reston, close to the Dulles Toll Road. A sister school, Chantilly Christian School, 13858 Metrotech Dr., Chantilly, (703) 968-3682, opened in fall of 1997.

Flint Hill School
10409 Academic Dr., Oakton, Va.
• (703) 242-0705

Flint Hill is a nondenominational, coed college prep school known for its lofty academic and competitive athletic programs. The student/faculty ratio is 9-to-1. Founded in 1956, the school also stresses community service of its approximately 600 students: Graduation requirements include 60 hours of service to be completed by the end of the first senior semester. Pupils can take a variety of honors and Advanced Placement courses, and all seniors design and complete three-week independent study projects. (Recent senior projects included such eclectic themes as living at a Buddhist monastery, working at a hospital in Uruguay and designing costumes and sets for The Shakespeare Theatre, among many others.) The 15-acre campus is a stone's throw from Interstate 66, in the upper-middle-class residential community of Oakton.

Foxcroft School
Va. Hwy. 626, Middleburg, Va.
• **(540) 687-5555, (800) 858-2364**

Founded in 1914, this small, residential prep school strives to foster self-esteem and strong moral character in 9th through 12th grade girls. Around 150 students attend Foxcroft, nationally recognized for its academic and athletic programs. The student/faculty ratio is 6-to-1. Educational highlights include an Interim Term, featuring nontraditional course offerings, guest lecturers and field trips; three-week, career-oriented senior projects; a fellowship program that brings to the school such notable visitors as Maya Angelou and Richard Leakey; an ESL program for international students; and an annual poetry festival. The beautiful 500-acre campus is slightly more than an hour away from Washington, in the heart of Virginia's hunt country; consequently, riding is a popular extracurricular activity here.

Gesher Jewish Day School of Northern Virginia
8900 Little River Turnpike, Fairfax
• **(703) 978-9789**

The only Northern Virginia Jewish day school for kindergarten through 6th grade, Gesher is conveniently situated in the bustling Jewish Community Center of Northern Virginia. Founded in 1982 by several community families, the school combines Jewish studies and general studies. The student/faculty ratio is 8-to-1. Curriculum highlights include all-day kindergarten, gifted instruction, accelerated reading, Hebrew study, computers, a science lab and art studio. The school also uses the community center's full-size gymnasium, indoor swimming pool and performing arts auditorium, and students can participate in the center's extended-day program. Bus service is available

Green Hedges School
415 Windover Ave., Vienna, Va.
• **(703) 938-8323**

Founded in 1942, this coed, nonsectarian school emphasizes a classical education for children in preschool through 8th grade. Children ages 3 to 6 attend a Montessori Early School, where French is introduced. Among curriculum highlights for 1st through 5th grades are phonics-based reading and a hands-on science lab. Middle-school students follow the University of Chicago Math Program of algebra and pre-algebra, participate in an environmental observation project via the Internet, perform community service and take field trips. All students study Latin. The school is in residential, centrally located Vienna.

The Langley School
1411 Balls Hill Rd., McLean, Va.
• **(703) 356-1920**

An independent, coed day school for preschool through 8th-grade students, Langley prides itself on its personalized and accelerated instruction. The student/teacher ratio is 9-to-1. A brand new 27,000-square-foot middle-school building features 18 computer terminals in every classroom. It also contains a greenhouse. The school offers all-day kindergarten, a structured extended-day program and summer school and day camps. Founded in 1942, Langley is set on a 10-acre campus in one of Northern Virginia's most exclusive neighborhoods.

Loudoun Country Day School
237 Fairview St., Leesburg, Va.
• **(703) 777-3841**

The mission of Loudoun Country Day is advanced instruction, including accelerated programs in foreign languages and the arts for more than 180 students in pre-kindergarten through 8th grade. Sports also play a major role at the school, located in quaint, historic Leesburg, the county seat.

The Madeira School
8328 Georgetown Pike, McLean, Va.
• **(703) 556-8253**

Founded in 1906, Madeira offers its 300-plus young women, grades 9 through 12, a challenging academic environment that includes advanced placement courses. The average student/faculty ratio is 6-to-1, and the average class size is 11. The school's unique, Wednesday Co-Curriculum is a required, non-credit, full-day program that fosters independence and leadership skills through such activities as public speaking, outdoor education, community service and Congressional and career-oriented internships. The boarding/day school's lovely 382-acre campus, one of the largest in Metro Washington, overlooks the Potomac River and houses such facilities as a 32,000-square-foot sports center, a riding ring and stables and an indoor, competition-size swimming pool. The school is set in well-to-do McLean, close to most points in the metro area.

Nysmith School for the Gifted
13525 Dulles Technology Dr.,
Herndon, Va. • **(703) 713-3332**

As the name implies, accelerated academics are the rule here. Nysmith's 450 students, ages 2½ to 6th grade, receive daily instruction in such subjects as computers, French, hands-on science and individualized math. Student/teacher ratios range from 7-to-1 for preschoolers to 9-to-1 for grade-school children. Students frequently go on field trips around the Washington area and to such places as Colonial Williamsburg and the United Nations. Extended-day and summer programs are available, as is van transportation. The school is in the northwest Fairfax County community of Herndon, one block from the Dulles Toll Road and near Washington Dulles International Airport.

The Potomac School
1301 Potomac School Rd., McLean, Va.
• **(703) 356-4100**

This prestigious, independent, coed day school places a premium on competitive academics and extensive community service. Its 875 pupils, pre-kindergarten through 12th grade, benefit from a student/teacher ratio of about 9-to-1 and average class size of 16. The school takes pride in its interscholastic sports, which include some of the area's top athletes. Founded in Washington in 1904, the school moved in 1951 to its current location, a 70-acre campus in a residential section of McLean. Bus transportation is available.

St. Stephen's & St. Agnes School
Grades JK-8, 400 Fontaine St.,
Alexandria, Va. • **(703) 751-2700**
Grades 6-8, 4401 W. Braddock Rd.,
Alexandria, Va. • **(703) 751-2700**
Grades 9-12, 1000 St. Stephen's Rd.,
Alexandria, Va. • **(703) 751-2700**

The emphasis behind this coed, 1,100-student Episcopal day school is balancing challenging academics with community service and other types of extracurricular activities. Courses in religion are required, as are 40 hours of community service. Some students participate in foreign or specialized summer study programs. Interscholastic sports are a vital part of campus life. The school was established in 1991 through a merger of St. Stephen's, founded in 1944, and St. Agnes, founded in 1924. After-school and extended-day programs are available. The 16-acre lower school, 7-acre middle school and 35-acre upper school campuses are minutes apart and easily reached via U.S. Highway 395.

Suburban Maryland

The Bullis School
10601 Falls Rd., Potomac, Md.
• **(301) 299-8500**

Students are immersed in a range of academic and extracurricular programs at Bullis. The 520-student coed prep school for grades 3 through 12, founded in 1930, boasts a curriculum that includes traditional subjects and a heavy emphasis on the fine and performing arts. Many Advanced Placement courses are offered. The average student/teacher ratio is 14-to-1. The school also takes pride in its extensive athletic program, in which a large percentage of the student body becomes involved. The Bullis Athletic Center houses a 1,000-seat gym, while the school's 2,000-seat stadium holds a football field and eight-lane track. The 80-acre, pastoral campus is nestled in the midst of Potomac, an attractive, wealthy community a short drive from Washington.

Capitol Christian Academy
610 Largo Rd., Upper Marlboro, Md.
• **(301) 336-2200**

Capitol Christian Academy offers both traditional and alternative academic programs for coed grades kindergarten through 12. Of special note here are the intimate tutoring and counseling programs for special-needs children.

Charles E. Smith Jewish Day School
1901 E. Jefferson St., Rockville, Md.
• **(301) 881-1400**

With 1,150 students in kindergarten through 12th grade, Charles E. Smith is the largest Jewish community day school in the country. This coed school, founded in 1966, blends a liberal arts curriculum with traditional Jewish studies programs. The 10-acre campus is conveniently situated in downtown Rockville, near the Montgomery County administrative complex.

DeMatha Catholic High School
4313 Madison St., Hyattsville, Md.
• **(301) 864-3666**

One of the region's true academic and athletic powerhouses, DeMatha is recognized by the U.S. Department of Education as an "Exemplary Private School." The all-male prep school, with more than 800 students in grades 9 through 12, is in Hyattsville, convenient to the District and most points in Suburban Maryland.

Georgetown Preparatory School
10900 Rockville Pike, Rockville, Md.
• **(301) 493-5000**

Founded in 1789 by the Jesuits, Georgetown Prep is one of the metro area's oldest private schools, and is the country's oldest Catholic secondary school. The 430 9th- through 12th-grade students who attend the all-male boarding school follow a curriculum steeped in academic and religious tradition. Honors and Advanced Placement courses are plentiful. Seniors are required to perform 40 hours of community service and participate in an ethics class. The 90-acre, college-like campus is just a mile from the Capital Beltway.

Holton-Arms School
7303 River Rd., Potomac, Md.
• **(301) 365-5300**

Holton-Arms is an all-girls college prep school that has a long-held reputation for its excellent liberal arts instruction. Subjects like computer science and African American history add a contemporary edge to the traditional curriculum. The Potomac-based day school, with more than 600 students in grades 3 through 12, excels in athletics and other extracurricular programs. Along with their traditional academic requirements for graduation, students must complete 50 hours of community service and pass a swimming-competency test. Seniors can participate in off-site senior projects and independent-study options. After-school programs are available for all ages. The school holds a coed summer camp for ages 3 through 13.

Landon School
6101 Wilson Ln., Bethesda, Md.
• **(301) 320-3200**

An independent, nonsectarian college prep school for boys, Landon is structured around rigorous academics and a variety of out-of-classroom opportunities in music, drama and art. Founded in 1929, the day school has 632 students in grades 3 through 12. The average class size is 15. The curriculum includes many Advanced Placement courses. Volunteer work and community service are valued traditions

INSIDERS' TIP

Many local community centers and recreation centers offer enrichment classes for adults and children, featuring such topics as crafts, performing arts, foreign languages and dog obedience. See our Parks and Recreation chapter for phone numbers.

here, as is an honor code among middle-and upper-school students. Off-campus learning opportunities include a semester spent on a working farm in Vermont and a summer language program in Spain and several French-speaking nations. The lush 72-acre campus is in Bethesda, not far from the National Institutes of Health.

Riverdale Baptist School
1133 Largo Rd., Upper Marlboro, Md.
• (301) 249-7000

Riverdale Baptist, with more than 1,000 students in preschool through 12th grade, is Maryland's largest Christian school. An outreach of Riverdale Baptist Church, the coed school offers academic and extracurricular programs that revolve around the Bible and fundamentalist Christian beliefs. Honors and Advanced Placement courses are available for academically qualified high-school students. The school's athletics department boasts 14 competitive varsity teams, including a baseball team ranked No. 1 in *The Washington Post*. The band, chorus and yearbook also garner honors on a regular basis. Riverdale offers extended-day care options and bus transportation for county students.

Colleges and Universities

Metro Washington colleges and universities attract students and faculty from all 50 states and more than 125 countries. A dozen of the region's leading schools are linked by the Consortium of Universities, (202) 331-8080, a network that allows for extensive cross-study programs and sharing of resources such as libraries, faculty and research facilities. Consortium members include the University of the District of Columbia and the University of Maryland, College Park; American, Catholic, Gallaudet, George Mason, George Washington, Georgetown, Howard and Marymount universities; and Mount Vernon and Trinity colleges. Of course, many residents or Northern Virginia and Suburban Maryland choose to attend schools in their states, but outside the metro area. The State Council of Higher Education for Virginia, 9th Floor, 101 N. 14th Street,

Richmond, Virginia 23219, (804) 225-2137, offers pamphlets with facts and figures about the state's public colleges and universities, as well as lists of private for- and not-for-profit institutions of higher learning. Virginia boasts 15 state-supported, four-year colleges and universities, including the highly respected College of William & Mary, (757) 221-4000, in Williamsburg; James Madison University, (540) 568-6211, in Harrisonburg; and University of Virginia, (804) 924-0311, in Charlottesville. Interested in Maryland schools? Obtain a copy of the Student Guide to Higher Education in Maryland through the Maryland Higher Education Commission, 16 Francis Street, Annapolis, Maryland 21401-1781, (410) 974-2971. The guide describes the 55 colleges and universities in the state, including such popular, nearby choices as Hood College, (800) 922-1599, in Frederick; Mount Saint Mary's College, (301) 447-6122, in Emmitsburg; and St. John's College, (410) 263-2371, in Annapolis. The booklet also includes information about all five U.S military academies, including the United States Naval Academy, (410) 293-1000, in Annapolis. The guide also lists private career schools offering training in fields from allied health to truck driving.

Washington, D.C.

American University
4400 Massachusetts Ave. NW,
Washington, D.C. • (202) 885-6000

"AU," as it's commonly known in these parts, attracts many who aspire to be diplomats and journalists. The independent, coed school, founded in 1891, offers competitive programs in arts and sciences, business administration, communications, international service and public affairs. American offers extensive study-abroad programs in Europe and Latin America. The campus also makes good use of its city as a learning lab: AU interns in the Washington Semester Program are almost as ubiquitous to D.C. as lawyers and lobbyists. The school takes pride in its university and law libraries, which contain thousands of volumes and up-to-date technical support.

Student life is surprisingly close knit, with

3,500 of the more than 11,000 students living on or very near the 76-acre campus, which is in a beautiful residential section of Northwest. Graduate students make up nearly a third of the enrollment, and various programs are available for working professionals. The university's athletic programs are gaining popularity, spurred in part by the fairly new on-campus gymnasium.

Catholic University of America
620 Michigan Ave. NE, Washington, D.C.
• (202) 319-5600

The Catholic Church's national university, founded in 1887, draws strength from the diversity of its students who come from all 50 states and at least 111 countries. Programs are offered through the schools of religious studies, philosophy, law, arts and sciences, engineering, social service, nursing, music, library and information science and architecture and planning. The university's 3,700 graduate students outnumber the 2,400 undergrads. The school's drama department is considered one of the nation's best, having produced the likes of Susan Sarandon and other stage and screen stars.

Housing on the 155-acre campus, adjacent to the stunning Basilica of the National Shrine of the Immaculate Conception, is guaranteed for freshmen and sophomores. Day care and kindergarten are available for young children of students and staff. Working adults can enroll in a bachelor of arts program through the Metropolitan College (call (202) 319-5256 for more information). Many students commute to the Northeast campus from the suburbs and other parts of the District. Catholic's highly acclaimed library contains more than 1.2 million volumes and is often frequented by students from other schools in the metro area. The Center for Planning and Information Technology offers a sophisticated array of computer equipment for use by students and faculty.

Corcoran School of Art
17th St. and New York Ave. NW,
Washington, D.C. • (202) 639-1814

This private professional art college, founded in 1890, offers fully accredited undergraduate programs for visual artists, photographers and designers. The 325 full-time students receive lots of personal attention: The student/faculty ratio is less than 7-to-1. More than 3,000 people annually register for the Division of Continuing Education's Open Program, filled with all kinds of nifty classes for children and adults. The school is affiliated with the venerable Corcoran Gallery of Art, near the White House and the National Mall.

Gallaudet University
800 Florida Ave. NE, Washington, D.C.
• (202) 651-5050

Gallaudet, which grew from a small school founded in 1856, is the nation's only university dedicated exclusively to the hearing-impaired. The private liberal arts college, in Northeast, awards bachelor's and master's degrees in more than 50 areas, such as business, biology, communications, the arts, computer science, education, engineering and environmental design.

The 2,000-strong student body is active in campus and community life. Fraternities and sororities, student societies and intercollegiate athletics are all vital components of the college. Gallaudet also operates model elementary, secondary and college prep schools for hearing-impaired students. The Visitors Center conducts, by reservation, tours of the school.

George Washington University
2121 I St. NW, Washington, D.C.
• (202) 994-6040

Like Catholic University, George Washington is a private, independent institution claiming more graduate students than undergrads, 10,845 to 6,582. Students hail from more than 130 countries. Graduate programs for working professionals are a growing commodity at GW. Bachelor-degree sequences, meanwhile, span the liberal arts and technical spectrum, with international affairs the No. 1 major; psychology, political science, international business, finance and electrical engineering also prove popular. The international MBA program is one of the best anywhere and the health professions school is bolstered by the university's highly acclaimed medical center.

Washington's biggest school of higher

education, GW started in 1821 via an act of Congress. Despite an urban setting, in the oddly named Foggy Bottom, the 45-acre campus maintains a distinctive collegiate atmosphere. Fraternities and sororities are big here, as are the more than 200 active student organizations, ranging from international and political societies to literary and theater groups. GW athletics are a growing attraction, especially the men's and women's basketball teams. Only freshmen are guaranteed on-campus housing. Not surprisingly, GW students are known to be avid commuters.

Georgetown University
37th and O Sts. NW, Washington, D.C.
• **(202) 687-0100**

Georgetown is undoubtedly Washington's — and one of the nation's — most visible and highly regarded universities. The 208-year-old school, the oldest Catholic college in America, has outstanding programs in the arts and sciences, business, engineering, the health professions, foreign service and nursing, to name a few. The 12,629 enrollment is nearly evenly split between undergrads and graduate students, who are drawn to Georgetown's fine law, business and medical schools, the latter of which includes a teaching hospital. The university also has one the area's most comprehensive continuing education programs, including dozens of interesting noncredit courses open to all adults.

Some may argue that the university's raison d'etre is its government department, which each year pumps out scores of budding lawmakers, policy analysts, advisors, researchers and diplomats. (The alumni list includes a guy named Bill Clinton.) And when it comes to sports, men's basketball, under longtime head coach John Thompson, reigns supreme. The program is a virtual breeding ground for NBA talent the likes of Patrick Ewing and Alonso Mourning.

Students come here from all 50 states and 84 countries, giving the beautiful 104-acre campus an unmistakably cosmopolitan air. As you can imagine, campus life is rich and intense. Undergrads tend to be the fashion- and trend-setters for Washington's 20-something set.

Howard University
2400 6th St. NE, Washington, D.C.
• **(202) 806-6100**

Howard is the nation's largest predominantly African American university — and one of the most respected. The school's list of distinguished alumni includes Thurgood Marshall, Andrew Young, Douglas Wilder, Jessye Norman, Roberta Flack and Vernon Jordan, to name a few. Sixteen schools and colleges, supported by nine research facilities, accommodate around 11,000 students. Medicine, law and engineering are among the top draws. Founded in 1867, the school has grown to include numerous resources, such as a hospital, radio and television stations and press specializing in African American-oriented topics. The school's athletic program includes champion football and women's basketball teams.

Howard students (80 percent African American) come from nearly every state and more than 100 countries. More than a third live in student housing, while most of the rest live in the neighboring LeDroit Park section of Northwest D.C. The 89-acre campus is just a couple of miles north of the Capitol.

Mount Vernon College
2100 Foxhall Rd. NW, Washington, D.C.
• **(202) 625-4682**

This small — approximately 600 students —private liberal arts school for women was founded in 1875 and became affiliated with George Washington University in the fall of 1996. Interior design is the school's flagship program, and the MBA program proves quite popular with international students, who make up about a third of the enrollment. The school offers undergraduate and coed graduate programs as well as evening and weekend undergraduate programs. Mount Vernon is situated on a gorgeous 26-acre campus in the city's wealthy Foxhall neighborhood.

Strayer College
1025 15th St. NW, Washington, D.C.
• **(202) 408-2400**

Strayer is a private, independent business college with campuses in the District (including Takoma Park), Maryland (Suitland) and Virginia (Alexandria, Arlington, Ashburn,

Fredericksburg, Manassas and Woodbridge). The commuter school, originating in 1892, offers associate, bachelor's and master's degree programs. Many of the students are working adults, most of whom take classes in the evenings and on weekends.

Trinity College
125 Michigan Ave. NE, Washington, D.C.
• (202) 884-9400, (800) 492-6882

Founded in 1897 by the Sisters of Notre Dame, Trinity is one of the first Roman Catholic women's colleges. The school boasts a personalized, liberal arts-oriented learning atmosphere and enrollment of around 1,500. Business administration, political science and information studies are the most popular degrees. Some of the school's graduate programs are coed.

About 95 percent of Trinity students live on the 26-acre campus just across the street from Catholic University.

University of the District of Columbia
4200 Connecticut Ave. NW, Washington, D.C. • (202) 274-5010

UDC is the only publicly funded college in the District and therefore its mission is a bit different than that of its neighbors. Many of its 5,652 students are D.C. high-school graduates. UDC offers two-year, bachelor's and master's degrees through its College of Arts and Sciences, College of Professional Studies, a graduate studies program and the Division of Continuing Education.

This is exclusively a commuter school, having no on-campus housing. In addition, the university is spread across several locations. Features include a media center, 1,000-seat auditorium and athletics facility.

Northern Virginia

George Mason University
4400 University Dr., Fairfax, Va.
• (703) 993-1000

Fast-growing George Mason is now the second-largest university in the Commonwealth. Since its founding in 1957, the college has undergone the transformation from a fledg-ling regional institution into a powerful national public university. Mason draws on a diverse and singularly impressive faculty (including Nobel Prize-winning economist James Buchanan), many of whom come from the public policy, business and political ranks of Washington. Undergraduate programs include studies in the arts and sciences, education, information technology, engineering, fine arts, business and nursing. The graduate school accounts for about 30 percent of the student body and contains rapidly expanding programs in business and international studies, public policy and biotechnology, among others.

The vast majority of Mason's 25,000 students attend classes on the expansive main campus just outside Fairfax City. The compact Arlington campus houses some professional programs and the law school. The school opened a campus in Prince William County in August of 1997. Almost 85 percent of GMU students are commuters and nearly the same amount are from Virginia. The school can, however, accommodate 3,000 people in university housing. Campus life is what you'd expect from a commuting school: sparse. The addition of a new fine arts center (see our Arts chapter for further details) and a growing slate of on-campus entertainment programming come with the promise of invigorating the social scene. The new George W. Johnson Center, with 8 acres of floor space, houses restaurants and a food/study court in addition to a library and media center. The sports program boasts 300 student athletes. But Mason students make no bones about it: They're here first and foremost for an education, and that they are getting.

Marymount University
2807 N. Glebe Rd., Arlington, Va.
• (703) 284-1500

Marymount began as a private Catholic college for women. In the late 1980s it went coed and today it seems to be expanding in every direction. (It even has a branch campus in Loudoun County.) The mission remains the same, though: to provide an intimate and accelerated atmosphere to grow and learn. The university offers undergraduate and graduate programs in such areas as nursing, business, education, human resource development, psychology and liberal studies. Day and evening classes are available for working professionals.

Virginia Tech/University of Virginia Northern Virginia Center
7054 Haycock Rd., Falls Church, Va.
• (703) 538-8324, (703) 876-6900

This jointly run, 105,000-square-foot center in Falls Church links Northern Virginia with two of the Commonwealth's largest and arguably most influential universities. The main campus of the University of Virginia is in Charlottesville, in central Virginia, while Tech is in Blacksburg, in the southwestern part of the state near Roanoke.

The Northern Virginia center offers adult students an array of undergraduate and graduate liberal arts and technical courses. Graduate degree programs are offered in urban planning, education and engineering.

The George Washington University Virginia Campus
20101 Academic Way, Ashburn, Va.
• (703) 729-8300

This satellite campus of GWU (see listing under Washington, D.C. in this chapter) is an innovative venture between industry and education.

Several courses and executive seminars are taught by area business and science leaders outside of academia. Master's and doctoral degree programs are offered in engineering, business, information systems and human resources. The center also conducts a number of non-degree professional development workshops. The campus is in the sprawling University Center, a corporate and research park that sits in the middle of eastern Loudoun County's rapidly growing Virginia Highway 7 corridor, convenient to Washington Dulles International Airport.

Mary Washington College
1301 College Ave., Fredericksburg, Va.
• (540) 654-2000

Thanks to the Virginia Railway Express and a large stock of affordable housing, Fredericksburg has become an exurb of Metro Washington. That being the case, we thought it only appropriate to include in this list the city's academic pride and joy: Mary Washington College. This publicly funded coed college is consistently rated among the nation's top regional liberal arts schools and one of the best buys in higher education. Undergrads number 3,700, and highly competitive admission standards will likely keep that figure stable in coming years. Students seem to migrate to the school's psychology, business and English departments. Bachelor's and master's degree programs in liberal studies are offered to working professionals. MWC's lush, tree-lined campus is a recruiting tool in itself.

Suburban Maryland

Bowie State University
14000 Jericho Park Rd., Bowie, Md.
• (301) 464-6570

Part of the University of Maryland system, Bowie State is a regional liberal arts institution that boasts strong undergraduate programs in business, education and computer science. The majority of the circa 1865 school's 4,900 students are African-Americans, but Bowie's enrollment is multicultural and international. About a third of all students are enrolled in the graduate school. The 312-acre campus includes such features as a learning-resource center, art gallery, radio and TV station and the Adler-Dreikurs Institute of Human Relations.

Capitol College
11301 Springfield Rd., Laurel, Md.
• (301) 953-3200

This college opened in 1927 as a correspondence school called the Capitol Radio Engineering Institute. Today, the private college champions "teaching tomorrow's technology," and awards bachelor's and associate's degrees in communications and engineering, including programs in telecommunications management, computer engineering, optoelectronics and engineering technology. The majority of students are professionals. Capitol is situated on a 52-acre campus in Laurel, a Prince George's County community between Washington and Baltimore.

Columbia Union College
Flower and Carroll Aves., Takoma Park, Md. • (301) 891-4232

Tiny Columbia Union (enrollment about

1,200) is a private liberal arts college affiliated with the Seventh-day Adventist Church. It's on a pretty, 19-acre campus in Takoma Park, a city known for its grass-roots activism and progressive politics. The student body represents all states and 40 countries. Business and nursing are popular programs. (There are no graduate programs.) Spiritual life and community service play active parts in extracurricular activities. Most students commute to campus.

University of Maryland at College Park
U.S. Hwy. 1, College Park, Md.
• (301) 405-1000

Maybe it's the proximity to Georgetown, or Baltimore's Johns Hopkins, or perhaps even the University of Virginia, some three hours to the south. Whatever the reason, the University of Maryland has never received its proper share of credit for being one of the nation's better state universities and one of the fastest-growing research institutions.

With nearly 33,000 students in its 14 undergraduate and graduate schools, Maryland has been criticized as being too large and impersonal. There may be some truth behind the claims, but with its size comes almost unlimited opportunities for academic and social life. Three-quarters of the students here are undergraduates, and they flock to the university's strong programs in engineering, computer science, physics, education and business management. Graduate programs in the physical sciences and engineering are bolstered by expanding research facilities on and off campus. *U.S. News and World Report*, in its 1997 rankings of graduate programs, lists the College of Business and Management as 25th in the nation, the College of Education as 25th and the Clark School of Engineering as 18th. When the magazine rated individual undergraduate programs in 1996, it ranked the school's engineering department 24th and its business school 20th among the nation's comparable undergraduate programs.

The University of Maryland's innovative University College was established in 1947 as one of the nation's pioneering adult education programs. Today it is one of the metro area's most popular continuing-ed programs, offering bachelor's and master's degrees in business, biology, communications, the arts, engineering and health professions, among others.

Campus life at Maryland tends to be pretty traditional. About 10 percent of the students are members of Greek societies, and those groups are joined by more than 400 social and professional clubs. Terrapins have always been bullish on their sports teams, particularly the men's basketball team, which has made six straight NCAA tournament appearances. New football facilities are aiding that team's rebuilding efforts.

Community Colleges

Northern Virginia

Northern Virginia Community College
4001 Wakefield Chapel Rd., Annandale, Va. • (703) 323-3000

Northern Virginia Community College, or "NOVA" in the local vernacular, awards two-year associate degrees in more than 130 occupational, technical and college transfer programs. The 60,000-plus-student school, the largest college in Virginia and the second largest multi-campus community college in the country, has campuses in Alexandria, Annandale, Loudoun County, Manassas and Woodbridge. The Extended Learning Institute provides credit and noncredit courses for study at home. Continuing-education programs abound on all five campuses and community facilities throughout Northern Virginia.

INSIDERS' TIP

The U.S. Department of Education provides written materials and videos on topics such as reading incentive programs, national education initiatives and community school involvement. You can call toll-free, (800) 424-1616, or write them at: U.S. Department of Education, 400 Maryland Ave. SW, Washington, D.C. 20202-4151.

Suburban Maryland

Maryland College of Art and Design
10500 Georgia Ave., Silver Spring
• **(301) 649-4454**

This small school, with about 70 students, has a two-year professional program culminating in an Associate of Fine Art degree. Students concentrate in fine art studies or visual communication areas like graphic design. Class sizes are small, and students spend a lot of time doing studio work.

Montgomery College
900 Hungerford Ave., Rockville, Md.
• **(301) 279-5000**

This community college, with 22,000 credit students and 10,000 continuing education students per semester, is spread across three campuses in Maryland's largest county. The Rockville campus, by far the largest with nearly 14,000 students, offers numerous technical and liberal arts transfer programs. The Takoma Park campus specializes in health studies and professional programs. The Germantown campus offers specialized career programs plus the gamut of arts and science courses. In addition to regular, for-credit courses, noncredit programs are taught at campuses and community sites across the county. These popular classes, ranging from auto maintenance to canoeing, enroll more than 17,000 students a year.

Prince George's Community College
301 Largo Rd., Largo, Md.
• **(301) 336-6000**

Another one of Maryland's fine community colleges, Prince George's, founded in 1958, has an open admissions policy and a menu of more than 60 areas of study including accounting, health sciences, education and law enforcement. Students, numbering more than 12,000, are as diverse as the curriculum, and class enrollment may include a mix of recent high school graduates, midcareer adults and senior citizens. Summer programs, contract training arrangements and extension and telecredit courses are all available here. More than half of all credit students transfer to four-year colleges and universities, with the University of Maryland being the top destination.

Most hospitals featured in this chapter offer community outreach programs, as well as speakers bureaus, outpatient testing, surgery and treatment programs and other services.

Healthcare

Anyone seeking medical care in the Metro Washington area can take comfort in knowing help is literally right around the corner. In D.C. proper, you can't travel more than a few blocks without encountering a hospital, medical clinic or a building full of doctors' offices.

The National Capital Area is home to some of the world's finest medical researchers and healthcare professionals, and four area hospitals are consistently ranked among the 100 best in America by *U.S. News and World Report.* Three of the four are Georgetown University Medical Center, Fairfax Hospital and Children's National Medical Center. The one with the most stellar reputation, however, is Johns Hopkins University Hospital, about an hour away in Baltimore, Maryland. Though it may be a little further, if you're struck with a serious illness, it's worth the drive. In many specialties, Hopkins is ranked No. 1 by *U.S. News Surveys* and is invariably in the top five.

Looking beyond Metro Washington and Maryland for a moment, there are two other acclaimed medical institutions: the University of Virginia Medical Center in Charlottesville and the Medical College of Virginia in Richmond.

This chapter, however, sticks closer to home and offers an overview of approximately 50 major hospitals and other medical facilities in Metro Washington, including the teaching and research hospitals affiliated with university medical schools that play a vital role in the training of future doctors, nurses and other healthcare professionals. We've also included some mental-health facilities and touched on the popular walk-in medical centers where minor illnesses and injuries can be quickly treated (see the emergency numbers graybox toward the end of this chapter). One caveat: By the time you read this, some of the names may have changed because takeovers by large managed-care organizations are ongoing.

We have intentionally omitted a list of hospices, since physicians or hospitals generally refer patients after initial medical treatment. There are, however, more than a dozen in the Washington metro area, and they are easily found in the yellow pages or through physician referrals. Also, an excellent clearinghouse for information on hospices and their services is the National Hospice Organization, 1901 N. Moore Street, Arlington, Virginia, (703) 243-5900. Don't forget that all local governments offer community health clinics and other local treatment facilities, included in the government listings in the phone book.

Finding the Right Doctor: Physician Referrals

While finding a hospital may be easy, the same doesn't always apply to finding the right doctor. So before delving too deeply into the hospital world, we've compiled a listing of some free dental and physician referral services — some of which are affiliated with area hospitals and some of which are financed by subscribing doctors. Aside from those listed here, almost every hospital we've named in this chapter has a referral service listed in the phone book along with the hospital's other departments. In most cases the referral services can provide access to hundreds of medical professionals in a wide range of fields and specialties. Caution: Since these services are often financed by those who stand to benefit, you may wish to check with the licensing board for credentials.

In Maryland, the state licensing board is at 4201 Patterson Avenue, Baltimore, MD 21215, (410) 764-4777. In Washington, D.C., write to 614 H Street NW, Room 108, Washington, DC 20001, (202) 727-5365; and in Virginia, 6606 W. Broad Street, 4th floor, Richmond, VA 23230, (804) 662-9900.

To get you started, here is a short list of some of the area's most popular referral services. It is by no means comprehensive, but it touches on most counties in Metro Washington:

Prologue, (202) or (800) DOCTORS

INOVA First Call, (703) 845-4848

Loudoun Physician Referral Service of Loudoun Hospital Center, (703) 771-7300 or (800) 732-3737

Montgomery General Hospital Physician Referral Service, (301) 774-8881

Laurel Regional Hospital's HealthMatch, (301) 262-7300

State hospital associations — smaller versions of the American Hospital Association — can be a valuable resource for information on medical facilities in Maryland, Virginia and Washington, D.C. Just contact the public relations office at the appropriate organization: Maryland Hospital Association, 1301 York Road, Suite 800, Luththerville, MD 21093-6087, (410) 321-6200; Virginia Hospital Association, P.O. Box 31394, Richmond, VA 23294, (804) 747-8600; District of Columbia Hospital Association, 1250 Eye Street NW, Suite 700, Washington, DC 20005, (202) 682-1581.

Most hospitals featured in this chapter offer many community outreach health and education programs (CPR, smoking cessation, weight reduction, family planning and child birth, stress management, etc.) as well as speakers bureaus, outpatient testing, surgery and treatment programs and other services beyond the usual realm of a hospital's everyday role. Many services are free, but call the individual facilities to find out more.

With one exception, we have not included any of the military or veterans hospitals since they don't serve the general public. If you are a newcomer seeking information on veteran's hospitals, contact the Veterans' Affairs Medical Center at (202) 745-8655.

Hospitals and Mental Health Facilities

Washington, D.C.

Children's National Medical Center
111 Michigan Ave. NW, Washington, D.C. • (202) 884-5000

When children are seriously ill or hurt, this is one of the top places they can go for treatment — and the patients aren't from just Metro Washington. Children's National Medical Center, often referred to as Children's Hospital, is recognized as one of the pre-eminent medical-care providers to infants, children and youths in the entire mid-Atlantic region. Some 75 percent of pediatricians in Metro Washington have trained here.

No one enjoys being hospitalized, particularly kids. Children's recognizes the trauma of hospitalization for children; Since 1910, there has been a "rooming in" program for parents. Founded in 1870 — although the present 279-bed facility opened in 1977 — Children's is a private, nonprofit hospital with two comprehensive-care branch clinics in Washington, D.C. and several suburban clinics in Maryland and Virginia.

Emergency trauma care is perhaps Children's best-known service, but the hospital's expertise extends well into other areas including cardiology, sports medicine, genetics, plastic and reconstructive surgery, infectious diseases, neonatology, psychiatry and physical therapy. Naturally, Children's is very active in the research field, with special emphasis on AIDS, sickle cell anemia and autism.

INSIDERS' TIP

Most community hospitals in the Metro area offer deluxe hotel-style wings suitable for those having elective surgery, or who simply wish for added comfort and better cuisine. Count on spending an extra $150 to $250 per day.

Columbia Hospital for Women
2425 L St. NW, Washington, D.C.
• (202) 293-6500

What Children's Hospital is to children, Columbia Hospital for Women is to . . . well, the name makes it pretty obvious. The present facility opened in 1874, and much has changed since. Columbia is now a leader in mammography and sonography, gynecological surgery, neonatal intensive care and reproductive endocrinology. The hospital has always maintained an unwavering commitment to women's health needs, including the birthing of babies, as many occupants of the 154 beds will attest.

Columbia's singular mission arose out of the federal government's concern for women's welfare following the Civil War. At one time a federally supported, charitable institution, Columbia evolved into a private, nonprofit, teaching medical center with a long history of making a difference in women's health, developing lifesaving delivery-room techniques, lowering infant and breast cancer mortality rates and making significant advances in reproductive health.

District of Columbia General Hospital
19th St. and Massachusetts Ave. SE, Washington, D.C. • (202) 675-5000

"D.C. General," a 404-bed hospital on the banks of the Anacostia River, was founded in 1806 when Congress appropriated $2,000 to establish the first institution for care of the poor, disabled and infirm. Like so many other older medical centers in Metro Washington, the hospital was a military hospital during the Civil War. It became the first charitable health institution in Washington, D.C. and also was the city's first training school for nurses. The present facility opened in 1929 and, since the adoption of its present name in 1953, has grown into one of the largest municipal hospitals in the nation.

D.C. General offers a full range of medical and surgical services and programs, including OB-GYN, pediatrics, neurology, orthopedics, internal medicine, ophthalmology, psychiatric services for adults and physical therapy. With more than 81,000 visits annually, D.C. General's emergency room is by far the city's busiest. Because of its inner-city location, many patients are victims of shooting and other crimes. As a result, the mortality rate in its emergency room is high. In recent years, there has been periodic grumbling from staff about the high-stress and limited resources of the hospital, so this is probably not the place to go unless you are in dire circumstances.

The George Washington University Medical Center
901 23rd St. NW, Washington, D.C.
• (202) 994-1000

One of the area's most comprehensive healthcare and education centers, 501-bed George Washington University Medical Center was founded in 1844 at the former Washington Infirmary on 16th Street NW. It moved to its present facility, in Foggy Bottom, in 1947. Private and nonprofit, the hospital also includes three other entities: the Medical Faculty Associates, a full-time physician group practice; the George Washington University Health Plan, a health-maintenance organization, or HMO; and the School of Medicine and Health Sciences.

A major teaching and research facility, not to mention a busy 24-hour emergency room, "GW" is involved in research projects costing in the tens of millions annually (see the Education chapter also). Special clinical programs include bone-marrow transplantation, gallstone lithotripsy and hyperbaric medicine. As could be expected from such a comprehensive healthcare facility, a broad range of services is offered including OB-GYN, neurology, orthopedics, internal medicine, cardiology, psychiatric services for adults, sports medicine, physical therapy, speech pathology and audiology.

Perhaps its most visible claim to fame is as the hospital to which President Reagan was transported when he was shot by John Hinckley. As you know, the president was successfully treated and went on to serve another term, a testament to the fine care he received from GW physicians.

Georgetown University Hospital
3800 Reservoir Rd. NW, Washington, D.C. • (202) 784-3000

Probably the city's most prestigious teaching hospital, Georgetown University Hospital was founded in 1898 and went on to break new ground by offering such conveniences as a special entrance for horse-drawn ambulances — modern indeed for its time. Today's 535-bed facility, which opened in 1948, is located in tony upper Northwest on a residential street lined with gracious mansions and diplomatic residences. The hospital, like its namesake university (see the Education chapter), is highly regarded internationally, and a top-flight team of doctors, nurses and other personnel have access to the most advanced technology in every clinical discipline.

The hospital has distinguished itself as a medical research hub and is known as an ultramodern teaching facility. Pioneering efforts at Georgetown led to later successes with heart-valve implants and hemodialysis, while work today continues in disciplines such as cancer treatment, shock-wave lithotripsy, magnetic resonance imaging (MRI) and specialized perinatal and neonatal care. The full range of services includes OB-GYN, pediatrics, neurology, orthopedics, emergency medicine, internal medicine and radiology.

Greater Southeast Community Hospital
1310 Southern Ave. SE, Washington, D.C. • (202) 574-6000

Greater Southeast Community Hospital, founded in 1966, is a 450-bed facility that today serves over 400,000 residents. It's the largest and most comprehensive hospital of its kind in the immediate area and continues to grow, adding equipment and personnel, and enhancing programs and capabilities.

GSCH offers a fairly broad range of surgical and medical services, including OB-GYN, pediatrics, neurology, orthopedics, emergency and internal medicine, radiology, family practice, ophthalmology, adult psychiatry, cancer screening, a diabetes management unit, geriatric assessment, oncology, neonatal intensive care, pathology, renal dialysis and cardiology.

Hadley Memorial Hospital
4601 Martin Luther King Jr. Ave. SW, Washington, D.C. • (202) 574-5700

Owned and operated by the Seventh-day Adventist Church and part of the nationwide Adventist Health System, Hadley has a history of compassionate service to anyone and everyone, especially the indigent. Its founder, Dr. Henry G. Hadley, started the Washington Sanitarium Mission Clinic in 1918 to treat the city's working poor and needy. He eventually bought the clinic and donated it to the church before setting out to build a much-needed hospital. The present building, one of the District's newest hospitals, opened in 1986.

Services offered at Hadley include OB-GYN, pediatrics, surgery, neurology, orthopedics, emergency medicine, internal medicine, radiology, family practice, ophthalmology, psychiatric services for children, adolescents and adults, physical therapy and sports medicine.

The Hospital for Sick Children
1731 Bunker Hill Rd. NE, Washington, D.C. • (202) 832-4400

The Hospital for Sick Children is another of the city's smaller (80 beds) healthcare centers with a unique role: that of a pediatric "transitional care" facility — the only one of its kind in Metro Washington — that serves as a link between hospital and home. Here, the young patients are treated for respiratory and chronic illnesses and a host of other disabilities.

Founded in 1883 as a "fresh air" summer home, the present facility opened in 1968. Services focus on a wide range of therapies including physical, occupational, recreational, nutritional, respiratory, speech and language.

Howard University Hospital
2041 Georgia Ave. NW, Washington, D.C. • (202) 865-6100

The second-oldest of Washington D.C.'s three major university-based teaching and research medical centers, 515-bed Howard University Hospital has come a long way since its founding in 1863 as Freedman's Hospital, a name that in itself speaks of history. The federal government created Freedman's as an emergency facility to treat the thousands of sick, destitute former slaves who poured into Washington after gaining their freedom. The Howard University Hospital of today opened in 1975 and remains synonymous with African-American advancement (some of the nation's top black medical professionals, beginning with Dr. Charles Drew, a pioneer in

Photo: Courtesy of the Richmond Times Dispatch

Aerobic exercise is an excellent way to stay fit and healthy.

blood-plasma preservation, have been trained here). The school itself, meanwhile, ranks as one of the nation's leading, historically black universities (see the Education chapter).

Howard is the third-largest private hospital and one of the four busiest hospitals in Metro Washington, with annual inpatient admissions of around 13,000 and emergency-room visits topping 53,000. Special services for the community include screening and counseling for sickle cell anemia, cancer screening, drug and alcohol addiction treatment and renal dialysis.

Underscoring its role as a major healthcare provider, the hospital's vast range of services includes OB-GYN, pediatrics, neurology, orthopedics, internal medicine, radiology, family practice, ophthalmology, oncology, dentistry, dermatology, plastic and reconstructive surgery, neurosurgery, radiotherapy, psychiatric services for children, adolescents and adults, physical and occupational therapy,

sports medicine, and areas dealing with infectious disease.

National Rehabilitation Hospital
102 Irving St. NW, Washington, D.C.
• (202) 877-1000

National Rehabilitation Hospital is a godsend for those severely disabled through accident or illness. It is the first and only freestanding facility in Metro Washington dedicated solely to thorough medical rehabilitation, with the aim of helping patients on to active and satisfying lives. The 160-bed hospital offers a host of inpatient and outpatient medical rehabilitation services including driver evaluation and training, social work, neuropsychology, nutrition, physical therapy, speech and language pathology, and therapeutic recreation.

The hospital is particularly designed for those who are physically disabled by spinal cord and brain injuries, stroke, arthritis, postpolio syndrome, amputation and other orthopedic and neurological conditions; a 40-bed unit is reserved solely for brain-injury patients. Besides its role as a rehabilitation center, NRH serves as a strong advocacy voice for the disabled.

Providence Hospital
1150 Varnum St. NE, Washington, D.C.
• **(202) 269-7000**

Providence is yet another District hospital with intriguing Civil War roots. Established in 1861 by four Catholic nuns in a renovated mansion, its original role was to care for the civilian population as the fighting between North and South raged. As luck would have it, Providence was the city's only medical facility not taken over by the military during the war. It is the only private hospital in Washington that has remained in continuous operation since.

Established at its present site in 1954, today's 382-bed Providence Hospital specializes in obstetrics and women's healthcare, geriatrics and a full range of acute and emergency services. Other programs include orthopedics, internal medicine, family practice, ophthalmology, infertility treatment, cardiology, psychiatric services for adults, substance abuse diagnosis, and physical and occupational therapy.

Sibley Memorial Hospital
5255 Loughboro Rd. NW, Washington, D.C. • **(202) 537-4000**

Sibley is yet another example of a truly "community" hospital, occupying a wooded parcel on a quiet residential street in upper Northwest. The 362-bed facility is also another example of a District medical center with a 19th-century heritage; It was founded in 1890 as a nurse-training school for deaconesses and missionaries. The hospital itself came later and was named in honor of William J. Sibley, an early supporter of the school's work, who donated $10,000 for the construction of the medical center in memory of his wife. The current building and site, however, date only to 1961. An extensive renovation and modernization program was completed in 1990.

Sibley has made its mark primarily as a surgical center, both inpatient and out. Specialties include eye and plastic surgeries, a wide range of programs for the elderly and a Sleep Disorders Center. Services include emergency medicine, family practice, internal medicine, neurology, OB-GYN, occupational and physical therapy, ophthalmology, orthopedics, radiology, and psychiatry for adults. Unlike the teaching hospitals, or publicly founded ones, Sibley is noted for more personalized attention to patients — maybe the word should be "pampering." So if you're having elective surgery, you might want to treat yourself to one of the private hotel-like "suites" that Sibley offers. After all, what better time to coddle yourself than when you're in the hospital?

The Washington Hospital Center
110 Irving St. NW, Washington, D.C.
• **(202) 877-7000**

Take three separate medical facilities, merge them, and what do you get? In this case, The Washington Hospital Center, the largest private teaching hospital in Washington, D.C. and a hub for research and education. Founded in 1958, the 907-bed facility has developed into one of Metro Washington's top medical centers with special emphasis on emergency shock-trauma care for the critically ill and injured, many of whom arrive via MedSTAR, the acclaimed air ambulance service.

Washington Hospital Center's expansive list of facilities and services includes a comprehensive burn center and cardiology unit, organ transplantation, high-risk maternal fetal care, cancer and eye disorders, neurology, OB-GYN, orthopedics, radiology, oral surgery, neurosurgery and treatment for diabetes, cancer, and eye disorders.

Northern Virginia

City of Alexandria

The Alexandria Hospital
4320 Seminary Rd., Alexandria, Va.
• **(703) 504-3000**

The Alexandria Hospital is the primary provider of medical services for city residents. It's also a primary provider of jobs, ranking as Alexandria's largest private employer with

2,000 workers and about 700 physicians. Established in 1872, the hospital occupied five sites before the present 414-bed, nonprofit facility opened in 1962. As part of its function as a teaching facility, the hospital maintains a partnership with the George Washington University Medical Center.

The hospital has one of the top cardiac-surgery units and a Level II trauma center that can handle most life-threatening illnesses and injuries 24 hours a day. Emergency medicine is also a specialty, and for good reason: Alexandria was the first hospital in the nation to staff its emergency department with full-time emergency physicians, a standard practice today at most major medical facilities. For minor emergencies when a private physician isn't available, the hospital offers an Express Care Center in the hospital's emergency department. There, you might be seen by a nurse or a nurse practitioner, although physicians are also on staff.

Cancer treatment is also a specialty at Alexandria Hospital, which houses the Northern Virginia Cancer Center. Other services include a birthing center, a neonatal intensive-care unit, dialysis, a blood donor center, respiratory therapy and a same day surgery center for outpatients.

Mount Vernon Hospital
2501 Parkers Ln., Alexandria, Va.
• (703) 664-7000

Alexandria's other major medical facility, Mount Vernon Hospital is a 235-bed nonprofit community hospital that opened in 1976. It's a member of the Inova Health System, a nonprofit, community-based organization that also includes Fair Oaks and Fairfax hospitals (see subsequent entries) as well as home healthcare, long-term care and behavioral services.

Located near its historic namesake, the hospital provides a full range of medical and surgical services, primarily to residents of Alexandria and southeastern Fairfax County. Services include 24-hour emergency medicine, a psychiatric unit for adolescents and adults, and a range of programs relating to cardiology, cancer, physical medicine and rehabilitation. Its 350 physicians represent a wide spectrum of the healthcare field. Diagnostic services offered include magnetic resonance

imaging, digital angiography, ultrasound, echocardiogram, cardiac catheterization, stress tests and mammography.

Perhaps Mount Vernon's broadest special service is the Inova Center for Rehabilitation where patients receive comprehensive care and therapy for stroke, orthopedic injuries, head and spinal cord injuries, amputation, multiple sclerosis, arthritis, workplace injuries and other neuromuscular disorders. The center includes an inpatient acute-care unit.

Arlington County

Columbia-Arlington Hospital
1701 N. George Mason Dr., Arlington, Va.
• (703) 558-5000

Arlington County's largest and most comprehensive healthcare facility is Columbia-Arlington Hospital, a 374-bed, nonprofit teaching hospital affiliated with Georgetown University's School of Medicine and several nursing schools. Open since 1944, it's well-known locally not only for fine medical and surgical services but also as the hospital of the Washington Redskins, because the team's medical staff has privileges here.

With more than 700 physicians, Arlington Hospital offers a wide range of services including a 24-hour emergency department, treatment for adult alcoholism and other drug addictions, OB-GYN, high-risk nursery, open-heart surgery, outpatient clinics, physical medicine and rehabilitation, psychiatric treatment, and numerous diagnostic and therapeutic services such as nuclear medicine, radiation therapy and respiratory therapy.

National Hospital for Orthopaedics and Rehabilitation
2455 Army-Navy Dr., Arlington, Va.
• (703) 920-6700

Looming over Interstate 395 near the Glebe Road interchange, it's hard to miss the National Hospital for Orthopaedics and Rehabilitation, a 115-bed facility that opened in 1951. As its name suggests, the hospital offers services and programs for those who sustain debilitating injuries and illnesses. Services for specific problems are a trademark; the Industrial Medical Services department, for example, deals with the prevention, treatment and rehabilitation of work-related injuries. The hospital also has a large orthotics and prosthetics department and is the only Virginia hospital to house an orthotics shop.

Services include a complete emergency department and a sports- medicine program at several satellite centers. Also offered are a range of specialized procedures including total joint replacement, microscopic hand and foot surgery, arthroscopy, a spine program, and neurologic and traumatic injury rehabilitation.

Vencor Hospital of Arlington
601 S. Carlin Springs Rd., Arlington, Va.
• (703) 671-1200

Arlington's third major medical facility used to be known as the Northern Virginia Doctors Hospital, and many still refer to it as such. Vencor, as it's now called, is a 206-bed medical/surgical and psychiatric facility that opened in 1961. The hospital offers a full range of medical/surgical and psychiatric services including ambulatory minimally invasive surgery, gynecology, urology, neurosurgery, orthopedics, gastroenterology and endoscopy, neurology and infectious diseases.

There's also an on-campus MRI center, computerized tomography, 24-hour emergency care, cardiac catheterization, nuclear medicine and an accredited diagnostic clinical lab service.

Fairfax County

Columbia-Dominion Hospital
2960 Sleepy Hollow Rd., Falls Church, Va. • (703) 538-2872

Columbia-Dominion, owned by the Columbia Healthcare giant, is one of Northern Virginia's leading mental-health care centers for children, adolescents and adults. "First Step," a free, confidential mental-health information, assessment and referral service, offers assistance in various crisis situations including suicide attempts and threats, sub-

stance abuse and other addictive illnesses, eating disorders, serious and prolonged depression, acute stress reactions, uncontrollable fears, behavioral problems in children and adolescents, sexual abuse, childhood trauma and sleep disorders.

Fair Oaks Hospital
3600 Joseph Siewick Dr., Fairfax, Va.
• (703) 391-3600

Fair Oaks Hospital was one of two hospitals built in Fairfax County in the 1980s — in this case, 1987. The other was Reston Hospital Center (see subsequent entry). Its newness is underscored in such design features as bed-mounted telephones and nurse call buttons, wall-to-wall carpeting in patients' rooms, private televisions with in-room movies, solariums, gourmet meals and rooms with deluxe amenities called The Oaks. The 160-bed, 900-employee facility is part of the Inova Health System that includes Mount Vernon and Fairfax hospitals. A western Fairfax location — just off U.S. Highway 50 at Interstate 66 — makes Fair Oaks Hospital convenient to many county residents beyond its core service area of Chantilly, Reston and Fairfax.

More than 700 physicians covering dozens of specialties have privileges at Fair Oaks, which can handle emergency, medical, surgical, critical-care, orthopedic, obstetric and pediatric patients. The 24-hour emergency department offers a helipad located just outside the doors. Two additions focus on the care and treatment of young patients: a 20-bed maternal and infant health center (which opened in 1988), emphasizing a family-centered approach to the birth process, and a Children's Unit (1990) specially equipped for infants and children through age 18. In-house pediatricians are available 24 hours a day.

Three programs at Fair Oaks Hospital deserve special notice: the International Diabetes Center of Virginia, designed for both inpatients and outpatients; the Pain Management Program — the only one of its kind in North-

INSIDERS' TIP

Each year, *Washingtonian* magazine publishes a rating of area doctors according to speciality. It's a good reference that is freely available in area libraries.

ern Virginia — that incorporates a multidisciplinary approach to the management and treatment of chronic pain; and Geriatric Psychiatric Services, a unique inpatient program in Northern Virginia that provides older persons with rapid diagnostic evaluation, stabilization and transition back to their homes.

Fairfax Hospital
3300 Gallows Rd., Falls Church, Va.
• (703) 698-1110

This 656-bed, nonprofit regional medical center, the flagship hospital of the INOVA Health System, is Northern Virginia's only Level I emergency and trauma center, meaning it can handle the most critical illnesses and accidents. Fairfax has Northern Virginia's only pediatric intensive-care unit with 24-hour care. Helicopters are a familiar sight here.

Opened in 1961, Fairfax Hospital has seen tremendous growth over the years during its emergence as one of Metro Washington's premier medical facilities. It's home to the nationally recognized Virginia Heart Center where the region's first heart transplant was performed in 1986. The hospital was also the site of the area's first lung transplant (1991) and first heart-kidney combination transplant (1992). An amazingly busy obstetrics wing (actually its own building) has earned Fairfax its local nickname, "The Baby Factory." Some 9,000 babies enter the world here each year, a figure that's among the highest in the Mid-Atlantic states. Indeed, babies are a specialty at Fairfax; there's even a unit for high-risk pregnancies, along with a neonatal intensive-care unit. The hospital offers the full range of other medical-surgical services and state-of-the-art technology, but it's also a major teaching hospital, affiliated with Georgetown and George Washington medical schools, the Medical College of Virginia, and nursing schools at George Mason and Marymount universities and Northern Virginia Community College.

Columbia-Fairfax Surgical Center
10730 Main St., Fairfax City, Va.
• (703) 691-0670

For outpatient surgical services without having to go to an actual hospital, many people opt for a facility such as Columbia-Fairfax Surgical Center, part of a national network. Offering what it calls "efficient, personal care in a pleasant atmosphere," the center charges a single fee that covers basic medical history, equipment and most supplies, routine drugs and anesthetics, recovery room services and operating room time. Be aware, though, that the price does not include the professional services of the surgeon or assistants, the anesthesiologist, radiologist, pathologist, physician consultants and pharmacist.

Columbia-Reston Hospital Center
1850 Town Center Pkwy., Reston, Va.
• (703) 689-9000

With the opening of Reston Hospital Center in 1986, many residents of western Fairfax County, particularly those in Reston, Herndon, Great Falls and parts of greater Vienna, realized the luxury of not having to travel across the county to Fairfax Hospital for comprehensive medical care. With 127 beds, it's certainly not the biggest hospital around, but its services are numerous and include most surgical and medical procedures as well as a 24-hour emergency room. Of particular note is its maternity center, the pediatric center and the kidney-stone treatment center — one of only two in the metro area.

Reston Hospital Center was the first hospital in Northern Virginia to offer laparoscopic cholecystectomy — gallbladder surgery through minor incisions. The same day surgery department has seen significant growth in recent years, reflecting a national trend toward outpatient services. Reston Hospital Center is the "official" hospital of Washington Dulles International Airport due to its proximity, easy access (just a couple of minutes off the Dulles Toll Road and parallel Airport Access Road) and wide range of services.

Loudoun County

Loudoun Hospital Center
44045 Riverside Pkwy., Leesburg, Va.
• (703) 858-6000

The county's primary medical facility is the 80-bed Loudoun Hospital Center. Founded in 1912 as a six-room rural hospital, LHC has had five names through the years and today is the flagship facility of the nonprofit Loudoun Healthcare Inc., a growing network of affiliated services located throughout the county. LHC offers most major medical and surgical services, including 24-hour emergency medicine. Special features include an intensive-care unit, an outpatient surgery department, comprehensive diagnostic imaging services, a birthing inn, a mental-health services unit, physical, occupational and speech therapy, and business health management services. Its cardiopulmonary health center was one of northern Virginia's first.

The hospital extends its community-outreach efforts to a new level with Lifeline, an electronic alert system that gives elderly residents or the severely disabled a direct connection to the hospital's emergency department (and no doubt provides family and friends with peace of mind). The Loudoun Long Term Care Center, a 100-bed residential facility, is near the hospital, at 224 Cornwall Street, Leesburg, Virginia, (703) 777-3300.

Affiliated services include the Countryside Ambulatory Surgery Center and Loudoun Pain Center, (703) 444-6060, in Sterling; the Loudoun Cancer Care Center, (703) 444-4460, also in the Countryside community, offering chemotherapy and radiation therapy; the Medex Immediate Care Center, (703) 430-7400, a walk-in facility in Sterling for minor emergencies; and the Sterling-Dulles Imaging & MRI Center, (703) 444-5800, for the diagnosis and treatment of a wide variety of disorders and diseases.

Prince William County

Potomac Hospital
2300 Opitz Blvd., Woodbridge, Va.
• (703) 670-1313

Potomac Hospital, established in 1972 with 29 beds, has grown into a 153-bed comprehensive healthcare facility with nearly 800 staff members. The hospital features a fully equipped pediatric unit, maternity unit and neonatology program, 24-hour emergency medicine, magnetic-resonance imaging and radiation therapy, and cardiac catheterization and angiography. Services include allergy and immunology, dermatology, family practice, internal medicine, neurology, OB-GYN, pediatrics, psychiatry, radiation oncology, general surgery, neurosurgery, ophthalmology, oral surgery, orthopedics, plastic surgery, thoracic and vascular surgery, urology, anesthesiology, pathology, physical medicine rehabilitation, and radiology and nuclear medicine.

Prince William Hospital
8700 Sudley Rd., Manassas, Va.
• (703) 369-8000

The county's largest medical facility is 170-bed Prince William Hospital, a private, nonprofit community facility established in 1964. The hospital features comprehensive medical and surgical services and includes a critical-care unit, inpatient and outpatient surgery, oncology, pediatrics, a 24-hour emergency department, a helipad, OB-GYN, cardiology, nuclear medicine, radiology and other diagnostic services, dialysis treatment, and physical, speech and occupational therapies.

Mary Washington Hospital
1001 Sam Perry Blvd., Fredericksburg, Va. • (540) 899-1100

Although located just outside the primary focus area of this book, Mary Washington Hospital merits inclusion for its size, services, branch facilities and accessibility to many residents of Metro Washington, particularly those in parts of southeastern Prince William County. The 340-bed hospital recently completed a major expansion and relocation and is part of the regional MWH MediCorp healthcare organization. It offers private rooms, intensive-care units (including neonatal ICU), neurosurgery, advanced cardiac technology and a 24-hour emergency department. The hospital also offers suites for labor, delivery, recovery and postpartum care for new mothers and their babies.

Affiliated facilities include Snowden at Fredericksburg, a psychiatric and addiction treatment center for adolescents and adults; the North Stafford Medical Mall, a freestanding facility that includes the ExpressCare outpatient emergency center; Carriage Hill Nursing Home and Mary Washington Health Center, providers of professional long-term care; Chancellor's Village of Fredericksburg, a retirement community; and Commonwealth Retirement Center, a modestly priced home for adults.

Suburban Maryland

Anne Arundel County

Anne Arundel Medical Center
64 Franklin St., Annapolis, Md.
• (410) 267-1000

The county's major medical facility, this acute-care hospital offers 209 beds, a full 24-hour emergency room and extensive inpatient and outpatient services, support groups and other programs at satellite locations. Outpatient services include physical therapy, cardiac rehabilitation, multiple sclerosis rehabilitation and intravenous therapy.

North Arundel Hospital
301 Hospital Dr., Glen Burnie, Md.
• (410) 787-4000

This 320-bed nonprofit hospital focuses on short-term acute care and features a 24-hour emergency room with an immediate-care center for minor injuries and illnesses, as well as a center for severe trauma and injuries. The hospital offers numerous outpatient support programs and services at various locations.

Major extensions of North Arundel Hospital include the Arundel Heart Center, 7649 Crain Highway, Glen Burnie, (410) 761-4000, specializing in cardiac rehabilitation; the Life Center, 200 Hospital Drive, Glen Burnie, (410) 768-6644, featuring a variety of wellness programs; and the Mammography Center, 301 Hospital Drive, Glen Burnie, (410) 787-4642, featuring excellent low-dose diagnostic equipment.

Montgomery County

Holy Cross Hospital of Silver Spring
1500 Forest Glen Rd., Silver Spring, Md.
• (301) 754-7000

One of Montgomery County's primary medical facilities, Holy Cross is a 442-bed nonprofit hospital founded in 1963 by Catholic nuns. Not only is this the largest acute-care facility in the county, it is also the only teaching hospital and boasts the largest medical staff in Montgomery with some 1,300 physicians enjoying privileges — a good thing since the hospital's chief service area of southern Montgomery County and northern and western Prince George's County is home to some 600,000 residents.

Holy Cross Hospital is a recognized teaching center through affiliations with George Washington University's graduate medical education programs in obstetrics, gynecology, medicine and surgery. The hospital works with GW as well as Children's National Medical Center in sponsoring a pediatric teaching program. Specialties include critical-care services, emergency medicine, OB-GYN, home care/hospice, pediatrics, psychiatry and a range of surgical procedures. A $24 million improvement program completed in 1992 significantly upgraded the hospital's technology, efficiency and aesthetics.

Montgomery General Hospital
18101 Prince Philip Dr., Olney, Md.
• (301) 774-8882

Founded in 1920, this 229-bed nonprofit community hospital is in the northern Montgomery County community of Olney, but it serves many residents of Howard and Prince George's counties as well. Montgomery General has a full range of inpatient and outpatient medical and surgical services and programs including obstetrics, pediatrics, 24-hour emergency and cardiac care, and cancer care. The hospital offers psychiatric and addiction treatment along with the latest medical imaging and diagnostic services, health education and screening programs. Some 500 physicians are on staff.

The National Institutes of Health
9000 Rockville Pk., Bethesda, Md.
• (301) 496-2351

Along with the Centers for Disease Control (CDC) in Atlanta, the National Institutes of Health is probably the best-known and most widely recognized of the medical field's distinguished "alphabet" agencies. Still, there's more to NIH than most people probably realize. Internationally renowned for its work, NIH is one of the largest biomedical research centers in the world and the principal medical research arm of the U.S. Department of Health and Human Services. Some 70 buildings, including the 500-bed hospital and lab complex known as the Warren Grant Magnuson Clinical Center, are scattered about the 300-acre Bethesda campus just 12 miles from downtown Washington; however, as mentioned in this chapter's introduction, not just anyone can obtain care at this hospital. You have to be referred by a physician, and even then you must qualify for a clinical trial that the center is funding.

Seeing the facility today, you'll be surprised to learn that NIH started out as a one-room hygiene lab in 1887. It now consists of 24 separate research institutes, centers and divisions. Special components include the National Library of Medicine (the world's largest reference center devoted to a single subject), more than 1,400 labs with some of the best science equipment ever developed, and the Fogarty International Center that houses foreign scholars-in-residence.

NIH focuses much of its efforts on combating the major life- threatening and crippling diseases prevalent in the United States today. These diseases include heart disease, cancer, arthritis, Alzheimer's, diabetes, AIDS, neurological diseases, vision and mental disorders, infectious diseases and dental diseases. Other work involves studying the human development and aging processes and exploring the relationship between the environment and human health.

A few numbers underscore the remarkable impact that NIH has had on the nation's health. As a result of NIH investment in research, mortality from heart disease — the nation's No. 1 killer — dropped 39 percent between 1972 and 1990, while death rates from stroke decreased about 58 percent during the same period; meanwhile, improved treatment methods have increased the five-year survival rate for cancer patients to 52 percent. Advancements don't come cheaply, though. The $300 annual budget from 1887 has grown to some $10 billion today.

National Naval Medical Center
8901 Wisconsin Ave., Bethesda, Md.
• **(301) 295-4611**

Another of Bethesda's healthcare icons, the 427-bed National Naval Medical Center provides care and treatment to active-duty military personnel and is not open to the general public. It does warrant a mention since this is where the president usually goes for annual physicals, routine examinations and surgery. Not surprisingly, this hospital offers all medical and surgical services and the latest in equipment and technology.

The hospital was founded in 1802 but has only been at the present location since 1942. The site was personally selected by President Franklin Roosevelt who actually sketched the design and grounds plans that the architect used as a guide. The National Naval Medical Center is among the 10 largest medical facilities in the nation and ranks as perhaps the best military hospital. About 17,000 patients are admitted annually, while its clinic sees a whopping 725,000.

Shady Grove Adventist Hospital
9901 Medical Center Dr., Rockville, Md.
• **(301) 279-6000**

Shady Grove Adventist Hospital is a full-service facility in transition, with expansions and/or renovations either underway or recently completed in the 24-hour emergency department (Montgomery County's busiest), the critical-care and maternity units, and the laser center. Open only since 1979, the 253-bed hospital delivers the second-highest number of babies in the state each year and is the only nonteaching hospital in Maryland to offer kidney transplant surgery. A full range of other inpatient and outpatient medical and surgical services are also offered including a Level II neonatal intensive-care unit and a coronary-care unit.

Suburban Hospital
8600 Old Georgetown Rd., Bethesda, Md.
• **(301) 896-3100**

Another of Montgomery County's comprehensive community hospitals, 338-bed, nonprofit Suburban Hospital opened in 1943 but has seen some dramatic changes. An extensive renovation completed during the 1980s included the addition of a luxury wing, the emergency and shock/trauma center, a pharmacy, a cafeteria and restaurant, and an addiction treatment center. Two additions completed in the '90s house radiology facilities, a medical library, the main entrance and admitting area, a 260-seat auditorium for medical and community education, and an elevated helipad.

The more than 850 physicians on staff at Suburban are trained in programs and services as diverse as orthopedics, cardiology, oncology (Suburban was the county's first comprehensive community cancer center), mental health, dermatology, gastroenterology, infectious diseases, and microvascular and thoracic surgery.

Washington Adventist Hospital
7600 Carroll Ave., Takoma Park, Md.
• (301) 891-7600

Located in what is nearly a tri-jurisdictional city — Takoma Park is actually in Montgomery County but is very near the Prince George's and District borders — this 350-bed, acute-care, church-affiliated facility has been in operation since 1907. Offering the most complete cardiology services in the county, Washington Adventist has been nationally recognized for innovative treatments in heart catheterization. The hospital's open-heart surgery center performs over 750 such procedures annually.

Other specialties include short-stay surgery (over 5,000 patients annually), maternity, radiation oncology, emergency medicine, rehabilitation medicine and pulmonary medicine. Psychiatric services are available on an inpatient or outpatient basis and include detoxification.

Prince George's County

Doctors Community Hospital
8118 Good Luck Rd., Lanham, Md.
• (301) 552-8118

Doctors Community Hospital serves a large portion of central Prince George's County, offering all major medical and surgical services except psychiatry and obstetrics. Open since 1975, the 250-bed adult, acute-care hospital underwent a major change in 1990, going from a national, chain-owned facility to a nonprofit

community hospital. The patient units and clinical areas were recently remodeled.

This hospital is renowned for its comprehensive emergency department, which sees some 30,000 patients a year and is the only unit in the county certified to handle victims of hazardous-materials incidents. The hospital also specializes in general and same-day surgery, ophthalmology, cardiology, physical and occupational therapy, and offers complete diagnostic services in radiology and laboratory work. The Home Care Program is available to many patients upon discharge, helping them adapt to being back home and recuperating successfully.

Fort Washington Hospital
11711 Livingston Rd., Fort Washington, Md. • (301) 292-7000

Fort Washington Medical Center, a nonprofit, 34-bed facility, is an entity of the Greater Southeast Community Hospital Foundation, whose flagship hospital is Greater Southeast Community Hospital, located in Washington. Serving residents of southern Prince George's and Charles counties, the center offers general and surgical services including outpatient surgery, a 24-hour emergency room, home-health services, a pharmacy, a complete laboratory, radiology testing, CAT scan and mammography testing, and community education programs.

Laurel Regional Hospital
7300 Van Dusen Rd., Laurel, Md.
• (301) 725-4300

Laurel Regional Hospital (formerly Greater Laurel Beltsville Hospital) is a private, nonprofit, 200-bed facility located in the heart of the Baltimore/Washington corridor, close to the Washington, D.C. line as well as the Capital Beltway and the Baltimore Washington Parkway. Open since 1978, the hospital offers the full spectrum of medical, surgical and testing services, a 24-hour emergency room that sees some 23,000 patients annually, intensive-care and

INSIDERS' TIP

Teaching hospitals may offer cutting-edge technology, but care will often be less personal than at community hospitals. If your procedure is simple, consider the latter.

coronary-care units, substance-abuse treatment programs, a new maternal and child-health unit, a mental-health unit and a comprehensive rehabilitation program. Because it is so conveniently located, the hospital is able to serve residents of Prince George's, Montgomery, Anne Arundel and Howard counties.

Prince George's Hospital Center
3001 Hospital Dr., Cheverly, Md.
• **(301) 618-2000**

Prince George's Hospital Center, with 450 beds, is the country's largest medical facility — and one of its most comprehensive. Private and nonprofit, PGHC is recognized nationwide for its outstanding 24-hour emergency care and is the designated regional trauma-care center for all of southern Maryland. Its Level 1 shock-trauma unit boasts an amazing 97 percent save rate for patients. PGHC also specializes in cardiac care and is the only hospital in the county with an open-heart surgery program. For minor emergencies and non-acute injuries and illnesses, the hospital offers an Express Care Center.

A wide range of obstetric services enables the hospital to handle high-risk pregnancies and difficult deliveries and to care for premature babies. A specialized unit called The Birthplace allows labor, delivery and recovery to take place in one area. For outpatient services, the hospital offers a newly redesigned short stay center. Other services at PGHC include family practice, gastroenterology, neurology, oro-facial plastic surgery, podiatry, psychiatry, sports medicine and urology. A new ambulatory surgical wing features 10 operating rooms.

Southern Maryland Hospital Center
7503 Surratts Rd., Clinton, Md.
• **(301) 868-8000**

"Southern Maryland" is certainly not a misnomer for this full-service, 338-bed facility that serves some 400,000 residents in parts of Prince George's, Charles, Calvert and St. Mary's counties — a big chunk of southern Maryland indeed, yet the hospital is located just five miles outside the Capital Beltway.

Open since 1977, Southern Maryland Hospital Center staffs over 400 physicians representing a wide range of fields including allergy and immunology, cardiology, dental surgery, dermatology, endocrinology, family practice, gastroenterology, oncology, neurosurgery, pathology, OB-GYN, pediatrics, podiatry, psychiatry, pulmonary medicine, radiology, thoracic and vascular surgery, urology, plastic surgery and emergency medicine.

Psychiatric Hospitals

Washington's psychiatric facilities have none of the celebrity cachet of places like the Betty Ford clinic. They are serious facilities for the seriously ill, and those famous figures who have problems — such as D.C.'s own Mayor Marion Barry — usually opt to go to places outside Metro Washington for treatment.

In the Metro area, facilities range from those treating substance addiction to those housing the criminally insane. No matter what the case, rarely does one become a patient in such an institution without a referral by a mental-health care provider — or a judge. The list below is meant to serve as an overview of Metro area psychiatric facilities, not a guide from which to choose, as that is a decision best left to the patient (if possible), the mental-health care provider, and the family. As in the case of other long-term care facilities, a personal visit before checking in is a must except in emergency situations. You'll note that our list is in alphabetical order, not subdivided by regions. The reason is simple: If you need a psychiatric facility, you will likely base your decision on the what kind of care the hospital offers rather than where it is.

Chestnut Lodge Hospital
500 W. Montgomery Ave., Rockville, Md.
• **(301) 424-8300**

Chestnut Lodge is a 132-bed private psychiatric hospital serving children, adolescents and adults. Founded in 1910 to care for the seriously mentally ill, the hospital is widely known today for its treatment of schizophrenia, severe manic and depressive disorders as well as borderline conditions. Varying levels of care and a variety of living situations are available. The residential program, for example, provides a homelike and family-oriented environment, with all activities geared toward moving the patient to independent life in a community.

Graydon Manor
801 Children's Center Rd., Leesburg, Va.
• **(703) 478-8767, (703) 777-3485**

Parents of children with psychiatric and other mental difficulties worked together to found Graydon Manor in 1957. A private, 61-bed, nonprofit residential treatment center, Graydon Manor treats children and adolescents (boys ages 7 to 17, girls 12 to 17) diagnosed with severe emotional or psychiatric disorders. While it does not treat those whose primary diagnoses are substance abuse, it does serve adolescents with secondary diagnoses of chemical dependency. Lengths of stay on the 100-plus-acre campus range from nine to 18 months, depending on need.

Operated by the National Children's Rehabilitation Center, Graydon offers outpatient services for adults and families in the community. An onsite school is accredited by the Virginia and Maryland departments of education.

The Psychiatric Institute of Washington, D.C.
4228 Wisconsin Ave. NW, Washington, D.C. • **(202) 965-8200**

The first private psychiatric hospital in Washington, D.C., the 201-bed Psychiatric Institute of Washington was founded in 1967 and moved to its present location in 1973. The facility treats children, adolescents and adults suffering from emotional and addictive illnesses, and even offers an intensive-care unit for especially serious cases. The hospital is acknowledged by the nation's psychiatric community as an education and professional development center for mental-health specialists.

Saint Elizabeth's Hospital
2700 Martin Luther King Jr. Ave. SE, Washington, D.C. • **(202) 562-4000**

For some 140 years, "Saint E's" has been perhaps the best-known of the District's mental-health facilities. Its reputation may have something to do with criminally insane patients such as would-be presidential assassin John Hinckley, who at this writing remains in residence. Still in the same place since its founding in 1855, the massive (1,500-bed) hospital actually sits on the grounds of D.C. General Hospital, but you wouldn't know it just by comparing addresses.

Formerly run by the federal government, Saint Elizabeth's is city-operated today under the purview of the Department of Human Services. Psychiatric services for children, adolescents and adults are offered in the form of acute care, long-term care, nursing care and residential care. The hospital also deals in forensic medicine. Services are being expanded for children and youth, in-home clients and multicultural and immigrant populations.

Saint Luke Institute
8901 New Hampshire Ave., Silver Spring, Md. • **(301) 445-7970**

This 35-bed, nonprofit psychiatric facility was founded by a minister/doctor and serves priests and other religious men and women active in church ministry. Initially treating only chemical dependency, St. Lukes has broadened its focus to include mood disorders, compulsive eating or compulsive sexual behaviors, and reactive or chronic depression. The major areas of service are in evaluation, inpatient treatment, aftercare, residential living, outpatient therapy and outreach.

Springwood Psychiatric Institute
42009 Charter Springwood Ln., Leesburg, Va. • **(703) 777-0800**

Springwood Psychiatric Institute offers comprehensive mental health treatment for adults, adolescents and children on either an inpatient or outpatient basis. The hospital specializes in the treatment of depression, substance abuse, co-dependency, suicidal tendencies, school failure, domestic problems, and stress and anxiety. Special services include 24-hour admissions, free evaluations, and extensive aftercare programs for patients and their families.

Nursing Homes

Nursing homes here vary widely in terms of atmosphere and services offered. A look in the Metro Washington phone book will lead you to two pages of listings and, indeed, you'll see many in your travels throughout the area — they are springing up everywhere to keep up with the graying of America. Some homes are actually luxury high-rises managed by hotel companies like Hyatt and Marriott, providing many of the same amenities. Others have the flavor of retirement communities in the degree of independence granted to patients and the number of activities offered. Some even look like summer resorts, complete with lush landscaping, wraparound verandas and cheerful color schemes.

A nursing home is ultimately a place for long-term care and choosing one is a highly individual decision. Prospective patients — or their families — must base their decisions on the degree of attention they need, amenities and specialized medical care offered, location and atmosphere. Choosing a nursing home requires careful investigation, personal visits and, as in the case of hospices, physician referral. Two services in Metro Washington provide information and referrals expressly for nursing homes — they are a starting point but ultimately the decision is too important to leave up to a third party. For more information, contact: American Healthcare Association, 1201 L Street NW, Washington, DC 20005, (202) 842-4444; Elder's Residential Facility, 10406 Thrift Road, Clinton, MD 20735, (301) 868-8843

Alternative Healthcare

Washington is a conventional, conservative town of blue pin-striped suits, pumps and pearls. People try to fit in rather than stand out, and their approach to medical care reflects this. Unlike Los Angeles and Santa Fe, you generally won't find the locals comparing the latest medical trends, or even such commonplace alternative practitioners as herbalists, nutritionists or chiropractors.

Washington's upwardly mobile prefer to expend energy on their careers. Meals are an excuse for networking, and workaholics live on hors d'oeuvres, fast food and liquor. Working out? Massages? Healthy cooking? Who has the time? To illustrate this, a 1997 nationwide survey ranked D.C. as No. 1 in couch potatoes — people who exercise rarely and eat all the wrong foods.

Washington is of course much too cosmopolitan and diverse to have completely avoided trends in alternative, holistic medicine and nutrition. People who admit to seeing a chiropractor may say it with a sheepish smile, but there are four pages of chiropractic listings in the D.C. yellow pages, so someone must be using them.

Delve a little further into people's backgrounds and they may even admit to popping daily multiple vitamins, though independent health food stores in Metro Washington — the few that exist — are mostly dusty little nooks with the hushed, abandoned atmospheres of the library on Tuesday morning. On the other hand, every Washington-area mall has a GNC vitamin store and gourmet groceries specializing in organic fare are cropping up all over. To top it off, the world-famous National Institutes of Health, a U.S. government agency, has established a specific office to investigate the value of vitamins, nutrition, biofeedback, acupuncture and more.

So where to go if you want to try something more holistic than a shot or a prescription? For vitamins and herbs, the aforementioned groceries and GNC stores are numerous and well-stocked, or you can search the phone book for independent health food stores. Massage therapists, unless you are working with a doctor-referred physical therapist, are most often found in Washington beauty salons and day spas, as they are still largely considered a frivolity — to be indulged in on rare occasions — rather than a necessity. If you're looking in the phone book, search under beauty salons rather than massage (unless you're really looking for a so-called escort service).

There are quite a few acupuncturists in Washington, but your first selection criterion should be that they use disposable needles. Most do. Second, a look in the yellow pages will reveal that some acupuncturists are actually board-certified medical doctors as well, and you may feel safer there. Finally, acupuncturists are licensed, so ensure that your practitioner's credentials are in order with the state licensing boards listed at the beginning of this chapter. If you choose carefully and get the proper clearances, you may even find that your treatments are covered by medical insurance. Indeed, acupuncture is a practice that many mainstream physicians, including the American Medical Association acknowledge as useful, so don't be embarrassed to ask your doctor, counselor or physical therapist for a referral.

Many nutritionists and holistic practitioners

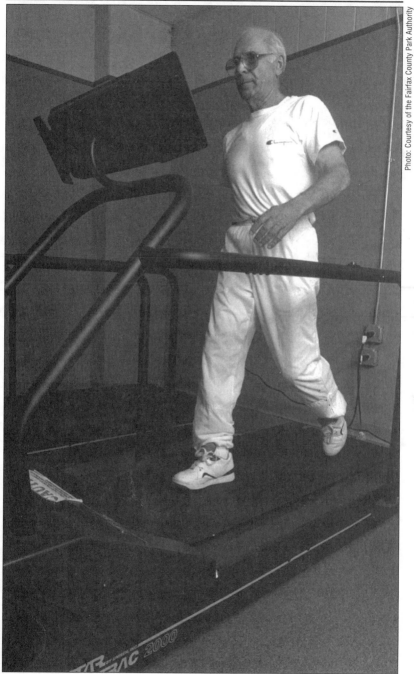

Daily exercise can help keep the doctor away.

now work on medical teams as adjunct therapy advisers, so check with your doctor about that too; and, don't forget that the Washington area is the home base for several organizations that can serve as useful resources for those seeking alternative medical care:

• American Association for Holistic Health, 1 Scott Circle NW, (202) 986-0850

• American College of Preventive Medicine, 1660 L Street NW, (202) 466-2044

• American Osteopathic Association, 1090 Vermont Avenue NW, (202) 414-0140

• International Massage Association, 3000 Connecticut Avenue NW, (202) 387-6555

• National Institutes of Health Office of Alternative Medicine, Clearinghouse, 9000 Rockville Pike, Bethesda, (301) 402-2466

Emergency Numbers

In dire emergencies, we've all been trained to call 911 from most places in the country, and the Washington Metro area is no exception. Still, other types of health emergencies may require more specific help. Here's a list of numbers for specific mental and physical health crises. (You may want to post a copy near your telephone, in case of emergency.)

Ambulance, fire department or police, 911

AIDS counseling and information hotline, (800) 590-2437

Alcoholics Anonymous area headquarters, (202) 966-9115

Battered Women's Bilingual Hotline, (202) 529-5991

Domestic Violence Hotline, (202) 347-2777

Dwelling Place Shelter for Abused Elderly, (202) 583-7602

Metro Area Poison Center, (202) 625-3333

Narcotics Anonymous Hotline, (202) 399-5316

National Organization for Victim Assistance, (202) 232-6682

For general mental-health crises, including suicide counseling, there are hotlines in Washington, D.C., (202) 223-2255 or (202) 737-2283; Virginia, (703) 527-4077; and Maryland, (301) 738-2255.

Walk-in Clinics

If you have a medical problem that is urgent, though not life-threatening, a walk-in medical clinic may be a good bet. Most walk-in clinics are found in Virginia-area shopping centers and other high-traffic areas. There is one clinic in the Maryland region that comprises Metro Washington, and, as of this writing, there is no such chain in D.C. Area hospitals, however — D.C. included — have jumped on the bandwagon and, to compete with the freestanding facilities, have in many cases opened their own walk-in centers right in their emergency rooms.

This chapter's section on hospitals makes mention of walk-in centers where they existed at press time, but please remember that these minor-care emergency rooms are a growing trend, and more are opening every day. Freestanding walk-in clinics are typically open seven days a week and into the evening, though hours vary from location to location. Call first to ensure that the office you want to visit is open.

No appointments are necessary, but waits can be long, as in hospital emergency rooms. With a small staff of doctors and nurses, the centers can perform some lab tests, blood work, sports physicals and other services not requiring the traditional hospital's resources or facilities; however, if you suspect a serious illness, it's probably best to go to a hospital.

Northern Virginia

INOVA Urgent Medical Care Locations

6045-KLM Burke Centre Pkwy., Burke, Va. • (703) 239-0300

14151 Saint Germain Dr., Centreville, Va. • (703) 830-5600

6370 Springfield Plaza, Springfield, Va. • (703) 569-7554

100 Maple Ave. E., Vienna, Va. • (703) 938-5300

The INOVA healthcare system includes several respected hospitals in Virginia, including Fairfax Hospital, so if it turns out you need more critical care, you'll be sent on quickly, perhaps by ambulance.

In response to the need for walk-in emergency care, many hospitals in the Metro Area have opened such facilities as adjuncts to their primary emergency rooms, but Mary Washington Hospital in Fredericksburg has actually set up a different facility similar to the shopping center walk-ins owned by the INOVA system. ExpressCare offers the minor services of the INOVA walk-ins, along with access to a hospital if needed. Contact them at: ExpressCare, 422 Garrisonville Road, Fredericksburg, VA 22554, (540) 720-0400.

ACCESS Emergency Care Locations
Access Emergency Care of Fairfax
4315 Chain Bridge Rd., Fairfax City, Va.
• (703) 591-9322

ACCESS Emergency Care of Reston/Herndon
11901 Baron Cameron Ave., Reston, Va.
• (703) 471-0175

ACCESS is a clever acronym for a very long name: Ambulatory Care Center Emergency Service System. As the name implies, they are hospital emergency rooms without the hospital. What these convenient and very efficient 24-hour facilities offer is a level of care somewhere between the walk-in shopping center facilities and regular hospitals. Part of the Inova Health System, ACCESS outlets also perform onsite lab and X-ray work and will arrange to transport you to a hospital if necessary.

Suburban Maryland

Secure Medical Care
803 Russell Ave., Gaithersburg, Md.
• (301) 869-0700

Secure Medical Care, like its counterpart operation in northern Virginia, known as Urgent Medical Care, is a convenient, cost-effective alternative to the hospital, best for treatment of minor illnesses and injuries. The center is staffed by a small team of doctors and nurses and is open late in the evenings, seven days a week. It can also perform a limited amount of lab work and diagnostic tests, physical examinations and other services.

As America's nearly 80 million baby boomers age, they bring with them new expectations. More want to be near family and close to business and volunteer activities.

Senior Scene

Metro Washington doesn't exactly top the list of the country's most popular retirement destinations. Certainly it's no Boca Raton, Florida, or Phoenix, Arizona. Pervasive national lifestyle trends are working in favor of dynamic urban areas like ours, however. Urban retirement is gaining steam today as more seniors look to metropolitan areas for their healthcare, transportation, recreation and education needs.

As America's nearly 80 million baby boomers age, they bring with them new expectations. More want to be near family and close to business and volunteer activities. Retiring to Florida's beaches or Arizona's deserts, while still a viable option, isn't for everyone in this new generation of seniors.

The implications of urban retirement are especially profound in the Nation's Capital, a region that's saturated in diversions and opportunities so craved by active seniors. Whether you're just visiting or considering the area as a permanent home, you may be pleasantly surprised at the variety of resources for people ages 60 and older. Housing options include luxury apartments and lush campus developments, geared toward both independent residents and those requiring varied degrees of assistance. Hundreds of senior and community centers offer classes, exercise programs and field trips, and numerous organizations and businesses feature volunteer and employment options. Meals on Wheels and Friendly Visitor programs provide nourishment and companionship to homebound seniors. Families facing difficult decisions regarding medical care, legal aid and financial management can find assistance through local agencies.

In this chapter, we offer an overview of helpful resources, as well as a sampling of retirement communities. See our Healthcare chapter for information about hospitals and urgent-care facilities, as well as suggestions on finding nursing homes and hospice care.

Area Agencies on Aging

Are you trying to locate a senior center that will meet your needs? Confused about housing options? Looking for home healthcare? Help is close at hand, through the nearest Area Agency (or Office) on Aging. Mandated by the Older Americans Act of 1965, these offices oversee federally and locally funded grants for programs serving citizens ages 60 and older. The agencies either directly provide or put seniors in touch with such services as Meals on Wheels, senior centers, adult day care, home health visits, long-term care concerns, transportation, discounts, volunteer programs, job banks, emergency aid, financial planning, moving assistance and numerous other resources.

Following is a list of Metro Washington's offices on aging and some of their programs.

Washington, D.C.

District of Columbia Office on Aging
One Judiciary Sq., 441 4th St. NW, Ste. 900 S., Washington, D.C.
• **(202) 724-5622 main office,**
(202) 724-5626 info and assistance

The office's Senior Service Network features 30 agencies that run more than 42 programs, a 262-bed nursing home, adult day care and meal delivery. The office's six Lead Agencies, listed below, coordinate many nutrition, social and health programs for residents in the city's eight wards.

Barney Neighborhood House Senior Citizen Satellite Center
7600 Georgia Ave. NW, Washington, D.C.
• **(202) 939-9020**

This agency serves residents in Wards 1 and 4.

Friendship House Services to the Elderly
619 D St. SE, Washington, D.C.
• (202) 675-9075

Friendship House serves residents of the Southwest section of Ward 2, and Ward 6, west of the Anacostia River.

Greater Southeast Community Center for the Aging/ Comprehensive Senior Services — Project KEEN
3242 Pennsylvania Ave. SE, Ste. 2, Washington, D.C. • (202) 584-0701

This agency serves residents of Ward 6, east of the Anacostia River; and Ward 7.

Greater Washington Urban League, Senior Neighbors and Companions Club
2900 Newton St. NE, 1st Fl., Washington, D.C. • (202) 529-8701

This agency serves residents of the downtown and Shaw neighborhoods of Ward 2 and all of Ward 5.

IONA Senior Services
4125 Albemarle St. NW, Washington, D.C. • (202) 966-1055

IONA serves residents of the Kalorama Heights section of Ward 1, the Foggy Bottom and Dupont Circle areas of Ward 2 and all of Ward 3.

Senior Citizens Counseling and Delivery Services Inc.
2500 Martin Luther King Jr. Ave. SE, Washington, D.C. • (202) 678-2800

This agency serves residents of Ward 8.

Northern Virginia

Alexandria Agency on Aging
2525 Mt. Vernon Ave., Unit 5, Alexandria, Va. • (703) 838-0920

Besides providing information and referrals, the agency operates a 10-bed assisted living facility and an adult day-care program, oversees two multi-service senior centers, runs an in-home respite program for Alzheimer's patients and their families, offers job training and counseling for low-income seniors and publishes a quarterly newsletter. The city council-appointed, 21-member Commission on Aging studies and makes recommendations regarding issues and programs for the elderly.

Arlington County Agency on Aging
1801 N. George Mason Dr., Arlington, Va. • (703) 228-5030

This information and referral agency also trains volunteers to provide more in-depth assistance to seniors. The agency offers details on such programs as Meals on Wheels, adult day healthcare and housing concerns.

Fairfax County Area Agency on Aging
12011 Government Center Pkwy., Ste. 720, Fairfax, Va. • (703) 324-5411, (703) 803-7914 TTY

A division of the Department of Family Services, this agency serves elderly residents of the county and the cities of Fairfax and Falls Church. It offers such services as job training for people ages 55 and older, volunteer visits to and assistance for homebound elderly residents, Meals on Wheels, the Seniors in Action volunteer program, resources for finding home healthcare and medical claims assistance. The agency also publishes a monthly newspaper featuring senior center program schedules and articles about topics and local events of interest to seniors.

Loudoun County Area Agency on Aging
102 Heritage Way NE, Ste. 102, Leesburg, Va. • (703) 777-0257

The agency's Elder Choices program provides information and referrals. Other services include a licensed respite center for Alzheimer's patients, home-delivered meals, four senior centers for ages 60 and older, a Retired Senior Volunteer Program for ages 55 and older, a discount program that includes some medical care and a free taxi service to and from medical appointments. The Commission on Aging serves as a citizens' advisory board to the agency and the county's board of supervisors.

Prince William Area Agency on Aging
7987 Ashton Ave., Ste. 231, Manassas, Va. • (703) 792-6400

Among the agency's services are home-delivered meals, two senior centers, two adult day-care centers, home-care assistance, chore and personal-care services for financially eligible seniors and a Bluebird bus program for day and overnight trips.

Virginia Department for the Aging
Preston Bldg., 1600 Forest Ave., Ste. 102, Richmond, Va. • (800) 552-3402

This agency directs state and federal funds to local programs. Call the toll-free number to voice concerns or receive information about long-term care.

Suburban Maryland

Maryland Office on Aging
**301 W. Preston St., Baltimore, Md.
• (410) 767-1100, (800) 243-3425**

This office offers information about state-funded programs for the elderly.

Montgomery County Commission on Aging and Disabilities
401 Hungerford Dr., 3rd Fl., Rockville, Md. • (301) 217-8500

This agency offers information and assistance as well as assessments and referrals to elderly residents and their families. The Commission on Aging, (301) 217-1120, researches pertinent issues and offers recommendations to local government.

Prince George's County Office of Family Services
**Aging Services Division, 5012 Rhode Island Ave., Hyattsville, Md.
• (301) 699-2696**

Besides offering an information and referral service, the agency provides such services as senior centers, a foster grandparents' pro-

gram, a Retired Senior Volunteer Program and assistance with housing issues.

Transportation

The following services are geared toward senior and disabled passengers. See our Transportation chapter for additional options.

Washington, D.C.

Call 'N' Ride Transportation Program
**Washington Elderly Handicapped Transportation Services (WEHTS), 2601 18th St. NE, Washington, D.C.
• (202) 635-3970, (202) 635-WEHTS**

Call 'N' Ride offers discounted door-to-door taxi rides, on a sliding fee scale, for D.C. residents ages 60 and older. To obtain discount coupons, contact the Lead Agency serving your ward (see the District of Columbia Office on Aging listing). WEHTS provides essential transportation for disabled seniors, through their local Lead Agency.

Washington Metropolitan Area Transit Authority (METRO)
**600 5th St. NW, Washington, D.C.
• (202) 637-7000, TDD (202) 638-3780**

Metrobus and Metrorail cars feature easily accessible priority seating for seniors and disabled passengers. Area residents and visitors ages 65 and older can buy discounted fare cards by showing a Metro ID card, available free of at public libraries and Metro sales offices. Disabled passengers may request a mailed application by calling (202) 962-1245, TDD (202) 628-8973. The public transportation system also offers special service for people whose disabilities prevent them from using the fixed-route bus or rail system. Call (202) 727-7178, TDD (202) 727-8062.

Northern Virginia

Senior Taxi Service
**121 N. Saint Asaph St., Alexandria, Va.
• (703) 836-4414**

Senior Citizens Employment and Services offers seniors inexpensive cab rides for essential trips such as medical appointments and grocery shopping within the city of Alexandria. Make a reservation by 3 PM the preceding work day.

Senior Trolley
2525 Mt. Vernon Ave., Unit 5, Alexandria, Va. • (703) 838-0920

Operated through the Alexandria Agency on Aging, this scheduled bus service transports passengers ages 60 and older to shopping and senior centers.

Suburban Maryland

Call-A-Bus
Prince George's County Office of Transportation, 9400 Peppercorn Pl., Ste. 320, Landover, Md. • (301) 499-8603, (800) 899-2287

This curb-to-curb bus service, available to county seniors and disabled persons, runs weekdays, 8:30 AM to 3:30 PM, with fares of 50 cents. Make a reservation up to 14 days in advance; same-day requests are subject to availability.

Call-A-Cab
Prince George's County Office of Transportation, 9400 Peppercorn Pl., Ste. 320, Largo, Md. • (301) 883-5656, (800) 735-2258 TDD

Prince George's seniors ages 55 and older and disabled residents can purchase discount coupon booklets to use for cab rides with participating companies. Eligible residents may purchase, during a six-month period, up to 12 booklets, each containing $20 in coupons, and priced at $10 apiece.

Publications

Goldmine Directory
P.O. Box 2227, Silver Spring, MD 20915 • (202) 724-5626

This annual booklet of the D.C. Office on Aging and Family and Child Services of Wash-

ington D.C. Inc., published by Senior Beacon newspaper, lists loads of restaurants, stores and services that offer discounts to D.C. residents ages 60 and older. Obtain a free copy at any public library or Senior Beacon distribution site, or send a $2 check or money order to the above address.

Guide to Retirement Living
P.O. Box 7512, McLean, VA 22106 • (703) 536-5150, (800) 394-9990

This twice-yearly magazine features a comprehensive guide to senior housing options, as well as lifestyle articles and information about helpful organizations. Call for a free copy.

Senior Beacon
500 23rd St. NW, Washington, D.C. • (202) 785-1151

Published monthly, this Mature Media award-winning newspaper focuses on national and local news and feature stories for the over-50 crowd. Ads include discount offers for restaurants. The paper is available free of charge at libraries, places of worship, banks, drug stores, book stores and restaurants.

Other Helpful Resources

Washington, D.C.

American Association of Retired Persons (AARP)
601 E St. NW, Washington D.C. • (202) 434-2277

This national nonprofit, nonpartisan membership organization, headquartered in Washington, offers many benefits for people ages 50 and older, retired or not. Members receive discounts on lodgings and car rentals, and are eligible for insurance, prescription and credit card programs. AARP's almost 4,000 local chapters provide tax and legal assistance, 55 Alive driving classes and social and volunteer opportunities. The $8-per-couple annual membership includes a subscription to *Modern Maturity* magazine and the monthly *AARP Bulletin*, special rates for online services and free publications on topics of interest to seniors.

The organization boasts 32,067,874 members nationwide, 84,954 in Washington, D.C., 790,389 in Virginia and 664,862 in Maryland. To contact the local office, see the listing under Northern Virginia.

Family and Child Services of Washington D.C. Inc.
929 L St. NW, Washington, D.C.
• (202) 289-1510

This agency, founded in 1969, offers a variety of services, including a Retired and Senior Volunteer Program with more than 500 participants, respite opportunities for Alzheimer's patients families, help for homebound patients and recreational and social activities. With the D.C. Office on Aging, Family and Child Services publishes the annual *Goldmine Directory*, a compact guide to area attractions and services, many of which offer 10-percent discounts to Washington seniors (see listing under Publications).

Gray Panthers
755 8th St. NW, Washington, D.C.
• (202) 347-9541

Members meet regularly to bring about beneficial changes for the elderly, focusing on such issues as Social Security, healthcare and housing.

IONA Senior Services
4125 Albemarle St. NW, Washington, D.C. • (202) 966-1055

This 23-year-old nonprofit community organization, largely supported by local churches and synagogues and volunteers, offers a large network of programs for residents ages 60 and older. Some of IONA's many services include an information and assistance specialist, (202) 895-0234; Healthy Aging Programs such as IONAcise, trips, classes and lunch clubs; a volunteer network featuring such activities as telephone calls and visits to homebound elderly, meal deliveries, help with medical claims and cleanup;

transportation; a long-term care ombudsman; an adult day-care program; and a resource guide jam-packed with information about helpful resources for seniors in Washington, D.C.

National Alliance of Senior Citizens (NASC)
1744 Riggs Pl. NW, 3rd Fl., Washington, D.C. • (202) 986-0117

This advocacy organization keeps track of important seniors' issues for its members and the general public. It offers a research library and several membership benefits.

National Association of Retired Federal Employees (NARFE)
1533 New Hampshire Ave. NW, Washington, D.C. • (202) 234-0832

This membership organization promotes legislation benefiting retired civil servants. Contact the headquarters for information about local chapters.

National Caucus and Center on Black Aged (NCBA)
1424 K St. NW, Ste. 500, Washington, D.C. • (202) 637-8400

Health, housing and other issues of concern to low-income and minority elderly receive this organization's focus. Membership is open to anyone. NCBA also offers a job training and location program, (202) 483-0220, for people ages 55 and older.

National Council on the Aging Inc. (NCOA)
409 3rd St. SW, Washington, D.C. • (202) 479-1200, TTY (202) 479-6674

NCOA produces programs and publications that educate seniors and those who work with the aging on such topics as retirement planning, job training and healthcare standards. The council holds their next biannual national conference in 1998.

Older Adult Service and Information System (OASIS)
Lord & Taylor, 2nd Fl., 5255 Western Ave. NW, Washington, D.C.
• (202) 362-9600 ext. 562

This educational program for seniors ages

Many visitors enjoy relaxing strolls on Alexandria's elegant waterfront promenade.

55 and older features classes, lectures and discussions on topics related to health, fitness, the arts, history, travel and other areas of interest. Hours are 10 AM to 3 PM Monday through Friday. Held at the Lord & Taylor department store in Friendship Heights, the program also is sponsored by the D.C. Office on Aging, IONA Senior Services and Suburban Hospital. Most classes are free, but registration requires a $10 semester fee.

Northern Virginia

All The Right Moves
3284 Laneview Pl., Herndon, Va.
• **(703) 758-2577**
Moving is stressful at any age, but the experience can prove extra unsettling for seniors preparing to relocate to a smaller home or retirement community. This company specializes in making the process go smoothly through such services as decluttering a household; holding moving or estate sales;

locating real-estate agents, moving services and contractors; coordinating moving arrangements; and unpacking and putting away items in your new home. The initial consultation is free.

American Association of Retired Persons (AARP)
Va./D.C./Md. State Office, 1600 Duke St., Ste. 200, Alexandria, Va.
• **(703) 739-9220**
Contact the organization's local office to locate an AARP chapter near you. For a complete description of AARP, see the listing under Washington, D.C.

Assistance for Seniors Inc.
1902 Trumpet Ct., Vienna, Va.
• **(703) 319-8787**
A member of the National Association of Professional Geriatric Care Managers, this company founded by a professional nurse assesses clients' needs and coordinates appropriate healthcare and assistance.

INSIDERS' TIP

Looking for a rewarding volunteer opportunity? Your neighborhood elementary school welcomes older adults to help students practice reading, assist teachers with projects and share talents with classes.

Elder Crafters of Alexandria Inc.
405 Cameron St., Alexandria, Va.
• (703) 683-4338

You'll find such handcrafted goodies as quilts, cloth dolls, stuffed animals, carved wooden miniatures, woven baskets, pottery and stitched, smocked, knitted and crocheted babies' and children's outfits at this nonprofit consignment shop, just across the street from historic Gadsby's Tavern in Old Town. It showcases an array of items created by area residents ages 55 and older. Hours are 10 AM to 5 PM Tuesday through Saturday, and 1 to 5 PM Sunday.

ElderSource
P.O. Box 23101, Alexandria, VA 22304
• (703) 370-7666, (800) 326-6001

This private company provides a resource and referral service for elderly adults and their families or caregivers, covering such areas as medical claims assistance, daily money management and geriatric care management and assessments.

Retired and Senior Volunteer Program (RSVP)
418 S. Washington St., Alexandria, Va.
• (703) 549-1607

If you're 55 or older and seeking an interesting volunteer opportunity, contact this organization for information about a variety of options in the Alexandria community.

Senior Citizens Employment and Services of Alexandria Inc.
121 N. Saint Asaph St., Alexandria, Va.
• (703) 836-4414

Local residents ages 55 and older who are seeking employment can visit this agency for job counseling and placement.

The Seniors Coalition
11166 Main St., Ste. 302, Fairfax, Va.
• (703) 591-0663

This conservative lobbying organization, with 2.4 million members nationwide, focuses on such issues as Social Security, healthcare reform and the Global Climate Treaty. Annual membership is $10 per person, $13 per couple, and includes a subscription to *The Seniors Coalition Advocate*, a quarterly magazine.

Telehelp and Friendly Visiting
American Red Cross, Alexandria Chapter, 123 N. Alfred St., Alexandria, Va. • (703) 549-8300

These programs offer reassurance to homebound or frail elderly residents by providing regular phone calls or visits by volunteers.

Suburban Maryland

Jewish Council for the Aging of Greater Washington
11820 Parklawn Dr., Ste. 200, Rockville, Md. • (301) 881-8782

This organization's Senior HelpLine, (301) 255-4200 in Washington and Maryland and (703) 425-0999 in Virginia, fields a wide array of inquiries regarding elderly concerns. The 25-year-old, nonprofit organization offers several other programs, including transportation, adult day care, in-home help with chores and personal care, aerobics programs, computer training, employment services and estate planning. All programs are open to people of all faiths.

Jewish Social Service Agency
6123 Montrose Rd., Rockville, Md.
• (301) 881-3700

Kosher home-delivered meals, home health and hospice care, counseling and long-term care planning are among the services this agency provides for elderly adults, their caregivers and families.

National Council of Senior Citizens (NCSC)
8403 Colesville Rd., Ste. 1200, Silver Spring, Md. • (301) 578-8800

NCSC informs members about pertinent legislation through a hotline and monthly newsletter.

INSIDERS' TIP

Before dining out, call ahead to find out if the restaurant offers early-bird or other specials for seniors.

The surrounding countryside is filled with interesting spots for seniors and others to visit.

Older Adult Service and Information System (OASIS)

Hecht's, Prince George's Plaza, 3500 East-West Hwy., Hyattsville, Md.
• (301) 559-6575
Lord & Taylor, Lakeforest, 701 Russell Ave., Gaithersburg, Md.
• (301) 947-0502 ext. 560

See the Washington, D.C. listing for information about this learning program.

Over-60 Counseling and Employment Service

4700 Norwood Dr., Chevy Chase, Md.
• (301) 652-8072

The Montgomery County Federation of Women's Clubs, Inc., sponsors this employment counseling and referral service for seniors ages 55 and older.

Pam Newton & Company

10121 Donegal Ct., Potomac, Md.
• (301) 765-9656

This interior design company specializes in working with seniors who are downsizing their residences. The firm helps clients choose furnishings to move and select colors and accessories for decorating their new home. Pam Newton & Company also oversees the move, organizes household goods and unpacks and puts away items in the new residence.

Senior's Interfaith Resource Center. Inc. (SIRC)

Chevy Chase Service Center, 4805 Edgemoor Ln., Bethesda, Md.
• (301) 652-9437

This nonprofit, volunteer-run organization offers information and assistance to elderly residents of Bethesda, Chevy Chase and Kensington. SIRC's Hands of Shared Time (HOST) program trains volunteers ages 15 and older willing to provide two hours of weekly service to frail or lonely seniors. Office hours are 9 AM to 1 PM Monday through Friday.

Community and Senior Centers

You'll find many senior centers by contacting the area agencies on aging listed earlier in this chapter. The following centers and recreation departments also offer numerous seniors' activities.

Washington, D.C.

District of Columbia Jewish Community Center

1529 16th St. NW, Washington, D.C.
• (202) 518-9400

DCJCC's Center for Active Living offers

numerous seniors' programs, including trips, classes, a retirement club and a lunch program, open to all faiths.

District of Columbia Department of Recreation and Parks
3149 16th St. NW, Washington, D.C.
• (202) 576-8677

The department's 17 senior centers feature fitness opportunities and special activities such as creative design classes and the Golden Age Theater Drama Group. Most centers are open from 10:30 AM to 7 PM on weekdays. Contact the Senior Services Division at the above phone number to locate the nearest center or specific programs.

Friends Senior Center
Friends Meeting House, 2111 Florida Ave. NW, Washington, D.C.
• (202) 483-3312

Tea and free activities such as films and lectures take place from 3 to 5 PM Wednesdays. Everyone is welcome.

National Capital YMCA
1711 Rhode Island Ave. NW, Washington, D.C. • (202) 862-9622

People ages 65 and older receive membership discounts, and members older than age 60 can participate in free classes and fitness programs.

Northern Virginia

Alexandria Department of Recreation, Parks and Cultural Activities
1108 Jefferson St., Alexandria, Va.
• (703) 838-4343

Oswald Durant Memorial Senior Center, 1605 Cameron Street, Alexandria, Virginia, (703) 838-6323, offers such activities as arts and craft classes, bingo, outings, films and meetings of organizations like AARP. Seniors' clubs and programs also take place at Mt. Vernon Recreation Center, 2701 Commonwealth Avenue, Alexandria, Virginia, (703) 838-4825; and Nannie J. Lee Recreation Center, 1108 Jefferson Street, Alexandria, Virginia, (703) 838-4845. Call for schedules.

Arlington County Department of Parks, Recreation and Community Resources
300 N. Park Dr., Arlington, Va.
• (703) 358-4744

Contact the Senior Adult Programs office for a newsletter describing activities at its six senior centers and some of the county's community centers.

City of Fairfax Senior Center
3730 Old Lee Hwy., Rm. 8, Fairfax, Va.
• (703) 359-2487

Residents ages 55 and older can visit weekdays and Saturdays for drop-in and scheduled activities, such as lectures, arts and crafts classes, games and trips.

Fairfax County Park Authority
12055 Government Center Pkwy., Ste. 927, Fairfax, Va. • (703) 246-5700

The park authority's eight full-service recreation centers offer several exercise classes for seniors ages 60 and older, who pay discounted fees. Call for the latest Parktakes schedule of classes and events.

Fairfax County Community and Recreation Services
12011 Government Center Pkwy. Ste. 1050, Fairfax, Va. • (703) 324-5544

The department's 12 senior centers, most of which are open 9 AM to 4 PM Monday through Friday, offer classes, games, discussion groups, outings and fellowship. Call a day in advance to reserve a hot lunch. Four other sites offer adult meals. Call for locations.

Falls Church Community Center
223 Little Falls St., Falls Church, Va.
• (703) 241-5077

The center hosts such seniors' classes as country line dancing, aerobics, exercise for people with arthritis , a walking group and a weekly Golden Age Club. Seniors ages 65 and older receive a 50 percent discount on class fee and supplies costs.

Falls Church Senior Center
401 W. Great Falls St., Falls Church, Va.
• (703) 241-5020

Watch free movies, from 12:30 to 3 PM

the first and third Tuesday of the month. Other programming highlights include a military history discussion group, backgammon, bridge, cribbage, canasta, legal assistance and German, Italian and French conversation groups.

Herndon Parks and Recreation
814 Ferndale Ave., Herndon, Va.
• (703) 435-6868

Senior programming highlights include art classes the first and third Tuesday of each month, requiring a onetime $2 registration fee; and free movies and refreshments at 2 PM the first and third Thursday of each month. The gym hosts an indoor walking program, from 7:30 to 9 AM weekdays, with mileage rewards for those seniors who pile up the most distance.

Ida Lee Recreation Center
50 Ida Lee Dr. NW, Leesburg, Va.
• (703) 777-1262

This facility of the Town of Leesburg Department of Parks and Recreation offers several fitness classes at half price to seniors ages 60 and older.

Jewish Community Center of Northern Virginia
8900 Little River Tnpk., Fairfax, Va.
• (703) 323-0880

Ongoing clubs, requiring an annual $40 Senior Associate fee, meet weekly on Mondays or Thursdays for lectures and seminars on Judaic issues and other topics. Other programs of interest to seniors include bridge, canasta, mahjongg, chess, discussion groups, Yiddish conversation hours, aquatic exercise classes and events for singles ages 55 and older. Activities are open to all faiths, and most are available to members and nonmembers.

Loudoun County Department of Parks and Recreation
18 N. King St., Leesburg, Va.
• (703) 777-0343

The department's 10 community centers offer a variety of fitness programs and leisure classes for seniors. Contact the Loudoun County Department of Parks and Recreation office for a schedule.

Prince William County Park Authority
14420 Bristow Rd., Manassas, Va.
• (703) 792-7060

Two Prince William County Park Authority facilities offer aqua exercise programs for seniors, as well as reduced admission and membership fees for people ages 60 and older: Chinn Aquatics and Fitness Center, 13025 Chinn Park Drive, Prince William, Virginia, (703) 791-2338, and Dale City Recreation Center, 14300 Minnieville Road, Dale City, Virginia, (703) 670-7112.

Town of Vienna Parks and Recreation
Vienna Community Center, 120 Cherry St. SE, Vienna, Va. • (703) 255-6360

The center hosts numerous senior activities, including Pickleball, Bocce Ball, mahjongg, fitness classes, blood-pressure checks, craft instruction, travel lectures, financial classes and meetings of clubs such as AARP and NARFE.

Suburban Maryland

Greenbelt Recreation Department
Greenbelt Community Center, 25 Crescent Rd., Greenbelt, Md.
• (301) 397-2208

A Senior Game Room and Lounge are open during regular hours. Other seniors' activities include hot lunches on weekdays, available by reservation at least a day in advance; a weekly Golden Age Club; monthly movies; craft and continuing education classes and a weekly intergenerational program with nursery school and kindergarten students. Call for the latest program guide.

Jewish Community Center of Greater Washington
6125 Montrose Rd., Rockville, Md.
• (301) 881-0100 ext. 3751

The Senior Adult Division offers activities and hot Kosher lunches Tuesdays, Thursdays and Fridays. Among senior-oriented programs are seminars, craft lessons, a chess club, cards and games, Yiddish, Seniors Organized for Change advocacy group meetings, a chora group, a quarterly magazine, Elderhostel classes, trips, water aerobics and arthritis exercise. Events are open to all faiths, members and nonmembers.

Maryland-National Capital Park and Planning Commission
Prince George's County Park and Recreation Administration Bldg., 6600 Kenilworth Ave., Riverdale, Md.
• **(301) 699-2407**

For information about seniors' activities at the county's 40 community centers, contact the above number or these area administrative offices: Central at (301) 249-9220, Northern at (301) 445-4500 and Southern at (301) 292-9006.

Montgomery County Recreation Department
12210 Bushey Dr., Silver Spring, Md.
• **(301) 217-6800**

Seniors' activities, including classes and fitness programs, take place at three senior citizens' centers and 13 community recreation centers. Call to obtain the latest schedule of events.

Rockville Senior Center
1150 Carnation Dr., Rockville, Md.
• **(301) 309-3025**

The center offers a variety of recreational programming for residents of Rockville.

City of Laurel Department of Parks and Recreation
Laurel Municipal Center, 8103 Sandy Spring Rd., Laurel, Md. • **(301) 725-7800**

Senior activities take place at Phelps Senior Citizens Center, 701 Montgomery Street, Laurel, Maryland, (301) 776-6168; Laurel Community Center, 7901 Cypress Street, Laurel, Maryland, (301) 497-0300; and Laurel Armory Anderson & Murphy Community Center, 422 Montgomery St., Laurel, Maryland, (301) 725-8088.

Takoma Park Recreation Department
7500 Maple Ave., Takoma Park, Md.
• **(301) 270-4048**

Bingo games for ages 55 and older take place regularly, along with daytrips. The Takoma Park Community Center, 7315 New Hampshire Avenue, holds seniors' arts and crafts programs.

Retirement Communities

These independent living sites include 24-hour security and safety features such as medical alert systems. Some also offer assisted living options for residents who require some degree of medical or personal care.

Washington, D.C.

Friendship Terrace
4201 Butterworth Pl. NW, Washington, D.C. • **(202) 244-7400**

Convenient to IONA Senior Services, this apartment complex includes a daily meal, health and fitness programs and cultural and religious activities in the $600 monthly rent. Features include a library, garden, sundecks, laundry and hair salon. Residents may have pets.

Methodist Home of the District of Columbia
4901 Connecticut Ave. NW, Washington, D.C. • **(202) 966-7623**

This nonsectarian apartment community offers independent and assistant living options, with sizes ranging from efficiency to four-bedroom. Rent starts at $1,600 and includes such amenities as three daily meals, housekeeping service, activities, transportation, a hair salon, library and chapel.

Northern Virginia

Caton Merchant House
9201 Portner Ave., Manassas, Va.
• **(703) 335-8401**

Affiliated with Prince William Hospital and Annaburg Manor Nursing Home, this facility offers four levels of care, from independent to intensive assisted living. Residents can choose from three floor plans among the site's 76 apartments. On-site amenities include laundry and hairstyling facilities, a library and activity and lounge areas. A certified recreation therapist leads optional educational and social programs. Nursing care is available 24 hours a day, and residents receive three meals daily. The facility does not require an admission fee. Monthly costs range from $1,495 for a studio to $2,095 for a one-bedroom apartment. Care fees range from no extra charge for independent living to $900 per month for intensive assisted living.

The Jefferson
900 S. Taylor St., Arlington, Va.
• (703) 351-0011

The Ballston Common Metro station and shopping mall are a block's walk from this striking Marriott condominium complex, which offers such services as daily meals, a weekly linen and housekeeping service, a hair salon and activities planned by a full-time coordinator. Residents can take advantage of a creative arts center, library, game room, exercise room, heated pool and Jacuzzi, lounge area and private dining room for parties. Choose from 10 floor plans, subject to availability, for one- and two-bedroom residences, with purchase prices starting at $155,000. Monthly service fees start at $1,142, and condo fees start at $89. The complex also offers assisted living and Alzheimer's care.

Retirement Unlimited Inc.
2917 Penn Forest Blvd., Ste. 110, Roanoke, Va. • (540) 774-4433

This company owns and operates two retirement communities for adults age 62 and older in Northern Virginia: Heatherwood, 9642 Burke Lake Road, Burke, (703) 425-1698, and Paul Spring, 7116 Fort Hunt Road, Alexandria, (703) 768-0234. Monthly rates include one daily meal, weekly housekeeping, a linen service, special activities, a wellness program and scheduled transportation to doctors' appointments and shopping. Rates, per single occupant, range from $1,780 for a studio to $2,995 for a two-bedroom apartment at Paul Spring; $1,800 to $2,810 at Heatherwood. Residents do not have to pay an entrance fee. Additional options include more comprehensive meal plans and assisted living care. The Retirement Unlimited sites also offer such amenities as

walking trails, individual gardening sites, picnic areas, hair salons, chapels and private dining rooms.

Senior Communities by First Centrum
Forest Glen at Sully Station, 14401 Woodmere Ct., Centreville, Va.
• (703) 802-9501
River Run at Prince William Commons, 13910 Hedgewood Dr., Woodbridge, Va.
• (703) 878-4618

These one- and two-bedroom apartments for active seniors range from $685 to $850 per month and feature such amenities as optional meal programs, hair salons, libraries, lounges and activities.

Sommerset Retirement Community
22355 Providence Village Dr., Sterling, Va. • (703) 450-6411

Set in eastern Loudoun County, this rental community includes in its monthly rental fees a daily meal, weekly housekeeping and linen services and scheduled transportation. Residents have access to hairstyling, a community store, a dining area, lounge areas featuring a fireplace and solarium, an arts and crafts studio, games and billiards, programs and free laundries. Pets are permitted for an additional fee. Monthly rent starts at $1,850.

The Virginian
9229 Arlington Blvd., Fairfax, Va.
• (703) 385-0555

This apartment complex, set on 32 landscaped acres, includes such services as two daily meals and housekeeping twice a month, and features such as a wellness center, chapel, library, arts and crafts and woodworking areas, hair salon, convenience store and hospitality suites. Rent starts at $2,120 for a one-bedroom apartment, single occupancy. The Virginian also offers assisted living options.

INSIDERS' TIP

If the weather's too unpleasant for walking, try a shopping mall. Many open their doors early just for walkers who want to avoid crowds.

Suburban Maryland

Charter House
1316 Fenwick Ln., Silver Spring, Md.
• (301) 495-1600

Convenient to Metro and numerous stores and restaurants, this apartment building for independent seniors also offers assisted living options. Residents do not have to pay an entrance fee. The monthly fee for single occupancy ranges from $1,260 to $2,900 and includes daily continental breakfast and one additional meal, weekly housekeeping, scheduled transportation, wellness and social programs, arts and game rooms, a library and an activity center. Among additional services are a hair salon and garage parking.

Classic Residence by Hyatt
8100 Connecticut Ave., Chevy Chase, Md. • (301) 907-8895

Daily breakfast and dinner and weekly housekeeping and linen services are included in the monthly rent, starting at $1,995, at this posh rental complex. Pets are permitted. Residents have access to a fitness center, indoor swimming pool, wellness center, transportation, hair salon and planned activities.

Collington Episcopal Life Care Community Inc.
10450 Lottsford Rd., Mitchellville, Md.
• (301) 925-9610

This 128-acre campus community in Prince George's County features garden apartments and cottages for independent seniors, as well as assisted living options and nursing care. Highlights include private balconies and patios, weekly linen service, housekeeping every two weeks and, in the cottages, washers and dryers. The Community Center includes a convenience store, hair salon, bank, an interfaith chapel, library, art and art rooms, exercise facilities and a heated pool and Jacuzzi.

Residents have access to recreational programs and scheduled transportation. Single-occupancy entrance fees range from approximately $66,000 to more than $211,000. Single-occupancy monthly fees, including three daily meals, range from around $1,700 to $2,800.

Leisure World of Maryland
3701 Rossmoor Blvd., Silver Spring, Md.
• (301) 598-1000

Geared toward active adults ages 50 and older, this huge retirement community — founded in 1966 by Ross Cortese — houses more than 7,000 residents in 19 condominiums and two cooperatives on a 620-acre site. The latest development, Turnberry Courts, includes four low-rise condominium buildings next to an 18-hole golf course. Prices start in the $130,000s. The recreation-oriented Leisure World community includes two clubhouses with features like dining, bowling, swimming, tennis, fitness rooms, spas and chapels. Residents can choose from more than 80 clubs and numerous activities. Close-at-hand Leisureworld Plaza offers a supermarket, restaurants, specialty shops, services and medical offices.

Maplewood Park Place
9707 Old Georgetown Rd., Bethesda, Md.
• (301) 564-5102

Managed by Marriott, a corporation known for its posh hotels, this cooperative in bustling Bethesda takes pride in its many features designed to make senior living worry-free. Homes cost roughly $185,000 to $465,000, and a monthly fee of $1,480 to $3,025 pays for taxes, utilities and such services as 27 dining-room meals, weekly linens and housekeeping, a heated pool and Jacuzzi, a fitness center, activities, a library and other club rooms and scheduled transportation. A hair salon, bank and general store are on the premises. Maplewood also offers assisted-living and nursing care as neede

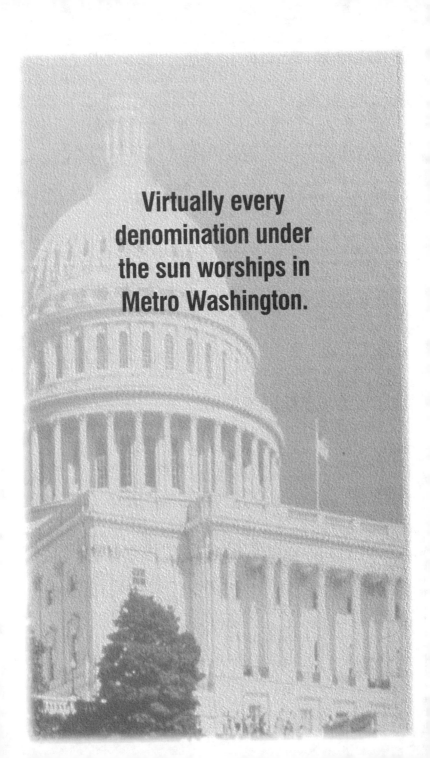

Virtually every denomination under the sun worships in Metro Washington.

Worship

There's an intense spiritual side to the Washington area that doesn't get a lot of attention. Maybe it's the American insistence on separating church and state that has kept the nation's capital from being recognized as an important religious center. Or maybe it's simply the image of hypocritical politicians topping off a week of hijinks with a showy church appearance, complete with bodyguards.

Nevertheless, behind the power struggles and political machinations, a religious current runs deep here, a kind of hidden moral checks-and-balances mechanism for the folks whose daily decisions affect the way more than 250 million people work and live.

Virtually every denomination under the sun — and then some — worships in Metro Washington. A quick scan through the Yellow Pages reveals everything from the mainstream to the obscure to the fringe: Catholic, Baptist, Jewish, Episcopal, Mormon, Quaker, Lutheran, Charismatic, Christian Scientist, Covenant, Church of God/Anderson, Indiana, Full Gospel, Open Bible, Self-Revelation Church of Absolute Monism and Unitarian, among many others. One church that gets right to the point (at least in name) is called God Is In Control in Waldorf, Maryland.

The Washington area's international character also is reflected in the way its citizenry worships. Throughout the region you'll find Korean Baptist and Greek Orthodox churches, Islamic mosques, Buddhist, Hindu and Sikh temples; and less-formal congregations representing religious practices from every corner of the globe.

Metro Washington was founded by WASPs — British Anglicans, to be exact — and the Protestant influence is still the dominant religious force in the region, especially in Northern Virginia. There are, however, some interesting dynamics here that newcomers should be aware of. In Washington, D.C., for instance, there is a large contingent of black Catholics,

perhaps even rivaling the number of Baptists. And in Maryland, a state that was founded as a haven for persecuted Catholics, the Catholic heritage is still very strong. In addition, Jewish families traditionally have migrated to the Maryland suburbs. These factors partly explain why Maryland and Washington historically have been more ethnically diverse than Virginia, but all that is changing as immigrant enclaves alter the face of even the most homogenous sections of the metro area. Drive through Annandale, Virginia, for example, and you'll likely see many traditional churches bearing signs in Asian characters. Korean, Vietnamese, Indian and Hispanic settlers all have established their own religious communities in the area. The Jewish community is now a significant presence in Northern Virginia, particularly in Fairfax County, home of the Jewish Community Center.

In this brief chapter, we want to introduce you to some of the more colorful, provocative and historical houses of worship in Metro Washington. Our purpose is to entertain, not recommend or list churches to attend. We'll leave that to ministers and the Yellow Pages. At the end of the chapter, however, we list some phone numbers of religious umbrella groups and associations that might help you get started in finding a specific church, meeting house, temple or synagogue that suits you.

Washington's Spiritual Legacy

Washington, D.C.'s, most prominent spiritual icon is also one of the city's newest churches. Well, it's new in the sense that it was recently completed — after 83 years in the making. Construction of the awe-inspiring Washington National Cathedral, at Wisconsin and Massachusetts avenues NW, was begun in 1907, with the laying of the first cornerstone, and completed in 1990. The cathedral, said to be the sixth-largest in the world, is widely revered as "the last of the great cathedrals," a church built in the Old World fashion — stone by stone. Worship services, concerts and recitals have been conducted here since Theodore Roosevelt's presidency.

The 14th-century, Gothic-style structure sits atop Mount Saint Alban, the highest point in the District of Columbia. Despite its recent vintage, the cathedral's soaring towers and room-size, stained-glass rosettes lend it the same grandeur — and the same graceful patina — as its centuries-old counterparts in Europe. The cathedral's commanding perch above the city skyline not only affords great views from its ornate bell towers, but also allows for the massive structure to be seen from miles around. On a clear day, one can discern the 200-yard-long cathedral from as far away as Fort Washington, Maryland, some 15 miles to the south.

Although officially known as the Cathedral Church of St. Peter and St. Paul, and affiliated with the Episcopal church, the National Cathedral is truly an interdenominational place of worship, serving as host for an array of Protestant, Catholic and Jewish services.

Among the interred in the cathedral are the bodies of President Woodrow Wilson, Adm. George Dewey, Helen Keller and her teacher, Anne Sullivan Macy, as well as Mabel Boardman, former head of the American Red Cross, and Cordell Hull, secretary of state during World War II. For tour and event information, see the Attractions and Kidstuff chapters.

The New York Avenue Presbyterian Church, at 1313 New York Avenue NW, is not as well known as the National Cathedral, but every bit as rooted in Washington history, if not more so. The Scottish stonemasons who built the White House organized the church in 1803, and both Abraham Lincoln and John Quincy Adams were members of the congregation. Visitors can thrill to the sight of Lincoln's original manuscript proposing the abolition of slavery, and other historical artifacts. In contrast, the building itself is of modern vintage, built in 1951. It contains 19 stained-glass windows, more contemporary than traditional in design. For tour information, see the Attractions chapter.

The oldest church in Washington is St Paul's (Episcopal), established in 1719. It's in the middle of Rock Creek Cemetery, at Rock Creek Road and Webster Street NW. (Despite the street and cemetery name, the church sits several blocks from Rock Creek Park.) On the grounds is one of the most artful and poignant sculptures in Washington: a bronze statue of a young women by Augustus Saint-Gaudens. Henry Adams commissioned the memorial in 1890 in honor of his wife who had committed suicide. Noted critic Alexander Wolcot called it "the most beautiful thing ever fashioned by the hand of a man on this continent."

A dominating presence in the Northeast quadrant of the city is the National Shrine of the Immaculate Conception, the largest Roman Catholic Church in the Western Hemisphere. The Romanesque- and Byzantine-style shrine, noted for its blue-domed roof, sits adjacent to Catholic University, a fascinating destination itself. The National Shrine's bell tower, reminiscent of St. Mark's in Venice, contains a 56-bell carillon. Carillon concerts are held year round on Sunday at 2:30 PM. In summer, there is also a 5:30 PM concert followed by an organ recital at 6 PM. For tour and concert information, see the Attractions chapter.

The greatest concentration of houses of worship in Washington can be found along 16th Street (a.k.a. the "Street of Churches") in Northwest — one of the city's widest, most stately north-south boulevards. Among the eye-catchers here is First Baptist Church, at 16th and O streets, built in 1955 in a pseudo-Gothic style. Presidents Harry Truman and Jimmy Carter frequented First Baptist while in office.

At 16th and P streets, Foundry Methodist Episcopal Church was founded by Georgetown businessman Henry Foxall, owner of the Foxall-Columbia Foundry on the Potomac River. Today, the congregation is one of the largest, wealthiest and most integrated in Washington.

The Jewish Community Center, a block

An Enlightening Experience

A dazzling holiday spectacle little known to Washington visitors is the Festival of Lights, held each Christmas season at the Washington Temple of the Church of Jesus Christ of Latter-day Saints. This seasonal extravaganza of lights, music and theater is sure to appeal to anyone, regardless of religious affiliation.

The Mormon Temple, as it's commonly known in the metro area, is just a 30-minute drive from downtown Washington — an Oz-like beacon high above the Capital Beltway in Kensington, Maryland. From early December until early January, the temple displays 300,000 multicolored lights topped off by the illuminated spires of the temple itself. So laborious is the illumination that stringing and testing must begin in September of each year to ensure completion in time for the holidays.

Besides the lights, visitors can enjoy the traditional life-size nativity, which features a live Mary and Joseph. The narration of the Biblical Christmas story takes place each evening (check at the onsite visitors center for the time and exact location).

Inside the visitors center, you'll discover 15 10-foot Christmas trees decorated in scriptural themes and adorned with thousands of ornamental lights. Among the most original are four international trees trimmed with dolls donated or loaned to the temple

— continued on next page

Photo: Courtesy of David Hofeling, Hofeling & Associates Photography

The Festival of Lights is featured at the Washington Temple visitors center of the Church of Jesus Christ of Latter-day Saints.

by more than 80 embassies in Washington, D.C. The trees also include dolls handmade by local young women of the Mormon church.

Artists from Europe, South America, Africa and Asia contribute to an international collection of nativity sets, also on display in the visitors center. The sets, or crèches, reflect a colorful blend of the traditional nativity scene and the cultural perspective of each artist.

In addition to the displays, nightly concerts feature choirs and instrumental groups from schools and area churches of many denominations. On Christmas Day, there is a special family presentation by a local theater group. As if that weren't enough, Christmas and holiday films such as *Mr. Krueger's Christmas*, starring Jimmy Stewart, are available in the center's five theaters, and there are even some presentations in Spanish.

All events are free and open to the public. Lights come on at dusk each evening. The center is at 9900 Stoneybrook Drive, Kensington, Maryland. For directions and visitor center hours, call (301) 587-0144.

away at 16th and Q, is an 83-year-old limestone structure built in the classical style. For several years the building was owned by the University of the District of Columbia, but was purchased by a local Jewish group in 1990 and returned to its original use.

At the southeast corner of 16th and Corcoran streets is the Church of the Holy City, a French Gothic-influenced building with a tower built in homage to the one that overlooks the entrance to Magdalen College in Oxford, England. Over a century old, the Episcopal church is graced by some rather intimidating gargoyles.

The Scottish Rite Temple, at 1733 16th Street, was designed by John Russell Pope and modeled largely after the Mausoleum of Halicarnassus in Greece. Pope, you may remember, was the same man who designed the Jefferson Memorial. The temple serves as the headquarters of the Supreme Council of the Southern Jurisdiction of the Thirty-Third Degree of the Ancient and Accepted Scottish Rite of Freemasonry. Try saying that two times really fast.

Also not to be overlooked on 16th Street at Harvard Street is All Souls Unitarian Church. The church, whose parishioners include some of the leading African-American powerbrokers

in Washington, was built in 1924 as a reproduction of London's St. Martin's-in-the-Fields.

Nearby, at 16th Street and Columbia Road, stands the Washington branch of the Unification Church, a denomination that was started by the eccentric South Korean Rev. Sun Myung Moon, who is also the owner of *The Washington Times* newspaper (see our Media chapter). Up until 1975, however, the church housed the Mormon Washington Chapel. The chapel was designed in the 1930s by Don Carlos Young, the grandson of Brigham Young.

At one time or another it seems that just about every church in Washington has been honored by the presence of an important politician, statesman or celebrity. We've already mentioned the case of First Baptist, which has been frequented by President Clinton and family. Teddy Roosevelt was a regular at Grace Reform Church (Dutch Reformed), at 15th and O streets NW. His wife and family, however, attended services at St. John's Episcopal Church, right across the street from the White House, at 16th and H streets NW. St. John's houses an extensive collection of Roosevelt memorabilia and to this day remains the church most visited by presidents.

St. Matthew's Cathedral (Catholic), downtown on Rhode Island Avenue NW, was where President Kennedy attended services; it also was the site of his funeral mass. This Renaissance-style structure also has an exotic hint of the Orient, thanks to the altar and baptismal font, gifts from India. Herbert Hoover, a devout Quaker, worshiped at the quaint stone Friends Meeting House, 2111 Florida Avenue NW.

Frederick Douglass, the famed abolitionist, journalist and scholar, was part of a congregation of free blacks and slaves who made up the Metropolitan African Methodist Episcopal Church, 1518 M Street NW, sometimes called the National Cathedral of African Methodism.

The first synagogue ever built in Washington was the Old Adas Israel. President Grant attended the dedication in 1876. The building nearly fell victim to the wrecking ball before being moved to its present location at Third and G streets NW, where it is restored as the Lillian and Albert Small Jewish Museum.

One of the most intriguing facades in Washington is that of the Islamic Mosque and Cultural Center, 2551 Massachusetts Avenue NW. Located in the thick of Embassy Row, the long white building and its 160-foot-high minaret are the religious and cultural focal points of the Washington area's Islamic community. The structure looks as though it belongs in a Middle Eastern oasis with its elaborate arches, mysterious courtyard and decorative tile work. Outside, worshipers — many clad in the traditional snowy white garments — can be seen leaving and entering the building. Inside are a library and a changing exhibit on Islamic culture and religion. Visitors are welcome, but proper attire is the rule here — arms and legs (and, yes, women's heads) must be covered.

Virginia's Colonial Churches

Across the river in Northern Virginia, one can peek into the world of colonial worship at Christ Church and the Old Presbyterian Meeting House in Old Town Alexandria. Built in 1773 by city founder John Carlyle, Christ Church was the regular place of worship for George Washington and, later, Robert E. Lee. The English country-style church sits in the center of Old

Town, at 118 N. Washington Street (also known as the George Washington Memorial Parkway). Its courtyard is graced by centuries-old poplar and oak trees that provide natural shelter for the graves of several Confederate soldiers who died in Alexandria hospitals. Just about every president has attended services at this historic Episcopal church.

Alexandria's Scottish forefathers also built the Old Presbyterian Meeting House at 316 S. Royal Street. George Washington's funeral services, originally scheduled for Christ Church, were held here because icy roads made the trip to the center of town impossible. Buried in the cemetery behind the meeting house is the Unknown Soldier of the American Revolution.

Latter-day Saints and Literary Landmarks

Suburban Maryland has its share of spiritual landmarks, but none is more imposing than the Washington Temple of the Church of Latter-day Saints, which towers above the Capital Beltway in Montgomery County like a vision of Dorothy's Emerald City. The $15 million white marble temple, complete with gold spires, is a sight to behold, especially after dark when it is dramatically lighted. But the outside is all that many people will ever see of this imposing structure since it's off-limits to non-Mormons (although public tours were given for a short time after construction was completed). However, during the winter holiday season, everyone is invited to the temple's Festival of Lights, a not-to-be-missed spectacle (see this chapter's Close-up). In addition, there is a visitors center on the grounds.

Literary buffs may want to venture up to Rockville, the Montgomery County seat about 40 minutes from downtown Washington, to view the grave sites of F. Scott Fitzgerald and his wife, Zelda, at the cemetery at St. Mary's Catholic Church, at Viers Mill Road and Rockville Pike. Their remains were moved here in 1975 from their original graves in Rockville Cemetery.

We have not yet even begun to scratch the surface of Metro Washington's fascinating spiritual landmarks. Should you venture into the Washington exurbs, you'll find more interesting religious sites, but we'll save that for another chapter (see Daytrips).

Christ Church in Old Town Alexandria was the regular place of worship for George Washington and later, Robert E. Lee.

Worship Resources

Interdenominational

**Council of Churches
of Greater Washington**
411 Rittenhouse Rd. NW,
Washington,D.C.
• (202) 722-9240

**Interfaith Conference of
Metropolitan Washington**
1419 V St. NW,Washington, D.C.
• (202) 234-6300

Protestant

**African Methodist Episcopal/
Second Episcopal District**
1134 11th St. NW, Washington, D.C.
• (202) 842-3788

Baptist D.C. Convention
1628 16th St. NW, Washington, D.C.
• (202) 265-1526

**Christian Churches
(Disciples of Christ)/Capital Area**
8901 Connecticut Ave.,
Chevy Chase, Md.
• (301) 654-7794

**Church of the Brethren/
Mid-Atlantic District**
300 N. Montague St., Arlington, Va.
• (703) 524-4100

Episcopal Diocese of Washington
Washington National Cathedral/Mount
Saint Alban, Wisconsin and
Massachusetts Aves. NW,
Washington,D.C.
• (202) 537-6555

**Evangelical Lutheran
Church of America/Metro
Washington, D.C., Synod**
212 E. Capitol St. NE, Washington, D.C.
• (202) 783-7501

National Capital Presbytery
4915 45th St. NW, Washington, D.C.
• (202) 244-4760

Society of Friends (Quakers)
2111 Florida Ave. NW, Washington, D.C.
• (202) 483-3310

United Church of Christ
110 Maryland Ave. NE, Washington, D.C.
• (202) 543-1517

**United Methodist Board
of Church and Society**
100 Maryland Ave. NE, Washington, D.C.
• (202) 488-5600

Roman Catholic

Archdiocese of Washington
P.O. Box 29260, Washington, D.C. 20017
• (301) 853-3800

Jewish

**Jewish Community Council
of Greater Washington**
6101 Montrose Rd., Rockville, Md.
• (301) 770-0881

Mormon

**The Church of Jesus
Christ of Latter-day Saints/
Washington Metropolitan
Area Regions**
529 14th St. NW, Ste. 900,
Washington,D.C.
• (202) 662-7480

Islamic

The Islamic Center
2551 Massachusetts Ave. NW,
Washington, D.C.
• (202) 332-8343

The winds of change are
forever blowing in our
fair city, and even
prominent media
are not immune
to their gusts.

Media

It's been said that information is a fundamental component of power. If so, residents of Metro Washington could be considered some of the most powerful people in the world. Indeed, many are just that, with No. 1 on the list living at 1600 Pennsylvania Avenue NW.

This chapter isn't about the political players, however, but rather the awesome presence of the information players. There are few places beyond Washington where the incoming and outgoing stream of information — specifically the written and spoken products of the print and electronic media — is as intense. There are also few places beyond Washington where citizens have as much interaction with and exposure to the conveyors of that information: literally thousands of reporters, editors, correspondents, broadcasters, freelance writers and others of the same ilk from around the globe who practice their trade here.

Washington has the highest concentration of journalists anywhere in the world, a staggering testament to the sphere of influence of the so-called "fourth estate," the term used to denote the public press (traditionally, the first three estates, each with its own influence in government, are nobility, clergy and townspeople). It's also a downright scary thought to many people (at least until they count the lawyers!) that there are all those nosy journalists running around. It's to be expected, however, since Washington plays the dual role of capital of the nation and capital of the free world.

When Local Means National

Living in Metro Washington, you soon get used to much of the "local" news also being national and international. Call it a blessing or a curse . . . it's reality. It's what happens when reporters have beats that include not only city hall, the county courthouse and the school board, but also the White House, Capitol Hill, the Supreme Court, the Pentagon and other focal points of the federal establishment.

Beyond the newspapers, magazines, radio and TV stations and other media based in Metro Washington, nearly every major (and some minor) news outlet in the world has a presence here, whether it's a full-blown bureau with two dozen staffers and a complement of high-tech machinery or a lone correspondent holding court at the National Press Building with little more than a desk, telephone and laptop computer.

Metro Washington is home to such media giants as The Washington Post Company, publisher of one of the world's most influential newspapers; Gannett Co. Inc., proud parent of "The Nation's Newspaper," *USA TODAY*, and a large stable of other print and broadcast properties; America Online, the popular computer network, with more than 9 million subscribers nationwide; United Press International, a Pulitzer-Prize winning news service; and the National Geographic Society, an American publishing institution that produces not only great magazines, but also maps, globes, books and TV specials. Numerous trade associations based here also represent the press in one form or another.

The winds of change are forever blowing in our fair city, and even prominent media are not immune to their gusts. Some longtime residents still mourn the loss of the popular afternoon daily, *The Washington Star*. *The Washington Times* has strived mightily since 1982 to fill the void, but it just hasn't been the same. *The Washington Post* has long been, and remains, the undisputed king of the local media hill. Local magazines that stopped their presses for good over the past few years include *Regardie's*, which profiled Washington's power hitters; *Dossier*, which chronicled the significant society and party circuit in the nation's capital; *Museum & Arts Washington*, an outstanding monthly that focused on the city's impressive arts and cultural scene; and *New Dominion*, a Northern Virginia lifestyle/business magazine. But Washingtonians also have witnessed the birth of new publications, such as *Washington Flyer*, the nation's first in-airport magazine and an official product of the Metropolitan Washington Airports Authority, launched at Washington National and Washington Dulles International airports; and, in the fall of 1997, *Capital Style*, devoted to "the art of political living."

It's All Within Your Reach

Whether scanning the radio or TV dial, or flipping through a newspaper or magazine, you quickly realize Washington media are diverse to say the least. The region's global influence is evident in the availability of foreign and domestic publications at neighborhood convenience stores, book shops, libraries and sidewalk newsstands. News junkies, students, academicians and homesick transplants will be relieved to know they can find numerous foreign and domestic reads at such publication sources as American International News, 1825 I Street NW, (202) 223-2526; Newsroom, 1753 Connecticut Avenue NW, (202) 332-1489, which carries scholarly journals and bilingual directories; and many large-chain book stores in the metropolitan area.

Several major newspapers based elsewhere, such as *The New York Times* and *The Wall Street Journal*, offer same-day delivery to certain areas of Metro Washington. Virginians wanting to keep close tabs on events in their state capital can pick up a current copy of the *Richmond Times-Dispatch* — one of the South's oldest and most respected newspapers — at some area newsstands; the paper also maintains a Washington bureau. Maryland residents keep up with statewide news by reading *The Baltimore Sun* and *The Capital*, a daily out of Annapolis.

As with other topics covered in this book, this chapter is intended as an overview, not an encyclopedic compilation. We've avoided, for the most part, mentioning any personalities and other details that could become outdated quickly. While we've tried to be as current as possible, bear in mind that publication titles, radio and TV formats and the ownership of such entities can and do change with little warning.

Newspapers

While TV and radio have come a long way since their inception in delivering the news with unprecedented speed and, in the case of television, amazing visual impact, the newspaper still provides expansive coverage and an overriding sense of permanence.

Dailies

The Washington Post
1150 15th St. NW, Washington, D.C.
• (202) 334-6000

Scan virtually any list of the most influential newspapers in the nation, even the world, and *The Washington Post* is sure to be there with domestic powerhouses such as *The New York Times*, *The Wall Street Journal* and *The Los Angeles Times*. It boasts a circulation of 818,231 Mondays through Fridays; 762,555 on Saturdays; and 1,123,305 on Sundays.

Like many publications, *The Post* is making high-tech changes: In a gradual makeover that began November of 1997 with new printing presses, the paper is changing its appearance, with the most notable difference being color photos on section front pages. The paper is also accessible online with current editions and recent articles. Another resource is Post-Haste, a free information service accessible by touch-tone telephone, (202) 334-9000.

No matter what you think of its liberal bent, you'll find *The Post* to be a top-notch major newspaper, with its wealth of resources, its worldwide presence and an immense staff replete with Pulitzer Prize-winning reporters, editors, photographers and even a cartoonist (the inimitable "Herblock"). After all, this is the paper that broke the Watergate scandal, propelling two formerly obscure reporters, Bob Woodward and Carl Bernstein, to international notoriety and forever changing investigative journalism.

Living in Metro Washington and reading *The Post* day in and day out, you come to expect what readers of many other papers do not: in-depth analysis and commentary, from both sides of the political fence, on a broad range of topics; reprints of the entire text of presidential speeches and news conferences; a Sunday magazine; stories and photos from the farthest reaches of the world provided by Post staffers, not wire services; heavy coverage of national and international news to complement local happenings; in-depth special series; and stimulating editorial and op-ed pages. The paper also boasts lively lifestyle pages; weekly food, health, business and community sections; and Friday's tabloid, *Weekend*, a comprehensive guide to upcoming events. It's easy to get spoiled; just a few days out of town can cause acute information withdrawal.

The Washington Times
3600 New York Ave. NE, Washington, D.C. • (202) 636-3000

If nothing else, *The Washington Times* gives conservatives a loud, colorful voice. Plucky and aggressive, *The Times* (which also publishes a weekly news magazine, *Insight*) has only been a seven-day-a-week daily since 1991, but you wouldn't know it from the way it challenges *The Post* everywhere in its marketing strategies and daily news coverage.

The Times distinguishes itself not only with its strong right-wing tilt, but by its ownership: the Rev. Sun Myung Moon's Unification Church. Controversy and circulation figures aside, *The Times* has come a long way in little more than a decade in making Washington a two-newspaper town again and in convincing

people to give them a try. With their own wealth of talented staffers, many of them former *Star* employees, *The Times* has earned praise for its visual appeal, outstanding sports and business sections, hard-hitting investigative instincts and for hustle, gumption and chutzpah in the face of a David and Goliath sort of rivalry with the Post.

The Times publishes its weekend section on Thursdays as a service to those who like to have Saturday and Sunday planned by the time Friday rolls around — a novel idea indeed. *The Times*, like *The Post*, can be perused online.

As long as the money doesn't run out, *The Times* will continue to be the proverbial fly in *The Post's* ointment and the darling of the conservative establishment. The battle is good old-fashioned newspaper competition at its finest.

The Journal Newspapers
2720 Prosperity Ave., Fairfax, Va.
• (703) 560-4000

The Journal publishes separate editions Monday through Friday in six area jurisdictions: the city of Alexandria plus the counties of Arlington, Fairfax, Prince William, Montgomery and Prince George's. It also produces four Sunday editions. Circulation is 126,649 Mondays through Thursdays; 178,743 on Fridays; and 386,000 on Sundays.

Suburbanites now depend on *The Journal* for in-depth coverage of their communities beyond what *The Washington Post* and *The Washington Times* provide. It takes a full-time presence to maintain the suburban readership, and *The Journal* certainly has that.

The chain does a respectable job of covering its own turf, particularly in the areas of news, sports and features, and has been known to scoop its two major competitors in bread-and-butter categories such as local government, crime and the courts. *The Journal* also produces two smaller weekly supplementary papers in Fairfax and Prince William counties.

INSIDERS' TIP

Check out your cable TV's public access station for an eclectic array of programming produced by and starring local citizens.

The Library of Congress is the world's largest library.

USA Today
1000 Wilson Blvd., Arlington, Va.
• (703) 276-3400

With its extensive use of color and digest-style news coverage, "The Nation's Newspaper" originated the look that's become the trend in print journalism. The locally headquartered paper, which published its first edition in 1982, is sold Monday through Friday in newsboxes almost everywhere. It boasts an average circulation of 2.1 million readers. *USA Today* is also online.

Community Newspapers

Residents of Metro Washington have dozens of community news outlets. The weekly chains in particular are vast, with virtually every enclave in Washington, D.C., Northern Virginia and suburban Maryland having some sort of newspaper to call its own.

Many publications are free and distributed either by mail or to the doorstep based on ZIP code.

Washington, D.C.

The Current Newspapers
5125 MacArthur Blvd. NW, Ste. 18,
Washington, D.C. • (202) 244-7223

The *Northwest Current* and *Georgetown Current* newspapers cover news and features in neighborhoods from Chevy Chase to Foggy Bottom. The free papers are distributed every Wednesday via bulk drop and home delivery. A yearly subscription is $42.

The Georgetowner Newspaper
1410 Wisconsin Ave. NW, Washington,
D.C. • (202) 338-4833

This free paper, founded in 1954, is devoted exclusively to Georgetown, featuring community news and features, historical lore, book reviews and an events calender. Published every other week, it's circulated throughout Georgetown and surrounding areas.

Hill Rag
224 7th St. SE, Washington, D.C.
• (202) 543-8300

This monthly magazine-style newspaper, founded in 1976, features neighborhood news, film and book reviews and editorials geared toward readers who live or work on Capitol Hill. Distributed the first weekend of each month, the free paper is widely available at restaurants, bars and in news boxes.

Washington City Paper
2390 Champlain St. NW, Washington, D.C. • (202) 332-2100

This hip weekly attracts predominantly young, single professionals, who are drawn to its extensive coverage of culture, the arts, music and nightlife. It gives a comprehensive rundown of upcoming events, covers controversial and newsworthy issues through in-depth features and runs personal ads like you don't usually see in mainstream publications. This free tabloid is published on Thursdays and is typically available at book and music stores in the metropolitan area.

The Washington New Observer
811 Florida Ave. NW, Washington, D.C.
• (202) 232-3060

This free weekly, billing itself as "the city's community newspaper," features general news, sports and entertainment. It's distributed throughout the city every Thursday.

The Washington Sun Newspaper
830 Kennedy St. NW, Washington, D.C.
• (202) 882-1021

This weekly targets the entire Metro Washington area, with a mixture of local and world news and information about community events. Published on Thursdays and distributed throughout the area, it costs 25¢ per issue, or $50 for a yearly subscription.

Northern Virginia

Arlington Courier
1600 Scott's Crossing, Arlington, Va.
• (703) 522-9898

Arlington community news is featured in this free paper that comes out every other Thursday. It is distributed free throughout the county.

DCI Publishing Inc.
7670 Old Springhouse Rd., McLean, Va.
• (703) 821-5050

The area's largest local newspaper publisher has numerous weeklies throughout Northern Virginia. *The Alexandria Gazette Packet* features news of the city of Alexandria, while *The Franconia Gazette Packet* reaches nearby parts of Fairfax County. The county's southern end receives coverage in *The Mount Vernon Gazette*, and the bustling western Fairfax communities of Centreville and Chantilly receive coverage in *Centre View*. *The Connection* weekly tabloids cover news and features in Burke, Fairfax, Springfield, Reston/Herndon/Fairfax West and McLean/Great Falls/Vienna/Oakton/Tysons. *The Manassas Weekly Gazette* publishes Prince William County news.

Falls Church News-Press
929 W. Broad St., Falls Church, Va.
• (703) 532-3267

The city's free "Independent, Locally-Owned Newspaper of Record" is published every Thursday and distributed throughout the city and neighboring areas. It is accessible online.

JGF Media Inc.
2710-C Prosperity Ave., Fairfax, Va.
• (703) 204-2800

This media group owns three newspapers. The monthly *Middleburg Life* specializes in features about the posh community in northeastern Loudoun County. *Northern Virginia Sun* is a small weekday paper out of Arlington, and *Sun Gazette*, a weekly, serves the communities of Great Falls, McLean, Vienna and Oakton.

The Metro Herald
901 N. Washington St., Ste. 603, Alexandria, Va. • (703) 548-8891

This weekly, published on Fridays, actually covers the entire Metro Washington area through regional news, commentary, business and sports updates, events listings and lifestyle and entertainment features. A single copy costs 50¢, and a subscription is $50 annually.

Old Town Crier
112 S. Patrick St., Alexandria, Va.
• **(703) 836-0132**

Another Alexandria-based periodical, this one covers lifestyle features, entertainment and restaurant news, business briefs and events listings, "From the Bay to the Blue Ridge." This monthly paper is "priceless," as described on the front page, and is available at the Alexandria Visitors and Convention Bureau and local businesses in Alexandria, Fairfax, Fredericksburg and the Blue Ridge area of Virginia; Annapolis, Md.; and Georgetown in Washington, D.C.

Times Community Newspapers
1760 Reston Pkwy., Ste. 411, Reston, Va.
• **(703) 437-5400**

ARCOM Publishing owns this massive, ever-growing newspaper group, featuring 14 community weekly newspapers, including the flagship *Loudoun Times Mirror* in Leesburg. Other links in this vast chain include *The Eastern Loudoun Times* and *The Times Community* newspapers in the Fairfax County communities of Burke, Centreville, Chantilly, Fairfax, Fairfax Station, Great Falls, Herndon, McLean, Reston, Springfield and Vienna. A bit more removed from the Metro Washington area are *The Fauquier Times Democrat*, *The Clarke Courier* and *The Front Royal News*.

Suburban Maryland

Almanac Newspapers
9910 River Rd., Potomac, Md.
• **(301) 983-3350**

Owned by DCI Publishing, Inc., a major force in Northern Virginia community news, these two weeklies carry local news about Bethesda and Chevy Chase and the Potomac vicinity. The papers earned six awards from the Maryland Delaware D.C. Press Association in 1997. Distribution is free, and it arrives by bulk drop.

Bowie-Blade News
Crofton News Crier
6000 Laurel-Bowie Rd., Ste. 101, Bowie, Md. • **(301) 262-3700**

Owned by Capital Gazette Communications Inc., which also publishes *The Capital* daily newspaper in Annapolis and *Maryland Gazette*, a weekly in Glen Burnie, these suburban weeklies cover news and features in their respective communities. Published on Thursdays, they're available at newsstands and by carrier delivery ($1.47 for four weeks) or subscription ($13 for six months).

The Enquirer-Gazette
14760 Main St., Upper Marlboro, Md.
• **(301) 627-2833**

This weekly covering Prince George's County and parts of nearby Charles, St. Mary's and Calvert counties was founded in 1851. Distributed on Thursdays by mail and at local newsstands, it costs 25¢ a copy. The parent company, Chesapeake Publishing, also owns weeklies in the three nearby counties previously mentioned.

Gazette Newspapers
1200 Quince Orchard Blvd.,
Gaithersburg, Md. • **(301) 948-3120**

They seem to be everywhere: The Gazette Newspapers cover news and features in the communities of Aspen Hill, Bethesda, Burtonsville, Chevy Chase, Damascus, Frederick, Gaithersburg, Germantown, Kensington, Mt. Airy, Olney, Poolesville, Potomac, Prince George's County, Rockville, Silver Spring, Takoma Park and Wheaton. The papers are published Wednesdays and distributed free to homeowners. The company also publishes a weekly *Business Gazette* and *Montgomery Gazette*, available Fridays for 50¢ a copy.

Local Newspapers Inc.
4307 Jefferson St., Ste. 608, Hyattsville, Md. • **(301) 927-0550**

Newcomers on the community scene, *Hyattsville Local News* (founded in 1995) and *College Park Local News* (founded in 1996) are published the second and final Thursdays of each month. The free papers cover local news, and are distributed by carrier and bulk drop.

Montgomery County Sentinel
615 S. Frederick Ave., Gaithersburg, Md.
• **(301) 948-4630**

Covering community news, the minority-owned *Sentinel* is the county's oldest weekly newspaper.

Prince George's Sentinel
9458 Lanham-Severn Rd., Seabrook, Md.
• **(301) 306-9500**

This minority-owned weekly features community news about Prince George's County.

African-American Newspapers

The African Shopper
P.O. Box 2540, Washington, D.C.
• **(202) 882-8840**

This free monthly newspaper includes international newsbriefs, columns on business and legal issues, a guide to African currency and assorted features. It's available locally and nationally at libraries, the African embassies, universities and various stores.

Capital Spotlight Newspaper
National Press Bldg., Ste. 202, 529 14th St. NW, Washington, D.C.
• **(202) 745-7858**

This free weekly, founded in 1953, focuses on noncontroversial, inspirational news and features geared toward the local African American community. The paper is distributed on Thursdays in bulk drops at apartment buildings, churches and schools throughout the metropolitan area.

The Prince George's Post
15207 Marlboro Pk., Upper Marlboro, Md.
• **(301) 627-0900**

Founded in 1932, this weekly newspaper serves the African-American community in Prince George's County. Distributed on Thursdays, free copies are available at county libraries, but most papers are circulated through subscriptions which cost $15 annually, and are half-price for senior citizens and students.

Washington Afro-American Newspaper
1612 14th St. NW, Washington, D.C.
• **(202) 332-0080**

Founded in 1892, the Washington Afro-American is one of the oldest newspapers in the city. It's published every Thursday and contains news and features aimed at Metro Washington's black community. It is widely distributed and costs 50¢ per issue, or $27.48 for a yearly subscription. This paper is also online.

The Washington Informer Newspaper
3117 Martin Luther King Jr. Ave. SE, Washington, D.C. • **(202) 561-4100**

This weekly newspaper, founded 34 years ago, features positive news aimed at the metro area's African American residents. Active in the community, the paper sponsors the annual city-wide spelling bee. It's available for 25¢ per copy, or $15 for a one-year subscription.

Business and Real Estate

Mortgage Banking
1125 15th St. NW, Washington, D.C.
• **(202) 861-1930**

Published monthly by the Mortgage Bankers Association of America, "the Magazine of Real Estate Finance" features topical articles and provides regular departments focusing on areas like training, technology, breaking news and noteworthy people in the field. A subscription costs $40 annually.

The Northern Virginia Association of Realtors Update
8411 Arlington Blvd., Fairfax, Va.
• **(703) 207-3200**

Geared toward real estate agents in Northern Virginia, this magazine contains newsbriefs, awards announcements, selling tips, market trends and a calendar of upcoming training sessions. It's published nine times a year.

Washington Business Journal
2000 N. 14th St., Ste. 500, Arlington, Va.
• **(703) 875-2200**

Published on Fridays, this weekly examines the local business scene with news and features and regular columns on subjects like advertising and marketing, banking and finance, healthcare, international business, real estate and tourism and hospitality. It costs $1.25 per copy.

Foreign

Asian Fortune
P.O. Box 222036, Chantilly, Va. 20153 • (703) 968-0202

Written in English, this monthly newspaper's news and features adhere to the motto "Where East Meets West," targeting Asian-Americans throughout the Metro Washington area. It is free, and can be found at libraries, book stores, oriental markets and restaurants.

El Tiempo Latino
1515 N. Courthouse Rd., Arlington, Va. • (703) 527-7860

This weekly for Hispanic residents in the Washington-Baltimore area covers local and international news, entertainment, sports and features. Published on Fridays, it's free at libraries, universities, restaurants and ethnic businesses. A yearly subscription is $35.

Washington Journal
1113 National Press Bldg., Washington, D.C. • (202) 628-0404

The city's oldest newspaper, established in 1859, publishes local and international news in German. This weekly comes out on Fridays and is available by subscription for $40 a year.

Lifestyles

Capital Style
900 2nd St. NE, Washington, D.C. • (202) 408-6100

The newest addition to the city's magazine scene seems a likely successor to the defunct *Dossier*. Glossy *Capital Style* bills itself as "smart, witty and provocative," and caters to a sophisticated audience through intelligent features and elegant ads. A single copy

costs $2.95, and a yearly subscription is $16.65.

The Medical News
9706 Pennsylvania Ave., Upper Marlboro, Md. • (301) 599-1100

In *The Medical News*, health professionals write about current health news, covering everything from coping with slipped discs to controlling weight through hypnosis. This is a free monthly, published by Hunter Management Consultants, Inc. Regionalized editions are distributed locally throughout Northern Virginia and Montgomery and Prince George's counties.

Pathways Magazine
4931 St. Elmo Ave., Bethesda, Md. • (301) 656-3023

Published quarterly, this unique journal focuses on New-Age topics such as metaphysical sciences, holistic health, vegetarian cuisine and spiritual awareness. Besides in-depth features on subjects like herbal health and becoming your own guru, the magazine features an exhaustive listing of resources and lots of intriguing advertising. It's circulated via direct mail ($10 for a two-year subscription) and free of charge at libraries and local businesses. It is accessible online.

The Washington Blade
1408 U St. NW, 2nd Fl., Washington, D.C. • (202) 797-7000

This free weekly for the gay and lesbian community offers comprehensive coverage of hard news and features, as well as entertainment reviews, commentaries, events calendars and a large classified and personal ads section. The paper, in its 29th year, is distributed widely at bookstores, libraries and businesses throughout the metropolitan area. Check it out online.

Washington Woman
6002 Gloster Rd., Bethesda, Md. • (301) 229-0247

This free newspaper covers a variety of

INSIDERS' TIP

Rely on the numerous community newspapers — many of which are free — for coverage of local events, people and places that you won't get from any other publications.

topics generally aimed at women in the 35- to 55-year-old age bracket. Regular features focus on unique events and businesses, arts programs, places to go with friends and expert advice on topics such as fitness and home decorating ideas. An extensive regional calendar lists scores of upcoming lectures, concerts, shows and other activities. Published every two months, the paper is widely distributed at area libraries, bookstores, doctors' offices and supermarkets.

Political

The Hill
733 15th St. NW, Ste. 1140, Washington, D.C. • (202) 628-8500

Specializing in behind-the-scenes coverage of Congress, this young weekly paper scooped the major players when it broke the story about a coup attempt against House Speaker Newt Gingrich. Founded in 1994, it's distributed free to congressional offices and is available at newsstands for $2.50 per issue or by annual subscription for $100. It is available online.

Legal Times
1730 M St. NW, Washington, D.C. • (202) 457-0686

This weekly paper focuses on "Law and Lobbying in the Nation's Capital" and its target readership naturally consists of lawyers, lobbyists, the Supreme Court and members of Congress. A single copy, available at newsstands, is $12.25.

The New Republic
1220 19th St. NW, Washington, D.C. • (202) 331-7494

Founded in 1914, this "Weekly Journal of Opinion" is one of the most highly respected periodicals of its type. It features an impressive array of political commentary, poetry, art news and reviews of films and books. It's available for $3.50 an issue, and $79.97 for a yearly subscription.

Roll Call
900 2nd St. NE, Washington, D.C. • (202) 289-4900

This biweekly (published Mondays and Thursdays), founded in 1955, covers Capitol Hill

in-depth and is distributed to all House and Senate offices. A subscription costs $225 annually.

The Stars and Stripes
P.O. Box 187, Thurmont, Md. 21788
• (301) 271-1145 (business)
P.O. Box 1803, Washington, D.C. 20013
• (202) 543-4740

This nationally circulated newspaper, available by subscription for $19 annually, focuses on veterans' affairs. The first issue appeared in 1861, during the Civil War. Published by the National Tribune Corp. since 1886, it comes out every other week and sometimes features themed issues on special events like monument dedications in Washington.

Washington Monthly
1611 Connecticut Ave. NW, Washington, D.C. • (202) 462-0128

Featuring commentary on current affairs, this magazine presents a monthly award honoring media stories "that demonstrate a commitment to the public interest" by chronicling such issues as successful or failing government programs. An issue costs $3.95.

National Membership Magazines

Air and Space Magazine
370 L'Enfant Promenade SW, Washington, D.C. • (202) 287-3733

Produced by the Smithsonian Institution's National Air and Space Museum, this magazine is just the ticket for flight enthusiasts. Published six times a year, *Air and Space* features news about upcoming special exhibits, a calendar of museum events and assorted features on both historical and current topics, with many photographic illustrations. An Air and Space membership, which includes the subscription, costs $20 annually. See the Attractions and Kidstuff chapters for museum information.

Civilization
666 Pennsylvania Ave. SE, Ste. 303, Washington, D.C. • (202) 546-6600

The Magazine of the Library of Congress contains eclectic features, tidbits on popular culture and puzzles, and a calendar of events and exhibits coming up at the library. It's published bimonthly and is included in a $20, one-year Associate membership. A single copy is $4.50.

National Geographic Magazine
17th and M Sts. NW., Washington, D.C.
• **(202) 857-7000**

With its incredible accounts and photography of people and places all over the world, not to mention those great maps, *National Geographic* is one of the country's oldest and most treasured periodicals. Published by the National Geographic Society, which was founded in 1888, the magazine is included in a 12-month society membership for $27. The society also publishes magazines for children, books and maps. See the Attractions and Kidstuff chapters for more about things to see and do at the headquarters.

Smithsonian Magazine
900 Jefferson Dr. SW, Washington, D.C.
• **(202) 786-2900**

For Smithsonian Institution members, reading this magazine is like making an armchair visit to the museums. Each monthly issue contains a variety of features, vivid photographs, intriguing profiles of Smithsonian exhibits and listings of upcoming events. See the Arts, Attractions and Kidstuff chapters for museum information.

Regional Publications

Washington Flyer Magazine
3104 Omega Office Park, Fairfax, Va.
• **(703) 359-8847, (202) 331-9393**

This glossy bimonthly owned by the Metropolitan Washington Airports Authority covers a range of business and travel topics pertinent to air travelers — locals and visitors alike. With complimentary distribution at Washington National and Washington Dulles International airports, the magazine occupies a unique market niche with impressive demographics and a high pass-along rate.

Washingtonian
1828 L St. NW, Washington, D.C.
• **(202) 296-3600**

The area's true city magazine — although its readership is predominantly suburban — is a slick, thick monthly known for its "best of" lists, dining/shopping guides, maps of the stars' homes, interesting features and personality profiles and the occasional hard-hitting investigative piece. High paid-circulation numbers, a well-heeled readership and a large staff have helped *Washingtonian* maintain its enviable position in the local magazine market.

Washington Jewish Week
12300 Twinbrook Pkwy., Ste. 250, Rockville, Md. • **(301) 230-2222**

Washington Jewish Week, founded in 1965, is chock-full of local, national and international news and features aimed at Metro Washington's ever-growing Jewish community. Published on Thursdays, each issue features an extensive calendar of events scheduled by area synagogues, Jewish community centers, museums and organizations; and regular departments devoted to sports, seniors, singles, food, travel, real estate and social announcements. In July, the paper publishes *The Guide to Jewish Life in Washington*, a comprehensive source of more than 200 pages. Other special editions focus on such topics as weddings, bar and bat mitzvahs and party planning. The paper costs $1 per copy, or $28.50 per yearly subscription.

Special Interest

Antique Traveller
P.O. Box 5216, Herndon, Va. 20172
• **(703) 437-4971**

"Free and Quite Valuable," this regional periodical is an antique hunter's dream. It features numerous entertaining little features about collectibles, local sights and activities, recipes, business profiles, events calendars and scads of ads for shops throughout the area. *Antique Traveller* is published every two months by PSC Publishing and distributed at area antique stores.

Washington ComputerUser
9001 Braddock Rd., Ste. 140, Springfield, Va. • **(703) 503-8677**

Computer enthusiasts will find plenty to download in this free monthly dedicated to "the future of computing." Besides special features on the latest technological wonders, the paper features plenty of ads and departments devoted to software, hardware, gadgets, career and training opportunities, Internet information and events. Distributed free to area businesses, the publication is also available to nonbusiness and non-local addresses through $24.99 yearly subscriptions.

Radio

Turn on your car radio and push the "scan" button. In a matter of seconds you will lock on a station. Push it again and again and you'll get the same result. Metro Washington is by no means New York or Los Angeles in terms of market size or listening choices, but it does offer more than 50 AM and FM stations with a wide range of formats.

Here's a look around the dial:

Adult Contemporary/Soft Adult Contemporary Stations
WASH 97.1 FM
WRQX 107.3 FM
WAGE 1200 AM

Classical Stations
WETA 90.9 FM (also information/National Public Radio)
WGMS 103.5 FM

Country Stations
WMZQ 98.7 FM
WFRE 99.9 FM
WUPP 107.7 FM
WXTR 820 AM
WPWC 1480 AM

Easy Listening Stations
WMJS 92.7 FM
WGAY 99.5 FM
WWDC 1280 AM

Jazz Stations
WPFW 89.3 FM (also community radio)
WJZW 105.9 FM

News/Talk/Sports/ Information Stations
WTEM 570 AM (all sports)

WMAL 630 AM
WBZS 730 AM (financial news)
WFMD 930 AM
WWRC 980 AM
WMET 1150 AM
WVPA 1390
WTOP 1500 AM
WAMU 88.5 FM (National Public Radio; also, folk and bluegrass music)
WCSP 90.1 FM (C-SPAN)
WJFK 106.7 FM

Oldies Stations
WARW 94.7 FM (classic rock)
WBIG 100.3 FM
WKIK 1560 AM (classic rock)
WINX 1600 AM

Religious/Inspirational/ Gospel Stations
WABS 780 AM
WCTN 950 AM
WFAX 1220 AM
WDCT 1310 AM
WYCB 1340 AM
WPGC 1580 AM
WGTS 91.9 FM
WAVA 105.1 FM

Rock Stations
WHFS 99.1 FM (modern/alternative)
WWDC 101.1 FM

Soul/Talk Stations
WOL 1450 AM

Top 40/Contemporary Hits Stations
WWVZ 103.9 FM
WWZZ 104.1 FM

Urban Adult Contemporary Stations
WKYS 93.9 FM
WPGC 95.5 FM
WHUR 96.3 FM
WMMJ 102.3 FM

Other Stations
WILC 900 AM (contemporary Spanish)
WKDL 1050 AM (Spanish)
WUST 1120 AM (multi-cultural)
WWDC 1260 AM (Big Band/original hits)
WKDV 1460 AM (Spanish)

WMDO 1540 AM (Latin music/news)
WMUC 88.1 FM (progressive)

Television

As you'd expect in this high-profile city, news coverage is a big deal at the major networks' local affiliates. The stations are highly competitive, whether trying to be first to break a story or attempting to put together the most comprehensive "team coverage" of an event. You'll find newscasts first thing in the morning, at noon, late afternoon and twice in the evening — and around-the-clock on cable's News Channel 8.

Virtually anything a television viewer wants is available in Metro Washington. Along with all the major networks, numerous independent stations and literally hundreds of cable channels are at your fingertips.

Local TV Stations

Following are Washington's major local TV stations and their network affiliates:

WRC Channel 4 (NBC)
WTTG Channel 5 (Fox)
WJLA Channel 7 (ABC)
WUSA Channel 9 (CBS)
WDCA Channel 20 (UPN)
WETA Channel 26 (PBS)
WHMM Channel 32 (PBS)

Others:

WMPT Channel 22 (PBS)
WBDC Channel 50 (WB)
WNVT Channel 53 (PBS)
WNVC Channel 56 (PBS)

Baltimore and Hagerstown TV

These stations are available to many residents of Metro Washington:

WMAR Channel 2 (ABC)
WBAL Channel 11 (NBC)
WJZ Channel 13 (CBS)
WHAG Channel 25 (NBC)

WBFF Channel 45 (Fox)
WNUV Channel 54 (UPN)
WMPB Channel 67 (PBS)
WJAL Channel 68 (WB)

Cable TV

Most Metro Washington residents are now able to get cable TV, although pockets remain where service has yet to be provided and may never be for various reasons. Surprisingly, the District is a fledgling cable community, with the first cable franchise having been awarded only in the late 1980s. Media General Cable of Fairfax, a subsidiary of the Richmond, Virginia-based Fortune 500 publishing and broadcasting conglomerate Media General, has been operating since the early 1980s and is by far the largest local cable provider, with nearly 200,000 subscribers in Fairfax County.

Cable offerings for local residents run the gamut, from local public-access channels that offer community and civic information to the major players such as premium movie channels (HBO, Showtime, Disney, etc.), the locally owned Black Entertainment Television (BET), CNN, Discovery, MTV, ESPN, TNT, USA Network, and Chicago and New York "super stations." Let's not forget C-SPAN (Cable-Satellite Public Affairs Network) and C-SPAN II, which offer live coverage of the U.S. House of Representatives and U.S. Senate, respectively, and related political programming; for some strange reason these channels seem especially popular around here.

The following companies provide cable TV service to residents of Metro Washington.

Washington, D.C.

District Cablevision L.P./TCI
900 Michigan Ave. NE, Washington, D.C.
• (202) 832-2001

This company offers more than 80 channels to homes throughout the city. Its ex-

---

INSIDERS' TIP

Check *Washingtonian* magazine and the weekend sections of *The Washington Post* and *The Washington Times* for helpful guides to local dining, shopping, nightlife and assorted recreational diversions.

panded basic package costs approximately $32.

Northern Virginia

Cable TV Arlington
2702 Wilson Blvd., Arlington, Va.
• **(703) 841-7700**

With 65 channels available to Arlington County residents, this company offers basic options ranging in cost from approximately $12 to $33.

Cable Vision of Loudoun
21545 Ridgetop Cir., Sterling, Va.
• **(703) 430-8200**

Providing service throughout Loudoun County, Cable Vision offers 55 channels to its 30,000 subscribers. The most basic service costs $16.78 monthly.

Jones Communications
617A S. Pickett St., Alexandria, Va.
• **(703) 823-3000**

Alexandria's cable company has 41,200 subscribers and 54 channels. A basic subscription costs approximately $28.

Jones Communications
12345 Sunrise Valley Dr., Ste. G, Reston, Va. • **(703) 716-9701**

Unlike the rest of Fairfax County, Reston receives its cable service through this company.

Jones Communications
4391 Dale Blvd., Woodbridge, Va.
• **(703) 730-2225**

This cable company serves most of Prince William County, as well as Fort Belvoir and

Reston. It boasts more than 90,000 subscribers, and offers more than 50 channels. Basic service costs approximately $27.

Media General Cable of Fairfax
14650 Old Lee Rd., Chantilly, Va.
• **(703) 378-8400**

Media General provides cable TV service to more than 234,000 subscribers throughout the county — including the incorporated towns and cities within — except in the Reston area (See Jones Communications). The company has the capacity for 120 channels, and basic full service starts at approximately $34, plus franchise and converter box fees.

Westgate Cable Company
8019 Ashland Ave., Apt. 4, Manassas, Va.
• **(703) 369-6213**

Residents of Westgate apartments and townhomes receive their cable service through this company.

Suburban Maryland

Cable TV Montgomery
20 W. Gude Dr., Rockville, Md.
• **(301) 424-4400**

Serving all of Montgomery County, this cable service offers up to 70 channels, with basic services costing approximately $16 to $18.

Jones Communications
9609 Annapolis Rd., Lanham, Md.
• **(301) 731-4260**

This Prince George's County cable service offers more than 72 channels in its preferred package, which costs approximately $35.

Index of Advertisers

Index

M

Going Somewhere?

Insiders' Guide presents 48 current and upcoming titles to popular destinations all over the country (including the titles below) — and we're planning on adding many more. To order a title, go to your local bookstore or call (800) 582-2665 and we'll direct you to one.

Adirondacks

Atlanta, GA

Bermuda

Boca Raton and the Palm Beaches, FL

Boulder, CO, and Rocky Mountain National Park

Bradenton/Sarasota, FL

Branson, MO, and the Ozark Mountains

California's Wine Country

Cape Cod, Nantucket and Martha's Vineyard, MA

Charleston, SC

Cincinnati, OH

Civil War Sites in the Eastern Theater

Colorado's Mountains

Denver, CO

Florida Keys and Key West

Florida's Great Northwest

Golf in the Carolinas

Indianapolis, IN

The Lake Superior Region

Las Vegas

Lexington, KY

Louisville, KY

Madison, WI

Maine's Mid-Coast

Minneapolis/St. Paul, MN

Mississippi

Myrtle Beach, SC

Nashville, TN

New Hampshire

North Carolina's Central Coast and New Bern

North Carolina's Mountains

Outer Banks of North Carolina

The Pocono Mountains

Relocation

Richmond, VA

Salt Lake City

Santa Fe

Savannah

Southwestern Utah

Tampa/St. Petersburg, FL

Tucson

Virginia's Blue Ridge

Virginia's Chesapeake Bay

Washington, D.C.

Wichita, KS

Williamsburg, VA

Wilmington, NC

Yellowstone

THE INSIDERS'® GUIDE

Insiders' Guide • P.O. Box 2057 • Manteo, NC 27954
Phone (252) 473-6100 • Fax (252) 473-5869 • www.insiders.com